For Martin — Captain of my flight to San Francisco and with thanks for showing me around during the stop-over.

[signature]

22.12.1995.

EAST AFRICAN
An Airline Story

EAST AFRICAN
An Airline Story

PETER J DAVIS

RUNNYMEDE MALTHOUSE
PUBLISHING

First edition
Published in 1993

Second edition published 1994
This revised edition incorporates the author's corrections to the first
edition, based upon new information received and some changes described
in *Notes to the Second Edition*, page 446.

by
Runnymede Malthouse Publishing
Runnymede Road, Egham, Surrey

Copyright 1994 © Peter J. Davis MCIT, AMRAeS

All rights reserved. No part of this publication may be reproduced or
transmitted in any form or by any means, electronic or mechanical, nor
may it be stored in any information storage and retrieval system without
prior permission in writing from the publisher.

British Library Cataloguing in Publication Data

Davis, Peter, 1935-
East African - An Airline Story

ISBN 0 9523047 0 8

Book design and typesetting by
Woodfield Publishing Services
Fontwell, Sussex UK

Printed and bound in Great Britain

*This book is dedicated
to those for whom these were the best days . . .*

Contents

Acknowledgements viii

Glossary ix

Chapter 1.   **In the Beginning** 1

Chapter 2.   1925-1939   **The Settler Aviators** 18

Chapter 3.   1945-1948   **The New Airline** 41

Chapter 4.   1949-1952   **Lodestars and Dakotas** 63

Chapter 5.   1953-1956   **Troubled Times** 119

Chapter 6.   1957-1958   **Overseas** 174

Chapter 7.   1959-1960   **Comets and the Jet Age** 204

Chapter 8.   1961-1965   **Uhuru** 232

Chapter 9.   1966-1970   **Super VC10s** 290

Chapter 10.   **A Coup in the Morning:** *From the Authors notebook* 356

Chapter 11.   1971-1973   **Africa claims its own** 366

Chapter 12.   1974-1977   **The End of a Dream** 419

Postscript 442

Notes to second edition 446

Appendix A   Log Book Pages: *Miss Kenya* 448

Appendix B   Air Agreement between Union of
South Africa and United Kingdom 450

Appendix C   Fleet Lists 454

List of Illustrations 460
Index 472

Acknowledgements

I have attempted to tell the story of an airline which, during the thirty-two years of its existence, employed many thousands of personnel. It has been possible for me to tell the story through the experiences of only a few of the those who served the airline. This in no way diminishes the work of the great majority, whose efforts helped make East African Airways so unique. There are very few of those, who experienced East African Airways' particular charms, who could not write a fascinating story. Those experiences which are told in this book should be regarded as representative of many other, untold, adventures.

I would like to thank Captains George Leslie, G.W. 'Mitch' Mitchell, Reg Cartwright, 'Tug' Wilson, 'Ginger' Brewer and Bob Ainsworth, without whom this story would have been a great deal less interesting.

There are many others to whom I owe a debt of gratitude for their kind assistance and guidance, I would like to thank Captain Peter Cunningham for kindly proof reading the draft manuscript; for technical advice, encouragement, or loan of photographs and other material my thanks to: Captain Arthur Ricketts, Mr Ian Francombe, Captain Alan Ratcliffe, Mr Tommy Webb, Mr Paddy Murray, Mr Charlie Nichols, Mrs Barbara Fumerton, Mr Stan Kingsley-Jones, for photographic services; Mr Brian Wexham and Mr Bob Holt of *The Standard* (Nairobi), Mr Joe Furniss, Mr Michael 'Spud' Murphy, Mr Tim Nightingale, Mr 'Jock' Hay, Mr Dick Whittingham, FRAeS, and Mr Harry Everitt.

I wish to give special thanks to Captain Eric Morris, MVO, to whom I am immeasurably grateful for his encouragement and wealth of memories from the far-off, pioneering, days of aviation in East Africa.

Excerpts from *The Flying Duchess*, by the Duke of Bedford, are by kind permission of the Marquess of Tavistock and the Trustees of the Bedford Estates. Excerpts from *West with the Night* are reproduced by permission of the estate of Beryl Markham. The article on Tom Cambell Black (Page 33), from *Flight*, 24th September, 1936, and the article May Day at Fort Victoria (Page 186), from *Flight*, 25th December, 1959, are reproduced with permission of the Editor of *Flight International*. The article on pages 400–402 is reproduced by kind permission of the editor of the *Daily Mail*. The extracts from *Kenyatta* by Jeremy Murray Brown, published by George Allen & Unwin Ltd, are by permission of Unwyn Hyman, an imprint of Harper Collins Publishers Limited. The portrait of Sir Malin Sorsbie is reproduced by kind permission of Mr Godfrey Argent, Baron Studios. The two colour photographs of R.A.F. VC10 K3s are Crown Copyright and are reproduced by permission of the Controller of Her Majesty's Stationery Office.

I acknowledge the published work of the following, to which I have referred for data and verification: Dr Norman Barfield (VC10); M.A. Ward, BSc (Eng), MICE (fleet lists); R.A.R. Wilson (VC10); Philip J. Birtles (DH Comet).

Peter J Davis, Fifield, July 1993

Glossary of Terms

CTM   Capacity Ton Miles: equals available pay load capacity of aircraft in short tons multiplied by the miles flown. A measure of transport production.

EAS   Equivalent airspeed; IAS corrected for position error and compressibility error.

Five 'Freedoms of the Air'   Proposed by the Roosevelt administration at the Chicago Conference on civil aviation in November, 1944, they were:

1. Freedom to fly over a nation.

2. Freedom to land in a nation (without picking up or putting down passengers or goods).

3. Freedom to carry passengers or goods from the home nation to a foreign nation.

4. Freedom to carry passengers or goods from a foreign nation to a home nation.

5. Freedom to pick up and put down passengers or goods belonging to a foreign nation between intermediate points.

The proposals were never fully adopted (Churchill saw an American plot, particularly in article 5, to encroach upon the air routes of the Empire). Air agreements continued to be made through bi-lateral talks.

HDI   Horizon Direction Indicator

I.A.T.A.   International Air Transport Association. Formed at the Hague in 1919 as the International Air Traffic Association, it was renamed at the Havana Convention of April, 1945. Also written IATA or Iata.

I.C.A.O.   International Civil Aviation Organisation. Formed, under the auspices of the United Nations, at Chicago in 1944, to co-ordinate international rules of the air.

ILS   Instrument Landing System

Load Factor: Percentage of Load Ton Miles carried to Capacity Ton Miles offered, or the percentage of revenue load carried to capacity provided.

LTM   Load Ton Miles: equals actual paying load of aircraft in short tons carried multiplied by the miles flown.

Maximum zero fuel weight	This is the weight of the aeroplane above which all weight must consist of fuel. This is a simplified definition which is satisfactory for current transport aeroplanes in which most of the fuel is contained in tanks in the wing. This limitation is always determined by the structural loading airworthiness requirements; unlike the other weight limitations, it is not associated with any handling or performance qualities. Its effect is to impose a limit on the amount of load which may be carried in the fuselage. A higher maximum take-off weight may be achieved by taking into account the relieving effect of the weight of fuel in the wing tanks on the loads imposed on the wing structure. Similarly, higher operating speeds are achieved by reducing the maximum zero fuel weight.
M.L.A.	Member of the Legislative Assembly.
M.L.C.	Member of the Legislative Council.
NDB	Non-directional radio beacon
V_1	Decision speed in the event of an engine failure on take-off; at which the take-off may be either abandoned or continued.
VOR	VHF Omni-directional radio beacon.
WAT	(limiting conditions) Conditions of aeroplane weight which, when combined with the aerodrome altitude and temperature, reduce the performance level to the airworthiness minima.

Place Names

Some countries and many of the towns and other features have undergone changes in name since independence.

Old Name	New Name
Northern Rhodesia	Zambia
Southern Rhodesia	Zimbabwe
Tanganyika	Tanzania
Zanzibar (State)	Tanzania
Lourenco Marques	Maputo
Nyasaland	Malawi
Lake Rudolf	Lake Turkana
Murchison Falls	Kabalega Falls
Salisbury	Harare
Wadi Halfa	Now beneath the waters of Lake Nasser, above the Aswan High Dam.
Lake Albert	Lake Mobutu

CHAPTER 1

"In The Beginning"

AT THE TIME OF ITS FORMATION, on 1st January, 1946, East African Airways was to serve the four Territories and almost three quarters of a million square miles which made up the countries of British East Africa.

These Territories consisted of Tanganyika, Kenya, Uganda and the Protectorate of Zanzibar and Pemba, two small islands off the coast of Tanganyika. They were bounded in the north by Ethiopia (then known as Abyssinia) and the Sudan, in the west by the Belgian Congo, in the south by Rhodesia and Nyasaland, and in the east by the Indian Ocean.

Between them, these four countries cover an area almost eight times that of the United Kingdom or nearly a quarter the size of the United States. Tanganyika, as it was then known, the largest of the Territories covered slightly more than half the total area. Now called Tanzania, it is almost 400,000 square miles in extent, four times as large as Great Britain.

Kenya covers 225,000 square miles and Uganda 94,000 square miles. Zanzibar Island is 640 square miles in extent and Pemba, twenty-five miles to the north-east, 380 square miles.

In 1946, these Territories were loosely spoken of as East Africa, there was no one single government responsible for the four countries and final responsibility rested with the Colonial Office in London.

The former German colony of Tanganyika was governed by Great Britain on behalf of the United Nations, as a Trust Territory, following the break-up of the German empire after the Great War. Dar es Salaam, the capital, was built by the Germans towards the end of the 19th century. It had about 100,000 persons living in the town. In earlier centuries the city-state of Kilwa had been "One of the most beautiful and best constructed towns in the world", according to the Moroccan scholar and traveller, Ibn Batuta, who visited it in 1331. In common with Mombasa and Zanzibar it became a rich Islamic trading state, thriving on the sea-borne trade with Egypt, Arabia and the Indies.

The fabulous Indian Ocean trading cities, such as Kilwa and Kisimani Mafia in Tanganyika, and Zanzibar, Pemba and other cities strung along the coast were completely unknown to the Europeans until the arrival of the Portuguese three-ship fleet in 1497. Their captains, Vasco da Gama, D'Almeida and Da Cunha, were awe-struck by these richly endowed cities, their tall, elegant buildings golden in the rays of the rising sun. Nevertheless, they were, in turn, plundered and razed to the ground by the adventurers, in acts of piracy clothed in Christian zeal. Kilwa, which had grown rich and powerful from taxing imports and exports and from the gold and ivory trade, was destroyed by D'Almeida, on a return visit to the coast in 1505.

Kenya was both a colony and a protectorate. Nairobi, the capital of Kenya, was also the largest city in East Africa and had an estimated population of 150,000. Over half were Africans, there being 15,000 Europeans and 45,000 Asians. Before the Uganda Railway was laid, from Mombasa to Port Florence, on Lake Victoria, the site of Nairobi was merely a watering place to which the nomadic Maasai herdsmen brought their cattle. Its very name being Maasai, *Engore Nyrobe*, meaning "A place of cold water". Early in the twentieth century, government headquarters was established here, when mile 327 was reached on the railway. It was not an ideal site. Among the many disadvantages, there was the black-cotton soil which, during the rains, turned into a sticky quagmire, turning the flat plain into a mosquito ridden swamp. When the rains departed, the earth would become a dust-bowl for months on end. Shortage of clean water was also a major drawback, as the population increased. Notwithstanding these obstacles, the city's growth continued steadily.

Mombasa, now East Africa's second city, also in Kenya, is the principal sea port and is of great antiquity. Prior to the construction of the Uganda Railway and the consequential growth of Nairobi, it was the port of destination for travellers to East Africa, where Swahili porters and askaris would be hired for the *safari*[1] up-country. It had, for centuries, been a major Arab city and trading centre, the undoubted richness of which can only be guessed at, since it was sacked by the Portuguese under Vasco da Gama in 1497. A cosmopolitan gateway to the East with markets in ivory, gold, cinnamon, sandalwood, rhinoceros horn and slaves, it was a thriving Afro-Islamic kingdom. The outstanding landmark of Fort Jesus, built upon the foundations of an earlier Arab fortress, and the navigation markers of Vasco da Gama are relics of the Portuguese conquest of the sixteenth century. North and south of Mombasa the coastline consists of sun bleached coral-sand beaches, fringed by coco-nut palms and casuarinas which whisper in the cooling breezes of the Trade Winds. The white breakers of the Indian Ocean crash upon a coral reef, nearly a mile off-shore, preserving the inshore waters from predatory sharks.

The old Arab dhow harbour was superseded by a deepwater harbour at Kilindini, to the south of Mombasa, where, at the beginning of the century, the liners of Union Castle and Messageries Maritimes would bring European passengers to connect with the railway. While the great ships of the world's merchant and naval fleets used the harbour facilities of Kilindini, the dhows continued to sail past Fort Jesus into the old harbour, overlooked by the Customs House and the cool haven of the Mombasa Club.

Uganda was a Protectorate with its capital at Entebbe, on the shores of Lake Victoria. It is situated almost astride the Equator at an elevation of 3,782 ft. Kampala, now the capital of independent Uganda, was the largest town and centre of commerce, some twenty-one miles from Entebbe.

Uganda had been fertile ground for Christian missionaries who had found the Baganda, in particular, willing converts and outstanding scholars. The competition

---

[1] A Caravan journey. Until the establishment of law and order, it would have been extremely unwise to travel far without an armed escort of askaris.

between Catholic and Protestant missionaries initially proved confusing to the Baganda king, or Kabaka, Mwanga, who sought to overcome the problem by raising three regiments, one Catholic, one Protestant and a third Muslim. Religious strife was unavoidable and led to British intervention in 1892, when the Imperial British East Africa Trading Company commissioned Captain Frederick Lugard to pacify the warring Baganda. Having succeeded, Lugard went on to crush the neighbouring kingdom of Banyoro. Lugard's levies, recruited from Sudan, were savage in their cruelty. Many remained in Uganda, creating a significant group of fierce, Moslem tribesmen. The seeds of this blunder would, nearly eighty years later, bring forth bitter fruit.

A great hindrance to early development in Uganda at the beginning of the twentieth century was the scourge of sleeping sickness, which killed many thousands of the native population, until controlled by scientific methods and medical care.

Zanzibar had been a city-state ruled by Arabs, who had settled centuries earlier. At the beginning of the nineteenth century, Arab subjects of the rulers of Muscat and Oman arrived under the Imam Seyyid Said. In common with the sailors from Arabia who had sailed in during the ninth and tenth centuries on the Trade Winds, they came to find the twin riches of Africa in olden times – slaves and ivory. The exploits of the Arab sailors were to be told in the *Thousand and One Nights*, and Sindbad would have sailed these waters and known Zanzibar at a time when it was an ancient Arab kingdom, minting its own coin, and importing porcelain from China to embellish the richness of its civilization. Together with Mombasa to the north, the city was destroyed in 1497 by the fleet of Vasco da Gama, who saw it as his Christian duty to put to the sword the heathen 'Moors', prior to plundering their riches. But the Imam Seyyid Said did not come merely to trade; he wanted to re-create the pre-Portuguese Arab empire of the coast. Slave trading had overtaken everything else by 1839, when it was estimated that between 40,000 and 45,000 slaves were bought and sold in the Zanzibar slave market.

Apart from creating one of the largest slave markets in the world, Seyyid Said was to import cloves from Mauritius in 1818, creating the world's biggest clove plantations, which would ensure the wealth of Zanzibar long after slavery had been abolished by the British in 1807, and which remain to this day.[2] Following the Anglo-French Declaration of 1862, binding both Powers to respect the Sultan's independence, British rule finally defeated the overt slave trade in 1887, following successful seizures of slave-ships by Royal Navy patrols. The Sultan of Zanzibar had 'agreed' to prohibit his subjects from exporting slaves overseas as early as 1873. As a form of compensation to the Sultan for the losses incurred in the cessation of the slave-trade, the then British East Africa Association obtained a concession, in 1887, of the mainland territories from the Sultan Seyid Bargash, for an annual rental. Following administration by the Foreign Office from 1890, when full protectorate status was established, the Colonial Office took control in 1905.

---

[2] In January 1974, Zanzibar had the first colour TV in Africa, while on the mainland there was not even black and white. This was due to earnings from cloves, which at £2000 per ton represented 90% of the economy.

The Island was still an Arab domain in 1946, although a British Protectorate, ruled by a Sultan and a Council, with the advice of a British Resident. The capital was Zanzibar Town, with a population of 50,000, comprising about half African and the remainder Arabs and Indians. There were few British or European residents on the Island.

The need for air transport across these huge territories was recognised long before the advent of East African Airways. Early pioneering flights had been carried out by the Royal Air Force after the Great War, although reports of an aircraft being seen in German East Africa during the first week of the war, in 1914, caused consternation in Nairobi. Early in 1914 the government of German East Africa was making arrangements to hold an exhibition at Dar es Salaam during August. One of the exhibits was to have been a civil aircraft. This was shipped to Dar es Salaam in the *SS Tabora* and arrived sometime in July. The machine, which was a bi-plane with a pusher type propeller, was requisitioned by the German army in the early days of the war and they subsequently tried to put it into service, but it crashed on 15th November, killing the pilot, Lt Hennesberger. This was believed to be the first aeroplane to fly over East Africa.

The next aircraft to arrive was an old Curtis hydroplane, which had been giving exhibition flights over Durban harbour during July 1914. The Admiralty purchased this aircraft, gave the pilot, Mr Cutler, a temporary commission in the Royal Navy and shipped the aircraft up to Mafia in the Union Castle liner *SS Kinfauns Castle*. She arrived off Mafia on 15th November, 1914, and it was intended to use the aircraft in locating the German cruiser *Koenigsberg*, and in directing the fall of shot.

Cutler, with no previous knowledge of the hazards which might await the aviator flying in the tropics, was a pioneer, learning and experiencing the difficulties which would be overcome in the years to follow. The aircraft was old, very fragile and the radiator leaked like a sieve. Cutler found that the three-ply on the hull was coming apart due to the heat from the iron decks melting the glue. The short rains were about to start, and there was no shelter for the aircraft.

He made his first flight from the water on 19th November, in bad weather, and landed successfully about fifty minutes later. He was apparently unaware that he had landed near Okusa Island about eighteen miles south of Mafia, and it was some hours before he was located. The radiator of his engine was leaking very badly, whereupon a Ford car radiator was obtained from Mombasa and fitted into the aircraft.

So urgent was the need by the Royal Navy to seek out and destroy the *Koenigsberg* that the *SS Kinfauns Castle* was sent down from Mafia to Durban to fetch a new hull. When the aircraft was repaired, Cutler was able to take-off with an observer and flights were made over the Rufiji delta on the 4th, 7th, 8th and 9th December; on the 10th he was shot down and taken prisoner and his observer was killed.

Early in January, 1915, it was learnt that some landplanes were likely to be available and on the 10th January, work was started on the construction of a landing ground at Mafia Island. This would appear to be the first landing ground to be constructed in East Africa. Two Sopwith seaplanes, however, were brought from Bombay. They were equipped with Gnome Monosoupape engines, which had no carburettor, and considerable difficulty appears to have been experienced in obtaining the right fuel mixture for them.

Flight Lieutenant John Tullock Cull, commanding the seaplane detachment, made several attempts to take off from the water in one of these aircraft carrying an observer, two 50lb bombs and two 16lb bombs. The aircraft failed to become airborne. After four days trials, Cull eventually took off without an observer or bombs and with sufficient petrol for an hours flight. With this reduced load he was able to reach an altitude of 1,500 ft. He was unable to obtain full power from the engine, and he experienced considerable trouble with leaking floats as the glued joints would not stand up to the heat, and he also found that the india-rubber tubing was perishing.

During June two Henry Farman and two Caudron landplanes arrived; a hangar which was prefabricated in Mombasa was brought to Mafia and erected in two days on the aerodrome. Of these aircraft, the first Caudron was wrecked in the trial flight, one Henry Farman crashed due to engine failure, but Flt Lt Cull and his observer were able to observe the fall of shot and to signal corrections by W/T until the third aircraft was shot down. By the end of the campaign there were three Short seaplanes remaining, and these were destroyed by the Navy off Mafia Island, before they left. In September, 1915, two Caudrons were railed up-country from Mombasa. There are no details of the use of these aircraft during the East African land campaign, but bombs were dropped on New Moshi and Handeni. It is thought probable that aerodromes were constructed at Moshi and near Same.

Early in 1919 the air route from Cairo to the Cape was surveyed and a number of airfields were cleared, including Shirati, north of Musoma, Mwanza and Tabora.

During the early part of 1920, five aircraft made attempts on the London to Cape Town flight. Only one of these reached East Africa; this was a Vickers Vimy Commercial, G-EAAV, powered by two Rolls-Royce Eagle engines of 350 h.p., giving a cruising speed of 85-90 m.p.h. The aircraft had been chartered by *The Times* newspaper to test the practical use of a Cairo – Cape Town air route.

The crew of the Vimy comprised Captain S. Cockerell, Captain F.C. Broome, Sgt Major James Wyatt (mechanic) and Mr C. Corby (rigger). Dr Peter Chalmers-Mitchell of *The Times* was to join the aircraft at Cairo.

Departing Brooklands on 24th January, 1920, they flew via Manston, Lyons, Istres, Rome, Malta, Tripoli, Benghazi, Sollum, Cairo, Luxor, Malakal, and Mongolla arriving at Kisumu, on the shores of Lake Victoria, on 20th February.

Arrangements had been made to ship new engines out by sea to East Africa and install them at Kisumu when the aircraft arrived. On arrival at Kisumu it was learnt that the ship carrying the engines had caught fire and sunk. As the engines in the aircraft appeared to be functioning satisfactorily, it was decided to continue the flight. The aircraft reached Mwanza, made temporary repairs and flew on to Tabora. Further repairs were made at Tabora, but on the 27th February, the aircraft crashed on take-off due to failure of the starboard engine and was a total loss. For many years one of the propellers of this aircraft decorated the bar of the Dar es Salaam Club. This was the first flight from London to East Africa, although it was planned to be an attempt from London to the Cape, and its failure in completing the journey overshadowed the fact.

The first flight from Cairo to the Cape was made by Wing Commander Pierre van Ryneveld and Flight Lieutenant Quintin Brand, but they used a number of aircraft to complete the journey. They started from Brooklands on 24th February, 1920, in a Vimy named the *Silver Queen* and reached Cairo on the 9th February. On the 10th February they attempted a night flight from Cairo, force-landed near the Nile early on the following day, and the aircraft was destroyed.

The undamaged engines were removed, and the party returned to Cairo. There the engines were installed in a second aircraft, a surplus R.A.F. Vimy, known as the *Silver Queen II*. This aircraft landed at Shirati, then flew on to Abercorn, and eventually reached Bulawayo. Continuing the flight, the aircraft failed to clear a low line of hills soon after take-off, and was written off. Another aircraft, a government DH9, was sent up from South Africa, and in this machine Van Ryneveld and Quinton Brand eventually reached the Cape on 20th March.

Sir Alan Cobham, during his undertaking to survey the potential air routes of the empire for Imperial Airways, departed from Stag Lane aerodrome on 16th November, 1925, spent Christmas at Khartoum and early in the new year flew his DH 50J bi-plane, G-EBFP, powered by an Armstrong Jaguar 385 HP engine, south to Malakal and on to Kisumu, from where he continued to Tabora, in Tanganyika. He landed in Cape Town on 17th February, 1926, having survived a near engine failure above the Victoria Falls, when spray from the Falls, rising hundreds of feet into the air, entered the carburettor.

On the 1st March, 1926 the first R.A.F. flight left Cairo for the Cape with the intention of investigating the possibility of a civil air service through Africa. The flight consisted of five two-seat Fairey IIIF bi-planes with Napier Lion engines. On the return flight these aircraft were fitted with seaplane floats at Aboukir and proceeded to Lee-on-Solent. A routine flight, Cairo to the Cape was made in each succeeding year up to 1931, in which year the flight was accompanied by a Vickers Victoria troop carrier, with a capacity for twenty-three passengers.

The Colonial Office, in London, decided that it would be of great benefit to examine the feasibility of an air mail service to Lake Victoria via Egypt, the Sudan and the valley of the Nile. On the 17th November, 1927, Sir Alan Cobham set out again, this time piloting a Short Singapore I flying-boat, G-EBUP, powered by two Rolls-Royce 700 h.p. Condor engines. Departing the winter waters of the River Medway, they set course for the River Nile and Africa. In the following seven months they traversed the vast, unknown skies of Africa, flying down from Khartoum via Butiaba on Lake Albert to Entebbe on the shores of Lake Victoria. At Entebbe, were decided the final details of the proving flight for the Colonial Office. Proceeding via Port Bell, Kisumu and Mwanza on Lake Victoria, the Singapore was to return to Khartoum and back to Entebbe, covering the 2,700 mile journey in only four days.

On the return to Entebbe, an armada of Baganda war canoes descended upon the "great bird" in a simulated war charge. The crew were afraid that the spiked prows together with the tribesmen's spears may puncture the wing floats, but the oarsmen skilfully avoided damaging the flying-boat. Cobham and his crew were to continue to Kigoma on Lake Tanganyika, thence to Mpulungu on the south shore of the lake to Vua and Fort Johnston on Lake Nyassa. They returned to England on 4th June 1928, via the West Coast, after a journey which had continued to Cape Town, having crossed the Zambezi to Beira, Lourenco Marques and Durban. The Short Singapore was the first flying-boat to be seen at the Cape. The great lakes of East Africa provided ideal alighting areas in the days when the future of civil aviation routes connecting the colonies and dominions of the British empire seemed to rest with seaplane and flying-boat development.

Another pioneer of that time, Captain T. A. Gladstone, A.F.C. had begun, in 1924, to explore the possibilities of marine aircraft on the African lakes. In 1926-27 he ran an experimental float-plane service for a company called North Sea Aerial and General Transport Ltd., in which the Territorial governments of Kenya and Uganda had each invested £2,500, and the Sudan £2,000, in order to evaluate a seaplane service between Khartoum and Kisumu. On 2nd January, 1927, Gladstone attempted a mail flight from Khartoum to Kisumu in a DH50J, G-EBOP. This ended in failure when the machine crashed on take-off. Gladstone then negotiated the loan of a Fairy IIID, G-EBPZ, from the Royal Air Force, in which he succeeded in completing a mail flight in February, departing Kisumu for Jinja on 12th February and continuing on to Khartoum on 15th. The mail was carried from Khartoum to Cairo by the R.A.F. The venture came to grief in October, when his DH50J sea-plane, G-EBOP having been repaired, sank in the deep waters of Lake Victoria, after a further flight from Khartoum to Kisumu.

Although this pioneer service was, perhaps, before its time, it pointed the way to the possibilities of the use of marine aircraft on the empire route through Africa. In a few years the flying-boats of Imperial Airways were to bring passengers and mail from Khartoum to Kisumu, en route to the Cape. It was, however, to be the land plane which would begin commercial aviation within East Africa, and to prevail, as it would do around the world in the years to come.

Captain Richard (Dick) Bentley M.C. had emigrated to Canada, at the age of fourteen, in 1912. Shortly after the outbreak of the Great War he enlisted in the Canadian army and served on the Western Front. After transferring to the Royal Flying Corps, he was commissioned as a pilot in 1917. After the war, in 1919, he emigrated, once again, to South Africa where, in 1924, he answered an advertisement for pilots to help build the emerging South African Air Force.

In 1927 he persuaded the *Johannesburg Star* to sponsor a solo flight from London to Cape Town. With an advance of £400 from the newspaper, he purchased a DH60 Moth, G-EBSO, which was fitted with an enlarged fuel tank. He left England on 1st September 1927 and arrived in Cape Town to a rapturous reception on 28th September. This epic flight of 8,300 miles established a record as the then longest

Alan Cobham's Short Singapore 1, G-EBUP, on the River Medway near Rochester, prior to departure for Africa. November, 1927.

The Short Singapore 1 at anchor on Lake Victoria off Entebbe, with Baganda war canoes. February, 1928

completed solo flight, and won Bentley the award of the Air Force Cross and the Britannia Trophy.

Following his arrival in London, after a leisurely three month honeymoon journey in the Moth together with his new wife, he was commissioned by Imperial Airways to survey the route from Nairobi to the south. The survey, which was jointly conducted by Imperial Airways, the Air Ministry and the successor to Gladstone's North Sea Aerial and General Transportation Ltd, Cobham-Blackburn Air Lines, commenced its work on 11th November 1929 and it was finally completed on 11th April, 1930.

Flights to and from South Africa were becoming almost commonplace, they were, none the less, dangerous adventures, across many miles of hostile territory. On April 10th, 1930, at 5.10 a.m., a Fokker 3-seater monoplane named the *Spider* and piloted by the Duchess of Bedford, aged sixty-five, accompanied by her co-pilot, Captain C.D. Barnard and navigator/engineer Mr R.F. Little, departed England for the Cape. They arrived at Cape Town's Maitland Aerodrome at approximately 4 p.m. on the 19th April. En route, they had passed through the East African Territories. The duchess remarked in her notes:

> "April 16th ... As we neared the lake (Victoria) we had to fly very low owing to low cloud. Very unpleasant for my pilot and navigator, but if one has nothing to do but pump petrol from the tank in the cabin to the wing tanks, it is better to forget the danger part of it and think about something else and when you see Equatorial Africa for the first time from just above the tree tops, there is plenty of diversion for those who desire it. For hundreds of miles we flew over forest and scrub and swamps with no possibility of landing for the Spider, but it was all very wonderful to see . . .
>
> Dodoma (Tanganyika) has a nice aerodrome and a nice climate and a perfectly detestable hotel. Uncomfortable, horribly dirty, a very unattractive bathroom with all sorts of evil-looking livestock creeping and flying about in it . . ."

On the return flight to England, they departed Dodoma on April 24th at 4.05 a.m. in unpleasant, cloudy weather. The duchess, who had been enthraled by the spectacle of great herds of game, fleeing before them in every direction, was attracted by the navigator:

> "Mr Little indicated that pumping was urgently required. My special task was to pump the contents of the big extra tank of petrol into the wing tanks daily, an operation which meant a quarter hour's pumping every hour until it was empty, 270 gallons, I believe. A thousand pumps took just about a quarter-hour.
>
> . . . whilst still on the shores of L. Victoria, Capt. B. handed me his 'Printator' slate on which he had written, 'There is a leak in our oil supply and we shall have to make a forced landing to examine it. Do you think it was hard ground where we saw all that game?' I replied that where zebras and ostriches were it ought to be, but did not look like it, though I did not see any splashing. However, he continued to fly straight on, and in a short time another note came down. 'We may just reach Kisumu, but it will be a matter of minutes.'
>
> So over the water of Lake Victoria and other impossible landing-places the old Spider sped on, till we had apparently only a pint of oil or less left, but we managed to reach

Kisumu at 10.30 a.m. We landed safely on this pretty little landing ground, right on the Equator, and there found that the oil supply was going strong, but that the oil gauge had gone on strike and given quite needless anxiety.

We were over Uganda about half-hour later, but our bad luck as regards weather pursued us, and we kept running into very heavy storms and bad visibility. I wondered what was going to happen, but the luck which failed us in the matter of weather on this flight seemed to be playing with us, and when it had made us sufficiently uncomfortable always provided a way out. The N'mule landing-ground was not far off, and to that we went. We were immediately surrounded by a weird collection of natives dressed in girdles of beads only, very black, but very cheerful-looking...The pilot's book of directions said that shelter might be obtained through the native doctor. So I wrote a note, which Captain Barnard managed to dispatch to this official. After a long wait, a man who spoke English and dressed as an Englishman appeared, and said the doctor had left two years ago, but there was a hut, apparently intended for sheltering stray aeronauts, to which he would conduct us."

They departed the following day, April 25th. The flight proceeded without further setbacks until near Sofia in Bulgaria, where they made a forced landing following engine trouble. There was no mechanical fault, so it was thought that poor oil circulation must be due to the cold northern climate. They arrived back in England on April 30th, 1930.

Towards the end of 1928, the Tanganyika government decided that air communications were necessary to the Territory, and Mr P.E.L. Gethin, then Director of Surveys, persuaded the government to purchase a small aircraft for survey duties.

Tanganyika's first aircraft, G-AAUN later re-registered VR-TAA, an Avro Avian IVM bi-plane with an Armstrong Siddeley Genet Major engine, arrived in Dar es Salaam and made its first flight in March, 1929, from Mkego landing ground.

Aubrey Francombe had first come to East Africa in that year, arriving at Dar es Salaam on Armistice Day on the Union Castle liner *Llanstephan Castle*. He had spent the previous three and a half years with 33 Squadron, Royal Air Force, on the North West Frontier of India. On leaving the Royal Air Force, he had to get a job quickly, as his funds were running out rapidly. After a short leave he was told by the Air Ministry that there were two vacancies for pilot surveyors in the newly formed Air Survey Department in Tanganyika. Having no idea where Tanganyika was, he was offered and accepted the post. By chance, on the same day, he met an old friend from Indian days, V. 'Lynx' Soltau, who was in the same financial situation as himself. He went straight off to the Air Ministry and got the other job.

They both had to do a ground survey course with the Royal Engineers at Bembridge on the Isle of Wight. As Francombe told later:

"This was a bit of a frolic, as neither of us was the slightest good at mathematics and we were not, in any case, going to do ground surveys. I could never understand why, standing on the top of Bembridge Fort, in the bitter cold all night, taking shots with

Armstrong Siddeley 'Genet' powered Avro Avian IVM of the Tanganyika Government Survey. One of two IVMs, G-AAUN, re-registered VR-TAA in September, 1931, this was the first civil aircraft to be imported into Tanganyika. This photo was annotated by Aubrey Francombe "Roberts doing a job of work!". Mr Roberts, seen swinging the prop' was one of three engineers working for the Survey Department. Circa 1930.
(Ian Francombe)

a theodolite, it then took two days and many sheets of calculations and logarithms to find the correct time two days before - or one's position, which one knew anyway!

"My first job in Tanganyika Territory was to be sent off by ship and train to dismantle and ship an Avro Avian, which Gethin, our Director, had forced landed and unavoidably damaged on the side of the Tanga - Moshi railway, between Mambo and Moshi. With about ten Africans, camping equipment and a knowledge of Swahili limited to about four words, we were decanted into the bush, in the middle of the night, in pouring rain - and I had my first experience of siafu (soldier ants). The job took about ten days, and I got back to Dar es Salaam just before Christmas. The repairs took some time and were carried out by our voluntary engineer named Parfitt, who had been in the R.F.C. in the war. Parfitt had a wife and daughter, and they were affectionately known as Parfitt, Mafitt and Misfitt."

The Tanganyika government subsequently acquired another Avro Avian IVM, VR-TAD (ex-G-ABIC), a Cirrus III powered Avian IIIA, VR-TAG, and three Avro 621 Tutor Armstrong Siddeley Lynx powered three-seater survey aircraft, VR-TAB (ex-G-ABAP), VR-TAC (ex-G-ABAR) and VR-TAE (ex-G-ABHA) and a single seater Comper Swift, VR-TAF. The Avian IVM, VR-TAD had made its way to East Africa via an attempt on the England to Cape record by Flt Lt T. Rose, who departed Lympne on 11th February, 1931, in an unsuccessful bid for the record. The Avians carried cameras for vertical photography and in the following few years they carried out many surveys. Area scales were worked out by including in the photographs white crosses, which were placed on the ground at known distances apart.

There were four pilots working for the Government Survey, all surveyors flying part time. They were J.H. Tanner, A.M.D. Howes, Soltau and Francombe. There were three full-time engineers, Mr Templeman, Mr Roberts and Mr Macpherson.

Navigation in those early days was a hit and miss affair. Of course, there was no radio, and the maps were highly inaccurate. But with a light aircraft one could land almost anywhere and ask a local native - if they did not run away, which they often did - *"Wapi Songea?"*.[3] Even Imperial Airways pilots on the central route in the early thirties had trouble in finding Dodoma, and there were one or two forced landings, until Francombe had the idea to paint white arrows on the roofs of stations either side of the landing field, pointing to it.

By 1929, Kisumu had become the southern terminus of the Nile route from Cairo and Khartoum. Large sheds and workshops were erected, and a substantial slipway up which flying-boats could be hauled for servicing. At the airfield, Handley-Page HP42 four engined bi-planes brought mail and passengers from London. They flew onward in the three-engined de Havilland 66 Hercules twelve-passenger bi-plane aircraft, which were later replaced by Armstrong Whitworth XV Atalantas, four engined monoplane airliners with a two ton payload, which continued on to Mwanza.

In October, 1930, an agreement was signed between the United Kingdom government and Imperial Airways Ltd " To operate an efficient and regular air

---

[3] "Where is Songea?"

service for the transport of passengers, mails and freight" between Alexandria or Cairo and Cape Town.

It was proposed to operate a weekly service in each direction. In the first instance it was intended to operate a section as far as Mwanza commencing on the 1st January, 1931. Due to a number of delays the first Short Calcutta flying-boat did not reach Mwanza until the 10th March, 1931. This service was supposed to connect with the mail train, but as the aircraft was two days late the train left without the mail. Air mails were similarly dispatched from Dar es Salaam by the up train to connect with the service at Mwanza.

The scheduled service from England was operated in three sections. London via Southampton to Cairo by flying-boat, Cairo to Khartoum by land-plane and Khartoum to Mwanza by flying-boat. There were frequent delays on one or other of these route sections, due to difficulties in providing back-up equipment when aircraft became unserviceable. On the first eleven services from the United Kingdom, only four reached Mwanza on time, and of the first ten inward services, again, only four reached London on time. Two of these missed connections at Cairo due to the unserviceability of the flying-boat, and in fact the mails reached England eight days late.

It had been intended that the extension to the Cape should begin three months after the inauguration of the service from London to Mwanza, but due to delays in acquiring new aircraft and in the installation of radio stations and aerodromes in Central Africa, the first through service to the Cape did not begin until January, 1932.

Owing to the bad weather experienced over Europe during the winter months, a winter timetable was introduced in October, 1931, in which the Paris to Brindisi sector was completed by train. The whole journey took eight days and the fare was £95.

The first return flight from the Cape to London left Cape Town on the 27th January, 1932. The de Havilland 66 Hercules, piloted by Captain R.F. Caspareuthus, routed through East Africa via Mbeya, Dodoma, Moshi and Nairobi. Caspareuthus had earlier attempted the record flight from England to the Cape in a de Havilland 80A Puss Moth, named *Springbok*. He had set out on the morning of October 5th, 1930, from Lympne, on the Kent coast. His route passed over Beauvais, in France, where the airship R101 had crashed only a few hours earlier. In his baggage were letters from Sir Sefton Brancker, the British Director of Civil Aviation, who had died in the airship wreckage below him. Caspareuthus was delivering the letters to the Union of South Africa's postmaster general, the Director of Civil Aviation and the mayor of Cape Town. He completed the 8,000 mile flight in eight and a half days, during which he spent 76 hours and 50 minutes at the controls, at an average speed of 105 mph. The earlier record, set by the Duchess of Bedford, had been broken by one and a half days.

Rheinholdt Ferdinand Caspareuthus was born in Cape Town on May 9th, 1899, and educated at the South African College. He learned to fly with the Royal Flying Corps, into which he was commissioned in 1917. He flew on bomber operations on the Western Front, during which time he was injured in a flying accident. Following extensive surgery on his jaw, he emerged with the nick-name of 'Long Chin'. On his return to the Cape he became one of the first pilots in the South African Air Force. In the course of his duties, Caspareuthus was selected to fly diamonds from the state diggings in Namaqualand to Cape Town, over the barren lands of the North West Cape Province, and deliver them to the office of the government diamond evaluator.

In 1929, he resigned his commission and joined Major A.M. Miller, who had established an air mail service in South Africa. After a spell with Union Airways (the forerunner of South African Airways), he moved, in 1932, to Imperial Airways. 'Caspar' Caspareuthus was to go on to become one of the famous names of Imperial Airways, before settling in Kenya, in a senior position as chief pilot for the East African Directorate of Civil Aviation.

Captain Francombe was one of the first to experience the new Imperial Airways service. He went on leave to the United Kingdom in 1932, and in his recollection "The trip was the best you can imagine. The fare was about £80 with no extras. One lived in luxury, but it was not always comfortable, flying for ten days. My trip was the second by Imperial Airways to London. One flew from Nairobi to Kisumu in a three-engined Hercules and there joined a Calcutta flying-boat. The flying-boat captain, Prendergast by name, was an old friend from India, and he invited me to the cockpit. The Kavirondo Gulf was dead calm, and a launch preceded us to make a wave, thus assisting the take-off. We trundled down the gulf, and towards the end, showing no sign of getting airborne, I asked Prendy if he intended to go all the way to Port Bell on the water. He shook his head, glanced at the fuel gauges, and said "We havn't used nearly enough yet." A little later, we were off and reached about 1,000 ft above the lake, which was the maximum ceiling attainable, until more fuel was used up.

"The Calcutta took us to Juba (they would sometimes route to Malakal) where we joined one of those monster four-engined Handley-Page 42s, maximum speed about 90 mph. They had a curious feature, when flying, a draught would blow forward, from the rear of the aircraft. One day an old lady called to the steward and asked why this was. The immediate reply from the little cockney was: "Following wind, madam.""

The journey continued from Cairo by train to Alexandria, where the passengers embarked upon a Short Kent[4] flying-boat to Brindisi, via Crete and Athens. At Brindisi they boarded the Grand Expresses des Wagon-Lits train to Paris. A night was spent in a Paris hotel, and the following morning they embarked upon the Handley-Page 42 bound for Hendon.

Towards the end of 1935, Imperial Airways decided that it would be preferable to replace the three types of aircraft now being used with the new 'C' Class Empire

---

[4] The Kent flying-boat was powered by four Bristol Jupiter engines giving a total of 2,400 horsepower. It carried fifteen passengers and two tons of mail or freight at 137 mph. Three machines, *Scipio, Satyrus* and *Sylvanus* operated the Mediterranean sector of Imperial Airways routes from 1931-1937.

flying-boats and operate these aircraft from Southampton to Kisumu and thence to Mombasa and along the coast to Durban.

The Kenya government objected most strongly to Nairobi being by-passed, but unavailingly, and on the 1st July 1937, the flying-boats started a bi-weekly service in each direction calling at Dar es Salaam and Lindi.

In October, 1937, an incident occurred, highlighting the perils of aviation on the route from Europe to East Africa. Following his success in coming second in the Kings Cup Air Race, Brig-Gen A.C. Lewin, accompanied by his wife, had set out from England in a Miles Whitney Straight single-engined monoplane to fly home to Kenya. Due to a compass error and failure of the aircraft's elapsed time clock, he overflew his en-route destination at Malakal, resulting in a forced landing due to lack of fuel. Unfortunately, they were over the vast Nile swamps of the Sudan Sudd. Lewin selected what appeared to be the driest patch on which to land. The undercarriage caught in the long grass and the aircraft turned over onto its back, injuring both occupants.

The injuries were not serious. Husband and wife sat on the upturned aircraft and considered their plight. They had only one gallon of water and a small packet of sandwiches. They were off track and unlikely to be located for many days, if at all. The rear end of the machine was clear of the swamp water and they prepared to spend the first night in this shelter, for rain was threatening and mosquitos were swarming round them. They draped mosquito netting inside the aeroplane and crept into the shelter, without eating any of the sandwiches, hoping for a night's rest.

Imperial Airways Armstrong Whitworth XV, G-ABTI, Atalanta, (the fourth of its class), at Mbeya, Tanganyika Territory. This aircraft, commanded by Capt H.G. Brackley, flew the first proving flight to the Cape, departing Croydon 31 December, 1932.

At sunset the mosquitos penetrated their shelter and made sleep impossible. The water rose inside the aeroplane and made it impossible for the occupants to sit or lie. The heat was intense. The stranded travellers could not speak without swallowing mosquitos and, although they killed handfuls of the insects, they had no respite. They dared not leave the aeroplane, fearing that the pests outside would be worse. The couple were exhausted when they crawled out at sunrise. They drank water but could not eat a sandwich.

With an umbrella and a waterproof they rigged a shelter on top of the machine, but Lewin preferred the sun to the flies. He searched in vain for a dry spot, but everywhere was swamp into which he sank up to his knees. Meanwhile Mrs Lewin sewed the mosquito netting into a bag, leaving an opening through which to enter. This mosquito sleeping bag was effective.

On the fourth day their food was exhausted, but they were too thirsty and feverish to feel the pangs of hunger. They strained the green slime from the swamp water and drank to assuage their thirst. At noon Brig-Gen Lewin was roused by the sound of an engine. Looking up he saw an aeroplane. He fired a Verey light, used one of his eight matches to light a fire and flashed a mirror – all to no purpose. The signals failed to attract attention. The aeroplane disappeared.

Within twenty minutes hope was revived again as they heard the sound of another machine. It was an Imperial Airways 'C' Class flying-boat, *Cassiopea*, piloted

Imperial Airways Handley Page HP42 G-AAGX, Hannibal, *being refuelled at Entebbe, Uganda. Circa mid-1930s.*

by Captain Caspareuthus. They renewed their efforts, this time with success. The flying-boat flew low and dropped food and a message for them.

Having dropped the food, Captain Caspareuthus turned back to Malakal. He remained there overnight while aircraft of No.47 Squadron of the Royal Air Force, under the direction of the Acting Governor at Malakal, Mr Macphail, prepared to leave at dawn. In the early light the great flying-boat lifted off from the Nile and Caspareuthus led eight service aircraft in the search. With remarkably accurate navigation he led the searching aircraft to the spot, where they were able to see mirror signals flashed by Brig-Gen Lewin.

Landing was out of the question. The rescuers dropped water, food, blankets, ground sheets, medical stores and a pole and flag, so that the position could be marked to guide a ground search party. They also dropped a message picking-up apparatus used for army co-operation exercises. The plight of the couple was still perilous. They were in a trackless swamp as large as Great Britain, and hidden by grass from four to eight feet high. They were finally rescued by Dinka tribesmen, who had crossed some seventy miles of swamps, from their home district of Bor, on the tenth day after the forced landing.

In the years following the Great War, civil aviation to the Middle East and India, and south to Africa had developed rapidly, spurred on by the British government's desire to secure the ties of empire, principally by means of the air mail service. The main arteries of the empire air routes were establishing themselves progressively with increasing reliability. But it had been left to others to open up the skies of the East African Territories.

CHAPTER 2

The Settler Aviators

SEREMAI LIES IN THE lush foothills of Mount Kenya, where the morning mists shroud the hillsides until burned away by the bright African sunlight. At an altitude of nearly eight thousand feet, it was ideal for the cultivation of coffee. At Seremai there lived a man who was to provide the accidental inspiration for the birth of an idea which was to grow one day into an international airline.

His name was John Carberry. Born John Evans-Freke in 1892, he had become the 10th Baron Carbery, inheriting the title during childhood. He had learned to fly before the Great War and, in 1914, had participated in the Schneider Trophy race at Monaco. During the war he joined the Royal Naval Air Service. On leaving the Navy, for some personal reason, he took a dislike to his country of origin and in 1919 took out American naturalisation papers. He failed in this ambition following difficulties with the law, in connection with 'bootlegging' during the period of prohibition. He moved to Kenya, dropping his title and changed his name to John Evans Carberry (inserting an extra 'r' in the family name). He settled in Kenya, creating a coffee plantation called Seremai, near Nyeri. It was Carberry who was to import the first privately owned aeroplane into Kenya. The de Havilland DH51, VP-KAA, was despatched from the de Havilland Stag Lane works to Mombasa on September 17, 1925 and, after a long passage by sea followed by the haul up-country on the Uganda Railway, it was finally carried on a cart drawn by an ox-team, on the last leg of its journey from Nairobi to Seremai, where it was re-assembled for flight.

At the same time, during the mid 1920s, another settler, who had been farming for several years between Rongai and Eldama Ravine, shared John Carberry's enthusiasm for aviation. He was, within a few years, to become a world famous aviator. His name was Tom Campbell Black. It was at the Nakuru Show in 1925 that he told of his ideas for commercial aviation in Kenya, to Mervyn Hill, later to become editor of the *Kenya Weekly News*.

> "...At the time, his ideas and his hopes were little more than pipe-dreams. That afternoon Tom Black had thrilled the crowd with one of the most remarkable if unorthodox exhibitions of show jumping that I have ever seen. He owned a black gelding that jumped like a stag and very fast, but he was as wild as a kite and the devil to hold. More often than not their way round the ring left a devastation of jumps behind them but on this occasion all went well. At a speed more suitable to the finish of a hurdle race, they never touched a jump and Tom retired to the Rift Valley Sports Club with a large cup which held an awful lot of liquor in the course of the evening. It was, indeed, a memorable night!
>
> Farming wasn't going too well so Tom Black set about turning the pipe-dreams into reality, with much of the drive and dash that he displayed in the show-ring. Soon he was flying with a purpose that began to take shape."

Campbell Black, together with two associates, G.T. Skinner, manager of the Thomson Falls sawmill and engineer and surveyor, A.E. Hughes, bought the DH51 from John Carberry and christened it *Miss Kenya*. They set up the Kenya Aircraft Company, a short lived enterprise which has left no trace of their exploits.

In 1926 the general manager of the Nairobi company Motor Mart and Exchange, Mr Alfred Vincent, appointed as chief engineer another person who was to fit into the emerging pattern of East African aviation, he was A.W. 'Archie' Watkins, an outstanding character who was to make a long and notable contribution to aviation in East Africa; and who would hold the No. 1 ground engineer's licence (Kenya) in categories 'A', 'B', 'C', and 'D' in addition to Pilots Licence No.27.

It was in January 1929 that John Carberry was contacted by a lady in a hurry to get to England by the quickest means. Florence Kerr Fernie was born in Liverpool in 1879. In 1902 she married Herbert Wilson and, after her husband's service in the Great War, they decided to emigrate to Kenya to try their hand at farming, in which they were highly successful. After her husband's death, she became convinced that air transport was vital in the colony, which had very few roads and where communities and farms were totally isolated at times of emergency or serious illness.

Carberry then owned a Wright Whirlwind powered Fokker Universal, VP-KAB, named *Miss Africa*, which he agreed to charter to her for the flight to England. He had offered to fly it himself, but on the death of his German-born mechanic, Mr Haeufl, tragically killed in a motor accident at Nyeri on January 20th, he contacted Mrs Wilson and said the trip was off. After she had considered alternative arrangements to motor via the Nile route, Tom Campbell Black, Mr Hughes and Mr Skinner tried to persuade her to go by air, using Carberry's Fokker. "...I refused, as I did not know them", she revealed later. "... They called to see me at the Norfolk Hotel, where I was staying at the time, and again tried to persuade me to fly, but I said I did not wish to do so.

"On my return to my farm, Messrs Hughes, Skinner and Black again called me with the same request, and as I preferred the idea of flying to motoring, I said I would think the matter over and then decided that provided a mechanic could be found and all arrangements be made with Mr Carberry, I would charter the aeroplane from Mr Carberry and I asked which of the three was the pilot and was told it was Mr Black."

Archie Watkins, the motor engineer from Motor Mart, volunteered to accompany them as engineer.

Departing from the old Nairobi aerodrome near the Ngong Road at 07.30 on the morning of 6th February, 1929, and averaging nine hours flying per day, they reached Croydon on 20th February, fourteen days after leaving Nairobi. They had spent some days sightseeing en route, which had extended their journey time. It was the first civilian flight from East Africa to the United Kingdom. This in itself was a notable event, but that fate had thrown together these three people was to prove to be the most significant factor in the story of East African aviation. As they circled over London, at the end of their journey, Mrs Kerr-Wilson tapped

Archie Watkins on the shoulder, "If I were to start an airline in Kenya, would you join me?" she asked him. Thus, Archie Watkins was to begin a lifetime career in East African aviation.

Accompanied by Tom Campbell Black, Mrs Kerr-Wilson visited a number of aircraft factories in Britain, eventually selecting a two seater De Havilland DH 60G Gipsy Moth, VP-KAC, which she named *Knight of the Mist*.

On their return to Kenya, the airline, called Wilson Airways, was formed, on 31st July 1929, with Mrs Kerr-Wilson as proprietor and chairman, Tom Campbell Black as chief pilot and manager, Mr C.W.F. Wood, pilot, and Archie Watkins as chief engineer.

Beryl Markham was a contemporary. A close friend of John Carberry and his circle of aviation enthusiasts, she was a pioneer aviatrix; later to become the first woman to fly the Atlantic solo from east to west. Taught to fly by Campbell Black, she describes her close association with him in her book *West with the Night*:

> "If the towns and villages of Kenya lacked roads to unite them, like threads in a net, then at least there was land enough for the wheels of planes and sky enough for their wings and time enough for their propellers to beat back the barriers of doubt they flew against ... Into this horizon Tom Black had flown his aeroplane. One day it would carry mail as he had intended it to. It would soar above old paths tramped by the feet of native runners, it would clear wakes in the wind ... There was never a more careful pilot nor a more casual one. His confidence never shrank beside the bullying roar of a plane. He wasn't a tall man, but he had a quiet convincing manner that made him look bigger than any job he ever held and more capable than any craft he ever flew.
>
> Wilson Airways - the first commercial enterprise of its kind in East Africa - had been the child of Tom's imagination and foresight.
>
> Tom's job was to pioneer new routes, to probe inland Africa, seeking foot-holds for the future. More often than not he took off from Nairobi, flying over country as unused to wheels as it was to wings, with not more than a modest expectation that there might be some place to land at the end of his flight.
>
> And not all of this was done by daylight; he flew without beams, without beacons or radio, through whatever darkness the night could offer - and through whatever weather. There was rarely a light of a village for guidance, nor any highways, nor rails, nor wires, nor farms. He did not call it blind flying; he called it night flying, though when fog or storm required it of him, he flew blind for hours without special instruments, yet not failing on his course".

The first noteworthy flight of Wilson Airways was made in October 1929, when Campbell Black flew the Gipsy Moth from Nairobi to England for an American, Capt. H.A. White of the Chicago Field Museum, who was anxious to accomplish the journey within a week. Loaded with a seventeen-and-a-half stone passenger, baggage and an extra fifteen gallon fuel tank, the little machine flew over bushland, desert, forest, and 10,000ft mountain ranges to the successful conclusion of a remarkable trip.

Campbell Black returned with the first Avro 'Five', VP-KAE named *Knight of the Grail*, from Heston to Nairobi, departing on 24th October 1929 and arriving some nineteen days later, 12th November - a leisurely trip even in those days. The

Puss Moth was flown back by Flt Lt F.A. Swoffer, formerly a flying instructor at the Hampshire Light Aeroplane Club, who had been engaged as a pilot.

First landings in Mombasa and in Zanzibar; the first non-stop flight from Zanzibar to Nairobi; from Zanzibar to Dar es Salaam; and the first flight from Nairobi to Mombasa and back in a day were all carried out by Campbell Black. Another 'first' was his flight from Nairobi to Zanzibar, Dar es Salaam and Mombasa, a distance of over 1,000 miles, completed in nine hours.

Tom Campbell Black was to fly many thousands of miles developing the air routes of East and Central Africa before leaving Wilson Airways to fly for Lord Furness in England.

His name was to be splashed across the headlines of the world's press, following his record breaking flight in the DH 88 Comet, racing from Mildenhall in England to Australia in the great MacRobertson Trophy Air Race of 1934. Together with C.W.A. Scott, he completed the distance of 12,500 miles in two days twenty-two hours and fifty-eight minutes.

Initially operating from a grass strip, kept short by grazing sheep, at Dagoretti Corner, which lies between the Ngong and Naivasha roads, they were to move after a year to the level grasslands on the western boundary of the colonial city, later to be known as Nairobi West. The small single engined bi-planes of Wilson Airways flew ad hoc charters wherever a strip could be cleared, to up-country farms, plantations and mines and across the wilderness of Tsavo to the Coast. Thus, the small band of bush pilots in East Africa, such as Campbell Black, Swoffer and Wood, were gradually, but surely, gaining the experience and developing the

Avro 619 'Five', VP-KAE, Knight of the Grail *at Nairobi, with Tom Campbell Black (nearest aircraft). Circa 1929.* (Capt Alec Noon)

techniques which were to continue far into the future, into the time, still undreamed of, when powerful, gleaming airliners would rend the skies with the sound of their powerful engines.

Within two years, Wilson Airways had expanded to a fleet of two Avro type 619 'Fives', two DH80A Puss Moths and three DH60G Gipsy Moths, with which they covered more than fifty landing strips throughout the region.

The Avro 619 'Five' started its history in Holland. In 1928 Avro acquired a licence to build the Dutch Fokker FVIIB3M for sale throughout the British Empire, excluding Canada. These British built machines were known as Avro 618 'Tens'. The 'Ten' referred to the fact that it carried two crew and eight passengers. The chief designer of Avro's, Roy Chadwick, developed a scaled down version, with the same power from the three engines, which was designated the Avro 619 'Five', because it carried one pilot and four passengers. Four of these machines were built, of which three were acquired by Wilson Airways.

In those early pioneering days, many famous people were carried to and from safari camp, including the Prince of Wales, the Duke of Gloucester, the Duke of Kent and American millionaires such as the Vanderbilts and Mr Marshall-Field. Big-game hunting was the primary purpose of travellers to East Africa, apart from traders and those on government service. An aircraft was an ideal means of transporting the wealthy big-game hunters from Nairobi into the bush, where tents and provisions would have been taken by an advance party, who would prepare the camp-site and later provide superb meals, hot baths and showers. They would clear a suitable landing site and ensure that it was clear of wild animals, which could, if necessary, be sent running by a low pass by the aeroplane, prior to landing. The Prince of Wales was one of Wilson Airways' clients, who, wishing to save time on safari, was flown by Campbell Black from Nairobi to the Serengeti Plains in Tanganyika, where his hunters had cleared a bush strip.

Beryl Markham, describing the early thirties in Kenya, wrote:

"It wasn't easy to get a plane in East Africa and it was almost impossible to get very far across country without one. There were roads, of course, leading in a dozen directions out of Nairobi. They started out boldly enough, but grew narrow and rough after a few miles and dwindled into the rock-studded hills, or lost themselves in a morass of red murram mud or black cotton soil, in the flat country and valleys . . . The more travelled roads were good and often paved for a short distance, but once the pavement ended, an aeroplane, if one were at hand, could save hours of weary toil behind the wheel of a lurching car - provided the driver were skilful enough to keep it lurching at all. My plane, though only a two seater (an Avro Avian, registration VP-KAN), *was busy most of the time in spite of competition from the then barely budding East African - not to say the full blown Wilson - Airways".*

The East African Airways referred to by Beryl Markham, had no connection, strangely, with the airline which was to come, many years later. A small company, it emerged to serve the gold mining areas and competed briefly with Wilson Airways carrying passengers and mail. Beryl Markham later free-lanced for the company until they went out of business, in 1936.

In 1930, Mrs Wilson, or 'Florrie' as she was called by her friends in Wilson Airways, accompanied her pilots on a survey flight from Nairobi to Johannesburg. It was there that she made the acquaintance of M.C.P. Mostert, a South African Air Force trained pilot who impressed her so much that she invited him to fly her back to Nairobi, where he joined Wilson Airways. The flight which took place between 29th April and 5th May 1930, was a route survey from Johannesburg via Messina—Bulawayo—Livingstone—Broken Hill—Ndola—Abercorn—Tabora—Arusha to Nairobi, in her Gipsy Moth, VP-KAG.

On 24th February 1931, they departed once more to survey the route from Zanzibar via Nairobi—Entebbe—Stanleyville—Bangui—Fort Lamy—Kano—Gao—Segou—Bamako—Kayes—Bathurst—Dakar—St Louis—Port Etienne—Villa Cisneros—Cape Juby—Las Palmas—Cape Juby—Agadir—Casablanca—Tangiers—Seville—Madrid—Biarritz—Bordeaux—Paris—Croydon, in the Puss Moth, VP-KAH. The first-ever aerial east-west crossing of central Africa, this was an epic flight of 80 hours and 40 minutes flight time. They spent long periods at some stops; fourteen days in Kano, eight days in Las Palmas. On some days they would fly legs of more than 1,000 miles. The sector between Entebbe and Stanleyville was more than 510 miles over jungle, with no airstrips and very little prospect of aid if they crashed. Careful pre-planning together with the Shell oil company ensured that there was fuel available at all the stops en route. "We always had plenty of petrol and oil, even in places which can be reached only by a journey of several weeks on camels. How they (Shell) do it I do not know", Mostert remarked later.

The *East African Standard* of 12th January 1932 reported a record flight made by Mostert during the preceding month:

RECORD FLIGHT IN AFRICA
From Nairobi to Johannesburg
A 36 – hour journey

FEAT BY KENYA AIRMEN IN A PUSS MOTH

In Nairobi on Sunday and in Johannesburg on Monday sounds like some vision of the future. But in actual fact this remarkable feat was accomplished less than a month ago by Mr M.C.P. Mostert and Mr R.R. Fiddian-Green. In an interview with the East African Standard, Mr Fiddian-Green stated that the journey had been an enjoyable one although it was very tiring. The aeroplane used was a Puss Moth belonging to Messrs Wilson Airways of which firm Mr Mostert is a pilot. Leaving Nairobi on Sunday, December 20, at 4.30 a.m. they succeeded in reaching Broken Hill, a distance of 1,200 miles, eleven and a half hours later. On the following day they left Broken Hill at 5 a.m. and after a halt of 65 minutes at Bulawayo they set out for Germiston, near Johannesburg, where a landing was made just after 2 p.m. The journey occupied some 21 flying hours and it is claimed that this is a record. The times made on the outward journey were remarkably good throughout and it is worthy of note that the average speed of the Puss Moth over the whole distance was 109 miles per hour. The two airmen spent Christmas in South Africa and then set off again from Roberts Heights. Leaving Roberts Heights, the headquarters of the South African Air Force, of which Mr Mostert used to be a member, at 10.05 on Thursday, January 7, the Puss Moth was escorted over the town of Pretoria by two S.A.A.F. machines. The first landing was made at Pietersburg, the flight taking an hour and a half. The next stop was at Bulawayo, and Salisbury was reached at 6 o'clock the same evening. No attempt was being made to rush the journey and there was no idea of creating any new records. After spending the night in Salisbury the machine left at 6 o'clock on the following morning for Broken Hill, the flight taking three hours. The next hop was to Mpika, where a stop was made for lunch. Leaving again at 1.30 p.m. they flew to Mbeya which was reached at 4 p.m. The night was spent at Mbeya and on the following morning the journey was continued at 6.30 a.m. Dodoma was reached at 9.10 and a non-stop flight was made from there to Nairobi, where they landed shortly before 1 p.m. Both the outward and return journeys were uneventful and the weather, generally was good. Very thick clouds were encountered between Broken Hill and Bulawayo both ways and on one occasion the Puss Moth was above them, without the chance of the ground being seen for four hours. Skilful navigation enabled them to reach their objective in spite of this. Curiously enough, very little game was seen throughout the flight. Some buffalo were spotted between Mbeya and Mpika and a herd of elephant was seen in Northern Rhodesia.

By 1934 Mostert was manager and chief pilot of Wilson Airways and he became a director of the company in 1935. During those formative years, Mostert increasingly displayed the fine qualities, including a rare talent for leadership and an ability to inspire others with his own zeal, that were to mark a notable career in aviation, both in peace and war.

On 28th February 1931 Imperial Airways had begun a weekly United Kingdom–Central Africa service, terminating at Mwanza via Kisumu. Passengers were carried only as far as Khartoum. Wilson Airways flew connecting services for air mail in both directions Kisumu–Nairobi, commencing 10th March 1931. By July, a full passenger service was in operation and on 8th July, 1931, Capt. Mostert flew the first connecting passengers to Kisumu in the Puss Moth VP-KAM. Gradually, additional scheduled air mail services were introduced. On 17th October, 1931, the first Dar es Salaam–Kisumu experimental mail service began, using the Tanganyika government aircraft on the sectors Dar es Salaam–Zanzibar–Tanga–Mombasa, from where they would be transferred to the Mombasa–Nairobi train to be carried by Wilson Airways from Nairobi to Kisumu. During the period of this experiment, which ceased on 22nd January, 1932, 26,000 letters were carried. In August, 1932, a once weekly Wilson Airways service from Nairobi to Mombasa, Tanga, Zanzibar and Dar es Salaam was introduced, using the DH Puss Moths, which carried two passengers, a small quantity of mail and very little luggage. Captain Mostert again flew the first of these services on 18th August, departing Dar es Salaam on 20th August in Puss Moth VP-KAM. Further links to Kisumu, Mafia and Lindi were later established. In 1933, a branch was opened in Dar es Salaam with two DH

Kisumu aerodrome, Kenya Colony. Handley Page HP 42, G-AAUC, Horsa, and Armstrong Whitworth AW XV, G-ABTH, Andromeda, in front of the Imperial Airways hangars. Prior to the introduction of the 'C' Class flying-boats in 1937, passengers for South Africa transferred from the HP 42s to the AW XVs for their onward journey. Mail for East African destinations was collected by Wilson Airways.

A DH84 Dragon, VP-KBA, of Wilson Airways at Zanzibar. Circa mid-1930s

Puss Moths and a Gipsy Moth. Three years later, Wilson Airways were also established at Entebbe.

By 1932, de Havilland's had produced an eight-seat twin engined machine to supersede the single engined Moths. Named the DH84 Dragon, it was powered by two Gipsy Major 130hp engines and became an immediate success in the United Kingdom and around the world. Never before had it been possible to carry eight passengers so economically with such an increase in operating safety. With a simple structure which could easily be repaired anywhere in the world and well tried engines, no more difficult to service than a motor car engine, this aircraft was the first airliner able to provide its owners with the opportunity to derive real profit from its operation in an era when air transport relied heavily upon subsidy, either directly or in the form of mail contracts from government.

Wilson Airways purchased one of these, VP-KAW, in 1934, which was initially used on the Kisumu–Dar es Salaam route. It was followed by VP-KBA and VP-KBG, a Dragon II.

At the end of 1933 de Havilland's had perfected a new engine, producing 205 h.p. at 2,350 r.p.m. This was the Gipsy-Six. Fitted to a new airframe developed from the Dragon, it was to be known as the Dragon Rapide. The DH89 Dragon Rapide first flew in April 1934. With a wing-span of 48ft and length of 34ft 6in, the DH89 had a maximum speed at sea level of 157 mph, normal cruising speed at 1,000ft. was 132 mph, it had a ceiling of 16,700ft. and could maintain 3,100ft. on one engine at a maximum all up weight of 5,500lb.

One other variant of the de Havilland Dragon, the DH90 Dragonfly, flew in October 1935, powered by two Gipsy Major engines. This was possibly de Havilland's one blunder. With a high-load wing, the aircraft had a quick stall, which could catch out the unwary in the tricky landing phase, when it would be discovered that the rudder was anything but efficient. Wilson Airways bought two of these machines, VP-KCA and VP-KCS, but it was the five DH89 Dragon Rapides, powered by the two De Havilland Gipsy-Six 200 h.p. engines, which were introduced in 1934 rather than the three less powerful DH84 Dragons, that enabled the little airline to operate profitably . With eight passenger seats, cruising at nearly 140 m.p.h. the Dragon Rapides proved to be very popular, so much so that it was often difficult to get a seat on the Nairobi–Mombasa route.

During 1933-34, Imperial Airways acquired a financial interest in Wilson Airways, emphasising the importance of the airline in providing support for the empire trunk routes. On 2nd October, 1934, services were extended Kisumu-Nairobi-Dar es Salaam through to Mafia. The Dragon service was terminated at Dar es Salaam, from where a Puss Moth would continue through to Mafia.

On 14th January, 1935, Wilson Airways began a service linking Kisumu–Kakamega-Eldoret–Njoro and Nairobi. On 13th April, 1935, a weekly service was inaugurated from Nairobi via Lolgorien–Watende–Kitere–Kisumu–Musoma–Mwanza to Nungwe, using Puss Moths. A service was also provided between Kakamega and Watende. The pilots of Wilson Airways, such as Mostert, Morris, Soltau, Pearson, Noon, Francombe, Kirkham, and Lovemore, were now flying

A DH89A Dragon Rapide of Wilson Airways (Mr I. Francombe)

A DH90 Dragonfly takes off from a typical bush strip (Mr I. Francombe)

thousands of miles across the territories of East Africa, gradually knitting together a reliable route structure, adding to the integrity of the society which they served, making innumerable friends, from the Coast to the great Lakes and the fertile Highlands, to lonely safari camps in the wilderness. The dispersed settler communities could now depend more often upon mail and newspaper deliveries, medicines, doctors and vets and quick delivery of essentials such as spare parts for vehicles or generators and farm machinery.

Alec Noon had joined Wilson Airways as a pilot in the mid-thirties. He recalled Mrs Wilson, above all as being a sympathetic boss. "I had three mishaps in quick succession. I wrote off a Leopard Moth, damaged a Rapide at Utete, and the left leg of a Vega Gull collapsed under me while taxying.

"I was on the carpet before Captain Mostert and Mrs Wilson and got a real dressing down from Mostert. Afterwards Mrs Wilson sought me out and said, "Don't take it too seriously. Just be a little more careful."

On another occasion Noon lost the tail wheel tyre of a Rapide to a hungry hyena at Iringa. Parked overnight on the airstrip, he found the tyre chewed to pieces the following morning. "I would have loved to have been there when its teeth reached the inner tube and the bang came", he said.

The two pilot surveyors, 'Lynx' Soltau and Aubrey Francombe, had joined Wilson Airways in 1933, having left the service of the Tanganyika Air Survey Department in 1932 when it was abolished during the great depression of that time. They had gained a an enormous amount of useful experience in Tanganyika, not entirely related to survey work. The Air Unit had gradually evolved to encompass

The sign-post near Mbeya aerodrome, Tanganyika Territory. Circa 1930s.
(Mr I. Francombe)

the carrying of mails, transporting officials and their wives on visits up-country, including the Governor, Sir Stewart Symes. Pilots often had to act as unofficial ADC. Flying in loose formation, a second aircraft would carry the baggage, usually including the Governor's be-feathered topi. Great embarrassment would be experienced if the following aircraft should force-land elsewhere. The pilots would carry a funnel and chamois-leather, with which they would refuel from four gallon debbies of motor spirit. It was customary in those days to take sausages or kippers as a treat for hosts up-country, as these small luxuries were otherwise unobtainable to those settlers and officials, far from the sea-port cities or Nairobi.

Francombe, with his local knowledge, had been asked to start up and operate the Wilson Airways Dar es Salaam branch. There were two pilots and an engineer, George 'Temp' Templeman, also ex-Tanganyika Survey. With two Puss Moths, they were at first engaged in charter flying for private and government clients. A great deal of assistance came from Sir Phillip Mitchell, who was then Secretary for African Affairs. In those days, officials who had to travel by road expected to buy a new car when they went on leave. The Airways became unpopular with many of them because Sir Philip made the cost of chartering from Wilson Airways ten cents less per mile than the car allowance, and if the departmental accounts did not show this saving he wanted to know the reason why!

Aubrey Francombe stands beside VP-KCA, first of the two DH90 Dragonfly, four-passenger aircraft which Wilson Airways utilised for government charters in Uganda. There is no record of the identity of these officials, photographed at Masindi, together with members of the Verona Fathers mission. Circa 1938. (Mr Ian Francombe)

To the two Puss Moths was added a single-seat Comper Swift, powered by a Pobjoy engine. This was used for aerodrome inspections and surveys. The first coastal service to Zanzibar, Tanga and Mombasa was started by the Puss Moths. The freight space was so small that 5lbs of mail would be all they could carry, and a night-stop bag would be kept in Mombasa, in case of emergency. Another mail service by Puss Moth was to Mafia Island, Kilwa and Lindi. There was no landing ground at Lindi, but a friend of Francombe in the African Wharfage Company calculated that if they landed on the beach at 9 a.m. on Monday mornings, they could do so whatever the state of the tides, neap or spring, all the year round. There was very little room during neap tides, and the Puss Moth, having no brakes, was apt to swing towards the sea in the cross-wind, so two askaris were trained to run out and catch hold of the wing tip, and swing the aeroplane up onto the soft sand.

At Mafia they landed alongside a swamp. There was no transport on the island, but the District Officer provided donkeys upon which he, his wife and the pilots raced to the Boma. There was betting on each race, which the District Officer or his wife always won – having the choice of mounts, but in return the D.O. would send the pilots out fishing in his launch for a few hours, while he read the mail and wrote his replies for them to take back to Dar es Salaam.

One of the regular passengers was a Mr Belart of the British American Tobacco Company. On the first tour of his area he asked Francombe what he should take as gifts for his hosts, apart from cigarettes. Francombe advised him that kippers

Watched by an askari, Aubrey Francombe fills in the paper work. The aircraft is the Wilson Airways DH84 Dragon 1, VP-KBA. Circa mid-1930s. (Mr Ian Francombe)

were always most acceptable at the remote up-country districts. They stayed the night at a remote village called Masasi, and were royally entertained by the D.O. On leaving the next morning, as Belart handed over his gifts, the D.O. enquired, "Excuse me sir, are you travelling in cigarettes – or *kippers*?"

In 1936, Francombe flew a twin engined de Havilland Dragonfly (VP-KCA) out from England. It was the year of the South Africa air race and he cabled Wilson Airways for permission to take part. He was very much disappointed to receive what he considered to be a rude and rather emphatic denial. He proceeded with his delivery flight alone, which allowed him to fly long hours, and he reached Nairobi comfortably in five days. The winner of the race took eight days to reach Nairobi, and ten days to complete the flight.

In the same year, Mrs Wilson was awarded the OBE, for her services to aviation in East Africa. Francombe said of her, "She never struck you as a businesswoman, but she was. She was feminine but had immense courage and knew everything that was going on in the business."

The Imperial Airways routes from London were extending via Khartoum and Malakal to Port Bell in Uganda, from where the Empire flying-boats would continue to Kisumu on the Kenya shore of Lake Victoria. From Kisumu, Wilson Airways would fly connecting passengers along the western shore of Lake Victoria to Lolgorien, Musoma, Mwanza and Geita. Another service connected directly with Nairobi and a third proceeded from Kisumu via Kakamega, Kitale, Eldoret, Nakuru, Nanyuki and Nyeri to Nairobi.

A DH90 Dragonfly of Wilson Airways lands in fading light. (Mr Ian Francombe)

From Nairobi, the feeder junction of the Wilson Airways network, passengers had the option of two further routes. One of these went to Mombasa, Tanga, Zanzibar and Dar es Salaam; the other followed a route inland through Moshi Dodoma, M'beya, M'pika and Broken Hill to Lusaka.

In April, 1937, the Imperial Airways Short Kent flying-boat, G-ABFC, *Satyrus*, commanded by Captain L.A. Egglesfield, made a proving flight to Lindi in Tanganyika, in advance of the introduction of the Short 'C' Class Empire flying-boats.

On the 15th May, 1937, the first 'C' Class flying-boat, G-ADUY, R.M.A. *Capella*, operated from the United Kingdom through to Kisumu. On 2nd June, the 'C' Class flying-boat G-ADHL, R.M.A. *Canopus* departed Southampton for South Africa, routing from Cairo via Wadi Halfa-Khartoum-Malakal-Butiaba-Port Bell-Kisumu-Mombasa-Dar es Salaam-Lindi-Mozambique-Beira-Lourenco Marques to Durban.

The trunk route from Kisumu via Nairobi and Mombasa down the beautiful palm-edged coast of white coral beaches and jade-green seas to Dar es Salaam and Lindi, in Tanganyika Territory and thence on to Mozambique in Portuguese East Africa represented 5,929 miles; four days travel for Imperial Airways passengers from London.

In 1938, the typical fare from London to Nairobi was £109 single, £196-4s return. The fare to Mombasa was £110 single and £198 return and to Dar es Salaam £112 single and £210-12s return.

At the same time, flights were pushing northwards from South Africa. South African Airways, formed in 1934, were operating Airspeed Envoy eight passenger, twin-engined airliners from the Rand, departing on Sunday mornings to Bulawayo, Livingstone, Lusaka and Broken Hill, where the passengers would stay overnight. On the Monday morning they continued to M'pika, M'beya, Dodoma and Moshi,

DH80A Puss Moths VP-KAK and VP-KAY and DH85 Leopard Moth VP-KBP of Wilson Airways, on the beach at Lindi. Circa late 1930s   Wing-Cdr A. Francombe

reaching Nairobi in the afternoon. The aircraft then continued on the Tuesday morning, completing the final leg to Kisumu in 70 minutes. Passengers were then able to connect with the Imperial Airways flights to Khartoum, Cairo and London.

While Wilson Airways was blossoming forth in the warmth of East Africa, a tragedy had struck, in the early Autumn of 1936, in England. An awful accident on 19th September, at Liverpool Speke Aerodrome had claimed the life of Tom Campbell Black.

The following obituary appeared in *Flight*, on Thursday, 24th September 1936:

THOMAS CAMPBELL BLACK

*It is with the deepest regret that **Flight** records the death, last Saturday, of Mr Thomas Campbell Black. He was involved in a collision on Speke Aerodrome, Liverpool, between his Mew Gull, which he was to have flown in the South Africa race, and a Service Hart. It appears that, as he taxied to take off for Gravesend, the airscrew of the slowly moving Hart cut through a wing and into his cockpit, inflicting terrible injuries which quickly proved fatal.*

The Short 'C' Class Empire flying-boat RMA Canopus. *This aircraft departed Southampton on 2nd June, 1937 on the first Imperial Airways flying-boat service to South Africa.*

34 · EAST AFRICAN: AN AIRLINE STORY

Wilson Airways advertisement, circa 1932.

Maasai warriors find shade beneath the wing of a DH85 Leopard Moth of Wilson Airways, circa 1935.

An inquest was opened at Liverpool on Monday but was adjourned for a week.

Tom Campbell Black was born in 1899 and served during the war in the R.N.A.S. and the R.A.F. In post-war years, while farming in Kenya, he was a pioneer of civil aviation, and, apart from making thirteen flights between that colony and England, founded Wilson Airways Ltd. In 1929 he flew from Nairobi to England in eight days. During the visit of the King, then Prince of Wales, to East Africa six years ago, Campbell Black was temporarily appointed his personal pilot. He was also engaged as private pilot to Lord Furness. In 1930 he made the first non-stop flight from Zanzibar to Nairobi, and in the following year rescued Herr Ernst Udet, who was starving on an island in the Upper Nile.

His most notable performance was in the MacRobertson England-Australia Race of 1934, when, as co-pilot with C.W.A. Scott, he gained first place, covering the distance from Mildenhall to Melbourne in 70 hr. 59 min. in a DH Comet. Subsequently the Royal Aeronautical Society awarded him the Britannia Trophy for 1934 and the British silver medal for outstanding achievements in aeronautics.

In 1935 he married Miss Florence Desmond, and that August he set out on a Comet to make an attempt on the Cape record, but was forced to abandon the journey at Cairo. During the following month he was off again, in company with Mr J.H.G. McArthur, on another attempt to lower the record, but, with his companion was forced to leave the machine by parachute 100 miles north of Khartoum.

In late months he has led British Empire Displays, and the following is a tribute from "J.A.T.", one of his colleagues:

" 'C.B.' was not with us all of the time, but each member of the staff looked forward to those long week-ends when he came on tour. The sight of his black-and-silver Puss Moth seemed to signify that all was well with the flying world; his presence was a tonic and an indication that we were going to have a successful week-end.

"Tom Campbell Black was one of the best 'mixers' with whom twenty years of flying has brought me into contact. Rank meant nothing to him, his smile and ready quip were for all. Generous to a fault, he had the happy knack of doing favours that were not recognised as such until long afterwards. The impish seriousness with which he would casually mention a 'sticky' journey, which you knew was more than 'sticky', endeared him to the hearts of other pilots. With an unusually good memory, 'C.B.' could keep the party in good humour without in any way usurping the conversation.

"I have a particularly happy memory of him somewhere in the North Country. The proprietor of our hotel had been telling us of the illness of her son, who was to enter the Royal Air Force at Halton in a very short time. The lad's principal distress was that he had been unable to see our show that day, and that he had dearly wanted the autograph of Mr. Black. Someone mentioned the matter to 'C.B.'- and we lost his company for more than an hour. Somewhere there is a boy mechanic who cherishes not only a famous autograph, but the memory of an hour of talk that encompassed the world.

"It would be intrusiveness on my part to write of Campbell Black's services to aviation, when so many famous pilots in the world will be prepared to pay homage to the master-hand. I need only say that on one occasion I heard him say 'This field doesn't look too good to me. Let me have a try with two of the staff.' Everyone within hearing moved as one man towards the famous Puss Moth."

Imperial Airways advertisement for Armstrong Whitworth XV Atlanta services ex Nairobi, circa 1934.

The 1938 advertisement for the Empire flying boat services.

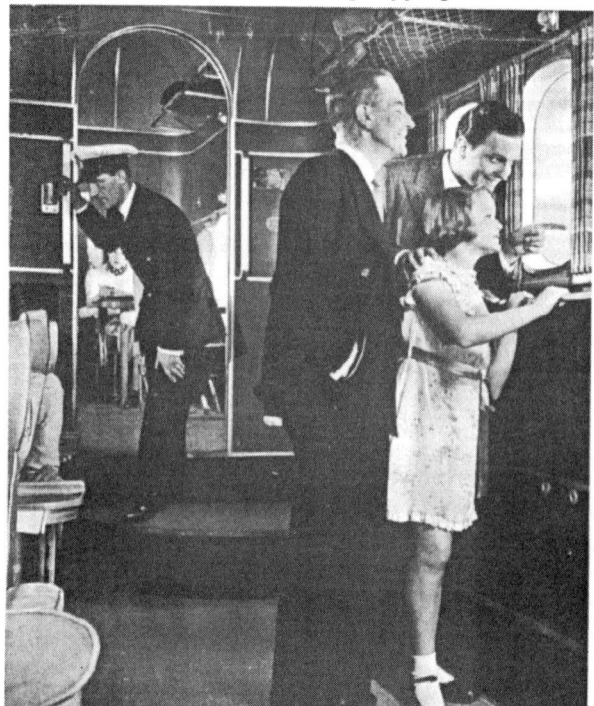

DH85 Leopard Moth, VP-KBP after a crash at Iringa, 25th January, 1939.

(Mr Ian Francombe)

So, Tom Campbell Black had gone, but he would be long remembered by those who had known him, and sorely missed by that little band of aviators who had, not so many years ago, sat talking far into the Kenya night, their dreams and ambitions as bright as the flaring embers of the log fire at the farm called Seremai.

❖ ❖ ❖

On 7th June, 1937, the Imperial Airways Armstrong Whitworth XV Atalanta, G-ABTG, commanded by Captain F. Dudley Travers departed Johannesburg northbound with the London mail. It was the last land-plane service for several years to do so, since with the inauguration of the Empire Air Mail programme, all services to South Africa would be operated by the Short 'C' Class flying-boats. This mail service commenced on 29th June 1937, with the departure from Southampton of G-ADVE, R.M.A. *Centurion*. The Empire Air Mail programme was a British government subsidised mail system which enabled first class mail to be sent to anywhere in the Empire at a flat postage rate of one and a half pence per half ounce for letters and a penny for postcards. The resultant increase in air mail[1]

---

[1]In 1931 212,380 letters were carried by Imperial Airways; by 1936 the numbers had increased to 34 million.

The African Routes of Imperial Airways, South African Airways and Wilson Airways, circa 1938

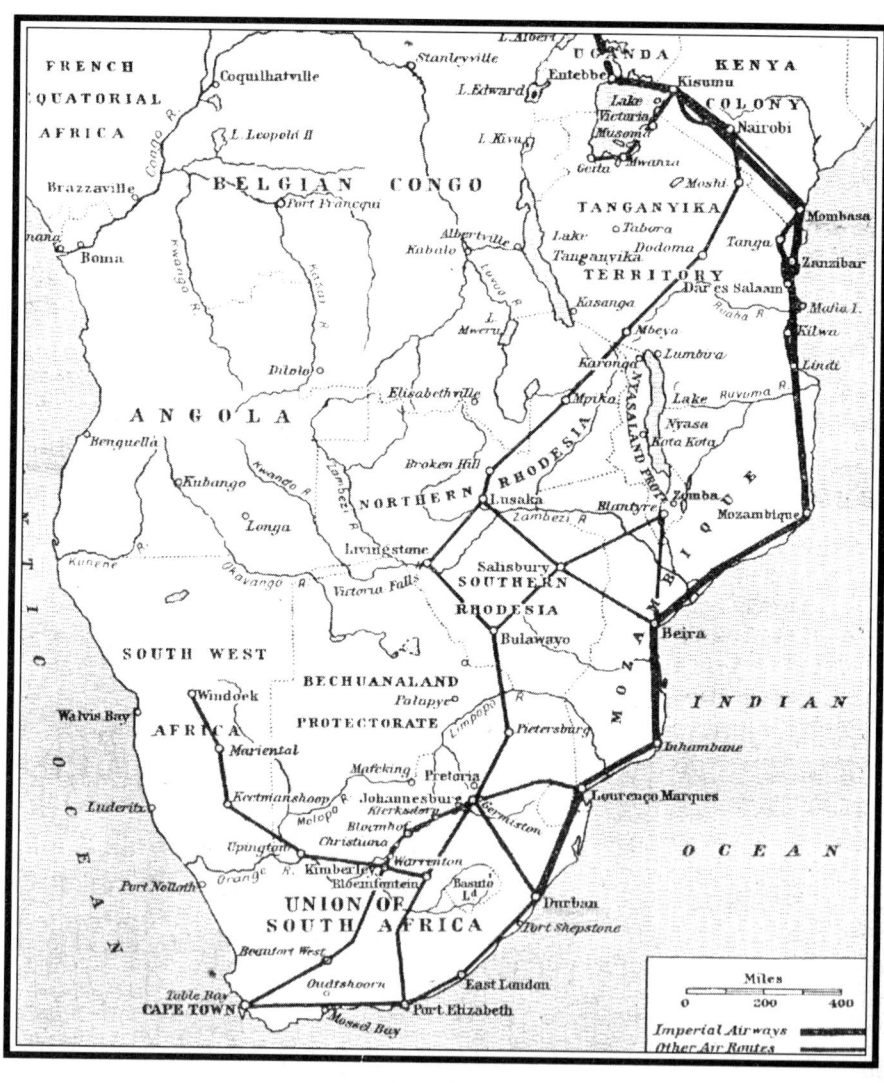

provided Imperial Airways, and its associated companies, with enormous Royal Mail revenues. Wilson Airways benefitted from this increase in revenues, flying all the East Africa mails on their twice weekly connection with the Imperial Airways flying-boat service transit through Kisumu. This commenced on 1st July 1937, with the first northbound mails ex Zanzibar departing on the same day. On 7th July a service was started once weekly from Lusaka, via Nairobi—Moshi—Dodoma—Mbeya—Mpika and Broken Hill, to carry mail connecting with Imperial Airways at Kisumu.

By 1939, the Wilson Airways fleet totalled sixteen aircraft, comprising five DH89A Rapides, two Percival Vega Gulls, two DH80A Puss Moths, two DH90 Dragonflies, a DH60G Moth Major, a DH85 Leopard Moth, a DH60 Gipsy Moth

With a few months before outbreak of war, there was still time for an off-duty flight with the ladies. Aubrey Francombe with a Wilson Airways Puss Moth. (Mr Ian Francombe)

On 1 July, 1937 a DH90 Dragonfly of Wilson Airways carried the first "all-up" or unsurcharged air mail from Nairobi to connect with the northbound "C" class Empire flying-boat at Kisumu. At Nairobi aerodrome, for the occasion are: (l.to r.): Mr F. Birkitt, deputy postmaster-general; Mr M.C.P. Mostert, manager of Wilson Airways Ltd; Mr V.G. Crudge, Central African area manager, Imperial Airways; H.E. the Governor of Kenya, Air Chief Marshal Sir Robert Brooke-Popham; Mrs F.K. Wilson, OBE, chairman of Wilson Airways; and Lady Brooke-Popham.

a DH84 Dragon and a Klemm L25A. With the exception of the Kenya Highlands Service (Nairobi–Nyeri–Nanyuki–Kitale–Kakamega–Kisumu and vice-versa), which was operated with Puss Moths and the Leopard Moth, all remaining scheduled services were then being operated by the DH89A Rapides. In this, the final year before commencement of war, Wilson Airways flew 4,794 passengers profitably over more than a million miles of East and Central Africa. The last services before the company ceased operations in September 1940, were Mombasa–Tanga–Zanzibar–Dar es Salaam and Kisumu–Nairobi.

CHAPTER 3

The New Airline

There is a tide in the affairs of men,
Which taken at the flood, leads on to fortune;
Omitted, all the voyage of their life
Is bound in shallows and in miseries.
On such a full sea are we now afloat,
And we must take the current when it serves,
Or lose our ventures

William Shakespeare
Julius Caesar IV. iii.

THE SECOND WORLD WAR brought Wilson Airways operations to an end just as negotiations were advancing to amalgamate with Rhodesia and Nyasaland Airways to the south, which would have created a major network covering a vast area of East and Central Africa.

As in the United Kingdom, all East African private flying was curtailed and commercial aviation was suborned by the Governor-General of Kenya, Air Chief Marshal Sir Robert Brooke-Popham, to the general war effort. The Kenya Regiment, as it then was, formed an Air Wing, the Kenya Auxiliary Air Unit, under the command of Captain Francombe, who was recalled to the R.A.F on the outbreak of war, into which aircraft of Wilson Airways were impressed in order to create a communications flight, a coastal reconnaissance flight and a flying training school. In addition, the commonwealth air force, which gradually emerged from the ranks of South African and Rhodesian volunteers, established flying training schools using Wilson Airways facilities.

Captain M.C.P. Mostert, who was then chief pilot of Wilson Airways, joined the Kenya Auxiliary Air Unit in October, 1939 and commanded the communication flight in Kenya. In the following year he transferred to the South African Air Force, and commanded units in Kenya, Abyssinia, North Africa, South Africa, Madagascar and Italy, before taking up management positions with B.O.A.C. in the Middle East. Twice mentioned in despatches, he was awarded the O.B.E. in 1942 and promoted to the rank of lieutenant colonel. Archie Watkins remained in charge of the repair section, was twice mentioned in despatches and achieved the rank of flight lieutenant.

In 1943, with the danger of enemy invasion no longer a threat to the East African Territories, the governors of the four territories appointed a committee to examine and report on the requirements for post war domestic air services. Wilson Airways had passed away with the turmoil of war, but it was realised that air travel would be vital to the economy and overall development of the immense region of East Africa.

The committee had little doubt that to succeed, a policy of advance was necessary that required efforts which the normal colonial administration would find hard to achieve.

The committee, noted that:

> *"It is apparent, both from general experience and from the estimates . . . that no air transport undertaking in East Africa can expect to be remunerative. It is, in fact, bound to require considerable subsidies from the East African Governments to bridge the gap between expenditure and revenue".*

It went on to recommend that a single inter-territorial authority responsible to the governments of Kenya, Uganda, Tanganyika and Zanzibar should be created, who should act as one for the control and development of air transport in East Africa, and the formation of an air transport service which should provide the following:

a) Feeder services to connect with trunk airlines
b) Stopping services along main trunk routes to serve intermediate points
c) Services for purely local traffic, including charters.

The resources of the territorial governments were barely adequate to provide the technical and commercial expertise to develop air services on the scale envisaged by the committee. This was accepted at the time and it was minuted that the committee attached importance to *"The closest co-operation between B.O.A.C. and the local undertaking".*

Two schemes were recommended by the committee for the initial formation of the airline. The first involved the purchase of 13 standard six-seater aircraft at a cost including spares and equipment of £130,000 and the second, the purchase of nine standard six-seater and five D.H. Rapides at a cost of £114,000.

Annual expenditure was estimated at £150,000 for the first scheme and £136,000 for the second with annual revenue of £100,000 in the first year, not including Air Mail receipts. These estimates required a provisional subsidy from the governments of Kenya, Uganda, Tanganyika and Zanzibar of £50,000. Furthermore, estimates of an extremely optimistic overall load factor of 85 per cent over an annual mileage of 900,000 route miles were produced in order to eliminate the requirement for government subsidies. However, the committee had no hesitation in recommending that the governments agree to the subsidies.

The report was presented to the four Territorial governments in 1943 and, due to the continuing war time requirements which diverted the energy and attentions of the colonial administration, it was not until 1945 that the East African Territories (Air Transport) Order-in-Council was drawn up. This provided for an East African Airways Corporation. The authority would consist of the governors of Kenya, Uganda and Tanganyika and the British Resident in Zanzibar, who would be responsible for the nomination of the chairman and five board members of E.A.A.C.

THE NEW AIRLINE · 43

The Order-in-Council was formally approved in London on 30th October, 1945 and the new B.O.A.C. Associate Company was launched with full technical and financial assistance of the direct descendant of Imperial Airways of pre war years which brought the travellers to Africa, who had then been carried across the lakes and plains, across the unmarked terrain of desert and bush by those frail single-engined machines of Wilson Airways. The dream of Tom Campbell Black was coming to fruition.

No time had been wasted. Already, six ex RAF DH89A Dominie (the Service name given to the Dragon Rapide) aircraft had been registered to B.O.A.C. and leased via Associated Companies to E.A.A.C. Six Kenya born R.A.F. pilots were seconded to B.O.A.C. purposely to fly air services in East Africa while they were awaiting their discharge from the R.A.F. Captains Lavers, Allison, Slade, Duncan, Davidson and Black flew the six aircraft, VP-KCT, VP-KCU, VP-KCV, VP-KCW, VP-KCX and VP-KCY, from Whitney to Eastleigh airport, Nairobi, at intervals during the summer of 1945. Although some proving flights were undertaken towards the end of 1945, the first scheduled service was not flown until 1st January, 1946.

On January 1st 1947, Sir Charles Lockhart became the first chairman of the Corporation. He was succeeded the following October by the vice-chairman, Sir Reginald Robins, former general manager of the Kenya and Uganda Railways. While holding that office he had urged strongly that the air service should be run by the Railways of East Africa. He had argued that the Railways already had the basic organisation of workshops, accounts, booking offices and so on, and that the plan which he proposed had worked well in South Africa. Sir Reginald's proposal

A DH89A Dragon Rapide, or Dominie, of East African Airways. The photograph has been autographed by the pilots who flew these aircraft. (R. Cartwright)

met with considerable opposition, even from within the railways, and it was set aside.

On 24th June, 1946, the following letter was signed by Philip Johnson, B.O.A.C. Manager, Nairobi, and posted to the first fifteen employees of East African Airways:

EAST AFRICAN AIRWAYS CORPORATION

From:Manager, E.A.A.C.	*To:*	*Capt. N. Kirkham*
Nairobi.		*Capt. A.M.T. Noon*
		Capt. E.E. Morris
		Capt. D.A. Lavers
		Capt. T.H.C. Allison
		T/O D.R. Brid
		Ch/Engr. A.W. Watkins
Ref.MEA.151		*G/E P.D. Wright*
		G/E D. Watson
		G/E A.R. Jenkins
		G/E G. Baudet
		D. Kelly
24th June 1946		*A.G. Mollison*
		H.T. Griffiths
		E. de B. West

Dear Sir,

Further to my letter MEA.461 of 7th May, to which I attached Terms and Conditions of Service with East African Airways Corporation, I have been instructed by the Chairman of the Board to inform you that the Corporation is prepared to offer you employment in the category of ( )
at a salary of ( )
in the salary scale of ( )

2. *Attached hereto is the formal agreement in duplicate. You are requested to sign and return one copy to me if you accept the offer made to you above.*

3. *The effective date of the agreement will be as from 1.7.46.*

Yours faithfully,

P. Johnson
Manager.

Nine of the addressees were former Wilson Airways staff – Kirkham, Noon, Morris, Bird (mis-typed Brid), Watkins, Wright, Jenkins, Baudet and West.

Eric Morris, who had joined Wilson Airways as a pilot in 1937, was born at Indwe, South Africa, on 9th August, 1912. Educated at Boys High School, Kimberley and matriculating from Palmer's University College in 1928, he joined his family's auctioneering business as a book-keeper. In 1936, he became the first pupil of the Witwatersrand Technical School of Aeronautics, at Germiston, Johannesburg, where he obtained his Commercial Pilot's Licence.

After a period of free-lance charter work in South Africa, he moved north to take up an appointment with Wilson Airways, and flew as an assistant instructor for the Aero Club of East Africa. He married in 1939, celebrating the occasion by taking his wife, May, up in a Puss Moth and dropping the bridal bouquet, (with the permission of Colonel Mostert), to the bridesmaids below. At the outbreak of war, Morris was commissioned into the Kenya Auxiliary Air Unit and was sent immediately to Dar es Salaam, where the original Avro Avians, from the old Tanganyika Survey, had been found stored in an old hangar. They had been quickly restored to flying condition and he and his fellow pilots were ordered to patrol out to sea, with instructions to seek out enemy shipping. Armed with nothing more than empty revolvers (there was no ammunition), and with no life-jackets, it was with great trepidation that they flew out over the shark infested waters of the Indian Ocean in the ancient bi-planes.

This period quickly ended and, together with Captain R.B. Lovemore, he formed a flying training unit at Nairobi, to train young Kenyans as war pilots. Some of these were to become captains in the post war East African Airways.

Following a posting to Gwelo in Southern Rhodesia in 1941, as officer in charge flying training, he went to the Middle East theatre as a ferry pilot with No 1 R.A.F. Ferry Unit, 216 Group.

On demobilisation, he was discharged in Cairo, where he and Norris Kirkham were immediately employed by B.O.A.C. as pilots for E.A.A.C., to assist in the formation of the airline. They were flown back to Nairobi, Kirkham in September and Morris on 10th October, 1945, where they both joined the Governor General's Communication Flight, which, under the commercial supervision of Philip Johnson, Manager B.O.A.C. in Nairobi, and with the technical assistance of Wing Commander Knowlden as technical manager, seconded from B.O.A.C., became the fledgling E.A.A.C.

The spaces on the letters of appointment were completed in the appropriate places which, in Eric Morris' case, were 'Pilot', and the salary was quoted as £850 p.a. in the scale £800 x 25 to £875.

This was little more than he had received before the war with Wilson Airways, when he was paid £30 per month retainer plus one penny (96 cents) per mile flown. In addition he had received thirty shillings per month petrol allowance and seventeen shillings fifty cents nightstop allowance.

Douglas Lavers, one of the R.A.F. seconded pilots, had spent some of the war years in the Middle East and found the prospect of returning to flying over the East African countryside, green and lush after the long rains, very pleasing, in contrast to the desert. He reported to Whitney in July 1945, together with Wing Commander Knowlden, to collect the first DH Rapide and fly it to Nairobi. They carried six passengers, mail and a small quantity of freight. The journey was uneventful, taking nine days with night stops, routing via Hurn to Le Bourget,

Istres, Cagliari, Castel Benito, Benina, El Adem, Almaza, Luxor, Wadi Halfa, Khartoum, Malakal, Juba, Kisumu and Nairobi.

During the year he went with some of the other new pilots to the B.O.A.C. base at Durban to obtain their navigators certificates, which formed part of the 'B' licence. On their return, they started services from Nairobi West to and from the three territories. There were regular night-stops away from base, and life was most enjoyable. One of the most popular stops was Kitale. They would land in the afternoon, after which they would repair to the Kitale Club where they stayed. Following 18 holes of golf, there was time for sun-downers, a good meal and, perhaps some pleasant company before turning in for the night. At Mbeya, another favourite, there was trout fishing to look forward to, when their flying duties were over for the day.

In those last days of Wilson Airways, before the war, Captain Eric Morris had flown regularly up the Rift Valley, flying the Highland service, Nairobi-Nyeri-Nanyuki-Nakuru-Eldoret-Kitale-Kakamega-Kisumu and return, the pilots nick-named it the 'London-Brighton all stops' service. Although crossing the Rift Valley escarpments forced them to climb to 10,000 feet or more at times, flight over the forests and plantations of beautiful farmlands, lakes and extinct volcanic craters, such as Menengai, invited the pilots to fly at lower levels, if the weather permitted. Many a passenger would thrill to the sight of tens of thousands of flamingo rising to the air and circling Lake Nakuru. A unique feature of this service was the crossing of the Equator four times on the outward journey and again on the return. Morris would pull and push the control column, just enough to cause unsuspecting stomachs to rise, then leaning back explain to his passengers, "Sorry about that – we just crossed the Equator".

Between Eldoret and Kitale, a twenty minute flight, lived a farmer and his wife whom Morris had got to know very well, although having never met them. It happened that one day as he was passing over their farm house, he saw the couple rush out and wave to him as he flew on track from Eldoret to Kitale. He turned above their lonely homestead to acknowledge their greeting, and continued on his journey. As the weeks passed this became almost a ritual, the little aeroplane a link with the outside world for the isolated farmer and his wife. The war came, and the friendly aeroplane did not pass by any more. Five years later, Morris found himself back, flying the DH Rapide up the Rift Valley on the E.A.A.C. Highland service – just as he had done with the Puss Moths of Wilson Airways. Nothing had changed as he looked for the little farm house. He circled, looking for his friends, but there was no one to be seen. With a feeling of disappointment, he levelled off to continue on his track, when he spotted them in a pasture – waving frantically were the farmer and his wife, with the addition of two small children.

Overcoming a host of complex problems, including inadequate airfields, poor communications, unreliable or non-existent navigation aids, shortage of spare parts and workshop facilities and extremely tight financial controls, the six aircraft and twelve B.O.A.C. pilots established, in the first year of operation, twenty-one services a week, serving Nairobi, Mombasa, Tanga, Zanzibar, Dar es Salaam, Lindi, Morogoro,

Nduli, Southern Highlands, Chunya, Mbeya, Moshi, Kisumu, Eldoret, Kitale and Entebbe. The DH 89A 'Bamboo Bombers', as they were affectionately known, had achieved by the end of that first year a total of 581,073 route miles flown carrying 9,403 passengers (at an average speed of 114 mph).

The governor's committee had not failed in their prediction that *"No air transport undertaking in East Africa can be expected to be remunerative..."* The operating deficit in the first year was a huge £25,483, considerably higher than the estimated £6000.

A factor influencing the airline's poor start was an unfortunate accident involving a DH 89A, VP-KCU. The aircraft, under the command of Captain Tommy Sack, had set out on 28th June, 1946, from Eastleigh bound for Mombasa, with six passengers, including a ten week old baby girl, on board. The pilot, with no navigational aids, and probably unknowingly or unwittingly setting an incorrect compass course, had flown a false heading and, as a result, became lost after descending through the stratus cloud at the point where he expected to find the coast and Mombasa. Instead, he could see only unfamiliar barren country, with no sight of the coast. Eventually, forced to make a descent, he crash landed the aircraft in wild bush country near Garsen, 130 miles north of Mombasa. The crew of two (a radio operator was carried at that time) and passengers were unhurt but there was little shelter from the elements and wild animals.

After two days, the crashed aircraft was found during an air search of 30,000 miles. It was spotted by the crew of an R.A.F. Baltimore on the 30th June. Captain Alec Noon flew a light aircraft to the area, with a doctor on board, but the rough ground made a landing impossible. On the third day, a ground party made their way to the group, to find that they had survived the ordeal of blazing hot days in the open, on a diet of 19 water biscuits, one bar of chocolate, a jar of marmalade and a bottle of whisky. Dew from the wings provided the only water available.

There was concern and public criticism following this incident. The ability of the new airline to perform to acceptable public transport standards was called into question. That the airline faced difficulties was accepted by everyone in E.A.A. There was a serious and dangerous shortage of radio navigational aids and beacons. In addition, the airline was receiving criticism for delays caused by the failure of so called 'overhauled' engines purchased from the R.A.F. in India. Not until they had been completely re-overhauled by E.A.A. engineers did they become serviceable. At one stage, there were only seven pilots on the Corporation's strength. In September it was touch and go as to whether all services should be suspended.

All the Rapides had been grounded while the engine modifications were carried out. The pilots were employed in ground jobs and in assisting the engineers. Douglas Lavers was given the opportunity of continuing to fly a small Auster aircraft which had been acquired, between Nairobi and Dar es Salaam, carrying the occasional passenger and mail. These small machines were hardly suitable for public transport over the great distances between the main cities of East Africa. However, the flying was very enjoyable most of the time. On one occasion, with the Chief Justice of Tanganyika as passenger, they encountered a severe thunderstorm en route from Dar es Salaam to Nairobi via Moshi. In blinding rain, Lavers force-landed the Auster in a football field near Mombo. They were put up for the evening and dried out by the District Officer and his wife, who, true to the up-country tradition, generously provided them with welcome hospitality.

On another day, as he prepared to take-off, his passenger, the writer Elspeth Huxley, asked if it was safe to fly from airfields at high altitudes, such as Nairobi. " Of course", he reassured her. They took-off. The little Auster had reached 50 feet, when the engine stopped. With skilful handling, Lavers managed to regain the runway and they landed safely, with the propeller windmilling uselessly. The lady's only reaction was to sigh sadly, her faith in the confidence of aviators, seemingly, lost for ever.

Due to the grounding of the Rapides, the crash at Garsen and the resultant bad publicity, there was a temporary loss of confidence in the embryo airline which was overcome by a reorganisation of the administration under Captain Malin Sorsbie as general manager, and Eric Morris as chief pilot.

Malin Sorsbie, although not universally popular with those who worked under him, due to a forceful style of leadership, was the ideal man to take charge of affairs at this stage. Prior to his appointment with E.A.A.C., he had already a varied and fascinating career behind him. Born in 1906, the son of a West Country vicar, he was educated at Brighton College and Manitoba University. In 1926 he enlisted in the Royal Canadian Mounted Police. After three years service with the famed 'Mounties', much of the time beyond the Arctic Circle, north of Hudson Bay, he returned to Britain in 1930 and was commissioned into the Royal Air Force as a pilot. His first experience of Africa was as a pilot with No. 216 Squadron, flying Vickers Victoria troop transports in Egypt and the Middle East. After six years service with the Royal Air Force, he joined Imperial Airways, flying the Hannibal airliners in Europe and moving, in 1937, to West Africa, where he pioneered routes from Lagos to Khartoum, flying DH 89A Rapides. His knowledge of this route was of great usefulness during the war, when the R.A.F. established the 4,000 mile ferry route from Takoradi, in the Gold Coast, to Khartoum, to reinforce the Desert Air Force in North Africa.

He gained further useful experience of air transport operations when called in to help run the Trans Atlantic Ferry Service, supplying aircraft from the factories of North America to reinforce Bomber and Coastal Commands.

With an invigorated management team, further strengthened by the appointment of former Wilson Airways pilot, Aubrey N. Francombe, returned from the war with the rank of wing commander and decorated with the DSO and MBE, as deputy general manager, 1947 brought new orders for a further six DH89A Rapides and an ex Wilson Airways Rapide to replace VP-KCU, following its misadventure at Garsen.

These were the years of post-war austerity in Britain, combined with exceptionally cold winters, shortages of every conceivable commodity and a growing sense of anti-climax for the victorious service personnel, slowly being demobilized from the army, navy and Royal Air Force.

To some of these, who had qualified as pilots during the war, the prospect of African sunshine and the appeal of colonial life far away from the dark, cold, austere British climate was overwhelming.

Bob Ainsworth was one of those who left the R.A.F. in 1946. Having trained during the war in Florida, he had developed a strong taste for the tropics.

"So, armed with my knowledge of Africa gleaned from Hollywood versions of *Trader Horn, Sanders of the River* and *Tarzan,* I decided that I must live in "The Dark Continent". I joined a charter firm called Congo Air and my first civil flight was in an ex-R.A.F. Airspeed Oxford, converted for civil use and renamed Consul. Together with a shareholder of the firm acting as navigator, we flew eight passengers, escaping the stringent conditions of post-war Britain, to Germiston near Johannesburg in South Africa.

"As there were insufficient scheduled airlines operating at that time, it was an easy task to fill a charter aircraft with eager immigrants. The trip took us twenty-eight days to Jo'burg and back, with eight days stay in South Africa for servicing. I earned a princely sum of £40 for the return trip, which was £10 more than my monthly salary as a Royal Air Force flight lieutenant.

"I thought it was wonderful. All the wonders of the world were within my grasp. There were no autopilots, no radios, no flight plans. The hours were long and the legs, in terms of distance, were short. I started from Croydon, proceeding via Paris, Lyons, Marseilles, Ajaccio, Cagliari, Benghazi, Mersa Matruh, Cairo, Wadi Halfa, Luxor, Khartoum, Malakal, Juba, Kisumu, Nairobi, The Rhodesias and on to South Africa.

Captain Malin Sorsbie.
(Baron Studios)

"I asked all the airlines en route if they wanted a pilot. At Nairobi I first saw Eric Morris and then Wing Commander Francombe, who said they would let me know.

"On returning to England, I joined a firm called Payloads at Gatwick, flying to Europe and North Africa. When this firm, in turn, failed, I wrote around the world for another job. British South American Airways offered me a job, but at the same time came an offer from East African Airways.

"I had already made up my mind that I was going to Africa, so I found myself aboard a de Havilland Rapide flown by Rex Sibson, on the way to Nairobi. Later I was not to regret this decision, when B.S.A.A. aircraft began to disappear into the Atlantic.

"Fellow passengers on the Rapide were Joe Furniss, later to be Director of Civil Aviation, and his family."

Joe Furniss, a former radio officer with Imperial Airways, was flying to Nairobi to take up the appointment of chief telecommunications officer with the Directorate of Civil Aviation. Although his passage to Nairobi had been secured, the possibility of getting his wife and two sons out was remote. By chance, he had heard that the Rapide, the last one to be ferried out to E.A.A.C., was due to be delivered. He knew that a radio officer would be required for the trip. As he still held a valid radio officers licence, he cabled Malin Sorsbie, whom he had known for some years, suggesting that he would act as R/O if he could bring his family.

Sorsbie agreed, so they found themselves travelling together with Bob Ainsworth and his wife on that last Rapide flight from England. It took eleven days, flying across North Africa, where the wartime airfields were still littered with abandoned Allied and German aircraft. They flew above the battlefields of the desert war, where tanks could still be seen, scattered across the landscape.

It so happened that when he got to Nairobi, both the Director of Civil Aviation, Stacey Colls and his deputy, Bobby Howes were away, so he immediately became acting D.C.A. The first decision that he had to make went against the interests of E.A.A.C. About a week or so after his arrival, a minute arrived on his desk from the secretary to the Governor's Conference (which was later to become the East African High Commission). A company owned by Charles Lloyd had complained that it had been given exclusive rights on the Nairobi-Aden-Nairobi route, yet they had learned that E.A.A.C. were themselves about to commence operating on the route. After searching through the relevant files, Furniss discovered that Sorsbie had given an undertaking, before the Licensing Board, that if rights were given to Lloyd's company, E.A.A.C. would not compete. Furniss reported these facts back to the Governor's Conference.

Shortly afterwards, he ran into Malin Sorsbie who was visiting the Directorate, and felt that he should make an apology. "Sorry I was not able to help you over the Aden business". Sorsbie snarled back "that's all right Joe, you got your family out here for free, didn't you?". Malin Sorsbie's memory was never too good and he soon forgot about the incident and they were later to become good friends – Sorsbie frequently insisting in conversation that they had flown together on the

Budapest and Atlantic routes of pre-war British and Imperial Airways. Furniss had, in fact, never flown with him in those days.

When Bob Ainsworth arrived in Nairobi in November, 1947, he found Eric Morris as chief pilot, with Captains Allison, Kirkham, Perry, Hall, Davidson, Fumerton, Watson, Lavers and Pat Travers who were all well established by then. Peter Duff joined at the same time and, "In fact, got to Nairobi before me. But as I had had my appointment confirmed in the UK at an earlier date, I was senior to him, although this was a point of discussion – it did seem to be so important at the time."

Bob Ainsworth goes on to describe his impressions of Kenya in those days. Impressions common to the great majority of pilots who had gone to settle and fly in the African sunshine.

" I loved everything about Kenya. It was everything that I had ever wanted. Almost perpetual sunshine, huge mountains, a marvellous coast, amazingly interesting variations of people; not least the intrepid colonial settlers who came to town in their ancient Fords. In Nairobi, still a small town, hyenas and the occasional lion would roam the streets at night, undisturbed. The natural population of Kenya, up until the coming of the white man, was half a million souls. There was space for everyone and it was a wonderful, relaxed way of life. Even in 1947, with the white man's order, law and medicine, the indigenous population was still only 3 million.

"We didn't have much money, £850 per annum, if qualified with a 'B' and 2nd 'N' licence. My first E.A.A.C. pay cheque came to 400 shillings, after deductions. But the cost of a night-stop and meals at the best hotel was only ten shillings."

Flying the de Havilland Rapides had not changed, substantially, from the days of Wilson Airways. Captain Ainsworth describes the difficulties and some of the incidents which occurred in the late 1940s.

"We flew the Rapides to Mombasa, Tanga, Zanzibar, Dar es Salaam, Gilgil, Naivasha, Eldoret, Kitale, Kisumu, Entebbe, Western Uganda, and all around southern Tanganyika. One day, at Mombasa, I met Eric Morris, on his way to Dar. I was going in the other direction and he briefed me that: "Negly Farson was on board, would I look after him". As I had never heard of this famous author, I thought Eric had said "Negro Parson". Although I looked over the six passengers carefully, I never found the one in question.

"Bush flying was exacting. We had radio, and were in contact with the ground at all times, but the radio direction finder (ADF) always seemed to show the station dead ahead, whichever way we pointed, so it was not a great deal of help. We seldom flew on top of cloud because there was no way down, except through holes, which could not always be guaranteed. Flying close to the ground, one got to know which ditch and which tree was the turning point. Sometimes we went through the Kilosa Gap or into M'beya with a few hundred yards visibility and a cloud base of a couple of hundred feet; and not for the last mile only but for the entire leg of the journey. It could be a highly stressful operation.

"One trip I remember well was from Nairobi to Kitale. I crossed the Escarpment at the lowest point near the Ngong Hills and descended into the Rift Valley, I knew it was always clear, once in the Rift Valley. But this time it was not. There was no way back, so I had to press on to the north, sliding past the hills until I was able to follow the road to Naivasha. There was no let up. On, I flew, to Gilgil and beyond, still just above the road. Finally we reached Kitale and managed to land in slightly improved weather conditions. I never forgot that trip. My only passenger was a lady who had been blind from birth, so she had no need to share my anxiety for our safety".

In the days of the Rapide, accidents seldom caused death or injury. A flat tyre on landing at Lindi brought Bob Ainsworth slowly into the Sisal crop at the side of the runway and Walter Hillary got hurt but not broken when his Rapide overshot the very short strip at Mafia, and was written off, on 13th May, 1950. Peter Cunningham wrote off a Rapide in a landing accident at Kasese on 15th October, 1951, with no injuries. In 1954, Reg Cartwright was to have an unfortunate take-off accident at Butiaba. Captain Drew ran off the runway at Kongwa, through a fence and into the bush. Captain Parker put one on its nose, due to sharp braking while parking the aircraft at Zanzibar.

A great advantage of the Rapide from the passenger's point of view was its low and slow flight characteristics. One could observe the remarkable view of great herds of elephant and other wild animals of the African bush. Captain Wilson tells of the flights en route to Mombasa in the late forties, when one could fly low over groups of up to two thousand elephant, shaking their trunks skyward, their young huddled against their mother's flanks, as the strange, huge bird cast its shadow over them. During the great annual migration, one could view the extraordinary sight of millions of creatures crossing the Bohara Flats, a 180 mile plain between Iringa and Mbeya, in Southern Tanganyika, which is laced by the meandering offshoots of the great Ruaha river. A forced landing at such a time would have been impossible to achieve, faced with that moving carpet of animals.

Captain Eric Morris, while flying low over the Flats, suddenly spotted a dry patch of land surrounded by the vast swamps. The swampy ground was marked by wet elephant tracks leading towards the dry island from all directions. On either side of the tracks they could see the carcases of elephants which had died after getting bogged down in the mud. Flying closer to the island, he could see hundreds of elephant carcases, some with enormous tusks. It seemed that he had discovered an elephants grave yard, where the old animals struggled across the swamps to die, isolated from hunters by the inaccessible mud Flats.

One night, Morris and a couple of colleagues, who were stopping over at the hotel in Dar es Salaam, discussed how they could get what must be an Aladin's hoard of ivory off the island. One of the group, a pilot named John Crewdson, had just joined the airline and had a helicopter pilots licence. They became quite excited as they evolved a plan to charter a helicopter from Crewdson's former company in England and recover the ivory, which would make them all rich men. Their dreams were shattered, however, when they later learned from a government official that all game, dead or alive, including especially ivory, was Crown Property. So the ivory was left on the island, to remain undisturbed, perhaps even to this day.

DH Dove Series 1, VP-KDF and VP-KDE, at Hatfield prior to delivery to East African Airways. February, 1948. (BAe Hatfield)

Lockheed L18 Lodestar, VP-KFC, RMA Lake Albert, *on arrival at Entebbe from Nairobi. August, 1949.* (Mr Tom Webb)

The airline was gradually making headway. In the year 1947, the number of passengers carried rose to 13,580, nearly a million miles were flown and the operating deficit was reduced to £19,617. Route planning was overhauled as the network patterns emerged. It became apparent that certain routes were uneconomic, in particular, Nairobi to Kitale via Eldoret, Dar es Salaam via Mbeya to Kasame and Nairobi to Dar es Salaam via Mwanza. These routes accounted for almost the entire deficit. If they were to be retained, the Corporation argued, then the government must subsidise them. This was agreed, together with an overdraft facility of £87,000 to enable the Corporation to order new aircraft, spare parts and workshop machinery.

In 1948, in a further significant move forward, the Corporation purchased five Lockheed 18-56 Lodestar aircraft from B.O.A.C. at a bargain price, at the time, of £6,000 each. These aircraft had been used on B.O.A.C.'s Middle East and North African network, based in Cairo. With their specially rated Wright Cyclone engines, they were well suited to the 'hot and high' conditions in East Africa. The first L18 Lodestar was flown from Cairo to Nairobi on February 22nd, 1948, under the command of Captain Monty Banks, of B.O.A.C., with 'Tug' Wilson of E.A.A.C. as first officer. Initial conversion training was conducted by Captain Alan Weston Tagart of B.O.A.C. The first scheduled service operated on March 21st, between Nairobi and Dar es Salaam, by VP-KFA, R.M.A. *Lake Victoria*, with Captain Tagart in command.

The Lockheed L18 Lodestar was a 12 passenger twin-engined airliner and was considered by its pilots a delight to fly. Developed from the Lockheed Electra of the pre-war years, it cruised at a true airspeed of 198 mph and was faster than any other commercial aircraft of its time. Once used to them, a competent pilot could land them 'virtually on a sixpence'. Touchdown with full flap (it was fitted with the first Fowler flaps) was at about 45-48 mph. They would get airborne at approximately 65 mph, with the assistance of 20 degrees of flap, which would be lowered as the speed was reached, combined with a gentle rotation to achieve full flight. The Pratt and Whitney 90C Double Wasp equipped models, which the airline would later acquire from South African Airways, were considered superior to the Cyclone powered machines, having quieter and smoother running engines.

In addition to the Lodestars, four de Havilland Doves were purchased from England, entering service on the same day as the Lodestars, on March 21st, 1948, when Capt. Phil Henn commanded a service from Nairobi to Mombasa carrying a party of M.P.s. The Doves were to suffer teething troubles from the start. Although no problems were found with the airframe, the cabin was free from vibration, with a low noise level, and the general performance and handling was found to be satisfactory, considerable difficulties were encountered with the maintenance of the Gipsy Queen 70 engines. Undue wear and tear was discovered in the working parts of the engines, when they were stripped down for overhaul, and serious faults were found in the controls operating the constant speed fully feathering propellers. A number of new engines which were shipped from the United Kingdom were corroded on arrival in East Africa. The carrying out of the necessary

THE NEW AIRLINE · 55

DH Dove, VP-KDE, at Mombasa. March, 1948   (BAe Hatfield)

DH Dove, VP-KDE, is refuelled at Nairobi West. March, 1948   (BAe Hatfield)

modifications was impossible in East Africa, and, following technical liaison by the B.O.A.C. engineering department, de Havilland's replaced all the engines, suitably modified and guaranteed.

There had been difficulties too in recruiting staff to maintain the Lodestars and Doves, which were a new type of aircraft, with metal skins, hydraulic and compressed air systems and with engine and propeller controls and instrumentation which differed on each aircraft type. The Corporation was fortunate in being able to obtain a number of staff who had maintained the Lodestars for B.O.A.C. in Cairo. Adequate workshop accommodation at Nairobi West for the necessary overhaul of all specialised items of equipment had been promised but had not been made available by the end of the year. The engineering department was forced to split its operation between Eastleigh and Nairobi West, as neither airport could accommodate the entire new fleet.

East African was now entering a new era. With the Lodestars and Doves replacing the old DH89 Rapides on all routes where airfield conditions allowed, the link with Wilson Airways and the pre-war pioneers was breaking. But not quite yet. Archie Watkins was still there; nothing came out of the maintenance hangar unless it had passed his stringent checks. It is undoubtedly true that the exceptional quality of East African Airways maintenance was due entirely to his high professional standards and engineering ability. Beryl Markham had met him in the old, pioneering days at Nairobi West..."*Tom (Campbell Black) leaned against a workbench in the newly built Wilson Airways hangar, jotting figures on a scrap of paper. Archie Watkins, high priest of engine magicians, a big blond man with a stutter and an almost holy reverence for the hymn of purring pistons, grinned good morning through a thicket of wires and bolts...*" He was to remain with E.A.A.C. into the age of the four engined turbojet airliners.

Another link with the past lay with the chairman of the board, appointed on 1st January, 1949. He was The Hon. Sir Alfred Vincent, M.L.A., M.L.C., the same man who had hired Archie Watkins as his chief engineer at the Nairobi Motor Mart all those years ago.

The new aircraft which entered service in 1948 brought the modern age of commercial aviation to East Africa. With these new aircraft, higher productivity, a route mileage of 1,656,986 miles, revenue of £295,178, and a reduced deficit at the end of that year of £11,391 was achieved. The Lodestars, cruising at 200 mph, maintained a Nairobi to Dar es Salaam route-time of two and a half hours, compared with the Rapides four hours forty minutes.

In January, 1948, the Corporation provided a capacity of fifteen seats weekly between Nairobi and Entebbe; by the end of the year this had increased to forty seats weekly after Doves had been introduced on the route on 14th April.

Staff levels totalled 594, comprising 155 Europeans, 118 Asians and 272 Africans. There were twenty pilots, all European, and forty-nine female staff, the majority in the traffic department.

The sales and reservations offices of East African Airways earned an international rate of commission, which was increased from 5 per cent to 7.5 percent for bookings between East Africa and all destinations outside the African Continent.

A DH Dove at Nairobi West in 1948. The maintenance crew are L to R: Ian Keith, Terry Brown, R. 'Dick' Wittingham, Terry McBreaty and Jack Marsh.

(R.A. Whittingham, FRAeS)

Engineer 'Dick' Whittingham attends to a troublesome engine on DH Dove, VP-KDF, while Captain Walter Hillary, R/O and young passengers seek shade under the wing. Tabora, December 16th, 1948.

(R.A. Whittingham, FRAeS)

Bookings within Africa and the Middle East remained at 5 per cent. The Corporation earned an overriding commission of 2.5 per cent on all bookings on those airlines for whom it acted as general sales agent, and the full commission for direct sales. The airlines concerned were: B.O.A.C., South African Airways, Central African Airways, Air France, Scandinavian Airlines System, and Skyways (E.A.) Ltd. B.O.A.C. were in pool with South African Airways, operating Avro Yorks and DC4 Skymasters respectively. B.O.A.C.'s York services were to be replaced by Solent flying boats, terminating at Naivasha and Dar es Salaam, during 1949. The total commissions earned on these agencies in 1948 was £35,973.

Malin Sorsbie wrote in his annual report for 1948 of the need for further replacement aircraft, but cautioned that, with aircraft prices soaring, services outside East Africa would have to be operated, to justify the expenditure. He estimated that a Lodestar type replacement would cost about £45,000 to manufacture, and in order to operate an aircraft of such a price, expansion into the Rhodesias and South Africa would be necessary.

The future beckoned, but the vast horizons of Africa alone were not to be wide enough for the energetic and ambitious airline which was coming out of Africa.

❖ ❖ ❖

Archie Watkins in the war time rank of flight lieutenant in the Royal Air Force. His pilot's wings show that he was a member of the Auxiliary Air Unit.
(Mr Cliff Sarginson)

THE NEW AIRLINE · 59

DH89A Dragon Rapide, VP-KED. Tanganyika, 1948 (R.A. Whittingham, FRAeS)

DH89A Dragon Rapide, VP-KEA and L18 Lodestar at Kongwa, October, 1948.
(R.A. Whittingham, FRAeS)

Captain "Pommy" Pomfret's Tale of the East African Coast

"It was my good fortune to make the acquaintance of Mr Singh during my frequent excursions down to the East African Coast from Nairobi in the company's old but reliable war-horse, the twin engined Rapide, which operated the Dar es Salaam, Zanzibar, Pemba and Tanga service.

Now Mr Singh was what one might emphatically call a "Contractor", a term covering a multitude of activities specialised in by Asians throughout East Africa, not least of which was house construction, followed by the dismemberment of decayed vehicles and their subsequent resuscitation into not-too-obviously decayed box-body buses and the like. All of this lay within Mr Singh's ambit, plus much more besides, including, one suspects, a judicious and discreet trade in "Black-Birding" up into the Yemen, where a good able-bodied slave fetched a high price.

Mr Singh was a man of substance who travelled far and wide up the Coast, invariably by air and, so it seemed to me, equally invariably whenever I was rostered to fly down the Coast on the Zanzibar – Pemba run.

Over the years, Mr Singh and I became firm friends and I looked forward to our regular meetings and, not least, to his morning greeting at the airport, or when he climbed on board the aircraft to take his seat of honour – the one adjacent to the cockpit door, which always remained open, to take advantage of any cool air.

"Ha, ha, Mr Captain Pomfret sir" yelled Mr Singh, (he never talked in whispers, for Mr Singh was large in every respect, almost larger than life, in fact). "So we go to Zanzibar, yes?"

"Indeed, Mr Singh", I replied, "And very happy to see you in such good health".

"You have good curry with me, tonight, Captain sir?" Mr Singh asked.

"Yes, indeed I will", I replied.

"And", Mr Singh hesitated, then his eyes twinkled like stars on a frosty night, he tapped me on the shoulder, "And I have very good girl for you, most beautiful girl in Zanzibar, you like, yes?"

"We'll see about that when the time comes, Mr Singh", I replied, not wishing to disappoint him and reject his hospitality, but inwardly fearful of the ramifications of such a liaison with the dusky beauties of the 'Land of Zanj', who were reputedly given to sundry fearful infections.

One morning in, I think, the month of May, Operations informed me that I had a special charter from Dar es Salaam to Zanzibar, with one passenger, none other than Mr Singh himself.

I duly arrived at the airport to carry Mr Singh to his appointed destination; but what a different Singh met my eyes in the passenger lounge. Not the laughing, yelling, cheerful Singh, greeting me with his usual "Ha, ha, Mr Captain Pomfret, sir, you take me to Zanzibar, yes?", but a downcast Singh, his turban awry, his face drawn and haggard as he sat clutching what appeared to be some sort of container on his lap.

Not a word could I get out of him, so I busied myself with other affairs connected with the flight, whilst wondering what ailed my good friend.

In due course all was ready. As I climbed on board, Mr Singh was slumped in his usual seat by the cockpit door. He still had the container on his lap, which I now realised was that universal object in Africa, the four gallon *debbie*, which, in various forms could be used to roof houses, when flattened, to build bus bodies or as a container of liquids, ranging from beer to paraffin. Indeed, this *debbie* bore the legend "Property of the Shell Company. Highly Inflammable Kerosine. Not for Human Consumption". If I had known what that *debbie* really contained, I would not, undoubtedly, have proceeded further.

Having reached cruising altitude, I decided it was time to determine what was afoot, so I turned my head towards the open door. Mr Singh was crying. The tears streamed down his cheeks into his voluminous beard. Wondering what to do, I decided to let well be, and busied myself with sundry self-inflicted tasks to do with aeroplanes.

Half way across the Zanzibar Channel, a claw-like hand suddenly gripped my shoulder. Mr Singh's face appeared in the door-way, he had a wild look in his eye.

"Mr Captain Pomfret, sir", he hesitated.

"Yes, Mr Singh".

"For how many years I have been travelling with you, Captain?".

"For more years than I care to remember, Mr Singh". "But why do you ask?".

Mr Singh hesitated, his hand gripped my shoulder like a vice. His hawk like eyes peered into mine.

"I ask great favour, very great favour indeed, a favour which only you can grant, will you please do this thing for me?".

"First you must tell me what it is, Mr Singh", I replied. He slumped back into his seat, gathering the *debbie* onto his lap at the same time.

"Sir", his forefinger tapping the *debbie* meaningfully, "Will you please throw my grandmother overboard into the Zanzibar Channel?"

This staggering and apparently unrelated request took me aback completely. My brain reeled. Was he mad, or was I? Gathering my wits, I addressed Mr Singh with as even a voice as I could muster. "But Mr Singh, how can I do this, your grandmother is not here and if she was, why should I do this thing that you ask?"

"Sir", he replied she is most certainly here".

He tapped the *debbie*. Then it all came out in a flood of words. His grandmother had died two days previously in Dar es Salaam and, as was the custom, had duly been incinerated and her ashes incarcerated in the confines of the *debbie*, but not before the old dame had, in her dying moments extracted a promise from Mr Singh to have her ashes cast into the Zanzibar Channel from the air.

Now here was a pretty kettle of fish, if ever there was one. My mind, no less than Mr Singh's was in turmoil. Suddenly I had the answer.

"Mr Singh, I cannot do the thing you ask, for the Air Navigation Regulations plainly state that only water or finely divided sand may be cast from a flying machine".

Mr Singh's eyes narrowed and his lips quivered. It was plain, I thought, this had stumped him. I was wrong, for, suddenly his eyes brightened once more, a toothless grin emerged from his beard. Once again he tapped the *debbie*, as if to emphasise what he was about to say.

"But sir, most honourable sir, she is most finely divided".

He picked the *debbie* up and rattled it around a bit. The contents were, I could discern, most finely divided.

What could I do? Opening, with great difficulty, the now dis-used drift sight hatch in the floor between us, we consigned the mortal remains of Mr Singh's grandmother to the waters of the Zanzibar Channel. His word had been kept. Honour was satisfied. Mr Singh had completed his contract."

It was fortunate that the old DH89A, VP-KEF, was the one remaining ex-R.A.F. 'Bamboo Bomber' with the drift-sight hatch fitted in the floor.

CHAPTER 4

Lodestars and Dakotas

1949 WAS A YEAR of continuing steady growth and route expansion for East African Airways. Following Malin Sorsbie's belief in the need to extend beyond the boundaries of East Africa, it was decided to purchase the first DC3 Dakota, which was delivered late in the year. Registered VP-KHK, it commenced proving flights in November and was augmented by a second aircraft, VP-KHN, a few weeks later. Planning had been initiated for a new route to Durban in South Africa to commence early in the year, using the Lodestars and DC3s.

April 3rd, 1949, had seen the first Lodestar service (VP-KFB) to Durban, under the command of Captain Phil Henn. With the crew consisting of co-pilot Captain H. 'Tug' Wilson and N/O Tim Nightingale, who was at the time working for Skyways and 'borrowed' for the trip, the flight routed Nairobi-Dar es Salaam (nightstop)-Lindi-Mozambique-Blantyre (night-stop)-Lourenco Marques (night-stop)-Durban. The return flight routed Mozambique-Nairobi direct with a flight time of 5 hours 30 minutes. This, the first international service of East African Airways, had been a major landmark.

During the year, the capital available to the Corporation was increased from £50,000 to £221,500. Kenya paid £150,000, Uganda £50,000, Tanganyika £20,000 and Zanzibar £1,500. Overdraft facilities for £230,000 were guaranteed by Tanganyika and Uganda.

The outstanding entry on the accounts for 1949 was the sum of £4.19 shillings and 98 cents, the airline's first ever profit. Passengers carried in 1949 rose to 36,132 and revenue was £473,144.

The main contribution to the move into profitability came from the Lodestars, which returned a cost per seat mile of nineteen cents compared with the Dove's thirty-four cents and the Rapide's forty-one cents. The Doves were proving unsuitable for the hot and high short field conditions encountered on many of the routes and a decision was taken to sell them and obtain more Lodestars. Three were subsequently purchased from the Congo.

The Corporation's Annual Report for 1949 gives an interesting insight into the growth of the airline:

"Accounting on the basis of the production of an accurate profit and loss account per mile operated per aircraft type is complicated by the continual changes that have taken place in the Corporation's fleet throughout the year. The Dominie fleet was reduced by 50 per cent, and the routes previously operated by them were taken over by Doves and Lodestars. Additional Lodestars were purchased, partly to meet increased traffic requirements and partly to act as a safeguard against the possible failure of the Dove fleet. The latter are referred to in a further stage of this report.

"A review of the operating costs of the three types of aircraft - Dominies, Doves and Lodestars - was studied by the Board towards the end of the year. With so many changes over a period of 12 months it is difficult to apportion overheads, but comparison in the basic operating costs is shown in Appendix iv. These produce startling results: Dominies, Shs. 2.06; Doves Shs 2.72; and Lodestars Shs. 2.24 per mile. The aircraft can accommodate 5, 8 and 12 passengers respectively, and the operating cost per passenger seat mile is as follows: Dominies, 41 cents; Doves, 34 cents, and Lodestars 18 cents.

"The route results show that the Lodestars made a net profit of Shs. 731,183/- on the commercial routes and lost Shs. 14,000/- on the uneconomic routes. The Doves lost Shs. 97,000/- on the commercial routes and Shs. 240,900/- on the uneconomic routes. It is particularly disappointing to note that the Doves even lost money on the twice daily coastal service Dar es Salaam–Zanzibar–Tanga–Mombasa. There is no doubt whatsoever that if this service had been operated with Lodestars it would have shown a handsome profit. For these reasons and for technical reasons the Corporation has decided to sell the Doves and to purchase additional Lodestar and DC3 aircraft.

"The Dominie (DH89A Rapide) is an uneconomic aircraft today, and has only been kept in operation to meet the needs of the public at those aerodromes which cannot accept the more modern types of aircraft due to length and surface limitations."

During the year an increase of sixty-three per cent had been achieved in passengers carried. This considerable increase had been gained during a period of serious engineering and technical difficulties. At the beginning of the year operations had to be conducted from both Eastleigh and Nairobi West, due to the lack of engineering accommodation at Eastleigh and the delay in completion of hangars at Nairobi West. This proved to be both costly to the Corporation and confusing to the travelling public. East African Airways operations from Eastleigh were finally closed in May, and the consolidation of technical equipment, supplies and servicing was completed at Nairobi West in August.

The new engineering base at Nairobi West consisted of four Bellman hangars and stores, workshops and office buildings. The organisation, under the chief engineer was made up as follows:

(1) The Certificate of Airworthiness Section, responsible for all major airframe checks and annual airframe overhauls.

(2) The Servicing Section, responsible for the day-to-day maintenance of both engines and airframes.

(3) The Workshop Section, responsible for engine preparation and overhaul, propellers, and all accessories, including hydraulics and compressed air units.

The sub-sections covering instruments, electric installations and sheet-metal work were controlled by the engineer in charge of workshops. This section also manufactured tarmac equipment.

Much of the overhaul equipment was purchased at cost when B.O.A.C.'s overhaul base at Cairo was finally dismantled. This helped to off-set the high cost and exceptional difficulties encountered in building modern facilities for advanced technical use in East Africa at the time.

The commercial department had been faced with three main problems; these were staff, communications, and airport handling facilities.

It had been found to be virtually impossible to recruit suitable staff locally, and recruitment from the United Kingdom had been far from satisfactory. Since East African Airways did not come into existence until 1946, it was unable to obtain a nucleus of trained commercial staff, as this type of work virtually ceased in air transport during the war, whereas trained pilots and engineers were obtainable from the Services. The position was aggravated by the general East African conditions, such as the cost of living and lack of accommodation.

Communications remained hopelessly backward from the point of view of fast air transport. Although the Corporation had received great assistance from the Post Office, in providing an adequate telephone exchange for the booking offices in Nairobi, fast communications between the principal traffic centres did not exist. This created aggravating delays in obtaining through and connecting bookings and return passages.

The increase in trunk route operations again underlined the inadequacy of the passenger-handling terminal buildings at Eastleigh. The buildings, just large enough to accommodate one main line service, were frequently faced with the influx from three to four Skymasters, Constellations or DC6s arriving together. This would result in the buildings being crowded by some 200 passengers and their friends, whereas they could only accommodate fifty if the services were to be efficiently handled. Nairobi West, Mombasa and Dar es Salaam airports were equally inadequate for the requirements of local services.

There had been very little investment in airfield improvements by the Territorial governments. Operations to Arusha had to be suspended until the aerodrome was improved, but it was still considered unsatisfactory for Lodestar or Dove operations. Moshi aerodrome became extremely rough, and vibration and bumping during take-off caused serious damage to instruments and radio installations. Some temporary improvement was made, but it was only of a short term nature. A new runway and airport buildings were under construction at Zanzibar, but during this work, the old runway became unserviceable due to coral outcrop, and operations were restricted to Rapides.

No improvements had taken place at Mtwara, and the airfield was not up to the standard required for Lodestars. This involved the Corporation in great additional expense, as special DH89A services had to be operated to Mtwara from Dar es Salaam, instead of being able to extend the Lodestar service only forty-three miles from Lindi.

The aerodrome problem was a constant worry. The technical equipment of East African Airways had outstripped aerodrome development, which largely remained on a pre-war basis. The future of the DH89A Rapide (Dominie) was inevitably limited and it was feared that a number of services would have to be curtailed unless rapid progress was made in aerodrome development. Even in Nairobi, the Public

Works Department could only lay murram (impacted soil) on the runways, instead of paving. The murram would be blown away by the engines of the Lodestars and DC3s and every few months would require replacing.

The Corporation had reported these facts to the proper authorities for the past three years, and was frustrated by the blame received from the general public for conditions which were outside its control. Airport buildings, it argued, were normally provided by governments all over the world, as essentially they must be on a common user basis and not operated exclusively by individual airlines. It is in this connection that the resolution passed by the Third International Congress of African Touring, which was held in Nairobi in October 1949, and presided over by Sir George Sandford, was of more than passing interest: "It is imperative to remember that the tourist's first impression of the country he is traversing, or proposes to visit, depends upon the aspect presented on his reception at the airport."

The Agreements with B.O.A.C. underwent changes as they were renewed in 1949. These Agreements were twofold: one covered the position of E.A.A.C. as managing, general and sales agents of B.O.A.C. within the East African Territories, under which, among other provisions was an arrangement for pooling certain non-technical costs; and the other by which B.O.A.C. acted as technical advisors to E.A.A.C. The opportunity was taken with effect from 1st April, 1949, to simplify the complicated apportionment of non-technical and indirect overheads in East Africa, previously pooled, and East African Airways would now carry such costs itself, receiving in return a fee for the services rendered to B.O.A.C.

East African Airways was now standing on its own feet financially, and would regulate its staff and other costs by the extent of the business agencies it held for other operators, together with its own internal requirements.

January 1950 found Captain Reg Cartwright on his way to Entebbe, four months after joining East African Airways from the British charter company Skyways of London, which had been flying early DC3 services from Nairobi to Durban. His brief from Malin Sorsbie was to operate charter flights with the DH89A Rapide on behalf of the Uganda Development Corporation and to try to establish a government communication flight.

The first regular charter was for the Kilembe mine, with a twice weekly supply flight to Kasese, in Western Uganda. It was Sir Charles Westlake, chairman of the Uganda Development Corporation, who had asked Malin Sorsbie to base an aircraft in Uganda. A number of charters were flown for the Corporation to the major developments of the time, the cement works at Tororo and the hydro-electric dam being constructed on the Nile at Jinja.

On 12th September, 1950, Cartwright started up the Uganda Communications Flight, on behalf of the government, which would create a regular network between the principal Districts. There were two services per week. On Monday the Rapide would depart Entebbe for Masindi–Arua–Gulu–Lira–Lolelia–Soroti and return to Entebbe. On Thursdays the route was flown in the reverse direction. Lolelia was a Tsetse fly control station and was fairly soon dropped from the schedule in favour of Moroto.

In 1951, surveys for the extension of the railway from Entebbe to the Kasese copper mines were begun, requiring a great many aerial survey flights, which were carried out by Cartwright with the Rapide. A site was also surveyed and selected for the construction of a support airfield for the G. Gascoine company, who had the contract for a section of the line over the eastern escarpment and the swamp area north of Lake George to Kasese. This airfield was subsequently developed to accept DC3s by October 1952.

Apart from the regular flights and varied charters, the Rapide was also used from the very beginning to provide a flying doctor service throughout the region. Doctors and nurses were flown to operate in the hospitals in the Provincial centres, in addition to responding to emergency calls, day or night.

The resident engineer at Entebbe during the early days of these operations was Charlie Carpenter of B.O.A.C., who serviced their Hermes aircraft, which were in use at the time. Later came 'D.B.', a great East African character. John Delves Broughton was the nephew of Sir John 'Jock' Delves Broughton, Bart., who was acquitted of the murder of Lord Erroll, a particularly notorious event among the Nairobi high-society, in 1941 (Later to be the subject of a book and a film entitled *White Mischief*). Rank was no protection against 'D.B.'s criticism and rhetoric. Captains disobeying his taxying signals could expect the marshalling bats to be

Captain Reg Cartwright with DH89A Dragon Rapide at Tororo, Uganda in 1950.

(Capt R. Cartwright)

thrown at the cockpit, followed by a lengthy and picturesque lecture. He did not suffer fools gladly. He was, none the less a first rate engineer of the old school. An aircraft snag would be considered for a little while, whereupon he would open his tool box, unroll a strip of green baize and then proceed to lay his tools out in the order in which he would require them. He was seldom wrong in his selection.

Later, the Uganda Rapide was supported by a Piper Pacer light aircraft, sub-chartered in October, 1953, which assisted with the scheduled communication flight in addition to the medical flights.

George Leslie had flown to South Africa in 1947, delivering a two-seat Auster from the factory at Leicester, in England, to Durban. He had passed through Kenya en route and was, as were so many others, attracted to the country. Hearing that E.A.A.C. was advertising for additional crews to operate the expanding routes, he forwarded his application for a first officer position.

On 2nd September, 1950, a telegram arrived, confirming his appointment as a first officer with the airline, with a salary of £66 per month. It was one of many telegrams he received that Saturday. It was his wedding day.

With his new wife, Loekie, George embarked on 26th September on the E.A.A.C. Lodestar from Durban to Nairobi. Whilst waiting at Stamford Hill airport, they met the other passengers. Among them were Gordon 'Mitch' Mitchell, Jock Glass and Wally Plunkett, all off to join E.A.A.C. The crew of the Lodestar were Captain Jack Bicknell and First Officer Peter Cunningham, the steward was George Matthews.

It was a two day trip up the East Coast to Mombasa, and then inland to Nairobi. They landed on the red murram runway of Nairobi West airport at five o'clock in the evening of Wednesday, 28th September.

After a long, tiring journey in the heat and humidity of the coast, stepping out of the aircraft at Nairobi was a delightful contrast, cool and fresh in the late afternoon, at 5,500 feet above sea level.

Full of expectations, they walked towards the airport buildings, large wooden huts, raised about two feet above the ground on sturdy poles. With only a couple of suitcases, customs formalities were brief, the Sikh customs officer waived them through. They were met by Captain E. E. Morris, the operations manager, 'Eric' as he was known to everyone. George, Loekie and the other new recruits were made to feel very welcome and were driven off to the Queen's Hotel to sort themselves out and make the acquaintance of this capital of the old Colonial Empire in Kenya.

The Queen's was a busy and lively place, not first class, but easy going and friendly. It was filled with people like themselves, in transit. The high-light of the day was tea time, at four o'clock. Everyone seemed to make an effort to be there to exchange stories on the progress of settling in. The big attraction was the fresh strawberry cream cake, served by the African waiters in their long white *Khanzus*, with a blue or red sash waistband, topped with a *Fez* above smiling faces.

Also living in the hotel at the time was another pilot, engaged in an aerial survey of the 'new' Nairobi city, which was expanding rapidly. He was Lou Starling, flying a de Havilland Rapide. When the survey was finished, he also joined the airline.

The first couple of weeks in Nairobi were full of adventure and fun. They were meeting new people daily, many of whom were to become life long friends. The centre of town was bustling by day, with popular meeting places for morning coffee and lunches, and well stocked shops.

When they were able to, they made excursions into the surrounding countryside and bush. Initially, George and Loekie walked everywhere in the city and suburbs, until they found a reasonably priced car, a pre-war Chevrolet, which cost six hundred shillings.

The population of Nairobi was a mixed lot. Africans of various tribes, from the Coast to the Congo, Indians of every hue, from Parsees to Goans and Sikhs, a mixed group of Europeans, up-country 'gentleman' farmers, Kenya cowboys, as the wilder colonial boys were called, civil servants seconded from London, a few 'ordinary' people, tourists and the elite white hunters, many of whom were larger than life characters, to be found, more often than not, propping up the Long Bar at the New Stanley Hotel, or telling highly embroidered tales of their exploits in the bush, down at the Norfolk Hotel, while casting a bloodshot eye out for new clientele.

For the new arrivals Life was Great. It was difficult to get to bed early. Everyone was having a good time. They discovered Swahili, the language of the Coast, which in various forms was the *lingua franca* of the people, coming from dozens of tribal groups with some 250 languages or dialects throughout East Africa. One of the first words they learned was *Maridadi*, which described everything which was lovely, fancy or beautiful. *Maridadi Memsahibs, Maridadi Gharries*, everywhere one looked, it was *Maridadi*.

Every one went to Ahamed Brothers, Tailors and Outfitters, who were the Nairobi equivalent of Moss Bros. Ahamed Brothers shop was the first stop for the tourists kitting out for Safari, for officers requiring a smart new tropical uniform, and it was an early venue for new pilots of E.A.A.C., where they would be measured up for their new uniforms. For domestic flying, the standard East African wear of heavily starched bush jacket and wide khaki shorts was the usual attire. For 'besters' a *maridadi* uniform was worn, with long trousers, it was thought that a certain dignity was required when 'going foreign' down to Durban.

After getting fixed up with uniforms, it took twenty four hours from beginning to end, a call was made to the offices of the DCA, where one met Joe Furniss, who was by then 'The Boss', Frank Moon, who validated one's licences and Doug Stewart, seconded from the UK, who represented the ARB – the Air Registration Board. One soon got to know a lot of people.

Following his check on the Lodestar with Captain Phil Henn, Leslie did his first airline flight as first officer, with Captain Eric Morris on 12th October 1950, in the Lockheed Lodestar VP-KHW, RMA *Tanga Safari*. They took a group of American tourists to view Mount Kilimanjaro, landing on the dried up bed of Lake Amboseli to stretch their legs and take photographs.

All the Tanganyika flights were real bush flying and could hardly be called dull. Most commenced from Dar es Salaam and, in those early days, the crews frequented a local 'pub' called the Maison Blanche. It was a popular watering hole, used by the locals, with a long bar and spacious verandas surrounding the building, in the old colonial style.

The Maison Blanche was owned by a mature French madame named Jeanette, who provided a *menu francais*, accompanied by suitable French background music. It was said, in her younger days, she was a much sought after young woman, in an establishment not far from the Champs Elysees. It was agreed by one and all that she ran a good bistro.

One of the dangers for those who wish to lead a quiet life is to meet up with young airline crews fresh from a trip, in a convivial bar. No doubt the madame proprietor of the Maison Blanche was well accustomed to the varied antics of the Lodestar crews, who passed through her establishment.

One evening, the usual party at the bar really got going, and the lads decided that a particularly large show-piece behind the bar, in the shape of a three foot high bottle of Amstel beer, should be seized as a memento.

The Lockheed L18 Lodestar, VP-KHX, RMA Uganda Safari, on the dry bed of Lake Amboseli, on 14th February, 1950. This aircraft was purchased from South African Airways. The vehicles in the photo are ex-WW2 trucks converted to safari cars, with racks on the roof to carry luggage and stores. The flight was carried out to inspect the landing strip before bringing in a group of American tourists the following day. This was, perhaps, the first tourist promotion in East Africa - prior to this, only big-game hunters were catered for. The vehicles pictured belonged to Kerr and Downey, pioneers of safaris and game-park tours. The figure on the right, with his arm on the propeller, was professional hunter Eddie Grafton; one side of his face was paralysed after being mauled by a buffalo, which hunted him after being wounded. The hoof tracks are from Maasai cattle. (B.O.A.C./Capt Morris)

With military style precision, a plan was laid and tasks allotted. Watches were synchronised to the second. At zero hour the main power switch, outside on the verandah, was to be pulled down. "Bloody hell, another power cut!" It was George Leslie's duty to hop over the bar in the ensuing black out, grab the bottle, which would be passed from hand to hand out to the parked car. The man outside, on the switch, was to allow forty-five seconds before restoring the power, whereupon everyone would be in exactly the same positions which they had occupied at the bar, prior to the power cut.

It all worked according to plan; except for one thing. The floor level behind the bar was lower. George could not climb back. The lads had to create a noisy diversion while he crept around and out the back. The barman and Madame were highly suspicious, though confused. The bottle had pride of place in a Nairobi 'pub' the next day.

Call time the following morning was 04.00 for a departure of 06.00, for Iringa, M'beya and Southern Highlands Club. All were patches of grass in Southern Tanganyika's mountainous terrain. Navigation was by map reading, they had to be good at that. There were only two radio beacons to tune into en route, for a bearing. The power supply for these was from Lister diesel engines, and provided these could be started, "You were in business."

Iringa was surrounded by mountains. The main Dar es Salaam to Iringa dirt road ran through the airfield, which was closed off for landing aircraft. There was a reasonable chance of finding Iringa by following the road below the mountains and clouds. The company agent at Iringa was a noisy, affable Portuguese gentleman called Joe. He seemed to be the agent for everything else locally, including Shell and Peugeot Motors.

M'beya was another tricky place to get into, particularly during the rains. Here the old Lister engine was usually working, there was a man in the 'control tower' to talk to and it was safe to go over the top of the airfield at 11,000 feet – one was clear of the mountain tops at 10,000 feet. The airfield was tucked below, the only gap in the mountains was to the south. "Another road following job". Here E.A.A. was looked after by a Mrs Montgomery, a little bouncy lady, who was also the local travel agent.

S.H.C. or the Southern Highlands Club, was special. The high ground surrounding the airfield was all at approximately the same height as the field itself, some 6,300 feet above sea level. It was undulating countryside, on which lay a number of large farms. The airfield, laid out on one of the farms, had no outstanding feature, except a small corrugated iron hut, which was the office. The runway was a grass strip, cut shorter than the surrounding meadow. It was three miles off the main road, which could and did create a problem at times.

The central point in the district was called Sao Hill, named after the post office, which was several miles away, surrounded by some half a dozen huts. S.H.C. could be a very difficult place to find. On one trip it was impossible to locate.

Loekie had gone along for the ride, which was quite normal in those days, and she was acting as unofficial liaison officer between the passengers and Leslie's crew up front. They could not find the S.H.C. airfield and were about to give up, when she came forward from the cabin and said "There is a man back there who says you have just passed over his farm house, which is next door, more or less to the airfield". They brought the farmer forward into the cockpit and sought his advice. He recognised the colours of barn roofs and the rose gardens. After that it was "A piece of cake". After landing, they found what had contributed to their difficulties. The P.W.D. (Public Works Department) had not cut the grass. This was important, as in the rainy season the high grass obliterated the white markers outlining the field.

Southern Highlands Club was a social club built alongside the airstrip founded by Lord Chesham after the war, for the settlement complex which encompassed the properties of mainly expatriate British ex-officers and their families, who had taken up farming in this former German tea plantation.[1] The local agent was a nearby farmer, who loaded the aircraft with the most superb fresh vegetables for the Dar es Salaam hotels. He and his wife used to set up tea and cakes for all, crew and passengers, during the turn-round.

S.H.C. was the last stop before the return flight to Dar es Salaam. At holiday times, the farmer's daughter, home from school, used to meet the aircraft. When she had grown up and left school, she married an E.A.A. traffic man, Jack Tonnet, in Dar es Salaam.

When it was time to depart S.H.C., the crew had given away all the extra newspapers which they had brought from Dar, and in return, had little jars of honey, packets of tea and other home produced goodies given them to take back home. There was always a stack of mail to be posted back at base. Another night would be spent in Dar es Salaam, the exhausted crew having worked perhaps fourteen hours since the 04.30 call time that morning. Then the long flight up the coast and inland to Nairobi the next day.

It was through flights such as these, all over the East African Territories, that the crews of E.A.A. would come to meet, over the years, so many of the settlers and residents. It brought a special relationship between the passengers and the crews of the airline which continued into the future. The airline's advertising slogan 'Fly Among Friends with E.A.A.'[2] held a special meaning, to those lonely up-country farming communities, to the business men flying between the Coast and Nairobi and, later, to those to whom the airline was a link with their mother country.

'Old Herbert' they called him. He was an old wildebeest who used to position himself on the far end of runway 14 of Nairobi West in the early morning. He

---

[1] It appeared to be ideal ranching and farming land. In fact, this former German tea and rubber planting district proved to be lacking in necessary nutrients and cattle raising proved to be a disaster. There was very little game in evidence. The soil was prehistoric and probably therefore devoid of life sustaining goodness. A few miles to the west, Dr Leakey had un-earthed the skull of earliest man. Tea plantations were successfully re-established where it was found that the old German neglected bushes had grown into trees. The seeds from these trees became sought after to cultivate hybrids with which to introduce new flavours.

[2] Sometimes corrupted to 'ly among fiends' by the mischievous.

used to stand there only during the winter months when the prevailing monsoon wind was from the south-east. In those days of DH Rapides, Lodestars and Doves, he probably saw them as some kind of wild creatures. He seemed to like the Rapides, didn't mind the Doves, but refused to accept the noisy L18 Lodestars. He showed his displeasure by facing head-on to the approaching aircraft, whipping his horse-like tail and poking upwards with his buffalo shaped horns as the aircraft passed low overhead on take-off. He would always provide the first laugh of the day on those early morning departures. No one ever discovered how he managed to penetrate the airfield game barrier fence, or why he only appeared during the south-east monsoon period.

There were hazards in flying the Lodestars in the hot, humid conditions of the Coastal routes. Shortly after Christmas, 1950, Captain Norris Kirkham and his radio officer, Clive Waite had flown the EC202 from Dar es Salaam via Zanzibar and Tanga to Mombasa. On the aircraft was John Carberry, who invited them to spend their lay-over rest period at his Manor Hotel, instead of the usual crew rest facilities at Port Reitz. Perhaps because of the post Christmas spirit, the two crew members fell into a trap, which was entirely of Carberry's making. Carberry was renowned throughout Kenya society for his sadistic cruelty both to Africans and animals. On one occasion, he threw his wife's pet hen from a light aircraft, "to see if it would fly". He was cordially disliked by the majority of those who came into contact with him. It was therefore, quite in character for him to ply the two crew with gin and tonic, rather than tea, coffee or fruit juice, knowing well that they could be in serious difficulty as a result. On their return to Port Reitz airport, they were probably both feeling that an afternoon flying in the tropical heat was something they could easily do without.

After take off, they climbed to 1,500 feet and selected the autopilot, which was universally known as 'George' in those days. The return flight between Mombasa and Tanga was uneventful, though wearisome in the afternoon sun. They accomplished the transit of Tanga and took off once more for Zanzibar, a flight of some fifteen minutes, they set course and again selected 'George'. Although the early autopilots were useful aids in reducing the pilot's workload, they required monitoring from time to time, particularly in the height mode. Soon the affects of their refreshments combined with the heat had it's effect and they both fell asleep, in the hot and humid air of the cockpit. As the Lodestar flew over the sea, 'George' elected to add to their troubles, and the aircraft gradually climbed higher and higher. As they crossed the harbour and the town and eventually passed over the airfield, the passengers looked down from an unaccustomed height upon Zanzibar, now gradually disappearing from view.

The Lodestar flew on to the south, over the Indian Ocean. After about ten minutes, the twelve passengers were visibly concerned, when the aircraft had not yet turned into the usual circuit pattern.

Concern soon grew into consternation, as one of the passengers, an Indian businessman who, among other things, owned an air charter company at the coast, moved quickly forward to the cockpit, to find out what was happening. He saw both pilots fast asleep, their heads lolling to and fro, as the Lodestar droned on through the hot afternoon.

"Captain, what's going on?", he shouted, shaking Kirkham's shoulder violently. He and the radio officer awoke with a start, as the passenger frantically beat him on the shoulder shouting that they had passed Zanzibar ten minutes ago and where did they think they were going?.

Kirkham looked out of the window and saw the town far below him, "There it is, directly below us" he said. "Nonsense" replied the Indian, "That is Dar es Salaam".

It was a tragic event in which a brilliant pilot, who had been one of the pioneers of East African Airways, was to face the loss of his career and eventually his life as a result of what was widely regarded as mischievous stupidity on behalf of Carberry, who certainly knew better than to tempt pilots with alcoholic drinks knowing that they were going on duty within a few hours.

Malin Sorsbie tried unsuccessfully, during the subsequent interview with Kirkham, to evince some reply to his questions which could be held as mitigating.

"Were you tired or fatigued?" "How many hours had you flown in the month prior to the incident?" "Had you, perhaps, unknowingly been given alcohol with your meal?" "Perhaps you had eaten something which disagreed with you?"

But Kirkham refused to see that he was being offered a life-line, simply replying that he fell asleep. Sorsbie was then left with no option.

"You are telling me Captain Kirkham, that you fell asleep while on duty in command of an aircraft?"

"Yes Sir."

"Then I have no alternative than to sack you."

It was at about this time that the Corporation bought a second-hand Link Trainer from the R.A.F. at Eastleigh, for, it was rumoured, one hundred shillings. 'Pommy' Ruthven Pomfret, who, it had come to Malin Sorsbie's notice, wore spectacles, was not permitted, as a result, to fly anything other than the Rapide. Pommy became the Link Trainer Instructor. This he got stuck into with enthusiasm. He was a great motor car enthusiast, general fiddler and do-it-yourself expert. He installed the Link in a disused garage at Nairobi West, and arranged for himself a nice little workshop.

For the pilots, it was always a pleasure to be rostered for the Link, it usually meant a day off from flying duties and there was a nice 'pub' on the airfield, called Dam-Busters, where all the intricacies of instrument flying and approach let-downs could be discussed over a few 'Tuskers', after a some practice sessions on the Link.

A most unfortunate event occurred in connection with Pommy's Link Trainer section. He started to miss tools from the workshop. This hurt his feelings, as he was, quite rightly very proud of his set-up. So, on leaving the Link Trainer section, one evening, without, perhaps, considering fully the consequences, he electrified a steel foot scraper mat outside the front door with the main power supply.* He then left for home.

Overnight there was a light fall of rain. When he arrived the next morning to open up his workshop, there was a very stiff and electrocuted black gentleman attached to the metal door handle and floor mat. This caused Pommy a great deal of trouble. However, the police found that the obvious cause of death was "heart failure from an unknown cause".

By now, East African Airways were carrying more passengers on internal routes than any other African airline, with the exception of South African Airways. During 1950, seven more Lockheed Lodestars were purchased from South African Airways. These were model 18-08 aircraft, with Pratt and Whitney R1830 14 cylinder engines. This brought the fleet strength up to fifteen Lodestars. Late in 1950, it was learned from South African Airways that they could not undertake the overhaul, as promised, of the Pratt and Whitney engines on the seven Lodestars. This was due to the impossibility of obtaining overhaul spares from the U.S.A., due to the increased pressure of the Korean war production requirements.

This was a bitter blow to the Corporation, as it seemed that the Pratt and Whitney R1830 powered machines would have to be grounded when the life of the existing engines expired. But by a stroke of good fortune, Malin Sorsbie had visited Lockheeds shortly before this news was received, and had negotiated with them for the manufacture of new spares, despite the Korean war, and at the same time he had negotiated the purchase of sixty Wright Cyclone R1820 nine-cylinder engines at an advantageously low price. After considerable investigation it was

The East African Airways servicing crew, Nairobi West, Christmas Eve, 1950. Back row: Sid Cox, Wally Plunkett, Dick Wright, Terry McBreaty, (not recognised), Eric Smith. Front row: Tosh Green, Dickie Maidens, Al Bennett, Gus van Schalkwyk, Ginger Brewer, Ron Herbert (?).
(Captain Brewer)

*This was the popular belief. In fact, the wiring up was done by an EAAC electrician.

decided to endeavour to re-engine the ex-S.A.A. machines bringing them in line with the E.A.A. Lodestar 18-56s.

With the greatest possible assistance of the B.O.A.C. supplies organisation in New York, the necessary conversion parts were purchased and flown to East Africa.

This was a major undertaking for Archie Watkins' engineering department, which was still small, compared with the facilities in South Africa or the United Kingdom, which had the only alternative facilities. It was probably the successful completion of this task over the next two years which set the seal on E.A.A.'s engineering competence.

With the successful integration of the DC3 Dakota services commencing from 2nd November, 1949, the replacement of Doves by Lodestars on the Nairobi – Entebbe route, which was now highly prosperous, and, a new venture for territories with a large Moslem population, the first *Hajj* flights, taking pilgrims to Jeddah, (from where they would make their journey to Medina and Mecca), a substantial rise in passenger loads was experienced. But there had been a sharp rise in costs, resulting in a deficit of £35,649 on revenue of £664,450.

With a new DC3 service to Salisbury via Mbeya, which commenced in August 1950, East African Airways was now providing the largest capacity and the highest frequency of services in any part of the colonial empire. In particular, Tanganyika was provided with a vast network of scheduled routes and twenty-two stations were now served in that Territory, compared with five in Kenya and one each in Uganda and Zanzibar.

East African Airways engineers at Dar es Salaam, 1953. Standing, L to R: George Templeman, Sid Cox. Seated: Edwin 'Tubby' Hobday, Tommy Webb, together with five African helpers. (Mr T. Webb)

During 1950 the engineering base had been hard pressed, due mainly to the problems with the re-engining of the Lodestars. An engineering section was formed at Eastleigh to undertake, on a contract basis, the turn-round maintenance for B.O.A.C. An E.A.A.C. engineer was sent to England for a course on Hermes aircraft, and passed his licence examinations with high marks, which was a creditable performance due to the fact that the technical aspects of pressurisation presented an entirely unknown problem to East African Airways. Additional skilled staff were employed for this section, which proved to be a great success. It also undertook maintenance and repair work for a number of other operators.

At Dar es Salaam, where the climate is hot and humid for the greater part of the year, the engineers had been working in the open for the past five years. At last, the Corporation had been able to obtain a hangar, rented from the Tanganyika government, although by the end of the year no power lines had been installed.

Unable to obtain accurate results from their obsolete weighing equipment, the engineering department purchased new electronic equipment, which enabled them to obtain accurate basic aircraft weights following major overhauls.

The overall performance of the three main sections of the engineering department, servicing, workshops and overhaul had been outstanding during 1950. The creation of an overhaul base in Africa capable of handling modern equipment such as automatic pilots and electronic units had been a major achievement in a country in which these aspects of engineering had never been undertaken before.

As with the previous years, communications, traffic handling facilities and staff remained the chief problems of the commercial department. Until such time as a first class network of teleprinter circuits between the main traffic generating stations would become available, there seemed no alternative to dividing up booking capacity into small allotments held by each of the main stations. Such divided control was not only cumbersome but wasteful. It entailed frequent interchange of messages between stations through the medium of the existing telephone and telegraph facilities, with the consequent delays in finalising through connections and round trip passages. The sales and reservations staff were continually frustrated as the delays in communications resulted in seats which became available due to last minute cancellations could not be offered to stations in time for them to be resold.

Traffic handling facilities at airports during 1950 were still of a deplorably low standard. Nairobi West was the main junction station for the passengers proceeding to and from international trunk route services. The general appearance of buildings, the amenities available (particularly sanitation) and the inevitable red dust through lack of tarmac in front of the buildings could only create a most unfavourable impression on visitors to East Africa. Airfield facilities at Mombasa, one of the premier ports of entry to East Africa were considered a disgrace. There had been little improvement at airports on domestic routes apart from Zanzibar and Entebbe, and East African Airways continued to bear the brunt of public criticism, which should have been more properly directed at the government. Plans for improvements at Eastleigh airport, the trunk route station for international carriers, were moving ahead, as was the new development at Entebbe. The airport situation during this period of the early fifties was a continuing irritant to the Corporation who, in 1949, paid over £10,000 and in 1950 £13,000 in landing fees, which were supposed to reimburse the provision of facilities and services.

Increased commitments not only in connection with E.A.A.C. services but also trunk services, had necessitated the engagement of additional staff. With the rapid developments in civil aviation it had been found difficult to find the right staff at a time of rising costs. The local labour market could not provide the categories required, so recruitment from the United Kingdom and South Africa, with the attendant cost burden was necessary. In Nairobi the enquiry centre which had been established at Shell House was supported by a new office at Mackinnon House, opposite the New Stanley Hotel. Plans were in force for new offices in Dar es Salaam and Kampala, to be opened in 1951.

E.A.A.C. now carried as many passengers by air as travelled first class by rail. New services were inaugurated to Mafia Island, Mombo (Lushoto), Tabora, Mpanda and to the Overseas Food Corporation stations at Kongwa, Nachingwea, and Urambo. By arrangement with the Overseas Food Corporation a Lodestar on charter to them for communication purposes was replaced in November by twice weekly services Nairobi–Kongwa–Nachingwea, Nairobi–Dar es Salaam–Nachingwea

Viewed across the four Bristol Hercules 637 engines of a B.O.A.C. Short Solent class flying-boat moored in Dar es Salaam harbour, the Lutheran church can be seen in the background. E.A.A.C. engineer Tom Webb would accompany the flight from Lake Naivasha for the Thursday night-stop. Circa 1950. (Mr T. Webb)

and once weekly Nairobi–Tabora–Urambo–Mpanda–Uranbo–Tabora–Kongwa–Dar es Salaam. The Overseas Food Corporation had, up until this time, acted as Agents for the Corporation at its stations in Tanganyika, during 1950 they were replaced by E.A.A.C. staff.

East African Airways continued to act as agents for the majority of the trunk route airlines operating through East Africa, and, therefore, were intimately connected with their developments. The previous year a new station was set up at Naivasha, including the construction of a new road, to service the B.O.A.C. Short Solent flying-boat service, routing through Lake Naivasha. But during 1950 B.O.A.C. discontinued their flying-boat services, and the marine stations at Port Bell and Naivasha were finally closed down. Four-engined Handley Page Hermes aircraft were introduced on the route from London, calling at Entebbe and Nairobi Eastleigh.

South African Airways replaced their DC4 Skymasters with Lockheed Constellations on the Springbok Route to London, at the same time they dropped Cairo from their timetable and routed through Lydda. Air India International commenced operations in February with a once-fortnightly Constellation service between Nairobi and Bombay, increased in June to once weekly. EL AL Israel National Airlines inaugurated a service in November in conjunction with that of South African Airways between Lydda and Johannesburg. Both Air India and EL AL appointed East African Airways as their general sales agents and traffic handling agents in East Africa.

Airborne from Lake Naivasha, the last B.O.A.C. Short Solent service, commanded by Captain Deadman, departs for Southampton. September, 1950. (Mr T. Webb)

In October 1950, B.O.A.C. operated to East Africa a special Hermes flight which brought a group of prominent representatives of the Press and travel industry in America, Britain and the Continent for a brief safari, which was hoped would have far-reaching effects in promoting tourist travel to the region. East African Airways played a large part in arranging this important promotion, in conjunction with the East African Tourist Travel Association and B.O.A.C.

As in the old days of Wilson Airways, there were charters flown for the rich and famous. On 3rd January 1951 the Lodestar VP-KHV was chartered by the Aga Khan's son, Prince Aly Khan, for his wife, the Princess Aly Khan, better known to the world at large as the beautiful film actress Rita Hayworth. The aircraft was commanded by Captain Jack Bicknell, with First Officer 'Mitch' Mitchell, Radio Officer Derek Rhodes and Flight Engineer 'Ginger' Brewer. The flight was to route Nairobi - Dar es Salaam - Lindi - Lumbo, where they would night-stop, continuing to Tananarive the following day. The prince would follow, in his own personal DH Dove, as the couple never travelled in the same aircraft. Rita did not like air travel, and would keep the cabin curtains drawn. For long periods she would keep her eyes tightly closed. There were long delays at Dar es Salaam and Lindi whilst the prince was greeted by enthusiastic followers.

On arrival at Lumbo, the aircraft was met by a large crowd of Ismailis, the Islamic sect of which the Aga Khan is spiritual leader. The crew, seeing that Rita was extremely unhappy about the constant attention her husband received from these crowds, who followed them about everywhere, suggested that she should accompany them on a boat trip out to Mozambique Island. She was delighted, and off they went to the pier where the boat was moored. Her freedom, however, was to be short lived, as Prince Aly appeared, surrounded by a fanatical crowd, just as the boat was about to be cast off. Aly boarded the boat and the followers were persuaded, with great difficulty, to remain ashore, where they continued with their incantations as the boat got under way. It was very obvious that tension was building up between the prince and Rita. On landing she refused to accompany him in a rickshaw, the only form of transport on the island, saying she would rather walk with "the boys".

The trip was not a success, their sojourn on the island was again marred by the fanatical attention of the Ismaili followers. The return trip was a disaster. Midway between the island and the mainland, out of the darkness appeared another boat, which, with a tremendous bump collided with them, and they were boarded by what seemed to be a hoard of shouting, screaming pirates. More religious followers, paying homage by touching their prince. Rita was quite hysterical by this time, and the Lodestar crew, unused to being in the midst of such religious fervour, were in a state of mild shock.

The following day the Lodestar was found to be very heavily laden with baggage, including that of Rita's friends, Jackson and Lola Lighter - the crew called them the Ronson twins. Jackson, seated in the aisle seat in front, always held Rita's ankle as they took-off to calm her fear; this practice was eyed with envy by the crew (who should have been concentrating on more serious things!). Captain Bicknell told Aly

Khan that some of the baggage must be off-loaded, or they would not be able to take-off. Aly Khan protested, saying, "I didn't ask for four big hairy pilots to come along." Bicknell replied, "OK, we'll leave Ginger behind, but if anything goes wrong, you'll have to pay for a charter flight to fetch him to Tananarive." They off-loaded some of the baggage and Ginger Brewer stayed with the crew.

The stay in Tananarive was much more pleasant and the crews were entertained like royalty. The highlight of the visit was a charity concert where the film *Gilda*, starring Rita Hayworth, was shown. She appeared on stage, dressed as she had been in the film, and made an appeal, in French, on behalf of the Ismaili charity, which was followed by a standing ovation.

Things were not going well, behind the scenes. Bicknell was called to the palace and ordered to fly Rita back to Nairobi direct. "No stops – just get her and her friends away!" This was impossible with the Lodestar's range, so they made a quick re-fuelling stop at Lindi and then flew on to Nairobi. Rita departed next day for Cannes, from where divorce proceedings began. On their arrival at Nairobi West, she posed for Ginger Brewer to take a snapshot of their world-famous passenger.

Several charters were to follow, to carry Aly Khan and his friends and also Karim Aga, who was to become the Aga Khan, and his brother Amin. Mitchell found them to be very nice people, and in particular, Karim, who was a "real charmer". He was always concerned about the welfare of the crew, and always had time for

At Tananarive, February, 1951. L to R: R/O from Prince Aly Khan's Dove, F/O G.W. 'Mitch' Mitchell, R/O Derek Rhodes, Captain Benjamin (of the DH Dove).

(Captain Mitchell)

82 · EAST AFRICAN: AN AIRLINE STORY

Rita Hayworth with her husband Prince Aly Khan at Tananarive, 4th February, 1951.

(Capt Brewer)

Rita Hayworth poses for Ginger Brewer at Nairobi West.

(Capt Brewer)

At Mombasa, 15th August, 1954. L to R: Steward Duffell, Capt G.W. Mitchell, Prince Karim Aga, Prince Amin Aga, F/O Pieter van Emmenis, Captain 'Dickie' Bird.

(Capt Mitchell)

a chat. He was very mindful of his future role, but a very humble person. Mitchell once accompanied him to an audience with the Sultan of Zanzibar, where they were entertained by a group of tumblers, performing on the finest Persian carpets, as the onlookers conversed and drank sherbet. It could have been a scene from the *Arabian Nights*.

In those days there were no stewardesses, so the ladies in the party would volunteer to serve the refreshments, and they would do a marvellous job. Radio Officer Derek Rhodes would tell how his transmitter would go wildly off tune every time one of the beautiful sari-clad ladies would squeeze past him, with bare midriff, to bring tea and sandwiches to the pilots.

Nairobi West was coming under intense pressure, with the increased activity brought about by a great expansion of air traffic. All the airport facilities throughout East Africa were feeling the strain, with the exception of Zanzibar, and Entebbe, where the new airports were to be completed in 1951. Estimates showed that to build a new airport at Nairobi would cost three million pounds, expenditure which was out of the question at that time.

The Dakota was proving to be a popular and superior aircraft to the Lodestar. With a twenty-eight passenger seating configuration, it cruised at 167 mph with nearly 33,000 lbs capacity for fuel and payload. It was the most widely used transport aircraft in the world, some 10,926 having been built.

The DC3 was first employed on local routes on 5th November, 1949, when the initial E.A.A.C. aircraft, VP-KHK, RMA *Kongwa Pioneer* was flown by Captain H. Wilson with co-pilot Captain A.N. Francombe and R/O 'Curly' Payne. Routing Nairobi–Tabora–Kongwa–Nairobi, it completed the round trip in seven hours.

E.A.A.C. first replaced the Lodestar with a weekly DC3 Dakota service to South Africa on May 12, 1950 on the route down the Indian Ocean Coast to Durban. Flight No EC103 departed Nairobi on Sundays, returning as the EC 104. The round trip journey took four days. The inaugural flight was commanded by Captain H. Tug Wilson with Johnny Webb as first officer. There had, however, been an earlier DC3 flight on the route using an aircraft leased from Skyways of London, on 6th August 1949, which was commanded by Captain Hawkins, with Tug Wilson as co-pilot.

For these services, E.A.A.C. employed an air hostess for the first time, overcoming Malin Sorsbie's strong objection to the employment of female cabin crew. Her name was Sheila McIvor. She was to be the only air hostess employed by the company for a period: later as the DC3 international flights became fully established, both stewards and stewardesses would be employed.

It was the responsibility of the first officer to pick up Sheila from home, driven in a yellow Vauxhall Velox crew car by an African driver. The flights departed Nairobi on Sunday mornings. The F/O together with the driver would help Sheila carry down all the cutlery, plates, cups, and saucers which she had taken home after the previous trip, to wash up. She preferred to do this herself, she said, as the canteen at Nairobi West was too rough and ready, and things got lost.

For these flights the crews wore their best uniforms, long trousers, jackets and ties. The absurdity of this was that they may have been leaving the cool climate of Nairobi and the highlands for four days of coastal heat and humidity.

The crew of four, two pilots, Sheila and a radio officer, who kept in touch with the stations on the long route by means of a Morse key, and took charge of the Very pistols. The trailing aerial, which pilots alone never used, was checked out, with lead weights and, with a large stack of charts for the long journey, they would board the passengers, fire up the engines and taxi to the take off position. With brakes on, out would come the check-list, "Flaps up, take-off trim set, seat belt sign on, carburettor air cold..." Each engine would be run up in turn to 30 inches of mercury, magnetos tested. "East African 103 ready to take-off".

The coastal journey via Mombasa, Dar es Salaam to Lumbo in Portuguese East Africa, was routine and visually beautiful. Most of the coastline was outlined in white coral sand beaches, the sea every hue of blue through turquoise to green. A line of lazy, white surf offshore delineated the coral reef, beyond which stretched the Indian Ocean, the sea of Sinbad, where the Arab dhows still sailed towards the African coast, as they had done for centuries past.

At Lumbo, 22nd September, 1954, prior to departure for Lindi-Dar es Salaam-Nairobi. L to R: Capt G.W. Mitchell, F/O Alan Handford-Rice, D.E.T.A. airport manager 'Louie', R/O Russ Blakely. (Capt Mitchell)

Over the Rufiji river delta, in the southernmost part of Tanganyika, they would circle above the rusty hulk of the old German battleship, the *Koenigsberg*. It had lain there for more than thirty-five years, after the naval action in 1915, when the Royal Navy had finally located and sunk her while her boilers were being repaired in Dar es Salaam. Her guns had been removed and hauled by four hundred chanting Africans to Dar es Salaam, where mobile gun carriages were improvised. The German land commander, Colonel (later Maj General) von Lettow-Vorbeck, then had ten new field pieces, the heaviest artillery in East Africa. Today they can be seen at the old fort at Tabora and one stands outside the walls of Fort Jesus in Mombasa.

They would arrive at Lumbo at about four o'clock in the afternoon, in time for tea on the verandah of the old B.O.A.C. hostel, dating back to the 'C' Class Empire flying-boat days, which was on the mainland off the island of Mozambique. Tea was always set in preparation for the crew and passengers. The conversation was pleasant and relaxed and they soon got to know one another. Later on, the locals, Portuguese residents, would arrive, dressed in their Sunday best, to look over the new faces that had arrived on the weekly flight.

The next morning the crew would hurry everyone up, so as to get an early start. They had to get to Durban before the shops closed. As always, the crews would have long shopping lists for bits and pieces for friends back in Nairobi, or at stations en route.

As the aircraft climbed away, in the early morning, from Lumbo, they passed over the island of Mozambique. It was the site of a large circular prison. The prisoners were housed in cages surrounding a courtyard, in the middle of which was a huge concrete feeding trough. Sometimes, as they circled above the prison, at breakfast time, they would see all the prisoners released at the same time from their cages, running, scrambling and fighting to reach the food trough.

After this thought provoking sight, they set course for Lourenco Marques and settled down for a long, six hour flight. To while away the time, they would tune the radio in to Radio LM, a popular radio station, playing lively, modern music. This was possible only when the radio officer was not using the 1154/1155 radio sets to send Morse signals. There were no radio beacons to tune into in this part of Africa. The radio officer would tune into a selected frequency, hold his Morse key down for long periods, while Portuguese ground stations attempted to fix their position. Sometimes this would take fifteen or twenty minutes. It was better than nothing and most of the time it worked well enough.

It was not always a tropical paradise. In the monsoon season the flying could be rough, with thick cloud cover and heavy continuous rain. Under these conditions all Dakotas leaked through the front windows and the opening clear vision panels. The sliding side windows leaked too. It would become most uncomfortable, the pilots would don raincoats, to try and keep the worst of the rainwater off. Quite often, after hours of torrential rain, it seeped through the ignition harness, causing the engines to run rough, which would add to the misery of the crew.

At Lourenco Marques, lunch would be provided in the airport restaurant, while the Dakota was refuelled and serviced by the local airline, D.E.T.A. The pilots would be fascinated by the ancient Junkers JU52 tri-motors, with their battered, corrugated fuselage, which operated the internal services of the Portuguese colonial airline.

On arrival at Durban, they all said good-bye to the passengers, whom they had got to know well over the past couple of days, then there was time for shopping and exploring the delights of the 'big city'. The crews night-stopped at the Park View Hotel, which was owned by Carl Erasmus, who had been a pilot before the war.

On the Tuesday morning they were ready to depart Durban's Stamford Hill Airport, often with a jolly crowd of no more than twenty passengers, in holiday mood, for the service was a popular excursion for South African tourists, who would fly up the coast to Mombasa and return some days later on one of the Lloyd Triestino or British India liners which regularly plied the route.

On the return trip, they would night-stop at Lumbo again. The evening would often be quite lively. Radio Officer Hank Close must be remembered by numerous passengers and crew for his impromptu cabaret act in which he played the double parts of Lord Nelson and Hardy at the Battle of Trafalgar, with the famous dying lines "Kiss me Hardy" and the reply of "Bugger you Nelson, I'm the Admiral now!" Sometimes, if the passengers were in a party mood, they would charter the ferry boat which, during the day plied to and fro between Lumbo and Mozambique Island. The hostel would provide a bar and snacks on the boat and they would enjoy an evening cruise, getting off on the island, for a stroll. The boat's captain would allow everyone a turn at the wheel.

It is now Wednesday afternoon, it has been a long flight and the last leg from Mombasa, in the bright sunlight, seems to last forever. They begin their descent, as the desert colours below slowly give way to the greener countryside of the high ground around Machakos, then Nairobi comes into view, beyond the Kapiti Plains.

"Before landing checks", calls the captain. "Brakes – system pressure 750 pounds. Undercarriage – down and locked" the first officer pushes down the lever which lowers the landing gear and, when the landing gear strut pressure reaches 750 pounds, locks the safety latch. "Wheels down and locked, two greens, pressure up" replies the F/O. "Mixture – fully rich. Props 2,300 rpm. Fuel selected main." The throttles are eased back, airspeed falls to 150 mph. Now at 6,700 feet, 1,200 feet above the ground, the pilot banks gently to line up with Nairobi West's murram runway "East African One Zero Four, clear to land", crackles the radio.

They are on final approach, lined up with the runway, speed down to 110 mph, descending. "Down flaps, three quarters", says the captain, there is a slight cross-wind, and he elects not to use full flap. The F/O lowers the flaps, returning the flap lever to neutral. "Flaps are down, three quarters", he replies, as he sets the engine cowl gills to trail.

The wheels touch the earth, the captain eases back on the control yoke, orders "Flaps up", then pushes the propeller controls ahead to full low pitch, returns the elevator trim tab to neutral, unlocks the tail wheel, opening the engine cowl gills to cool down the engines, and they taxi slowly towards the terminal buildings, opening the side windows, to catch the cool high-altitude Nairobi air.

With the passengers on their way and the paper-work completed, there would be time to greet the off-duty chaps in the bar of the passenger lounge, have a few beers and tell a few tales. Happy days...

By November, 1951, George Leslie was a Dakota first officer. On Sunday, 18th November, 1951, he accompanied Captain Lou Lewis, taking the EC001, which operated seven days a week, from Nairobi to the Coast. It was during the short rains, the rainy season from mid-October to December. It had poured all night and was still raining when they reached Mombasa. The weather on the entire route that morning was forecast rain.

"We got wet, sitting up front," Leslie recalls. "Some people would wear a Mac, but this was cumbersome and a bit too warm. We stuffed paper towels where the rain bubbled and sprayed in through the front windows. The side windows were opened a fraction, to suck out some of the water.

"We left Mombasa for Tanga, and flew over the sea, parallel with the coast, where the rain was less. Tanga had a control tower and the man there said they had had a lot of rain overnight, he had been stuck in his Land Rover whilst inspecting the field and the grass was under water in most places.

"Lou, the captain, sitting in the left hand seat, twirled the end of his large walrus moustache, as was his habit when about to make a decision. We circled the airfield to have a look. There was certainly a lot of water everywhere, the trees and clouds reflected in the water, where we would normally have landed on the grass.

"Shall I tell them that we'll continue on to Zanzibar?" said Leslie. He thought it was a foregone conclusion. "Wheels down", said Lou. He intended to land.

Leslie continues, "On the final approach, I tightened my seat belt an extra notch or two, hoping that the passengers in the back had understood the sign which was illuminated, for there was no cabin attendant, on these coastal runs, and many of the passengers could not read or understand English.

"We touched down; the deceleration was tremendous. I thought Lou had the brakes on already but the tail did not sink as it should, in fact the reverse was happening, we were nosing over. Just before it appeared we would tip upside down, the momentum was lost and the tail settled down with a squelch. The master ignition switch had cut both engines. I think I must have pulled it. There we sat, in the middle of the airfield, which resembled a sleepy lagoon surrounded by palm trees.

"The passengers, comprising Arabs, Indians and one or two white men, did not seem unduly perturbed. The arrival was a bit unusual. It was a *Shauri ya Mungu*, loosely translated as an Act of God, which was quite appropriate, since captains, it was well known, regarded themselves as no less than God Almighty".

Act of God or not, it was clear that something had to be done. Being a Sunday, and by now about lunch time, there was only one place to seek assistance. The Tanga Club. Everyone would be there, enjoying drinks or the traditional Sunday curry. It was a foregone conclusion that, once informed of the sticky problem, the members would rise to the occasion, with a variety of talent.

Preparations took up the rest of the day. Fuel was drained from the Dakota, baggage and mail off-loaded, channels were dug and drained. The real job of shifting the aircraft was to commence the following morning, provided there was no more rain overnight.

Happily, the rain held off and, at about seven o'clock hundreds of native convicts arrived from the local prison. The railway's chief engineer outlined how the prisoners were to lift the aircraft out of the soggy ground. This was translated into Swahili, for the warders, headmen and "choirmasters". In East Africa, wherever a communal physical task was performed, such as pulling the Kilifi chain ferry, or pushing a disabled locomotive, a headman was required and "choirmasters", to provide a conductor and leader of the work-songs. This ensured that everyone heaved in concert and avoided wasted effort.

"The empty aeroplane weighed about 11,000 pounds. Each man could contribute an average of 50 pounds of lift or shove, so, the railway engineer had calculated, three hundred men would provide 15,000 pounds of combined effort. This man really knew his stuff, a real *Bwana M'kubwa* ("*Big Boss*" or "*Great Master*").

"They got under the wings, under the belly and the tail. They pushed up with their backs and lifted with their hands. The choirmaster got them going, and after a little preamble with a sing song, everything was repeated by the assembled company and on the final word "Sasa *HIVI*", "now *HEAVE*", up went the Dak,

The Dakota, VP-KIF, stuck firmly in the mud, with the local labour preparing to start work.

(Capt Leslie)

The problem is assessed by the experts while the convicts and their guards look on.

(Capt Leslie)

and moved a couple of inches. This routine was repeated for the next three or four hours.

"Thanks to the efforts of the experts of the Tanga Club and the prisoners of the Tanga prison, that afternoon we flew off to Zanzibar, completing the service just a little late."

Wherever a group of East African Airways people got together, it would not be long before the name Tug Wilson was mentioned.

Herbert Wilson was the eldest of a family of six, brought up in the hard environment of a Cumbrian farm, near Kendal in Westmoreland. His childhood was spent, outside of school, in the endless tasks of farm life. From the age of seven he would deliver six quarts of milk on a three mile round before running the last mile and a half to school. If he were late home, to help with the evening milking, he would receive a thrashing from his father. On his fourteenth birthday, he was no longer obliged by law to attend school, whereupon his father, responding to his wish to play professional football, answered "You have kicked enough bloody boot toes out, I need you on the farm!" He then proceeded to help the young Herbert yoke up two ill matched horses into a plough. "That's the way I learned and that's the way you'll learn", he shouted as he left Herbert to plough the fields alone for ten hours.

When his younger brother, Reg, left school, Herbert went to work for neighbouring farmers for a wage of £8 for six months of fourteen hour days. The six months pay usually went to his father, to help pay the rent on the farm.

In 1938 he started studying at the Radio College at Preston, in Lancashire. He was determined to escape from the drudgery of tenant farming and find a means of discovering the world beyond the English Lake District. He would ride his bicycle 40 miles to the college in Guildhall Street every Monday morning, returning the following Friday night, often through driving rain or snow. Week-ends were spent working on the farm, the evenings studying by candle-light as there was no electricity on the farm.

He sailed on the P&O *Stratheden* on the first day of September, 1939, two days before the declaration of war. He was third, or junior radio officer. As they cleared the Thames Estuary, on the first stage of the voyage to Australia, the ship rammed and sank a semi-submerged German U boat, the first enemy casualty, before a state of war had been declared. His twenty-first birthday, uncelebrated, co-incided with his arrival in Liverpool, following two Atlantic crossings in the *Duchess of Richmond*, which rolled so badly that on arrival all the lifeboats on the port side were missing, the davits "twisted like wet spaghetti". Wilson survived being hurled from the top bunk unscathed.

After sneaking out of Dunkirk just in time, he found himself on the *SS Baltanic*, 1,000 tons. The ship survived mines and enemy dive-bombing in the English Channel, following which they berthed in Liverpool. They were to load up with shells for the defence of New Zealand. For eight nights the docks were bombed, from 10pm to 6am, on one occasion the *Baltanic* was lifted out of the water, with enough shells and explosives on the quay to "wipe Liverpool off the map".

It took about two months of solitary sailing to reach Wellington, New Zealand, via the Panama Canal. Wilson and some of his shipmates then took the train to Auckland where they boarded the *SS Rangitane*, to begin the long voyage home. On the second night out she was sunk by two German 'Q' ships, escorted by a supply vessel. Wilson scrambled aboard a lifeboat, but it had been holed by the shelling. He was plucked out of the water by the Germans, as was a companion, whose arm was wrenched from its socket in the process, the poor mans wounds slapped against Wilson's face as they struggled aboard the raider. Both the man and his father were buried at sea that night. Those who were not killed by the shelling were taken aboard the supply ship and locked between decks, where they were kept for about two months, after which they were released on the Pacific island of Emirau, northwest of New Ireland, close to the Equator.

They were rescued after a week or so on the beautiful but mosquito ridden island by the *SS Nellore* of the Eastern Australasian Steamship Company. There were about 500 of them by then, as the raiders had sunk more vessels. Wilson was taken from Townsville to Melbourne, where he was hospitalised with malaria, contracted on the island.

On his recovery, he joined the *SS Koranui*, 1,200 tons, plying between Melbourne and Hobart. After about a year, it was decided to arm the ship. A condition of the release onto the island by the Germans had been that all the seamen should sign a release document that they should not go to sea on armed vessels. This seemed to Wilson to be an extremely good, if totally illegal and absurd, excuse to give up seafaring and he moved on to the mines at Broken Hill, New South Wales, where he could double his wages as a radio officer at sea.

He had saved most of his wages while at sea, and with his pay of £6 per week as a miner, he found that he could afford to learn to fly at the local aero club.

A year later, with a brand new Commercial Pilots Licence in his pocket, he joined, on 1st August, 1943, Guinea Airways at Adelaide where he commenced flying as first officer on Lockheed 10 Electras, and Lockheed 14 Hudsons. They flew between Adelaide and Katherine, south of Darwin, on trooping flights. Darwin was not used as a destination due to Japanese bombing. His first 'command' was with Guinea Airways, flying a DH Fox Moth. After nearly a year, at the end of July 1944, he decided to return to England and joined the *SS Port Huron*, a rusty old tramp, as an unpaid deck hand.

He had been promised a flying job by B.O.A.C., but after eight frustrating months of writing and telephoning from the farm, he was finally told that they "had plenty of pilots already, but radio officers were as scarce as hens teeth". Reluctantly, as he was now penniless without work, he accepted the R/O position and after a short refresher course at Bristol, was posted to Iraqi Airways, a B.O.A.C. subsidiary company, in Baghdad.

'Tug', as he became known, due to his seafaring background, now found himself as a fully licensed pilot, with navigators certificate and marine and air radio licences, working as a radio officer on DH Rapides. There were times when he found this particularly hard to bear. On one occasion a captain ground-looped the Rapide on landing at Baghdad, swung off the runway and by pure luck careered back onto the runway in a cloud of dust. The general manager, who was none other than Colonel M. C. P. Mostert, asked him, "Tug, as a pilot, please put in a report on the incident". This rubbed salt into the wound. Wilson told him in no uncertain terms that he had "No bloody intention of reporting on a captain while on a radio officer's salary", adding as he left the room, "but I'll tell you this, I've just done my last flight with Captain X!".

Early in May 1946 Wilson left Baghdad, unhappy with B.O.A.C. and his lack of progress to a pilot's position. He went to Cairo and renewed his licence on an old DH Dragonfly, "tied up with string and wire". Within a short time he had obtained a Rapide command with Middle East Airways, another company connected with B.O.A.C. at the time. During his first eighteen months he had logged 1,800 hours, and had loved every minute of it. At the end of 1947, B.O.A.C. severed their connection with M.E.A. and all their pilot's contracts were terminated. Although Wilson had joined locally, and was not a B.O.A.C. employee, he received a letter of termination also. As he climbed aboard the Rapide to return to England, the M.E.A. chief executive, Fowzi Hoss, asked him to return to the airline. But he had already been in touch with East African Airways, and explained that he felt obliged to take a job with them, should it be offered.

Tug Wilson took up his employment with East African Airways on 1st January, 1948, with a new bride. They were housed in basic accommodation near Eastleigh airport. It was not what they had expected and Wilson began to regret leaving the exciting and sophisticated city of Beirut, with his salary of £2,400 which he had exchanged for these colonial African backwoods and a salary of £800.

Nothing seemed to go right. The Baghdad ground-looper had also been hired by E.A.A., only to be fired soon afterwards for getting lost. His wife spent long, miserable, hours at the airport waiting for him to return from flights, but it was better than staying at home in the "dog box" (Wilson's description) which had been provided for them. Things improved when they found their own house, which they bought with Tug's savings from Beirut.

Perhaps due to Wilson's own character and background, there seemed often to be a conflict between him and those who held his interests in thrall. Soon after joining the airline, he had written a comprehensive route information booklet, something which was put to great use by the crews and which pre-dated the manuals which would follow. He did not seem to get fair recognition for his efforts. He considered leaving the airline, and wrote to several prospective employers, but was offered only junior first officer positions, as the strong pilot's unions would never permit direct entry captains.

By the early 1950s, Tug Wilson was a Lodestar captain. One of his experiences at that time concerned a green mamba, one of the deadliest snakes in Africa.

It was on 25th April, 1952, the passengers had been boarded, doors closed, and the Lodestar was ready to commence its flight. The two radial engines pulsed and throbbed, the propeller blades glistening as they scythed through the warm air. Wreathes of moist air curled lazily up from the tall grass, wet from recent rain, at the edge of the airfield. A warm, humid breeze did little to alleviate the discomfort of the sticky heat. The temperature in the cockpit was like an overheated greenhouse.

The flight, from Dar es Salaam, was a short one, some thirty minutes, over shark-infested waters, to Zanzibar. Every seat in the Lodestar was full. Captain Tug Wilson and his radio officer, Alan Handford-Rice, completed their cockpit checks and, following a crackling on the radio, thumbs up from the R/O, indicated that they were clear to taxi to the take-off position.

The muted throb of the engines gave way to a growl, as the throttles were pushed open. The propellers made silvery discs as the revolutions increased. On releasing the brakes, the Lodestar ambled forward, reluctantly at first, then gradually built up taxying speed over the rough surface. Reaching the end of the runway, the pre take-off checks were quickly completed, the radio crackled again and they were cleared for take-off. Wilson pushed the throttles open, the engine's growl changed to a powerful roar, and the plane started to roll down the runway, which held a certain fascination for all pilots, as it ended on a cliff top, on the edge of the harbour. The airspeed indicator rapidly moved upwards through seventy, eighty, ninety miles per hour. The hydraulic rams in the undercarriage were beginning to thump up and down, indicating a semi-airborne state. Taking a final scan across the instrument panel, before rotating, Wilson's eyes were attracted to something unusual, a movement which he quickly discerned was a snake, a green mamba, wriggling round the radio officer's control column. None of his emergency drills had taken account of such an eventuality. One of the worst scenarios is loss of an engine on take-off, something which all professional pilots are tested on regularly. That was something Wilson would have willingly exchanged for this. Struggling with the now airborne Lodestar, one eye on airspeed the other on the wriggling green mamba, Wilson shouted to the terrified radio officer "Get out!" This order was totally unnecessary, for he had already unfastened his seat belt and was, ashen faced, scrambling past Wilson, even as he spoke.

Wilson was now alone in the cockpit, with the mamba. He selected wheels up and eased the throttles back to climb power, as the speed built up to 150 mph and the altimeter needle struggled to touch two hundred feet. Throwing the aircraft into a steep turn, he picked up the hand-mike, "East African zero zero one, we're coming back in, we have a snake in the cockpit". There followed a few seconds of silence. "Why don't you take more water with it, Tug?", was the reply from the tower. Wilson gave them full marks for sympathy and understanding!

He turned to Handford-Rice, now standing in the radio compartment behind him, "For God's sake keep the communication door shut, if the passengers catch on to what is happening, they'll panic and run to the back, we'll go way out of trim". It was not necessary to explain the result of such an occurrence.

The mamba, in the meantime, had leapt from the control column to the top of the instrument panel and across to Tug's side of the cockpit, where its diamond shaped head, with baleful eyes, was weaving sinuously from side to side, about eighteen inches from his face. "Stay there, you little devil", he thought, "and we'll all stand a chance of survival". He tried hard, as he flew the Lodestar back into the landing pattern, to remember how long the venom of the green mamba would take to transfer one to the next world, three minutes, five? It was vital to get the Lodestar down on the ground as soon as possible, fifteen lives were at stake.

Banking steeply, the lower wing seeming awfully close to the tops of the palm trees, he turned on to base leg, continuing the turn onto final approach, "East African zero zero one, finals", he called. "Clear to land", replied the controller, the low circuit and steep turns close to the tops of the palm trees having convinced him that all was not as it should have been.

The airspeed indicator was moving down to 100 mph and the ground was rushing up at an alarming rate, when the mamba made its next move, suddenly dropping down from the instrument panel, towards Tug's bare ankles. Due to the particularly hot weather, he had pushed his long socks down for comfort. Even bush shirt and shorts can prove uncomfortable in the African rainy season. Questions flooded into his brain. Should he continue with the landing, although it seemed that a snake bite was imminent? Would it be better to abandon the approach, climb away and try to deal with the snake? In the time it took for these messages to flash through his mind, his professional training kept him physically working and thinking about flying the Lodestar. They were close to the runway threshold. The airspeed indicator was falling through ninety, eighty five, eighty. He opened the throttles slightly, pressing forward on the control yoke, much lower than eighty and a subsequent stall would have them all dumped in a mass of flames among the trees.

The altimeter needle was passing the fifty feet mark when he felt the mamba's passage from right to left across his bare ankles. The velvet caress seemed yards long. As the runway threshold slipped beneath the plane, Wilson closed the throttles and a lifetime of three seconds passed before the last part of the mamba slid off his naked flesh, as the rubber of the tyres kissed the runway and he concentrated on keeping the Lodestar straight, down the undulating surface.

He did not remember much about the fast taxi to the ramp, the hurried shut down of the engines and cutting of the switches. The passengers were disembarked, with the excuse that there had been some technical fault, then, with the help of the ground staff and engineers, the baggage was gingerly unloaded from the nose locker. As the last suitcase was removed, there it was, one metre of green mamba. One of the engineers held it down with a long broom, another dispatched it with a panga.

Some days later, Wilson was sitting in the cockpit and saw through the windshield the coil of a snake. "Oh hell, not another one", he thought and, leaping out of his seat grabbed a newspaper from the hands of a passenger - who must have thought he had gone berserk - left the cabin and jumped on the wing with the paper now rolled ready to swipe the creature off the windscreen. The snake was tied to the aerial by a piece of string. Looking across towards the terminal he saw a group of crew members "laughing their damn fool heads off". He thought the slipstream would soon sever the string, but it thumped on the roof all the way to the landing at Mombasa.

The first flight of East African Airways to operate to the United Kingdom was chartered at the end of April, 1950 to take a load of "groundnutters", (contract staff from the Tanganyika Ground Nut Scheme), home to England. With Wilson in command, Johnny Webb as first officer and Curly Payne the radio officer, they departed from Kongwa on the first stage of the long journey. The flight made it's way northwards across the wilderness of East Africa and the Sudan. After refuelling at Khartoum, they set course for Benghazi.

At 10,000 feet they hit an 'air pocket'. Wilson's head sank into his neck, Johnny Webb, who had just left his seat in order to visit the toilet, "was glued to the ceiling from head to backside". When they hit bottom, he was spread-eagled in the passageway behind the cockpit and was lucky not to have broken a limb on one of the various cockpit protrusions. The altimeter read 1,000 feet lower. Several passengers, who had ignored the seat belt sign, had their heads pushed through the overhead wire luggage rack. George Boursnell, the steward, reported that he had been glued to the roof with a case of beer in his arms, causing some breakages. Using his captain's discretion, Wilson instructed him to issue a free beer all round. On arrival in London, the passengers 'passed the hat round' and the princely sum (in those days) of £10 helped the crew to celebrate the first E.A.A. flight to the United Kingdom.

There was an occasion in the spring of 1951 when Wilson and his crew, F/O George Leslie, R/O Paddy Murray and F/E Ginger Brewer were at Lumbo, on the night-stop down to Durban. Tug Wilson had been invited on his own to a beach party the previous evening and, when he was called in the morning, he was not at all well. The three members of his crew stood round the bed surveying their captain, who looked quite green, and suffered severe stomach gripes. As they commiserated with him, he looked up at them through bleary, blood-shot eyes and, raising his head said "You lot of bloody vultures! Standing around waiting for me to die just so you can have a day off here! Well, I won't - I will be up soon - just get me to the aircraft". He recovered by the time they got to Durban, but George Leslie was the virtual commander of that part of the flight.*

Until the advent of the high flying turbo-jet airliners, the weather was an enduring hazard. The Lockheed Lodestar and the DC3 Dakota, with all its merits, were still lonely islands in the sky on many of the journeys, through those great tropical storm belts, undertaken by East African Airways. Captain Wilson's log book shows one such long distance charter flight, again in April 1950, from Tananarive to Nairobi, a distance of 1,414 nautical miles. Wilson (with Johnny Webb as co-pilot), recalls the flight, of some eight and a half hours duration, in which they encountered cumulo-nimbus over Madagascar rising to forty or fifty thousand feet. The aircraft "shook and shivered like a frightened horse", although at least twenty miles from the base of the storm cloud, which was sprouting forked lightning in a continuous curtain. Wilson says that he has never seen the equal of that storm and would have taken his chances landing in the dense, undulating jungle below, rather than stick his nose into that fiery curtain.

---

*See Notes to second edition, page 446.

On the delivery flight of DC3, VP-KJQ, from Nottingham in August 1952, with Pommy Pomfret as first officer and Frank MacNabb as R/O, they were inbound for Khartoum, (it would seem to Wilson that Khartoum was his Nemesis). It was night and all around them were great black, solid masses of cumulo-nimbus, lit by a barrage of lightning. The aircraft was fully loaded and the passengers were already worried when, at 2,000 ft they hit an updraught from a nearby cumulo-nimbus storm cell. Within a few seconds they were at 8,000 ft. The Dakota "was stood on its tail, still rising, with all power off and the airspeed indicator reading zero". They landed that night, 2nd August, 1952, in heavy rain with a blustering cross wind and "barely enough fuel for another circuit". They had completed the leg from Benghazi to Khartoum, some 1,422 miles, in nine hours.

Due to its short range capability, the Lodestar used to stop at Quelimane on the Durban service, to refuel. Prior to the DC3s taking over the service, Captain Roger Drew was landing in a Lodestar when a tornado hit the airfield, completely destroying the control tower. It was a stroke of incredible luck that the aircraft escaped damage. With the introduction of the DC3s, Quelimane was dropped, since they could fly direct Dar es Salaam – Lumbo and later, Beira, which replaced Lumbo on the route.

1951 had been a bad year, financially, for East African Airways. The deficit had risen from £35,649 in 1950 to an alarming £76,000. Fuel costs had risen substantially during the year, (the first of many fuel crises had occurred in May, when the Anglo-Iranian Oil Company was nationalised, together with the Persian oil industry). Four of the DH89 Dragon Rapides were sold, one each to Caspair and Noone and Pearce Air Charters, of Nairobi, and two were exported to Israel. Another, VP-KEB, piloted by Peter Cunningham, was involved in an accident at Kasese on 15th October, when the port wheel struck a patch of soft earth, probably the result of some aggressive behaviour by buffalo the previous night, swung and hit a bank at the side of the runway. Fortunately, there had been no casualties among the two passengers, but the aircraft was subsequently written off.

On 15th November, 1951, the new airport at Entebbe was formally opened, East African Airways provided an exciting flying display by a Lodestar, piloted by Captain Tug Wilson, accompanied by R/O Frank MacNabb. For a temporary period during that month, Eastleigh airport had become unserviceable due to heavy rain, and all international trunk services were diverted to Entebbe. This required a rapid deployment of staff and the introduction of a special airlift between Nairobi and Entebbe.

The year had been an excellent one from an operational aspect. 13, 700 services were operated and there were only four technical cancellations, one due to weather and three due to aircraft unserviceability. With the fleet reduced and redundant aircraft sold, the capacity was increased by 32%. Revenue remained buoyant and was increased by 29% and the number of passengers carried by 31%.

For the second year in succession East African Airways undertook *Hajj* flights for pilgrims to Jeddah. This year the charters were conducted in partnership with Aden Airways, who carried the passengers on to Jeddah from Aden, where the East

African service terminated. Lodestars and DC3s were chartered by the British government to fly Army personnel to Khartoum, where there were disturbances and to Rhodesia for National Service exercises.

Towards the end of 1951, three of the Lodestars were flown to Blackbushe in England from where they would be ferried to the USA, where they had been sold. Among the Lodestars, which had been standing neglected for some time outside the hangars at Nairobi West were VP-KHA, VP-KHB and VP-KHE, irreverently termed 'How Awful' 'How Bloody' and 'How Evil' by the crews. Warnings were issued by operations management that correct radio procedures should be followed, and the practice should cease. (The international aviation phonetic alphabet at that time designated the letter 'H' as 'How'). 'How Evil' together with VP-KFC and VP-KFF were prepared for flight by the engineering department, given new American registrations, N94536, N94537 and N94538. The route to England was via Juba – Wadi Seidna – Wadi Halfa – El Adem – Malta – Nice – Blackbushe. Captain Eric Morris, Radio Officer Derek Rhodes and Flight Engineer Ginger Brewer were to fly N94538 in the rear, carrying a selection of spares which may be required en route. Eric Morris had not flown anywhere north of Cairo, but Derek Rhodes had flown with Malin Sorsbie before the war with the old British Airways.

Problems began, however, before they even left Nairobi. Each of the Lodestar's four fuel tanks held 125 gallons. In normal E.A.A.C. service, to allow for payload, they were never filled beyond 100 gallons. As a result the integral wing-tank seals had perished and when the fuel level passed the 100 gallons mark, it started to seep into the belly freight and baggage lockers. As the delivery deadline was fixed, there was no time to drain and re-seal the tanks. It was decided to leave the tanks full for the first leg and at Juba top-up to the 100 gallon mark in each tank. They would select each tank in turn, to use up the excess twenty-five gallons as quickly as possible. With normal care and attention, this procedure was considered to be quite safe.

They had been airborne for a couple of hours when Derek Rhodes went back to the rear of the aircraft to smoke a cigarette. It was not long after he returned to the cockpit that Ginger Brewer smelt smoke. Rhodes was sent back very smartly, with a fire extinguisher, everyone suddenly concerned about the fuel leakage earlier. He had used a waxed cup as an ash tray, and had stubbed out his cigarette in it before returning to his seat – or he thought that he had, for it was smouldering in the bottom of the cup, in a hold-all behind one of the seats.

After they had recovered from this upset, things went smoothly, flying across the North African desert until, just as Malta came into sight, the port engine started to cut out. There was no electric fuel pump on those Lodestars, they were equipped only with a hand operated 'wobble' pump situated beneath the throttle quadrant. As they made their approach into Luqa, Brewer pumped energetically, but just as they were on short final the engine gave up completely. They made a successful landing, but it was impossible to taxi with one engine inoperative and they were towed to the apron. When the carburettor filter was checked, it was found to be completely choked with mud. The starboard filter was nearly as bad – they had been very close to disaster. The sludge had accumulated in the fuel tanks during the months that the aircraft had stood un-attended at Nairobi and had eventually worked its way into the carburettors.

With cleaned-up carburettor filters, they were soon on their way to Nice, where they night-stopped. The next morning they found the tail-wheel had a flat tyre. The spares list showed '1 tail-wheel assy'. Unfortunately for Ginger Brewer, it was dismantled in its component pieces plus tyre. By the time it had been assembled and fitted, the weather had deteriorated making it impossible to clear the mountains behind Nice. They decided to follow the coastline to Marseilles and then route via Bordeaux. The weather continued to deteriorate further and they were losing sight of the ground. It became imperative to land. They had no VHF radio and no HF frequencies for the area. They spotted an aircraft which was obviously letting down for landing, so following it in, they landed at Bordeaux. Air traffic control were very kind to the naive African colonials and B. E. A. arranged accommodation for them for the night. Next day they departed in good weather and heading for England they passed over Mont Saint Michel and across the Channel. Once again they were in trouble with their radio, but after a great deal of trial and error Derek Rhodes managed to raise GPO Birdlip on W/T, who passed their messages to Blackbushe.

Relations between E.A.A.C. and its political masters was becoming strained as the Corporation tried to maintain financial viability. The accounts for the year 1951 were summarised as follows:

Revenue
Passengers, Freight, Mail, Contract and Miscellaneous £845,000
Estimated due from Kenya and Tanganyika
Governments 10,279
                                                                                                                                £855,279

Expenditure
Cost of all Operations £922,916
Operating Loss £67,637

To which must be added Interest at £3. 5%
on Government held Stock and Loan charges 7,753
Board Expenses 622
                                                                                                                                (£76,012)

The East African governments had been paid by the Corporation in landing fees some £20,000, in rentals some £7,000 and in interest on their stock almost £8,000, a total of approximately £35,000 (and it was known that landing fees were to be further increased in 1952). Against this the Corporation expected to receive for 1951 only some £10,000 from Kenya and Tanganyika, in roughly equal proportions, against the cost of operating the uneconomic services, the Corporation having to include a heavy shortfall of £31,834, being the difference between the gross deficit resulting from operating the uneconomic services and the expected payment, as a loss within its ordinary trading results.

The position of East African Airways was clearly supported by the original East African Territories (Air Transport) Order in Council, 1945, Section 20, which stated:

"The Corporation shall not be required by any of the respective Governments of the East African Territories to provide air transport facilities gratuitously, or subject to preferential conditions or at a rate of charge which is insufficient to meet the cost involved in the provision of such facilities, unless the Government concerned undertakes to pay the amount of loss incurred by reason of the provision of such grant of facilities."

If this Section had been properly implemented over the years to the end of 1951 the Corporation would have received £145,032 from the governments of Kenya and Tanganyika, whereas it had only received £61,476, a shortfall of £83,556. Full implementation would have resulted in the Corporation showing an accumulated surplus of £19,046 to the end of 1950, and an accumulated deficiency of £26,474 to the end of 1951.

The position at the end of 1951 was that approximately £110,000 of capital had been spent, and the Board of East African Airways made strong suggestions to the Territorial governments that the Corporation should be reimbursed in accordance with the Order in Council, and that they should also meet the actual loss incurred in the years 1945-51 of £26,474 by a division between the Territories, to be agreed.

The Corporation continued to act as general agents for B.O.A.C., general sales and traffic handling agents for Aden Airways, Air India International, Central African Airways, El Al, Sabena, Scandinavian Airlines System and South African Airways, and as traffic handling agents for Ethiopian Airlines and certain charter companies. B.O.A.C. had increased their frequency to a daily service and introduced special round trip and family excursion fares for East African residents. Trial flights with Comet 1 aircraft had been undertaken on an ad hoc basis and it was anticipated that a regular thrice weekly service through Entebbe would be inaugurated in April 1952.

The political situation in Egypt (In October The Egyptian Parliament had passed unanimously Bills abrogating the Anglo-Egyptian Treaty of 1936 and the 1899 Sudan Condominium Agreement) caused a temporary dislocation of B.O.A.C. timetables – with the independence of Libya in December, it was an indication of the enormous changes which were to create a permanent change in the way in which the British viewed the world.

Outside of East Africa, the world was in turmoil. Still unrecovered from the deprivations of the second world war, the bitter, costly, disengagement from Palestine in 1948, and the on-going fight against communist terrorism in Malaya, Britain was again engaged in combat, together with the United States, with the forces of North Korea, in the Far East. In East Africa, the cosy world of those who had migrated to find a better life in the sun, was beginning to see the tip of a long shadow.

During 1950, sporadic outbursts of violence had been experienced in the Rift Valley and the White Highlands of Kenya. These were attributed to an organisation called Mau Mau, an African secret society, composed mainly of Kikuyu. The aims were not clear, but it was believed by the government to be political in its intentions and a threat to the wellbeing and government of the colony. It was, as a result, proscribed. At the same time, a political organisation, which had been in existence for several years, the Kenya African Union, was openly recruiting membership from all tribal groups, under the leadership of a Kikuyu leader. His name was Jomo Kenyatta.

In 1951, Jomo Kenyatta was addressing meetings of 30,000 people, or more, claiming political rights and justice for the African people. Across the African Continent, in Ghana, the first general elections had been permitted in February. Kwame Nkrumah was appointed Leader of Government Business. It was inconceivable to some and disquieting to many of the white settlers of Kenya Colony that this event in far away Accra could foretell an end to their dreams and ambitions in the country which they had fashioned with English farmsteads and mock-tudor leafy suburbs, carefully separated from the garish architecture of the Indian sub-continent which, in turn, shielded them from the hovels of the native people.

In those busy days of the early 1950s, a few burned huts, or panga attacks 'up country' was of little significance. The white population was growing constantly, from 12,000 in 1945 to nearly 50,000. Capital was pouring into Nairobi from Britain and the United States. The Colonial Development Corporation, financed partially by the British government and partly by loans raised on the government's guarantee, was supplying finance and expertise to build new roads, supply electricity, water, irrigation and forest management, throughout East Africa. In the wake of these development plans came the passengers and cargoes which would help to boost the fortunes of East African Airways.

In Tanganyika, in the late 1940s, hundreds of British workmen, mostly ex-service men, had been flown down to Dar es Salaam and thence on to Lindi and Nachingwea following the inception of the British government inspired Ground Nut Scheme. Bush was cleared for miles to make landing strips for the Dakotas. A new port was built at Mtwara, to handle the fuel required by the hundreds of vehicles engaged on the massive project. The bush clearing machines were very thirsty. They were war surplus Sherman tanks, converted in England by Vickers Armstrong and re-christened 'Shervic'. They were reputed to consume one gallon of petrol per mile.

The pilots of East African Airways, flying into the cleared strips at 'Nach', Songea, Kongwa, Urambo, Mpanda and others long since forgotten and returned to the bush, could see, on clear, dry days the 'Shervics' working from, perhaps, thirty or forty miles away. A giant pall of red dust would rise high into the sky as half a dozen of the tank-like vehicles would churn through the bush, squashing everything they rode over. They would be stationed forty or fifty yards apart and between them would be a ship's anchor chain, uprooting the bush down to the bare earth. Then the planting would begin.

After two or three 'long rains' the scheme was wound up. There would be no cheap margarine and cooking oil for the British housewife and Tanganyika would not become a great oil producer. The scheme had been disastrously ill-prepared. The soil was infertile, no one had taken into account the rains and the tropical pests.[4] In all, £36 million had been spent. The few nuts which had been harvested had cost an estimated one shilling each, in the currency of the day and not one had come to market. But it helped to put East African Airways on its feet, the Colonial Office and the Overseas Food Corporation in London paid for many hundreds of air fares and the air mail revenues were considerably increased. The last O.F.C. charter flight was operated by DC3 VP-KIF with Captain Bob Warder-Griffin in command, First Officer George Leslie and Flight Engineer Ginger Brewer on 8th December, 1950. It was well remembered by everyone involved – part of the cargo consisted of the O.F.C. manager's baby grand piano which was flown from Natchingwea to Kongwa. The greatly diminished revenue of East African Airways at the end of 1950 was attributed to the drastic reduction in the operations of the Overseas Food Corporation, which previously had made a "substantial contribution to the revenue."

By the end of 1951, the Dakotas had extended their routes into Rhodesia and Nyasaland, in addition to the service to Durban in South Africa. They were demonstrating their superiority over the Lodestars, returning a lower passenger seat mile cost by virtue of better fuel consumption and higher payload capacity. The Lodestars had been now put on the market and plans were effected to replace the entire fleet over the following two years with Dakotas.

In February 1952 East African Airways became the first commercial airline to carry a reigning British Monarch. King George VI died in London, during the royal honeymoon tour of East Africa by Princess Elizabeth and the Duke of Edinburgh. On 12th February, the Royal couple were viewing game at the Treetops hotel, near Nyeri, when the tragic news was brought to them.

The original plan had been that East African Airways were to fly The Princess Elizabeth and the Duke of Edinburgh from Nanyuki to Mombasa, where they were to board the *Gothic* for their voyage to Australia. A Dakota, VP-KHK, named RMA *Sagana*, had been extensively overhauled during the last months of 1951 and polished to a near mirror finish in preparation for the royal couple.

When the sad news of the death of H. M. King George VI was received, it was obvious that Her Majesty the Queen might decide to return to England by air. B.O.A.C. had positioned the Argonaut which flew the royal couple from England

---

[4] The few farmers trying to cultivate the land in the Dodoma and Masasi regions had warned the authorities at the start that the scheme would fail. They foresaw that by clearing those hundreds of thousands of African thorn bush, the end result would be a dust-bowl. Some years later, when cattle ranching was tried in a further experiment, the north-east monsoon and its whirlwinds created a man-made navigational beacon for airmen – great pillars of dust.

to Mombasa, and instructions were received by radio telephone from London to have the aircraft standing by at Nairobi. Later in the day the royal equerry informed the Corporation that Her Majesty wished to fly home that night. The Argonaut could not leave direct for El Adem from Nairobi due to the limited length of the runway, and any intermediary landing was undesirable. With Her Majesty's approval a co-ordinated operation to ensure the earliest possible departure from Entebbe was arranged.

The Queen and the Duke of Edinburgh had been presented upon their arrival, by the people of Kenya, with a beautiful private lodge on the slopes of Mount Kenya. With its delightful surroundings and secluded wilderness it was named Sagana Lodge. From the lodge, it was now impossible to reach Nanyuki, the nearest aerodrome, before dusk. It was decided that a night operation could be safely planned between Nanyuki and Entebbe, but due to the high mountains intervening, it was necessary that the all up weight of the specially prepared Dakota VP-KHK should be reduced. Within an hour the Dakota was despatched to Nanyuki, together with a Lodestar carrying a flare-path kit and emergency ground radio equipment. The royal baggage would be carried to Entebbe in the Lodestar, thus reducing the take-off weight of the Dakota.

The Queen and the Duke of Edinburgh and their suite were finally embarked at dusk and were served with dinner on board. The royal visitors were to have dined with the General Officer Commanding East Africa that night, and due to the hurried plans for departure, East African Airways were unable to provide a suitable menu, for the dinner between Nanyuki and Entebbe, at such short notice. Malin

Dakota VP-KHK, RMA Sagana, with the crew of the royal flight: Captain A.N. Francombe, Captain W. Watson, Radio Officer Ivan Morris, Steward George Matthews. Behind them the engineering personnel who had completely overhauled and prepared the aircraft. (Capt E. Morris)

Sorsbie overcame the problem by having the general's dinner placed aboard the aircraft. The Royal Flight was commanded by Captain A. N. Francombe, with Captain Bob Watson as co-pilot, Radio Officer Ivan Morris and Steward George Matthews. In the meantime, contact was made with Captain R. C. Parker,[5] the commander of the B.O.A.C. Argonaut, G-ALHK, and the flight plan for the passage from Entebbe to London was arranged. The departure from Mombasa was synchronised with the arrival of the East African Airways aircraft, and all three machines arrived within minutes of each other at Entebbe.

Special arrangements had to be made to unload certain baggage from the *Gothic* and transfer it to the Argonaut. In addition, all the stations on the route had to be warned and the special safety precautions, which had been used on the outward flight, brought into force at short notice. This was achieved by the excellent co-operation between the departments of the Postmaster General, the Director of Civil Aviation and the Air Officer Commanding East Africa. The operations room at East African Airways had never known such a high level of activity – at one time three simultaneous telephone calls were taking place, one to the royal equerry, another to the operations director of B.O.A.C. in London, and to the captain of the *Gothic* in Mombasa. It was with a great sense of pride that East African Airways recorded that all arrangements went without a hitch, despite a night of violent tropical storms, which delayed the departure of the B.O.A.C. Argonaut from Entebbe.

The crew of the royal DC3, *Sagana* stayed overnight at the Lake Victoria Hotel, at Entebbe. There was a small group of American tourists staying at the hotel, prior to flying to Nairobi the following morning. As *Sagana* was empty on her return flight to Nairobi, the Americans were offered the opportunity of flying on the now famous aircraft. During the flight, one of the Americans asked steward George Matthews which seat had the Queen occupied. As Matthews pointed out the royal seat, the American stood up and quickly went back to sit in it. He was followed, reverently, by each one of the party. Excited by the prospect of recounting this memorable experience to countless audiences back home, the American then asked Matthews whether any of the royal party had used the toilet. With a straight face the steward replied: "Only the Queen." The man was out of his seat in an instant, and ran quickly down the aisle to the toilet. Within seconds, he emerged carrying a slip of toilet paper. "The *next* sheet, the *next* sheet!", he declared, his face beaming with delight.

That evening, East African Airways and the Tourist Board of East Africa hosted a sundowner at the Stanley Hotel, to which the same group of Americans, together with passengers from the world-cruise ship *SS Caronia*, were invited. To the mixed astonishment, amusement and horror of the assembled guests, the American pulled out his wallet and drew out his treasured curio to show to anyone who would listen to his story.

---

[5] Captain Parker would later, in 1956, be seconded to E.A.A.C. to train the Canadair pilots.

In accordance with the planning decision taken the previous year, during 1952 the Dakota fleet was substantially increased by the purchase of six ex-Royal Air Force C47B Dakota Mk 4 aircraft. These aircraft were overhauled, the cabins configured to twenty-eight seats and new radio equipment fitted by Field Aircraft Services Ltd., in England, prior to delivery to Nairobi. With the introduction of a standardised DC3 fleet it became possible, with the approval of the Air Registration Board, to make important changes in the system for complete overhauls to airframes and major checks. Under a revised system, DC3s no longer required a complete overhaul annually, unless a utilisation of 2,400 hours was achieved; as the average utilisation at the time did not exceed 1,400–1,600 hours per annum, complete overhauls fell due at approximately 18 months, as opposed to the previous system of every 12 months. In addition, all major checks were revised, the Check IV previously carried out at 480 hours was extended to 800 hours, and re-certification previously carried out at 30 hours was extended to 50 hours. These changes, through more efficient engineering practices, effected substantial labour economies.

The engineering department experienced serious difficulties at this time in obtaining supplies from the United Kingdom due to poor shipping facilities. Pratt and Whitney engines were sent to the B.O.A.C. factory at Treforest for overhaul, sometimes taking up to nine months to travel from East Africa to the United Kingdom and back via Mombasa.

Steps were taken towards the end of 1952 to establish a field force of sales representatives to provide an improved service to the public in general and to the Corporation's agents. Various fare rate incentive schemes were considered, particu-

Dakota VP-KLA, RMA James A. Grant, at Moshi, Tanganyika, 1953. Mt Kilimanjaro visible in the background. (Captain Leslie)

larly to improve cargo revenues, now that the DC3s provided additional capacity. It was believed that the new DC3 fleet would soon be able to play a large part in developing and facilitating the bulk distribution of commodities throughout the Territories.

The Emergency in Kenya was having an effect and there had undoubtedly been some hesitation on the part of would-be tourists from outside East Africa to visit the Territories, and locally there had been a tendency on the part of the public to defer their normal business safaris until satisfied with measures put into force for the protection of their families and homes. There was a marked decline during the months of September, October and November in passenger bookings, which was undoubtedly due to the activities of the Mau Mau terrorists.

At the end of 1952 there were 899 staff employed by East African Airways. The statistics for the year show the considerable effect on productivity during the year, in comparison with the previous years of the 1950s:

Year	Staff	Capacity Ton Miles Per Employee	Load Ton Miles Per Employee
1950	851	3001	1573
1951	861	3907	2190
1952	899	4270	2079

There was still no sign of government action in regard to construction of a new international airport, or "trunk route aerodrome" in the parlance of the day. Land at Embakasi had been acquired, however, and it seemed likely that action would follow soon, in view of the considerable difficulties encountered at Eastleigh, where the murram portion of the main runway continued to deteriorate and was made unusable after heavy rains. This occurred on several occasions, and had caused great inconvenience and expense to the international airlines, and even more inconvenience to the passengers who had to be transhipped at Entebbe, where the hotel accommodation was quite inadequate for such large numbers of extra people arriving at short notice. East African Airways operated both by night and by day between Entebbe and Nairobi West to overcome the difficulty.

The case for a new airport was underlined by the fact that Nairobi had now become a great traffic centre in air transport, producing no less than £1,500,000 worth of passenger traffic per annum. It was already being by-passed by the Comet aircraft of B.O.A.C., and Eastleigh was barely satisfactory for the latest generation of piston engined airliners. Grave doubts existed as to whether the airport could accommodate the B.O.A.C. Britannia aircraft, the prototype of which flew for the first time on 16 August 1952, and which was to replace the Hermes during 1954 and 1955.

During the early 1950s there were two Rapides based at Nairobi to operate the service to Dar es Salaam via Musoma, Mwanza, Tabora, Dodoma and Morogoro. It took two days each way, night stopping at Mwanza. It was a long, dreary trip for the pilots, one could see the Ngong Hills shortly after take-off from Musoma and a couple of hours later they would seem very little closer. Another Rapide was based at Entebbe, where Reg Cartwright resided on semi-permanent posting to operate the Uganda Communications Services.

Attempts had been made at the end of 1951 to replace the ageing Rapides with more up to date machines. Lord Waterpark, who farmed in Kenya, had been given an Italian Macchi MB320 as a wedding present. The local agents, Campling Brothers, persuaded Malin Sorsbie that these machines would be ideal to replace the Rapides in Uganda. Ginger Brewer, who was both a qualified aircraft engineer and a senior flight engineer, was sent, in mid-December, 1951, to Italy with vague instructions to look at the aircraft being built, check that they were modified to airline standards and generally represent the airline at Macchi's. For Brewer, getting to Rome that winter was a problem. It was at the time of one of the periodic Arab/Israeli upsets and the B.O.A.C. Hermes was delayed transitting Cairo. From Rome he flew to Milan, where he had been told the Macchi factory was situated. On making enquiries, no one could help him, until he discovered that the factory was at Varese, some 50km from Milan.

He arrived in Varese, which was covered in deep snow, still dressed in his East African light-weight clothing, and was introduced to the managing director, General Illari. "You have brought the 16 million lire for the payment for the aircraft?", he asked. Brewer disappointed him, making a vague promise, whereupon he was asked to come back in two weeks, as the factory was closing down for Christmas.

Having spent Christmas in England with his mother, Brewer returned to Varese in the New Year to find that one of the aircraft was nearly complete and two more were in an advanced stage of construction. Brewer was able to inspect and, with the aid of an interpreter, check the airframe construction, controls, hydraulics and all the many individual items which went into the manufacture of the aeroplane. The Italian aircraft industry was slowly recovering from the effects of the war. Whilst the wooden airframe construction was of first class quality, some of the other materials were of a poor standard, as it was to be discovered later. The engines were Continental 185hp and the designer, Eng Bazzochi, told Brewer that the aircraft had been designed for 225hp engines, but these had been unobtainable. This would severely affect the single-engine performance in African conditions.

Captain Phillip Henn together with Radio Officer Handford-Rice arrived in March for the first delivery flight. Commandante Carristiato, who had competed in the pre-war Schneider Trophy races, carried out the first flight, with Henn, Handford-Rice, Brewer and an Italian engineer as passengers. The aircraft performed well, maintaining height, in the cold March air, with one engine shut-down.

Brewer had borrowed, when he first arrived, a very old Olivetti typewriter and, working at night since he was in the factory every day from 08.30am until 6.30pm, typed out the Maintenance Manual and the Flight Manual. He had great difficulty in obtaining fuel flow figures, without which it was impossible to calculate range and endurance flight plan figures. It was necessary for the flight test centre to fit fuel flow test equipment on an aircraft and conduct air tests. Since the aircraft was due to depart for East Africa in a few days, it was necessary to carry out the flight tests on a Saturday. When General Illari, who was in his office, saw the aircraft flying overhead, he wanted to know what was going on. All hell broke loose when he discovered that the English engineer had required the tests to be carried out! As it turned out, a possible disaster had been averted, since the figures showed that the fuel consumption was considerably higher than on the earlier model owned by Lord Waterpark. Had these figures been used for flight plan purposes, the engines would have run dry en route.

On another occasion, Brewer was checking the blue-prints and after double and treble checking he was certain that from the plans the controls operated in reverse. He pointed this out to the chief draughtsman who said "Impossible!" A little later he overheard heated exchanges coming from the drafting office. He had made a lot of work for himself, as he was then asked to check all the drawings. The hydraulic system was made up as one unit in a Milan factory and it transpired that no one at Macchis knew how it was internally routed – as demonstrated on the gravely suspicious blue-prints. Brewer was asked to go to Milan, sort out the system, re-draw the plans and pass them on to Macchis.

It soon became apparent that the Macchis were by no means dependable alternatives to the venerable old DH 89s. The first aircraft, VP-KJD, was delivered without incident to Nairobi, but the second machine, VP-KJJ, flown by Captain Lavers and R/O Ivan Morris ran into difficulties. About 100 miles south of Khartoum, the system oil pipe burst and the starboard engine failed, as well as the hydraulics. Lavers performed a successful wheels up landing on an island on the Nile near Kosti and they were eventually rescued by the Sudan Desert Rescue Organisation.

Ginger Brewer with Macchi test pilot Commandante Carristiato, and the MB320 VP-KJD, at Varese. February, 1952. (Capt Brewer)

In May, Captain Cartwright took delivery of another machine, VP-KJG, and en route, while letting down in a sand storm at Khartoum, the trim wheel came off in his hand. On the 30th May, 1952 Cartwright carried out the first proving flight with VP-KJD on behalf of the Uganda Communications Flight, with Brewer as flight engineer/radio officer, and the aircraft performed up to expectations. However, on subsequent Tuesdays, on 4th and 11th June, Cartwright came to grief, making forced landings first at Tororo, with Brewer on board, and then at Naivasha, after engine failures. These events were followed by three similar incidents, all involving wheels up landings, after which the DCA became interested in the shortcomings of this, a brand new aircraft. It was arranged for Jerry Ames from the ARB and Capt Pat Travers to accompany Capt Lavers as he carried out tests at MAUW (with ballast), to evaluate the single engine performance of the Macchi. When the starboard engine cut and would not restart, they were cleared for a forced landing on Eastleigh's reciprocal runway. Ames tried unsuccessfully to pump down the undercarriage, but Lavers brought the Macchi to rest with the wheels partially down and little damage done.

It was discovered that the basic problem with the aircraft was that its engine oil system was badly designed and was inclined to fail in an area which resulted in the engine oil being pumped overboard. Feathering action would be taken, which then resulted in two things. The propeller would feather and then, when the button was released, it would un-feather again. Back to square one. But then there appeared another design fault, because after the propeller feathered the first time, the oil in the propeller feathering mechanism would flow into the sump, to join the oil being pumped overboard. The result of multiple attempts to feather the propeller, which was windmilling and causing drag, would be eventual seizure of the engine due to loss of oil. A stopped propeller, then causing greater drag, would result in failure to meet the single engine performance.

After considerable investigation, it was found that, when feathering action was carried out in flight, it was necessary to keep the button pressed until the propeller

Archie Watkins and Douglas Stewart at Nairobi West.

actually turned in reverse. This would engage a lock so that when the button was finally released, the propeller would take up the feathered position, and the pilot had a chance of landing in a place of his own choosing.

After a short period, during which at least one such machine carried H.R.H. Princess Margaret during a visit to East Africa, the airline disposed of the three Macchis to a local air safari company, and the dependable old Rapides continued in service. From February 1953 the Entebbe based Rapide was scheduled to operate Entebbe–Tororo–Kitale–Eldoret–Nairobi, returning in the opposite direction the following day. This enabled routine maintenance to be conducted at Nairobi.

John "Ginger" Brewer had been working as an outstation engineer at Nairobi Eastleigh for South African Airways in 1950. This brought him into contact with the E.A.A.C. chief engineer, Archie Watkins, overhaul workshop engineer 'Taffy' Brammer and the engineering manager 'Bunny' Wright. Before joining S.A.A. he had started up the small charter company in Margate, Natal for which George Leslie and 'Mitch' Mitchell had flown prior to joining E.A.A.C. During the war, Brewer had been an R.A.F. engineer and had trained South African pilots in their ground subjects. He had met his wife-to-be in South Africa, where he married and settled after the war.

Not only did he hold British and South African licences for all the E.A.A.C. aircraft types, but he also held a British Flight Engineers Licence. There was no possibility of his getting an aircrew job with S.A.A., so when Archie Watkins suggested that he should join E.A.A.C. as a ground/flight engineer, he resigned from S.A.A. and started working for East African Airways in mid-1950.

Brewer worked in the hangar at Nairobi West as a servicing engineer on the DC3s, Lodestars, Doves and DH89A Rapides for a short time. His first flight as a flight engineer was on 13th November, 1950, on a DC3 charter for the Overseas Food Corporation – the ill-fated groundnut scheme. The aircraft was based at Kongwa, from where it operated a supply shuttle between Natchingwea, Dar es Salaam and Urambo. At Kongwa the crews lived in tents. One day someone picked up a human skull beside the camp. On examination it was found to be the skull of a woman with a musket-ball hole through it. They were told that it had belonged to a woman slave, shot on the way to the coast – Kongwa had been on the Arab slave trade route[6]. The head had been placed on a wooden post to ward off spirits. The only off-duty entertainment at Kongwa was a bar and an open-air cinema, showing mainly Indian films.

During this period, Brewer who had ambitions to become a pilot, took advantage, while a flight engineer on the O.F.C. charters, to practice some dual. He still remembers the bruises on his left arm where Tug Wilson pummelled him for being too tense on the control column!

---

[6] Further north, near Tabora, one of the navigation aids was a scattered line of mango trees. The Arabs had fed their captured slaves with mangoes on the long walk to the coast. Over the years, the discarded seeds had grown into trees along the path.

Back at Nairobi West he continued to work on ground duties, sometimes working night-shifts in the hangar. The aerodrome adjoined the game park and one of the hazards was the frequent visits of wild animals. He often had to lend his 9mm Mauser rifle to the air traffic controllers to frighten the Thomson's gazelles away. On a night-shift, when the work had been completed, he and his companions were about to leave the hangar when a lion appeared at the door – which was closed very quickly. There was no telephone, so they could not call for help. After a couple of hours, when they were sure it had gone, they furtively opened the door and made a dash for their cars. There was also another night when a hyena took a bite out of a Lodestar tyre, resulting in a wheel change and, quite probably, a very sick hyena. Airborne again, he was flying with Captain Phil Henn into the strip at Kasese, at the foot of the Ruwenzori Mountains. It was a very narrow strip then, carved out of the side of a hill, which served the railway construction from Kampala to the nearby copper mines. It was standard practice to fly down the runway to check that there were no buffalo grazing on the strip. On this occasion Captain Henn carried out the procedure and, sure enough, there was not simply one or two buffalo, but a herd. When they sensed that the Dakota was approaching, they charged off ahead of the aircraft. As they passed low overhead, Henn and Brewer were aghast as they spotted a survey crew working in the path of the thundering herd of wild buffalo. Henn swung the Dakota round in a tight turn and circled the group of men, trying to warn them of the on-coming herd. They returned to the now clear strip and, after landing, their enquiries drew no reports of death or injuries, so they assumed the survey party had escaped.

It had been decided that from 1952 the minimum crew for the DC3 should be captain and a co-pilot first officer. As a result, the redundant radio officers were offered re-training as pilots or, in some cases, flight engineers. A.N. Francombe called Brewer in and detailed him to re-train a group of radio officers to be flight engineers. He was given two weeks. Protesting that if he were to do this, he would lose his own job as flight engineer, Francombe promised him that he would become permanent aircrew, and would be relieved of hangar duties. In order to train and certify the radio officers, he was required to convert his United Kingdom licence to a Kenya flight engineer's licence and thus became the holder of Kenya flight engineer licence Number 1.

In September of 1952, Captain Eric Morris flew, with Roger Drew as co-pilot, to Blackbushe, in England, in the Dakota VP-KIF, on a delivery flight, as the aircraft was to be sold through the airline's broker, 'Slick' Goodlin. On the way from Nairobi they had routed through Malmo, in Sweden, to drop off two Pratt and Whitney 90D engines, which had also been sold through Goodlin.

They were to return to Nairobi as supernumerary crew on a Swedish registered PBY Catalina 3 amphibian flying-boat, SE-BUB, which was owned by Goodlin and used for charter work. He employed a captain, Peter Holmes and an engineer, Swen

Swenson, as the crew. Morris and Drew were expected to assist Holmes with the route planning and navigation on the positioning flight to Nairobi.

Malin Sorsbie was a man of considerable foresight. He had registered a new company, Seychelles and Kilimanjaro Air Transport Services Ltd, (S.K.A.T.) some weeks earlier, as a subsidiary of E.A.A.C. The Catalina was to be chartered by S.K.A.T. to check on the feasibility of flying-boat services on the East African lakes, to the Seychelles and other Indian Ocean islands.

Morris and his co-pilot met their new skipper and Swen, the engineer, at a hotel near Blackbushe. He was most casually dressed in a sloppy shirt, old grey flannels, sandals and a tartan tweed cap. A swarthy Welshman who Eric Morris judged to be a typical free-lance pilot, a "press-on regardless" type – as he proved to be. Swen was the complete opposite – a fair haired, strong, clean looking young Swede.

When they arrived at the airport the following morning, October 3rd, 1952, the aircraft was on the tarmac, refuelled, loaded and ready for flight. There was a great deal of freight on board, the middle section of the fuselage was packed with loose boxes, packets and sacks. A small space was left to allow access through to the long rear section, where there was a narrow emergency exit. It was only at this point that they learned that there were eight passengers accompanying them on the flight. These were to be accommodated in the rear area – in which there was only space for them to sit or lie among their baggage, the ceiling was too low for anyone to stand.

What a motley crew emerged from the terminal building – possibly they were seamen, or workers employed by the groundnut scheme – they were obviously taking advantage of a low price fare, and must have been partly briefed on what could only be described as 'steerage accommodation'. Air safety regulations had not yet caught up with these sort of operations in those early post-war years.

The first shock of what they were to experience on the trip was the sight of about a dozen iron or steel 10ft bars lying length-wise along the flight-deck floor. They stretched from the front mooring-hatch, ran directly under the instrument panel (on which the compass was mounted), through to the cargo loaded behind. Morris asked Captain Holmes if the compass had been swung, since the metal bars would almost certainly create magnetic fields resulting in compass deviation, which should have been recorded on the correction card. "They have had no effect" replied the skipper, curtly. Morris was sure that he was lying and made a mental note that they would learn the truth sooner or later.

As they trundled down the taxi-way to the take-off position, the Catalina was like a duck out of water. It seemed to waddle along, its backside barely clearing the ground. Holmes opened the throttles, which were mounted, in flying-boat fashion, above their heads and they started a slow rumble down the tarred runway and gradually gained take-off speed. With the aircraft so heavily loaded they could achieve only a slow rate of climb. At 500ft a slow turn to port brought them on to a southerly compass course for their destination, Marseilles. Over the channel it became cloudy and by the time they reached the French coast there was 10 tenths[7] stratus below. The cloud cover persisted until they neared the Mediterranean.

---

[7] The practice of measuring cloud cover in tenths had not then been superseded by the current measurement in 'octas' or eighths.

It was not until they were some 20 minutes from their ETA that a check could be made on the accuracy of the compass heading. They had drifted considerably to starboard, but some ten minutes later, they saw Marseilles through broken cloud. It was worrying that they could not tell whether it had been the wind which had blown them off course, or compass error. With long flights ahead over desert and wilderness, it was a worry which would stay with them until they reached Nairobi.

The next leg of their flight took them across the Mediterranean islands to the airport at Benina near the city of Benghazi. The weather was clear and map reading easy. There did not appear to be much wrong with the compass. Captain Holmes vacated his seat and handed over the controls to Eric Morris while he attempted to fiddle with the aircraft's long-range radio, without any success. They carried a Bendix VHF set, for short-range R/T communications, but for the long crossing of the vast African Continent, with its deserts, swamps and mountains the Collins long-range set was vital.

Benina to Wadi Halfa, on the east bank of the Nile, would take seven to eight hours. The Catalina was fuelled to the brim. Roger Drew and Morris were convinced that the aircraft was heavily overloaded. They seemed to run for miles before scraping off a few yards before the end of the rough runway. There were moments when both the East African pilots wondered if the flimsy folding undercarriage would collapse under the loaded weight of the aircraft, as it hammered against the uneven runway surface. They started a slow climb on virtually full power until, at 500 feet, it was reduced to achieve a best climb speed of 95 knots. After a long time they reached 7,500 feet, where they levelled off and at normal cruising power settled into the cruise at an astonishing 90 knots Indicated Airspeed. It would gradually increase as they consumed fuel over the next four or five hours.

Their captain had set a compass course measured from an Admiralty chart of the Eastern Mediterranean African Seaboard! The two pilots could only surmise that this was a correct navigation aid for the flying-boat which he was commanding. Apart from the coastline and sea bed fathom depths, the only other feature on the chart was the river Nile (water again, of course), with Wadi Halfa on its eastern bank.

Soon after settling into the cruise, the skipper handed over to Captain Drew and returned to tinkering with the Collins radio, with no further success than previously, he soon gave up and began to read a paperback.

Swen was situated in his engineer's hutch in the large aerodynamically shaped turret in the centre section, which joined the wide wing above, carrying the two engines and fuel tanks to the fuselage hull section below. After a while he reported that engine oil was leaking from the back of the starboard engine. They gave it some thought, and decided that it was nothing to worry about. Oil frequently leaks from topped up or overfilled tanks. At least this is what they hoped was the case.

An hour or so later the Sahara's Great Sand Sea was on their right. The other sea, which the boat could use, had disappeared far to their left. They were now over the true desert, and lonely, empty and forbidding it was. It was time for some serious navigation and the skipper was asked for a map. To their horror the two pilots learned that he did not have one – apart from his Admiralty chart. It was unbelievable. Admittedly a topographical chart could not provide much detail, but the odd oases and landmarks could help with navigation.

So there they were, miles and miles from anywhere, their only aid being a suspect compass. It was late afternoon and their ETA was two or more hours after dark. Morris thought he saw the edge of the Qattara Depression, in the far distance to their left, as the daylight was failing. Holmes broke the silence by saying "All we have to do is stick to our course until we hit the Nile river running at right angles to us - we should pick out the lights of Wadi then".

There was no moon that night but, as often during desert nights, the stars were bright enough for them to discern the ground below. They descended to a lower level and waited, watched and stared out into the night, hoping for a glimpse of the great river, or a cluster of lights. They had passed their ETA when suddenly they saw the stars reflected in the waters of the River Nile ahead. There were no clusters of lights which might be Wadi Halfa. As soon as they closed upon the Nile, Roger Drew swung around and shouted "Which way now?" Calmly and deliberately their captain put his hand in his pocket, pulled out a coin and said "Heads starboard, tails port along the river". Heads it was. "Hell's Bell's", mumbled Drew, as he turned them south, up the river. "What if we should have turned left?" asked Morris. "Don't worry", Holmes said, "you have forgotten, we have a flying-boat - I can land on the river in an emergency". One could not help admiring the man; a true Captain, allaying the fears of his charges and avoiding possible panic.

They were now well past their calculated flight time. Minutes dragged past. They stared forward in silence. That compass was imprinted on their minds. Holmes was listening and calling on the VHF channels; he had had no contact as yet. Perhaps they were flying too low to receive the line-of-sight waves. After an agonizing, long wait they saw a faint glow on the horizon, and then they heard the answering calls of the controller at Wadi Halfa. They sank back in their seats, relaxed with relief and joy. Swen, in his turret nest started to sing. Perhaps it was the circumstances which caused them to think that he had a nice voice!

The captain climbed into the pilot's seat and within about fifteen minutes they were entering the circuit pattern of their destination. All was well, or so they assumed. Roger Drew and Eric Morris had no other thoughts than for a bath, a cold beer and bed at the Nile Hotel. On the downwind leg of the circuit Holmes selected undercarriage down. They heard the mechanical links working as the wheels came out of their nacelles on the side of the fuselage, drop down and fall into their final extension. The red lights shone brightly as the undercarriage went down - and they continued to shine after they should have turned to green, indicating a safely locked undercarriage. Holmes activated the emergency hydraulic system. Still no greens. He told Drew to grab a length of piping secured below the starboard window and insert its end into a socket of a mechanical device which would lock the undercarriage down. Drew could not force the undercarriage into the required position. Morris joined him in the effort. No luck. It was beginning to look as if they would have to land on the Nile in the dark after all. Swen climbed down to join them. He was a strong man. With his back against the bulkhead, both feet upon the lever and Drew and Morris pushing with all their might, the mechanism clicked and locked. They whooped with delight, as the captain turned the aircraft onto the landing approach. The undercarriage held – it had not been damaged on the take-off from Benina – Thank God!

As soon as they had their feet on the ground Morris and Drew headed for the airport cafe – they were famished and were dying for some tea. They left the skipper and his engineer to see to the off-loading of the crew baggage. After their refreshments they went out expecting to set off for the hotel. The passengers were standing around, wanting to know what was going to happen. They eventually found Holmes in the control tower talking to the official in charge. He was explaining that he intended to depart for Aden immediately. Drew and Morris were speechless. Morris could not believe it. "You can't possibly be serious", he said. "After a long day flying with no proper maps, and without proper radio, you cannot expect air traffic control here to give you clearance to proceed!" "I shall take-off without clearance, if I decide", declared Holmes. "Well then", replied Morris, "I shall certainly not share in your madness. The flight time to Aden is nearly ten hours, after about half way you will be flying over very high ground in the dark. What will you do in the event of an engine failure, or something serious?" "Don't forget that I can land on the Red Sea", he almost shouted in reply. Roger Drew broke in saying, "Well, I'm not going to go with you. The Swedish authorities should be asked to withdraw your Commercial Licence". That settled the issue.

The following day they encountered strong headwinds, forcing them to divert to Port Sudan to refuel. There was a simple landing strip with no night flying facilities. Had they been foolish enough to depart Wadi Halfa the previous night, fuel shortage may well have forced them to make a night landing in the dark on the Red Sea.

The remainder of the journey home to Nairobi was uneventful. All of the cargo and some of the unfortunate passengers were dropped off at Aden. Peter Holmes was much more pleasant and affable after the trials of the journey to Wadi Halfa, with the subsequent outburst. They flew through a deluge of heavy tropical rain on the run-in to Nairobi. When, at last they came to rest, outside the East African Airways hangars, the battered old flying-boat seemed to succumb to its weariness; water and oil started to drip from the back of the wings, and the undercarriage legs stood weakly akimbo.

It had entered East Africa with the Swedish registration SE-BUB and was later re-registered VP-KKJ. In an experiment to test the suitability of the amphibian for services connecting the East African Lakes, it was used by E.A.A.C. for the delivery of cement to Kabale, and cargoes of fish were brought from Lake George. The aircraft was also modified for the carriage of passengers, and proving flights had been made to the Nile below the Murchison Falls, but had proved too hazardous due to the debris in the river, in addition to the vast numbers of crocodiles and hippopotomi.

At the end of 1952, Malin Sorsbie, following discussions with the Directorate of Civil Aviation, made arrangements for a proving flight, with the Catalina, to the Seychelles. Apart from the possibility of tourist flights to the 'paradise islands', and the feasibility of continuing through to Mauritius and Durban, the DCA were interested in surveying the main island, Mahé, to find out whether an aerodrome could be constructed there. Captain Bill Fumerton, an experienced flying-boat pilot, together with R/O Brian Close and the aircraft's captain and engineer formed the crew. Malin Sorsbie together with an E.A.A.C. traffic official, officials from the Public Works Department, a forecaster from the Met Office in Nairobi, and a representative of the DCA, formed the passenger complement.

New Zealander Michael 'Spud' Murphy was chief telecommunications officer at the Directorate of Civil Aviation in Nairobi. Ordered by Joe Furniss to interest himself in the forthcoming proving flight, he was eventually told to participate in the operation as a member of the crew – supernumerary radio officer. There was no ground to air radio communication with the Seychelles, so it was decided to use the facilities of the French naval station at Diego Suarez, at Antsiranana, on the northernmost tip of Madagascar. Murphy had been to school in French speaking Tahiti, so being fluent in the language, he wrote to the French admiral and made provisional plans for communication procedures. Arrangements were made through the Nairobi office of Cable and Wireless for the flight inbound to Mahé from Diego Suarez, to contact their station on the island.

On 14th January, 1953, they took-off from the waters of Kilindini harbour, Mombasa and set course south-east, across the Indian Ocean. The flight was uneventful and they made land fall at Diego Suarez as arranged. They were met by the local airline agent, a Malagassy, and a large limousine from the French admiral's H.Q. Spud Murphy, the radio officer, was whisked off to have dinner with the admiral, while the general manager was entertained by the local representative. Malin Sorsbie was hopping mad, but could do nothing about it. There was no hotel accommodation, so the party had to sleep in the maternity ward of the local hospital.

The next day, 16th January, they set off on the last leg of their journey for Mahé. Radio communication with the Cable and Wireless shipping station was good, and after passing over an island on which they found a small aircraft, which seemed to have forced landed safely, they spotted the main island of Mahé and landed on a still sea outside the small harbour of Victoria, the capital of the islands, after a flight of five hours and twenty-five minutes. The Catalina taxied towards the shore and gained dry land near the wharf. In those days the Seychelles were sleepy tropical islands, undisturbed by the world at large, isolated by their position in the middle of the vast Indian Ocean. Sailors returning from a call at Victoria would bring back tales of the 'love islands' where the totally amoral local beauties offered indiscriminate hospitality to those fortunate to sojourn in the delightful islands, where there was nothing to do but listen to the pounding surf and to relax beneath the palms, refreshed by the caress of the Trade Winds. The arrival of a flying-boat from who-knows-where beyond the blue horizon brought the lovely maidens running down to the beach, as the travellers walked ashore. "Come with me, come with me", they called enticingly, but to no avail, there was work to be done, and time was short.

Mahé Island is made of basalt rock, rising steeply out of the sea. There were some sandy beaches and undulating rocky ground, covered with tropical vegetation, but there was nowhere a suitable, flat area of sufficient size to build an aerodrome. The party found, however, a narrow strip of land a few miles south of Victoria. It ran parallel to a small beach, and at its southern end stretched a large flat area of tidal coral reef. They all agreed that there was space for a single runway, if an extension could be created by constructing a built up causeway on top of the coral reef.

The day was spent in surveying the island, during which the Catalina flew some two hours, and in discussion with various local authorities and after a night in the delightful local hotel, the next day January 18th, they, reluctantly one can imagine, set off again on their long return flight to Kenya.

The total flight time recorded was twenty-six hours forty minutes, routing: Nairobi—Mombasa—DiegoSuarez—Seychelles—Seychelles—local—Seychelles—Mombasa—Nairobi. The return flight was logged as ten hours forty-five minutes flight time from Seychelles to Nairobi.

Following their recommendations to the colonial government, the airport was constructed, which in years to come would eventually accommodate the world's largest airliners, disgorging thousands of tourists seeking the long lost magic of the islands.

Regrettably, the Catalina had proved to be uncommercial, despite the enthusiasm of the old flying-boat brigade. It was slow, noisy and uncomfortable, with no suitable toilet and galley space for the kind of travel expected by passengers becoming more demanding and sophisticated in their requirements. The days of flying-boats were coming to an end, as land planes, with increasing range and payloads, multiplied, and airports around the world, following the American models, constructed miles and miles of concrete runways which could accommodate any airliner imaginable.

But the old flying-boat was to prove useful, before being sold in the United States.

Following a series of charters in 1950 during the filming of *King Solomon's Mines*, further charter flights were conducted during June and July, 1951, in Uganda, for the film *The African Queen*, starring Humphrey Bogart and Katherine Hepburn. An airstrip at Butiaba, on Lake Albert, was cleared for this film, to enable the Rapide, flown by Reg Cartwright, and a charter aircraft flown by Alec Noon, who had left East African Airways to form Noon and Pierce Air Charter Services, to serve the location. The ancient hull for the *African Queen* was found at Butiaba, and the boat was reconstructed by local carpenters.

Aircraft were used extensively to bridge the three locations used for the film, Butiaba, the Ruiki river near Ponthierville in the Belgian Congo, and Murchison Falls, where the film was completed.

On their return to Entebbe from their up-country expedition shooting the film, the entire cast and crew, including Humphrey Bogart, Lauren Bacall, Katherine

Hepburn, John Huston and Sam Spiegel came to the party which Cartwright and his wife Sheila organised at the Lake Victoria Hotel.

Towards the end of 1952 and into 1953, E.A.A.C. were again engaged to operate a number of charter flights for Metro-Goldwyn-Meyer. An African adventure film called *Mogambo* was being shot at Buffalo Springs and various other locations in East Africa, starring Clark Gable, Ava Gardner and Grace Kelly (Ava Gardner's current husband at the time, Frank Sinatra, also tagged along – it was thought to keep his eye on her and newly-divorced Gable).

A location was set up on the Kagera river, in north-western Tanganyika. Unfortunately, there was no airstrip nearby, so it was decided to overcome the problem by constructing one. Pat Travers flew with Peter Holmes and Swen Swensen up to Bukoba, on Lake Victoria, with the Catalina flying boat, since this was a task eminently suited to it. After alighting on the lake, it was found that the only means of gaining the shore was to anchor the Catalina and swim for it. A suitable site was found near the *Mogambo* settlement, and within six days a 1,800 yard landing strip was ready.

The settlement, cut out of the bush, was no rough safari camp, it amounted to a luxury hotel under canvas. It had lavishly upholstered sleeping tents, thirteen dining tents, a portable cinema, an entertainment tent with pool tables, and a hospital tent complete with an X-ray unit. The women's tents included bathrooms with hot and cold running water, this was provided by two large oil drums at the back of each tent, one containing 'cold' water and the other, set above a wood fire, providing the hot, in the fashion perfected by the Kenya luxury safari operators.

On 14th December, 1952, Captain Peter Hall and F/E Ginger Brewer flew in DC3 VP-KJP on a charter to carry fresh supplies from Nairobi to Mogambo, as the strip had now been named. Although the camp was on the bank of a river, the director, John Ford, refused to drink the water, so fresh water was flown from the New Stanley Hotel, a flight of some two hours. When they arrived, 'Bunny' Allen the professional White Hunter, introduced them to Ava Gardner. They told her that they had heard on the company radio frequency that her husband, Frank Sinatra, had arrived at Entebbe, and was being flown to Mogambo. Ava appeared to be less than excited about the news.

A week or so later, on 21st December, the same crew, in DC3 VP-KJC, flew Grace Kelly, Ava Gardner, Clarke Gable and Sinatra from Mogambo to Nairobi for the Christmas holiday period. There had been persistent rumours that Grace Kelly had been enjoying an affair with Gable during the period on location. There were a number of E.A.A.C. employees working as extras on the film, in addition to the coming and going of the aircrews, none of them were aware of anything untoward or promiscuous in Miss Kelly's conduct.

One day, during this time, Reg Cartwright had been off duty in Nairobi, where he had called into the Long Bar at the New Stanley Hotel. He spotted a lone drinker whom he vaguely recognised, and introduced himself, "Sorry, I've forgotten your name" he said. "I'm Clark, I don't recall yours either". "Reg". "Well Reg, have a beer". The two of them got on well and Reg showed Clark all the bright spots of Nairobi.

A day or so later, Cartwright, who was attempting to gain experience, with a view to getting the flying-boat endorsement on his licence, accompanied the flying-boat crew, together with Pat Travers, in the Catalina to the location at Bukoba. They anchored the aircraft off-shore and rowed to the beach in the aircraft's dinghy. Overnight the wind had risen and by early morning the lake was extremely rough, Travers and Cartwright saw the Catalina dragging its anchor and drifting away. They launched the dinghy through the breakers off the lee shore beach, but in their haste they broke an oar, and the dinghy capsized. They were obliged to strip to their underpants and swim for it in order to rescue the aircraft. They had left their clothing and shoes on the beach. When they returned after securing the Catalina, they were nowhere to be seen. Unseen natives had taken them. There was nothing they could do other than fly back to Entebbe dressed only in their underpants.

On arrival at Entebbe, they parked the amphibian on the tarmac and tried to make a discrete exit, but as luck would have it, Clark Gable, accompanied by the lovely Ava Gardner, recognised his drinking companion of some nights before and called out a greeting, whereupon all eyes were turned on the two cringing, half naked pilots. Gable wanted to thank Reg Cartwright for the night out in Nairobi, which he had enjoyed, free of the usual atmosphere surrounding his celebrity status.

Mogambo was a logistical nightmare. The production involved 175 American and British actors and film crew members, more than 100 vehicles and an assortment of chartered aircraft. A thousand Africans were recruited as extras, MGM was anxious to avoid a repetition of its earlier problems while making *King Solomon's Mines* in Kenya, when Maasai and Kikuyu tribesmen appearing in the film, forsaking the play for reality, entered into violent tribal clashes, resulting in four deaths. On this occasion, Maasai and their cousins the Samburu were employed for the fighting scenes.

For one scene in the film, director John Ford required a tropical storm to add to the thrills of a torrid love scene. Since the local weather at the time proved uncooperative, the mechanical skills of the perennial Archie Watkins were called upon. Not wishing to cause disappointment, Archie rigged up two time-expired Wright Cyclone Lodestar engines, arranging for the prop wash to blow a fierce storm across the set. Alas, in his enthusiasm to provide a first rate storm, he had underestimated his powers. The slender Grace Kelly, required by the story to be blown into the arms of Clark Gable, was swept off her feet, and together with the hero, blown into the nearby Kagera river.

In another scene, shown in early versions of the completed film, Clarke Gable is seen grabbing Grace Kelly as in a thick storm of dust, created by the engines, stampeding game charge across the screen, and he pulls her down behind a fallen tree for safety, as a zebra jumps over them. A close look will reveal that it was a curious looking zebra. It was actually a donkey painted with black and white stripes.

The narrow grass airstrip at Bukoba ran uphill from the lake shore, ending at a cliff face. The largest aircraft to land there had been a Rapide, until the film people insisted on using modern, larger aircraft. There was no room for the slightest error, once below 500 feet, you were committed to land. On approach to land in a Lodestar, in November 1952, Captain Wilson recalls that his R/O, 'Curly' Payne looked back to see Gable, who was well aware of the inherent dangers of the situation, and losing no opportunity in his attempts to gain her favour, holding the hand of Grace Kelly across the aisle, "Giving her the confidence he didn't appear to have himself", as Payne put it. The prop-wash disturbed the crocodiles on numerous occasions, as the Lodestars made their precautionary approach to that runway.

The Hollywood romantic view of Africa, never very close to the real thing, was now, towards the end of 1952, even more remote from reality.

On 22nd October, 1952, Jomo Kenyatta and five of his colleagues, all leaders of the K.A.U. were detained, to be charged, on 18th November, with managing Mau Mau. Widespread terrorism swept through Kenya. When the security forces, composed of troops from the United Kingdom and loyal Kikuyu retaliated, the terrorists formed guerrilla bands, and the country was in a state of civil war. The happy times were over. There would be no alternative to violent change, which would create a new world in Kenya and the other East African countries.

Wing Commander Aubrey Francombe, who had experienced continual disagreements with Malin Sorsbie, resigned from East African Airways at this time in order to form and command the Kenya Police Air Wing, which was to come into being as a result of the Emergency.

To observers on the ground in Kenya, during the summer of 1952, there could be seen, high in the stratosphere, a tiny silver speck, speeding south, its tantalising shadow flitting down the Great Rift Valley. On 2nd May, the B.O.A.C. de Havilland Comet 1 four-jet airliner, G-ALYP, under the command of Captain A. M. A. Majendie, had commenced its first flight on the London to Johannesburg route. Calling at Rome, Beirut, Khartoum, Entebbe and Livingstone, it completed the journey in twenty-three and a half hours. Until a new airport with hard runways of suitable length was constructed, the Comets would continue to overfly Nairobi. Thus, the lake-side airport of Entebbe, with its new runway, would continue to be the only call in East Africa for this, the world's first jet-propelled airliner.

CHAPTER 5

Troubled Times

ON 8TH APRIL, 1953, JOMO KENYATTA was finally convicted of the management of Mau Mau, and sentenced to seven years imprisonment. People now thought that after a little mopping up, things would get back to normal up-country. But they didn't. The war became more bitter and drew further upon British resources.

Later that year, on Tuesday 14th July, George Leslie was off duty at home in Nairobi. He was outside, tinkering with his car, when he was called to the telephone. It was Johnny West, the operations crew controller. He had a charter flight booked to Kitale and return for the following day, the 15th, could George take it? It would make a pleasant change from the hot and steamy coastal trips. Kitale was high up, at 6,200 ft in the 'White Highlands' of Kenya, an airfield normally served only by the DH Rapides.

The next morning Leslie boarded the crew transport, stopping on the way to the airport to pick up Dave Dempster, his first officer. They arrived at Nairobi West at about seven o'clock and went in for their crew breakfast, a routine practice on those early morning departures.

No one could tell them very much about the forthcoming flight. They were to fly up to Kitale empty, pick up a passenger and return to Nairobi. A rather curious requirement for a twenty-eight seat Dakota, but these were strange and troubled times and E.A.A.C. was in business to provide a service, whatever the customer demanded.

It had rained overnight, and the morning was crystal clear, fresh and brisk. The sort of Nairobi morning which made one feel good to be alive.

They got airborne and set course northward. There was no need to look at the maps, one needed only to follow the road and railway line. Soon they could see the crater of Longonot ahead as the Dakota climbed slowly to cruising height. They passed abeam Limuru and then Lake Naivasha, shimmering in the centre of the Rift Valley, and continued towards Nakuru and the great crater of Menengai. The Aberdare mountains were over to their right, obscured by clouds. On the left, the Mau escarpment, in the clear.

They were still following the railway line and main road but the ground was rising below them, as Eldoret came into view. At 10,000 ft, they were about level with the tops of the high ground. Just beyond Eldoret the railway line forks, continuing left to its destination in Uganda and right to Kitale. Leslie banked the Dakota to the right and commenced a slow circle of the town and aerodrome, the usual signal to those below that an aircraft had arrived overhead and any cattle should be moved off the airfield, prior to its landing.

As they taxied across the field to their parking position, the pilots remarked to each other that there seemed to be some kind of welcoming committee waiting for them. A group of uniformed Kenya Police officers and askaris stood waiting for the Dakota to come to a halt. The engines were shut down and Dave went back to open the door and put down the steps - Kitale had no passenger steps, being served usually by the little DH Rapides.

A very senior police officer approached, accompanied by two civilians, easily recognisable as British civil service types. These were the clients who had chartered the aircraft.

"Good morning, captain, we would like to have a few words in confidence, if you please." They sat together in the back of the Dakota, and one of the civilians explained what was required. To their surprise, Leslie and Dempster learned that they were to transport Jomo Kenyatta and five of his close colleagues to an undisclosed destination. They were told that there should be sufficient fuel for six hours flying. One of the officials, dressed in a suit and wearing a tie, which was quite remarkable in up country Kenya, produced an envelope and explained that it contained sealed instructions which would be handed to them after take-off by the senior police officer, who would be accompanying them on the flight.

In addition to the six prisoners, there were two European police officers and four Kamba police askaris, sergeants and corporals of long standing in the Kenya Police, twelve passengers in all.

After Dempster had checked the fuel, dipping the tanks and topping up from the hand-hauled bowser, they were ready to go. Within a few minutes the police trucks and escorts arrived and were driven straight to the steps of the Dakota. The prisoners were all handcuffed and chained together. They were immediately hustled aboard the aircraft. Jomo Kenyatta easily recognisable, wearing his familiar leather jacket, featured frequently in newspaper and magazine photographs.

The two pilots boarded the aircraft, walking past the six policemen and their prisoners, who were now being handcuffed to the seat arm rests. The chain was then removed. The African askaris, dressed in regulation khaki shorts and navy blue woollen pullovers, sat at the rear of the aircraft, holding their .303 rifles. The two officers sat in front, armed with side arms and rifles. One of them held the sealed orders.

The aircraft was light, and they quickly took-off towards the east, then turned south, in the direction of Nairobi, as they had, so far, no knowledge of any change to their flight plan. Both Leslie and Dempster had unspoken thoughts that in the ten minutes or so it would take to climb away out of sight, those on the ground would assume that they were heading for Nairobi, whereas the envelope still remained sealed, in the hands of the policeman.

Once they were established on a southerly course, the police officer handed the envelope to the captain. There were covering letters with impressive seals of the Foreign and Colonial Office in London and the Department of Justice of Kenya, giving detailed instructions to various persons connected with the operation. They quickly discarded most of these documents as they searched for their instructions.

Finally they found what they were looking for. They were to fly to Lake Rudolf, in northern Kenya. Putting aside the papers, Dempster quickly calculated a course for the lake and Leslie took up a new heading, turning left some ninety degrees, to cross the Cherangani Hills, their peaks rising to 11,000 ft, before plunging down into the Great Rift Valley, which the Dakota now followed northward, towards the NFD, the Northern Frontier District of Kenya and the great expanse of Lake Rudolf, some 150 miles in length.

With a course set for the lake, they turned their attention to the details of their instructions. They were to proceed to the most northerly part of Kenya, to position 'X', designated by latitude and longitude. It was north east of Lokitaung, a police post, by some twenty-five miles and a couple of miles from the borders of Ethiopia and the Sudan. They were to land on the dried out portion of the lake shore, where an area would be marked out as safe and free of obstructions, such as rocks, gulleys and soft sand. A trail of engine oil would mark the safe limits, and a temporary windsock hoisted on a pole from a Land Rover would indicate the landing direction. A sketch map of the area was attached to the instructions.

After about an hour they were over the southern shore of the lake. The country leading to Lake Rudolf was barren and remote. There were no signs of habitation. They flew along the shore line, looking for signs of life. There was nothing. A couple of desert islands passed below. They descended after a further hours flight up the lake. At 7,000 ft the heat was unbearable, they opened the windows and scooped the air in with their hands, in a vain hope of relief from the blazing heat which enveloped them from this terrible place.

Dempster had marked the map with some precision, but on the ground there was nothing to which one could relate. They descended lower, both police officers now joined in the search for the oil slick markers. The visibility was poor in the heat haze, with rising sand and swirling dust devils. They weaved to and fro across the area in which the landing site had been located on the map. Leslie was getting worried. To return to Kitale now, to arrive during the afternoon thunder storm having failed in their mission, would be a disaster; to return to Nairobi was not even worth thinking about.

They were now very low. Suddenly someone shouted "What's that over there?" As they looked, the aircraft brought them closer to the large black forty-four gallon oil drum, and they saw the 'runway' marked out on the sand. There was no sign of life – no Land Rover – nothing. They could not remain airborne for much longer. "Let's give it a go" said Leslie, after they had searched without success. The lake bed was as smooth as a tarmac runway. He gently brought the Dakota to a stop and switched off the engines. The ground was shimmering in the heat haze. It was quiet and totally deserted. The temperature in the cabin was unbearable. Since it was apparent that they would have to wait, they climbed out of the aircraft and settled down under the wings, where the shade and cooler air from the fuel tanks would provide some relief from the heat.

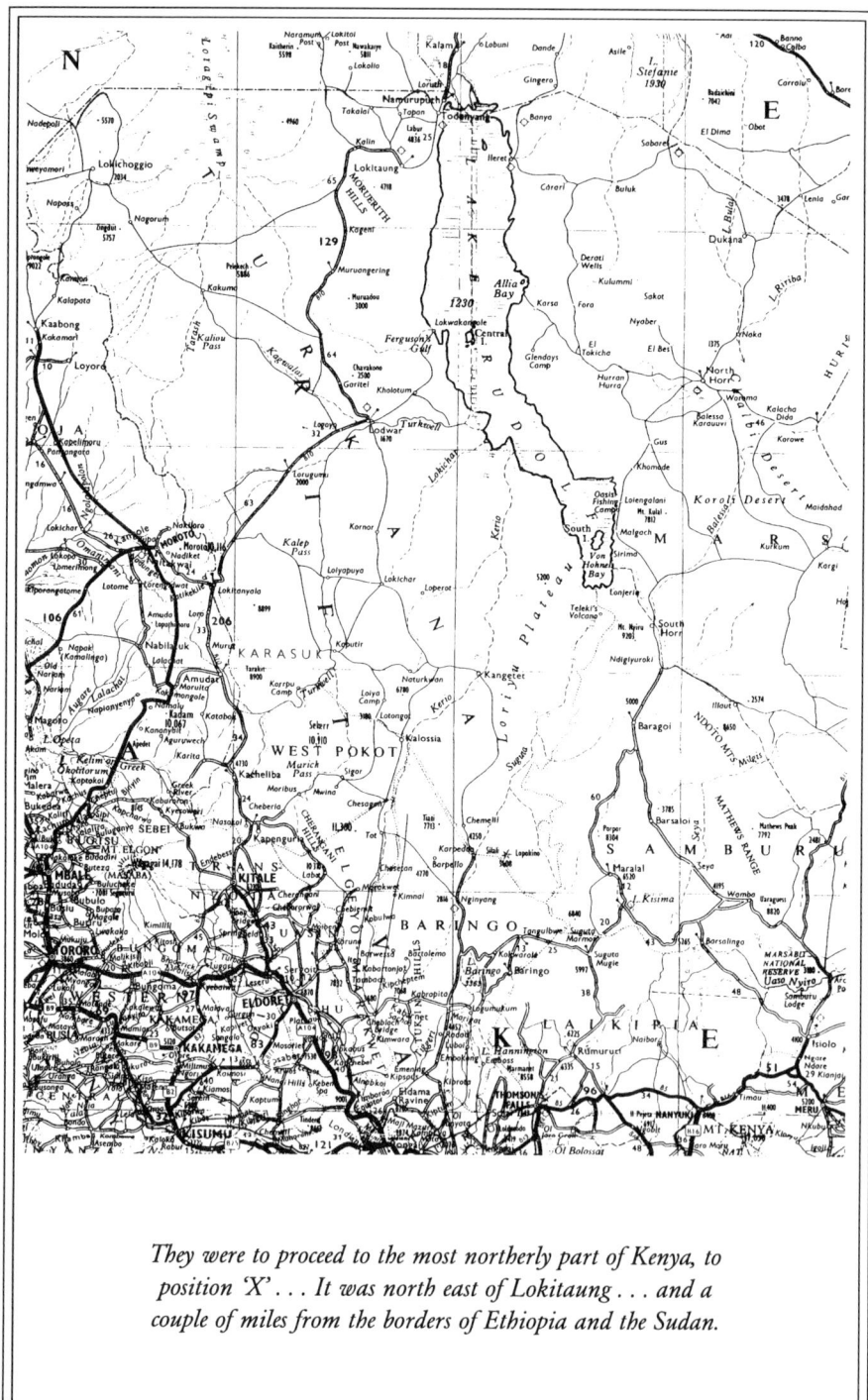

They were to proceed to the most northerly part of Kenya, to position 'X'... It was north east of Lokitaung... and a couple of miles from the borders of Ethiopia and the Sudan.

The prisoners, after a short time, indicated that they wanted to relieve themselves. The policemen unshackled them from their chains and handcuffs, and told them to walk away from the aircraft. Kenyatta and his five companions ambled, in the searing heat, some hundred yards or so, talking and gesticulating together, no doubt wondering where on earth they had been brought to, and what fate might have in store for them.

The four askaris had succumbed to the heat and slept in the shade of the starboard wing. The four white men sat beneath the port wing, watching the prisoners. The policemen conversed quietly, oblivious to the listening pilots, who slowly came to realise that they were to be party to a terrible deed. As the realisation of their predicament surfaced, George Leslie and Dave Dempster got up, saying that they also wished to relieve themselves, and walked off into the desert, in the opposite direction to the prisoners. They did not wish to be witnesses to the shooting of the prisoners, 'while trying to escape'.

Whether it was the click of a rifle bolt, or simply luck, we shall never know, but one of the askaris stirred and sat up, yawning. The plan could not have worked with a native police witness. The future President of Kenya had survived a murder apparently planned thousands of miles away by nameless men in the corridors of power...

A convoy of three Land Rovers eventually arrived. They had heard the Dakota's engines an hour before, but progress had been slow in the sand. The policemen handed over the six convicts, receiving in return signatures to the effect that they were alive and well.

In his book *Kenyatta*, Jeremy Murray-Brown gives the background to the events which occurred on 15th July. Kenyatta had been brought from his imprisonment at Lokitaung to the Supreme Court sitting at Kitale to hear his appeal against the original conviction. His defence lawyer, D.N. Pritt, Q.C., established that the original verdict was illegal, due to a technicality concerning the territorial jurisdiction of the magistrate. Kenyatta was therefore a free man. Murray-Brown wrote:

> "By now the atmosphere at Kitale was very bad. The settlers were threatening to shoot Pritt, let alone the African prisoners. It was market-day; many of them had been drinking and they all carried guns. The police quickly served new detention orders on Kenyatta and his colleagues and smuggled them away, while they got Pritt out of his hotel in a hurry by the back door, and even packed his luggage for him". Kenyatta and the others were loaded into a lorry within five minutes of the end of the judgement and driven off as fast as the roads permitted. Not only did the police pack Pritt's bags for him, they also provided him with a car to take him to Nairobi".

It was not until some considerable time later that Eric Morris learned about this charter flight from George Leslie. "But how was it, that as ops manager, I was not informed of this charter?" he asked. It was only when he consulted his log book that he realised that he had been on long leave at the time. He was particularly interested because he had performed very nearly the same task in December, when on 17th of that month he had flown Kenyatta and his fellow convicts from Nairobi

West to a strip at Todenyang, on the northern tip of Lake Rudolf. His account has many similarities with that of Leslie's and is worth recounting for historical reasons.

> "The Kenya Police called on me to prepare for a highly secret air charter flight... the five passengers would be Mau Mau leaders. It was arranged that I would have a Dak on the compass swinging base, well away from hangars and buildings, and make out as if a compass check was in progress. While there, an army truck would arrive with the five prisoners, escorted by two armed police officers and three askaris. Embarkation and the following take-off would be carried out as quickly as possible.
>
> When things were eventually ready on the compass base next day (17th December 1953), a covered army truck arrived and the rear canvas flaps were drawn apart... Jomo and Fred Kubai were told to get out. The floor of the truck was a good three and a half feet off the ground, and Kenyatta made a sign for steps. An officer told him to jump and, as he hesitated, a Turkana askari gave him a push. Kenyatta fell out, pulling Kubai with him, as they were linked by handcuffs. During the Mau Mau rebellion you often saw deep hate in the eyes of the rebels. It was frightening to see the anger and hate in Jomo's eyes on this occasion!
>
> The three hour flight, in VP-KJU, was uneventful. We picked up a smoke flare which was started as we circled the dry, barren and flat edge of Lake Rudolf. The landing strip

Year Month Day	Aircraft Type	Markings	Time of take-off	Single-Engined Dual	Single-Engined First Pilot	Multi-Engined Dual	Multi-Engined First Pilot	Multi-Engined Second Pilot	Pilot or First Pilot	Second Pilot, Pupil or Passenger	Nature of Flight
				Brought forward			·05 3·15				
July 8	DC3	VP-KLA	0550				2·10		SELF	PINSCOW	LUMBO–LINDI
8	"	"	0755				1·20		"	"	LINDI–DSM
9	"	"	1055				2·40		"	"	DSM–NAI
10	"	VP-KJT	0320				4·10		"	CLOSE BREWER	NAI–SALISBY
11	"	"	0540				4·10		"	"	SAL–NAI
15	"	VP-KJO	0550				1·20		"	DEMPSTER	NAI–KITALE
15	"	"	0855				1·45		"	"	KITALE–POS
15	"	"	1200				1·35		"	"	POS X–KITAL
15	"	"	1340				1·20		"	"	KITALE–NAI
20	"	VP-KJS	0420				1·45		FLANNEGAN	"	NAI–MOM
20	"	"	0645				·45		"	"	MOM–TAN
20	"	"	0745				·45		"	"	TAN–ZAN
20	"	"	0845				·30		"	"	ZAN–DSM
21	"	VP-KJS	1025				·25		"	"	DSM–ZAN
21	"	"	1105				·35		"	"	ZAN–TAN
21	"	"	1200				·35		"	"	TAN–MOM
21	"	"	1255				·45		"	"	MOM–TAN
21	"	"	1400				·40		"	"	TAN–ZAN
21	"	"	1455				·30	65·00	"	"	ZAN–DAR
	Carried forward										

The pages from Captain Leslie's Log Book, with the entry for 15th July, 1953.

was marked out with strips of used black motor oil. After landing and coming to a stop, a lone askari, who had obviously been sent to light the smoke flare, approached. The prisoners were disembarked and the handcuffs removed. They were allowed to move around freely but not far, being followed by an askari with a rifle, bayonet fixed. Most of us sheltered under the aircraft's wing because of the merciless sun and heat. Jomo Kenyatta moved off alone, clearly to urinate; an askari walked a few paces behind with a lowered bayonet, pointing threateningly towards his prisoner. Kenyatta stopped at a short distance away, for his purpose - but what man, under such circumstances, in flat, open, stark surroundings could relieve himself?

"After a wait of about half an hour two vehicles arrived, more police and askaris climbed out, a few words and greetings passed and off went the poor unfortunates to start seven years of imprisonment at Lokitaung Outpost, situated atop a high table top mountain. It was a Post established to watch the border area, where the Kenya, Uganda, Sudan and Abyssinian territories meet.

"First Officer Fuller, myself and a police officer flew out of Todenyang and 'shot-up' the trucks as they struggled along the rough tracks".

Captain Morris went on to say: *"We felt proud that we had had a part in taking the criminals, who had been tried and sentenced by a High Court . . . to justified punishment".*

(This would have been following an appeal by the Kenya government to the Privy Council in London over the East African Court of Appeal reversal of the Kitale judgement. The Privy Council, heavily influenced by Lord Goddard, the Lord Chief Justice, overturned the decision of the East African Court of Appeal, after only twenty minutes. Pritt wrote later: *"I fear I was wrong in thinking that when it came to politics the Privy Council would behave any better than anyone else".*)

On 29th March, 1953 Captain Roger Drew was operating DC3 VP-KJP on the coastal service, when he heard the last position report of a Central African Airways Corporation Viking, call-sign VP-YEY. Later on air traffic control could be heard attempting to contact the aircraft, but with no success. Drew tried to call the aircraft also, but there was no reply. They learned later that the main spar had failed, due to corrosion and the aircraft had crashed just inland from Tanga. As a result of this two of East African Airways DC3s were operated for a period of some six weeks between Nairobi and Salisbury, following the grounding of all the C.A.A. Vikings. Up until this time the E.A.A.C. cabin crew had been European males, with the exception of the early flights on which Sheila McIvor and some of the secretaries had been conscripted. On the chartered flights, C.A.A. loaned some of their air hostesses, but it was to be nearly three years before E.A.A.C. employed hostesses on a regular basis.

In February 1953 the last Lodestar service was flown. The aircraft had played an important part in the development of E.A.A.C., with a remarkable operating record. In the years between 1949 and 1952 records reveal that the fleet had flown 32,000 hours, covering five and a half million miles, with only one minor accident, caused by a brake failure. With only three in-flight engine failures during this period, it proved to be a tribute not only to its manufacturers, but also to the excellent engineering practices in the E.A.A.C. workshops.

It was during 1953 that the airline's planners first began to talk seriously about a service to the United Kingdom. Perhaps as a result of the stresses and strains of the emergency, the government in Kenya was considering the introduction of shorter tours of duty for government officials. E.A.A.C. was asked to examine the possibilities of an air service to the United Kingdom and the feasibility of fares below those of B.O.A.C. and S.A.A. There was no question of B.O.A.C. accepting such an arrangement, so following protracted discussions, it was agreed that all government leave traffic would be shared on a pooled basis and that E.A.A.C. would as a result of the negotiations, lease-purchase three Canadair DC-4M Argonauts. This fitted in with the Corporation's requirement for a DC3 replacement, i.e. an aircraft which could use the airfields currently in use, with the versatility of the DC3, but with greater pay-load and more speed, a pressurised cabin and with four engines for the projected overseas routes. B.O.A.C. had proved the aircraft, both in Africa and on the North Atlantic.

The original delivery date for the first aircraft was to be 31st March 1956, but there were to be numerous delays caused by technical faults with the B.O.A.C. Britannias, which were to replace the aircraft being sold to E.A.A.C., and it was revised to October 1957.

During 1953 a service pattern, operated entirely by a fleet of nine DC3s and two DH Rapides (or Dominies as they were often referred to) was introduced. By virtue of larger load and passenger carrying characteristics, it was possible, through

DH89A, VP-KCY, shown at Dar es Salaam, with engineer Tommy Webb and local helpers. Circa mid-1950s. (Mr T. Webb)

careful planning of aircraft utilisation, not only to offer to the public improved service facilities, but also to make the aircraft available for the ever increasing demand of charter flying.

A new pattern of services was introduced in February, the main feature of which was the linking of certain stations in Tanganyika by circular routes. Passengers travelled clockwise or anti-clockwise to certain destinations at the shortest distance fares. This maintained frequencies at the desired level, but permitted economy in the use of aircraft.

An important revenue earner over the years had been the Jeddah pilgrimage operations each year at the time of the annual *Hajj*. The charters had started in 1951, with the acquision of the DC3s. East African Airways was a pioneer in the *Hajj* charter market, drawing not only upon the large number of moslems in Kenya, Uganda and Tanzania, but also from the Rhodesias, the Comoros Islands and even South Africa. From a small beginning, the *Hajj* traffic grew annually to become a significant factor in the airline's plans. Although a good revenue earner, all airlines involved in the *Hajj* flights had to cope with the special problems associated with this operation. The handling and reception facilities at Jeddah were primitive and disorganised. Most of the passengers were from poor and backward communities – many having invested their lifetime's savings in this holy pilgrimage. As a result, the aircraft suffered from their ignorance and un-trained manners.

The standard average male passenger weight had been established as 75kgs and this was an international norm. It was soon found that the pilgrims were on average much lighter, averaging 65kgs., some of them weighed only 50kgs. This enabled E.A.A.C. to fit an additional four seats in the pilgrim Dakotas, increasing the passenger load to thirty-two from the normal twenty-eight. The aircraft were flown on scheduled services between charters. Soon complaints came in from passengers who had been bitten by fleas, or collected 'crabs' from the seats. After this, every cabin was scrubbed and fumigated after a charter flight.

The pilgrim's sanitary habits caused difficulties in the small DC3 toilets. They were not accustomed to using a lavatory pan and thus the floor of the toilet would soon become awash with urine and water. This would, in time empty away through a drain hole in a corner of the flooring, to escape into the atmosphere. Captain Warder-Griffin on returning from one of the Jeddah charters wrote in his Flight Report: *"I have seen many things during my flying days, but I have never seen a fountain of urine such as I saw in the toilet of this aircraft during flight, nor can I offer any explanation for the phenomenon"*. The aircraft had just come back on line following a complete overhaul. Evidently, the toilet air-extractor fan had been replaced by a larger unit, which was so powerful that it sucked air up through the floor drain-hole, creating a fountain effect!

Other difficulties encountered included the vast quantities of water required for ritual washing, which again added to the floods in the toilet area. On at least one occasion, the captain discovered pilgrims sitting on the floor, brewing tea over a primus stove. Sector times had to be carefully scheduled, so that transit stops allowed time for prayers.

The return flights would lose many of the passenger weight gains, as each pilgrim would be loaded with flasks of holy water from the well of *Zam Zam*. Unless, as sometimes happened, some of the frail and elderly *Hajjis* had succumbed to the terrible heat and arduous conditions.

In addition to the Jeddah *Hajj* flights, the *Mogambo* film charters, and the two DC3s operated for a period of some six weeks between Nairobi and Salisbury on charter to Central African Airways, Kenya Regiment personnel undergoing training in Salisbury were carried by E.A.A. aircraft and several flights to Khartoum, Blantyre and Lusaka were undertaken. Several of the charters were conducted under military secrecy. On one occasion a company of Tanganyika Police were flown to Nyasaland within three hours of the airline receiving a request from the authorities.

The *Hajj* flights to Jeddah were never a very pleasant experience. Conditions in Saudi Arabia were primitive and uncomfortable. It was still a country where slaves were sold openly, heads were cut off by sword wielding executioners and limbs severed as punishment for stealing. On one flight, Captain Pat Travers and F/E Ginger Brewer were crossing the Red Sea, having departed Hargeisa, in Somaliland, when on changing fuel tanks in DC3 VP-KJP, the fuel booster pump failed. They completed their journey to Jeddah, where they found that the handling agent could not provide an engineer to replace the pump. Since it is not possible to start the DC3 without a fuel pump, Brewer had to set to and do the job himself. They had started out from Nairobi at 6.30 a.m. that morning – it was dark before Brewer had finished removing the hundreds of wing-root cowling screws and he asked for someone to hold a torch. They found him an Arab with one hand – the other had been cut off for stealing!

Dakota VP-KKI, *RMA* Sir Richard Burton, *being refuelled at Hargeisa, British Somaliland, 1953.* (Captain Mitchell)

It was 4 a.m. the following morning when he finished work. When he arrived at the hotel, hot, exhausted and sticky he was delighted to find a bath, ready filled with cool water. He pulled the plug after a refreshing bath, and turned in. About two hours later, he was awakened by a tumult in the hotel corridor – "Some bastard has emptied all the water out of the bath!" The following day's supply of washing water was emptied into the bath every night. Brewer thought "Some bastard!" and went back to sleep.

The year was marked by the introduction of a network of Tourist and Colonial Coach Class services to and from Africa. In September, Comet services between Johannesburg and London via Entebbe were increased from three to four a week, two being operated by B.O.A.C. and two by South African Airways in partnership. B.O.A.C. withdrew their Hermes and replaced them with Argonauts in October.

By the end of 1953, the corporation had achieved the first significant profit of £26,360, carried 73,062 passengers, and 1,395,797 kg of cargo over a total of 2,355,422 miles.

During May 1952, a number of E.A.A. captains left to join the Belgian airline Sabena, in the Belgian Congo. As a result, several pilots were upgraded to the DC3. One of these was Captain G.W. 'Mitch' Mitchell, who had accompanied George Leslie on the flight from Durban in 1950. On the 20th June 1952 he had received his roster, giving him command of the service EC033 routing Nairobi-Mombasa-Tanga-Zanzibar-Dar es Salaam – the 'Puddle Jumper', as it was known. There was only one problem. Mitch did not have the DC3 on his licence. He took himself off to see Eric Morris, the operations manager, who very quickly commandeered a DC3 from the departure terminal apron and they took-off for a circuit, completing the single engine performance and emergency drills. After landing, the forms were completed and Eric Morris sent him off to the D.C.A. in town to get his licence endorsed. This achieved, he had to make a mad dash home to get his uniform and back to Nairobi West, just in time to walk calmly, and with some pride, out to his first DC3 command.

It had been common practice during the Lodestar period for the radio officer to act as unofficial co-pilot, since there was no provision for two pilots. The radio officer held an Ops Licence, which meant that he had passed a type technical examination, which qualified him to carry out cockpit checks and emergency drills. With the disappearance of W/T communications, radio officers were virtually redundant. E.A.A.C. had evolved a scheme, approved by the D.C.A. whereby these experienced air crew could be trained as assistants to the captain, which resulted in the 'O' licence. Later a selected few of these were offered flying training to second officer standard, providing that they obtained, at their own expense, an 'A' Private Pilots Licence, which could be done at the flying club. Other R/Os advanced to become flight engineers. The airline was to reap the rewards of this foresighted move in the loyalty and eager service of the aircrew. Some of these, such as Curly Payne and Hank Close were to become senior captains with the airline. The DC3 was similarly crewed on the domestic flights, but both types required a pilot first officer on international flights. Base checks carried out on the L18 Lodestar were permitted by the D.C.A. to cover the DC3, as long as the type was on the pilot's licence.

In 1954, following new government legislation, it was decided to build up an improved training scheme, under Captain Douglas Lavers, as chief flying instructor. An Airspeed Consul twin engined aircraft, VP-KMI, was purchased from B.O.A.C. and ferried from the United Kingdom to Nairobi by Captain Ian Ainscow and Alan Burkitt. The flight, which involved twenty stops, including a forced landing at Ateara, in the Sudan, where they were reprimanded for landing at a non-Customs airfield, took thirty-six hours and fifty-seven minutes flying time. A number of radio officers were then trained as pilots on this machine until it was found to be beyond repair

At Chingola copper mine, Northern Rhodesia. The Dakota was chartered by a United Kingdom Parliamentary group touring Central Africa. The crew used the DC3 wing as a diving-board. Seated by the pool: R/O Curly Payne, Stewardess Dora Young, F/O Alan Burkitt. 5th September, 1954. (Captain Leslie)

in 1955. The foundations had been established for what was to become an extremely busy and efficient training establishment, without which the forthcoming transition to inter-continental airliners would not be possible.

Ken Fuller came from South Africa in 1954, to join East African Airways. He had already logged many hours in the DC3, with Africair, and quickly settled into the routine of his new airline. " We certainly earned our money in those days. A typical log book entry shows Nairobi–Entebbe–Juba–Khartoum–Jeddah–Khartoum. Total time sixteen hours thirty minutes. As for duty time, well forget it, that came later.

> *"On my command check, which involved a night-stop at Dar es Salaam, it was normal for the crew to have a drink or two at the airport, before the drive to the hostel where we stayed. I seriously declined the offer of a beer; was I not on a command check? In no mean or uncertain manner, I was informed by the check captain "We are not interested if you can fly sober, we want to see how you operate with a hangover."*
>
> *"There were some great parties in those days. In Dar es Salaam, I can remember Princess Margaret being told not to visit a certain night club which was over frequented by air crew members! Passenger ships in the harbour were also fair game when it came to parties. Our ops manager had a clever way of writing to us. "Were you responsible for the debacle; if not, what did you do to prevent it?*
>
> *"Unusual happenings did indeed occur. One of our crews[1] saw a flying saucer over Kilimanjaro; the passengers actually verified the phenomenon. I can recall, on the descent into Mombasa one day, we entered cloud at about 7,000 ft and were thrown up to 14,000 ft in a tremendous storm. A moment in time which belonged only to us and our aeroplane.*
>
> *"Landing and take-off accidents always carried the fear of the port propeller coming adrift and tearing into the fuselage, either killing the captain or cutting the control cables. With a runaway propeller we had a theory - fly just above the stall, fly at low altitude where the air is denser. Just before the propeller breaks off, if the nose is pushed forward, the gyroscopic effect will let the propeller clear the aircraft. Fortunately, I never had to test this theory."*[2]

One of the first Air Hostesses, Nicky Proctor, joined E.A.A. at Dar es Salaam, in the early 1950s. The E.A.A.C. town office was in the old Customs House, at the jetty, just off Acacia Avenue. It was merely a medium sized hall, with a small private office leading off at one end, which was occupied by the station manager, Dennis Lloyd, and his secretary, Red Watson. The ticket office and freight section were both housed in this hall. The staff consisted of one ticket clerk, 'Gilly' Gilfillan, and a mail and cargo officer, Chick Evans. At the airport, she recalls three traffic staff, two of whom were named Stockman and Jack Tonnet.

---

[1] It was Captain Bicknell and his crew who saw the flying-saucer. It was fully investigated and well documented at the time.

[2] A senior training captain expressed doubts about this theory, which he regarded as aerodynamically unsound.

There were not many services per day. There was an arrival at 11.00 from Nairobi, which departed at 14.00, routing Zanzibar, Tanga, Mombasa and Nairobi. The afternoon service from Nairobi arrived at 18.00, departing at 07.00 the following morning on the 'milk run' as it was known, back to Nairobi. The groundnut scheme was in full swing at the time, and one aircraft used to fly back and forth to Kongwa and Lindi with personnel, mail and cargo.

Nicky was employed at first in the office. "There was little enough typing to keep me busy as a full time typist", she remembers, "and I spent a great part of my first few months in the bowels of the jetty, in a damp and dark store room, sorting through papers, checking flight coupons against receipts and pay-in slips for the auditors. Great piles of them had to be checked, and I did this accompanied by the spiders, centipedes and other creepy-crawlies, until a messenger would come down, having been sent with news of something more urgent for me to do upstairs."

"Some months later, Stockman left for Nairobi, and Mr Schubert, or 'Shuby',[3] as he was universally known, was posted as senior traffic officer to the airport, and I was transferred there to be his secretary. This was at the old airport, which seemed to be a jumble of old huts, which housed various offices, charter companies, the airport canteen and a hostel. Then the airline started to expand very rapidly, and the DC3s made their appearance, with new faces among the crews, new traffic officers, and then two or three ground receptionists to meet the aircraft and conduct the passengers to and from the wooden terminal building.

"Shuby was great fun to work for, and never ceased to play pranks and tease. I never knew whether he was joking or not. Every morning Templeman,[4] or 'Temp', the chief engineer, would come to the office for coffee and a discussion with 'Shuby' regarding the serviceability state of the aircraft. One morning, while they were busy with their figures, I went into the adjoining office to do some filing. The box files were kept on wooden shelves lining the walls, under a makuti roof. As I pulled down a large file, something fell from it and down the front of my dress, as it disappeared I had just caught sight of a very large, evil looking centipede. Rushing into the office where 'Shuby' and 'Temp' were having their coffee I shouted 'Help, Help, there is a centipede down my bosom, what shall I do?' 'Get your dress off, get it off quickly', said 'Shuby' and 'Temp' in unison, and they helped me undress in a second. One of them grabbed the dress and shook it vigorously, and out fell the large and colourful centipede, which was swiftly annihilated by a large male shoe.

"When it was all over and I collected myself together, I suddenly realised that, in full view of a large audience of passers-by, made up of passengers, crews, airport staff and indigenous Africans, who had all stopped to watch the fun through the door way, I was standing in nothing but my pants and bra! I hastily retired and clothed my rather scantily clad body, while 'Temp' appeared with a glass of brandy in his hand, which he had brought from the canteen, to help me recover from the shock. Sometime afterwards 'Temp' came to me, took me aside and said, in a very confidential manner, that I was not to be embarrassed by what had happened,

---

[3] Schubert was one of those killed in VP-KKH on Kilimanjaro
[4] Ex the Tanganyika Survey Department of 1930s

as he was a married man . . . 'Shuby', on the other hand, never ceased to pull my leg and make ribald remarks about my state of undress in the course of duty.

"The free and easy way of life in Dar came to an end in 1952, when I was transferred to Nairobi West to work for Reg Silverlock, the station manager. We still only had little huts for offices, and the traffic terminal was a larger wooden building, with a small crew room at one side and the mail and cargo section behind it. We worked for a long time before it became quite impossible to cope with the volume of traffic in and out of this small shed. During this time we employed a couple of Sikhs as traffic clerks, they worked as receptionists, leading the passengers to the aircraft, ensuring that their safety belts were fastened, and giving a rudimentary briefing. One day, for some reason, I was on board the DC3 - one of my jobs as Jill-of-all-trades was to complete the load sheet, maybe I had taken it to the aircraft, and this delightful young Sikh was just finishing his briefing. As he walked down the cabin to where I was standing, he said to each row of passengers, in a sombre and doleful voice "Good Luck, Good Luck". Some of the passengers looked quite alarmed while others saw the funny side of it - but not Sarjit Singh.

"It was about this time that stewards were employed to work on the DC3s on the Durban run, once a week. This was not altogether successful at first, as they would go sick, fail to show up and for various reasons there would be a last minute panic to find one. As a result, the three secretaries of the station manager Eastleigh, station manager Nairobi West and operations manager were roped in as part time stewardesses for these services, and to help with charters which required catering on board. I was one of these stewardesses and was continually being called out at a moments notice to go to Durban, or on a charter to another part of East Africa. It was fun and I enjoyed it. Now, when I see the catering equipment, galleys, microwave ovens and the whole paraphernalia, I have to laugh to myself. Before my first trip I was 'briefed' by a Mr Matthews from the Nairobi West canteen. There was no training, or anything like that. He told me, "There is nothing in it, just collect your bar and catering and the flasks, see them onto the aircraft and give it out".

"It sounded easy, so the next morning at the crack of dawn I was at the canteen collecting my catering. Lunch boxes, bar box, soft drinks, six large flasks, containing soup, boiling water, cold water, tea, milk and ice. A box of sandwiches, a box of cut cake, biscuits and a packet of sugar. This all had to be loaded into the rear baggage locker, from where I worked.

"It was not at all easy. Being bumped about in the tail of a DC3, with all that loose catering equipment, rushing backwards and forwards with sick bags, cups of tea and coffee, beers and cold drinks. I remember one hopeful passenger asked me for a Manhattan cocktail - I'm afraid it had to be a plain G&T - nothing fancy. It was really quite tiring after about eight hours, and that for three days running. In addition, at each stop I had to organize the catering on and off the aircraft, to ensure that everything was present, that there was sufficient and at the same time looking cool, calm and collected.

"At first, there was no remuneration for this extra work and, further, I would get back from Durban and hand in my catering equipment and stores, check the bar boxes and do all the fiddly things which had to be done and it would be quite late by the time I got home. Nonetheless, I was expected to be in the office the next morning to catch up with the three days work which had piled up while I had been away. It never occurred to me that there was anything unusual about this arrangement, someone had to do it, so why not me. Later, as a special concession, we were paid 10 shillings per hour for the time spent in the air.

"One day I was called out after I had arrived at my office at Nairobi West. There was no one available to cover the Nairobi - Dar sector of the Durban service. I was asked to cover this sector and hand over to a steward who would join the flight at Dar es Salaam. Off I went, in the belief that I would be back home in Nairobi that evening. On disembarking at Dar, there was consternation. There was no sign of the promised steward. The aircraft had to depart on time. "Couldn't you possibly go?" I was asked. But I had no clothes with me - but this was a minor problem in the circumstances. So I went, and washed out my clothes at each night-stop and managed to get my uniform dress, (it was in the days when ground staff wore fawn linen dresses), ironed ready for the flight the next morning.

"On the way back, we night-stopped in Salisbury and I happened to mention to the station manager there that I must rush off to the hotel in order to do my laundry, as I had no change of clothes with me and I must be ready for the next morning. He retorted with a long diatribe on how irresponsible it was of me to leave Nairobi without proper clothes, and I was advised not to let it happen again. " Just imagine someone had spilled tomato ketchup over you and you had no clean dress to change into, what a bad impression that would have created among the passengers". Little did he know what things I had spilled over me on that trip, and I wondered if he seriously believed that I would leave intentionally without my kit.

"With the advent of larger aircraft, proper cabin staff were engaged, with three week training courses, up-to-date equipment and safety procedures were introduced. Necessity is the mother of invention - we had to invent a lot of things ourselves and learn the hard way, before E.A.A.C. became the efficient and friendly airline which so many of us knew."

Captain George Leslie recalls how the inclusion of stewardesses in the crew brightened up the routine of flying for the pilots. "These girls would do a few days ground training before getting airborne to complete their education. The aircrew were expected to help out with this aspect. One of the more intricate duties was to complete the load and trim sheet. Now, this was one thing in the calm of the class-room, but quite another thing with the rush of a thirty-minute turn around on the ground with people coming and going, freight on and off, refuelling and so on. But it was done, and the captain had to sign the load sheet when it was ready. The first officer would dip the four fuel tanks on the DC3, and the readings were entered on the load sheet. Immediately prior to departure, with the pilots sitting up front, the hostess, (the terms air hostess and stewardess were interchangeable, stewardess being somewhat more acceptable to some), would bring the completed loadsheet up to the cockpit. "Ah - fuel O.K., so many passengers, er, but what about the toilet reading?" This of course was something the poor girl had never heard of before, so it was carefully explained to her. As with the fuel levels, the toilet had to be dipped to see how many gallons were in there. Back she would go to the rear of the Dakota, dip the bucket, and the reading would be noted by the pilots. She would do this until she was told, or realised that her leg was being pulled.

"Another trick was the speciality of First Officer Handford-Rice. The new girl would come up front just prior to take-off to give her usual checks – all secure aft, twenty-one passengers strapped in, ready for take-off. She would then go back and strap herself in. As soon as the wheels were up, the captain would press the hostess call button before the No Smoking and Fasten Seat Belts sign was switched off. She would dash up, sensing something urgent. "Where is the first officer?" – his seat now being empty – "tell him to come here at once, he should be here for take-off." The girl would rush back in a panic, check all around the cabin, but of course, no first officer. On her return to the cockpit she would then get a stern lecture from the captain about how it was her responsibility to not only count the passengers on the aircraft, but also to ensure that the crew were on board and how very cross the company would be if the first officer were left behind, and how illegal it was to be flying with only one pilot.

"All of this would take some thirty minutes on a short leg of the journey. Alan Handford-Rice would have arranged the baggage container up front and, secluded by the cabin door in such a way that he could hide from sight. He would perform his take-off and landing duties as required. After landing he would leave his seat and disappear until the hostess went ashore, a very worried young lady indeed. At the right moment, he would appear, running into the airport building, jacket undone, no cap, out of breath and hair dishevelled. As he approached the now shocked and totally confused girl, he would gasp "Jesus – don't do that to me again . . . long run . . . g-give me . . . a c-cold drink!" It would take a moment or two before she realised that she had been had, but not before everyone had collapsed with mirth".

Captain Harry Allison came from an old settler family; wherever he went he seemed to have a cousin or another relative to visit. He lived in the style to which the old families had become accustomed. One day, Aubrey Francombe and Captain Phil Henn were having breakfast at the Nairobi West staff canteen, just prior to departing on the early morning service. Harry Allison came in late, looking rather flushed. "Alarm didn't wake me" he said. Phil Henn looked at him for a while and then said "Harry, are you pulling our legs?" Allison then explained that his house servant had laid out his freshly laundered khaki uniform, but with the pilot's brevet on upside down, medal ribbons the wrong way round and even his captain's epaulette bars upside down!

In August, 1953, the African Games took place at Ndola in Northern Rhodesia. Allison flew a series of flights throughout Tanganyika, Kenya and Uganda, carrying the sports teams to the games. He was determined to ensure that the Kenya team should arrive in good shape, so was careful to fly as low as possible, since in those days there was no cabin oxygen, and no rules about what height one should fly. When he picked up the favourites, the Uganda team from Entebbe, he flew the Tabora to Ndola sector at 17,000ft. But to no avail, they swept the board at the games! Harry Allison and his wife were to be tragically killed some years later, as the DC6 in which they were passengers, swung off the runway at Casablanca, and hit a hangar. They might have escaped, but he remained on board, to assist with the evacuation, and the aircraft blew-up.

Peter Cunningham and John Crewdson, followed by Gordon Mitchell and George Leslie, were the first pilot first officers that E.A.A.C. had recruited and they were employed specifically for the DC3 international services, as the captain/radio officer crew arrangement on the Lodestars was of doubtful legality on long international flights.

'Mitch', as he was to be known, had been a pilot with the Royal Air Force during the war and had completed his training at Benoni and Nigel, in South Africa. It was during this time that he got married to a South African girl and when the war ended he returned there to start his civil flying career. It was in

The acceptance of DC3 VP-KJR at Tollerton on 3rd June, 1952. Captain Pat Travers shakes hands with Captain G.W. 'Mitch' Mitchell, accompanied by N/O Paddy Murray. Two Field Aviation staff look on. (Captain Mitchell)

Durban, in 1947, that he first met George Leslie and joined him in a company called South Coast Aviation, flying a schedule between Durban and Margate, on the Natal coast, with light aircraft.

Having flown up with Leslie on the Lodestar to Nairobi, 'Mitch' set about renting a house and getting things organised, between the flying and familiarisation with his new airline. Just before Christmas, 1950, he had everything ready for his family, and he arranged to be rostered as first officer on the DC3 scheduled to depart Nairobi on 24th December, bound for Durban. The captain was Bob Warder-Griffin whose wife, Mavis went along as stewardess. They encountered foul weather due to a cyclone in the Mozambique Channel, but they arrived in Durban on time on Christmas Day.

They left the following day on the return journey, together with Mitchell's family. When they reached Lourenco Marques they were told that it would be unwise to continue, due to the cyclone. One of the D.E.T.A. DH Rapides had reportedly overshot its destination by many miles flying down-wind in the cyclone, in weather

Dakota VP-KJT, RMA Joseph Thomson. The eternal snows of Mt Kilimanjaro (19,340ft), in the background.

(Captain Brewer)

so rough that the pilot had great difficulty in turning the aircraft, and when he did he was flying backwards. Another of their pilots had made a precautionary landing on the beach because he was getting low on fuel due to the head-winds.

They all retired to the Aviz Hotel for two days, while the cyclone blew itself out. Mitchell's son, at that time under three years old, was, one day, to fly beside his father as first officer on the Super VC10s, which were to come in the distant future, yet undreamed of during that stormy interlude.

In retrospect, most of the flying was pretty humdrum, with relief from the local flights provided by the Durban and Salisbury services. Even so, most of the crews would not have changed their job for anything. There always existed a great spirit and a sense of loyalty in the company, and few doubted that the management was good, by any standards.

Mitchell was involved with two of the DC3 delivery flights from England. The first was in May, 1952, when chief pilot Pat Travers and he delivered a Lodestar to Blackbushe, and then travelled up to Tollerton to collect the DC3. During the stop-over, they did their initial Instrument Rating test at Stansted, as the new I.C.A.O. flight crew licences were being introduced. Their flight home routed via Rome-Malta (where they spent a pleasant two days while awaiting a replacement inverter), El Adem-Wadi Halfa, (night-stop), Juba-Nairobi.

His second delivery flight came as a complete surprise when, during his long leave in England in August, 1953, he was contacted by Eric Morris, and asked to proceed to Tollerton to pick up another DC3 for delivery to Nairobi. On this occasion they routed via Benina instead of El Adem.

1954

On Sunday, 24th January, 1954, Captain Reg Cartwright had the day off and was enjoying a lazy breakfast with his family, when he received a telephone call from Johnny Cox in the Entebbe control tower. A single engined Cessna had left from Nairobi the previous day, on a flight to the Murchison Falls. The aircraft was missing and he was asked to join in the search which was being organised. The passengers on board the Cessna were Ernest Hemingway and his wife Mary.

The Rapide, VP-KEA, was quickly prepared and checked, and Cartwright got airborne to fly to his allocated search territory, which was a large area to the east of Masindi between the River Nile and Lake Victoria. For over three hours he flew a square search pattern. Unknown to him at the time, a B.O.A.C. Argonaut, en route from Nairobi to Khartoum, had reported seeing the wreckage of a small plane near the Murchison Falls. On arrival at the aerodrome at Masindi, where he had landed to refuel, Cartwright learned that Howard Iliffe and Dickie Bird, who had flown up from Nairobi, had got airborne in the Piper Pacer. They had been directed to the Murchison Falls area and had identified the wreckage as that of the missing aircraft. They could not, however see any sign of the occupants.

In the meantime, the world was being made aware of the incident, involving the famous author and personality, who had the previous year received the prestigious Nobel Prize for Literature. The teleprinters and ticker-tapes were carrying the story from Reuters.

> *"Kampala Uganda Jan 24 Reuter... Plane carrying the novelist Mr Ernest Hemingway and his wife crashed over Murchison Falls, where the River Nile plunges four hundred feet down through a rock chasm in north west Uganda yesterday... after a search by police and aircraft, wreckage of a plane, believed to be the Hemingway's was sighted today three miles below the falls and a search plane reported there was no sign of life... more ... A police rescue party immediately set out to battle up the Nile by launch from Butiaba on Lake Albert to the wild country where the plane came down... It is the least accessible part of Uganda, thick with big game, including Elephants, Hippopotomi, Buffalo, and Crocodiles... more... Search for the Hemingway's plane, which was on a charter flight, began when it failed to arrive at Masindi to refuel... Passengers on a British Overseas Airways Corporation airliner flying over the area were warned to keep a look-out for the wreckage... The search plane which spotted the aircraft on the ground reported that it was on the south bank of the Nile..."*

The wreckage had been reported as being close to the boat landing stage near the base of the falls. Cartwright knew that a boat based at Butiaba was available for charter and it was soon discovered that it had been chartered by Dr Ian MacAdam of Makarere University, who was well known to him through their contacts in connection with the Flying Doctor Service.

After a long series of conversations by HF radio link with Entebbe and Nairobi, Cartwright was given permission to search the lake for this craft, to see if they had picked up any survivors. He spotted the boat as it was leaving the Nile estuary, heading south across Lake Albert for Butiaba. As the Rapide approached, three people went to the front of the craft, and the remainder of those on board pointed towards them. Cartwright reported to search control and informed them that he would land at Butiaba and confirm that the three people had been picked up. Should all be well, the huge, expensive, rescue operation both on the land and in the air, could be called off.

Reg Cartwright had not used the strip at Butiaba since the charter flights in 1951 for the film *The African Queen*, and had no idea of its condition. He made a careful inspection before landing, but apart from being bumpy and somewhat overgrown, it was not beyond the capabilities of the Rapide.

By now it was late in the afternoon, the Rapide had completed some six hours flying, with two refuelling stops. The local police had met Cartwright at the airstrip and he was driven down to the pier to meet the boat. It was soon established that Hemingway, his wife Mary and Roy Marsh, the pilot of the Cessna, had been rescued without serious injury. As he was climbing back into the police vehicle to return to the airstrip, Cartwright was approached by Hemingway, who asked him if they could fly with him back to Entebbe. On the face of it this was a reasonable request. However, the Rapide was a public transport aircraft, operating within the constraints of the Air Navigation Order. Butiaba was an unlicensed airfield from which the aircraft was not permitted to carry passengers, within the terms of the

Corporation's insurance cover. Cartwright explained this to Hemingway and refused his request, excusing himself, as darkness was approaching and he needed to check both the aircraft and the strip prior to take-off.

Again, as Cartwright completed his detailed pre-flight inspection at the airstrip, Hemingway approached him. He said that they had spent a poor night in the open, following the crash, and they were anxious to get back to civilization as soon as possible. Cartwright was in a very difficult spot. With his professional pilot's hat on, he knew that he should refuse. But it did, on the other hand, appear unreasonable to depart in the Rapide alone, leaving the three unfortunate victims of what must have been a shocking escape from death, to their own devices in a remote part of Uganda. Reluctantly, he agreed to take them, and they quickly boarded the Rapide.

The light was failing fast as he taxied to the end of the strip and lined up for take-off. In the short equatorial twilight, even in the period spent taxying, the runway had become featureless against the last of the sun's light. Cartwright eased open the throttles and the two Gipsy-Six engines roared as the aircraft gradually built up speed down the uneven surface.

They were three quarters of the way down the strip, perhaps a second or two before rotation speed, at which the Rapide would have sufficient speed to leave the ground, when the wheels sped over a large bump, which, while probably not effecting a lightly laden machine, bounced the aircraft prematurely into the air, in a tail down attitude. The Rapide, groping for lift, was staggering as Cartwright fought to gain speed. There was just insufficient to gain enough height to clear a thorn bush, about four feet high, which now lay in their path. The fixed undercarriage of the Rapide passed through the bush, which decreased its already critical airspeed resulting in a return to earth. The next few moments were extremely busy for Cartwright, as he struggled to prevent the Rapide from hurtling to destruction. When they finally came to rest, he had completed the necessary emergency drills, throttles closed, fuel turned off, electrical switches off. The aircraft was more or less intact and he undid his safety harness and climbed out of his seat to look aft, hoping that his passengers were unhurt. In the gloom he could not make out much, except to see that the cabin door was open. He quickly discovered that Hemingway had already left the scene of the accident. Returning briefly to the cockpit, Cartwright saw that fuel was leaking from the starboard engine onto the hot exhaust. Within moments it had caught fire and he struggled in the small cabin to drag Mary Hemingway and the other pilot out through an emergency exit. The fire quickly engulfed the Rapide as the fabric on the starboard side caught fire and the cockpit was ringed with flames. Cartwright made an attempt to salvage the baggage, but was forced back by the flames and managed to get away before the fuel tanks exploded, together with the Very cartridges stored on board.

In his own words Cartwright remembers, "Safely out of the aircraft my first concern was for the missing Mr Hemingway. I'm sorry to report that he had departed at great speed, making no attempt to help anyone else. My day had not gone well, and my relationship with Hemingway became thorny".

Tired and despondent, they were driven to the small hotel at Masindi, where they met up with some of the colonials who had been out all that day searching the ground for the Hemingway party. As they partook of welcome food and refreshment, Hemingway, who soon became worse for drink, began to change from bluff geniality to offensiveness, to such a degree that even the fact that he had survived two serious aircraft accidents within a short time could not excuse him in Cartwright's view. There is no record of what was said by Hemingway that night, but Cartwright counts the episode as one which he does not like to remember, even some forty years after the event. But it convinced him that the man, famous for his self proclaimed bravery and macho image, was a coward and a sham.

The ticker-tapes were still active, as the news of the rescue had not yet reached the world at large. Reuters transmitted the message:

> "... New York Jan 25 ... American newspapers today splashed the news that Ernest Hemingway, the novelist, and his wife were feared dead in a private plane crash in Africa ... The New York Daily News printed photographic scenes from the novelists life with the caption "A Farewell to Hemingway" ... The New York Daily Mirror said that Mrs Hemingway, the former Mary Welsh, "tough minded, only daughter of a wealthy Minnesota lumber man" had been the only woman correspondent assigned to the Royal Air Force during the war ... "Hemingway wrote so much about bravery and violence and his own exploits that there were some people who doubted he could be that virile", the Daily News said ... "He flattened an inebriated broker in the Stork Club some years ago because the broker called him a professional he-man"."

Reuters went on to report:

> "Hemingway long had a fear of flying", Mr William Lowe, former Executive Editor of Look Magazine said here. "That is why the author had insisted on using surface transport for his trip last September to Africa, and travelled by land whenever he could" ... "But only last month the novelist chartered a small plane for easier spotting of game" ... He explained that Hemingway had gathered much material for fiction writing while on his trip but that he planned to publish a non-fiction picture book on his African experience ... In one of his last letters, Mr Lowe revealed, Hemingway wrote that he was preparing for a trip to the East coast of Africa before sailing home on March 10 from Mombasa ... He said the flight on Saturday might have been the author's departure for the East coast and the boat trip home".

Newspapers were comparing the author's fate with the fictional scenarios in his books:

> "When rescuers reach the plane in which Ernest Hemingway and his wife crashed in a most inaccessible part of North-west Uganda, they may, suggested the **Daily Mail**, find a scene reminiscent of the American author's story The "Snows of Kilimanjaro". The story is set in Tanganyika, some 500 miles from Murchison Falls. The "Snows of Kilimanjaro" and the Technicolor film which followed it tell of a novelist who lies at the foot of the Mountain, waiting to die. He is nursed by a loyal and loving wife, but in his delirium keeps jerking with each and every fevered toss and turn to the other loves of his life. In

the film – though not in the book – the rescuing aircraft arrives in time, and the vultures fly away."

At the time of the crash, *Look* Magazine, which had commissioned his visit to East Africa, had published Hemingway's most recent work, a travel article titled *Safari*. The article, with many photographs dealt with the first five weeks of his 2,000 mile trip with his wife through the wild Maasai country of Southern Kenya.

The cause of the original accident to the Cessna was low flying. The pilot did not know the area and had not been told of the telephone cable which passed over the top of the falls. In the event, they had been lucky to come to rest in fairly thick bush, above the river bank, where they had spent an uncomfortable night. The river at that point teems with large crocodiles and hippos, and their fate would have been sealed had they not been able to camp on the high ground.

Cartwright's opinion of Hemingway was not changed by the great writer's response to his request for a report on the accident, to corroborate his own report to the D.C.A. Hemingway gave him a dirty piece of crumpled paper, with some barely legible words scratched upon it.

One of the high-lights of the year 1954 was to be the visit by Her Majesty the Queen and the Duke of Edinburgh to Uganda, in which the great hydro-electric plant and dam at the Owen Falls, on the River Nile, would be officially opened. In addition, the vast big-game area bordering the Nile in western Uganda would be dedicated as the Queen Elizabeth National Park. As with the previous visit, which had been the royal honeymoon, tragically cut short by the death of her father, King George VI, East African Airways were given the singular honour, for the time, of conveying the Queen within East Africa.

A Dakota aircraft, VP-KJU, named *Sagana II*, had been selected for the flights, which had been subjected to a complete overhaul, every component and working part was overhauled or replaced. A special interior was fitted to the aircraft with a separate compartment, to seat eight, for the royal party, provided with fully adjustable and swivelling chairs and tables. The engineering work was carried out under the supervision of engineering manager A.E. Robinson, with J. Walsh responsible for upholstery and interior, and Andy Ross-Marsh in charge of the airframe overhaul. Decorative panels depicting typical scenes of Uganda life were painted by the Kenyan artist, Miss Robin Anderson.

The first flight that took place was from Jinja to Entebbe on the 29th of April. The aircraft left Jinja at dusk and the short night operation was carried out on schedule. The second operation was to Kasenyi on the 30th of April, where Her Majesty opened the new Queen Elizabeth National Park, and returned to Entebbe the same day. Both flights were carried out with faultless precision. In addition to Her Majesty and His Royal Highness, the passengers were the Secretary of State for the Colonies, the Rt Hon. Oliver Lyttleton and Lady Moira Lyttleton, Sir Andrew and Lady Cohen, Lord Althorp and Sir Michael Adeane.

The cockpit of DC3, VP-KJU Sagana II, photographed during a demonstration flight to Salisbury in July, 1954, two months after the royal flights.

(Capt Morris)

The Royal Flight aircraft VP-KJU, RMA Sagana II, at Jinja, Uganda, on 29th April, 1954. The crew L to R: E/O Cawthorne, Captain Pat Travers, Captain Eric Morris, R/O Derek Rhodes, Steward George Matthews. Although the Royal Standard is flying, the Queen was inspecting the 5th Battalion, Kings African Rifles at the time the photograph was taken. (Captain E. Morris / B.O.A.C)

144 · EAST AFRICAN: AN AIRLINE STORY

The royal party including the Governor of Uganda, Sir Andrew Cohen (in full dress), followed by his ADC, board Sagana II. *They are seen off by Captain Malin Sorsbie, Sir Alfred Vincent and Mr Hugh Dawson (airport manager, Entebbe). A security officer stands near the tail.* (B.O.A.C./Captain Morris)

Her Majesty the Queen and Prince Philip board Sagana II *at Entebbe, saluted by E.A.A.C. senior station officer Entebbe, Robin Grant. 29th April, 1954.* (B.O.A.C./Captain Morris)

Chocks away, as Sagana II, *Royal Standard flying, prepares to taxi at Entebbe, bound for Jinja. 'Spud' Murphy supervises the ground-crew. For moments during take-off, Lake-birds and shrike, seeking worms after a series of showers, presented a hazard to Captain E. Morris. 29th April, 1954.* (B.O.A.C./Captain Morris)

The internal territorial ticket issued to Her Majesty the Queen. Written in the days before ball-point pens, it was completed in indelible pencil. The fare paid is shown as 'Free'!

(Captain E. Morris)

The interior of Sagana II, *looking forward. The telephone intercom to the cockpit can be seen, between the Queen's and the Duke of Edinburgh's seats.*

The interior looking aft. The Queen sat facing forward, opposite the Duke of Edinburgh (left of picture). Decorative pictures can be seen in the window recesses. The linen head rest covers were embroidered with the ER monogram. Steward Matthews served only canned orange juice during the flight, opened in the cabin, as a security precaution against poisoning.

(Captain Morris)

Form No. E.A.A. 95

PASSENGER MANIFEST

Owner or Operator EAST AFRICAN AIRWAYS CORPORATION

Aircraft VP — K.J.U. Flight No E C Royal Flight Date 29th, April 54.
(Registration marks and nationality)

Point of Embarkation ENTEBBE. (UGANDA) Point of Disembarkation JINJA. (UGANDA)
(Place and Country) (Place and Country)

	Surname and Initials	a	b	c	d	e	f	g	For official use only
1.	H. M. QUEEN.	F		–	65				8-40512
2.	H.R.H. THE DUKE OF EDINBURGH	M		–	75				8-40513
3.	H. E. SIR ANDREW COHEN	M		–	75				8-40514
4.	LADY COHEN	F		–	65				8-40515
5.	MR. LYTTELTON O.	M		–	75				8-40516
6.	LADY LYTTELTON	F		–	65				8-40517
7.	LORD ALTHORP	M		–	75				8-40518
8.	SIR MICHAEL ADEAN E	M		–	75				8-40519
9.	SUPT. CLARK	M		–	75				8-40520
10.	LADY ALICE EGERTON	F		–	65				8-40521
11.	SIR E. FIELDEN	M		–	75				8-40522
12.	MR. GRIFFITHS O.	M		–	75				8-40523

CREW.
CAPT. MORRIS. E.
" TRAVERS. P.
R/O. RHODES.
E/O. CAWTHORN.
ATW. MATHEWS.

Prepared by .... Page ..... of ..... Pages

The Passenger Manifest issued on the occasion of the Royal Flight from Entebbe to Jinja, 29th April, 1954. (courtesy of Captain E. Morris)

An additional service provided by East African Airways was a luncheon for Her Majesty the Queen and the Duke of Edinburgh and 180 guests at the Mweya Lodge in the Queen Elizabeth National Park. This required considerable ingenuity as the supplies had to be flown packed in dry ice from Nairobi to Kasenyi. Fruit was specially flown to Nairobi from South Africa, delicacies from the United Kingdom and hors d'oeuvres from Scandinavia, with the assistance and co-operation of B.O.A.C., South African Airways and S.A.S. The meal was prepared by the E.A.A.C. catering manager, Charles West Thomas, often irreverently referred to as the "Kitchen Group-Captain", due to his eccentric habit of wearing, quite unofficially, four silver-lined red bars on the epaulettes of his uniform.

The menu, served at the lodge, surrounded in the great park by some of the greatest elephant herds on earth, was quite incongruous, in those surroundings:

> A Luncheon
> on the occasion of
> The Royal Tour of Uganda
> 30th April 1954
> Menu
> Iced Melon PawPaw Grape Fruit
> Tomato Juice Cocktail
> Iced Fruit Juice
>
> ---
>
> Fresh Scotch Salmon Lobster Mayonnaise
> Smoked Scotch Salmon
>
> ---
>
> Roast Stuffed Turkey Uplands York Ham
> Roast Duck Roast Sirloin of Beef
> Stuffed loin of Veal Roast Saddle of Lamb
> Glazed Ox Tongue
> Roast Pork Melton Mowbray Pie
>
> ---
>
> Avocado Pear Asparagus Tomato Cucumber
> Lettuce Beetroot Celery Stuffed Egg
> Russian Salad Potato Salad
>
> ---
>
> Pear Cardinal Sherry Trifle
> Mango Fool
>
> ---
>
> Assorted Cheeses
>
> ---
>
> Coffee
>
> ---
>
> *Dessert*

The Queen's interest in the sport of kings was, even then, highly developed, remembering, while in the National Park, that the Thousand Guineas had taken place in England, she asked for a special message to be sent by police radio to Government House, Entebbe, asking for the result of the race.

With his experience in the development of air routes in Uganda, Reg Cartwright was a natural choice to crew the royal DC3, *Sagana II*. It was a crushing disappointment, therefore, when the incident at Butiaba disqualified him from flying as co-pilot to Captain Eric Morris. He was replaced by Captain Pat Travers. The remainder of the crew were Radio Officer Derek Rhodes, Flight Engineer Bill Cawthorne and Steward George Matthews.

The flights had gone smoothly, without incident. The Queen and the Duke were fascinated by the game on the last afternoon of their visit. The departure was delayed by some twenty minutes, as they watched, in the last of the evening sun, the great lines of elephants moving majestically across the hillsides. When they landed at Entebbe airport, after dark, the Duke, who had been reading a Penguin paperback edition of *Death in a White Tie* by Ngaio Marsh, during the short flights in *Sagana II*, dashed off for a meeting at Government House, leaving the book on his seat, with a bookmark in the page near the end. A little while later an African traffic policeman on a motorcycle roared back to the airport with the message, "His Royal Highness wants his book, please."

On that night of 30th April, the crew were summoned to Government House, Entebbe, where Her Majesty bestowed upon Eric Morris the Victorian Order, M.V.O., an honour within the Sovereign's personal gift, together with autographed portraits of the Queen and the Duke. Each member of the crew received a signed photograph.

On May 3rd, The chief secretary of Uganda, Mr Colin H. Thornley[5] wrote to Malin Sorsbie:

"I am directed to convey to you the grateful thanks of His Excellency the Governor for the most efficient arrangements made by you and your staff in connection with the flights made by Her Majesty the Queen and His Royal Highness the Duke of Edinburgh during the course of their visit to Uganda. The excellence of these arrangements reflects the greatest credit on all who were responsible for them".

Progress and development in 1954 had been satisfactory, despite the continuation of the Emergency in Kenya and a fall in the value of exports throughout the East African Territories. The capacity offered to the public on scheduled services was increased by nearly one and a quarter million ton miles to 5,643,464, and although costs continued to increase, revenue remained buoyant and exceeded expectations. Progress was maintained with similar results to 1953. An operating profit of £7,817 was made, and after providing for interest on the East African Government Stock and other charges, the aggregate deficiency carried forward had been reduced to £1,554.

---

[5] Later Sir Colin Thornley

(Left) George Leslie bought this 1951 Standard 8 tourer at a bargain price - £75, in Tanga. With no seats fitted in the Dakota, he was able to bring it home to Nairobi as 'crew baggage'. 12th September, 1954.
(Captain Leslie)

(Below) Dickie Waters supervises the off-load of the Standard 8 at Nairobi West.
(Captain Leslie)

Since the formation of East African Airways 18,000,000 aircraft miles or some 720 times round the world had been operated without serious incident. In 1954, 14,000 flights were operated on scheduled services, and nearly 1,000 on charter. With the exception of the accident during the rescue of the Hemingway party (which was not on an authorised flight), no accidents or incidents occurred on scheduled or charter services.

The number of passengers carried reached a new peak of 93,427 on scheduled services alone, being some 20,000 more than the number carried in 1953. The quantity of cargo carried was nearly doubled at 2,118,337 kilos, which represented some 700 full Dakota loads per annum, or nearly two per day.

Although there was a relatively small increase of 1,344 hours in the total number of hours flown by the fleet, the overall utility of the service to the public was considerably improved by improvements in the general pattern of service operations, and the replacement of some Rapide services by DC3s. The capacity ton miles increased by almost 28% and this in turn resulted in more traffic being carried and better schedules.

Improvements at the airfield at Mwanza permitted the introduction of a DC3 service on the central line route between Dar es Salaam and Nairobi via Dodoma, Tabora and Mwanza. As had been experienced in the past, the replacement of the Rapides by DC3s on this service resulted in a marked increase in the traffic offered.

A new regional service linking Nairobi and Dar es Salaam with Salisbury and Durban via Blantyre was introduced in May.

Captain Eric Morris commanded the DC3, VP-KJU, on this inaugural service, EC115/116, which departed Nairobi on 21st May, 1954. They picked up members of the press and a number of travel agents on the Salisbury - Durban - Salisbury sector, on what was the first airline service between the two cities. There were soon to be difficulties, however, as the traffic rights were rescinded by the governments of Southern Rhodesia and South Africa, following the inauguration of South African Airways and Central African Airways services on the route.

In Uganda, the internal Communications Flight previously operated on a charter basis to the government, was taken over and operated as a bi-weekly scheduled service.

During the third quarter of 1954 there was a concentrated period of charter flying, which included fourteen flights to Jeddah for the annual *Hajj* pilgrimage, and to destinations such as Damascus, Teheran, Salisbury and Khartoum in addition to extensive operations in connection with the Commonwealth Parliamentary Association, whose members were carried throughout East Africa and the Rhodesias.

By the end of 1954 there were sixty-two flying staff. Six new captains, ten co-pilots, one European flight steward and three African stewards had been recruited during the year (on one flight a passenger beckoned to the African steward, addressing him as "Boy". The steward replied forcefully "Bwana, mimi hapana *Boy* - mimi *Hostess!*).[6] The comparatively large increase in pilot strength was due to a shortage at the commencement of the year due to increased DC3 operations

---

[6] Grammatically incorrect up-country Swahili translated as "Sir, I am not Boy - I am Hostess!"

towards the end of 1953, the introduction of new legislation requiring two pilots on all DC3 operations, and increases to DC3 operations during the year.

The Emergency in Kenya was affecting the airline personnel in that conscription had now been introduced, which caused considerable dislocation among the staff. At the end of 1954 some 6% of Kenya based supervisory staff were serving full time in the military or police, and a further 7% were due to be called up in 1955, while part-time service made further calls upon resources. Special measures had to be taken to protect the aircraft standing outside at the airports. At Wilson Airport, which adjoined the Nairobi game reserve and the Athi River plains, the askari guards had more than the Mau Mau rebels to concern them. One morning, as the early shift arrived for duty, they saw a pride of lion resting beneath a Dakota; on top of the fuselage sat two very frightened askaris.

The Mau Mau method of operation was to terrify the great majority of peaceful African citizens, in order to turn them against the British, hoping that this would further their aims in quickly gaining independence, when their leaders would seize power. One day, it was the turn of one of the African stewards to be coerced into

The crew of VP-KJU at Durban during 'Wings Week' in July, 1954. L to R: R/O Paddy Murray, F/O Pieter von Emmenis, Captain Eric Morris. "By this time Sagana II (VP-KJU) was part of me" said Morris "She seemed to have accepted me and we just throbbed a singular beat together. She seemed to glide herself to a 'kiss' landing, quite differently to that first at Jinja with the Queen on board, when she (Sagana) made it known that it was neither Her Majesty nor the fellow controlling her that was playing the most important part of the whole pageantry." (Captain Morris)

showing allegiance to the terror gangs. He was a Kikuyu named Mwangi who reported to operations that he was frightened to carry out his flight to Mombasa that afternoon. He explained that the "Mau Mau people had come to him" and told him that "unless he obeyed their instructions, his wife and children would be killed". He had been asked to carry something with him, to be collected at Mombasa. The police were called in, who advised that he should not continue working as a steward. Security checks were carried out on the remaining stewards, who were warned to report any Mau Mau threats. Mwangi went to work in the catering unit and eventually was employed running the duty free liquor shop at Nairobi Airport.

During the year Board meetings had concentrated on the vexed question of re-equipment and future development. Sir Alfred Vincent and Captain Malin Sorsbie had spent a frustrating year discussing proposals with B.O.A.C. and the Territorial governments the various options which would best meet the needs of East African Airways. At one stage, following Central African Airways lead, in March, £55,000 was paid to Vickers Armstrongs, as an initial instalment on Viscount aircraft. This was followed by an offer of second-hand DC4-M Argonaut aircraft from B.O.A.C. at a "very reasonable price", but with no firm delivery date. The issue was further confused by an offer from Pan American of three Convair 240 aircraft, which was highly recommended by Captain Malin Sorsbie.

On June 11th, Sir Miles Thomas, chairman of B.O.A.C., wrote to Sir Alfred Vincent

". . . its (Convair 240) range-payload is even more critical than the Viscount and, in our opinion, it would not be suitable for trunk route operations. It follows that we would not be justified in investing money in E.A.A.C. for the specific purpose of purchasing these aircraft . . . we should, therefore, have to oppose any application by E.A.A.C. for a licence to the U.K. to operate with Convairs".

It was only after the intervention of the Commissioner for Transport of the East African High Commission, Maj Gen D.A. Williams, who wrote to the Secretary of State for the Colonies, that a meeting was convened on 20th September at Airways House in London, between East African Airways and B.O.A.C., where an agreement was reached for the 50/50 share of government leave traffic based upon a chartered B.O.A.C. Argonaut once-weekly service between East Africa and the United Kingdom and two weekly Argonaut services Nairobi-Durban, effective June, 1955. Agreement was reached for the sale by B.O.A.C. of three Argonauts at £93,000 each, for delivery to E.A.A.C. on 31st March 1956.

As it became evident that government leave traffic alone would not be sufficient to support a weekly Argonaut service, it was proposed that some seats would be sold to tourist class passengers. This was initially opposed by B.O.A.C. Mr Basil Smallpeice wrote to Sir Alfred Vincent on January 18th, 1955,

". . . after six to twelve months...we could consider changing it to a scheduled tourist class service if it became apparent that a once a week service provided greater capacity than we needed to move approximately half the leave traffic."

This was resisted by Sir Alfred Vincent until, on January 25th, B.O.A.C. agreed to a scheduled service.

1955

An interesting diversion from the routine line flights came in March, 1955, for Tug Wilson and Curly Payne. 'Slick' Goodlin had asked Malin Sorsbie's help in delivering a Lockheed Lodestar, which Goodlin had purchased from Sabena, to New York from Leopoldville, in the Belgian Congo. The flight routed Leopoldville – Accra – Roberts Field, Liberia,- Fernando de Noronho Island – Natal, Brazil – Georgetown, British Guiana – Nassau, Bahamas – New York.

The journey, which commenced on 6th March, in Lodestar N2744A, went smoothly and without incident – which was fortunate, since their only emergency equipment across the vast south Atlantic was a tractor inner-tube – until they arrived at the Brazilian island of Fernando de Noronho, where the authorities refused them fuel, due to lack of "correct papers." Forced to continue to Natal, after ten hours and twenty minutes crossing the south Atlantic, they were placed under house arrest while the local officials perused the paper-work, trying to find some infringement of arbitrary rules. Frustrated by the indifference of the officials and some fairly unsubtle indications that the offer of dollar bills would ease their situation, the two aviators attempted to steal away, hoping that their captors would not detect them.

As they furtively walked around the aircraft, the military guard must have sensed their purpose, and they were confronted by a rifle pointed at them, then, as they stood, horrified, the soldier slid the bolt, injecting a round into the breech. Wilson spoke out of the corner of his mouth, "I think discretion is the better part of valour, in this case..." and they walked, defeated, back to the terminal building.

Finally, after a week or so in "a disgusting hotel", they were released, and continued for mile after mile, hour after hour, for nine hours over solid, impenetrable jungle, and across the mouth of the Amazon, to Georgetown, British Guiana. For most of the flight they were in thick, wet, stratus cloud. Holes in the cockpit roof allowed a continual drip of water onto their legs. The aircraft was at all up weight, with fuel carried in two huge containers in the passenger compartment. It was not a comfortable flight, the last hour of which was completed in total darkness. In contrast to their last accommodation, they spent that night in the comfort of the Royal Air Force mess, where they enjoyed a hot bath, a meal and a good night's rest.

The next leg of the journey, from Georgetown to Nassau was more pleasant, they completed it in nine hours and forty minutes of pleasurable flying, over the myriad coloured seas and islands of the Caribbean. A night-stop at Nassau, and the final sector of the flight brought them, in cold, fine weather, to New York, La Guardia, in six hours fifteen minutes – forty-six hours in total since they left Leopoldville.

A gum-chewing ground engineer came out to meet them on arrival, "Where you from, Bud?" "Africa" replied Tug. Surveying the oil-smeared, weather beaten Lodestar, N2744A, the American replied "What - in *that?*" He was still staring in bewilderment as Wilson and Curly Payne walked wearily to the terminal buildings.

After a rest in New York, Wilson returned in a leisurely fashion to the United Kingdom aboard the *Queen Mary*, while Curly Payne flew the Atlantic in order to take further Civil Aviation examinations in London.

First Officer Ken Fuller looked at his flight roster for the first two weeks in May, 1955, and was surprised to see that he had been allocated the Nairobi - Lumbo - Durban service, since he had flown the route on his previous flight. It was soon changed, when this was discovered and he was replaced by First Officer Cairncross.

Curiously, the radio officer also had to be changed, when he stated that he had had a premonition of disaster and that he would never fly again; even as a passenger. He was replaced by 'Greg' Gregory, a ground radio officer with the D.C.A., who was so keen to fly that he volunteered for the flight during his period of local leave. On the 15th May, the DC3, VP-KKH, departed for Durban under the command of Captain Jack Neville Quirk assisted by First Officer Cairncross. Much to the relief of the crew, there was nothing out of the ordinary during the flight, and it arrived in Durban on schedule.

On Wednesday the 18th May, Captain G.W. Mitchell was on DC3 standby duty at Nairobi West, where the routine was to be available in the crew room at the traffic terminal for all departures. During the early afternoon, the traffic superintendent, Reg Silverlock, called him to one side and said that he had just learned from air traffic control that the Durban flight, EC 104, had not called 'top of descent' as instructed by the controller, and that by air traffic's calculations it should have landed ten minutes ago, at 13.20.

Mitchell hurried to the telephone to obtain specific information from the controller, while Silverlock went to report to Captain Malin Sorsbie, the general manager, who was waiting in the terminal to meet his wife, Betty, returning from a shopping expedition to Durban.

Mitchell had spoken to the controller who confirmed that all contact had been lost with the DC3. The last message received from the aircraft was at 11.56, when Captain Quirk had reported his position as Lake Jipe at 10,500ft, flying on course in visual flight conditions on top of cloud. There was no doubt that something had happened, and Mitchell quickly telephoned the hangar giving instructions for the standby aircraft to be fuelled and prepared for departure as soon as possible. Malin Sorsbie appeared in the crew room, and asked what Mitchell proposed to do. He explained that he intended to fly along the incoming aircraft's reciprocal track, to the last reporting point, to see if they could locate the DC3 before dark. There was about ninety minutes daylight still available. They would be listening out on the emergency frequency and liaising with other aircraft in the area. Malin Sorsbie agreed with the plan and decided to come on the flight. The first officer was 'Pablo' Johnson.

Flying along the reciprocal track was probably easier said than done because in those days the route between Nairobi and Dar es Salaam, the last departure point, was nominally direct, with a 'dog-leg' at the captain's discretion if it was likely that the flight would be in cloud when in the vicinity of Mount Kilimajaro. The normal flight levels used were 95 (9,500 ft) or 115 (11,500 ft) Nairobi – Dar es Salaam and 105 (10,500 ft) in the reverse direction. Mount Kilimanjaro is 19,340 ft., just to the west of track. If, in fact, you were dead on track, it would take you over the lower slopes of the mountain.

Mitchell had a problem, in that he did not know exactly where Captain Quirk had initiated his 'dog-leg', if he had decided to make one. What he did known was that there was cloud in the vicinity of the mountain, for one of Quirk's last calls was to request flight level 125, as he entered the area.

They scoured the region, as best they could, choosing altitudes which offered the greatest area for visual inspection. As they flew into the darkness, hoping to see, perhaps, a flare, they told each other that Kilimanjaro was too big to hit, but they all had secret fears that the mountain had claimed the lives of the twenty passengers and crew of flight EC 104. After some five hours of fruitless searching they returned to Nairobi West. In the meantime, they had been joined in the search by four E.A.A. aircraft and a Royal Air Force Lincoln, which flew non-stop for nine hours on its mission. They continued throughout the night, and the following day a full-scale ground and air search covering an area of 27,000 miles was launched.

Snow covered Kibo and Mwenzi, the twin peaks of Mt Kilimanjaro. The crash site is on the top of the left-hand ridge of Mwenzi. (Captain Brewer)

It was not until 07.15 the following Sunday, May 21st, that Captain 'Laddie' Richter and F/O 'Pommy' Pomfret, while on a positioning flight from Nairobi to Dar es Salaam, decided to fly over the saddle between the twin peaks of Kilimanjaro, Mwenzi and Kibo. They examined what appeared to be a heap of rocks, when suddenly they saw something glint in the sun. Flying with extreme care, Captain Richter selected flap and lowered the undercarriage for a slow fly-past, as low as he dared, From 200 ft above the high ground, which was at 14,500 ft above sea level, they recognised the remains of the Dakota, a charred silhouette on top of a rock escarpment, on the Mwenzi peak, which had been shrouded in cloud for days.[7]

A rescue party of nine trained mountaineers of the Mountain Club of Kenya left a few hours later by air from Nairobi West, for Moshi. With them were a doctor and six technical experts from the Directorate of Civil Aviation, the Air Registration Board and East African Airways, who were to investigate the cause of the

[7] The dangers of mountain-wave conditions were not as widely known then. An interesting phenomenon experienced by pilots when flying in the vicinity of Mt Kilimanjaro, was the loss of sense of distance and proportion, due to the vast mass of the mountain. Great boulders could be mistaken for small stones. Often they would take avoiding action several miles away in the belief that they were too close.

A photograph of the snow clad crater of Kibo, taken from a Lancastrian (4 Rolls-Royce Merlins) of Skyways of London, by C.E. Smith, at that time a flight engineer with the airline. Circa 1947. (Mr T. Nightingale)

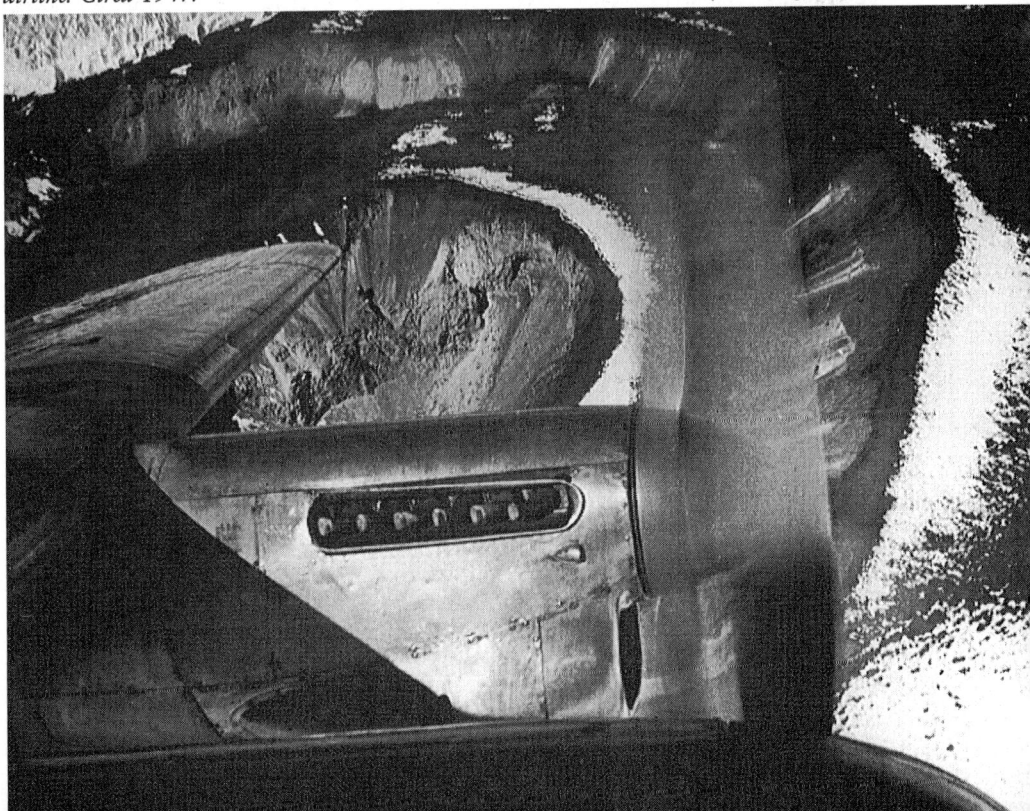

accident. Together with a policeman from Moshi they made up the official search and rescue party. They took with them food, medical equipment and a two way radio to report progress and to communicate at pre-arranged times with a Cessna 180 aircraft flown by Michael 'Punch' Bearcroft, the commandant of the Kenya Police Air Wing. This was to prove invaluable to the climbing party, who were dropped supplies of food and the latest aerial photographs of the scene of the crash.

On Monday morning there were forty police constables standing by at the Kibo Hotel, in case their help was needed in carrying equipment 9,500 feet up to Bismark hut, the first of the climbers huts on the route up Kilimanjaro.

The advance climbing party, including the doctor, left at the crack of dawn with fifteen porters. They toiled up through the thickly forested slopes of Kilimanjaro on to the moorlands, walking a distance of about twenty miles and to a height of 13,000 ft. up the mountainside, before camping for the night.

On Tuesday they set up a base camp further up the valley close to the south-east ridge, and climbed to the scene of the crash.

The charred remains of the aircraft were spread over a considerable distance; twisted pieces of metal clung precariously to the rocks, while some lay in deep, inaccessible ravines.

There could have been no survivors from this, the first and only fatal accident, to date, for East African Airways. After collecting some items of freight and examining the few accessible parts of the aircraft the search party erected a cairn in the valley below and a cross and wreaths of everlasting flowers, made by the African porters, were placed over it.

The whole party then moved down to Bismark hut, and tired, weary and footsore, they walked down to Kibo Hotel the next day. Members of the Mountain

The scene of the wreckage of VP-KKH, at about 17,000ft up on Mwenzi peak. The separated tail-plane can be clearly seen. (Capt Brewer.)

Club then flew the same day to Nairobi and were among the congregation who attended the memorial service at All Saints Cathedral.

The subsequent Public Inquiry attributed the crash to navigational error. "There was obviously a navigational error, but the degree of this error is immaterial – the final tragedy is mute evidence that adequate precautions were not taken". On 23rd July, Captain Malin Sorsbie gave instructions for an internal inquiry into the accident. Captain P.E. Henn and chief engineer A.E. Robinson reported: "The captain cannot be exonerated because he was in command of the aircraft at the time of the accident. The degree of blame is difficult to assess, but the evidence tends to show that the accident may have been caused by faulty navigation in that the captain identified Lake Jipe incorrectly. The assertion in the findings of the Court of Inquiry that 'the captain did not show regard for the safety of his aircraft and his passengers, that could be expected from a man of his training and experience' cannot be accepted as there is no evidence to substantiate such a statement".

Direct flights were immediately forbidden by E.A.A.C. on this sector and it was very soon after the tragedy that an NDB was installed at Manyani, some eighty miles East of Mount Kilimanjaro, with the Morse code callsign Romeo Alpha. All flights on the Dar es Salaam – Nairobi – Dar es Salaam services were then routed via Romeo Alpha.

As a result of the loss of VP-KKH, efforts were made to purchase a replacement Dakota, but to no avail. There being no suitable replacement aircraft, a DC3, G-AMYB, was hired from Eagle Airways in the United Kingdom and another, VP-KNU, was leased from South African Airways, until 1956.

There were heavy charter commitments which required all the available aircraft, making it impossible to cover the loss of VP-KKH by intensifying the utilisation of the remainder of the fleet. The *Hajj* was a major revenue earner, in addition to government charter flights for the police and security forces continuing the battle against Mau Mau. There were also some overseas DC3 charters to the UK, on government business.

It was on one of these flights to the United Kingdom that George Leslie, with Howard Iliffe as first officer and Frank MacNabb the flight engineer had an extraordinary experience.

Half way between Khartoum and Wadi Halfa a passenger remarked upon the stream of oil running back over the starboard engine cowling. Captain Leslie made nothing of it, in response, explaining that it was merely 'heavy breathing', not uncommon on the Pratt & Whitney engines. Returning up front to the cockpit, he slid open the first officer's window and stuck his head out to get a good look. Over the cylinders and exhaust he could make out a broken pipe which was spewing oil and he could see a long trail of black smoke.

They limped in to Wadi Halfa, from where they signalled to Nairobi for spares and an engineer. This would take several days, so they had to make their passengers and themselves comfortable for as long as it would take. This was not so bad, Wadi Halfa was a lovely stop-over on the Nile and the amenities were acceptable enough.

In the hotel bar that night they chatted with the air traffic control officer (who dealt with some three or four aircraft a week) and a couple of engineers from the Sudan Railways. On hearing of the problems with the Dakota, the railway men remembered that they had, during their forays into the desert, seen the wreckage of an old Dakota, which had probably run out of fuel on one of the Cairo to the Union flights. They thought the engines were intact, being of no use to the desert nomads.

They offered to search for it there and then. it would be cooler in the desert during the night, with good visibility. Two Land Rovers were refuelled and spare petrol cans loaded in the back, and with two Sudanese firemen who knew the desert, they set off on the search. They found the wreckage at about 1 a.m., and the engines were indeed in good condition and, it seemed, the parts which they needed were still in place. They decided to return at dawn, with tools, and dismantle the components.

After working all day, they assembled the oil pipe together with the fasteners and seals, which had been stripped from the wreck. That evening Leslie took the Dakota up on an air test, there was no sign of any further leak; they had been completely successful. A signal was sent to Nairobi to cancel the requirement for spares and an engineer, and the following morning they continued on their way to England.

As a result of this incident, it was decided by E.A.A.C. to provide a tool kit on each Dakota, to deal with minor break-downs at stations where there was no resident engineer. A green canvas bag of assorted tools became part of the crew's personal kit.

One day a Dakota landed at Tabora with a rough running engine. Out came the tool kit and the captain and first officer fiddled with the magnetos and re-set the points (the passengers were always impressed with the versatility of the E.A.A.C. aircrews!). They decided to run the engine on the ground, and the first officer went into the cockpit to start-up. The captain remained on the steps to watch the engine, with the cowlings off. The engine roared into life – and promptly burst into flames. Fortunately, a fireman was standing by with a high capacity wheeled extinguisher. He blasted off the foam; the captain, being between the extinguisher and the fire, was then blown off the steps onto the tarmac. Picking himself up with what little dignity remained, he watched, thoroughly soaked, as the fire was quickly put out. A fuel pipe had sheared – no one was to know whether this had occurred before or after the tinkering with the engine by the two pilots.

The loss of VP-KKH reduced the Corporation's potential output and capacity by some 10% for nearly eight months of 1955. At the close of the year the fleet consisted of nine DC3 and four DH89A Rapide aircraft, plus the Airspeed Consul used for training purposes. The fleet achieved a total of 20,279 flying hours, of which 17,140 were on scheduled services, representing an increase of 1,130 hours over 1954.

Scheduled services were operated to a pattern best calculated to satisfy each territory's requirements, within the limitations set by financial and operational conditions. Some alterations to service patterns were made as a result of airfield restrictions. Pemba was withdrawn from the coastal pattern operated by DC3s, and Rapides were introduced to maintain the light transport needs between Zanzibar,

Pemba and Tanga. Kilwa was introduced into the southern Tanganyika coastal pattern towards the end of the year.

Pemba Island, which lay between Mombasa and Tanga, was probably the worst of the aerodromes on the East African Airways routes. The runway was just on the limits for the DC3, with the threshold at either end dropping away steeply – the pilots compared it with an aircraft carrier. With the heat and turbulence and a wind which was invariably across the runway, very few pilots enjoyed the experience of landing the Dakotas there and there was considerable relief when the services were returned to the DH89 Rapides.

The two regional services to Durban, one via the Portuguese East African coast and the other via Salisbury, continued to operate with increasing success, whilst a third regional service was introduced in December, operating from Nairobi to Salisbury via Abercorn and Lusaka in Northern Rhodesia.

Charter operations continued to be dominated by the annual pilgrimage to Mecca. Twenty-one *Hajj* flights were made from East Africa to Jeddah in July and a further twenty-one return flights were made in August. In addition, E.A.A.C. aircraft assisted in the repatriation from Khartoum to Uganda of some 400 pilgrims who were stranded on their return by Nile steamer from Jeddah, as a result of a revolt in the Southern Sudan.

The Northern Frontier District of Kenya was well off the tourist track. In fact no one could go there without a Government Permit and the protection of armed askaris. The reason for this was that for centuries, probably since man first existed, nomadic tribesmen crossed and re-crossed this area which bordered present day Kenya, Somalia, Sudan and Ethiopia. One of the day to day problems of the Administration was the activity of these armed tribesmen, or *Shifta*, who would cross the international borders to steal cattle and women from the Kenya side. The administrative centre for the district was at Lodwar. One day, it was 15th September, 1955, Captain Peter Duff flew the Police Commissioner and twenty-four armed askaris on a charter to Lodwar, for a conference with the local police commander, in connection with an increase in *Shifta* raids.

They flew up from Nairobi in the DC3, VP-KLC. Duff had not been to Lodwar before (few people had), and he had instructions to look out for the airstrip, located on the western side of Lake Rudolf. If he failed to spot it the first time, the procedure was to continue towards the top of the Lake, when he would spot a Beau Geste type fort, then fly back five miles, where the airstrip was located. In the event there was no difficulty in finding the strip, since they could see the white dust from the police commander's Land Rover, which they followed until the white circle denoting the landing strip came into sight.

While they waited for the police to conduct their meeting, Duff and his flight engineer, Ginger Brewer, examined the white circle. It was constructed of bones – animal, crocodile and human – all bleached white by the sun.

1954 had seen the introduction of the East African Air Navigation (General) Regulations, which were brought into force on 1st July of that year. These Regulations replaced and consolidated previous piecemeal legislation, bringing the colonial rules into line with UK legislation. The effect was to raise the standard of operational qualifications and both training and check flights were, as a result, more rigorous and comprehensive. The full impact of these regulations was not felt until 1955, as exemption for a period was granted from the provisions of the regulations, in the normal way, in order to permit operators affected either to qualify or to comply with requirements.

As a result of the new regulations, flying training increased substantially, totalling some 610 hours, 449 of which were flown on the Consul. Despite a world shortage of pilots, six new entrants arrived in 1955, bringing the total to sixty-seven, sufficient to meet the expansion demands of the forthcoming year.

Ginger Brewer was now in a difficult situation, since the new regulations required two pilots at all times on the DC3 and he could no longer fly along as a flight engineer in the right-hand seat. Although he had obtained his Commercial Pilot's Licence, E.A.A.C. refused to release him from his engineering role. As a result he had applied to B.O.A.C. for a job as flight engineer on the Lockheed Constellations. They had passed his application to Wing Commander Francombe for approval. After listening to his dilemma, Francombe agreed to accept him for training and he did a conversion course on the DC3 with Captain Lavers and Captain Iliffe, becoming a second officer pilot. He flew with Captain Mitchell during the search for VP-KKH and also with Captain Leo Davidson in one of the Macchis, VP-KJD on the same mission.

On 11th and 12th November, 1955, Brewer completed his twin-engine instrument rating on the Airspeed Consul, with Captain Bill Fumerton. He had the distinction of being the last person to fly the Consul. They had been doing training in recovery from unusual attitudes and, after landing, he noticed that the fabric strips round each wing root centre section showed signs of fraying. The fabric was re-doped and the next day he completed his tests. But the fabric strips were even worse than the previous day. He reported this to "Taffy" Brammah, who was then the C of A hangar foreman. When they checked the main spar, they saw that there was a complete wood and glue failure. The aircraft was grounded and declared beyond repair, and subsequently broken up.

With the first fatal accident in its history, the airline had highlighted the need for radio aids throughout the territories. There is no doubt that the introduction of NDBs and VHF direction finding aids introduced during 1955 was as a direct result of the tragedy. In addition Advisory Routes were established by the Directorate of Civil Aviation on some sectors of the East African routes. Of the thirty-five airfields used by E.A.A.C. at the time, no less than seventeen had no radio of any description. There was no airfield equipped with a runway approach aid, as a result of which no operations could be carried out in conditions of low cloud or poor visibility. Most of the late departures which occurred from Nairobi West were due to low cloud and poor visibility, resulting in disruption to services and low esteem from the travelling public. Sir Alfred Vincent, in his Report on the Administration for 1955 "... *hoped that with the opening of the New Nairobi Airport these aids will become immediately available".*

At about this time, facilities for air to ground communication by wireless telegraphy were gradually being withdrawn, world-wide, and wireless telephony was taking its place. The problems facing operators during the change-over period were appreciated by the Director of Civil Aviation in East Africa, who had agreed not to withdraw wireless telegraphy until such time as wireless telephony had been fully evaluated and proved to be a suitable substitute. Communication was often difficult, due to static interference, particularly during the rainy seasons, with their build up of great thunder storms.

Two major difficulties faced East African Airways in regard to airfields in East Africa; the absence of night flying facilities at airfields other than Entebbe, Eastleigh and Dar es Salaam, and the bearing strength on runway surfaces at other airfields. Expansion of DC3 services would largely depend upon E.A.A.C. being able to introduce night flights, thereby increasing fleet utilisation and creating new demand. The large four-engined aircraft which were expected to be introduced the following year would be confined to the three main territorial airports, both Mombasa, the principal port, and Zanzibar, a thriving large centre of population, would remain dependent upon daylight flights with the DC3s.

Cargo was advancing at a remarkable rate. With an increase of 24% over 1954, some difficulties were being encountered in the physical handling of the greatly developed volume of traffic and in the increased size and weight of heavy consignments, which was then being carried on freight services. Loading equipment had to be designed and produced in the Corporation's workshops to ensure that loading and unloading was done with the minimum of delay, and that aircraft spent the shortest possible time on the ground at transit stations. Loading ramps designed by the engineering department were positioned at various stations and more equipment was being built. To overcome shortages of experienced air cargo handling staff, some recruitment was carried out in the United Kingdom to fill the requirements caused by the introduction of Hunting-Clan Air Transport cargo flights operating through Eastleigh.

The gradual development of international air services through East Africa was highlighting the inadequacies of the facilities at all the stations. At Nairobi West, the terminal building, although improved, was totally inadequate at peak periods, although the government authorities had finally agreed to construct urgently needed additional toilet accommodation for passengers, and a secure transit shed for cargo was in place. There were serious difficulties in the provision of housing for African staff and at the base there were extreme difficulties in maintaining the sanitary arrangements in the absence of water borne sanitation, which the Corporation was prepared to partially fund in co-operation with the government, once the protracted negotiations ended. Much the same story could be told about the conditions at the main international entry airport at Eastleigh, although government funding had been obtained for improvements.

The parking ramp at Eastleigh was already inadequate and, with B.O.A.C. planning to operate the giant Bristol Britannia aircraft new problems were foreseen. Government funding had been obtained for an extension to the concrete apron, to overcome this particular problem. In the meantime, with possibly another three years before the move to the New Nairobi Airport, East African Airways decided to fund improvements to the restaurant and kitchen facilities, which could no longer meet the requirements of passengers in transit. Additional space for another fifty persons was created by an extension to the restaurant, and extra kitchen space for the preparation of meals for uplift by the many airlines for whom the Corporation acted as agent.

One of the tasks inherent in operating an airline is the provision of meals or refreshments both in the air and on the ground. E.A.A.C. had been doing this for ten years, to meet both its own requirements and that of many other international operators, and had accordingly invested capital in this aspect of its affairs, as well as incurring an additional commitment in staff. There was, as a result, some concern that the airline would be permitted to transfer its Eastleigh catering unit to the new Nairobi Airport. Kenya government policy was eagerly awaited, not only by E.A.A.C., but by those businessmen who realised that airline catering was an extremely profitable enterprise. In the event, the government decided in 1956 that the contract for catering in the public restaurant and the Terminal canteen used by employees other than those of E.A.A.C. at the new Nairobi airport, should be determined by public tender.

This came as a disappointment to the Corporation, who felt that as the government sponsored airline, it should be permitted to transfer its activities to one centre at the new airport, to facilitate catering for the many international airlines operating through Nairobi. Following negotiations and, in the conviction that the needs of the airlines and of the public would best be met by a separate catering organisation to undertake what was to be a project of major proportions, a tender was submitted jointly by E.A.A.C. and Block Hotels Limited.

The Blocks were a Kenya pioneer family who had succeeded in creating one of the colony's principal business empires. Abraham Block had been born in Vilna, Lithuania in 1883. He followed his father, Samuel to South Africa, from where he worked his way, by salvaging wool from barbed wire fences and selling it sack by sack, from the Cape to Johannesburg. In March 1902 he sailed with a party of Jewish settlers for Mombasa. Abraham Block arrived in the frontier town of Nairobi on 15th April, 1902, some four years after the town had been created. Block set his hand to whatever opportunities for making money came his way. The Hotel Stanley, named after the explorer, was opened by the owner, Mayence Bent in 1903. There was one problem. Mattresses could not be obtained anywhere. Block had noticed how grass which had been cut by the railway constructors was left lying to dry on either side of the railway. He found some ticking in the Indian bazaar, made needles from bicycle spokes and manufactured twenty-four mattresses, which he sold to Mayence Bent.

In 1947 Block's eldest son, Jack, bought the New Stanley Hotel from Mayence Tate (*nee* Bent) on his father's behalf, just twenty years after Abraham Block had purchased his first hotel, the Norfolk, in exchange for £500 and a parcel of land.

In 1950 Block Hotels, owners of the most prestigious hotels in East Africa, became a public company. Block had in addition to the hotel business, built up

DC3 Dakota 4, VP-KLC, RMA *Alexander M. Mackay*, at Dar es Salaam.

(Mr T. Webb)

the United Africa Company, and created African Representatives Ltd, the sole distributor of Lever Brothers products, which was to become East African Industries, the largest manufacturing company in modern Kenya.

The combination of Block's business prowess and the airline's expertise in the field of in-flight catering won the new company, named Caterair Limited, the contract. The Corporation and Block Hotels Limited with an equal share in the capital requirements each appointed two members to the board of the new company, under the chairmanship of The Hon. Sir Charles Markham, Bart.[8]

1956

East African Airways, in conjunction with the East African Tourist Travel Association, was increasingly aware of the need to promote tourism in the Territories. In 1956, with a basic travel allowance still imposed upon British citizens, Anglo-French and Israeli military action against Egypt and the Soviet's crushing of the Hungarian revolution, few American or European travellers were disposed to visit East Africa. South and Central Africa were still the only regions from where substantial tourist growth could be expected. All the efforts, including advertising and promotional flights by the DC3s, were hampered by the severe lack of modern

---

[8] In November 1965 a new company was formed together with Nairobi Airport Services Ltd (NAS), called NAS-Caterair. The UK branch of NAS took over the E.A.A. aircraft catering ex London. As with Blocks, NAS was founded by a Jewish entrepreneurial family. Robert Seeman was chairman and managing director.

hotels on the entire coastal stretch from the borders of Portuguese East Africa to Mombasa. Tourists were becoming more sophisticated and they would not return to hotels comprising *makuti*[9] roofed bandas with bucket sanitation, whose sole facility was a bar. Resorts were springing up on the African coast from Beira to Cape Town with the most modern of hotels. Unless the government did more to encourage the development of modern hotels in Nairobi and along the coast, there were those in the airline who felt all their efforts were in vain.

Similarly, the condition of airfields such as Mombasa and Pemba for the operation of Canadair and DC3 aircraft respectively, and others such as the Kenya Highlands airfields and several in Tanganyika and Uganda, was not only affecting the airline's earning capacity, but was forcing it to operate a fleet of small, uneconomic aircraft exclusively for the purpose of serving those airfields which could not be used by DC3 aircraft. The Territorial governments were being urged by the board of E.A.A.C. to give urgent consideration to the improvements necessary and, in the case of Kenya, to bring the standard of Mombasa up to the requirements of Canadair type aircraft. It was a situation which required delicate timing, for in the matter of increased tourism to the coast, the requirement for a larger airport would need to be balanced by the provision of suitable hotel accommodation.

In a way, 1956 brought to an end the formative years of East African Airways. At the end of the year it stood at the threshold of a new, wider world. In his summing up of the year, Sir Alfred Vincent made the following comments:

"In the immediate future, the Corporation, with the help of B.O.A.C., will be introducing the 4-engined and well-tried Canadair as another progressive step forward in the development of East African aviation where modest enterprise and government co-operation has seen the capacity ton miles available to the public climb from 254,200 in 1946, to 6,930,992 eleven years later with much more to come.

" Relatively heavy expenditure must be faced with the introduction of a new type which, with staggered delivery dates, cannot for some time achieve proper utilisation and thus full revenue. Nevertheless the Corporation looks forward with confidence to the ultimate result.

"To ensure a high standard of operational efficiency a study of the Corporation's aircraft requirements over the next ten years has been made, and it is clear that to meet the requirements both within and without the Territories at least two types of aircraft will be required. Modern aircraft are very expensive, so much so that internal operations alone could not adequately support the investment without the prospect of subsidy.

"A suitable replacement for the DC3s may be an aircraft with an all up maximum weight of 30,000 to 35,000lb, while for regional and any trunk services, an aircraft of about 80,000lbs would seem desirable. Both types should be pressurised, and it would be desirable that advantage be taken of the turbo-prop engine development which is taking place.

---

[9] *Palm-leaf thatch, common to the coastal region for roof cover.*

"To buy, say, four of a DC3 type replacement and, say, three to replace the Canadair type now to be introduced, would mean placing orders in 1958 and 1959 to obtain delivery in 1960 and 1961 respectively. The cost of such a modest replacement programme would be something like £3,500,000 and this may be required within the next three to four years.

"The problem requires considerable study and the Territories have been made aware of the finance required, if East African aviation is not to lag behind in developing and catering for its own considerable potential of internal and external air traffic.

The main highlight of the year 1956 was the visit of Her Royal Highness the Princess Margaret to the East African Territories. Months of detailed planning by E.A.A.C. and the Government ensured that the successful programme of charter flights and airport arrangements gained high praise. A Royal Air Force Heron of the Queen's Flight is seen at Mwanza, where the Princess was greeted by Sir Edward Twining, Governor of Tanganyika. The senior officer responsible for E.A.A.C. ground handling arrangements was Bill Ainscough, seen here presenting a smart salute. (Mr W. Ainscough)

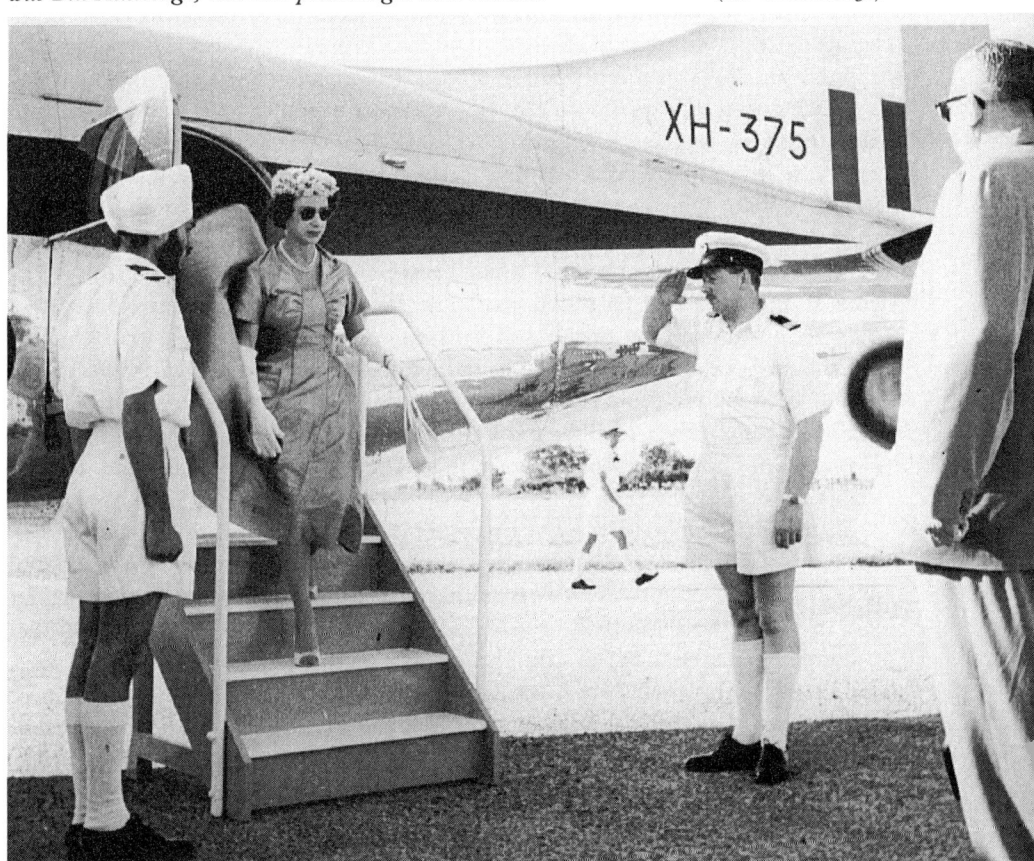

"It is felt that aviation should have at least equal opportunity with other requirements in these rapidly advancing Territories, but if capital of this order cannot be made forthcoming, then the Corporation will have to consider operating Canadair aircraft for a longer period than is envisaged at the present. There is, however, no alternative to the DC3 replacement programme, as some of these aircraft will have to be replaced in 1960 with a new type of pressurised aircraft. This may be the wisest policy for the future, provided that the Corporation is able to maintain its competitive position on those routes which will be operated with Canadairs. It must also be realised that there are very distinct advantages, economical and otherwise, to be derived from the operation of modern turbo-prop engined aircraft, and it is, therefore, possible that it may be considerably more economical in the long run to introduce to the Corporation's fleet turbo-prop aircraft at an early date.

"It must be appreciated that the Corporation, as required under its Mandate, does carry out a very great deal of development, and that its ability to develop has till now been limited by its capacity to pay for development out of income; the less economic routes being carried by the profits on the main routes and ancillary activities such as agency services to the trunk route operators.

"The staff have worked exceedingly hard and faced many problems to bring the airline to its present pitch of efficiency, and the Corporation wishes to record its deep appreciation of the great contribution the staff have made and will continue to make".

East African Airways did indeed show its appreciation to loyal staff – after some fairly energetic nudges, at times.

A case in point concerned Ginger Brewer, who, during the early part of 1956, flew as co-pilot with Captain Howard Iliffe, still with the peculiar E.A.A.C. classification of 'Second Officer'. It was on the Durban service, in the Dakota VP-KJS. They were returning northbound when, between Salisbury and Blantyre, one of the port engine magnetos failed. At that time there was no engineering back-up at Blantyre but fortunately Brewer still held his engineering licences and after about four hours work, he had replaced the magneto with one from his spares pack. Had he not been on the flight, it would have meant a night-stop plus the expense of engineers being flown to Blantyre. Earlier, during the flight, he had been telling Howard Iliffe how unfair he found it as a second officer, when his salary was less than that of a steward.

Iliffe had remembered what he had told him and reported it to higher authority back in Nairobi. As a result, Brewer was promoted to first officer and given a bonus of four hundred pounds as an ex-gratia payment for saving the Corporation a great loss in money and good-will.

Lumbo had been dropped from the schedule on the Durban service during 1955, and crews would night-stop at the Grand Hotel at Beira. The Grand was a magnificent hotel in the old tradition, but with few guests, apart from the airline passengers. Each room had an open balcony with a separating wall between them. The wall was only about seven feet high and it was difficult not to hear the conversations next door.

Captain Roger Drew and F/O Ginger Brewer at the controls of Dakota VP-KKI, RMA Sir Richard Burton. The panel indicates that the aircraft was in flight. (Captain Brewer)

On the late afternoon of 10th January, 1956, Captain Mitchell overheard the following exchange:

Ginger Brewer's voice: "Please let me do it".

Portuguese girl's voice: "No, No, No".

"Come on, I'll feel much better if you let me do it".

"No, No, No".

Unable to overcome his curiosity, Mitchell stood on a chair and peered over the wall, only to see R/O Russ Blakely looking over from the opposite side. They saw Ginger Brewer attempting to wrest his shoes from the clutches of a chambermaid, who was trying to polish them. Obviously Brewer thought it too embarrassing for a young girl to perform this task – or he could not afford the tip for the service!

On May 2nd, 1956, the Eagle Airways Dakota, G-AMYB, which had been leased following the loss of VP-KKH on Kilimanjaro twelve months previously, departed from Nairobi on its return flight to England. With a degree of foresight in leave planning by the administration, some fourteen staff passengers took advantage of the otherwise empty seats for passage home on leave. With the crew comprising Captain Drew, Chief Radio Officer Rhodes and F/O Brewer, they routed via Juba-Khartoum-Wadi Halfa-Benina-Malta-Nice to Blackbushe. They were two hours late in departing Nairobi due to an engine starter problem. As a result, they were told on arrival at Khartoum that their accommodation was no longer available. All the rooms at the Grand Hotel and the houseboat *Omdurman* had been given away to other people. Their only option was to continue on to Wadi Halfa, where, they were assured, accommodation would be available.

It took another three hours night flying to reach Wadi Halfa, where they had to land in a sandstorm. By the time they reached the hotel the crew had been 'on duty' for seventeen hours. They had intended to route from there to transit Benina and night stop at Malta. With headwinds of 100kt or more, they had to call at Mersah Matru to refuel then continue to Benina where they spent the night. The following day, the winds were still against them, so they were forced to spend a night in Nice. Finally, they arrived in UK airspace, only to find that the multi-channel VHF radios were of little use; in the previous months in East Africa someone had mixed up all the crystals. They were able to communicate on some basic frequencies, but were unable to speak to the Airways controllers and, finally, had to rely upon a green Aldis lamp signal to land at Blackbushe.

In 1956, the Islamic month of *Dhu'l-hijja* in the Hejira calendar fell in June of the Gregorian year. East African Airways had been looking forward to another profitable pilgrimage charter season for the annual *Hajj*. The Middle East had been in turmoil for several years, with aggressive nationalism in Egypt, Syria, the Sudan, and Jordan provoking aggression and hostility in Israel. In April, there had been a cease-fire between Egypt and Israel, and in June, shortly after the last British troops had left the Canal Zone, Colonel Nasser was elected President. One month later he declared that the Suez Canal was to be nationalised. Within a very short time the region was at war, with Britain, France and Israel involved in a messy conflict with Egypt and by association with the entire Islamic world.

For East African Airways the result of the strife, although it had not come to war in June and July, was a huge down-turn in pilgrim traffic. In 1955 ten full return flights were operated from Uganda; in 1956 there were only two.

The effects of the Arab – Israeli conflict was felt by the crews of E.A.A.C. who were obliged to stick their heads into the 'lions den' of Arab territory. Being a British colonial airline made matters worse. The anger of Arab nationalism, fuelled by Nasser in Egypt, was turned on the former colonial masters, even by countries which had never been colonised by Britain, such as Saudi Arabia, where the pilgrim flights were destined.

Photographed at Dar es Salaam in February, 1956, Edward Onyango Were was the first African steward to be employed on international services. He is shown with Captain Roger Drew and F/O Ginger Brewer.

Twice in the course of the 1956 *Hajj*, Ginger Brewer was faced with unpleasantness from the Arabs. On 27th June, with Captain Tom Dornan, they had landed with a group of pilgrims in DC3 VP-KJU, and Brewer was tidying up the aircraft. Suddenly, the E.A.A.C. traffic clerk, who had been posted to Jeddah for the

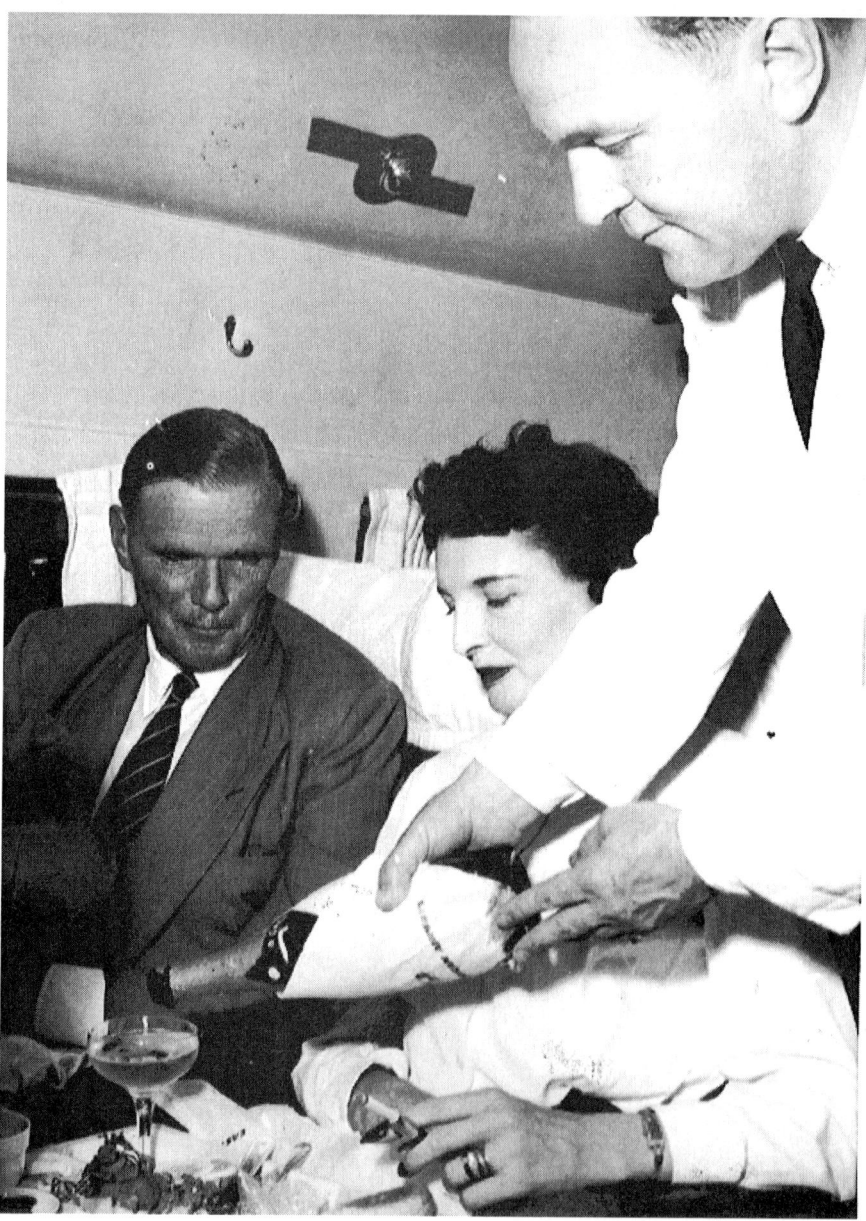

Captain Phil Henn, enjoying the luxury of first class travel, accompanied by Diana Howard-Williams (E.A.A. public relations officer). The steward is Arthur Street.

duration, appeared together with two Saudi soldiers, who grabbed Brewer and told him he was under arrest. Apparently, his South African passport, which the clerk had taken with the ships documents for clearance, had Israel among the countries listed as valid. Captain Dornan told them that he would be prepared to leave for Khartoum, but they would not agree, saying that Brewer should be jailed. Finally making him swear that he would not approach or speak to any Saudi citizen, they stamped his passport 'Undesirable', and allowed him to depart with the aircraft. To overcome the problem of operating into Saudi Arabia on future occasions, he later obtained another passport.

On 26th July, with Captain Laddie Richter and R/O Paddy Murray, Brewer was *en route* for Damascus, to take pilgrims on a visit to an Islamic shrine and then to pick up another group of pilgrims returning from Jeddah. They routed via Entebbe–Juba–Khartoum–Wadi Halfa, where they night-stopped and continued the following day via Luxor to Damascus. On their day of departure (26th July), Nasser had announced the nationalisation of the Suez Canal, and on arrival at Luxor, passengers and crew were refused permission to leave the aircraft and were even denied refreshments. In a distinctly unfriendly atmosphere, they were lucky to be permitted to uplift fuel, following which they were told to depart without further delay. The next day they left Damascus for Jeddah, and returned to Nairobi, via Juba and Khartoum, thankfully with no further incident.

CHAPTER 6

OVERSEAS

THE CANADAIR DC–4M–2 incorporated features of both the Douglas DC4 and the DC6, but was powered by four Rolls-Royce Merlin 620 engines of 1,760 h.p. each. The original Douglas DC4 was powered by four Pratt and Whitney Twin Wasp R–2800–2SD13-G engines of 1,450 h.p. and the DC6, which was a larger and more powerful aircraft, came fitted with, variously, four 2,100 h.p. or four 2,400 h.p. Pratt and Whitney engines.

B.O.A.C. had taken delivery of twenty-six of the Canadair C4-M 'North Stars', which they called 'Argonauts'. In the lean post-war years, with currency controls imposed upon a near bankrupt economy, the fitting of Rolls-Royce engines to a Canadian-American aircraft was an enormous cost benefit, saving precious dollars. The Argonauts were fully pressurised and had proved reliable and popular on the long Atlantic ocean crossings. The Performance figures were impressive: Max. cruising speed 325 mph; initial climb rate at 78,000 lb, 680ft/min; max. range 3,440 miles; service ceiling 29,500 ft.; empty weight 46,832 lb.; loaded, 82,300 lb. The dimensions were equally impressive. Span, 117ft. 6in.; length, 93ft. 7in.; height, 27 ft. 6in.

East African Airways had been waiting for the delivery of their Canadairs, which had originally been planned for 31st, March, 1956. This had been put back to October and, finally, a year later than planned, the first aircraft, VP-KNY, left Heathrow on Saturday, 30th March, 1957, crewed by Captains Parker, Lavers and Fumerton, N/O Warren, Chief R/O Rhodes and Steward Arthur Street.

There had been months of delays to the agreements and in getting B.O.A.C. to set a firm date for the release of the Argonauts. At the last minute the British Ministry of Aviation and the Treasury had held out for 5% on the Guaranteed interest-bearing stock to be issued to B.O.A.C. as part of the purchase agreement, whereas E.A.A.C. considered three and a half percent an adequate return. Captain Eric Morris had been to London to negotiate the difficult arrangements for crew training and secondment to B.O.A.C. while the protracted negotiations continued. Captain Malin Sorsbie concluded an agreement with Sir Victor Tait, B.O.A.C.'s operations director, for the secondment of a B.O.A.C. check captain and route inspector for at least a year. Captain Morris also concluded an agreement for the recruitment and training of nine stewards and five stewardesses, to be trained by B.O.A.C. *"The general manager"*, he wrote, *"was extremely anxious to employ staff in this category who will be up to the same standard as those of B.O.A.C."*

Training for the initial crews took place at London Airport, conducted by B.O.A.C., under training captains C.P. Houlder, C. Butler and Laurie Arthur. Four E.A.A.C. captains, Lavers, Fumerton, Davidson and Ainsworth were converted in preparation for the initial aircraft.

Until the advent of these large airliners East African Airways had continued to conduct their operations from their base at Nairobi West. There had for several years been an East African Airways handling unit at the airport at Eastleigh, situated approximately five miles to the north-east, which was the Royal Air Force base. Due to the provision of runways of sufficient length to accommodate the Lockheed Constellations, DC6s, and other large intercontinental airliners of B.O.A.C., South African Airways, K.L.M. and the other major international carriers transiting Nairobi, Eastleigh had become the International Airport. A major drawback, however, for the future of Eastleigh Airport was the steady encroachment of the city, making for difficult and potentially dangerous approach and departure profiles.

Nairobi West airport, looking north. The cars indicate that the photograph was taken on the occasion of an annual air-show.   E.A.Standard.

Now, with the coming of the Canadairs, which would operate from Eastleigh, Nairobi West was to remain the base for the domestic DC3 operations of E.A.A.C., until the new airport, which was under construction at Embakasi, was completed, when the entire operation would move to new headquarters, which would bring them together with all the foreign operators, enabling much greater efficiency and convenience for the interlining of passengers to the domestic and regional services.

It was during this period that, late one afternoon, a few of the E.A.A.C. crew were relaxing in the crew room at Nairobi West, having completed their flights, when Captain John Bunstead appeared at the door and said, "If you guys want to see something funny, come quick!" They tumbled out of the door just in time to see a B.O.A.C. Constellation on short finals for runway 07. It touched down on the short tarmac section and then disappeared in an enormous cloud of red dust with engines roaring and propellers screaming in full reverse pitch. It stopped with its nose almost hanging over the edge of the runway. It stayed there for quite a few minutes before turning to backtrack. The East African onlookers found the entire performance enormously entertaining and could only imagine at the content of the conversation taking place on the flight-deck, as the crew tried to figure out how they had arrived at runway 07, Nairobi West instead of their destination, runway 06, Eastleigh.

The next amazing thing to happen was that it taxied all the way back to the take-off position of runway 07 and there it sat for some considerable time while, the onlookers presumed, the crew got the manuals out and scratched their heads over the take-off calculations. Discretion took over in the end and a red faced B.O.A.C. captain taxied the aircraft to the terminal.

The B.O.A.C. Constellation back-tracks past the Nairobi West control tower Capt Ratcliffe

But his problems were not yet over. The real fun started when it was realised that Nairobi West did not possess steps which reached the passenger doors of this huge aircraft. The DC3 steps just about reached the top of the main wheels. The entertainment continued for the onlookers as the assorted passengers, fat people, thin people, little old ladies, sari clad ladies – were all handed down gingerly from the door to helpers below via a precarious maintenance stand, normally used for working on engines. Station manager Reg Silverlock, with great presence of mind, soon had them all despatched by Eboos' Taxis to Eastleigh, to clear Customs.

The Constellation, G-ALAK, had been en-route from Entebbe to Eastleigh and was descending through cloud, using the Eastleigh NDB. Nairobi West would have been just to the right of track, and, as has so often happened, the crew saw a runway,

The giant airliner in front of the E.A.A.C. maintenance hangars, workshop and administration building at Nairobi West. (Mr John Hudson)

albeit five miles short, but in all respects just like the one they were looking for. With no further reference to the ADF, tuned to the Eastleigh NDB, they hurriedly performed their pre-landing checks, dropped the wheels, selected flap and in no time at all they were busy stopping the aircraft on the short runway.

Franz Margadant, an E.A.A.C. ground engineer who had been to Entebbe to service the Constellation, was on the flight-deck at the time and realised the mistake on late finals, but did not dare to interrupt the captain's concentration during the critical landing phase. To make matters worse, there were two captains, one being checked by the other.

1957 – 1959

From the start, the Canadair C4Ms were crewed by E.A.A.C. pilots, trained initially by B.O.A.C. Captain Joe Parker came from B.O.A.C. to head the fleet as chief pilot, Syd Hannaford conducted the technical courses and Captain Douglas Lavers, assisted by Captain Howard Iliffe, an ex-R.A.F. instructor, was responsible for flying training.

The first scheduled Canadair service, EC501, was scheduled to depart Nairobi for Durban on Saturday, 13th April, 1957, initially on a weekly basis, supplementing the Monday DC3 prestige 'Coastliner' EC103/104 international service to South Africa. Routing via Dar es Salaam and Salisbury the Canadair would complete the round trip in two days, with a night stop in Durban. This would be a great improvement on the four day trip of the DC3. To the great embarrassment of all concerned, with board members Sir Charles Phillips and Mr J.C. Mundy, due to travel on the flight and Colonel Mostert and Mr G.D.H. Nicol already in Durban hosting celebrations, an accident at Eastleigh delayed departure by twenty-four hours. A member of the ground staff, carrying heavy equipment, accidentally walked into the wing trailing-edge and damaged the flaps.

But the Corporation had planned far more adventurous things for these aircraft than the old trail down to Durban. On 15th September, 1957, a Canadair, flown by Captain Parker and Captain Reg Cartwright as his first officer, ventured on the first scheduled flight to Karachi and Bombay via Aden. This followed the EC602/024 service to London via Entebbe, Benina and Rome commanded by Capt Bob Ainsworth on 5th September and an extension of the southern route, to Johannesburg via Salisbury.

Later in the year, as more crews became available, these services were increased to twice weekly. This had been a quantum step for the airline. New horizons had been opened up almost overnight. For the Canadair crews the Bombay service was regarded as "a real killer" by comparison with their previous experience. The duty time on the Bombay service was seventeen hours forty-five minutes each way. In order to do this legally three pilot crews were used. The minimum requirement was for one captain and two first officers with a group one rating on type. There was a so called bunk on board, to provide for crew rest. It consisted of a wooden board mounted above the invertors in one of the forward baggage compartments, just behind the flight deck. In order to allow maximum baggage space, the board

The East African Airways DC4-M Canadair, VP-KNY, starting engines at Dar es Salaam. (Mr T. Webb)

with a Dunlopillo mattress on top was placed about two feet below the ceiling. There was very little room in which to squeeze, without hitting the roof.

In addition to this claustrophobic discomfort, the invertors provided a built in heating system, which was on at all times, whether needed or not. To add to the discomfort, the humidifiers had been removed from the aircraft, due to difficulties in keeping them serviceable, with the result that 'when you broke a bread roll, the remaining half was like toast by the time you had eaten the first half'.

To add to the fatigue problems there was a five and a half hour time change on the Bombay route which meant, in the worst case, taking off from Nairobi in the dark and flying through the night and the next day, and arriving in the late evening, after dark. Bombay State was 'dry' in the early days, so the crews got up to all kinds of tricks to get their liquid nourishment through customs. One individual attempted to smuggle miniature bottles of liquor stuffed into long stockings with elastic tops – until the elastic broke as he strode through the customs hall.

The Indian customs officers often turned a blind eye to the infringements of regulations, and were usually rewarded by a pack of cigarettes placed casually on top of an open flight bag. Later, 'permit rooms' were opened in the hotels, where one could buy a drink at great expense, provided you were in possession of a permit, which could be obtained by the simple procedure of declaring that you were an alcoholic and paying a fee. As the layover period could be anything from two to five days, it was essential for normal, red-blooded aircrew to need a drink during their relaxation.

Bombay was an eye-opener to the East African crews, who had, up until now, experienced only the efficiently run British colonies of East and Central Africa and the equally acceptable big city of Durban. If they arrived in the evening, and provided it was not during the monsoon season, as they drove to the hotel, they saw the pavements crowded with sleeping bodies. An even more incredible sight, if they arrived in the morning, was a swamp area, just past the airport, where enormous sections of sewer pipe had at some time been deposited ready for installation. However, the locals had commandeered them and sealed the ends in one way or another, and were using them as houses, no matter the position or the angle of the pipe. It would seem that the local authority had given up trying to evict them and had provided electricity.[1] Small children would be playing in the slimy green water and almost every dry area would have men, women and children of all ages, squatting on the ground, with dhotis and saris pulled up, performing their morning toilet – just the thing to provide an appetite for breakfast after a long night flight!

When they reached the West End Hotel, they would find people living on the pavement outside. One resourceful family had built a number of platforms in the branches of a tree, and it appeared that it was necessary for one member to be present at all times, to avoid being dispossessed. There was not much to do in Bombay, except for shopping, which was very good, with cheap and plentiful cotton goods – sheets, tablecloths and other materials which the crew members took home.

---

[1] Incredibly, thirty-five years later, these pipes are still there and inhabited.

There was the luxury of the Bombay barber-shops, where one could spend up to two hours in air-conditioned comfort, receiving the full treatment of haircut, shampoo and shave for just a few rupees. On one occasion, Captain Mitchell noticed a young man, naked and covered in sores, lying outside the door of the barber-shop. On enquiring, he learned that the man had died in the night, and the body would be collected by the cart. It was still there when he left.

The rest of the days would be spent by the hotel swimming pool, followed by a visit to the cinema in the evening.

By comparison, the EC602/601 London service was extremely popular. The Canadairs would depart Nairobi in the mid-afternoon for Entebbe, Khartoum and Benina, where they would arrive just before dawn. The crew would slip at Benina and await the next service, which they would take on to Rome and London. Sometimes the roster would require them to return to Nairobi from Benina, or they may slip again in Rome. After a period of trial and error, it was decided to retain a resident crew at Benghazi, who would operate the sector Benina – Rome – London. This was a very popular slip station, with a generally pleasant climate, a very good sailing club next to the hotel, where many of the crew members learned to sail, and a golf course, which was quite acceptable, despite the lack of greens.

The hotel was the Berenice, situated next to a huge mosque with two enormous domes. The crews with typical irreverence nicknamed it St Sabrina, after a well endowed English actress of the time. The hotel manager, 'Morsie', was everyone's friend. He was an Egyptian of the old school, his smooth urbanity would not have been out of place in the court of King Farouk, or in one of those old Hollywood movies located in Cairo. Within the hotel the East African floor was known as 'Skid Row' and a popular 'snake-pit' bar and an all-night casino ensured that the statutory 'rest period' between flights was not taken in a manner most generally required for airline crews.

There was plenty of company at Benghazi because Airwork, Hunting-Clan, B.O.A.C. and Central African Airways also slipped their crews there. Socially it was a paradise. As one pilot put it, "Girls, girls, girls – for the single men, of course!"

The Canadair had been a great step for everyone. With its four mighty Rolls-Royce Merlins, it was not a difficult aircraft to fly, but more complicated than they had been used to, with its pressurization, de-icing systems, hydraulics and electrics. This was also the first time that the American idea of check-lists had been employed. It was, after the initial resistance to the idea of reading from a card what any self respecting pilot should know without hesitation, (or so it was perceived by some), found to be the only way to ensure a standard check within the cockpit, or flight-deck as it was soon to be called.

The aircraft, until introduced to the hot, high and humid East African routes, was basically reliable, and, of course, the emergency drills had to be learned off by heart. This was done by use of mnemonics, most of which were invented by F/O Bruce Barnard, who spent a great deal of time working on them. Those pilots who flew the Canadairs would have little difficulty in recalling, for example, the engine fire drill mnemonic, "Throttle, Bottle, Button, Bulkhead, Ref, Big, Bas." This was interpreted in the following drill:

Throttle	-	Throttle closed
Bottle	-	Fire No 1 Extinguisher
Button	-	Press Feathering Button
Bulkhead	-	Bulkhead (Firewall) Valve closed. This cuts off fuel, oil, and hydraulics to the engine.
R	-	Radiator Flap closed
E	-	Electrics off-loaded
F	-	Fuel Off
B	-	Fire No 2 Bottle if necessary
I	-	Ignition Off
G	-	Generator Off
B	-	Booster Pump Off
A	-	Air conditioning Adjust
S	-	Prop Synch selected to live engine if applicable

Passing Mt Kilimanjaro, the view from the cockpit of a Canadair. (Captain Brewer)

Some of the take-offs were way outside the since acceptable WAT (Weight/Altitude/Temperature) limits, although at the time they were quite legal. Khartoum was a good example. The service would arrive at midnight, departing for Benina an hour later. In summer the surface temperature would be about 30 deg C., and after getting airborne the Canadairs would skim the tops of the sand dunes for some distance, before slowly climbing away into the cooler air. For the pilots it was a 'Catch 22' situation, having to inch open the radiator flaps, to keep the radiator temperatures within limits, thus creating more drag, which prevented the much sought after increase in height. As soon as the radiator temperature dropped, the radiator flaps would be closed again slightly, to recover the lost airspeed. It seemed an age before they got to the cooler air and the aircraft started to show its true performance.

The Canadairs were designed for operations in cold or temperate climates. In E.A.A.C. service they proved to be a continuous source of trouble. With liquid cooled engines, electric propeller controls and two speed superchargers, where, on the climb one throttled back, changed gear and accelerated again, causing the passengers to fairly jump out of their skins, they provided some exciting moments when the engines failed under the pressure of tropical conditions. Captain Mitchell was in command of one such flight on the eastern route, when, about two hours out of Aden en route to Karachi, there was a banshee scream from number three

First Officer Ginger Brewer in the right-hand seat of a Canadair. (Captain Brewer)

engine, and something hit the fuselage with a discernable 'clunk'. The engine RPM went 'off the clock' and the aircraft yawed violently. The immediate action was to reduce speed as quickly as possible in order to get the propeller RPM back into the feathering range. In the event of this not being successful and the propeller remaining un-feathered, the propeller shaft could seize, resulting in the propeller flying off, possibly resulting in disaster. Fortunately, they managed to feather the propeller and returned to Aden. While over South Yemen, a distinctly unfriendly tribal territory, an Army officer passenger remarked that, even if they had them, *goolie chits* were not recognised by the tribesmen down below – they were doubly relieved upon their safe arrival at Aden.

On inspection it was found that a reduction gear tooth had broken away, causing the entire assembly to disintegrate and a part of it had broken through the casing and hit the fuselage.

One day, in late 1959, Franz Margadant, then a flight engineer on the Canadairs, was on the EC508, VP-KOI, out of Johannesburg bound for Salisbury and Nairobi, commanded by Captain Peter Cooke. Some time after take-off the oil pressure in number one engine fell. He was unable to feather the propeller and there was fear that it would fly off, due to lack of oil in the reduction gear. Salisbury was still some distance away and Captain Cooke decided that a landing was required without

Captain G.W. 'Mitch' Mitchell in the new B.O.A.C. style uniform which was introduced for the overseas Canadair services.

(Captain Mitchell)

delay. They decided to make an approach and land at Fort Victoria, although under normal circumstances the runway was far too short for a Canadair.

The landing, which had to be made with as little forward speed as possible, in order to contain the RPM on the runaway propeller, and the need to stop on the short runway, was successful. The airfield authorities had, helpfully, removed the fence at the end of the runway, just in case they should over-run.

After the passengers had been transferred to a Central African Airways flight, preparations were made for an engine change. An engine had to be flown down from Nairobi, so there was not much they could do until it arrived. The crew were entertained that night by the kind and friendly local people, who laid on a party for them. The following day some of the ladies organised an outing to the nearby Zimbabwe ruins, which was much appreciated by everyone.

Early the following afternoon a DC3, flown by Captain Peter Cunningham, arrived with a gang of engineers and a replacement engine. With a huge crowd of local African onlookers, who had never seen such a large *Ndege* at the airfield before, the engineers set to, and by nightfall the job was done.

In the cool of the next morning, Capt Cooke with only Franz Margadant aboard, taxied the Canadair to the extreme end of the runway. The aircraft had been lightened as much as possible to allow for the short take-off distance available. The throttles were opened, brakes released and they accelerated down the runway,

Engineer Officer Franz Margadant

Captain Peter Cooke

gradually gaining speed as the limited strip disappeared behind them. Capt Cooke, with a quick glance at the airspeed indicator, eased back the yoke and they were airborne, skimming above the ground to climb gently over the trees. They made one low pass above the onlookers massed below them, before turning on course for Salisbury, to continue their interrupted journey.

The Christmas 1959 edition of *Flight* magazine carried an amusing account of this incident, written by Mr. S.G.H. Williams, then a meteorological officer at Fort Victoria aerodrome.

"To B.O.A.C. and other crews commuting between London and Johannesburg there are but two airports after Entebbe southbound, namely, Salisbury and Jan Smuts. There are others; but these are for the use of *les autres*, and have no significance other than a dot on the map.

"Such a field is Fort Victoria aerodrome in Southern Rhodesia. Situated 150 miles south of Salisbury, it is on the direct route from Salisbury to Johannesburg and provides a non-directional radio beacon as its contribution to the facilities of the route. It is manned by one European who, although primarily employed by the Federal Meteorological Department, carries out his duties of meteorological officer, radio operator, aerodrome controller, Shell refuelling agent, aerodrome manager, fire officer, Vacuum Oil refuelling agent, information officer, aerodrome maintenance officer and provider of light refreshments with impartiality. He lives on the aerodrome in splendid isolation, and, theoretically, is available for twenty-four hours of the day on most days of the year.

"It is a well known concept that familiarity breeds contempt and, to those of his ilk toiling in their spacious, air conditioned and upholstered offices in Salisbury and Bulawayo, the sights and sounds of large, four engined aircraft are commonplace. Even a stately Comet taxying past the windows would occasion no remarks other than an anguished expletive from the briefing officer in the middle of a telephone conversation.

"Not so in Fort Victoria. Work is carried out in a rather more tranquil atmosphere. Surrounded by b-b-b-bundu and mealie patches as it is, the total absence of noise and distractions often make it possible to distinguish the African met observer's snores, emanating from the office next door, above the mutter of the point-to-point radio and the occasional buzzing of a trapped bee on the windowpane.

"At intervals, a light aircraft – usually of the Cessna or Piper breed – arrives, bringing businessmen, dam-builders, engineers, and the occasional American tourist bound for the Zimbabwe Ruins and loaded with five year's salary in photographic equipment. Even commercial air services occasionally operate their daily schedule and arrive and depart in their usual frantic rush. Other than that, however, the only view we ever have of the larger aircraft is when they float majestically overhead at their 10,000 – 15,000ft, bound for Johannesburg or Salisbury. It is doubtful whether the captain even looks up from his Agatha Christie to note that he is passing over Fort Victoria.

"But it was rather a different story one day earlier this year – a day which will doubtless go down in the annals of Fort Victoria.

"It started normally. For the first part of the morning, the officer in charge was buried quietly under a mountain of ledger sheets, returns, charts, monthly reports and unanswered H.Q. correspondence which constitutes the normal end-of-month anguish. He could have been working hard. Or asleep. Or dead. Or merely dreaming of his long-awaited leave. It is a moot point. But tea time was looming on an otherwise black horizon when the information was received on the point-to-point radio that an East African Airways Argonaut (the B.O.A.C. name was used, even among E.A.A.C., although the Corporation had decided to adopt the name Canadair for their DC-4Ms), en route from Jan Smuts to Salisbury, was in trouble and wished to make a forced landing on Fort Victoria aerodrome in twenty minutes.

"At this point a few details of the facilities at Fort Victoria may not come amiss. Situated two and a half miles from town, we possess a fairly level grass runway 4,200ft in length. The grass is kept reasonably short with the aid of a prehistoric mowing machine drawn by two extremely patient oxen and manned by two Africans, who yield easily to the gentle swaying motion and are normally in a state of complete somnolence by 0800 hr.

"Fire equipment was evolved by Mr Heath Robinson in his heyday and one of his lighter moments. It consists of a cylindrical tank, mounted on two wheels, which is reputed to emit foam when three cocks are screwed in, two screwed out – and a little brass handle at one end wound furiously in a clockwise direction. As this was the original equipment that stood by for Bleriot's landing on the Cliffs of Dover, some pardonable doubt does exist concerning its efficiency. In any case, it requires fourteen men and one horse to move it from its resting place – provided that the tyres are inflated.

"However, a 222 call to the Town Police produced some quite remarkable results. Within fifteen minutes, arrivals at the aerodrome included: one limousine and the Police Officer in Charge; three Police Land Rovers and seven large policemen; one red Morris Ten van containing two men, 800ft of hose and ten pairs of asbestos gloves and aprons (the town fire engine); three doctors; one ambulance and three nurses; one half-ton pick-up loaded with axes; one half-ton pick-up loaded with fire extinguishers; four other cars loaded with eager-beavers; 357 Africans (walking or running).

"By this time the Argonaut was well in sight, limping slowly over the town on its downwind leg. The suspense mounted as we dispersed everything and everybody on the secondary runway near the end of the main runway to await the almost inevitable overrun. Neither was the atmosphere eased at the sight of the aircraft well down on its final approach with the undercarriage still retracted – although visions of unpleasant belly-landings were dispelled when, at approximately 300ft the wheels were lowered. And then the value of reversible-pitch propellers was demonstrated in no uncertain fashion. Brought into play at the moment of touch-down with a roar from the two inner engines, a perfect landing was effected, with room to spare. Not a lot of room. But some – slightly to the disappointment of the town's fire fighting crew, to the relief of the meteorological officer, and to the very obvious relief of the 27 passengers who clambered down a pair of kitchen steps to firm ground. These were transported quickly into town to make appreciable inroads into the stocks of alcoholic stimulants of the local hotel and to await the arrival of a charted Dakota to ferry them on to Salisbury.

"The Argonaut provided a show-piece for two days, together with two Dakotas that arrived on the scene the following day, containing a spare engine and a remarkably hard-working ground crew. Working under adverse conditions (which included a horde of spectators, gaggles of sticky children and numerous dazed Africans, who thought they had now seen everything), the crew completed an engine change in slightly over six hours – a considerable part of the task being the removal of the new engine from its stowage in the Dakota. In this, they were aided by some remarkable co-operation from Rhodesia Railways, who supplied a mobile crane of dubious vintage which eased the task considerably, but which also removed most of the main telephone lines to Umtali during its passage to the aerodrome.

"The removal of the faulty engine was carried out in a very short time and it was discovered that one piston, connecting rod and bearing had rolled themselves into unrecognizable chunks of metal and battered numerous holes in both sides of the crankcase of an extremely expensive product.

"For the whole of that day Fort Victoria aerodrome resembled a big fairground, with new crowds arriving in a continuous stream of cars, bicycles, scooters and even a large yellow bus operated by a local opportunist. Children from six years of age to sixty clambered over every inch of the aircraft, while dogs fought and chased each other in circles around the undercarriage. The local hotel-keeper transformed his battered Dodge saloon into a delivery van to maintain a steady supply of solid and liquid refreshment for both crew and privileged onlookers, while the town's electrician rigged floodlights so that darkness should not interfere with activities.

"The meteorological officer meanwhile rebuilt his mountain of returns in a remote corner of the office and spent hours at the telephone answering queries. And it is worthy of note that, less than one hour after the landing, he was asked to supply details of the Constellation that had just crashed in flames with 72 people on board!

"However, the coming of night saw the end. At eleven p.m. the last panel was replaced and the night shattered by a roar from the new engine – saluted by a raising of numerous bottles of refreshment grasped firmly by the hard core of spectators.

"An even smaller group was present the following morning at 0630 hr to watch the Argonaut use almost every foot of the runway to continue on its way to Salisbury. And it was with a sense of real regret that the met officer watched the two Dakotas follow on later in the morning – leaving the aerodrome to regain slowly its general air of tranquillity".

The Canadairs continued to misbehave in the exotic climate into which they had been introduced.

Captain Laddie Richter, en route from Aden to Karachi, did a forced landing on the island of Masirah, off the Arabian coast.

Captain George Leslie experienced a loss of power on all four engines, with smoke in the cockpit and made a MAYDAY call picked up by the R.A.F. at Aden. He landed at a small R.A.F. airfield at Riyan, 300 miles from Aden on the South Yemen coast, with only paraffin lit goose-neck flares to illuminate the runway.

Captain Tug Wilson continued his battle with the elements over Khartoum when, in command of a Canadair, he was making a let down on a stormy night, after a flight from Entebbe. At 4,000 ft, on the final approach to Khartoum airport, with the power throttled right back, the aircraft was struck by a powerful up-draft associated with a nearby cumulo-nimbus. Within seconds they were at 20,000 ft. Overhead the airport, they were still at 15,000 ft. and it was necessary to make an orbiting descent to land.

East African Airways was still on the anvil. The expansion into overseas routes with these complex four-engined airliners was stretching the crews, building their experience and expertise through trial and error – it was the required schooling for what was to follow in the years ahead. Sometimes things went wrong which could not be attributed to the machines alone. One night the experienced pilot of a Canadair was cleared to take-off by the Bombay control tower. As he climbed away, he received a further clearance to turn left and continue his climb en route to Karachi. Tug Wilson, who was in the jump seat behind the pilots, immediately realised that the controller had given wrong instructions. He leapt up, flicked on the landing lights, which illuminated a tree clad hillside ahead of them. He grabbed the control yoke and, giving the four Merlins full throttle, pulled the Canadair into a steep climbing turn to the right.

On another night, this time between Karachi and Aden, Wilson was resting in the crew bunk when he sensed that something was wrong. He got up and made his way to the flight-deck. He studied the compass and cross checked with the north star. The indications were wrong.

"Where are you going?" he asked the acting captain.

"Why, to Aden of course, Tug, you know. Why don't you go back and get your rest."

It was a most embarrassed man that disengaged the auto pilot and did a 180 degree turn on to the correct heading. Probably they had dozed and the auto pilot had slipped out and had been re-engaged when on a reciprocal heading. There

Captain Tug Wilson (1960)

would have been considerable confusion when they called up Aden for landing and Bombay answered them! The flight landed at Aden an hour late - evidence that they had flown a reciprocal heading for thirty minutes.

On the 24th March 1958, Captain Joe Parker was in command of VP-KNY when, shortly after take-off from Khartoum bound for Benina, an engine failed. The aircraft was fuelled 'to the top' and was very nearly at maximum weight. Before they could land it was necessary to dump fuel to maintain height and get down to maximum landing weight. They circled out over the desert and the first officer, who was Ginger Brewer, carried out the drill. Prior to pulling the dump levers, he looked at Captain Parker, ex-chief pilot of the B.O.A.C. Argonaut fleet, and asked him if all was in order to dump. "Go ahead", he said, "I have never dumped fuel before!".

"With these aircraft we commenced a service to India", recalls Captain George Leslie. "The routing, from Nairobi, leaving at ten o'clock at night, to Aden, Karachi and Bombay, arriving there the next afternoon, Bombay time. It was always hot, hot, hot - on the ground and in the air. It played havoc with the engines. Take-offs took the engine temperatures to the maximums, we couldn't climb high enough to get into the cooler air, eight to ten thousand feet being the limit."

On one of his first Canadair trips he flew with the Chief Pilot, Captain Leo Davidson. They left Nairobi on Christmas Eve, December 24th, 1959, a little late, at 22.45. The navigator was Paddy Murray, and before take-off, he gave the entire crew, boys and girls, a little present marked 'not to be opened until Christmas'. They all wondered what the surprise was. Midnight came during the cruise between Nairobi and Aden. The presents were opened - sweets, balloons, little Christmassy nick-nacks - and a 'French Letter' for each of them!

After take-off from Aden and having settled down on the cruise once again, they passed their point of no return when they had a second surprise that Christmas Day. Number two engine started playing up. Long streams of flame from the exhausts started to stream out, beyond the tailplane. The cabin was illuminated by the flames, and the passengers became very anxious - as indeed were the crew. The tropical daylight came up and the day quickly became warmer, as a result, the engines began to run hot, and the Canadair gradually lost height. Visibility was good and eventually the outskirts of Karachi came into sight. The disused airfield at Drigh Road came into view, they could see the huge hangar which had been built for the ill-fated R101 airship.

They were drifting down steadily, with still some fifteen minutes to go before reaching the International Airport on the far side of the city. They quickly decided not to risk continuing, as the engines were running hot, well out of limits, with the cowls fully open. They called Karachi, advising them that they were landing at Drigh Road. They touched down at 12.10 local time on Christmas Day 1959. The passengers were extremely relieved as the aircraft was taxied to a stop and the engines shut down.

Their problems were not entirely over, however, as the aerodrome was totally deserted, there was no sign of life anywhere in their field of view. Grass was pushing up through the cracks in the tarmac and weeds grew in the dusty soil. There was no means of descending from the Canadair, even if there had been somewhere to go. It soon became uncomfortably hot in the cabin and the crew opened all the doors, hatches and emergency exits. As there seemed no sign of help coming, and they were well into Christmas Day, they opened up the generously stocked bar and free drinks were served all round, very soon everyone was enjoying quite an extraordinary party in the Canadair's cabin.

Still no help arrived, so the cabin crew served up the contents of the galley – a full Christmas dinner of turkey and trimmings, champagne, hats and crackers. It was five o'clock in the afternoon when a B.O.A.C. team arrived to take care of everything.

The following day, after a replacement engine had been fitted, they took off for Nairobi, via Aden. It had been decided to cancel the Bombay sector. The replacement engine began to give trouble fairly soon into the cruise. They struggled on to Aden where they were delayed another two days. It had been just another Canadair flight – full of the ups and downs of life!

The Canadair service to London proved to be more reliable, but it was a long flight – something in excess of twenty-four hours was spent in the aircraft, longer in the winter when they would encounter the strong northerly winds for the last ten hours or so. The ground speed would drop from 240 mph to 170 mph, no faster than a Dakota. The journey, however was broken by the Benina stop-over, where they would arrive at about four in the morning, when they would be driven the fifteen miles into Benghazi by the most arrogant and dangerous taxi drivers they had ever encountered. It was generally acknowledged that the taxi ride was the most hazardous part of the job.

There were other problems associated with flying into London. Although Heathrow Airport was to become a great deal more busy in the years to come, even in the late fifties it was an airport which, for the un-sophisticated colonials, was a source of constant bewilderment and exasperation as they encountered the work practices and union power which existed at the time, particularly among the huge B.O.A.C. engineering organisation, upon which they depended for ground servicing at London. Things which could be done in a very short time in Nairobi, if everyone set-to to accomplish them, would take many hours at Heathrow, often undertaken with little enthusiasm. It was a reflection upon the social conditions of the period, rather than upon the engineers concerned.

One night, on September 12th, 1958, Captain Les Pink took over VP-KOI on the northbound service at Benina. The incoming captain had reported flying through severe hail storms after leaving Entebbe, but no serious damage was apparent. John Delves-Broughton, then resident station engineer, discovered, as he checked the aircraft over, that the radiator cores had been damaged. Captain Pink decided that, since the logistics of getting replacement cores to Benina were quite formidable, the risks of overheating were very slight, as they were now flying into the more temperate European skies. The remainder of the flight went without further trouble and, on arrival at London he asked B.O.A.C. to repair the radiators, since they would need to be working efficiently on the flight south into the African high temperatures.

Prior to departure, the next day, as the flight engineer performed his walk-around checks, he saw that the radiator cores were still flattened and nothing had been done to replace them. The word came from B.O.A.C. that since these were listed as "base snags", they would have to be repaired in Nairobi. Captain Pink refused to accept this explanation. The Canadair's cooling system was difficult enough, departing from the hot route stations, in normal circumstances. With defective radiator cooling it would have been foolish to continue. " Well, it will take five hours to complete, and you will have to apply for another departure slot, probably eight hours", Pink was told. This would mean that the crew would be out of flight time limits before they reached Benina, so it was decided that everyone should return to the hotel and departure should be delayed for twenty-four hours.

It was when air traffic control were asked if VP-KOI could be taken up for an air test that Pink and his crew discovered how differently things were done at London, compared with Nairobi. That an aircraft departing Heathrow went lumbering about the sky on an air test within the tightly controlled London zone was completely unheard of. After all, had not the engineers of B.O.A.C. signed that the work was completed and that the aircraft was fit to fly? Pink was adamant that he wanted an air test, and air traffic control reluctantly agreed to fit his Canadair into their pattern, but East African Airways were not popular that day.

There have been several occasions when airliners have disappeared without trace, with no rational explanation for their loss. On the evening of 19th December 1959, such an event came very close to occurring to the passengers and crew of the Canadair VP-KOI. It was a hot, sticky evening when Captain Jack Bicknell took-off from Bombay at the start of a long night flight to Nairobi. The first sector to Karachi was scheduled to take two and a half hours. As they flew on through the tropical night, no one noticed the odour which slowly increased in pungency throughout the cabin. About half an hour before top of descent, Dave Dempster, the handling first officer, looked at his captain and saw that he didn't look at all well. He then realised that he himself was feeling sick. Quickly grabbing an oxygen mask, he slapped it over Bicknell's face, and then donning his own mask, commenced a fast descent, until the cabin could be depressurised. They forced as much fresh air through the aircraft as possible. Sensing that the worst of the vapour was in the forward part of the aircraft, they figured that there must be cargo loaded in the forward hold giving off the noxious fumes.

They called P.I.A. on the company frequency, asking them to find out what had been loaded in the forward area. Shortly before arrival they learned that the cargo consisted of cellophane bangles, used as cheap costume jewellery by the Asian women. When the cargo handlers at Karachi removed the bales and carried them on their shoulders, they began to stagger, and nearly collapsed before reaching the cargo building. It was discovered later that the bangles had been coated with amyl-acetone, which, when heated, gives off highly toxic fumes.

The long night passages provided opportunities for entertainment. A favourite prank among the cabin crew, when a new stewardess was on board, was to pretend that a 'sleeping roster' required the crew to rest in the crew bunk, which in fact was only for the use of the operating crew, to allow mandatory crew rest away from the controls. The 'chief,' or purser, would write down the names of the crew, instructing the new girl to be the first to rest in the bunk. The Corporation, he would tell her, insisted that no one slept in their uniforms, as it would crease them. Underwear, pants and bra would be OK. The aircraft would reach top of climb, and with up to twelve hours level cruise, it would be time to commence 'crew rest'. Unknown to the poor girl, the cockpit crew would be co-conspirators in this practical joke. On one occasion the captain was lying in the bunk, feigning sleep, when the stewardess climbed up the ladder, to find the bunk occupied. She reversed down quickly, only to be told by the Purser that it was the Corporation's instructions that crew must take their rest, and that all was in order. She went back up the steps, reluctantly.

It was dark, the cockpit was lit only by the instrument lighting, everyone tried hard not to give the game away, but someone failed to suppress a giggle and suddenly the entire crew burst out laughing as the master top dome light was switched on, revealing the unfortunate victim on top of the ladder, dressed only in bra and briefs, quickly realising, to her dismay, that she had been set up for the amusement of one and all!

On one occasion the tables were turned. A check-captain was part of the crew on the eastern route service to Bombay. He had taken the opportunity of a rest in the crew bunk during the night sector to Aden. The bunk was a portable device, which was comprised of three planks of wood, fitted onto brackets and was curtained off from the aisle. Just aft of this was the curtain shielding the first class passenger cabin. If the planks were not positioned correctly on their brackets, it was easy for the plank nearest the aisle to collapse and dump the mattress and occupant on the floor. The Canadair had a master RPM synchronising switch which, if switched off when the engines were not quite lined up, caused an unpleasant, unsynchronised noise. On this occasion the handling pilot, Captain Drew, reached up and switched off this master switch. The check-captain, disturbed by the resultant noise, leaned out of the bunk to find out what was going on. Unfortunately, the bunk was not secure and the whole device collapsed, dumping him into the aisle. The accident would not have been so bad if the passenger compartment curtain had not been drawn back and if, sad to relate, the unfortunate man's pyjama trousers had not fallen down round his ankles. This performance was greeted with great delight by the passengers and a loud cheer went up throughout the cabin.

There was a stewardess on the Canadairs at that time who was the sister of a leading Anglo-Irish film star. She was acclaimed to be a devastating beauty, with typical Irish colouring and dark hair, with blue eyes. She had a boy-friend who was so besotted with her that he sold up his business in England and followed her out to Nairobi. The result of this rash decision was that within a short time he became destitute and was deported back to the United Kingdom. After a while the girl became engaged to a millionaire, whom, she admitted, she had decided to marry for his money. On one of her London stop-overs, the old boy-friend rang her up to congratulate her, and asked her out to dinner, for 'old times sake'.

During the course of the meal he asked her to remove her very expensive engagement ring, so that he could admire it.

With the ring in his hand, he quickly left the restaurant, leaving her high and dry. She called the police, in panic and for the rest of the evening she was in a state of great distress. The next day she was due to depart for Nairobi as a member of the Canadair crew. But she was more concerned about her engagement ring. The service departed without her, and upon hearing that she had failed to show, Eric Morris in Nairobi, suspended her (at that time cabin crew came under the jurisdiction of the operations manager).

She turned up a week later in Nairobi, having traced the former boy-friend got him arrested and recovered the ring. She cried on Eric Morris' shoulder, who, melted by her charms, re-instated her.

She used her charms to great effect on Paddy Murray, who, being a bachelor at the time, knew her fairly well. She used to borrow his car in Nairobi when he was away on trips, but he decided that it was not a good idea, since she regularly failed to meet him on return, or turned up late at the airport. The car would be filthy and the fuel tank empty. She begged him to let her borrow it again, but he said "NO".

Then she said, with beguiling Irish charm, "We could come to an amicable arrangement - for every 100 miles I do in your car, you can make love to me once". Paddy Murray claims that he was so taken aback that he did not take her up on the offer. She married her millionaire and no one heard any more of her.

One first officer had become a pilot almost by default. He was originally a radio officer and elected to become a pilot when the old practice died out with the Lodestars. He sat the pilot's exams nine times - on one occasion Captain 'Caspar' Caspereuthus, who was then the invigilator for the Ministry of Civil Aviation, asked "Where is our friend, is he sick? He has not sat his exam this morning - the Ministry will want to know what had happened to him - they have got so used to receiving his papers every month."

Eventually he received his licence - some said, unkindly, for good attendance. His airmanship was of the casual variety, there was no question of actual negligence, things simply happened to him. On one occasion, flying from Durban in a Dakota, Captain Jack Bicknell decided to have forty winks after lunch. He took a look round, noted the coast line on his left and handed over to his first officer. The aircraft was on autopilot, and he became engrossed in a novel. Unfortunately, the autopilot faithfully followed the precessing directional gyro several degrees and Jack Bicknell awoke to find blue sea outside his window and the coastline on the other side. They had no idea how long they had been off heading, so there was controlled panic while the very unreliable map was scoured for clues. They eventually landed at Lumbo just before last light with fuel barely above scavenging levels.

One morning Captain Bill Fumerton commenced take-off from Nairobi in a Canadair, with the unlucky fellow sat beside him as first officer. The large four-engined airliner was speeding down the runway when, moments before V_1, he said "My rabbit died last night."

Because of the mighty roar of the four Rolls-Royce Merlins, Bill Fumerton could not understand him.

"What's that?"

"My rabbit died last night."

Fumerton still could understand nothing, or perhaps could not believe his ears, so assuming that the F/O was reporting some catastrophic failure, he closed the throttles, threw the propellers into reverse pitch and with full braking action he aborted the take-off, and brought the Canadair to a stop. As the engines ticked over while they parked in the loop, there was a scene of dumbfounded incredulity as the crew gradually understood the innocent remark which had so quickly terminated their flight!

❖ ❖ ❖

Looking across Nairobi towards Ol Donyo Sabuk, which rises 2,144ft above ground level. From the roof of the New Stanley Hotel. (Author)

In those days it was common practice for the crews to find themselves rostered on DC3s or Canadairs - or even Rapides, in the case of several pilots. Later on, the procedure of operating crew staying on the fleet to which they were allocated, was adopted by the Corporation.

In the same year that the Canadairs commenced service, EAA introduced a very popular Sunday excursion by Dakota to the Serengeti National Game Park. It was an extremely popular flight amongst the crews, a welcome alternative to the trip to Karachi and Bombay. The *Guide to East Africa* at the time described the excursion:

> "This one hour flight is a popular Sunday excursion with resident and visitor alike. The inclusive cost 150 Shs [£7.10s.]. The plane leaves Nairobi airport at 6.30 a.m. and at 7.30 a.m. lands at the Serengeti airstrip. Here passengers are met by a park warden and transferred to safari vehicles to commence a 100 mile trip through excellent game country, with ample opportunities for photography. A picnic lunch is served in the Park at a spot chosen by the warden. At 5 p.m., in the cool of the evening, the return flight is made, arriving back at Nairobi airport at 6 p.m."

To arrive at the airport at about six on a Sunday morning was not the best time, after a Saturday night in Nairobi, but this was one trip that everyone looked forward to. One could see more wild life in this one day than most people would see in a lifetime. Once airborne, they would set course to the south west, with the rising sun behind them. They passed over Lake Magadi, a soda lake, with its soda factory and little self-contained township, skirting to the north of Lake Natron and the extensive soda swamps, into the vast bushland of northern Tanganyika, which was virtually uninhabited. This was the region known as the Serengeti. Five thousand five hundred square miles of bush, reaching almost to the shores of Lake Victoria - this was what they called a Park!

They would land at a clearing in the bush, called Seronera. This could not be seen easily from the air, but to the north, about eight miles away, there was a pimple standing above the plain, it was called Banagi Hill, famed for its lions. To find the landing strip was the most difficult part of the day's work. If they should ever 'hit it on the nose', it was put down to exceptional good luck. When time was up plus, say, five minutes, they would turn 180 degrees and commence a reverse search. But this would mean flying into the sunrise and haze. The maps which they used were hopelessly out of date, although the ground features would constantly change from season to season, the appearance of the plains after the rains would bear little relation to the long months of dry weather. During the months of April and May the Serengeti would be closed, after the rains all the old tracks or roads would be obliterated. New ones would be formed as the ground dried out, and they would follow a different path. Some pilots used the AA road maps, compiled after the war - the aviation charts in use at the time were of 1930s vintage. Sometimes Seronera could not be found on the first attempt, and a diversion would be made to Arusha, to refuel before setting out for another attempt.

Miles Turner was the game warden at Seronera. When he heard the sound of the aircraft's engines, he set off in the Land Rover, to tear up and down the airstrip,

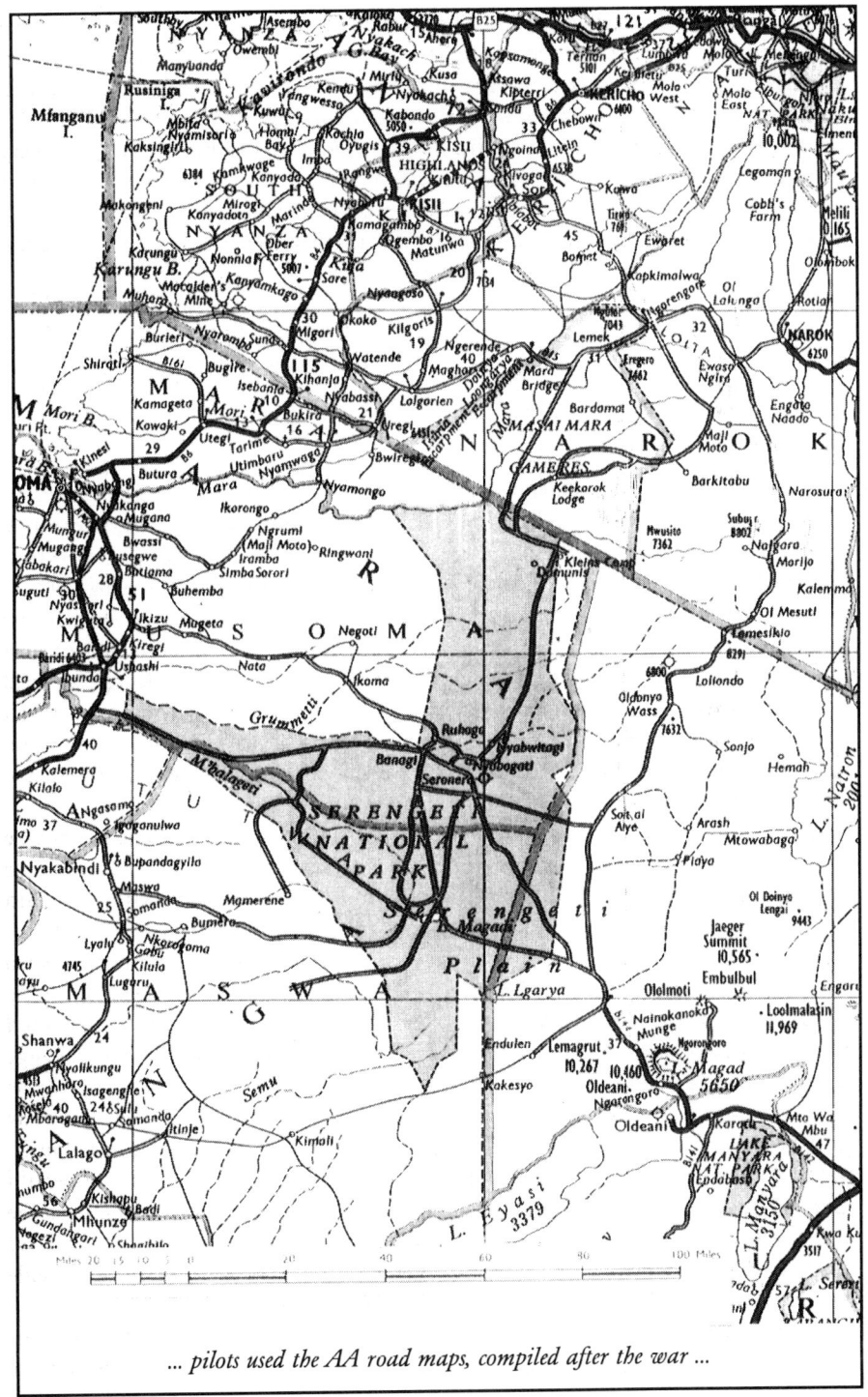

... pilots used the AA road maps, compiled after the war ...

raising a lot of dust, if there had not been an overnight shower. This was to shoo away the ever present zebras and wildebeest. The dust was a great help to the pilots in locating the airstrip. After landing and switching off the engines, the catering was off-loaded. The picnic, provided by the catering manager, Charles West-Thomas, was for everyone on board, including beer, wine and champagne – it was all included in the fare.

Miles and his charming wife, Kay, would always be there to greet the passengers and outline for them what he had planned for the day. He was regarded as a *fundi* – an expert – on the wild life of the Serengeti.

For the next four or five hours they would meander through the countryside. Sometimes following a Land Rover track, but for most of the time across country, or along and through dry river beds. Miles and his scouts knew the country like the backs of their hands – where certain animals would be, which trees the leopards were sleeping in, where the water holes were – one could guarantee to see everything. The herds of zebra and wildebeest were common, there were also gazelle, eland, elephant, rhino, hippos, lion, and monkeys. They would find the leopards sleeping lazily in the trees, there would be families of warthogs trotting in file, and there would be snakes and tsetse flies. They might be passing through a thicket of thorn trees when, suddenly the tsetse flies would attack. Their red-hot needle stings would penetrate a couple of layers of khaki drill. The discomfort, however, soon passed.

The picnic lunches were jolly affairs. The Land Rovers would have split up to make individual safaris – there is nothing worse in Africa than following a vehicle ahead and sitting in its wake of dust and stones. At lunch time they would all meet at a pre-arranged spot, somewhere cosy, in the shade, by a water hole. An hour or so for lunch, resting from the heat of the mid-day, and they would be ready to set off again. They could be sixty or seventy miles away from the aircraft by now, none of them would be able to say in which direction to go, their safari had taken them in all directions. Fortunately, their guides would have no difficulty in leading them back, wandering across the bush, and finding more groups of animals on the way.

On one occasion, at the end of a day's outing, the Land Rovers returned to the airstrip and, as they approached the Dakota, which had been sitting there all day, some movement was noticed in the shadows under the belly and the tail. A group of lions with their mates and teenage cubs were dozing. They had seen the approaching people, but were obviously not at all worried, and they were not very interested in moving either. This was great fun for the tourists, but the crew knew different. Lions had an appetite for the fabric and dope covered elevators on the Dakota's tail-plane. This had occurred in the past at Nairobi, when the aircraft scheduled for the early morning flights had been left out overnight, lions would wander into Nairobi West from the Athi Plains and the Nairobi Game Reserve on the other side of the airfield and chew away at any DC3 elevators they could find.

The lions were finally made to feel unwelcome by revving the engines of the Land Rovers until the foul smelling fumes got up their noses, and the pride reluctantly moved off from their shady repose. The tired but happy group of crew and tourists climbed aboard the hot Dakota and within a few minutes were climbing away into the cool evening air, soon to be back in Nairobi for a refreshing shower in the New Stanley or the Norfolk, prior to the first sundowners of the evening.

In 1957, the first year of Canadair operations, an overall increase of 7.6 percent or 114,182 passengers was achieved by external operations, compared with 106,162 passengers in 1956. It had been a remarkable year in the progress of East African Airways. For the first time it had entered fully into the sphere of international activities and showed itself capable of operating on equal terms. With an increase in revenue estimated at one million pounds per year from the two services per week to the United Kingdom, it could be optimistic about the future, knowing that the funds could be generated for future re-equipment and that given support it could increase its share of this valuable market.

The extension of operations to the United Kingdom and to India by Canadair aircraft had brought with it those problems of route facilities commonly encountered by international airlines. It was not economically possible to provide staff at all stations on those long routes, so it was necessary to rely upon local organisations for ground handling services at each airport. East African Airways had entered into a number of agreements for the provision of the necessary facilities at route stations. On the United Kingdom route at stations outside the East African Territories, all facilities were provided by B.O.A.C., or their agents. On the Eastern Route, ground handling was carried out by Aden Airways, Pakistan International Airlines Corporation and B.O.A.C., at Aden, Karachi and Bombay respectively.

Embakasi was a small railway siding on the Nairobi – Mombasa line, about four miles east of Nairobi. The main road to Mombasa ran parallel, alongside the railway and, to the north of both, lay a large, flat, tree-less grass plain. During the second world war R.A.F. training flights from Eastleigh would conduct simulated emergency landings on a rough but safe patch on the plain. Probably with a memory of those flights, plus the obvious advantages of the flat terrain and unimpeded access, this area was selected by the government for the new Nairobi Airport.

Work had begun during 1953, at the height of the Mau Mau emergency and large numbers of these Mau Mau supporters had been rounded up and held in detention camps throughout Kenya and were employed to excavate and prepare the long single runway. These labourers would use picks, shovels and *kerais* (a kind of plough share disc), two men would loosen the soil and fill a *kerai*, which would be carried to be dumped on a mound about 100yds away, parallel to the

060/240 runway. This seemed a most ingenious way in which to construct a new airport at minimal cost. The contractors rubbed their hands and thought of the profits. That is, until the rains came.

Although it was known that the surface of the plain had considerable areas of black cotton soil (a very heavy clay-like substance, becoming sticky and adhesive when wet), it was apparently, not considered to be a serious obstacle by the constructors. The long rains came, and the labourers began to get bogged down. As the prisoners dug, shovelled and filled their *kerais*, the black-cotton stuck hard to the implements and made it almost impossible to use them. The poor Africans were carrying more soil around their ankles and bare feet than in the *kerais*. Bulldozers and lorries became stuck fast in the awful, adhesive soil. As a result, there was considerable delay to the construction of the airport, only when the rain ceased and the earth began to dry, several weeks later, could work re-commence.

The black cotton soil was three to six feet thick and lay upon bed-rock which acted as a seal, thus creating pools of water below the surface. Frogs and other hibernating creatures were unearthed during the excavations, and the workmen were astonished to find small fish swimming in the underground pools, as they exposed them.

On Sunday, March 9th, 1958, Nairobi was in festive spirits as crowds flocked to witness the official opening of the new Nairobi Airport at Embakasi by Her Majesty the Queen Mother. The opening had been originally scheduled to take place on the Saturday, but engine trouble had caused the royal Super-Constellation to be delayed at Mauritius on its journey from Australia. There was further disappointment when it was learned that the aircraft could not reach Nairobi in time and as a result the opening ceremony was conducted by the Governor of Kenya, Sir Evelyn Baring, who arrived from Government House by helicopter, to read a message from Her Majesty:

"I am greatly distressed that it has not been possible for me to perform the opening ceremony at the Nairobi Airport. I send my warmest congratulations to all those who have been engaged in this project and I look forward to the day when, on another voyage which I hope will not be too far in the future, my aircraft will land at your new airport."

The subsequent route of the royal flight by-passed Nairobi to re-fuel at Entebbe late on the night of March 10th, en route to Malta. Hurt feelings in Nairobi were not soothed by an official who stated that there was 'no point' in landing twice, as the aircraft could not reach Malta non-stop after re-fuelling at Nairobi.

The 20,000 people at the ceremony, however, were not disappointed as they were thrilled by flying displays from the Royal Air Force and by various civilian aircraft, while the music of the Kenya Police band took turns with the Kenya band of the Kings African Rifles to create a holiday atmosphere. A Vickers Viscount turbo-prop airliner took parties on flights over Kilimanjaro during the morning, prior to the arrival of the Governor. As the day wore on, traffic jams built up on the road to the airport, cars were bumper to bumper, stretching the length of the approach road. On the apron, sharing the glory beside a Royal Air Force Avro Vulcan V-Bomber and a gleaming new B.O.A.C. Comet 4 airliner, stood the little de Havilland DH51 which John Carberry had imported into the colony and Tom Campbell-Black had christened *Miss Kenya* all those years ago.

The following day, Nairobi West airport was officially renamed Wilson Aerodrome, in honour of Mrs Florence Kerr Wilson, the aviation pioneer who started it all.

Ray Lambeth had come to E.A.A.C. in 1950 as a trainee station officer. After eight years of postings at Nairobi, Dar es Salaam and Zanzibar, he was appointed the first station manager of the newly-named Wilson Airport. His happiness at acquiring a station of his own was cruelly interrupted at midnight on his first day, when Bill Richer, the cargo officer, came to his house to say that the airport was on fire. They raced to the scene to find that the wooden accommodation blocks, the 'labour lines', were ablaze. The authorities had closed an eye to the violation of the rule that the African workers should not have wives and children living in the accommodation, where no cooking fires were allowed. The sun-baked wooden buildings were totally destroyed. The fire service saved the wooden terminal buildings, and none of the aircraft were endangered. For Lambeth, it was an inauspicious start to his new promotion, but the inquiry board took account of the fact that he had been in charge for only one day, and his career was salvaged.

The road junction familiar to passengers and crew driving from the airport at Embakasi during the 1950s and 60s. (Author)

At the end of 1958, East African Airways could take stock of a most satisfactory period of growth and a future which was to take it out of the back-woods of a colonial African country into the limelight of international civil aviation, equipped with the best that the world could produce in the way of modern airliners.

The Board of Directors of the Corporation, under the Chairmanship of Sir Alfred Vincent, M.L.A., M.L.C., were now The Hon Sir Charles Phillips, CBE, M.L.A.,M.L.C., Major J.F. McCrindle, CMG, OBE, MC, The Hon J.T. Simpson, CBE, M.L.A., Col. The Hon. B.R. Mackenzie, DSO, DFC, M.L.C., The Hon. H.J. Hinchey, CBE, M.L.A., and J.C. Mundy, Esq., CMG.

Reporting to the Board, under the General Manager, Col. M.C.P. Mostert, OBE, were Secretary and Assistant General Manager, A.V. Gill, OBE, Chief Engineer, A.E. Robinson, BEM, Operations Manager, Captain E.E. Morris, MVO, Sales Manager, Captain P.A. Travers, Chief Accountant, S.G. Choppin, Manager, Stations and Traffic, A.G. Molison, MC.

A notable addition to the board was Colonel Bruce Mackenzie. Born at Richmond, Natal, in 1919, he had joined the South African Air Force at the outbreak of war, and was seconded to the R.A.F. for the duration. At the age of twenty-four

Col M.C.P. 'Mossie' Mostert stands between Mrs Gay Ainscough and the millionth E.A.A.C. passenger, Mr Stan Young, who was presented at a small reception with a silver cigarette box. On the right stands E.A.A.C. Chief Engineer, Mr A.E. 'Robbie' Robinson. Circa 1958. (Mr W. Ainscough)

he was promoted to the S.A.A.F. rank of colonel. He was awarded the DSO and DFC and bar. He had arrived in Kenya in 1946, where he purchased some undeveloped land near Nakuru, and built up one of the best farms in the Rift Valley. A tall, portly man with charismatic presence, he sported a full set of sandy 'handle-bar' whiskers. A member of the Legislative Council, he joined the board of E.A.A.C. in 1957, only to relinquish the position in 1959, in order to take up the appointment of Minister for Agriculture, Animal Husbandry and Water Resources in the Kenya government. He was to return to East African Airways during the 1970s.

Captain Malin Sorsbie had resigned as general manager following the death of his wife in the crash on Kilimanjaro in May 1955, whereupon Colonel Mostert had been appointed to replace him. Archie Watkins was still at the engineering base, with the post of plant and maintenance engineer. Another member of the management team was a long serving ex-Wilson Airways man, Mr A.V. Gill, who had been seconded to Wilson Airways by Imperial Airways in 1934–1935. From 1941 to 1944 he had served with B.O.A.C. in Nairobi and joined East African Airways at the beginning as secretary and accountant. Mr S.G. Choppin had joined E.A.A. in 1951 as an assistant accountant. His career had begun in 1933 with Imperial Airways at Croydon, from where he went on to the B.O.A.C. 'C' Class flying boat base at Durban, followed by Cairo, Khartoum and Asmara, before returning briefly to Croydon in 1944.

The airline's fleet now consisted of three Canadairs, nine DC3 Dakotas, and four DH89A Rapides. The total unduplicated route mileage in 1958 was 22,977 miles. It is interesting to compare the figures with those of 1947, the second year of the airline's existence:

	1947	*1958*
Passengers carried:	13,580	117,294
Freight (tons):	59	2,051
Mail (tons):	45	479
Miles flown:	998,242	4,150,229

The timetables now included a comprehensive list of services between East, Central, Portuguese East and South Africa, in addition to Somaliland, Aden, Karachi and Bombay to the east and from Dar es Salaam via Nairobi to Entebbe, Khartoum, Benghazi and Rome through to London, in the west. The Canadairs would depart Nairobi at 14.30 on Sunday afternoon, arriving in London the following morning at 11.40. By comparison, the B.O.A.C. Britannias would leave Nairobi at 19.15 on Thursday, arriving at London at 10.45 on the Friday morning. The Comets would, in turn, shrink the journey times to an even greater extent, in a few years to come.

CHAPTER 7

Comets and The Jet Age

SHORTLY AFTER 09.30 G.M.T., on Sunday, January 10th, 1954 the B.O.A.C. Comet 1, G-ALYP, left Rome's Ciampino Airport on the last leg of its journey from Singapore to London. Within a few minutes it had come down in the sea off the island of Elba. There were no survivors from the crew of six and twenty-nine passengers. Three months later, on Thursday, April 8th, 1954, the B.O.A.C. Comet 1, G-ALYY, on charter to South African Airways, left Ciampino Airport for Cairo. Again there was tragedy as the aircraft disappeared into the sea near Naples. These two accidents, coupled with the loss of an earlier Comet, G-ALYV, at Calcutta, on May 2nd, 1953, which was found by the Indian court of inquiry to be caused by structural damage occasioned by a severe thunderstorm, brought about the cessation of Comet public transport flights by B.O.A.C. and the Ministry of Transport and Civil Aviation withdrew their Certificates of Airworthiness.

This terrible set-back to Britain's undeniable lead in turbine powered airliner development was tackled with the utmost urgency and no efforts were spared in the immense task of determining the cause of these accidents. As a result of the work of the de Havilland stress engineers and the scientists at R.A.E. Farnborough, where an enormous water tank had been built in which to immerse a complete Comet fuselage, it was found that the skin, close to a window frame, had failed, due to fatigue following repeated pressurization cycles.

Modifications followed on the Comet 1A and Comet 2 aircraft being operated by the R.C.A.F. and R.A.F. A Comet 3 prototype, with four Rolls-Royce Avon 26 10,000 lb thrust engines was built, but with a new Rolls-Royce Avon engine offering 10,500 lb. thrust, twice the power of the original Comet 1 Ghost engine, a larger and far more useful aircraft emerged in the Comet 4. In March, 1955, B.O.A.C. ordered nineteen of these improved 81 passenger machines. The first of these flew on Sunday, April 27th, 1958 when chief test-pilot of de Havilland, Group Captain John Cunningham, took G-APDA into the air from Hatfield aerodrome.

The Comet 4 was a medium sized aircraft designed for the world's trunk routes. It was designed to operate on stages ranging from 2,950 statute miles with 81 passengers to 3,225 statute miles with 60 passengers. Powered by four Rolls-Royce Avon R.A.29 engines, delivering 10,500lbs static thrust, it had a span of 115ft., length of 111.5ft., and height (empty) of 29.5ft. It had a wing area of 2,121 sq.ft. and a total tankage within the wings of 8,898 Imp. gallons. The maximum all up weight was 162,000lbs, with capacity payload ranging from 16,800lbs to 20,290lbs, depending upon seating configuration. Maximum still air stage length with capacity payload and fuel reserves was 3,225 statute miles. It cruised in the height band 28,000 to 40,000ft at 500 miles per hour.

It had become obvious to the Board of East African Airways that if they were to succeed as an international airline, it must purchase more modern aircraft, to compete with the Britannias and Comets of B.O.A.C. on the routes to which E.A.A.C. was entitled to 50% of the traffic. After Colonel Mostert and Mr J.C. Mundy (who, in addition to being a member of the Corporation's board, was Finance Member of the East African High Commission) had visited de Havillands in May, a bold and far-sighted decision was taken to order two Comet 4s. This move more than any other was to prove to be the beginning of the period of outstanding success and international growth which was to follow.

In August, 1958, Sir Alfred Vincent appended his signature to the contract for two machines to be delivered in July and September 1960. Reporting to the October board meeting, Sir Alfred Vincent told the members that, following negotiations with the Colonial Development Corporation, de Havillands and Barclays bank, the latter had agreed to provide a loan at an interest rate one percent above the ruling Bank Rate, with a minimum of five per cent. It would be necessary to borrow nearly £2 million for the project and the need for guarantees would have to be put to the Legislative Councils of the East African Territories. It had been arranged that the Avon engines (eight installed and two spares) for the Comets would be hired from B.O.A.C. over a period of seven years, during which time they would remain the property of B.O.A.C. At the end of the seven years E.A.A.C. were to purchase the engines at their written down value, approximately 25 per cent of cost. By this time it was estimated that B.O.A.C. would have furnished assistance to E.A.A.C. to the tune of nearly £1 million in loans, advances and technical aid.

At the same time, it was decided to replace one of the Canadairs (VP-KOT, which, after being used for B.O.A.C. apprentice training, became a familiar, if gradually diminishing sight, to passengers landing at Heathrow, as the airport fire service used it for emergency practice drills) by chartering a Bristol Britannia 312, from B.O.A.C., to operate a weekly service on the London route, in order to maintain a higher level of competition and service, until the advent of the Comet 4s. This service was to commence in October 1958, flown by B.O.A.C. crews, with East African cabin crew.

Throughout Africa there were great changes taking place. By 1959 the state of emergency in Kenya had been in place for seven years, and it would be another year before it was lifted. Elsewhere there were movements and upheavals which would soon bring about chaos and misery, elation and joy, in equal measures.

In the spring of 1958 the South African electorate returned the pro-Apartheid Nationalist Party to power with an increased majority, effectively disenfranchising the liberal English speaking minority for the foreseeable future. Throughout East Africa, from Zanzibar through Tanganyika, Uganda and the settlers' paradise of

Kenya, the inexorable movement towards self-rule was being encouraged by the British government. These movements were being given impetus by events elsewhere. In August 1958 General de Gaulle paid a visit to Brazzaville and offered the French Congo the choice in a referendum between membership of the French Community as an autonomous republic and complete independence. This was to have terrible repercussions across the river in the Belgian Congo where the speech fuelled the movements of different factions in their demands for 'the elite and the masses to take control of public affairs' in a united Congo, with Lumumba on the one hand and the tribal federalists supporting Kasavubu and Kanza on the other. It would not be long before 'the Congo' became synonymous with the horrors of rape and pillage and the total failure of the colonial ideal.

In the British territories of Central Africa, Northern and Southern Rhodesia and Nyasaland, African political movements were struggling for independence based upon tribal affinities, contrary to the white settlers' and the British governments' proposals for a Federation. States of emergency were imposed early in 1959 in Southern Rhodesia and in Nyasaland.

The British political theory of Federation, which was thought to provide a more viable economic and political entity than the alternative 'Balkanisation' of the various African territories, was anathema to the Africans themselves, whose leaders based their power upon the tribal system stemming from the grass roots of the villages and the land, and sustained in the migration to the cities. The African leadership in Uganda, primarily from the elitist Baganda, the largest and most advanced regional group, favoured by the British administration (who admired and recognised their system of government under a king, or Kabaka), were particularly active in their demands for independence, from the end of the second world war. The Kabaka, Cambridge educated and an honorary captain in the Grenadier Guards, where he was known as King Freddie, was exiled to London by the British government in 1953 for demanding independence for Buganda, fearing that the British had plans for a 'federation' of the kingdoms of Uganda – which, in effect, they had.

Tanganyika had never been a British colony, as such, but was administered as a United Nations Trust Territory. Julius Nyerere, who had been the first Tankanyika African to go to a British university, (he took an Arts degree at Edinburgh), found it relatively easy to organise the restive Africans of the Territory in his political group, the Tanganyika African National Union. With few European or Asian settlers, this organisation became the vehicle to bring about electoral reforms which eventually brought him to chairmanship of the Legislative Council. In 1959 Tanganyika was on the threshold of independence.

One of the more curious aspects of British rule in the territories was the existence of the Coastal Strip. Since 1895, as part of the agreements made in connection with the cessation of the Arab slave trade, Britain had leased a strip of the Indian Ocean coast, ten miles deep and 300 miles long, from the Sultan of Zanzibar. This strip, stretching from Vanga on the Tanganyika border to Chiamboni on the Somali border, was ruled, nominally, by the Liwali of the Coast, a vassal of the Sultan, but, with the vital port of Mombasa within its borders, it was totally British controlled and administered, with the exception of religious affairs. However, under the terms of the treaty, the British government paid a rental £11,000 per year to the Sultan of Zanzibar for the lease.

The Arabs who populated this predominantly Muslim strip demanded autonomy within an East African federation, whereas the Sultan of Zanzibar agreed with British proposals that the area should become an integral part of a future independent Kenya.

In Nairobi, people were still meeting at the New Stanley's Thorn Tree for afternoon tea with Webley revolvers hanging from their belts, or for the ladies, something lighter in their handbag. Mau Mau was being defeated, with bombing raids by Lincoln bombers, derived from the Lancaster of the war years, on the Aberdare forest retreats of the remaining terrorists. Prior to the opening of the new airport at Embakasi, passengers arriving at Eastleigh would see, through the windows of their Constellations, Canadairs and DC6s, Harvard trainer aircraft, impressed into the bombing effort, with 500 lb bombs loaded beneath the wings, as they taxied past. The Emergency had been an ugly period in British colonial history. The conflict between London's acceptance of inevitable multi-racial rule leading to independence, and the colonial government's stance, influenced by the white settlers who had their land, the lush 'White Highlands', and way of life at stake, had led to an unnecessarily violent revolution fed by the desperation of the Kikuyu. Gradually, from June 1955, when the government allowed limited political activity to the Africans, political groups formed throughout Kenya. By 1958 there were 14 African elected members of the Legislative Council, which comprised a Speaker, six ex-officio civil servants, 37 nominated members, 12 Specially Elected members, 14 elected Europeans, six elected Asians and two elected Arabs. The African members militantly boycotted the Legislature in support of the countrywide demand for the release of Kenyatta, who was by now coming to the end of his term of imprisonment. Complicated political divisions between the white settlers, themselves divided into liberal and extreme right groups, and the African, Asian and coastal Arabs finally led to the government agreeing to a constitutional conference in London to be held early in 1960.

It was in this atmosphere of unprecedented change in East Africa that East African Airways was planning its future, with the eagerly awaited Comet 4s and preparing for a courageous leap into a the new, technological age of the 1960s.

1959 was a year in which all departments of East African Airways were busily preparing for the advent of the Comets. In addition, E.A.A.C. had entered into the Colonial Coach Class fare structure, formerly only applicable to UK registered operators, applying 'cabotage' rights. With fares to the United Kingdom some 15% below the normal full fare, sales were greatly increased, the total overall for the year being 33,831 on all international routes (an increase of 26.7% on the previous year).

Even more remarkable was the increase in cargo, an enormous 72.3% jump to 674 tons. Mail, similarly was up by 34.3% at 135 tons.

Charter flights, too, had shown a great increase during the year. Apart from the normal run of charters within East Africa which included groups from round the world cruises, package tours, wedding parties and sports teams, there were a series of nine Canadair charters to Mauritius, carrying soldiers of the Kings African Rifles from Dar es Salaam, in order to relieve the garrison there. More significantly, the first trans-atlantic flight by the airline was flown in September when a Canadair was chartered to carry a party of students for the Africa-America Student Foundation from Nairobi to New York.

To overcome difficulties with the accommodation of African staff, East African Airways, in collaboration with the Nairobi city council had embarked upon a scheme to build permanent staff housing in the Embakasi village. This scheme eased the difficulties encountered in providing staff at all hours with the attendant transport difficulties.

The staff numbers and make-up at the end of 1959 was as follows:

	European		*Asian*		*African*	
	Male	Female	Male	Female	Male	Female
Flying Crew	81	-	-	-	-	-
Cabin Crew	16	10	2	3	4	-
Operations General	10	1	2	-	1	-
Engineering & Supplies	114	4	155	1	184	-
Sales & Reservations	34	46	16	18	25	-
Stations & Traffic	71	49	154	9	404	-
Accounts	8	3	40	5	35	-
Gen Management/Admin	5	5	2	1	22	1
Total (1,541)	339	118	371	37	675	1

East African Airways was furthering its local national character by no longer filling station officer vacancies from experienced airline staff from overseas, since the start of a station trainee scheme, intended for the training of young (white) men resident in East Africa. Staff relations in general were good, but with most of the pilots being members of the British union, BALPA, the airline had been forced during 1956 into a dispute requiring arbitration, the resultant decision cost the Corporation some £52,000 per annum compared with their offer of £23,000. Further flying staff reviews followed and labour costs continued to make excessive inroads into the Corporation's income. A policy of joint consultation evolved and increasingly, the powerfully politicised African trades unions were becoming involved.

Planning for the forthcoming turbo-jet airliners meant a shake-up in the training of all categories of staff. The selection of suitable, experienced crew caused a considerable movement of crew members between the different fleets and involved a large increase in technical and flying training. Behind the practical steps taken to ensure the competency of crews lay a mass of planning and compilation of data and new operations and flight manuals, which had, with the advent of more sophisticated aircraft, become items of increasing importance.

A considerable amount of development work was carried out by the engineering department during the year, particularly in the new engineering workshops, which had been successfully transferred to new accommodation at Embakasi during 1958. A more comprehensive range of Canadair components and accessories could now be overhauled at the base. Additional test rigs necessary for this work were designed and manufactured by staff technicians. Since April, 1959, with the exception of the basic Merlin engine, which was overhauled by Rolls-Royce, all other power-plant work associated with it had been undertaken in the workshops. A high degree of productivity and operational serviceability was achieved and maintained. The overhaul of Pratt and Whitney engines continued, with the addition of contract work on those of Aden Airways, bringing the total annual output to 80 engines.

As with other departments, plans were well in hand for the introduction of the East African Airways Comet 4s. B.O.A.C. had introduced Comet 4s on the African routes during the latter part of 1959, and East African Airways engineers took over full responsibility for their maintenance throughout the territories from the commencement of operations.

"I shall always remember the day, if not the date, when my love affair with the Canadair was ruined forever", Captain Mitchell recalls. "It was a Sunday, sometime in 1959 and I had been invited to join a Comet 4 demonstration flight with Sir Geoffrey and Lady de Havilland. John 'Cats Eyes' Cunningham was the captain and Des Watts the flight engineer. The F/O I cannot remember. I sat on the flight-deck for take-off and couldn't believe the effortless power and grace of it all. We flew to Dar and back, without landing and also circled Mt. Kilimanjaro in about half the time it took us to fly to Dar in our Canadair. The same evening I took-off for Bombay on our regular schedule, which very much highlighted the difference between 'them' and 'us'. As we clambered into the night sky I wondered what possible chance any of us would have of flying an aeroplane like that - never dreaming that we would be doing just that in less than two years."

1960

July 1960 saw the first contingent of E.A.A.C. pilots and engineers depart for England to commence their training on the Comet 4s. They were to undergo a very tight ground training schedule, with one week on the airframe at the de Havilland training school at Hatfield, followed by a week at the Rolls-Royce Derby factory, learning about the Avon engine. This was followed immediately by the UK Board of Trade examinations. From the 1st to 9th August they trained night and day at Shannon, in Ireland in the first E.A.A.C. Comet, VP-KPJ, under the B.O.A.C. training captains Wallace, Holder, Howard and Jenkins.

The B.O.A.C. training captains did not at first regard these pilots from the 'African bush' very highly. Captain Phil Henn was a case in point. On the occasion of his final check, which required an asymmetric approach and landing at night with two engines out on one side, the B.O.A.C. instructor became reluctant to continue with the flight as the weather deteriorated. He called the tower as they made their approach from out over the Atlantic and was told that the cloud base was lowering, it was raining heavily and the wind was off the runway. "I think we had better scrub it", he said to Henn. "In my experience", Phil Henn replied, "when you have lost two engines, it is at night, it is always raining, the cloud base is on limits and the wind is off the runway. I shall continue with the approach and landing." The B.O.A.C. captain nervously kept his hand above the closed throttle levers as the Comet pitched and bumped through the storm clouds and crabbed into the cross-wind, to make a perfect landing. "You have passed", was all he said, now with a great deal more respect for the 'African bush pilot'.

Having obtained their licences and instrument ratings on the Comet, they flew from 19th August until 3rd September on the B.O.A.C. routes, as supernumerary crew. They flew to destinations such as Johannesburg, Montreal and New York. Making an approach and landing a Comet into New York, as first officer, was an exciting, albeit awesome, experience for a pilot from the 'African bush' – a taste of things to come.

With the second Comet 4, VP-KPK, delivery in September, the inaugural Comet passenger service, EC715, operated by VP-KPJ, departed London at 18.30 on the evening of September 17th 1960, commanded by Captain Jack Bicknell. Captain Phil Henn and Captain Peter Duff took the service from Rome to Entebbe and Nairobi. The service routed London-Rome-Khartoum-Entebbe-Nairobi. The first northbound service with VP-KPK, commanded by Captain Roger Drew, with co-pilot F/O John 'Ginger' Brewer, departed Nairobi at 10.00 on 19th September. Drew was somewhat apprehensive, since he had not landed at Entebbe at night,

Captain Jack Bicknell.
(Capt Ratcliffe)

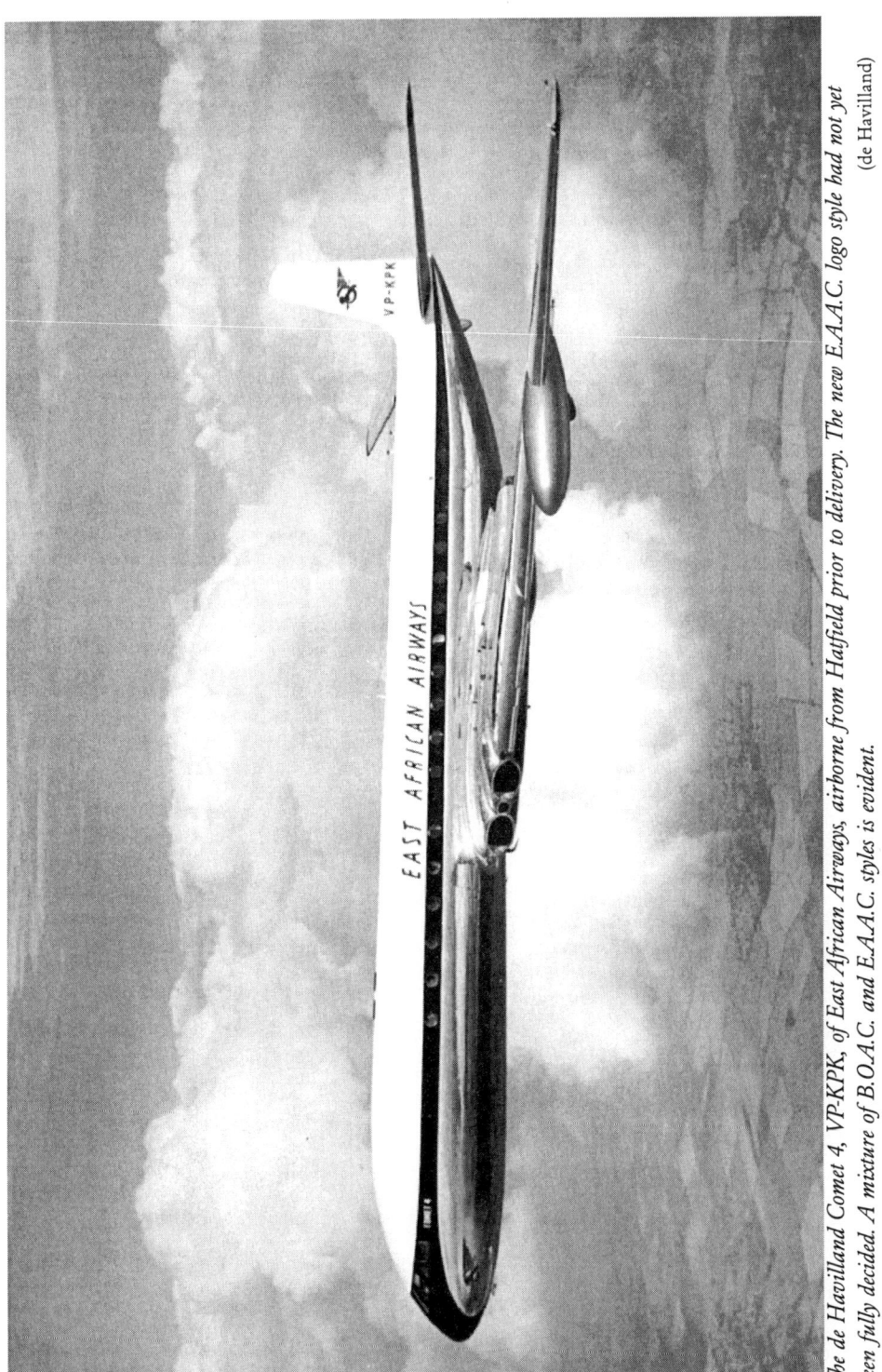

The de Havilland Comet 4, VP-KPK, of East African Airways, airborne from Hatfield prior to delivery. The new E.A.A.C. logo style had not yet been fully decided. A mixture of B.O.A.C. and E.A.A.C. styles is evident. (de Havilland)

and his first experience was to be in the brand new Comet. Each one of the operating crews viewed their task with a degree of trepidation, but everything went as planned. The northbound crew slipped at Rome, where Captain Jack Bicknell, F/O Jeff de Jager and F/E Paddy Murray operated the Rome-London sector.

On October 6th, Captain Roger Drew took VP-KPJ to Johannesburg on the inaugural E.A.A.C. Comet service to South Africa, completing the pattern of three services weekly in each direction between London and Nairobi, calling at Entebbe, with one service extending to Dar es Salaam and another to Johannesburg. A Comet service to Karachi and Bombay would commence in January, 1961.

For those early Comet aircrews, it was as if they had entered a different world. The Comets, direct from the de Havilland factory, gleamed with an almost mirror finish, their shiny aluminium highlighted by the tasteful blue and white East African Airways paint scheme, with the Corporation's leaping lion emblem proudly displayed on the side.

Members of the East African Airways course at Hatfield, March, 1960. L to R: (Partially obscured) Capt Bill Fumerton, (leaning on wheels) ex-N/O Frank Warren, ex-N/O Tim Nightingale, DH Instructor, Capt Roger Drew, Capt Leo Davidson, F/E Bill Cawthorne, ex-ground engineer Derek Taylor, ex-N/O Paddy Murray, F/O Larry Allen, Capt Reg Cartwright, F/O Dave Dempster, F/O Ginger Brewer. F/O Ivan Morris stands hidden behind Brewer. The N/Os and Derek Taylor had been selected for training as flight engineers. It was thought navigators would become redundant with the advent of the Comet. (de Havilland/Capt Brewer)

The pilots had been amazed to find that much of their experience of flying the Canadairs was now irrelevant. After the piston engine propeller flying, the turbojet opened up a completely new concept in aviating, from start-up through to landing. Things were done differently, and a lot of the old practices gave way to new techniques. The basic principles of flight, they were pleased to find, remained the same. After their battered old second-hand Canadairs, standing with pools of black oil under each engine, the Comet was a joy to behold – sleek, shining, brand new, and an object of beauty.

The flight-deck was quite small, and visibility out of the sloping wind-screens was not what they had been used to. One could not, from their forward position, see any exterior part of the aircraft, the engines and wings were out of sight – a completely new experience to pilots and engineers accustomed to visible reassurance that the wings, engines and propellers were still all in place.

The old standard blind flying panel, which many pilots had been used to reading like a well worn book since their R.A.F. days, was now transformed into a complicated array of dials, needles and switches, including a new Flight Director System. From the ceiling above their heads were more little switches and multi-coloured levers – various alternatives for the powered controls.

Engine start was simplicity itself. No more juggling with the throttle to get an engine to start, the coughing and spluttering, fiddling with mixture levers – was it too weak? was it too rich? No more of those failed starts followed by the bangs

Comet 4, VP-KPJ, landing at Shannon during crew training. August, 1960.

(Capt Brewer)

and clouds of blue smoke when they finally caught and ran, the propellers blasting the smoke across the apron.

The Comet start-up was barely audible in the cockpit, just the rising needles of the engine instruments and flickering fuel-flow meters until the rush of cooling air came through the air-conditioning ducts. Again, there was a departure from tradition, as the chocks were pulled away, and the brakes were released, they could taxi uninterrupted to the take-off position – no more the time-worn performance of parking somewhere between the apron and the runway to exercise each engine in turn, checking the power and the 'mag-drop'. It was almost with a guilty feeling that they abandoned the old ways, swinging the aircraft on to the runway, lining up and with a gentle forward movement of the throttle levers, releasing a surge of power.

The take-off was quick and effortless. There was no feeling that the machine should be nursed into the air, with concentration on the rate of climb versus air speed. With power to spare, the Comet simply pointed upwards and ascended, if cleared to do so, straight up to 30,000ft, whereupon a simple power setting would adjust the cruise at around 420 knots. The normal Comet practice was to throttle back all engines from take-off power to normal power after leaving the ground. Apart from relieving the engines of wear and tear it would lessen the noise nuisance to people living near the airports. In typical conditions, and loaded to maximum weight, it would reach a height of 1,000ft when only two and a half miles from start of take-off, less than twice the length of an average runway.

de Havilland Comet 4, VP-KPJ, showing the definitive E.A.A.C. blue and white livery and logo style. (BAe Hatfield)

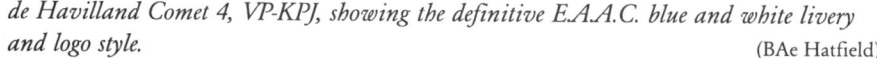

Of course, nothing could be quite so straight-forward, as Captain Peter Duff discovered on leaving Rome on November 18th 1960, in VP-KPJ. One new procedure which the Comet demanded of the pilots was the elevator gear change. As part of the after take-off drill, the tail plane setting which limited the elevator control movements at high speeds, is adjusted. This initially gave a nose-up attitude, which was allowed for, followed by a nose-down into normal flight. On this occasion, Captain Duff may have switched off the seat belt signs a little early, before the tailplane had settled into its cruise position. Ginger Brewer, who was the handling pilot, suddenly found that as he pushed the nose forward, nothing happened, and the nose continued to rise. With the control column fully forward,

Passengers disembark from VP-KPJ, the inaugural Comet 4 arrival at Nairobi on 18th September, 1960. (E.A. Standard)

he trimmed wildly, until the nose began to fall to an acceptable level. It was not until they had time to speak with the chief steward that they discovered that they had picked up the South African Springbok rugby team in Rome. When the seat belt lights had gone out, they leapt up to a man and struggled madly to the rear galley for a beer. With an average weight of some 220lb, they were enough to upset the trim of the Comet 4, despite the power of its four Rolls-Royce Avon turbo-jets.

For the passengers, the Comet was something quite extraordinary. Many pilots had experienced the sensation of flight at great altitudes in their military flying. Not so the civilian traveller. For the first time one could sit comfortably in the cabin of an airliner – the Comet has never been surpassed for comfort, its twenty first class seats, set at forty-seven inch pitch would recline to forty-two degrees. Seated four abreast, the small cabin had a club-like atmosphere in which the two or three cabin crew attended to their passengers in an unhurried and friendly manner. With operating altitudes up to 40,000ft, passengers could view the earth from a totally different aspect. The night flight from London would be smooth and quiet as the Comet ate up the miles high above the deserts and mountains far below. Those who cared to open their eyes to the dawn breaking above the

The crew of VP-KPJ, the first East African Airways Comet into Johannesburg. L to R: Steward J. Malyon, Steward P.J. Maclaughlin, E/O Watts, Stewardess Barbara Seymour, F/O J.H. 'Ginger' Brewer, Captain Roger Drew, Stewardess L. Strang, N/O D.J. Griffiths, N/O R.A. Foster.

curvature of the earth, far to the east, beyond the Valley of the Nile, would be entranced by the razor edge of crimson which would gradually fill the eastern sky with blush, until it pushed before it the opal coloured morning sky. Never before had mere travelling mortals witnessed such breathtaking sights. They were an appropriate introduction to the African adventure.

The economy class cabin was only slightly less comfortable, with forty-three seats at thirty-eight inch pitch, which would recline to forty-two degrees, the same as in first class. There were seven rows of five-abreast seats with one forward and one aft row of four-abreast. As travel became more affordable to greater numbers of

Comet 4, VP-KPK, airborne from Entebbe. 1964. (Mr T. Webb)

Comet 4, VP-KPJ, at Entebbe. 1964. (Mr T. Webb)

people, never again would these standards of comfort be experienced by the low-fare passengers. These were still the days of business or official travel, with a small number of private travellers, and government leave takers.

Few private individuals could afford the fare to Europe. A trip 'home' was frequently accompanied by a send-off party, which would continue in the warm tropical night at Embakasi, where, from the waving base above the terminal, friends and relatives could still call to the passengers as they walked across the dark apron to the waiting bus and the Comet parked not far away, its lights a welcoming glow and the cabin prepared for its passengers. Many years later, Lord Deedes, writing in the *Daily Telegraph*, recalled such a scene:

> *"Years ago, I went with my host to Nairobi airport at midnight to see off one of his guests returning to London overnight. He was flying home on that beautiful, ill-starred plane, the Comet, which was coming up from Johannesburg via Salisbury. To see the London-bound Comet go through was an event in Africa in those days, and many expatriates were at the airport to wave it through.*
>
> *I glanced at the face of a man standing a pace ahead of me. He was English. Long ago he had made his life in Kenya. He would never return to this country. He was an exile.*
>
> *Yet as the Comet ran down the flarepath on take-off, there entered his face a look which forever etched itself in my mind. By breakfast time those passengers would be back in England, which he would probably never see again. So near and yet so far."* *

Maybe he did make it, later on, when the Comets of East African Airways carried affinity charters of groups such as the Kenya Farmers Association and the Friends of the Donovan Maule Theatre.

Eric Morris, chief pilot and operations manager was forty-eight years of age. It was thought that to continue in his position, without converting to the Comet, would not be appropriate and with relatively few years to retirement, he decided that it was time to resign his position. He handed over to Captain Phil Henn on the 31st October, 1960 and took up a senior position in Durban, as regional sales manager for E.A.A.C. Later, as relations between the East African Community and South Africa deteriorated, all E.A.A.C. offices were closed and he transferred to B.O.A.C.

Captain Pat Travers, who came to E.A.A.C. from B.O.A.C. in 1946, and had made a remarkably successful transition in 1954 from flying to the commercial side of the airline, became the commercial manager in 1960, after a period, since 1958 as sales manager. It was Travers, apart from anyone else in the management team who would be primarily responsible for the remarkably successful process of change to the new world of turbo-jet airliners.

The purchase of Comet aircraft involved E.A.A.C. in a heavy programme of recruitment and training. Before the Comet training could begin, it was necessary to train pilots on DC3s, thereby releasing pilots for training on Canadairs, and,

---

* © *The Telegraph* plc, 1992

in turn, Canadair pilots could commence training on Comets. It was soon found, that with the more complex aircraft, the planning and training programmes became more complicated. The initial Comet training taking place in the United Kingdom, all DC3 and Canadair ground and flying training, bi-annual checks and Instrument Ratings were completed at Nairobi. With the introduction of the Comet, pilot strength increased by fourteen, navigation and radio officers were reduced by two, and there were nine engineer officers.

The new aircraft again highlighted the poor state of airfields outside of the three principal cities. Mombasa had finally been upgraded to allow Canadairs to operate from its runway, but could only accept a Comet in an emergency situation. With the turbo-jet aircraft it was increasingly obvious that the state of affairs could not continue. With high rates of fuel consumption, the diversion planning for a London – Nairobi early morning arrival could provide a head-ache if both Entebbe and Nairobi were fog-bound, which was sometimes the case. The only other possibility then would be to divert to Mombasa. This highlighted the need for an adequate instrument landing system at these aerodromes. VORs had been installed at Entebbe and Nairobi during 1960 and an ILS for Nairobi was planned for the following year. Both Entebbe and Dar es Salaam airports had found that, although the runways were adequate for Canadairs, the high-speed four wheel bogies of the Comet suffered damage to tyres and threw up pieces of runway surface, damaging the flaps.

There *was* another alternate landing field, of sorts, for the Comets. Way back in 1952, in order to provide an emergency diversion for the B.O.A.C. early Comet I services, a huge runway was constructed at Kasenye, on the shores of Lake George, in Uganda. The runway was over 10,000 ft in length, about 150 ft wide and was graded out of solid, hard-baked earth. It was reputed to have cost all of two hundred pounds – having been constructed by local native labour. It was never used for the purpose for which it was intended, but a frozen fish company called TUFMAC

Captain Pat Travers.
(Capt Ratcliffe)

had set up a factory nearby, paying the local fishermen one shilling per fish caught. The DC3s were re-routed on their Entebbe-Kasese trips to pick up the consignments of frozen fish. The runway was superb for training purposes, the DC3s could do two or three "touch and go" landings during one approach.

Captain Ainsworth recalled the changes which had occurred over the years, culminating in the arrival of gas turbine-powered aircraft. . .

> "So, after the Dakota and Canadair days, flying changed. . . with high technology, weather and mountains became less important and life was more sedate. VORs, VHF, radio altimeters became the norm. . . not much fun any more. Except - just once - I had the chance. One day a letter came from the operations manager, Phil Henn; there was a flying display at the newly named Wilson Airport - would I please do a low fly-past and climb away steeply, to show how well the Comet performed.
>
> "While the aircraft was being started by Dave Dempster, I briefed the passengers, bound for Dar es Salaam, very carefully about my intentions. I took-off from Embakasi, lined up with the main runway at Wilson, over the Eastleigh beacon. With the runway in sight, the Comet flew at maximum speed, a touch of trim, steady at 100ft over the centre of the airfield, then nose up, full power and a steep climb to 10,000ft, with the spectators looking at the fire in the jet pipes. Poor passengers - perhaps they had not listened to my briefing. I gave them a tour of Kilimanjaro. . . chatted to them. . . even invited them to the cockpit - but nobody came. No one would speak to me."

Ainsworth would take particular delight in arriving down-wind at Dar es Salaam at 10,000ft, pulling back the throttle levers, and not handling them again until touch-down. First officers were forbidden to touch the levers, they would get a sharp reminder should he see a hand nervously hovering close to them.

The introduction and transition to the Comets went remarkably smoothly and contributed to the 1960 end of year sales target being comfortably overshot, the figures being:

Target figure set £3,490,000
Achieved figure ... ...   £3,906,000 (33.4% increase on the previous year).

The world increase in airline traffic during 1960 had been estimated to be 15% - East African Airways had achieved 13%, despite the numerous difficulties normally involved in the introduction of new equipment.

After almost twenty-five years of un-interrupted service, with the exception of the war years, the venerable old DH89A Rapides were finally withdrawn from line service, since all airfields on the route enabled services to be undertaken with DC3 aircraft, with the exception of Eldoret in Kenya, which was taken out of the network, Pemba Island, which was now only suitable for light aircraft, and Malindi, which was, after some two years of sporadic work to bring it up to DC3 standard, soon to reach the improved level. The Rapides were to continue in service with

Seychelles and Kilimanjaro Air Transport, operating the coastal island routes between Zanzibar and Pemba, connecting with Tanga and Dar es Salaam.

The local network of services maintained a largely unchanged pattern, with the DC3s taking over from Rapides, and, in October the inter-city routes between Nairobi and Entebbe and Nairobi - Mombasa - Dar es Salaam were taken over by Canadairs, providing increased speed and capacity.

The East African Comet 4s were originally planned to commence operations between Nairobi and the United Kingdom in July, and due to delivery delays these services did not commence until mid-September, but by October the complete pattern of services between Nairobi, Dar es Salaam and Johannesburg, to London was in operation. As a result of the satisfactory introduction of the Comets, the Britannia chartered from B.O.A.C. was no longer required, and was taken out of service.

Charters performed by the Canadairs during the year included more flights to Mauritius, to bring troops of the Kings African Rifles back to Dar es Salaam, and the transport of the Kenya and Uganda teams to the Olympic Games in Rome, and return. Other charters performed during 1960, however, were not of such a peaceful nature . . .

1960 was notable for the speed with which colonial Africa was being demolished. With the exception of South Africa, where black African freedom was not only harshly resisted (in March a state of emergency would be declared following the shooting dead of sixty-seven Africans by the police in Sharpville), but where new laws were being enacted to prevent the freedoms which, north of the Zambezi, were being seized greedily. British Prime Minister Harold Macmillan made a speech on a visit, in February, to South Africa, where he referred to a "wind of change" blowing throughout Africa. This was less than a month after the state of emergency was ended in Kenya.

The French Cameroons, Togoland, Ghana, Somalia, Ivory Coast, Dahomey, Niger, Upper Volta, Chad, Central African Republic, Nigeria, Mauritania, and the French Congo all achieved independence during 1960 and, on 30th June 1960, the Belgian Congo was proclaimed independent, becoming the Congo Republic.

Independence had come to the Belgian Congo with no preparation. For over eighty years a ruthless Belgian rule had shut off the Congo from most of the outside world. During the first thirty years, when the territory was the personal domain of the king of the Belgians, Leopold II, the native population was drastically reduced by an estimated third (this was a territory of some 904,754 square miles).

Royal agents drove Africans in search of ivory and rubber, claiming limbs and lives as a punishment for their unfulfilled quotas. After international pressure, in 1908 the territory was surrendered to the Belgian government, who continued to exploit the people with forced labour, and punishment by death or imprisonment for political activity.

The country was the richest in natural resources of all the African colonies. It was divided into dozens of quarrelling tribes, speaking nearly a thousand languages and dialects. The Belgians, ruling the territory with some ten thousand colonial administrators had, in the period of eighty years, produced just thirteen university graduates by 1960. There were no African doctors, lawyers or architects; there was one solitary African engineer.

Independence was conceded with little grace after a series of deteriorating meetings between the Belgians and the discontented Africans. The principal African adversaries were Joseph Kasavubu who was to become President and Patrice Lumumba, Premier, in a short lived entente. Five days after independence, the Force Publique mutinied against its Belgian officers and anti white violence broke out, with scenes of terrible bloodshed, accompanied by rape and destruction of property. The Belgian government flew troops into the country to protect and evacuate the white people. The government of Kasavubu called for United Nations assistance. On July 11th, the province of Katanga was declared independent by Provincial Governor Moise Tshombe

A DC4M Canadair of E.A.A.C., VP-KNY, at Plaisance airport, Mauritius, where, prior to independence from Britain, trooping contracts were undertaken in 1960 to fly British officers and NCOs and 250 soldiers of the Tanganyika Battalion of the Kings African Rifles, and their families, back to Dar es Salaam.

VP-KNY flew ten 14 hour round trips on ten consecutive days without a minutes delay. This remarkable achievement by an elderly aircraft was tribute to the airline's maintenance excellence and the work of Ron Gander and his crew who carried out the daily maintenance at Dar es Salaam and Plaisance. Ground Engineer Jock Glass, in white overalls, supervises the departure. (Mr J.H. Glass)

who was supported in his secessionist stand by the Belgian residents in Elisabethville. The country was at a stroke, cut off from its richest source of revenue, the great copper mines of the Union Miniere in Katanga.

On 15th September, with fighting taking place throughout the Congo, accompanied by continuous violence towards the whites, Colonel Joseph-Desiree Mobutu, Chief of Staff of the Congolese army, seized power, and suspending both Kasavubu and Lumumba, quickly consolidated his position. Lumumba fled, in an attempt to reach Stanleyville, but was captured by Mobutu's troops and would be murdered within six months, Kasavubu went to the United Nations to gain support for his government. Katanga remained seceded, controlled by Belgians and mercenaries from Europe and South Africa. The stage had been set for a period of bloodshed and terror which made the Congo a byword for horror for years to come.

East African Airways became heavily involved in the rescue of refugees from the Congo crisis. By setting up special handling units, with considerable extra effort by the staff of the airline, the evacuation of some 1,500 men, women and children was achieved from Stanleyville and Bukavu. A co-ordinating committee was set up between the government and East African Airways, who were appointed the sole agent to handle the movement of the evacuees to Belgium by air. A total of 3,778 people were repatriated on charter flights, with a further 541 being flown on scheduled services.

During this time Captain George Leslie had returned to flying the DC3s, prior to commencing Comet training. He, among many other DC3 crews, was involved in the air evacuation.

"In Kenya... independence was next on the cards. However, in the Congo, their problems were just beginning. By the July of 1960 a call went out to rescue the white people, and the Congo Belge evacuation began.

EAA were involved, and quickly put a DC3 operation together, to airlift people out and drop them off at Entebbe, where a tented camp had been set up near the airfield. On 23rd July, information was obtained that there were groups of people who had fought their way to a couple of airfields in the eastern Kivu Province of the Congo, at Bukavu and Usambara, which, for the time being, were safe to operate into. We went off, in an empty aircraft, bound for Bukavu. Flying initially along the railway line that runs from Entebbe to Kasese, where it terminates at the Kilembe copper mine, we flew an indirect route, looking for the point where we could weave between the snow covered peaks of the Ruwenzoris, the Mountains of the Moon, towering to nearly 17,000ft. These fabled mountains often remain hidden in clouds for weeks on end, giving no intimation of their existence.

Visibility was normally terrible after leaving Entebbe. There was a brown dust and smoke haze which persisted to perhaps eleven or twelve thousand feet, where there would be an abrupt, clear cut-off line parallel with the horizon. One could not see ahead at all, only vertically below. There were no radio aids in this part of Central Africa. After the flattish country along the railway line, and after the copper mine, the vegetation changed, eventually becoming thick jungle, with misty valleys. It was, we were told, the thickest and tallest jungle in Africa. The home of the mountain gorillas. Some years before joining EAA, 'Mitch' had crash landed an Anson there and, leaving the aircraft in the bush, had walked out".

The Mountains of the Moon, or *Lunae montes*, were so named from an ancient map drawn by Ptolemy in 150 AD, which showed the Nile flowing northwards, based upon the report of the Greek explorer Diogenes, who had seen the snow covered mountains after a twenty-five day journey from Zanzibar in the first century AD. It was not until 1888 that Henry Stanley re-discovered the mountains, although they were reported as having been seen by Sir Samuel Baker in 1864 while on an expedition which discovered Lake Albert. He did not realise that he saw the northern extension of the *Lunae montes* bordering the western shore of the lake when he named them the Blue Mountains.

> "On the other side of the mountain range, lies the vast expanse of the Congo. There is a valley running more or less north to south; one could now descend a little, turn left and fly over Lake Edward and on down to Lake Kivu. Lush and green, the country is beautiful. And now, with clear visibility, one could see the deep blue lakes, reflecting the mountains on the left. Bukavu is situated at the southern end of Lake Kivu, and the airfield is easily spotted. We were not going to do more than a quick turn-round and get the hell out of it again. I knew the town from a stay a few years previously, before the troubles began. It had a lovely continental charm, with vermilion bougainvillaea cascades draping the colonial villas, and a relaxed atmosphere in which one could enjoy the refreshingly cool evenings.
>
> There were crowds of people in the parking area. We cut the port engine, but kept the other one going. A man met us, who seemed to be a spokesman. We thought, perhaps, one of the Sabena Congo staff. The idea was to take as many of the refugees as we could. There was no baggage for the holds, just bits and pieces of hand-baggage and kikapus. We had 28 seats, but what with small ones squeezing together, kids on the floor, and a few in the toilet, we were full, and the doors were closed. We took-off towards the lake, which was quite a bit below the level of the airstrip. The downhill gradient helped us to get going with, I do not know, perhaps 50 persons on board. We weaved our way among the mountain peaks back to Entebbe.
>
> There was another quick turn around. And now to repeat the process again - this time to Usambara. What a sorry state of affairs!"

In tribute to the magnificent effort in difficult and somewhat dangerous circumstances, Captain Peter Cunningham, chief pilot of the DC3 fleet since 1958, was awarded the Queens Commendation for Valuable Services in the Air. The E.A.A.C. rescue operation, delivered over 1,500 refugees to safety, during the former Belgian Congo crisis. The citation read:

> "Mr Cunningham is a senior pilot with East African Airways. He is a most able and experienced pilot who, as flight captain, both supervised and participated in the successful airlift of Belgian refugees from the Congo. Forty-five such flights were made by East African aircraft under his command."

❖ ❖ ❖

H.E. the Governor of Kenya, Sir Patrick Renison, awards Captain Peter Cunningham with the Queen's Commendation for Valuable Services in the Air, at Government House, Nairobi, 27th May 1961.

With the introduction of the Comet, 1960 was a year of significant change in the progress of East African Airways. It is interesting to review, in detail, the Corporation's vital statistics at the end of that year.

COMPARATIVE STATISTICS

FINANCIAL	1960	1959	% Var.
Traffic Revenue	£3,906,067	£2,927,818	+ 33.4
Operating Revenue	£4,340,069	£3,322,140	+ 30.6
Operating Expenditure	£3,879,386	£3,282,449	+ 18.2
Net Operating Profit	£ 460,683	£ 39,691	+1,060.7
Total Expenditure	£3,887,381	£3,292,002	+ 18.1
Surplus	£ 452,688	£ 30,138	+1,402.1
TRAFFIC			
Capacity Ton Miles Offered	24,672,375	22,020,517	+ 12.0
Load Ton Miles sold	15,700,130	12,026,029	+ 30.6
Revenue Weight Load Factor	63.63%	54.61%	+ 16.5
Load Factor Required to cover net expenditure	56.26%	54.05%	+ 4.1
Net Cost per CTM	Shs. 2/80	Shs. 2/63	+ 6.5
Traffic revenue per CTM	Shs. 3/17	Shs. 2/66	+ 19.2
Traffic revenue per LTM Scheduled services	Shs. 5/07	Shs. 5/14	- 1.4
All revenue operations	Shs. 4/98	Shs. 4/87	+ 2.3
Passengers carried	149,419	130,402	+ 14.6
Revenue Passenger Miles	120,839,104	84,260,955	+ 43.4
Available Seat Miles	196,401,520	162,306,315	+ 21.0
Passenger Load Factor	61.53%	51.91%	+ 18.5
Mail carried – tons ...	735	602	+ 22.1
Mail Ton Miles.	840,728	512,460	+ 64.1
Cargo carried – tons...	2,896	2,543	+ 13.9
Cargo Ton Miles	2,388,161	1,911,069	+ 25.0
OPERATIONS			
Revenue Hours flown ...	26,615	26,200	+ 1.6
Net Cost per Revenue Flying Hour	£ 129.75	£ 110.60	+ 17.3
Traffic Revenue per Revenue Flying Hour ...	£ 146.76	£ 111.75	+ 31.3
Revenue Miles Flown ...	4,804,029	4,449,575	+ 8.0
Net cost per Revenue Mile flown	Shs.14/38	Shs.13/02	+ 10.4
Traffic revenue per Revenue Mile Flown ...	Shs.16/26	Shs.13/16	+ 23.6
Stage flights completed -Scheduled services and charter operations.	18,288	18,654	- 1.9

* East African Pound equalled £1 Sterling, with Sh. 20 = £1

The net operating profit for the year of £460,683 compared dramatically with the previous year's £39,691. Although several factors contributed to this satisfactory result, the principal cause was the all-round increase in traffic on the scheduled services. Traffic carried, measured in Load Ton Miles, on domestic services increased by 13.2%; on regional services to Rhodesia and South Africa by 21.2% and on international services to the United Kingdom, Aden, Pakistan and India by 57.2%. The overall increase for all scheduled services over 1959 was 40.3%. Apart from the greater capacity available, factors which influenced these increases were a better than average number of passengers on the annual *Hajj* pilgrimage, and additional traffic created by the Congo crisis.

To the net operating profit of £460,683 was added dividends and debenture interest received from associated and subsidiary companies of £5,025, and a deduction of a subversion payment to the subsidiary company, Seychelles and Kilimanjaro Air Transport Limited, of £3,486 to reimburse its losses incurred for the period July to December 1960 in operating the Rapide services Zanzibar – Dar es Salaam and Tanga – Pemba Island. Fees and expenses to East African Airways board members amounted to £1,781 for the year. After payment of interest on the East African government's holdings of E.A.A.C. Stock 1975 of £7,753, the resulting surplus for the year on operations was £452,688.

With the balance brought forward from 1959 of £23,199, the adjustments to accounts of previous years of £1,027 and the difference between proceeds of assets on disposal and book values of £13,831, there was an available balance of £490,745.

The Board had considered it appropriate to write-off immediately the unamortised balance of £129,319 at the end of the year, which represented the total expenditure incurred on the initial aircrew and engineering staff training, and the development costs for the Comet 4 operations, rather than amortising the sum over a seven year period. The sum of £325,000 was transferred to the aircraft replacement reserve, as an initial contribution towards the cost of new aircraft and equipment.

The amount of £490,745 was therefore appropriated as follows:

> Written off Comet 4 development expenditure £129,319
> Transferred to general revenue reserve .... £ 13,831
> Transferred to aircraft replacement reserve £325,000
> Balance of surplus carried forward .... £ 22,595

The details of the Operating Account for the year, with variations on the previous year were as follows:

	1960 £	Var %	1959 £
Passenger fares, excess baggage and charter revenue	3,235,102	+34.7	2,402,475
Cargo revenue	316,344	+25.2	252,719
Mail revenue	354,621	+30.1	272,624
Total Traffic revenue	3,906,067	+33.4	2,927,818
Other revenue	434,002	+10.1	394,322
Total revenue	**£4,340,069**	**+30.6**	**3,322,140**

An analysis of traffic revenue earned by domestic, regional and international services showed the groups of services contributing to the overall revenue increase of 33.4 per cent on 1959's figures:

	1960 £	1959 £	Var. %
Domestic services	1,113,648	8,495	+12.7
Regional services to Rhodesia & S. Africa	396,077	338,110	+17.1
International services	2,264,260	1,399,343	+61.8
Charters including Pilgrim flights	132,083	201,870	-34.6
Total traffic revenue	£3,906,067	2,927,818	+33.4

Traffic revenue earned by groups of scheduled domestic services during 1960 as compared with 1959 was as follows:

	1960 £	1959 £	Var %
Kenya – Tanganyika Coastal	679,599	597,024	+13.8
Kenya – Uganda inter-territorial	191,902	165,618	+15.9
Nairobi or Entebbe – Tanganyika Central	151,227	138,223	+ 9.4
Tanganyika Internal	81,900	79,404	+ 3.1
Uganda Internal	5,705	5,482	+ 4.1
Seronera (Serengeti) Flights	3,315	2,744	+20.8
	£1,113,648	988,495	+12.7

Traffic revenue per load ton mile for scheduled services had fallen; for 1960, the figure was Shs 5/07 per short ton mile from all scheduled services as compared with Shs 5/14 for 1959. The decline reflected the increased proportion of E.A.A.C. operations on long haul services, giving lower unit returns, and the introduction of reduced 'economy' and 'skycoach' fares between East Africa and London. These latter had replaced the colonial coach class fares and were some 16% lower.

The capacity produced for the year was employed as shown:

	1960 CTMs	1959 CTMs	Var %
Domestic services	5,555,856	4,890,994	+13.6
Regional services to Rhodesia & S. Africa	3,399,897	3,503,529	– 3.0
International services	14,897,760	12,209,641	+22.0
Charters including Pilgrim flights	818,862	1,416,353	-42.2
Total capacity produced	24,672,375	22,020,517	+12.0

The increase in capacity on the domestic services almost coincided with the increase in load carried; the increase in load carried on the international services was proportionally greater than the increase in capacity, while for the regional services, there was a slight decrease in capacity offered, due to the suspension of DC3 services to Blantyre and Salisbury later in the year, in favour of a Central African Airways Viscount service, but nevertheless there was an increase in loads and revenue. The decrease in charter capacity for 1960 over 1959 was explained by the extensive series of charter flights carried out in 1959 on behalf of the Ismaili community, in connection with the burial of the late Aga Khan.

The airline's expenditure was summarised under the following heads:

	1960 £	1959 £	Var %
Pay and allowances	962,289	866,168	+11.1
Other staff costs	257,315	231,877	+11.0
Fleet obsolescence and depreciation of property & equipment	248,866	169,839	+46.5
Aircraft fuel & oil	470,956	383,950	+22.7
Charter & hire of aircraft	667,787	692,455	- 3.6
Other technical expenditure less misc. recoveries	595,357	426,938	+39.4
All other expenditure	684,811	520,775	+31.5
Totals	£3,887,381	£3,292,002	+18.1

The increases in staff costs reflected, in part, the recruitment of staff required for the operation of the United Kingdom services with E.A.A.C. aircraft, as did the expansion in expenditure under fleet obsolescence, fuel and oil and technical expenditure headings. The item 'all other expenditure' was greater than for 1959 because of the larger amount of commissions paid out on account of the greatly enhanced traffic revenue, increased passenger costs and traffic handling expenses, due to expanded loads and higher finance charges.

The balance sheet for 1960 showed an excess of assets over liabilities of £1,123,691, an increase of £590,571 over the 1959 figure. Fixed assets at net book values of £3,814,175, an increase of a staggering £2,401,255, reflected the purchase of the Comet 4s. Capital expenditures, exclusive of aircraft spares purchased during the year were:

	£
Aircraft and engines under hire purchase	2,364,471
Other engines	4,852
Freehold & leasehold property	20,874
Plant & equipment	26,489
Furniture & office equipment	2,321
	£2,419,007

E.A.A.C. had an overdraft facility of £230,000, guaranteed by the governments of Uganda and Tanganyika, with a further £200,000 secured on staff houses owned by the Corporation, should it be required. There were loans made up of £107,000 from B.O.A.C. (later converted to Stock) and £8,000 from the subsidiary, Caterair. In addition B.O.A.C. took up a further £143,000 of E.A.A.C. 3.5% Stock 1975, this being of a loan nature carried no voting rights. The Corporation's loan capital structure was now based upon £471,500 E.A.A.C. 3.5% Stock 1975 with £230,000 guaranteed overdraft facility. The relative holdings of the stock and participation as guarantors was as follows:

	3.5% 1975 Stock £	Overdraft Guarantor £	Total £
Kenya Government	150,000	–	150,000
Uganda Government	50,000	100,000	150,000
Tanganyika Government	20,000	130,000	150,000
Zanzibar Government	1,500	–	1,500
Territorial Participation	221,500	230,000	451,500
B.O.A.C. Participation	250,000	–	250,000
	£471,500	230,000	701,500

The final item on the financial agenda for 1960 was the provision made for the order of a third Comet 4 in 1961, for delivery in 1962, at a value of £1,169,000, for which finance had been arranged on favourable terms, secured on the aircraft itself.

In a further move to rationalise the airline's structure, the responsibility for the cabin crews was removed from the operations department, which, logically, was principally concerned with flight operations and aircrew recruitment and training. A new cabin services department, under Mr Bill Ainscough, was established, which under its own management would be responsible for the running of all catering establishments and all aspects of cabin service. It was considered essential that the stewards and stewardesses should be transferred to the commercial side of the organisation and that the operations department should no longer be responsible for their administration.

By the end of 1960 the cabin crew numbers had risen to 49, made up in the following groups:

	European	Asian	African
Stewards	21	2	4
Stewardesses	18	4	0

The airline had continued with its stated policy of training and recruiting Africans, but it reflected badly upon the colonial education system that, with rapid expansion and the need to find new recruits, it still found it impossible to recruit suitably qualified local staff. With an improved training organisation and management structure, it was felt that, in the course of time, suitably trained staff of the right calibre would be made available. It is well to bear in mind, that, until very recently, it was not uncommon for B.O.A.C. to recruit its stewardesses from among the upper classes of British society. The standards were set extremely high – and East African Airways were not looking for lower standards. The problem could only be overcome by setting new standards of training. East African Airways, in direct competition with the airlines of Europe and South Africa, were having to break completely new ground by introducing African staff into one of the most sophisticated environments in the world – the passenger cabin of an intercontinental airliner. Some of these new recruits would be coming from an unchanged tradition reaching back thousands of years, completely alien to the culture they would find both in their work, and at the places where they would stop-over on the routes. The training stewardesses would often find that explanations of the significance of table knives and forks would be as important as instruction in how to walk in court shoes. The Africans had a great advantage, however, and that was their natural feeling of hospitality and friendliness, which when combined with appropriate cabin service training, enabled them to make the passengers on East African Airways feel that they were already welcome visitors in the African sunshine. Even if the passengers had not understood the welcoming *"Karibu"*, the accompanying smiles were, more often than not, genuine.

Towards the end of 1960, with more than satisfactory revenue results and with the prospect of similar earning levels in the foreseeable future, the board allocated £325,000 towards an aircraft replacement fund. A committee was appointed to study suitable types for replacing the Canadair and DC3 aircraft by the end of 1962, their recommendations to be made available to the board by early 1961.

CHAPTER 8

Uhuru

INDEPENDENCE FIRST CAME to the East African Territories on December 9, 1961, when Tanganyika became a sovereign state under the leadership of President Julius Nyerere. In Kenya, torn by the tragic Mau Mau campaign, the end of colonial rule would be delayed until the end of 1963, five days after the island state of Zanzibar. Jomo Kenyatta had, however, been freed from detention on 14th August, 1961, and was to become the first President of independent Kenya.

Independence came on October 9, 1962, to Uganda, Winston Churchill's "Pearl of the Nile", which seemed, to those unaware of the deep undercurrents of dissent among the great diversity of tribal people, to be the most fortunate of the East African Territories. A wonderful climate in which no one should ever starve, due to the fertility of the soil and the abundance of both rain and sunshine, an educated African elite (the first university between Cairo and the Zambezi opened at Makerere, in Kampala as far back as the 1920s), and an economy which rested soundly on a cornucopia of produce from copper, beryl and tin to cotton, coffee (accounting for 95% of the country's foreign earnings), tea, sugar, tobacco, maize, ground-nuts and timber. Perhaps not altogether to the general good, excellent lager, and a local gin – a great deal more refined than the Nubian gin of former times – distilled from bananas, called *Waragi*. In addition, the potential for tourism in the vast National Parks, teeming with elephant, buffalo and all forms of game; great forest reserves, with countless varieties of bird life and some of the last chimpanzee and gorilla sanctuaries in Africa. The Mountains of the Moon, The White Nile, Murchison's Falls – the list of exciting tourist opportunities seemed endless.

Britain had provided a benevolent rule during the years of the Protectorate. Generally, the British were liked, particularly among the Baganda tribe whom the British administrators and missionaries had favoured, to the exclusion almost totally of the untamed, partly Moslem tribes in the less accessible north of the country. However, this did not protect the British officials from the zealous Africanisation policy of Benedicto Kiwanuka, the first Prime Minister. Although he lost his seat to Dr Milton Obote in April 1962, he had set the course for the policy of Africanisation, which would continue until long after Britain had departed from government in East Africa.

East African Airways had reason to be wary of the speedy Africanisation of the airline, which had been built up over the years on firmly based training requirements, experience and demonstrated ability. As far back as the 1950s, an American initiative was put to the corporation, suggesting that they would train a number of African pilots, on condition that the airline employed them. Captain Eric Morris, who was then chief pilot, agreed that there would be no objection, subject to the new pilots passing a flight check. The Americans would not agree to this commonsense proviso, and the offer was withdrawn.

The broad policy which the Corporation developed was stated in its annual report for 1960:

"The Corporation recognises the need for localisation of staff as quickly as is practicable, and has set up a Commercial, Engineering and Accounts Training Scheme. Details of vacancies were circulated to all schools. At the same time, the progressive training of existing staff has continued.

"It has been the Corporation's policy and practice to recruit staff from within the East African Territories whenever candidates possessed of suitable qualifications could be found, but due to the very rapid expansion of the Corporation's activities it has at times proved impossible to recruit staff locally of sufficient experience to fill the posts necessary to maintain this rate of expansion. The training organisation now set up is designed to produce in the course of time trained personnel, particularly Africans, of the required calibre.

"It will be recognised that more senior posts in any airline must be occupied by persons of many years specialised experience, such as can be acquired in the highly developed countries. Experience of this kind gained in the ordinary course of employment, is not available on a sufficiently large scale in the East African territories, and it is this deficiency that our Training Schemes, which will be conducted by experienced and specialist staff of the Corporation, seek to remedy.

"No course of instruction, however well conducted, can replace steadily acquired experience, which alone befits a man for the assumption of responsibility, for the taking of well-judged decisions, and for dealing confidently with the unusual.

"It will be appreciated that in the airline business the first consideration is safety. No other fact, however expedient it may appear can be allowed to influence this prime consideration, and staff whose duties are in any way connected with aircraft operation must necessarily reach a very high standard."

There is no doubt that any of those educated, confident and ambitious Africans who read this, would see it as yet another 'colonialist' attempt to hang on to power and exclude from office those Africans who saw all employment within their country of origin as theirs by birthright.

However, behind the statement lay the fact that major difficulties had been met by the corporation, in the implementation of its policy. It was accepted then, as now, that it is imperative in the operation of costly aircraft, with the attendant risk of serious loss of life in accident, that international standards, most of which are prescribed by law, should be adhered to strictly, in fact, aircraft could not operate commercial services unless this were done. These standards require that all personnel concerned should hold recognised qualifications or licences, most of which can be obtained only after long periods of training and experience. In the case of East African Airways pilots, for example, some ten to twelve years of flying experience in conjunction with rigid and searching training courses were required as a qualification for a captain of Comet aircraft.

Against this background of thinking, it was felt that the corporation would have to rely upon its existing experienced staff for a number of years to come, and it made a point of repeating these points in 1961, in the face of calls for Africanisation from independent Uganda and those impatient for Uhuru in Kenya and Tanganyika.

On 1st January 1961, the sales department and the stations and traffic department were merged to form the commercial department, with sales manager, J.W. Baines reporting to the commercial manager A.G. Molison. During the previous year the airline had entered into an association with B.O.A.C., South African Airways and Central African Airways, in a quadripartite pool. The new department was busy during the year, in discussions with the partner airlines on subjects ranging from basic policy decisions; pool agreements; accounting procedures and scheduling to commercial policy and advertising. Towards the end of the year, negotiations were concluded with Aden Airways for the pooling of the joint services between Aden and East Africa. Despite the fact that early in the year fares to the United Kingdom had been reduced by 16%, the estimated revenue for 1961 was exceeded by some £232,000. All aspects of the airline's traffic showed satisfactory increases, particularly within the East African territories themselves:

> Passenger traffic being .... 16.3% up to 173,811 passengers
> Cargo .... 18.3% up to 3,425 tons
> Mail .... 11.4% up to 819 tons

The established pattern of local services remained unchanged, with the exception of the introduction of a scheduled service, in April, between Arusha and Mwanza, which linked the two provinces for the first time, and during the same month, a scheduled service was introduced to Malindi, where the airfield had finally been brought up to DC3 standard. At Embakasi, ILS equipment had been installed, its introduction coming some 11 years after it had been made a requirement by I.C.A.O., listing minimum equipment for international airports. The ability to make standard precision approaches, together with the facility, newly installed, of search radar equipment, meant that diversions were reduced considerably, with the concomitant savings in time and expense.

The international pattern of services in operation at the end of 1960 was continued with the addition in January 1961 of Comet services between Nairobi, Karachi and Bombay, this being the first jet airline service across the Arabian sea. Planning was in hand to increase the frequency of Comet services between East Africa and the United Kingdom and also to Pakistan and India via Aden, when the third Comet was delivered in April 1962. Aden would be introduced into the Nairobi-Karachi-Bombay sector, on 2nd January 1962, when Captain Howard Iliffe commanded VP-KPK on the first Comet service.

Towards the end of the year, unprecedented rains disrupted rail and road communications, and East African Airway's resources were fully mobilised in a concentrated effort to meet the demand for air transport, particularly between Mombasa and Nairobi. The situation, following severe flooding which cut the rail link between Nairobi and Mombasa, became a matter of great concern when deliveries of aviation fuel began to dry up. By government order, fuel rationing was imposed, and it was necessary to introduce an emergency pattern of international services, by re-scheduling a number to overfly Nairobi.

In April, Khartoum and Rome had been taken out of the schedule and the Comets were routed via Benina to London, providing the fastest service between Nairobi and London.

Benina was a borderline airport to get into, at the best of times. B.O.A.C. operated their Comet 4s through there for a short time, but abandoned it. United Arab Airlines (formerly Misrair of Egypt, who had combined during a period of political brotherhood with Syrian Arab Airlines) had purchased Comets and operated them on their Cairo – Benina – Tripoli service. One aircraft undershot the runway, ploughing into the desert and losing its undercarriage; the second one, having learned from the mistake of his friend, landed further down the runway, and ran off into the desert at the other end. They did not try it again.[1] The single tarmac runway was almost too short for Comet operations, unless pilots, aware of the limitations, adopted careful operating techniques.

A new phenomenon to the crews of the Comets, now operating in the high levels where the tropopause met the stratosphere above 30,000ft was the jet-stream. On the flights to Benina they would encounter these winds, flowing in a narrow track at about latitude 20 North. During the winter months they could expect winds of up to 150kts, varying in direction between 240 and 300 degrees. It was very difficult to predict these winds, and it was normal practice to fly as far left of track as possible, so that when the jet-stream was intercepted, a gentle right turn towards Benina increased ground-speed, improving the sector time and, ultimately, ensuring an early arrival at London.

There were no approach aids to Benina, apart from the NDB, a form of radio aid classed as 'non-precision' for approach and let down purposes and subject to static interference and loss of signal strength at night. NDBs also suffer from station interference, mountain effect and coastal refraction. Radio communication was poor and the weather unpredictable. Flying north, it was usual to get a good 'fix' passing Lodwar radio beacon, but after that it was no use depending upon anything until the radio beacon at Benina was picked up.

At about the time of these Comet services, the crews began to notice lights in the otherwise black void of the desert above 20 deg North. They learned that these were American oil exploratory camps. Later, the oilmen used radio beacons, which the navigators tried to use, until they discovered that they were mobile. Later on, some of these radio beacons became fixed features, marked on the navigation charts. A new aid fitted to the Comet was weather radar, intended for the location of storm cells. It could also pick up certain ground features, such as coastlines. On the still terrifying fifteen mile taxi ride into Benghazi, the crews would litter the roadside with empty beer cans, as they consumed their 'after landing' refreshments. Some

---

[1] United Arab Airlines operated 9 Comet 4Cs. Of these, five crashed between 1963 and 1971.

earnestly believed that, eventually, the uncollected mass of metal would enhance the signals, as they searched for Benina on their radar screens!

Radio communications on the Marconi HF sets were exhausting, with the two main control centres on the route, before reaching European airspace, being Khartoum and Malta. It was not unusual for it to take half an hour to get a brief position report through. Under those conditions, the obtaining of weather reports was pretty well out of the question. In spring and summer, hot dry winds would cause rising sand, cutting forward visibility to zero at times. In winter the Mediterranean can show some remarkably rough weather, with storms, high winds and driving rain. The coastal regions sometimes experience rolling sea fogs, which creep a few miles inland.

Benina is ideally placed to experience all of these weather conditions. In addition, it had an unpleasant surprise for incoming aircraft when, from time to time, following torrential rain, the runway lights would fail without warning.

With this in mind, the cabin crew were a little apprehensive about landing at Benina, particularly during the winter when it suffered from the *ghibli*, a strong desert wind, causing rising sand, reducing visibility and making a tricky landing even more difficult. East African Airways continued to use it, since it was advertised as the fastest service to London, and the crews were anxious to prove it. The station had been used by the airline for many years. Ron Gander, the resident station engineer would always be there as the aircraft arrived, usually at about 03.00. The airfield would be otherwise deserted at that time in the morning, they would be in, fuelled, and out within thirty minutes.

It was on one such occasion that Mary Quill, a young impressionable stewardess, was one of the crew. As usual, on the descent, Mary came up front to report all was secure at the back, and asked the navigator what the weather was like. He just said, "shitty". But before she went back to tell the other girls the bad news, the captain asked for a bottle of HP sauce and a wad of cotton wool. She brought it up to the cockpit, and retired aft to strap herself in for the landing.

The arrival was uneventful, there were no problems. It was blowing sand, but the wind was thirty knots, right down the runway.

Mary had to find out why the captain had requested the HP sauce. She collared the navigator and first officer, as they were drinking coffee in the transit lounge. They explained that in sandy desert conditions the first officer would, just prior to landing, open up the clear vision panels on the front windscreen and smear all the windows with the sauce, causing a brown film to form – this reacted with the similar colour sand, causing a neutralising reaction – very technical stuff, actually – which permitted the pilots to see clearly through the filthy dust and sand. HP sauce had been proved to be just the right consistency, Worcester sauce was too thin, and blew away too easily. Mary was visibly impressed by this explanation.

The next stop was Heathrow Airport, London. The weather was thick fog. Just on limits. Again, Mary came forward to the cockpit, prior to landing. She was told that the weather was borderline, but that they were commencing their descent into London. This time the captain called for Nivea creme and cotton wool, and explained to Mary that the first officer would adopt the same procedure as before, but using the creme, being a similar colour to the fog to be encountered.

The approach and landing was again routine. A combination of London's superb approach radar, and precision radar talk-down from ten miles out, coupled with the ILS to confirm everything, guarantees success – with the indispensable aid of the Nivea.

Later, in the hotel bar, Mary was bubbling with the discovery of how wonderful East African crews were, to have discovered the secret of these sauces and cremes. In the meantime, it was hinted that chili paste was being developed for the Indian run. All the foreign crew members in the bar listened with astonishment to her revelations, until they could no longer hold their mirth. After she found out how she had been fooled, Mary never trusted air-crews again.

East African Airways had established over the years a natural ability to promote friendliness and comradeship, from the chairman, Sir Alfred Vincent, down to the newest recruit, who would feel, from the first moments, that he was welcomed into a close family of colleagues. The reward for the airline for this corporate atmosphere, was tremendous loyalty, and among the aircrew in particular, there was an outstanding esprit de corps which created a magnificent, supportive team. The early years of the Comet services probably represented the zenith of this general feeling of esprit. Now they had joined the 'Jet Set'. There was tremendous excitement – the up and coming airline had got there and was going places!

Paddy Murray summed it up, "I think the happiest days of East African Airways were during the Comet era. We were all one big happy family, with great pride and enthusiasm – but little money. The cabin service was wonderful. The airline always showed a profit during those days, even though one year it was only 100 shillings – but it was still a profit. Maintenance was first class, as were the pilots." There was keen competition between E.A.A.C. and 'big brother' B.O.A.C. In addition to being quicker into London, East African Airway's Comets were achieving 10 – 15% more landings per tyre, and the highly polished E.A.A.C. Comet hulls gave them 0.5 to 0.75% higher performance than B.O.A.C. These small things added up to more than lower costs, they were the product of a special kind of spirit of cooperation, which cannot be bought.

Captain Peter Cunningham remarked many years later how, as chief pilot of the DC3 fleet, he "regularly had complaints from colleagues who thought they were not flying enough, even though we were a hard working bunch." He went on to describe how the ground engineers "were fantastic in the pride they took in getting the aircraft ready on time, not so easy with the quirky old piston engines. More than once I recall them working through the night changing an engine at some grass airfield where we had broken down, and taking them beer and sandwiches from the local hotel! They made sure we were ready to roll by eight o'clock."

The colonial informality of the East African Airways aircrew was regarded by some as verging upon the eccentric. In an airline which was small by international standards, there was not much chance of getting away with anything smacking of pomposity, unprofessional conduct or poor airmanship without it becoming common knowledge fairly soon. Respect was earned, and where it was given, it was genuine. As a result there were none of the airs and graces which were still preserved by the successors of the great Imperial Airways. There were still those in B.O.A.C. who could remember the redoubtable Captain O.P. Jones, who would never depart without donning a pair of impeccable white gloves, maintaining a regal distance at all times between his position of command and those lowly persons ordained to serve him. It is said that upon one occasion, at the end of one of the early pioneering Atlantic crossings, his navigator said, very pleased with himself, "Excuse me Captain Jones, I hope you noticed my ATA was within 30 seconds of my ETA". Captain O.P. Jones glared at him and said, frigidly, "To what do you attribute the error, Mr Navigator?"

Early one morning, a B.O.A.C. Britannia had arrived at Entebbe from Khartoum on its way to Nairobi. The captain was standing outside the main entrance, admiring the sunrise when his first officer came up to him and said "Captain, Sir, do you want to take flight plan fuel, or would you like some extra?" The captain replied, "Mister First Officer, as the weather in Nairobi is OK, flight plan fuel will do fine, thank you". While this little exchange was taking place, round the corner came an E.A.A.C. DC3 crew - Captain Ian Ainscow and Second Officer Mike Rigby, who were dressed in the old uniform of khaki bush jackets and shorts. They had night-stopped at the Lake Victoria Hotel, where, if one did not know better, judging by their rather scruffy appearance, one might think, erroneously, that they had had a fairly late night in the bar.

"Hey Shag, go and kick the tyres, while I go and file the flight plan" said Rigby, a very junior second officer to his captain. "OK Knocker", came the reply, as Ian Ainscow ambled off towards the dew soaked DC3.

The B.O.A.C. captain, whose admiration of the sunrise was disturbed by what he had just overheard, was horrified. He called to Rigby and asked him if he was a *second* officer with East African Airways, to which Rigby replied, "Yeh". The captain then proceeded to lecture Rigby on decorum and the standards which should be observed in the airline. Discipline dictated that you should not, especially in a public place, call your captain "Shag". Rigby replied, "Well, he called me Knocker, didn't he? Anyway, what has it got to do with *you* - Shag?"

As Rigby disappeared round the corner, leaving the captain speechless, he heard someone running behind him, and turning round, he was grabbed by the B.O.A.C. first officer, shaking him by the hand he said, "Congratulations, that was marvellous, I would have given a months salary to have said what you just said to that b*****d captain!"

The captain was sufficiently angered to write a letter of complaint to Peter Cunningham, chief pilot DC3s, giving a full account of the incident, with a description of the two E.A.A. crew. Of course, no action was taken.

A great deal of friendly ribbing went on, to relieve the boredom of long passages, or the tension at the end of a difficult flight. Bob Ainsworth had the reputation of being something of a ladies man. Whether he was or not, he did nothing to disabuse his colleagues of this belief. He was also very health-conscious (long before cigarette smoking fell out of general favour, he would forbid smoking on the flight-deck, when he was in command). On one of the first Comet flights he was together with Dave Griffiths (chief navigator), who told him that it was unhealthy flying jets. A significant hazard, Griffiths told him, was that it made your head grow larger, because of the high pressure differential in the cockpit and cabin. On the first sector, the crew managed to get hold of his hat, and put a single layer of newspaper in the sweatband. When he put his hat on, on disembarking at Entebbe, he thought his hat felt tight, and was visibly worried. On the next sector, another layer was added, and his concern became extreme when he put his hat on to walk around the aircraft at Benina. It was not until they reached London that the penny dropped.

Bob Ainsworth's interest in his health led him to investigate an article in the *Sunday Times* magazine supplement, showing photographs of a group of dignified old men in Samarkand who looked fit and healthy despite their ages, which were reputedly 110 years or thereabouts. On his return from a holiday trip to the Samarkand region of the U.S.S.R., he was none the wiser, but suspected that the reporter, or the old folk themselves had been adding a few years on to their age.

In the early years of the United Kingdom services, the East African Airways crews would stop over at the Mount Royal Hotel in London, as did South African Airways. In the early sixties a new hotel was constructed by the Bath Road, opposite the north side of London Airport, this was the Skyway Hotel. Soon after the introduction of the Comets, E.A.A.C. decided to accommodate all their staff at the Skyway Hotel, which was only some five minutes bus journey from Terminal 3. From the point of view of some, this was a very popular move since it cut down the time between arrival and their getting settled into the bar. Others would have preferred to remain in the West End.

A favourite lunch time meeting place in those days, and for many years, was a pub which stood a few yards west of the hotel, called 'The Air Hostess'. On most days, from opening time until after lunch, one could find a crowd of East African crew members, their tables laden with rounds of Watney's bitter. It was here that the latest news would be exchanged, friends would meet up, perhaps after weeks of speaking, in passing, via the radio channels in the sky, and stories would be told and re-told to gales of laughter.

One day, Paddy Murray and Frank MacNabb were sitting on the crew bus at the hotel, waiting for the captain to make an appearance. It was Bob Ainsworth, who had just bought a fire-engine red Jaguar E type, for which he had paid £1,800, plus an enormous insurance premium of £250, because he parked it at the hotel. As Ainsworth climbed on board the bus, Paddy Murray remarked to MacNabb that the only reason that he had bought the car was to attract the 'birds', and that by his calculations it cost him £50 every time he bedded them. Captain Ainsworth then turned and addressed the entire crew in his measured, polite and gentlemanly manner, saying: "For your information – and anybody else in this crew who is interested, I have just had £250 worth", whereupon he took his seat, and they drove off.

1961

Reporting early in 1961, the committee appointed to review replacement aircraft for the Canadairs and DC3s, which was headed by Chief Technical Officer Johnny Johnson, Captain Peter Cunningham and engineer C. E. Smith, with the assistance of Mr J.C. Dykes, an independent advising aeronautical engineer who had been recommended by B.O.A.C., presented their conclusions to the board of East African Airways. After considering the options, the possible types of aircraft were narrowed down to three, the Avro 748, the Handley Page Herald and the Fokker F27 Friendship. The outstanding aircraft which fulfilled the performance requirements for the regional routes, outclassing the other aircraft was the twin Rolls-Royce Dart turbo-prop powered Friendship. Three Series 200 Friendships were ordered for delivery in October, November and December 1962, with an option on a fourth machine.

This decision was followed at the end of the year by a new Colonial Air Navigation Order which was introduced on December 6th, 1961, which imposed many performance penalties on the DC3s. For many years East African Airways had been safely operating the Dakotas, paying particular attention to performance safeguards when operating from hot and high airfields. This had not always been the case with other operators flying charter services, or those operated by mining companies and other private operators.

Government legislation was, year by year, tightening its hold on public air transport, with regard to safety performance. The emergency single-engine performance after take-off out of the high airfields of East Africa at maximum weights could approach the dangerous category if restricted take-off limits were not applied.

The problem was not new, some ten years previously United Kingdom M.C.A.R.s (Ministry of Civil Aviation Regulations) had been passed on to the East African D.C.A. which showed relevant graphs, figures and charts governing British registered aircraft. The restrictions were quite alarming, with the regulated take-off weight being reduced from 28,000lbs to approximately 26,000lbs to meet calculated slide-rule single-engine performance requirements. If adopted, these new regulations would practically have put E.A.A. out of business. Since there was no evidence of flight tests to uphold the new regulations, it was decided that some tests should be carried out. Eric Morris and Phillip Henn carried out flight tests with VP-KJQ at Dar es Salaam in September, 1952. At maximum all up weight of 28,000lbs they established straight and level cruise on one engine with 2,300 RPM at 7,000ft. After a report was submitted to the D.C.A. in which it was shown that the DC3 could be operated at 28,000lbs maximum, even in East African conditions, approval was received to continue as before.

By the end of the 1961, no decision had been made by the authorities, but the Corporation was concerned that should it not be able to obtain exemptions based upon past performance, the DC3 would no longer be a viable proposition. The Nairobi – Mombasa route would, for example, suffer a reduction of more than 50% of its payload:

Seating Capacity	Less Restriction	Seats Available
30	16	14

These considerations made the re-equipping with the Fokker F27 an even more pressing requirement. In fact, there had been very little delay in considering the F27 and the initial order for three aircraft had been placed on 23rd August, for delivery in October, November and December, 1962. The Fokker F27 was a high-wing aircraft with a seating capacity of 40. It had a comfortable modern cabin, with air-conditioning and a superb view for the passengers through large windows, with no wing to obscure the scenic views below. A rugged, durable and easily maintained aircraft, the F27 would prove a superb replacement for the DC3.

There were disappointing charter and tourist booking cancellations during 1961, as a direct consequence of the bad publicity around the world arising from the Congo crisis. This was to affect tourism throughout the region quite dramatically – the visitors from South Africa, which had declared itself a Republic, withdrawing

The third production East African Airways Fokker F27 'Friendship', VP-KSC (re-registered 5H-AAI). This photograph was taken prior to delivery, the aircraft being test flown with the Dutch registration PH-FEC. (Fokker)

from the Commonwealth, in May, would diminish and very soon cease altogether in the wake of political change.

Within Kenya, however, the airport at Malindi was finally improved to DC3 standard and, in April, Sir Alfred Vincent, who had said he would only visit Malindi when it had a scheduled air service, was on board the inaugural flight, which was followed on the same day by four Dakota services carrying holiday-makers for the Easter week-end.

During July, British forces were rushed into Kuwait as it became a target for Iraqi aggression. Both the Canadair and Comet fleets were called upon to transport troops from East Africa to reinforce the British presence in Aden and Bahrain.

With political upheavals taking place throughout Africa many of those who had come to East Africa, particularly Kenya, to settle and enjoy a new life in the sun, became increasingly concerned that the future would not bring the security which an earlier colonial ideal had promised. The Congo experience, coupled with the surge of nationalism and independence, was unsettling to many. The domestic problems associated with living in a country in which the living standards of the European settlers could not be guaranteed were too much for many of them. East African Airways suffered a loss during the early sixties of a number of staff, who had decided that their future would be better taken care of further south, or away from Africa altogether. During 1961, some twelve pilots, one navigator and two engineer officers resigned. Although pilot applicants during the year were few, by comparison with previous years, the airline was, however, able to recruit twenty-one pilots, five navigators and eleven engineer officers to replace those who had left and to permit the expansion of services planned for early 1962.

The Comet services were now well established on the London, Johannesburg and Eastern routes to Pakistan and India, operating seven flights a week to London via Rome, two flights a week to Karachi and Bombay and two flights a week to Johannesburg. Throughout the year large scale conversion training had been undertaken at Nairobi with the assistance of de Havilland pilot Captain Peter Wilson. A further five Comet crews were trained at Nairobi early in the year and further training was carried out as crews became available for conversion towards the end of 1961.

On August 7th 1961, Captain Tug Wilson completed 2,702 hours on the Canadair. He had been chief pilot of the fleet since June, 1960, and was now overdue for conversion to the Comet. The delay in his introduction to the Comet was a source of discontent. He believed, in moments of introspection, that the reason why his seniority in the airline was consistently overlooked lay in the event, on 14th November, 1955, when his little daughter, Denise Jane, aged two and a half was killed in a motoring accident. Cleared by the court of any blame, nevertheless, to Wilson this was a tragedy of immense proportions which would lie like a black cloud over him for the remainder of his life. He harboured the belief that the airline management took the view that a captain who could not ensure the safety of his own child in a car would not have one of the principal qualities for command, namely that of the care and safety of his passengers. In fairness to the operations managers under whom he served, there is no evidence to support this belief. In fact, Captain Eric Morris expressed great sympathy and understanding for Wilson over this tragic event.

He was certainly more correct when he surmised that "my trouble was lack of diplomacy – a spade is a spade is a bloody shovel!" but adding, "I might be hard-assed, but will always apologise when in error".

Wilson was chosen to convert to the Comet in September 1961, commencing line checks with Captain Roger Drew, who he regarded as "junior in E.A.A.C. service", albeit by only one or two places on the list. (Captain Roger Drew was an outstanding ex-R.A.F. pilot who held the Distinguished Flying Cross and bar. The first DFC was awarded to him when he was with No. 69 Squadron in Malta in 1941, where he carried out 120 sorties and destroyed three enemy aircraft. His second DFC was awarded for piloting a Baltimore aircraft which shadowed the Italian fleet, culminating in the Battle of Taranto. Anxious not to lose contact with the enemy until assured that the location of the fleet had been noted, he flew beyond the endurance of his aircraft and was unable to return to base. He safely landed at a desert airstrip. Prior to joining East African Airways he had flown with B.E.A. He was, in fact a highly experienced and competent airline captain).

The Canadairs were now used only on the regional routes, flying short sectors which provoked them into frequent displays of mechanical temperament. On a couple of occasions though, the aircraft could not be blamed. Captain Mitchell had just landed in a Comet from London and was holding in the loop at the far end of runway 07 at Embakasi for a Canadair to take-off. He recognised the voice of its captain, Mike Russell, as he made his pre take-off radio calls. As the aircraft accelerated down the runway, thick black smoke could be seen coming from the exhausts. It got airborne, but there was an obvious problem, as it was unable to climb. Captain Russell called that his engines were overheating and were not producing normal climb power and he requested an emergency landing clearance. He then proceeded to perform a low circuit, at tree-top height, and completed a successful approach and landing, with black smoke continuing to pour out of the engines.

An investigation soon found that the aircraft had been re-fuelled with AVTUR jet fuel instead of AVGAS, giving a mixture of approximately 50/50 petrol and paraffin. It was unfortunate that, although measures had been taken to fit incompatible fuel couplings between the aircraft and different types of fuel dispensers, the tanker on this occasion had not yet been modified – resulting in the loss of four Merlin engines.

This was not, regrettably, the only incident of this nature, for, on May 23rd, 1961, on a flight from Nairobi to Salisbury, shortly after take-off Captain Leslie had been forced to shut down a rough running engine and turn back to Nairobi. The fifty or so passengers were disembarked and taken to the restaurant while engineers tried to discover what had been the cause of the engine trouble. Having found nothing obvious, it was decided to do an air test. The aircraft was fully laden with baggage and cargo and, as a result, was well out of trim. In order to overcome this, volunteers were called for and within no time a good crowd of passengers was made up of the hangar boys, who were enjoying their tea break at the time.

Leslie, with co-pilot John Wilson, Flight Engineer Alan James and chief ground engineer Ron Barton proceeded to taxi to the take-off position. Again a Comet landed and held in the loop while they lined up and commenced the take-off roll. As the wheels left the ground, No.3 engine began to vibrate, "It seemed to be shaking itself to bits before ending with a bang and stopping" recalled Leslie. Captain Cartwright, observing the departure from the Comet could see black smoke pouring from the engine. This was confirmed by the control tower. They landed with no further delay; the hangar lads were delighted with their trip. Ron Barton was shattered. There were holes in the engine. They worked on the problem for a week, ruining two more Merlins in the process, before an engineer, cleaning his hands from the fuel drain cock under the starboard wing noticed something 'funny' about the fuel. It was found to contain paraffin, or more correctly AVTUR jet fuel, which had mistakenly been dispensed into the starboard fuel tanks, probably from the same tanker as in the other incident.

It was some ten months later that a Canadair was destroyed in a training incident involving captains Tom Dornan, D.R.'Dickie' Bird and George Atchison. VP-KNY was taking-off on a beautiful day (March 4th, 1962), from Embakasi, with Captain Bird at the controls and Captain Dornan was the Instrument Rating examiner, carrying out local training. Following retraction of the gear, the aircraft, for reasons never properly established, sank back onto the runway. With the propellers slicing

Captain Tom Dornan.
(Capt Ratcliffe)

into the tarmac the Canadair slid on its belly off the end of the runway and quickly began to burn. The pilots got out smartly, (not forgetting to collect their briefcases), and ran clear of the smoking wreck. The ground engineers had watched the display from their hangar a couple of miles away and, collecting the chief engineer 'Robbie' Robinson on the way, they were quickly on the scene, ahead of the fire engines. Seeing that the crew were safe, Robinson, no doubt pleased to see the end of this ancient source of trouble, advised the firemen, as the fire spread out of control, to "let the f*****g thing burn!" After it was well under way they set about their fire-drill.

It was a cold, wintry night, the 15th November, 1961, and everyone was looking forward to getting airborne from London on their journey to the warm south. Captain Phil Henn opened up the power on Comet VP-KPJ and the aircraft surged smoothly down the runway. All seemed to be fine, as the runway lights sped past, and the speed increased with gathering momentum. "100 knots" called the first officer. Then "Abort take-off!" came a shout from the flight engineer. They were close to V_1, but with more than half the long Heathrow runway ahead of them, Henn brought the Comet safely to taxi speed and turned off at the far end. With embarrassed apologies, the flight engineer explained that the wing leading-edge de-icers (feeding hot air to the wings from the turbines) had come on, and he thought that he had inadvertently switched them on.

They were lucky and the tower was able to give them clearance for an immediate second take-off. Lining up once more, Henn and his crew repeated their take-off routine and the Comet swept into the night sky. But their problems were not to be over so easily. Almost as soon as they were airborne, the flight engineer reported that the wing leading-edge heaters had gone to "full heat" and there was no way to control them without reducing power. It was imperative that they landed without delay. They had taken-off at close to maximum take-off weight for the sector non-stop to Benina. There was a considerable difference between the maximum take-off weight and the maximum landing-weight. They needed to dump fuel. Flying at minimum power at slow speed they were cleared by air traffic control to Beachy Head, where a series of radar headings enabled them to dump fuel without flying into the fine spray as it filled the air. They were given a straight-in approach back to Heathrow. An overshoot, although possible, would be most inadvisable, the resultant power surge necessary would send the temperature of the heated air over the wing leading-edge soaring.

The Comet landed safely and their journey was postponed for a couple of days. The B.O.A.C. engineers found that the cause was due to a small valve which had been installed incorrectly during a recent overhaul. Why it had not misbehaved earlier was an unsolved mystery. VP-KPJ was flown back to Nairobi two days later by Captain Peter Duff, when the Comet performed like a perfect lady.

The results of the year 1961 were generally very satisfactory. An operating profit of £263,927 was achieved from a total revenue of £4,925,785. Profits could have been higher had new economy fares not been introduced in 1960 , costing some £150,000 in the first full year of implementation. There was concern, too, about the levels of landing charges set by the East African governments, of a total of £307,000 paid in landing charges, £184,000 was to the East African governments, the 'owners' of the airline.

Revenue for 1961 showed remarkable percentage increases in most areas, but particularly on the international services where the increase was 64.1%. This would be the last year in which services to South Africa and the Rhodesias would be categorised separately as 'Regional' services, the increase of only 8.1% in traffic revenue gave an indication of the way things were going.

Staff numbers grew from 1,759 to 2,110 during the year. A number of Africans achieved artisan status in the engineering section, but the airline was still finding difficulties in fulfilling its policy of introducing local Africans in all departments. In the non-operational departments it was felt that some fifty trainees per annum should be required. To this end, the Territorial governments and the East African

East African continued to provide charter aircraft for the spiritual leader of the Ismaili community. The new Aga Khan is shown shaking hands with Asian Stewardess Zarina Keshavjee after a two-week charter covering some 2,560 miles and 15 hours flying throughout Kenya, Uganda and Tanzania. The remainder of the DC3 crew are: L to R: Captain Alan Ratcliffe, F/O Jim Cole and Purser Roy Prout. May, 1961.

(Capt Ratcliffe).

Super VC10, 5X-UVA (BAC)

Super VC10, 5X-UVA BAC

Fokker F27 Friendship, 5Y-AAB, at Moshi, Tanzania, 15th Sept 1969. (Author)

McDonnell Douglas DC-9, 5H-MOI *(MD/Capt Ratcliffe)*

Super VC10 5H-MOG at Filton after delivery to BAC, the last flight in East African Airways colours. 3rd August, 1977. *(Capt Ricketts).*

5H-MOG parked beside a British Airways Concorde at Filton. *(Capt Ricketts).*

Formerly 5X-UVJ, one of four ex-East African Airways Super VC10 K3 tankers in service with the Royal Air Force.
(© British Crown copyright 1992/MOD reproduced with the permission of the Controller of her Britannic Majesty's Stationery Office.)

Flanked by a Tornado, Super VC10 K3 tanker ZA 149 (5X-UVJ) takes up station to receive fuel from a Tristar tanker of the Royal Air Force.

Common Services Organization gave assurances that they would assist with the search for suitably qualified Africans for further training.

The composition of the Corporation's manpower at the end of 1961 was as follows:

	European		Asian		African	
	Male	Female	Male	Female	Male	Female
Flying Crews	122	-	-	-	-	-
Cabin Crews	21	37	2	6	12	6
Operations	13	2	4	2	1	-
Engineering & Supplies	129	6	238	2	251	-
Sales & Reservations	41	48	60	16	40	-
Stations & Traffic	64	50	184	13	573	10
Accounts	8	2	45	5	57	-
Management, Administration & General	6	5	-	1	27	1
	404	150	533	45	961	17

This staff total equated to a racial percentage breakdown as follows:

Colonel M.C.P. Mostert and Mr A. Gill represented E.A.A.C. at the Tanganyika independence celebrations. Shown at Dar es Salaam, a Comet 4 in the background, are L to R: Capt R. Drew, Mrs Gill, Col M.C.P. Mostert, Mrs Joan Mackenzie, Mr A. Mackenzie (manager Tanganyika) Capt P. Cooke, Mr A. Gill. (Mr A. Mackenzie)

European 26%
Asian 28%
African 46%

That single African female, employed in Administration in 1959, could, no doubt, feel a little less lonely at the close of 1961.

In 1960 an economic and fiscal commission was appointed under the chairmanship of Sir Jeremy Raisman to examine the existing East African common market, economic coordination and fiscal uniformity. The main concerns were in connection with fiscal policy and distribution of wealth between the territories, through revenues to the East Africa High Commission. Together with the East African Railways and Harbours, East African Airways was a major asset of the territories, which, during the period of British rule, could be adequately administered through a corporation answering to the Commission of Governors. With the advent of independence, the countries of East Africa were looking forward to total freedom, some having quite opposite views concerning the nature of their government and fiscal and economic policies.

The commission, after deliberating upon the tangled web of inter-territorial differences, presented a report on 1st July, 1961, which proposed the establishment of a distributable pool of revenue made up of fixed proportions of certain income tax and customs and excise receipts. Half would go to the High Commission to finance the non-self contained services, and half would be equally distributed among the three territories. Thus the High Commission would be guaranteed its own revenue, independent of the three territories, and Uganda and Tanganyika would receive a re-distribution of funds to off-set the disproportionate levels of benefit gained by Kenya, being the most highly developed economy and sole sea port (at Mombasa) for land-locked Uganda.

The report of the commissioners declared:

Delegates agreed that it would be in the interests of all territories to ensure that whatever constitutional changes might take place in the future in East Africa, common services at present provided by the East Africa High Commission should continue to be provided on an East African basis. They further agreed that the arrangements made must be fully compatible with the sovereignty of Tanganyika when Tanganyika became independent.

The East Africa High Commission of Governors was to be replaced by the East African Common Services Authority, consisting of the three leading elected Ministers in each of the territories. Under these Ministers would be four Ministerial departments concerned with communications, finance and commerce and industry, and social and research services. Each of these departments would be headed by three Ministers, one from each of the territories.

From 1961, the Board of East African Airways would be reporting to the newly formed East African Common Services Organisation. Some observers may have reflected upon the questions arising from the dependence of the airline upon the continuing future success of the E.A. Common Services Organisation, but in those heady days of freedom in the air and independence, these thoughts would be quickly submerged.

Sir Alfred Vincent, summed up the year in his report:

"The problem of how best to serve the Territories and public is always before the Executive Management and the lack of adequate finance is a stringent and compelling factor.

"The Corporation feels that aviation should have at least equal opportunity with other requirements in these territories rapidly advancing to independence.

"In the absence of capital in amounts justified by the size and stature of the Corporation, we are committing earnings to fleet replacement projects, as it is vital to maintain a competitive position and the need for continuous development must not be stifled by lack of funds.

". . . As the year closed, Tanganyika achieved independence, and the airline welcomes the opportunity to be regarded as her National Airline as well as that of the other emerging Territories, and looks forward with interest and confidence to a tradition of continued service."

1962

The East African Safari rally took place during April, in 1962. George Leslie had been competing since 1959, and this year participated with Roger Eastell, who worked for East African Railways. They did not finish the circuit, their car crashed spectacularly in part of the Tanganyika section. Leslie was severely disabled, requiring speedy repatriation to the United Kingdom as a stretcher case on a Comet. Among other things, he had a detached retina. This was serious for an airline pilot and extremely worrying for Leslie, who imagined that his flying days may be over.

It was July before he had recovered sufficiently to return to flying. He had suffered from double-vision long after the other injuries had cleared up. His Harley Street consultant had re-assured him that it would get better, given time. He managed to get past his medical checks and recommenced flying. During the day there was no problem, but at night he found he could see four sets of runway lights. This made it very difficult to judge the flare correctly on landing. With an airliner such as the Comet, it was not necessary to judge the height of the flare in terms of inches, but pilots prided themselves on a smooth landing. Leslie evolved a technique whereby he maintained speed and virtually flew the Comet onto the runway. Captain Roger Drew, route checking him over six sectors, following his return, remarked on this "new procedure", but could not fault the smooth touchdowns. He didn't ask Leslie what he was up to, and Leslie didn't tell him anything about the four sets of runways lights out there. Fortunately, the consultant's promise came true, and the runway lights soon returned to their normal pattern.

Engine failures were almost unheard of with the Rolls-Royce Avons. Most of the in-flight incidents were hot air leaks, which could be blow-lamp hot, from the engines buried in the wings – in which all the fuel was carried. A serious wing leading-edge overheat, or fire warning would require an engine shut-down, to quell the escaping blast of hot air – but this was not classed as an engine failure.

An engine failure did occur on 29th September, 1962, on the Comet VP-KRL, which had entered service in April. On the EC720 daylight flight to London, the No.4 engine seized soon after take-off, and began to burn. The aircraft returned to Nairobi, making an emergency landing with the fire still burning fiercely. After the fire was put out, it was discovered that the oil-filler plug was lying in the bottom of the engine cowlings. Evidently, during an earlier routine service, the filler plug had been replaced and left finger tight. It had vibrated loose and then blown off with the pressure of the lubricant, which then escaped.

A Comet, commanded by Capt Dave Power, returning from Bujumbura, was in difficulty on the approach to Nairobi. It had lost all its pressure instruments. This placed the crew in a potentially disastrous situation. Fortunately, another Comet was on local training, flown by Captain Jeff de Jager. He flew in formation with the crippled aircraft, calling out airspeeds as they descended to the runway. As the engineers checked the airspeed indicators and the system behind them, they discovered that bees had entered the pitot tubes, blocking them, and, as a result disabling the instruments.

In keeping with the usual airline practice, pilot upgrade from first officer to captain would always entail moving to another type of aircraft of which the new captain had previous experience. In the case of E.A.A.C. Comet first officers, the distinction of command was a mixed blessing, since, for the time being, it meant returning to the DC3 Dakota, after experiencing a totally new world of flying. As Ginger Brewer sat in the right-hand cockpit seat of the Comet, next to Captain Peter Cooke on the night of 30th January, 1962, his thoughts reflected upon the path which had brought him from an engineering beginning some twelve years ago to the point where he had been offered his command as captain of a DC3. As the Comet made its journey high above the Arabian Sea, en route from Aden to Nairobi, he wondered when again, if at all, he would experience the power of this magnificent aircraft, responding to his commands.

There had been very little change on the internal DC3 routes over the years. Brewer commenced his first service in command of VP-KJR on 23rd July 1962, with F/O Becker, operating the EC033, Nairobi-Mombasa-Tanga-Zanzibar- Dar es Salaam, the old route, just the same as it always was. They didn't go down to Durban any more, much to the disappointment of the DC3 crews, but they operated to Ndola in Northern Rhodesia, via Mbeya and Abercorn. The airport at Malindi was improved and opened up to DC3s in October, 1962, which was a boon to the steadily growing tourist resort. The game viewing flights to Seronera, in the Serengeti National Park, were still popular, during the dry season. That year Brewer took some twenty-five

American tourists one Sunday who were lucky enough to see the annual migration of the wildebeest and zebra herds. The game park wardens, who did aerial spot counts, estimated that on that day there were more than one million animals on the move. On the bumpy, hot late-afternoon flight, returning to Nairobi, Brewer reflected, happily, that this was what made East African Airways so unique in character, and, on that day, the customers had, most surely, had their money's worth.

On 1st October, 1962, he had an opportunity to re-visit Tananarive, in Madagascar, for the first time since he had taken Prince Aly Khan and Rita Hayworth there eleven years previously. The charter was in VP-KLC, with F/O Malcolm Mounter. They routed via Mtwara with a cargo of translating equipment for an international conference. All went well until about half way across the Mozambique Channel all the vacuum instruments failed. With poor weather forecast at their destination, they were obliged to let down into the airfield at Ivato, tucked between hills at 7,000ft amsl, without an artificial horizon, or turn and slip indicator. The landing was accomplished using the restricted panel and, on finding that the vacuum pump had failed, they were happy to spend twenty-four hours on the Island, awaiting repairs.

Despite its noise and comparative lack of comfort for both crew and passengers, compared with the more up to date Fokker F27, the DC3 was a wonderful aeronautical workhorse and did yeoman service for E.A.A.C. On the coastal services and when working from the inland aerodromes with long runways, its performance was adequate. But the WAT limitations when operating from the interior airfields presented many problems for the DC3 captains. The service from Mbeya, close to the Northern Rhodesia border with Tanganyika, to Dar es Salaam via the Southern Highlands Club and Iringa could provide typical examples of the kind of operating conditions encountered at the time.

Mbeya airfield was at a height of 5,600ft amsl, with a runway length of 1,350 metres and a typical summer air temperature of 20 deg C. One day, a DC3 had been loaded to nearly maximum WAT take-off weight, with perishable cargo and a number of passengers transferred from a connecting Air Rhodesia aircraft, including the Archbishop of Tanganyika and his personal staff. The first stop, to off-load about 50kg of mail and freight, was SHC, which was at 6,300ft amsl., with a similar air temperature of 20 deg C. The grass runway at SHC had a marked uphill slope, in the prevailing wind – if there was little wind, a down-hill take-off was the norm. A very difficult airfield to operate from, at the best of times.

The DC3 landed at SHC, the captain noting that his landing weight was almost the same as maximum take-off weight. As the freight was being off-loaded, a car drew up with three African government officials who demanded to be taken to Dar es Salaam for a meeting. The captain explained that the aircraft was at maximum weight, despite the empty seats. The 'officials' insisted that they be taken, and that some of the transit passengers should be thrown off. When they were told who the passengers were, they replied, "Throw off the Archbishop!" The captain resolved the dilemma by off-loading as much of the non-perishable cargo as possible, and delaying departure until the afternoon temperature eased. He could not afford to wait for the cool evening air since they had to get in and out of Iringa before dark.

A small coterie of pilots and engineers had been training at the Fokker factory in Amsterdam, after which the four pilots, Captains Peter Cunningham, Tom Dornan, Lou Starling and 'Dickie' Bird ferried the aircraft to Nairobi. Dornan and Starling trained subsequent courses at Embakasi while Cunningham, nominated as chief pilot of the regional and domestic fleets (F27, DC3 and Rapides), had overall responsibility for the operations. Johnny Johnson organised the engineering and maintenance programmes and was responsible for the high technical standards that E.A.A.C. insisted upon.

1962 had presented the airline with substantial challenges. With the delivery of the third Comet aircraft, VP-KRL, the services to the United Kingdom and Europe were increased from three to seven per week, while those to Pakistan and India were increased from one to two. This imposed a heavy load of responsibility upon the airline's staff to ensure the smooth, efficient and viable introduction of this greatly increased capacity. Under general manager Captain P.A. (Pat) Travers, chief engineer A.E. Robinson, operations manager P.E. (Phil) Henn and commercial manager A.G. Molison, who had been joined by deputy E.F. (Ted) Bates, the transition was, in every respect, achieved successfully; traffic revenue increased markedly by £1,409,539 to £5,791,271 while, despite increased expenditure, the cost per unit of production (the capacity ton mile), fell from E.A.S. 2/71 to E.A.S. 2/62.

The result for the year was a net operating profit of £312,060 (after taking into account a shorter amortisation period, of five years, for the Comets, leaving them after that period with a residual value of 15%). The domestic passenger traffic was up on that for 1961 and there was an improvement in the overall load factor from 55.4% to 57.5%. With the ad hoc introduction of the Fokker F27 Friendships, following the delivery of the first, VP-KSA, on 5th November, towards the end of the year there was a marked upswing in passenger bookings.

At this stage in East African's development, it is interesting to reflect that at that time the loss of only four passengers per service on each of the seven flights per week to Europe and the United Kingdom would result in a loss of revenue of nearly £300,000. Conversely, an increase in the cost of a capacity ton mile of only 14 cents, representing a mere 5% of the unit cost for the year 1962, would result in an increase in expenditure of £300,000.

With the transition from colonial rule to full independence throughout the East African Territories, the requirement for training and Africanisation was paramount. The training organisations concentrated on courses designed to introduce students to airline commercial procedures, but the facilities available were restricted by the need to conserve funds to meet previous commitments for aircraft, spares, and equipment then in use. With the aid of an aptitude testing unit, a great deal of progress was made during the year in recruiting Africans to train for employment with the airline. It continued to be difficult to obtain an adequate number of suitable candidates with higher educational qualifications for training in positions of greater responsibility, but efforts continued to locate and interest suitably qualified Africans.

It was felt that, particularly in engineering, there was little possibility of bridging the gap between artisans and professionally qualified engineers; there seemed to be no flicker of interest in engineering from the higher qualified Africans, many of whom had their eyes firmly focused on political or government appointments.

A great deal had already been done in employing trainee African passenger assistants at main stations and stewards and stewardesses on the aircraft. Training courses for reservations, counter and traffic assistants were in constant progress. It was recognised that success could only be achieved by attracting candidates of a higher educational standard than had been forthcoming in the past, while giving existing staff the opportunity to improve their positions. There always remained the fact that the airline must continue, in the public interest, to maintain the highest international standards, most of which, in the operating field, were prescribed by law.

At Schipol, following the signing of the F27 acceptance, L to R: Captain Lou Starling, Mr Ron Gander (EAA engineering), Captain Tom Dornan, Mr C.E. Smith. November, 1962. (Fokker)

In the engineering department the training of engineering apprentices had continued throughout the year, with response from African students eligible to take up apprenticeships rather disappointing. Every effort had been made to attract young men into this branch of engineering, with comprehensive training facilities at the base qualifications could be obtained locally without the need to use overseas training establishments.

With the third Comet put into service in April, and with the experience gained on the operation of the first two aircraft, it was possible to introduce a new type of maintenance schedule which offered a higher annual utilisation than was possible in the original schedule. The utilisation of each aircraft averaged just over 3,000 hours per annum. Development of the workshop's facilities for the major overhaul of the majority of Comet components and accessories had worked well. The small amount of rectification work required at base and en route still remained an outstanding feature of the Comet 4 aircraft. The approved life of the Avon engine stood then at 3,800 hours between overhauls.

The overhaul of Pratt and Whitney engines for the DC3s continued to function well, although it was now becoming difficult to obtain spares, which increased the cost of overhauling each engine by 35%. This section of engineering had proven to be a good training ground for the African trainees who had progressively been raised to artisan status.

The Canadairs, now with some 30,000 hours flying each since the date of manufacture, were planned to be phased out of service the following year, having

Fokker F27 Friendship, VP-KSA, at Dar es Salaam, 1962.

given good service to the airline, for their class and vintage. They had been the means whereby East African Airways had emerged from a regional African airline to one with successful international routes.

With the introduction of the F27s, at the end of 1962, the preparatory work, such as the drawing up of the maintenance schedule, designing and manufacturing equipment, and re-organising the workshops to deal with the overhaul of practically all the components and accessories of the aircraft, required a considerable effort on behalf of the executive engineers responsible for the forward planning. Plans were drawn up at the end of the year to re-organise the engine overhaul workshops and the test bed site for the overhaul of the F27's Rolls-Royce Dart R.Da.7 propeller turbine engines and it was hoped to have the first of these on the production line by June or July 1963. Important considerations were the economies achieved by doing the work in East Africa and the benefits of apprentice training being extended to encompass turbine engine overhaul.

As the Comet services to the United Kingdom were progressively increased from three to seven flights per week during April, a popular daylight flight was introduced in May, departing Nairobi at 10.15 on Saturdays and reaching London, via Entebbe and Benina, at 20.30 in the evening. Rome was re-introduced into the route pattern in November, in order to meet the increasing demand for European destinations. Benina then ceased to be a crew slip station, crew rest was to be taken in Rome and London.

Uganda became independent on 9th October and East African Airways was put under great pressure with the many extra services and charter flights to convey passengers to and from Entebbe. Staff were posted from other stations to Kampala and Entebbe to cope with the additional traffic. These celebrations preceded the introduction of the Fokker F27 Friendships, which were soon brought in to the inter-city services following their arrival in November and December.

On 24th January, 1962, a small ceremony had taken place at Wilson Airport. In the presence of Sir Alfred Vincent and many of her friends and colleagues of Wilson Airways days, Mrs Florence Wilson watched as the Minister for Commerce, Industry and Communications, Mr Masinde Muliro unveiled a plaque commemorating her services to aviation. He said: "We have come here to do honour to a very great and dear lady. Mrs Wilson's name is a household word in civil aviation circles. Her story is one of great courage, imagination and determination. It is a story of conspicuous and noble services to Kenya and to all East Africa... Wilson Airways was a very successful and a most significant venture. It laid the foundations and largely set the pattern for the future development of air transport in Kenya and in the whole of East Africa".

256 · EAST AFRICAN: AN AIRLINE STORY

Mrs Florence K. Wilson receives a tribute from Mr Muliro, Kenya Minister for Commerce, Industry and Communications, at the unveiling ceremony at the re-named Wilson Airport. Sir Alfred Vincent stands on the left of the picture. 25th January, 1962.
(E.A. Standard)

The plaque which was unveiled by Mrs Wilson. (E.A. Standard)

1963

The past year, 1962, had been the final year in which East African Airways was managed by a purely colonial Board of Directors. Sir Alfred Vincent, however, continued to preside over a board onto which the independent East African governments had nominated their representatives. The changes were as follows:

	1962	1963
Chairman	Sir Alfred Vincent	Sir Alfred Vincent
Members	H.J. Hinchey	H.J. Hinchey
	J.C. Mundy	Abdu C. Faraji
	R.S. Alexander	P.K. Jani
	J.T. Simpson (Uganda)	J.T. Simpson
	K.G. Granville (B.O.A.C.)	K.G. Granville
	W.D. Murray	W.D. Murray
		J.J. Nyagah
		S. Nyanzi
		H.M. Barwani (Zanzibar)

The executive management had not yet been affected by the requirements of Africanisation, due mainly to the continued difficulty in obtaining suitably qualified African candidates to understudy the European management.

The very successful Executive Management team had remained unchanged for several years, and was made up of the following:

General Manager	P.A. Travers
Secretary & Assistant Gen. Mgr.	A.V. Gill
Chief Engineer	A.E. Robinson
Operations Manager	P.E. Henn
Financial Controller	S.G. Choppin
Commercial Manager	A.G. Molison
Sales Manager	J.W. Baines

Colonel M.C.P. Mostert had handed over to Captain Pat Travers during 1962, when after some thirty-two years service to East African aviation, dating back to the day, in 1930, when Mrs Wilson invited him to become a pilot, leading to manager and finally a director in Wilson Airways, he retired to the Cape Province of South Africa.

1963 had opened on a sad note. Captain Bill Fumerton was chief pilot Comet fleet and had converted many of the current pilots onto the type. A no-nonsense Canadian, he was extremely popular with all the crews. It was on a Comet flight to London, where he was travelling as supernumerary crew for a medical check-up, that he began to feel unwell. It was during the five and a half hour Nairobi to Benina sector that one of the stewardesses came forward to the flight deck to report that Bill was not looking too good. The two stewardesses, Barbara Seymour and Heather Jordan, tended to him, while the cockpit crew called Malta for medical advice. The normally busy radio channels quietened as, with one of the girls donning a head-set, a doctor passed what advice he could. Malta would have been the ideal diversion, with its first class hospital facilities, but it was just beyond the range of the Comet. They had to continue to Benina. Watching the fuel, they increased power to the maximum possible in order to speed up their arrival.

It was no good. At just about top of descent the girls reported that Bill was dead. They had called Benina and advised them of the medical emergency, requesting an ambulance to be there on arrival. It was fortunate that the ambulance was provided by the British army that night, as the Comet landed at 02.15, otherwise there would have been severe difficulties. The young R.A.M.C. doctor confirmed that Captain Fumerton was dead on arrival and, in strict confidence, explained the international health and local legal problems that lay before them. To begin with, the aircraft could not proceed. An inquest would have to be convened, which could take several days. Evidence would have to be given by all the crew, who would have to stay in Benghazi until it was completed.

As the group of men stood discussing the problem, it soon became apparent that they could not allow their aircraft and passengers to be marooned in Libya while the local authorities performed obscure legal processes. The army doctor and the crew of that night's Comet service never disclosed to anyone that Bill was taken to the British Military Hospital "unconscious", where he "died" some time after their departure for London.

They landed at London Airport at 06.20 in thick snow. The B.O.A.C. man who met them handed over a message received from Benghazi with the news that Captain Fumerton had passed away in the British Military Hospital.

Captain Bill Fumerton
(Mrs Barbara Fumerton)

In those days the crews were small, very often made up of four male flying crew and four stewardesses. They were very close knit groups, often they led a double life, a stable domestic life while off duty, which would completely change as they worked hard and played hard together. As they travelled up and down the routes they would often talk about their innermost thoughts, which they would never discuss at home. Many crews were able to use the flights as a kind of emotional safety valve, before returning to the reality and pressures of life at home. Often they would make friendships which would last a lifetime.

It is in this context that the shocked and saddened crew of Flight EC718 came together later in the Skyway Hotel for drinks, which developed into a riotous party, or more correctly, a wake. The sadness and gloom which they all felt within them had to be erased and the tension released somehow. One member of the crew, after consuming a number of beers, descended from the fourth floor of the hotel by means of knotted bed sheets. Unfortunately there were not enough of them and his fall was cushioned by the snow on the roof of the car below him. The two girls, who had comforted Bill Fumerton in his last moments released their emotions in the bar lounge as Clive, the resident pianist, accompanied them on the honky-tonk piano. As they departed on the following evening's service, they all felt that they had given Bill the sort of send off which he would have appreciated. Captain Bill Fumerton lies buried in a cemetery near Benghazi, where only the ghosts of the Canadairs and Comets, with their crews of long ago, pass overhead.

On 29th August, an E.A.A.C. DC3, VP-KJT, which had been chartered to carry refugees from Bechuanaland to Tanganyika was burned out, mysteriously, while on the ground at Francistown. A relief aircraft was recalled to Dar es Salaam when it had reached Mbeya. This helped to spur on the demands for action by the African states to the north against the perceived enemy, South Africa.

The event which would probably have the greatest effect upon the future economic strength of the airline occurred in October of 1963. The quadripartite pool, whereby revenues were shared between East African Airways, B.O.A.C., Central African Airways and South African Airways on their common route sectors had provided significant financial advantages to E.A.A.C., it could be argued that being small by comparison with B.O.A.C. and South African Airways, it was the principal beneficiary. On the 12th October, 1963, on instructions from the East African governments, all connections with South Africa were broken, as part of a concerted attack on the apartheid regime. The following day the South African government announced a ban on all East African Airways flights to the Republic. During August, the Security Council of the United Nations had passed a resolution to stop the sale of arms and ammunition to South Africa, but the newly independent African states wanted to demonstrate their "strength" and freedom from the influence of their former colonial masters by taking more resolute action.

So, there would be no more Durban or Johannesburg flights, South African Airways would no longer be permitted to fly north across Africa to Europe, but would be forced to discover new routes with long range aircraft, but they would continue to carry full passenger loads on the long but lucrative route which was to be for them and B.O.A.C., and its successor British Airways, a massive revenue earner for decades.

With the dissolution of the quadripartite pool, new arrangements were made with B.O.A.C. and Air France for the conclusion of bi-partite agreements covering the services between East Africa, Europe and the United Kingdom. At a sweep, all revenue from the passengers through to South Africa, and the former visitors from South Africa, which had been shared with the two major carriers connecting with the south would be lost to E.A.A.C. The network which had held the old British Empire together, which had been pioneered by aviators such as Alan Cobham, Florence Wilson, Mostert, Tom Campbell Black, Aubrey Francombe, Caspareuthus and pilots who still flew the African routes, was unravelling as fast as the old Empire was fading away.

However, the problems still remained in the future. The outstanding feature of 1963 for E.A.A.C. was the substantial increase in East African domestic traffic, of which the principal advance was 26.8 per cent in passenger miles flown over 1962's record. Load ton miles carried on all domestic services jumped by 22.3 per cent, the largest contribution being from the Kenya/Tanganyika Coastal group of services, which had gained 27.3 per cent in 1962. The importance of the latter advance was that those services provided 58.5 per cent of the capacity for all the domestic services and on them was carried 62.7 per cent of the total domestic service's load.

The operations of the international services continued to produce a high level of revenue, with increases in passenger miles of 15.8 per cent, cargo ton miles by 56.1 per cent and mail ton miles by 20.6 per cent. The break up of the quadripartite pool had affected only ten weeks of 1963, so it was not possible to evaluate the losses which may occur as a result. Figures had been influenced by the political changes taking place during the year, bringing about a large number of visitors to the territories. It was appreciated that the severe reduction in the scope of the partnership alone would bring about a reduction in revenue in the immediate future. In addition, other advantages which operated in East African Airways' favour had been lost. Apart from revenues sourced from the pooling of fares on common sectors, losses would be incurred on cargo sales, ground handling services, marketing and ticket sales within South Africa through to the domestic difficulties of losing South African staff, who would be difficult and expensive to replace.

In September E.A.A.C. had entered into a pooling agreement with Air India, which, with increases of 26.4 per cent over 1962 on the Eastern route, promised to reduce competition and bring overall future benefits.

The 1960s had seen, finally, an end to the post war shortages, rationing and general air of austerity in the United Kingdom, by 1963, ten years had passed since sweet and sugar rationing was ended. There was an air of prosperity and large numbers of people were ready to travel on package tours, which the airlines had created to fill the increasing number of seats on the new airliners. There had been investment in the coastal areas of Kenya, at Mombasa and Malindi, to provide modern hotels for the overseas visitors. With an end to unrest in the country, travel agents had created safari excursions to the Mara, Tsavo and outlying areas of the country, giving the tourists a taste of what it had been like for the millionaire big-game hunters of thirty years ago. In fact, a whole industry was being created to foster the legend of the "East African Safari". A holiday in East Africa became synonymous with the Swahili word *Safari*, many package tourists would return home believing that they knew what a *Safari* was. It has now come to mean, universally, a particular form of holiday in East Africa, listed in the travel brochures in addition to the Caribbean or the Costa Brava, advertised by the marketing men as "Sun, Sea and Safari".

A typical 25 days holiday package at that time costing £340 per person for two persons from London on the East African Airways Comet, economy class, was advertised as follows:

Under a darkening sky, the gleaming white upper surfaces of Comet 4, VP-KRL, are displayed in this photograph taken at Embakasi in 1963. Parked alongside is F27 Friendship, VP-KSA, which had been delivered the previous year. (Mr Tim Nightingale)

*Nairobi - Nyeri - Nakuru - Limuru - Namanga - Arusha
- Ngorongoro - Lake Manyara - Mombasa - Malindi*

ITINERARY

1st day .... Leave London by E.A.A.C. Economy jet air service.

2nd day .... Arrive Nairobi (Norfolk Hotel)

3rd day .... Nairobi. Drive by car to the Nairobi National Park.

4th day .... Leave Nairobi for four day tour via Thika, where the Chania Falls will be seen, to Nyeri, arriving at the Outspan Hotel for lunch. In the afternoon proceed to the famous Treetops Hotel built in the branches of a giant forest tree, where visitors can spend a fascinating night watching big game.

5th day .... Return to Nyeri (Outspan Hotel).

6th day .... Drive from Nyeri via Thomson's Falls to Nakuru. Night at Stags head Hotel.

7th day .... Drive to the Lake Nakuru bird sanctuary. Lunch at Nakuru, then continue along the Rift Valley to the Escarpment, Limuru and back to Nairobi (Norfolk Hotel).

8th day .... Leave Nairobi for six-day tour. Drive through the Masai Reserve to the picturesque Namanga River Hotel, for the night.

9th day .... Namanga. Early morning game-viewing drive in the Amboseli National Reserve. Among the animals most frequently seen are rhino, elephant, lion, wildebeest, hartebeest, Grant's gazelle, Thomson's gazelle, etc. Return to the Namanga Hotel for the night.

10th day .... Drive from Namanga via Longido to Arusha, situated at the foot of Mount Meru (14,979ft) for lunch. Continue though a spectacular mountain area to the rim of the Ngorongoro Crater (the second largest in the world) and one of the most wonderful sights in Africa (Ngorongoro Lodge).

11th day .... Ngorongoro. Whole day drive in the 120-square mile crater to view game.

12th day .... Continue to the wonderful surroundings of Lake Manyara, where the hotel has unparalleled views of the Great Rift Valley. (Lake Manyara Hotel).

13th day .... Return via Arusha to Namanga for lunch and continue in the afternoon to Nairobi. (Norfolk Hotel).

14th day .... Leave by plane for Mombasa (Nyali Beach Hotel).

15th day .... By air to Malindi (Sinbad Hotel).

16th-21st day ...... Malindi. At Leisure.

22nd day .... Leave by plane for Nairobi. (Norfolk Hotel).

23rd day .... Nairobi. At Leisure.

24th day .... Leave Nairobi by air.

25th day .... Arrive London.

Everything on the tour was included, all air travel, surface transport, full-board accommodation, meals en route and sightseeing tours.

Whatever the entrepreneurs did to capture the tourist market, Africa was unchanging, and the visitors went home satisfied, for no one could visit the extraordinary countries of East Africa, each different in its majestic beauty, without being moved by the immensity of its horizons, the magnificence of the natural surroundings, the empty, palm-fringed coral sand beaches and, inland, the grandeur of the animal life, roaming freely as no where else on earth.

With the introduction of the F27 Friendship aircraft, the package tours could take advantage of the increased capacity available and enhanced comfort of the modern cabins compared with the DC3s. With the opening of embassies following independence, an increase in inter-territorial travel was experienced during the year, which added to the overall growth in both local and overseas travel generated by the changed status of the territories.

H.R.H. Prince Philip, representing the Queen at the independence celebrations in Kenya and Zanzibar, was flown throughout the territories in an F27 Friendship of E.A.A.C. Elaborate preparations were made for these historic occasions.

A representative from the R.A.F. Queen's Flight visited Nairobi to brief the airline on royal protocol and conventions, and to vet the pilots and engineering standards. A crew of six was selected under the command of Captain Peter Cunningham with Captain Lou Starling as his co-pilot and Senior Purser Gordon Evans in charge of the cabin, assisted by Kenyan Steward John Muthiani. Every effort was made to ensure an efficient operation. The airline was told that H.R.H. wished the aircraft to start as soon as he boarded, no matter whether this meant that he would arrive early at his next stop. On the other hand, the crew was well aware that the dignitaries waiting at Zanzibar and Nairobi would confidently expect the aircraft to arrive on time.

The first short sector, on 9th December, 1963, from Dar es Salaam to Zanzibar operated precisely on schedule. Two days later, however, when preparing for the flight to Nairobi, the crew were surprised to hear the sirens of the prince's motor cycle escort approaching the airport some thirty minutes earlier than anticipated. Hastily moving out to the aircraft, on which all pre-flight checks had been completed, the pilots watched in consternation, as H.R.H. quickly shook hands with a line of officials and immediately boarded the aircraft.

The starboard engine was started as he did so. As soon as the steps were removed, the port engine burst into life. Moments later, as the prince's personal standard was lowered from the cockpit window, and the F27 taxied slowly to the runway. Captain Cunningham looked at his watch and calculated that he had twenty-seven minutes to lose. He instructed Lou Starling to re-plan the flight to overhead Mombasa, instead of the direct track to Nairobi. That would take an extra twelve minutes. A slow climb would add a little more time.

As it happened, the aircraft arrived over Mombasa a minute earlier than estimated; another thirteen minutes had still to be lost, somehow. Lou Starling calculated the airspeed that would have to be flown from there to Embakasi. This was slower than the aircraft could safely fly. Slight diversions from track and an unusually wide circuit on arrival would be necessary but the prince must not know his flight was being manoevered in this way. As soon as he was able to contact the Nairobi radar controller, Captain Cunningham told him he wanted radar steers that would bring the aircraft over the ILS outer marker at precisely four minutes to six. He instructed the controller to make no comment other than to advise each new heading and clearance.

No sooner had he done so than H.R.H. appeared on the flight deck. Purser Evans made sure he was safely strapped in the third crew seat and Captain Starling gave him a headset so that he could follow the progress of the flight. There were numerous thunderstorms in the area and the pilots hoped that these, coupled with normal radar approach procedures, would explain the circuitous routing they were about to take.

Fortunately, the controller juggled the aircraft so that it arrived exactly as requested. Consulting his stop-watch, Peter Cunningham was determined to bring

HRH the Duke of Edinburgh takes leave of the crew at Khartoum, following the Fokker Friendship flights associated with independence celebrations in Zanzibar and Kenya. L to R: Captain Peter Cunningham, Captain Lou Starling, licensed ground engineer Ray Kearns, (in uniform for the occasion, on which he accompanied the aircraft to Khartoum, in case repairs were necessary), Purser Gordon Evans, Steward John Muthiani. The obscured figure last in line was David Drummond, the EAA chief of security.

(Capt Peter Cunningham)

the aircraft to a halt at exactly 6 p.m. He knew which parking position had been planned for his arrival and judged his taxying route and speed accordingly. What he did not know until the last moment was that the airport authorities had decided that he should park elsewhere, on the edge of the apron, close beside the VIP enclosure, in view of the torrential rain which was falling. As he switched the engines off, he was disappointed to see that he was fractionally late. Although the media credited him with a faultless on-time arrival, he later received a telephone call from his boss, Captain Phillip Henn, asking why he had been thirty seconds late!

After such complications, the final sector to Khartoum where H.R.H. was due to be met by B.O.A.C., was plain sailing. Only the cabin crew were disappointed as the prince ate very little from what must have been one of the finest meals ever served on this comparatively small aircraft. On disembarking, H.R.H. shook hands with the crew, each of whom was presented with a signed photograph.

There had been a number of meetings during the year to decide upon new aircraft paint schemes and corporate logo for the airline. In December the DC3 and F27 aircraft were seen emerging from the engineering paint shop with new tail logos, depicting the E.A.A.C. lion in the sun emblem above the four flags of Kenya, Uganda, Tanganyika and Zanzibar. This was one of several experimental paint schemes which were to emerge over the following months, which would be finalised after twelve months of trials. Since 1962, the Corporation's house style had been changing, in keeping with the 1960's fashion. The formal E.A.A.C. had given way to E.A.A., and would later, following the marketing adviser's proposals, be written without punctuation, EAA, before the final "East African" was adopted.

The beginning of 1963 saw the three F27 Friendship aircraft phased onto scheduled services at a fairly high utilisation for aircraft used on domestic and regional services. Utilisation was at the rate of 6.15 hours per aircraft per day per annum. The maintenance of the Friendships was carried out on an equalised plan, which had been evolved to give the best flexibility for high utilisation. In these first months the aircraft had proved to be very reliable on the routes and had required very little maintenance away from base.

The development of the engineering workshops to overhaul practically all the accessories and components of the Friendships had gone smoothly during the year. One of the more important developments was to extend the base facilities to include the overhaul of Rolls-Royce Dart turbine engines for the F27s. The Comets had operated very satisfactorily during the year with the cost of spares being little more than estimated and the engineering manpower requirements being less than was originally anticipated. Utilisation of the Comets had been a consistent nine hours per day per aircraft per annum. There had been no change in the overhaul procedures for the Pratt and Whitney engines of the DC3s for E.A.A.C. and Aden Airways, which continued to function smoothly. The DC3s continued to operate satisfactorily during the year and were still in excellent condition, having been constantly maintained in accordance with manufacturers Douglas and F.A.A. directives, so far as those publications affected DC3 aircraft.

There was, in fact, one serious incident concerning a DC3, VP-KKI, on 9th April, during take-off from Mafia Island, on a flight to Lindi. Captain Brewer and First Officer Fleming experienced an engine failure shortly after leaving the ground. The port engine failed, one cylinder of the radial Pratt and Whitney blew off and, at the same time, moved the cowlings forward, so as Brewer feathered the engine, the cowlings fouled the propeller and split open, "rather like peel from an orange", as he described it. The weather at the time was poor, and as he turned the aircraft to return to Mafia, a storm had moved in and completely closed the airfield. The only option was to divert to Dar es Salaam, flying on one engine. The fire warning light had come on, but it went out again after a short interval. There was no need to fire the extinguishers. The drag from the cowlings was tremendous, making the task of controlling the aircraft and maintaining single-engine safety speed extremely difficult. At intervals the cowlings would inch open even further, reducing the airspeed each time. It took them about an hour to fly the ninety miles, "the longest hour I have ever experienced", said Brewer.

The weather at Dar es Salaam was marginal, with rain and minimal visibility. Brewer decided that if he should miss the approach, an overshoot on one engine under the circumstances would be impossible, so he would land on the grass alongside the runway, if necessary. Fortunately the landing was successfully accomplished on the runway where the aircraft was brought to a halt. It being impossible to taxi a DC3 on one engine, it had to be towed away. The engine and cowling assembly were damaged beyond repair and immediately written off.

The Canadairs were phased out of the scheduled services at the beginning of the year and both remaining aircraft, VP-KOI and VP-KOJ, were hired to another operator, Britair (E.A.) Ltd, on a bare hull basis for fairly long periods during the year. Both aircraft were advertised for sale, together with spares, but it was felt that with so few of these aircraft in operation, there was not a good chance of selling them.

On the night of 30th May, the airline's staff celebrated the departure of the Canadairs with what was described as the "biggest company party we ever had". Planning for the party included a special draught beer produced by the "Tusker" brewery, normally only a provider of German-style bottled lager. The theme had been devised as an Italian street, together with genuine street signs, dustbins and whatever else the crew members had been able to spirit out of Rome. Under a banner emblazoned "FINITO CANADAIR", the assembled guests danced through the night to the music of two live bands.

Later in the year, the Canadairs disappeared. They had been acquired by the Rhodesian Air Force, whose pilots, under their C.O., Harry Coleman, stayed in Nairobi for a couple of weeks, prior to flying the aircraft back to Southern Rhodesia.

At the end of a momentous year, during which the Union Flag of Great Britain had been lowered for the last time over the countries for which E.A.A.C. was now the National Airline, it was able to report a record net operating profit of £461,071. During the year, since E.A.A.C. continued to undertake all transit maintenance and rectification for B.O.A.C., several of the airline's engineers were sent to England to be trained on the new B.O.A.C. airliners which would be operating through East Africa. They were the Vickers VC10s. The training of these engineers on the VC10s underlined the statement of Sir Alfred Vincent at the end of 1963:

> "The Corporation is very much aware of the necessity to remain competitive, especially in the field of international operations, and to this end a technical committee is to be set up which will be charged with the duty of making recommendations in respect of the ultimate replacement aircraft for international operations. This task on the surface may appear comparatively easy - an evaluation of the various types of aircraft contending for such a role. However, the underlying implications are much wider, some of the points to be considered being: the long term requirements of the East African countries in regard to forecast traffic potentials and new points of call: the future plans of aircraft manufacturers in production of new types which can so quickly and easily render a fleet obsolescent before its allotted time: the provision of finance for such a project which would require a minimum of £9,000,000 for three aircraft and spares".

With the coming of independence to Kenya on 12th December 1963, many Europeans believed that scores would now be settled. Some had already departed, fearful of what may happen. East African Airways had suffered the loss of a number of staff through the unsettled atmosphere and the need to change attitudes at independence. The new President, Jomo Kenyatta, had taken cognisance of these fears and, although it could be said that he was being pragmatic, needing the expertise of the Europeans for many years to come, there would be no known instance of revenge towards the British, who had exiled him for so long in the barren wastes of Lodwar.

Speaking to a group of white farmers, shortly after independence Kenyatta said: "If I have done a mistake to you in the past, it is for you to forgive me. If you have done a mistake to me, it is for me to forgive you. The Africans cannot say that the Europeans have done all the wrong and the Europeans cannot say that the Africans have done all the wrong. The good thing is to be able to forget and forgive one another. You have something to forget, just as I have."

Mzee Jomo Kenyatta was a giant among men; it is doubtful if Kenya would have achieved the orderly development which followed independence without his leadership and his constant cry of *Harambee* - "Let us all pull together".

1964

Although, nominally, Britain had now washed its hands of the East African Territories, with the granting of full independence there were still large investments of British capital in addition to massive aid, to bolster the infant nations. The world was split between the communist powers of the Soviet Union and China, and the West. Each would attempt to exert influence in the interests of its own ideology.

Britain had undertaken to protect the new Commonwealth countries of East Africa, if *in extremis*, it were to be called upon for assistance. At the beginning of 1964, the lights were burning late in Whitehall as the generals and Foreign Office officials calculated how to gather forces to deal with the worsening situation in Cyprus. As attention was distracted by the possibility of a Greek - Turkish conflagration in the Mediterranean, horror struck on the Indian Ocean island of Zanzibar, in January, where African rebels, backed by the communist powers, rose up and, in an orgy of bloodshed, massacred thousands of Arabs and Indians within the space of hours. The British were taken by surprise, their forces spread thinly - almost as if it had been planned, British troops still in East Africa were otherwise engaged putting down mutinies of the former Kings African Rifles, now the Kenya, Uganda and Tanganyika army, who, no longer officered by Britons, suffered tribal and other grievances over pay and promotion.

East African Airways suffered some dislocation to its services due to the military unrest and a number of special flights were undertaken for the governments. Confusion and lack of information at specific airfields required a high level of courage, tact, and common sense on behalf of the crews. In one instance a DC3 crew at Dar es Salaam were forced out of their crew-bus at gun point by mutinous soldiers, and by removing their uniform jackets and badges, they managed to avoid further trouble.

Alistair Mackenzie was manager for Tanganyika and Zanzibar at the time of the revolution. On the morning of 17th January he had received instructions to organise two shuttles to rescue stranded passengers from Zanzibar. The E.A.A. station superintendent in Zanzibar, Mr Hasham, stressed that the aircraft should arrive empty. The first Dakota arrived back at Dar es Salaam just after mid-day. A further two, a DC3 and a Friendship were organised for the afternoon. At about three o'clock in the afternoon, Mackenzie received a telephone call to transport seventy 'passengers' to Zanzibar. The Tanganyika government official, Mr Maggidi, confirmed that these were Police Field Force.

This 'request' contravened the conditions which Zanzibar had imposed upon the flights, in addition, there were no satisfactory guarantees, as to the safety of the aircraft and the legality of such an undertaking (it was in contravention of the civil Air Navigation legislation to carry armed police or troops in a civil aircraft). Mackenzie and everyone else knew that the Government of Zanzibar had been taken over by force of arms. No clear decisions could be obtained from Mr Molison or Mr Bates in Nairobi or the government officials concerned. Despite threats from the Minister of Home Affairs, Lusinde, Mackenzie refused to clear the flight until he had received proper guarantees. Lusinde then proceeded to instruct the captain of the DC3, Captain L.N. Anderson, to depart, with himself and twenty-five armed police on board.

At 11.15 p.m., Mackenzie was served with a Deportation Order to leave the country within twelve hours.

After consultation with the chairman, belated permission had been passed to Dar es Salaam, but not until Lusinde had pressurised Captain Anderson to depart.

Submissions to President Nyerere by the Corporation eventually permitted Mackenzie to return to East Africa from England, where he spent six months waiting for the outcome. It was, however, thought wise not to return to Tanganyika, and he was appointed manager Uganda before taking the post of traffic manager, based in Nairobi.

The African population of Zanzibar had, in the past, been dependent upon the Arabs for their economic wellbeing, such as it was, and, although they were the descendants of slaves who had been cruelly imported from mainland Africa, there had not until now been any sign of an uprising. When it came, it was probably the worst example of indiscriminate slaughter seen in Africa in modern times. In the narrow alleys of Zanzibar, the open drains ran with the blood of the descendants of the slave-masters. The British, who could have stopped the uprising with a battalion of troops, were otherwise engaged, and by the time they were in a position to act, the Sultan had been overthrown and had fled with his wives to Hastings, and the country was in the hands of a communist protege, Abeid Karume.

Zanzibar had a population of 300,000 at independence, no one could estimate how many thousands had died or fled the island during the Revolution. But it was clear that the majority of those who ran the island's economy, which, in any event, was primarily based upon clove production, had vanished. The East Germans and Chinese were moving in fast, the mainland Rulers, Kenyatta and Nyerere were extremely worried about the nature of the Revolution on the off-shore island, which was becoming an armed camp of the communist powers. There was a great deal of diplomatic activity, with British and American intervention.

Karume found that his position as President of Zanzibar was extremely precarious, depending upon the support of a hardened Marxist, Abdul-Rahman Mohammed Babu, who was virtually a front-man for the Chinese. President Nyerere of Tanganyika, fearful of the consequences to his own country of this situation, offered Karume to form a union between their two countries. Karume saw this as a safeguard and an escape from the jaws of the Chinese and East German political commissars, and accepted. In April the Union of Zanzibar and Tanganyika came into being. The new country was to be called Tanzania.

In pursuing the policy of training and Africanisation, vigorous efforts continued to be made and some progress was made during the year. Africans possessing the basic educational qualifications necessary to absorb the technical knowledge and ability to gain experience so essential in the highly specialised airline industry continued to be in short supply. Nevertheless, special recruitment drives to attract into the airline more Africans with School Certificate or Higher School Certificate qualifications were undertaken. Visits and lectures to students in secondary schools resulted in interviews being conducted in Kenya, Uganda and Tanzania and in all cases the outcome seemed at the time to be encouraging. The 'on the job' training being undertaken in various departments was not showing very positive results, but it was accepted that the acquisition of skills was a long process. A good example of the special airline task to be encountered lay in the accounts department, where knowledge of specialised techniques was required, connected with the rules and regulations governing passenger fares and freight rates, most of which were governed by the IATA Resolutions, as well as the relevant background information for the efficient conduct of normal day to day accounting practices.

Additional Africans continued to be employed as stewards and stewardesses. A mock-up of the Comet interior was on order to assist with training in cabin procedures. There were difficulties in recruiting aircrew, due mainly to the unsettled political atmosphere and the general feeling that the future in Africa was uncertain. In addition, the world's airlines were busy re-equipping with new and larger airliners and there was not, during this period, an over supply of pilots. The significant event of 1964, in this respect, was the recruitment of the airline's first two trainee African pilots. Basic pilot training, with further training to Commercial Pilots Licence was contracted with the Airwork school at Perth, in Scotland and in October the first four African cadet pilots commenced their training.

Pressure was being put on the management to fill with Africans the middle and higher executive posts, which had, in the past, been filled by expatriate officers, and were now continually falling vacant due to the Europeans resigning from the airline. The problem then arose that the posts had to be filled; there were few suitable Africans, so the pressures dictated either a replacement European, which would require an explanation to disapproving African board members, or employment of an unsuitable African candidate. Plans were laid to recruit up to eighteen Africans to be sent to Airwork for pilot training in 1965, under a government scheme, to which the airline would contribute £14,320 plus free transportation.

Captain Pat Travers resigned his position as general manager on 31st August, taking up the newly created position of technical director. The new general manager

Captain Leo Davidson at the controls of the Comet 4.

was Ugandan Wilson Kyobe. Kyobe had had no experience in the airline industry, but was one of a small number of Africans with an impressive CV. He had been engineer-in-chief to the Uganda Ministry of Works prior to his appointment. From 1949 to 1951 he had attended the Public Works Department Engineering School in Kampala, from where he went on to obtain his B.Sc. in engineering at the University College, Cardiff in 1954.

Captain Phil Henn resigned from the airline at the end of October and was replaced as operations manager and chief pilot by Captain Leo Davidson, DFC. Leo Davidson, as one of the six Kenya born R.A.F. pilots selected to fly the first East African Airways DH89A Rapides from England in 1945, had been in the airline from the start. A dark curly haired, quietly spoken, totally competent captain and a thorough gentleman, he was liked and admired by all those who knew him.

With a Ugandan heading the executive management, the board continued to change throughout the year, Keith Granville, the B.O.A.C. designate, departed in May, to be replaced by Mr Gilbert Lee. The final change, which came on 31st December would put the seal upon the new order, and close a chapter of history. 1964 had been the most successful year in the history of East African Airways, a year in which it recorded a net operating profit of £510,373. It was a fitting tribute to the departure of Sir Alfred Vincent as he stepped down from the chairmanship of the airline he had served for over nineteen years, during fifteen of which he had been chairman.

It had been agreed by the East African Community heads that the senior executives of the airline should always be allocated in the following manner: the chairman should be provided by Tanzania, the general manager by Uganda and the assistant general manager by Kenya. This tended to reflect Kenya's other advantages in having the headquarters of the airline based on its territory. Sir Alfred Vincent was replaced by Chief Abdulla Said Fundikira. A Cambridge graduate, Chief Fundikira had a sound background in African administrative and political affairs. He had was a member of the Tanganyika Legislative Council and had been Tanganyika's Minister of Justice from 1961 to 1963. Other appointments included chairmanship of the Tanganyika Development Corporation, and presidency of the Tanganyika Red Cross.

It seemed, that with the appointment of Chief Fundikira, a man with discernible presence, a suitable conduit had been found for the difficult business, for the airline, of serving three masters, although there were whispers from those who followed the affairs of Tanzanian politics that Fundikira was not on good terms with President Nyerere, who had appointed him in order to "get him out of Tanzania". The lines between truth and bazaar gossip were very difficult to identify. The third government nominee, for the post of assistant general manager would be Musa Amalemba from Kenya. Amalemba had been the only African in the colonial cabinet, holding the portfolio of Housing Minister in 1958. After working for the Army Education Corps, he became a journalist on the *East African Standard* and was a councillor on the Nairobi City Council. He joined East African Airways in 1963 as an international relations officer, and was later appointed international relations manager. His main brief was the implementation of Africanisation throughout the airline.

With the coming of independence, all Air Service Agreements had been suspended and, consequently, delegations had been busy renegotiating agreements with a number of states. In October a new commercial manager, R.E. Young, took over

A highly polished Comet 4 is admired by three young passengers. Nairobi, 1964.

from the outgoing E.F. (Ted) Bates and was immediately engaged in implementing new agreements which were concluded with the United Kingdom, United Arab Republic, Ethiopia, Scandinavia, the Federal Republic of Germany and the Republic of the Sudan, Italy and Belgium. M. Amalemba's rather grand title of International

Stewardesses Rosie Chettyar, Naomi Amakowa and Sheila Smith in the B.O.A.C. style uniform in April, 1964. Note experimental logo on the fin of F27, 5H-AAI.

Relations within the commercial department did, in fact, embrace a field of quite busy activity, necessitating a good deal of travel, meetings and subsequent paper work.

Special tariffs relating to the empire cabotage status were swept away in April, when fares between Kenya, Uganda and Tanzania on the one hand and the United Kingdom on the other, were adjusted to fall into line with international fares between East Africa and Europe.

On all scheduled services during 1964 the total number of passengers carried rose by 2.9 per cent over the previous year to reach an all time record of 236,407. Post Office mail at 1,134 tons showed an increase of 11.7 per cent over the previous twelve months. Cargo reflected a 21.3 per cent improvement with 4,857 tons carried.

Other than the acquisition of the fourth Friendship in February, the composition of the airline's fleet remained unchanged, as did the overall load factor at 56.3 per cent. With more capacity on offer the available seat miles showed a considerable increase from 403,767,000 to 413,718,000.

On the international routes passengers carried rose by 4.1 per cent to 74,326. In October, twice weekly Comet services were introduced to Cairo and a once weekly Comet frequency to Addis Ababa.

Within East Africa 2.4 per cent more passengers were recorded with a total of 162,081 being carried during the year. A special night tourist service was introduced in May between Nairobi and Mombasa primarily for the carriage of newspapers

After a Comet night-flight from London, stewardesses Janet Chamberlain and Mary Loe on arrival at Nairobi.
(Mrs Mary Breuker née Loe)

and with limited passenger accommodation. The early timings and experimental low fare attracted a number of people who might otherwise have taken the overnight train.

With the introduction of Comets onto the Cairo service, crews were accommodated at the Nile Hilton. One night, Paddy Murray and two or three of his crew colleagues decided to go next door to the Semiramus Hotel for a drink. Several drinks later, in a merry mood, they emerged into the night, and walked towards their hotel. As they approached the entrance, Murray noticed a large shiny limousine, which he recognised as that of the American ambassador, parked outside. Presuming that the ambassador was inside, attending a cocktail party, Murray approached the Egyptian chauffeur saying that they had just come down from the party and the ambassador had said that he should drive them to a restaurant, then return to collect him. The chauffeur swallowed the story, hook, line and sinker. The crew, now intoxicated by their audacity, piled into the ambassador's car. The two stewardesses, sitting in the front, discovered a red telephone and picking it up, one of them shouted, "Is that the White House? I wish to speak to the President!" The chauffeur was not at all impressed by this and by now had smelt a rat. Realising that he was in serious personal trouble, he attempted to turn round, but Paddy Murray told him they were nearly there. On arriving at the restaurant, he was in a dreadful panic, "I have worked eighteen years for the Americans, and now I will lose my job", he wailed. He even refused the ten Egyptian pounds they offered him, so he must have been genuinely worried.

On another night, Murray, who seemed frequently to participate in those more outrageous escapades, was dining at a smart French restaurant in Cairo together with Captain Drew, Frank MacNabb and a stewardess, Dorothy (Dot) Cooper, who was a ball of fire and as full of fun as Paddy Murray. Sitting opposite them was a tall, handsome man, who they were fascinated to see was spoon feeding his beautiful female companion in an obvious demonstration of affection. This soon proved to be too much of a performance for the irreverent aircrew onlookers and they fell about themselves in fits of giggles. The gentleman opposite quickly became angered by this display of bad manners, and, getting up from his table, he approached them and said, "You all seem to be very interested in what is going on at my table, so, for your information, my name is ***** and that pretty lady with me is my wife. I am forty-nine years old and I am an English actor taking part in a film called *Gordon of Khartoum* – and I have a black belt in Judo."

The four crew looked in silence as the actor spoke to them. There was a pause after he had finished, then Dot Cooper said, "My name is Dotty Cooper, and I am a stewardess with East African Airways. I am twenty-five years old and I also have a black belt – a suspender belt." This took him aback, and not wishing to get embroiled with what appeared to be a group of rough unsophisticates, he returned to his table. Murray, who had an ability to pour charm onto choppy waters, asked Roger Drew if he should go over and "sort him out". Without waiting for a reply, he went across and invited the actor and his wife to join them, which, after a few moments, they did. The company proved to be congenial, and, as the evening passed, they all had a most enjoyable, although unexpected, night out in Cairo.

In April, tragedy had struck as Captain Gene T. Brokensha operated the service connecting the small Indian Ocean islands. On landing a DC3 at Kilwa, on 27th April, in a difficult cross-wind, the aircraft swung off the centre-line of the runway. There had been heavy rainfall during the previous night and the sides of the crushed coral runway, inside the edge markings, had softened, and the port wheel sank in, whereupon the propeller struck the ground and broke off. The broken propeller penetrated the cockpit and Brokensha was killed instantly. The aircraft was brought to a stop by his first officer, Tommy Turk. Understandably, it took First Officer Turk a long time to recover from the shock of this terrible accident.

1965

East African Airways had been one of the last airlines to purchase the de Havilland Comet. While it was a superb aircraft, with an almost perfect power to weight ratio, it was unable to carry enough fuel to make the long flights to Europe without intermediate stops. The airlines competing on the routes were equipped with Boeing 707 and DC8 aircraft, which, with runway improvements being made all the time, were becoming able to lift greater passenger loads, making the Comet, with its small cabin, less competitive. On the special 'hot and high' African routes a new threat to East African Airway's competitive position emerged as B.O.A.C. and B.U.A. brought their Vickers VC10s into operation through Nairobi.

East African Airways had been engaged in a long study of the future requirements, needing vast financial investment in order to replace the intercontinental fleet of Comets. The considerations were heavy and required a great deal of faith in the ability of the airline to continue earning profits sufficiently large to repay the huge loans which would be required. The fact that the British government was still behind the emergent countries of East Africa, enabled Vickers Armstrong (British Aircraft Corporation) to present the VC10 as a natural progression from the Comet, with a lease purchase plan backed by British Government guarantees. The technical committee which had been formed to find a solution to the problem had reduced the selection to one of three types – the Douglas DC8, the Boeing 707-320C and the Vickers VC10. In March, 1965, the committee, unsurprisingly, recommended that the corporation purchase three Super VC10 aircraft, worth, together with spares, nearly £11 million. Before the end of the month an agreement was signed between Chief Fundikira and the vice-chairman, Air Marshall Sir Geoffrey Tuttle, of the British Aircraft Corporation, Weybridge Division, for delivery commencing August and September, 1966, with a third in March, 1967.

Chief Fundikira said "This is an historic moment in the development of East African Airways... the acquisition of the Super VC10 will enable our airline to more than treble its capacity".

Perhaps it was the competitive spirit enhanced by B.O.A.C.'s superior VC10 aircraft which provoked Captain Leslie and his crew to consider a direct flight on 24th February, 1965, after a delay to their Comet operating the EC705 service, scheduled to route London-Rome-Nairobi. There was no record of a Comet having flown non-stop the 4,250 statute miles which separated London and Nairobi.

After checking that there were no passengers for Rome, or to be picked up, Leslie gave instructions for the Comet to be refuelled to the top of the tanks, and they prepared to depart. In addition to Captain Leslie, the crew were First Officer Jerry Sirley, E/O Tim Nightingale and N/O Barry Oram.

Climbing unrestricted to high altitude, they set course for Nairobi. They flight planned so that if there was insufficient fuel to reach Nairobi, routing abeam Khartoum, they would land there, if necessary. With a continuous, high altitude cruise the fuel flow was reduced to a minimum, so that continuing with their flight, they saw, as the dawn came up, the glistening snows of Kilimanjaro from 250 miles away. They landed at Nairobi some nine hours and five minutes after leaving London the night before.

Even with the non-stop flight, Tim Nightingale, the engineer, found that when he got home his wife had left for work. Deciding that he deserved his after duty beer even more than usual, he went to the fridge to select a cold Tusker and, on opening the door, was confronted by the family dog, staring at him from the shelf. His wife, in the week during which he had been away, had failed to save the poor animal from some illness and it had passed away. She had put the body in the fridge to await her husband's return.

When news of the Super VC10's imminent arrival percolated among the crews, there was a general belief that with its superior range, there would no longer be a requirement for the northbound crew slip at Rome. This urged everyone to make an effort to see more of Italy while it was still possible. The Pilots' Association produced a typed brochure, with the title *High Flying and Low Living*. This guide gave all the information one might need to find restaurants, congenial 'pubs' and establishments off the beaten tourist track. Taxi fares and bus routes were quoted, allowing the brave to venture beyond even Rome to the nearby towns of Ostia, Lido de Roma, Civitavecchia, Anzio and Frascati. Winter skiing trips to Termonila were extremely popular, until Paddy Murray broke his leg, following which Andrew Gill, the Corporation's secretary and assistant general manager, let it be known that he would frown heavily upon sports which might prejudice the Corporation's operations. Visits were made to all the islands, Elba, Giglio, Ponza, Ischia and Capri. With excellent train services, they could visit Naples in two hours, Florence and Pisa were a little further.

Navigator Bob Gallon recalls the morning that the entire crew got up early to visit the grave of Robert the Bruce at Frascati.* They popped into a local bar on arrival to revive their spirits after the early start and, they later admitted to their

---

*In fact, it was the tomb of Bonnie Prince Charlie, which they had failed to visit.

shame, they never did get to find the grave. Crews would stay at the Hotel Commodore, near the central railway station in Rome during the winter months. In the summer they would move to the Hotel ENALC (Every Night A Little Crumpet was the favoured acronym) in Ostia. The hotel was an Italian government training establishment for hotel staff, who came from all over Europe, including some from the United Kingdom. Next door was the popular "Silver Wings Club", the social club of British European Airways. It is not difficult to imagine why Rome was a popular crew slip station.

After nineteen years' service with East African Airways, the former general manager, Captain Pat Travers, left the corporation in June to take up the position of managing director of Bahamas Airways. With the conclusion of the Super VC10 agreement, his guiding position as technical director and close involvement with the project, was ended and the affairs of his office would be dealt with by Mr Kyobe and Mr Amalemba. Since he joined the airline as a pilot in 1946, Travers had seen the airline's revenue grow from £450,000 per year to £8,500,000 in 1964. "I cannot think of any other airline which has shown a profit for the past ten years" he said, "I don't think I can ever remember a time when we have sat back and said 'That's it' – that is why the Corporation is in the position it is in at the moment". Captain Travers stayed only a few months with Bahamas Airways before returning to Africa to take up the position of chief executive and general manager of Central African Airways, in September, 1965.

In January, 1965, following a constitutional committee's findings, the aircraft belonging to East African Airways were divided up between the three states, since prior to independence they had all been registered in Kenya. The old British Empire registration letters of VP, which had been allocated to the East African Territories in the early 1930s, was now abandoned, and the new I.C.A.O. airframe identification codes were allocated. The aircraft would now be identified by the following codes:

Tanzania	5H-
Uganda	5X-
Kenya	5Y-

The training and Africanisation was accelerating and the programme had been reinforced by the appointment of a sub-committee of the Board charged with the duty of constantly reviewing progress, to enable the Board to report regularly to the Common Services Organisation. In addition to standing commitments, a further sum of £25,000 was put aside with the general purpose of 'supplementing the requirements of Africanisation'. Africanisation was a political priority, which took precedence over the sensible requirements of the airline. As the months passed, it became clear to those who were charged with the operation of the airline, and the future operational planning, that their task was to become ensnared with difficulties as the Africanisation policy came into conflict with real manpower requirements.

With the expansion of the airline the labour force had substantially increased, shown as follows:

	Africans	Asians	Europeans	Total
1965	1859	669	514	3042
1960	756	481	522	1759

The figure of 514 Europeans includes 387 expatriate staff living in East Africa. In 1960 the figure was 381. During a period during which the revenue had grown from £4 million to nearly £9 million, it is surprising that only six additional expatriate staff were employed.

Expatriate staff by departments was shown as follows:

Flight Operations	
Flying Crew	161
Ground General	17
Engineering	102
Commercial	99
Accounts	5
Administration	3
	387

The airline continued to sponsor, jointly with the three East African governments, *ab initio* training of up to eighteen African pilots per annum and would provide employment to the successful candidates. It was hoped that this scheme would gain momentum in 1966, when the first group of cadet pilots returned. Two pilots who had been flying on the DC3 (Kiwanuka) and F27 (Kitende) were sent for further training, in order to upgrade their basic Commercial Pilots Licences. In the graduate category, two African engineers were recruited and sent to the United Kingdom for further training. One graduate engineer was appointed purchasing and supplies manager (designate) and one engineer, recruited as an apprentice, became the first African to obtain a licence in aircraft maintenance. Further training facilities had been arranged with Rolls-Royce at Derby, but problems arose, when at least two trainees had to be escorted home, having experienced psychological disorders attributed to 'culture shock'. It was a long way from home in a great many ways for the African young men visiting the industrial heartland for the first time.

In the commercial department an intensified programme for the recruitment, aptitude testing and selection of Africans, mainly of School Certificate and higher academic standards, for appropriate commercial appointments, had been followed throughout the year. Nearly 2,000 applicants were called forward of whom some 1,500 were tested, 800 interviewed and 300 selected. Despite these efforts the airline's requirements were not achieved because of the paucity of suitable material and the relatively high turnover rate in staff due mainly to the opportunities offered for higher education.

In addition to several conversion and mandatory refresher courses, thirty-two newly recruited stewards and stewardesses were trained, and two stewards were promoted to chief steward. The special Comet cabin mock-up was installed during the year, assisting considerably with the training techniques. It was generally felt that whilst the airline was faced with a shortage of experienced staff, it had to take into account the need to prepare for the introduction of the Super VC10s in the latter part of 1966. Therefore, recruitment should not be confined to the need to satisfy the Africanisation programme alone, but must also take into account the requirements of expansion.

On the routes, a new runway was opened at Benghazi, and better radio facilities installed. Cairo had runway repairs, resulting in improved landings but it was reported that the surfaces still left something to be desired. F27 Friendship services to Arusha were suspended due to the poor state of the runway. Mombasa was still below standard for Comets and it was urged that improvements should be made to enable the airport to be included in the inter-city pattern. In Tanzania, Mtwara and Mwanza had been given priority for improvements to enable the Friendships to operate on a wider basis. A VOR was about to be installed at Mombasa. Radio communications were now excellent throughout the area; reports of poor communications continued to be made about Khartoum, Cairo and Malta.

The F27 Friendships had entered service in a most un-dramatic way. The pilots regarded it as a great leap forward from the DC3s which they had been used to flying, the Canadair was a couple of generations back. "A gentleman's aircraft" was the view of those who flew the new Friendships up and down the local route pattern. The chief engineer was critical of the pilots, at one stage, about the frequency of brake lining changes. The manufacturer had provided figures based upon the brake lining changes in other parts of the world. Evidently, in Malaysia the frequency was a great deal less. It was pointed out to him that the airfields in Malaysia, and elsewhere, such as Cox's Bazaar, had sealed runways of over 10,000ft in length at sea level, whereas the pilots of East African had to contend with operating into airfields such as Mbeya at 5,600ft with a 4,050ft runway, of which only 1,500ft was sealed. Apart from the coastal aerodromes and Entebbe and Nairobi, all the aerodromes operated by the F27s were on a par with Mbeya and no blame could be placed upon the pilots for increased brake usage.

Zanzibar was still heavily under the influence of the Chinese communists and had long since become a place to avoid for the tourists and other visitors to East Africa. The pilots of East African were not able to avoid it, since the schedules still required them to operate the coastal services stopping at Zanzibar. Ginger Brewer had converted to the F27 in August, 1964, training under Captain Alan Ratcliffe. On 6th June, 1965, he was detailed to fly the Chinese Prime Minister, Chou En-lai and his retinue from Dar es Salaam to Zanzibar. Chou En-lai was on an official visit to Tanzania, which involved a visit to the island, during which he would inspect a military parade and attend a reception, followed by a return flight to Dar es Salaam via a circuit of the island, seeing the main points of interest.

Brewer immediately had recollections of a previous flight into Zanzibar, one night about three months ago. After landing he had entered the terminal, only to be accosted by an irate army lieutenant who was demanding to see, in his own words "the airman who had blinded his anti-aircraft gunners with his headlamps"! This was reported to the airline headquarters, and enquiries revealed that the Zanzibar government had acquired some Chinese anti-aircraft guns and were using the E.A.A. aircraft on normal scheduled flights for gunnery training. It was discovered that an anti-aircraft gunnery school was being built on ground in the centre of the north-south airway, furthermore, the shells had fuse details written in Chinese and no one could decipher them. The result of this would be shells exploding quite haphazardly, since the trainee gunners would be unable to fuse them for a given height. The airway was quickly given a temporary dog-leg track adjustment in the interests of safety. In the very volatile political atmosphere of the times – no one knew whether some trigger-happy gunner might let off a round – all night flights into Zanzibar were cancelled.

Brewer agreed to operate the special flight on the understanding that the anti-aircraft guns were not trained on his aircraft (although the loss of the Chinese head of state would cause a major international incident, Brewer was primarily concerned with not being a part of it!). No assurances were forthcoming, so he declined to agree to undertake the flight. After about an hour, during which telephone lines buzzed between E.A.A. headquarters and the various officials involved with the protocol arrangements, a message was received confirming that anti-aircraft units would be stood down. This confirmed the worst suspicions of the pilots who had been operating into Zanzibar.

On 6th June, 1965, accompanied by First Officer Alan Martin, Brewer departed in F27, 5Y-AAC for Zanzibar, with the prime minister. They had decided to do the sight-seeing first, following which the aircraft returned to Dar es Salaam for a party of press reporters and photographers. In the event, all went well, there were no incidents and Brewer received a parting gift of a tray, cigarette box and ashtray from Mr Chou En-lai. He was probably among a very small group of Western pilots who had flown the Chinese prime minister.

Mr A.E. Robinson, the airline's chief engineer reported that during 1965 the Comet, Friendship and DC3 fleets had produced utilization figures of 3,913, 2,444 and 1,480 hours per aircraft respectively. A fourth Comet, which had become necessary due to the commitments in 1966, had been hired from B.O.A.C., and was in the workshops undergoing extensive overhaul and re-painting in East African Airways colours. Following the decision to purchase Super VC10s, a base development project, costing some £200,000 was planned. This would comprise an electronics hall, housing a Super VC10 flight simulator, flight procedure trainers, an IBM computer for accounts purposes and an Avionics workshop, including an area on lease to International Aeradio (East Africa) Ltd for use as a radar workshop.

The Dakota, VP-KJP, at Kilwa following the accident on 27th April, 1964, in which the propeller blades sliced through the fuselage, killing Captain Gene Brokensha. The aircraft was repaired by East African Airways and was later sold, in 1968, to Zambia Airways.
(Mr Cliff Sarginson)

As at Tanga, thirteen years earlier, convicts were employed to assist the engineers in pulling VP-KPJ out of the soft ground on the verge of Kilwa's grass runway.
(Mr Cliff Sarginson)

The necessary upgrade in base facilities would further include, within the fully air-conditioned hall of 14,000 sq. ft., a great deal of modern and sophisticated electronics equipment. A 60ft high extension to the maintenance hangar was commenced, to accommodate the Super VC10. A new general workshop of 15,000 sq.ft. was to be constructed to contain a motor transport garage, ground equipment facility, repair shop and cleaning section for aircraft engines.

New bi-lateral agreements proliferated. Alitalia and United Arab Airlines established new services to Entebbe and Dar es Salaam in addition to Ethiopian Airlines and Pan American Airways inaugurating services from Nairobi via Entebbe to the West coast of Africa and, in the case of Pan American, onward to the United States. East African Airways inaugurated new services to Bujumbura and Frankfurt and increased the Eastern route service with an additional Comet to Karachi and Bombay via Addis Ababa.

There had been a consistent and integrated advertising campaign carried out in East Africa, Europe, Asia, the Far East and the U.S.A. to keep the public fully informed on services, the facilities and the special attractions of East Africa as a tourist centre. Besides using the press as the main advertising medium, emphasis was also placed on radio and, where possible, television. There was a noticeable cumulative press coverage both in East Africa and overseas as the Super VC10 introduction programme became more sustained.

Sales promotion activities were strengthened by the appointment of district sales representatives in Rome, Cairo, and Addis Ababa and by increasing representation in London, Paris and Frankfurt. The inclusive tour market in terms of East Africa, ethnic and missionary traffic were each given special attention in sales presentations and activities. During the 1965 *Hajj* season, a record number of 1,500 pilgrims were carried by charter services, underlining the importance of this annual event as a revenue earner for the airline.

Another step, which together with the repainting of the aircraft in a bright, modern style, which would identify them as coming out of Africa, was the introduction of new uniforms. Initially the stewardesses were issued, towards the end of the year, smart, light-weight beige linen dresses, with a matching jacket, brown gloves and high quality leather handbag. They wore a pill-box hat in brown, edged with simulated leopard skin. It was a complete break away from the traditional navy-blue uniforms which had been purchased from the B.O.A.C. uniform stores in the past. Male uniforms were again a total change, being tailored from a quality light-weight dark-green cloth, with white shirt, green knitted tie and gold badges of rank.

A final aircraft paint scheme had been evolved, which again, was a departure from the fairly conservative designs of the time. Aircraft were painted white on top with a cheat-line consisting of coloured lines in green, yellow, red, white and black (representing the green forests, yellow sun, red earth and white and black, the 'two races living in harmony'. Blue would represent the sea and the sky). The blue lion-in- the-sun symbol remained, situated in front. On the tail of each aircraft was painted, on the white fin, a yellow sun design, within which were the three flags of the East African countries, the flag uppermost being the one representing the country of registration of the aircraft concerned. Above the window line (below, in the case of the Friendships) was painted the airline name, in light blue, now shortened to read *EAST AFRICAN*. The overall effect of the new designs both in uniforms and aircraft gave a bright, modern, thoroughly with-it impression, perfectly in keeping with the times (these were the 'swinging sixties'). East African was showing the world proudly, where it had come from. If the people who had created this sparkling international airline could maintain their course, the professionals, both on the ground and in the air, were motivated to give of their best.

Following the increase in sales activity, there was a corresponding increase in the traffic handling activities, particularly overseas, where traffic liaison officers were recruited from, in most cases, the national airlines, to ensure that the local handling of East African's services went smoothly. Reporting to traffic manager Alistair Mackenzie, traffic liaison officers were appointed at London (where a

The new uniforms, shown by Iris Breidenbend and an Asian and African stewardess. The sign-post was a familiar land mark to travellers, as was the waving base above the departure gate at Nairobi's old Embakasi airport.

traffic office was opened at Heathrow), Aden, Bombay, Cairo, Karachi and Paris. With traffic superintendent Mike Hall, traffic services officer John Betts and traffic standards officer Tony O'Donoghue, Mackenzie was at the centre of a well controlled system, maintaining continuity and high standards of service throughout the route system. A reporting procedure ensured that a traffic handling report, which included a full breakdown of the load, and details of any problems encountered, on every flight, was despatched to Nairobi on each following service.

1965 had been a troubled year around the world. In Britain the old order had finally passed away with the death of Sir Winston Churchill in January. In February, the United States was entering into the first stages of its long years of intervention in Vietnam. War was in the air also between India and Pakistan, over territorial claims concerning Kashmir. In November, an event would occur which would have an impact upon East African Airways services to the territories to the south – Mr Ian Smith would announce UDI (Unilateral Declaration of Independence) in Rhodesia. In common with the United Kingdom and many countries around the world, economic sanctions were imposed upon the illegal regime. East African Airways would no longer fly to Salisbury and Bulawayo – another link with its past

With a Comet 4 in the background, stewardesses: Mary Muganga, Jennie Dickson, Chief Stewardess Una Buchanan and, showing the specially designed sari uniform for the Asian girls, Priscilla De Souza, (Mrs Jennie Hartley née Dickson)

had gone, and the economic advantages which accrued from this wealthy region of Central Africa. The former Northern Rhodesia had become independent Zambia in October 1963, with its own airline, Zambian Airways, operating out of Lusaka.

In September, relations between India and Pakistan had deteriorated to such an extent that it was no longer possible to operate the Karachi - Bombay sector. Since the Indian route was a major revenue earner and there was still considerable traffic on the route, it was decided to continue operating by flying Nairobi - Bombay direct. The flight time was approximately six and a half hours and the crews would return with the Comets, as it was considered dangerous to remain in Bombay, not knowing how the war would develop. To overcome this problem, it was decided that no first class passengers would be carried, so that a second crew could be accommodated in the forward cabin. Camp beds were secured to the floor and provided with sheets and blankets, so that the crews could get their mandatory rest prior to flying the aircraft back, with the other crew now replacing them in the cabin.

The passengers in the rear, economy class section, would be screened from the crew rest compartment by curtains, for safety reasons nothing more substantial could be fitted.

On one memorable occasion, when the Comet arrived at Bombay, the local handling agent, which was Air India, could only provide one pair of passenger steps, which they positioned at the front, first class, door. As a result the entire fifty passengers from the rear cabin trooped forward through the crew compartment, where the scene was very hard to explain - both male and female crew in various stages of undress, as they prepared to exchange places with the now off-duty crew who were already preparing to relax. The majority of the passengers were an American tour group, who are probably still regaling their friends with the story of the East African Airways flight into Bombay in '65 and what they saw in the front cabin as they got out.

Back in 1962, an incident occurred at Rome's Fiumicino airport, which although seemed funny at the time, was soon forgotten by those involved. After landing, the Comet commanded by Captain Leslie, with Bill Careful acting as co-pilot, taxied in, behind the "follow me" jeep. For some reason, after stopping the Comet, the marshaller indicated that it should make a turn, necessitating engine power and a 360 degree turn, before he was satisfied and waved chocks into place. When the crew disembarked, they found total chaos reigned on the apron. Un-noticed by the marshaller, and completely out of sight to anyone on the aircraft, a tractor pulling the joining baggage train was close behind the jet pipes when the engines were powered up for the turn. The resultant jet-blast had blown over the tractor and the baggage carts, spilling bags all over the apron. No one was hurt, thankfully, and no damage was done to the luggage. The B.E.A. handling staff were in fits of laughter, this being the funniest thing they had seen since they could not remember when. Apart from a brief entry in the aircraft log book the incident was forgotten.

Exactly two years later, in November 1965, a summons was issued to Captain Leslie and Bill Careful to attend a court in Rome. The tractor driver, through his trade union, had lodged a huge claim for damages. Since under Italian law they would have to prove their innocence, and would be arrested on arrival at Rome, the crew rostering officer had to ensure that neither of them were routed through Italy for several weeks, until it was sorted out. With the assistance of the Italian pilots' union the matter was resolved; the driver was 'trying it on', since both he and the marshallers were at fault.

In December the last payment was made on the Comet fleet, which together with the back-up stock of spares and associated equipment had cost some £4.2 million, all of which had been paid out of revenue earnings over the past seven year period. With unrest in Aden, India, Pakistan and UDI in Rhodesia, the year had shown a drop in traffic revenues, resulting in a down-turn in operating profit over the previous record breaking year.

Considerable competition was encountered in the year on the Europe and United Kingdom route, not only from the long established operators but also from African airlines operating between East Africa and Europe through their own territories. The VC10 was the main competitive aircraft and without doubt attracted many passengers away from EAA's Comets.

Although total traffic expressed in load ton miles increased for 1965 over 1964, this increase was almost wholly attributable to a greater carriage of lower rated cargo on capacity purchased from pool partners, contributing to the dilution of the revenue return per load ton mile to Shs. 4/74 from 1964's rate of Shs. 4/99. Passengers carried and passenger miles were only marginally changed on 1964's traffic:

>   Passengers carried 242,480   up 2.6%
>   Passenger miles 224,066,000   down 0.2%
>   Average journey .... 924 miles   down 2.7%

The significant figures for the year were still impressive:

>   Output .... 61,836,000 ctm   up 14.8%
>   Traffic .... 33,897,000 ltm   up 11.8%
>   Operating Revenue .... £8,852,815   up 6.9%
>   Total Expenditure .... £8,460,954   up 8.6%
>   Surplus on Operations .... £391,861 down by £95,284

The Corporation had set itself a target for 1965 of a surplus on operations of £331,106 from a total revenue of £8,738,644 to give a return on net assets after depreciation and interest of 12.7 per cent. The years results showed an achievement of a surplus on operations of £391,861 from a total revenue of £8,852,815 and a return on net assets (mid-1965) after depreciation and interest of 13.8 per cent. The airline proudly reported to the East African Common Services Organisation that it had fulfilled its task.

Captain Malin Sorsbie, following the untimely death of his wife and his subsequent departure from East African Airways, had remained in Kenya, where he had taken an interest in wildlife conservation. He had married again, an old friend, Connie Beech, heiress to the American Beechcraft aircraft manufacturers. With the aid of his wife's fortune he created a company called Munitalp (which was Platinum spelled backwards – thought to be a reference to his wife's wealth). Through the Munitalp Foundation he bestowed a new wing for the Nairobi hospital, ambulances for the St John's Ambulance service and aircraft for the Kenya flying doctor service. In the conservation field he built Treetops and established the Samburu Game Reserve. Sorsbie had been awarded the O.B.E. in 1942 and in 1956 the C.B.E. He was knighted in 1965.

At this stage in the development of East African Airways, it may be well to reflect upon the part played in its success by the British Overseas Airways Corporation. Since the days of Wilson Airways when B.O.A.C.'s predecessor, Imperial Airways saw the importance of the successful colonial airline and purchased equity in it, the requirement to feed the trunk routes from outlying areas was regarded as vital in the vast expanse of regional East Africa. But East African Airways could not be sustained as a viable business if it were to depend upon the inter-territorial and regional routes alone, as was foreseen by Captain Malin Sorsbie. B.O.A.C. ensured the success of the early post war period, supplying through B.O.A.C. Associated Companies Ltd, both aircraft and personnel. Malin Sorsbie himself came via B.O.A.C., as did Colonel Mostert, Steve Choppin and Andrew Gill who came in as accountant and later became administration manager and assistant general manager. B.O.A.C.'s non-voting shares in the airline represented a higher value than the holdings of the three colonial territories combined. At every stage in the progress of the airline, B.O.A.C. supplied expertise, technical and engineering services, stores procurement and shipping and, through Associated Companies, they selected and engaged many pilots, other aircrew and staff. In South Africa they assisted with personnel recruited there.

Without the willing and friendly assistance of B.O.A.C. neither the DH89A, Lodestar, DC3, Canadair nor Comet projects could have been undertaken. When the Canadairs were introduced and East African Airways commenced services to the United Kingdom, 'competing' with B.O.A.C., crews were converted to type, ground engineers were trained, the Rolls-Royce engines overhauled. Their senior Canadair captain, Captain Joe Parker was seconded to E.A.A.C., to supervise the flight deck operations and undertake the route checks. Similar arrangements followed the introduction of the Comet 4. Extensive use was made of B.O.A.C.'s flight simulators for training and statutory annual checks for pilots and flight engineers.

East African Airways, however, could never have been called a subsidiary or client airline of B.O.A.C. It had an indefinable quality of its own, not to be compared with the rather stuffy descendant of the grand Imperial Airways. There were discernable types of East African employee among the Europeans. Some had come via the B.O.A.C. Associated Companies route or were ex-R.A.F., and then there were the 'colonials', who were easy going, slightly irreverent white Kenyans, Rhodesians, South Africans and others from as far away as Australia and New Zealand and who contributed to the different persona of East African Airways. It was their pioneering, adventurous spirit which had not only played a stimulating part in the development of the airline, but also was at the heart of the strong *esprit de corps* which existed among the crew, engineers, traffic staff and, indeed, throughout the entire airline. Combined with the exotic mixture of races from Africa, India and Arabia, the traveller found himself entering an exciting, different but comfortably familiar atmosphere created by East African Airways. It was the personification of the old Empire ideal.

When the Comet 4 was introduced on the East African routes, South Africa, the Rhodesias and East Africa were all within the British Empire. Apart from sharing this common heritage, the citizens of these countries could benefit from British cabotage fares, a kind of Imperial preference, outside of the international fare structures arranged between the airlines at I.A.T.A. Thus the quadripartite pool initiative came from B.O.A.C., permitting low fares and common routes and accounting between the partner airlines. It was the successful operation of the United Kingdom – South Africa routes of the quadripartite pool that gave the Board of East African Airways the confidence to engage upon the replacement project of the magnitude which resulted in the Super VC10 acquisition. Had the pool continued, the Super VC10s of E.A.A. would have shared the benefits of operating through from London to Durban, Johannesburg and the Cape; these would remain the greatest revenue earning routes in the world for at least twenty-five years in the future. With the banning of South African Airways services through Central and East Africa after independence, this pool was dashed to pieces, never to be replaced. From there on, it was 'open skies'. The African airlines had effectively lost the game – for the planners had already seen what was to come and, alone, the new nations could never afford to re-equip with the emerging Jumbo jets, and they would not unite effectively. But this takes us too far into the future. At the end of 1965, it was the ultimate in its generation of airliners which occupied the minds of those guiding East African Airways.

Chapter 9

Super VC10s

THE VICKERS SUPER VC10 came about following a series of studies leading from the Valiant bomber, which was produced in quantity for the R.A.F., to a military intercontinental jet transport, which was far ahead of its time, the Vickers V1000, and a civilian version, the VC7. Development of these aircraft was cancelled in 1955 following withdrawal of government support, even though the first airframe was 80% completed.

In 1956, B.O.A.C. underwent major changes in top management and a great deal of attention was paid to future fleet requirements. The Comet 1 disasters and Britannia late deliveries had caused extreme planning difficulties in the past few years. It was now vital to get the decisions right in regard to the various fleet replacements. By March, 1957, a specification for a Comet and Britannia replacement had been formed. This called for a payload of about 35,000lb to be carried over 2,500 mile sectors on the airline's routes to Africa and Australia. This implied the combination of high ambient temperatures, high altitude and short runways, plus difficult route sectors with headwinds of 35 knots or more. These were the basic parameters around which Vickers Armstrongs pursued their design studies. In the interval since the cancellation of the V1000 project, Boeing in the United States had successfully introduced the Boeing 707 airliner and B.O.A.C. had been authorised to purchase fifteen of these machines, but the Treasury would not permit further dollars for additional aircraft. It was universally recognised that with their huge home market and marketing power, the American machines would soon set the trend for international air travel. Vickers, meanwhile, had completed their development studies and had evolved a four-engined intercontinental airliner capable of meeting the most stringent operating conditions in the world – the VC10.

With government pressure, B.O.A.C., who would rather have purchased the Boeing 707 and standardised its fleet structure, signed a contract with Vickers Armstrongs for thirty-five VC10s. The first of these aircraft made its maiden flight on 29th June, 1962, powered by four Rolls-Royce Conway 42 turbofans of 20,400lb thrust.

Despite the reluctance of B.O.A.C. to purchase them and some adverse comparisons with the Boeing 707 (they were heavy, thirsty, expensive – and late) the VC10s soon became extremely popular with the travelling public, some passengers preferring to change their flight in order to fly VC10. The reason for this became clear when one first entered the spacious, elegant cabin, low-lit from tiny pin holes in the ceiling panels, the decor custom-designed by Charles Butler Associates of New York. For the first time, passengers boarding in tropical conditions experienced the comfort of the 30 ton freon cabin refrigeration system. Departure was preceded by a low hum, from the rear mounted engines. A superb advanced-design landing gear provided a feather light ride as the aircraft taxied to the runway threshold. As the thrust levers were opened, the sound from the engines, far back in the tail, approximated nothing more than a neighbour's vacuum cleaner, the runway was eaten up swiftly, and the only indication of the transition from ground to air was the angle at which the curtains dividing the cabins fell.

The VC10 was the last in a line of airliners designed and built for the air routes of the British Commonwealth and Empire. Since the days of Imperial Airways, the requirements for the long empire life-lines were served by the MRE, Medium Range Empire, aircraft. For many years these requirements had been met by a mix of land-planes and flying-boats; most of the British possessions were open to the sea, many capitals being built close to harbours. East and Central Africa were obvious exceptions, where, on the many lakes, the flying-boats were not found to be a great success. One of the things which these colonial territories had in common was the lack of money to build extensive airports, whereas in the United States, modern airports, with magnificent, long runways were abundant.

An advanced feature of the VC10 was the totally new wing design. This concept, known as the 'supercritical peaky (referring to the distribution of lift profile) wing design theory', was the result of the work of a distinguished aerodynamicist, H.H. Pearcy of the National Physical Laboratory, Teddington, and Barry Haines of the Aircraft Research Association wind tunnel establishment, Bedford. Their aerofoil design concept gave a two dimensional transition from supersonic to subsonic flow, without creating a strong shock wave, common to conventional aerofoil sections, which provided benefits in both drag and buffet reduction. With the VC10's four engines mounted high in the tail, it was then possible to place complete, continuous lifting devices incorporating highly efficient leading edge slats and 65 per cent span Fowler flaps on the trailing edge of this wing. With its 'clean wing' and high lift capability, the VC10 could land about 20 knots slower than the Boeing 707, which allowed it to operate into and out of less spacious airports with a full payload, which the 707 was unable to achieve.

Another advantage of the VC10 were the specially designed Vickers 4-wheel bogie main gear units, incorporating large, low-pressure tyres and fully duplicated main wheel hydraulic braking systems. Combined with the superb take-off and landing characteristics, these undercarriage units were designed to operate from the secondary, un-developed airports of the Commonwealth, which had low runway load-bearing classifications. The follow-on advantage of these units, combined with the low speed, ground-effect cushioned landings was to give the passengers and crew an unprecedented silky-smooth arrival – frequently accompanied by cheers and hand-clapping from the appreciative passengers. The Rome published *Daily American* commented, *"The landing was such a masterpiece of perfection that the travel-hardened passengers burst into applause".*

The rear-mounted engines followed from the requirement for a high-lift clean wing. The concept had been used with success by the French on the Caravelle twin engined airliner. Further, the British ideas of aerodynamically burying the engines in the wing, as on the de Havilland Comet, the Vickers Valiant and Avro Vulcan were becoming outdated as wing design advanced, bringing thin section, high speed wings to the fore. Engine design was also moving ahead with larger diameter turbofan and bypass engines. Numerous advantages for rear-mounted engines were put forward:

- Greatly improved airfield performance, giving higher payload uplift, hence better operating economy.
- Greater versatility of operation for an airline such as B.O.A.C., with its world-wide route network embracing virtually every kind of operational problem.
- Improved control characteristics and lower approach speeds.
- A new standard of passenger comfort derived from the drastic reduction in cabin noise level and vibration.
- Reduced fire hazards in a wheels-up landing because the engines were well isolated from the main fuel tanks.
- Excellent ditching characteristics.
- Structural surfaces less likely to incur fatigue failure from the effects of jet efflux.
- Reduced risk of damage to engines by the ingress of runway debris.

The VC10 had an overall length of 158ft 8in, a wingspan of 146ft 2in and a height of 39ft 6in. With up to 151 passengers, it had a maximum take-off weight of 312,000lb, maximum landing weight of 216,000lb and a maximum zero fuel weight of 188,400lb. It cruised effortlessly at 550mph with a nil reserve maximum payload range of 5,040 miles.

This was indeed a superb airliner; but it was not the finish. As a result of the spread of the American Boeing machines, airports around the world had, of necessity, been forced to extend their runways. This had reduced the competitive edge of the VC10, except in Africa. In order to enhance their commercial potential, Vickers had evolved an improved design in which the fuselage was extended by 13ft. This meant that the B.O.A.C. version VC10 with 135 economy seats was increased to 163 economy seats, with the subsequent decrease in seat mile costs.

With an uprated Rolls-Royce Conway engine delivering 21,800lb thrust, this new aircraft had a maximum take-off weight of 335,000lb, maximum landing weight of 237,000lb and maximum zero fuel weight of 215,000lb. This was the Super VC10.

The comparison with the Boeing 707-320B was very interesting. The Super VC10 gave 87,200lb static thrust from its four Rolls-Royce Conway R.Co.43 engines compared with the Boeing's 72,000lb. The Super VC10 used more fuel, but it was quicker. The 707 APS weight, however, was some 7 or 8 tons lighter. Maximum power loadings were 3.84lb per lb static thrust for the Super VC10 against 4.54lb for the 707-320B. At maximum take-off weight, the Super VC10 grossed 8,000lb more than the Boeing and got airborne to 35ft in some 2,000ft less. The only thing which would, in the end, remove the Super VC10 from the world's airline routes would be the price of fuel, burned at a rate of some 3,533lb to 3,830lb per engine per hour.

It was, perhaps ironic, in view of what was to come, that East African Airways should find itself equipped with the ultimate mark of this superb aircraft, the Super VC10-1154. In order to meet the airline's specifications, which required a take-off from Nairobi (5,327ft AMSL), with maximum payload at surface temperatures of up to 28 degrees Celsius, with a flight direct to London, using Prestwick as the fuel alternate, the aircraft were fitted with the most advanced Rolls-Royce Conway R.Co.42-550-B engines, of 22,500lb thrust. This would permit complete freedom of scheduling, day or night, winter or summer. It was a capability that no other civil airliner had at the time. (Later, Boeing 747 Jumbo jets were restricted on payloads, by up to 50 seats ex Nairobi due to WAT while E.A.A. Super VC10s departed at maximum take-off weight). The penalty paid for these, the most powerful civil engines in service in the world, with a fuel maximum uplift of 19,325

The contract for the Super VC10s is signed at Nairobi, March, 1965. L to R, seated: Mr A.V. Gill, Capt P.A. Travers, AVM Sir Geoffrey Tuttle (vice-chairman BAC), Chief Fundikira, Mr P.K. Jani. Standing are members of the British Aircraft Corporation, including Mr Ron Bailey and Mr R. Phillips next to Mr S.G. Choppin, E.A.A.C. financial controller, on the extreme right. (E.A.A.C.)

At Brooklands, 1966. 5X-UVA prior to completion. (Capt Leslie)

gallons, was an average consumption of 30 gallons per minute, or 3 gallons per mile.

The Performance Guarantee flight, prior to acceptance by East African Airways, entailed taking-off from London Airport, with full tanks, the cabin loaded up with electronic equipment, and climbing to virtually maximum ceiling. For several hours 5X-UVA carried out cruise-climb procedures, on circuits between Le Havre and Stornaway. Both the cruise-climb procedure and the maximum ceiling were unnecessary for airline operations, but on completion, it proved that the aircraft could satisfy the airline's requirements, with an additional 50% payload over maximum – had this been possible.

Another feature of the East African Airways Super VC10 was the provision of an upper deck freight compartment which contained four 56in x 49in non-standard size pallets, loaded through a hydraulically powered cargo door measuring 140in by 84in. This allowed for up to 6,000lb of bulk or palletised freight to be carried, in addition to the normal hold stowage, which was often subject to volume.

The passenger seating configuration was fourteen first class seats with 111 economy class seats beyond the curtained-off cargo area. The cabin decor was chosen to high-light the East African character of the airline, with tastefully etched motifs including typical animals, shields and the familiar silhouette of Mt. Kilimanjaro, on the light coloured side panels. The gold coloured bulkheads in first class were

Facing page: East African Airways' first Super VC 10, 5X-UVA, lands at Wisley on its maiden flight from Brooklands. 15th September, 1966. 5X-UVA was fitted with a set of Conway 540 engines, borrowed from a Standard VC10, for the maiden flight, as her 550-B engines were not ready in time. (BAC/E.A. Standard)

The interior, looking aft, of 5X-UVA, prior to the fitting of seats. The cargo door lifting arm can be seen above the windows on the right of the picture. (Capt Leslie)

decorated with picture maps of the East African countries (Chief Fundikira had ordained that on the map, Tanzania should be labelled by the old name of Tanganyika). The overall effect was one of sunshine and light, which was further enhanced once the aircraft was cruising in the brilliant upper atmosphere of the tropics.

Captain G.W. Mitchell had been given the appointment of chief instructor Super VC10 fleet at the beginning of September, 1966. This included responsibility for the operational introduction of the new aircraft, involving flight-deck layout, flight acceptance tests including performance guarantees, aircraft documents, conversion and route training and simulator specification. He spent many weeks with the British Aircraft Corporation, in a liaison capacity. The East African Super VC10s were being built at the Vickers factory at Brooklands, near Weybridge. As the weeks passed, one could follow the stage by stage construction of the magnificent aircraft in the old construction hangars beside the now crumbling Brooklands racetrack of 1930s vintage.

The factory was built on what was the Brooklands race track of earlier years and space was a problem. The hangars were too small for anything as large as the Super VC10 and this was evident when it came to fitting the wings to the fuselage. This was accomplished under cover, by manoeuvring the fuselage so that it, and the wing to be fitted, were inside the hangar; when this operation was completed, the aircraft would be turned round so that the other wing could be fitted under cover. When the aircraft was ready to fly it was basically an empty shell and would be completed at the nearby facility at Wisley. Minimum fuel would be loaded and the Super VC10 would be ready for its maiden flight, which was also an exercise in manipulation. The runway was of minimal length and bounded by the old banked motor racing track. As a result the take-off run had to be started on the taxi-way, requiring a swing of some 30 degrees onto the runway, where the taxi-way met the threshold. There was plenty of power available for a successful take-off, but some had doubts about what would have happened should an aborted take-off close to V_1 been necessary.

Most of these departures were made on a Saturday morning, if the wind and weather were suitable. They were a popular event among the local people, many of whom had participated in the construction of the aircraft, and who would turn out in large numbers to witness the spectacle of this giant, and tremendously noisy, aeroplane as it accelerated down the short runway towards the race-track banking and, as a crash seemed imminent, rotated and climbed skyward at 28 degrees, the thunder of its four Rolls-Royce Conway engines drowning all other sounds.

The aircrews selected to fly the Super VC10s were sent to Weybridge to attend the ground school, followed by long visits to the construction hangars to watch the assembly. Training and conversion flights were conducted by the BAC pilots, Bill Cairns, Dennis Hayley-Bell and the test pilot in charge of the project Lew Roberts. Although deeply involved with the Concorde project at the time, chief test pilot Brian Trubshaw and John Cochran were always ready to have a chat and answer questions raised by the East African pilots.

The first East African Airways Super VC10, 5X-UVA, was handed over at a ceremony at Wisley on 30th September 1966. The delivery flight, which departed from Heathrow, was on 11th October 1966, with Captain Mitchell in command, assisted by Lew Roberts of BAC. The flight was delayed by the appearance of a bowler-hatted gentleman[1] who boarded the aircraft just before start-up and apologetically explained that the documentation could not be handed over until certain necessary guarantees in connection with the lease/purchase agreement had been given. After dashing to and fro for about an hour, he finally gave the thumbs up and start-up commenced for the flight to Nairobi, which was routed via Rome and Cairo, to 'show the flag'.

1966 had been a year of intense activity culminating in the arrival of the first two Super VC10s in October (5X-UVA) and November (5H-MMT). The new aircraft were put into scheduled service (the first on 13th October) and crew training immediately after delivery and in the last two months of the year accumulated 1,000 hours of trouble free flying. All departments had participated in the increased work which the Super VC10s created. In sales, an advertising campaign led by commercial manager Mr R.E. Young, embraced not only the East African countries but also Ethiopia, Sudan, Zambia, Malawi, Aden, Pakistan, India, United Arab Republic,

---

[1] Mr Frank Collier, MVO, B.O.A.C. Manager London Stations.

Italy, Germany, France, the United Kingdom, the U.S.A. and to a limited extent, certain countries in the Far East. A special feature of the programme was a successful "Stopover" (in Cairo, Rome, Frankfurt and Paris en route to London) campaign throughout East Africa and a general build up coverage for the introduction of the Super VC10. To strengthen the airline's selling position abroad, sales shops were opened or planned, in Cairo, London, Karachi and Bombay. Some of the early Super VC10 operations carried inaugural guests, comprising officials of other international airlines and travel agents, so that they could experience the considerable attraction of the new aircraft in addition to the tourist potential of East African Airway's countries of origin.

Following the bi-lateral agreements which had been concluded after independence and the break-up of the quadripartite pool, new services were inaugurated by Lufthansa and Pan American to Nairobi, Entebbe and Dar es Salaam. Additional services were introduced by Ethiopian Airlines and Sabena to Dar es Salaam, by S.A.S. through Entebbe and by Pakistan International Airlines to Nairobi. Commercial arrangements continued to exist between East African Airways and B.O.A.C. on the routes to and from Europe and with Air India and Aden Airways on the Eastern routes. New agreements were concluded with Zambia Airways and Air Malawi, with regard to the regional routes between East Africa, Zambia and Malawi and with Ethiopian Airlines in respect of traffic between East Africa and Ethiopia.

Super VC10, 5X-UVA lands at Entebbe's lake-side airport. 1966. (E.A. Standard)

East African Airways was at this time acting as general sales agent for fifty-two airlines and as handling agents for twenty-four airlines operating into the three countries. In 1966 the revenues from ticket sales commissions yielded £239,470 and for services to other operators £361,853.

The introduction of the Super VC10 necessitated changes in handling procedures at all the stations served by the new aircraft. Special loading devices such as high-loaders to handle the palletised cargo loads (the use of fork-lifts was very much frowned upon, although these were a favoured means of dealing with bulk loads and pallets at some less well provided stations, a small mistake could cause piercing of the skin and even serious damage to the pressurised cabin), the belly holds could not be easily reached from the ground, as could the Comet's tiny compartments. The rearmost hold had a small ventral hatch which could only be reached by using a specially introduced loading vehicle fitted with an extended motor driven belt which would carry the baggage or cargo up or down. These baggage conveyor vehicles became common world-wide within a few years. Of course, B.O.A.C. and British United Airways had introduced standard model VC10s on the routes in advance of East African Airways, so much of the necessary equipment was in place. These changes in handling techniques provided difficulties at many airports, requiring a great deal of liaison between the airline's representatives and the local airport authorities, since more men were required to turn the aircraft round and handle the new equipment, handling charges were expected to rise as a result.

Traffic, during 1966, improved steadily, although the Super VC10s had only been in service for two months of the year. They were introduced on the East Africa

Captain Bob Ainsworth at the controls of Super VC10 5Y-ADA.

– London route, operating turn and turn about five days per week, with the Comets gradually phasing out. Even for an aircraft of the Super VC10's excellent breeding, it was asking a lot of it to maintain this schedule without the odd hitch occurring. There were a number of delays to services as a result of this tight scheduling, which drew a certain amount of criticism from passengers accustomed to the Comet's regularity in the past. The three E.A.A. Comets had been withdrawn from the UK route after six years of service in which they had accumulated a total of 57,730 hours, with a peak utilisation of 11 hours per day, prior to being replaced by the Super VC10s. The delivery of the third Super VC10, 5Y-ADA, would relieve the scheduling difficulties in April, 1967.

Passengers carried during 1966 had increased by 16.2 per cent to 281,836 and passenger miles by 21.5 per cent to 272,163,000. Cargo ton miles went up by 6.2 per cent to 11,062,000 while mail ton miles at 1,719,000 were 6.6 per cent down. The overall load factor improved to 56.3 per cent and the passenger load factor went up to 53.9 per cent from 50.5 per cent in 1965. While the traffic handling units continued to serve an increasing number of services (thirteen foreign scheduled airlines at Nairobi, twelve at Entebbe and eight at Dar es Salaam, in addition to non-scheduled charter operators), the provision of satisfactory facilities at the

Comet 4, 5H-AAF, at Blantyre, Malawi, 17th February, 1966. (E.A. Standard)

various airports continued to cause dissatisfaction. The booming tourist industry and increase in arriving and departing airliners, requiring simultaneous handling of large numbers of passengers, was not matched by the airport accommodation and services.

Africanisation was now in full swing. The regular review of posts for the purposes of Africanisation at various times during the course of the year ranged from top management to officer grade and covered all the five departments of the corporation. The recruitment of applicants for training as pilots continued vigorously and a further three trained African pilots were engaged on their successful return from Perth, with brand new Commercial Pilots Licences, obtained after 250 hours flying experience. The casualty figure for those trainees not completing the courses, due to disqualification on medical grounds, inability to assimilate and various other reasons was high (83 per cent), but it was hoped that with improvements in selection processes and an increase in numbers of applicants, the position would improve. (It could be assumed that there was a truly desperate shortage of pilots from this. Of course there was not – only a desperate shortage of African pilots. This is an outstanding example of where the policy of Africanisation was leading).

Two African graduate engineers who were taken on in 1965 were thought to be making good progress, two more graduates and one Fokker Friendship licensed engineer were recruited during the year. Eight engineering bursaries were offered by Air India and taken up and a selection panel from the British Aircraft Corporation and from Rolls-Royce chose eight apprentices for specialised training in the United Kingdom.

A Comet 4 arrives at Entebbe from London. 20th May, 1966 (Author)

Charles Semogerere, a Ugandan, was appointed purchasing and stores manager in March. A graduate of Roorkee University, Delhi, he had worked as an apprentice in the Uganda civil aviation department and at Bombay's Santa Cruz airport before joining Shell International for training on oil industry equipment. A.G. Muteshi was appointed personnel manager, having worked in that department since 1962. He was formally an employee of the East African Tobacco Company. Further posts such as housing officer; sales office superintendent, Kampala; assistant manager (designate) Uganda; assistant manager (designate) Tanzania; staff travel officer; publicity officer; assistant to area sales manager (East Africa); assistant to commercial planning manager and assistant passenger handling instructress, were filled by Africans.

Both DC3 and Friendship fleets were now operated entirely with African stewards and stewardesses. Twenty-three stewards and nineteen African stewardesses had been trained for service on Comet and Super VC10 aircraft. Recruitment in cabin services was being pressed forward as rapidly as possible, limited only by the availability of suitable recruits, and the time taken to train them to replace experienced staff (twenty-three African stewards and stewardesses left the airline's employ during 1966).

The number of commercial instructors, especially in the field of on-the-job training was planned to be increased early in 1967 together with more class room facilities. This would include a mock-up of the Super VC10 cabin to supplement that of the Comet. It was hoped that the extra training aids would enable the gap between training newcomers and the growth/wastage rates to be spanned, while managing to maintain commercial competency in the face of growing international competition.

In the accounts and administration departments Africanisation was proceeding quickly, with vacancies created by expatriates leaving being filled by recruits from the three African countries.

London was the main destination for the airline, and the route was the predominant revenue earner. It was decided during 1964 that African staff should be employed, to 'show the flag' and assist the handling agent, B.O.A.C., with passenger handling. Many African passengers, almost all of whom were officials of one kind or another, welcomed the appearance of uniformed staff who could speak Swahili, Kiganda or maybe Kikuyu. Staff could be quickly provided from the large numbers of Commonwealth students, nurses and residents in London. Two male and three or four female traffic staff were recruited and took up their duties under two British traffic liaison officers.

When the second Super VC10, 5H-MMT, was ready to depart for Nairobi in November, Captain Mitchell was back at Weybridge in his liaison capacity. It was necessary for him to pass the details of the crew by telephone to the E.A.A. traffic office at London Airport. The call was taken by one of the new African female receptionists, who wrote down the names as Mitchell gave them to her. All went well until he came to the purser, Russell (Russ) Molyneux. There was a short silence, then she said, "Would you spell it please". Mitchell spelled the name, using the familiar phonetic alphabet, "Mike, Oscar, Lima, Yankee, November, Echo, Uniform" - "What was that?" interrupted the young lady. "Uniform", said Mitchell. "Would you spell it, please", said the receptionist.

The end of 1966 saw a year in which the Super VC10 had arrived on the international routes. Elsewhere, on the domestic services, a remarkable fact stood out - the basic fares and rates had been maintained for ten years, since July 1956. It must have been a bargain unmatched anywhere else in the world during those years of inflation and upwardly spiralling costs.

The total number of staff at the end of 1966 amounted to 3,451 compared with 3,042 the previous year. With 380 expatriates still employed, an overall reduction of Europeans was a mere seven. In crude terms it would appear that 409 Africans had replaced seven expatriates. This was not the case, however, since many of the Africans were understudying expatriates - but it was a rough indicator which could have provided distant warning bells, had anyone an ear to listen.

Mr A.V. Gill retired from service at the end of the year after 20 years employment as secretary to the corporation while holding the positions of chief accountant 1947-55 and assistant general manager 1955-65.

With the redemption of the £250,000 B.O.A.C. holding of E.A.A.C. 3.5% Loan Stock 1975, the final links with B.O.A.C. were now nearly broken; the B.O.A.C. board delegate, Mr Gilbert Lee would remain for a further year then there would be no requirement for a B.O.A.C. connection; the only remaining member of the

DC3 Dakota, 5H-AAJ (formerly VP-KLA, RMA James A. Grant) at Entebbe, May, 1966. (Author)

executive management who had B.O.A.C. and Imperial Airways connections was Mr S.G. Choppin, who continued as financial controller.

East African Airways had made further progress in 1966, the twenty-first year of its existence. Traffic revenue was £9,504,139, an increase of 18.3 per cent and total revenue aggregated £10,411,674, an increase of 17.6 per cent. Growth in traffic was experienced over all groups of services compared with 1965 except that from the Europe/Britain services, constituting *two-thirds* of the airline's output of capacity, *the earning potential*, it was admitted, *for which had been adversely affected by the increasing exercise of traffic rights to and from East Africa by more international airlines.*

The surplus on operations, assisted by a total depreciation charge less than that of past years, was the highest East African Airways would ever record – £705,394.

Among the other news during all the changes which 1966 brought to the East African aviation community was that of the death of Mrs Florence Wilson. The lady who began it all died at her home at Karen on September 29th, 1966, at the age of 88.

1967

During 1967, the United Kingdom devalued the pound sterling, which resulted in the outstanding amount owed by East African Airways of £8,864,985 on the Super VC10s being reduced by K£1,266,407. This could be regarded as a very acceptable twenty-first birthday present, for, in January, 1967, East African Airways came of age. The event was celebrated by the issue of a set of four commemorative postage stamps by the East African joint postal authority, featuring the DH89A Rapide, Super VC10, Comet and F27 Friendship. The *East African Standard* of Friday, 6th January,1967, carried a comprehensive supplement devoted to the growth of East African Airways, as it evolved from the post-war years to the era of the Super VC10. The newspaper also carried a message from Mr J.M. Lusinde, chairman of the Communications Ministerial Committee, East African Common Services Organisation:

> "Members of the East African Common Services Communications Ministerial Committee have reason to be proud of the 21st anniversary of East African Airways.
>
> "While it is only proper that a message should express congratulations, we are of the opinion that congratulations alone are not enough.
>
> "The core of the staff of East African Airways have a heavy responsibility to justify and an important role to play in the furtherance of our national airline.
>
> "Flying, as East African Airways does, to important cities within Africa, Europe and Asia, the people of these countries have begun to appreciate the united efforts of the East African Governments to forge ahead and to develop their countries in a manner that will be second to none.
>
> "It is only natural that there will be new routes and more frequencies for East African Airways seriously to give thought to and. in time, there is no doubt that there will be

an even keener interest in acquiring aircraft superior and more spacious than the present Super VC10s now flying on E.A.A.'s international routes.

"The East African Common Services Communications Ministerial Committee is very appreciative of the work done by the pioneers in developing East African Airways. We send every one of them and the present members of the E.A.A. staff our good wishes.

"As a symbol of solidarity and a mark of faith in the future, we expect East African Airways to blaze even more successful trails in the years ahead, and to bring a good name to the airline which will be a constant reminder to people in East Africa and overseas of dedicated efforts and a constant awareness in projecting an East African image denoting safety, speed, service, comfort and efficiency".

Thus were the *raisons d'etre* and the goals for the airline spelled out by the spokesman of the Authority to which it answered.

In May, it was announced that a fourth Super VC10 would be ordered, together with the option on a fifth. During the previous year it had been decided to purchase two de Havilland (Canada) DHC6 Twin Otter aircraft to replace certain DC3 and the last remaining DH89A Rapide S.K.A.T. services. It was further decided in 1967 to increase this order to four Twin Otters. The first of these, 5H-MMK, was ferried across the Atlantic by Captain Leo Davidson, transiting Heathrow on 15th/16th July, en route to Nairobi. The 19 seat Twin Otter, with its twin Pratt and Whitney

A Twin Otter, Comet 4 and two Super VC10s on the apron at Nairobi's Embakasi airport. 1967.

PT6A-27 turbo-prop engines, 210 m.p.h. cruise and tricycle undercarriage was believed to be "an even better aircraft perhaps than the DC3 for training future cadet pilots". It was easier to fly than the 'tail-dragger' DC3.

The ever widening bi-lateral air service agreements which had been negotiated brought additional competition onto the East African routes as the months passed. New services were inaugurated by T.W.A. to Entebbe, Nairobi and Dar es Salaam and by Aeroflot and Somali Airlines to Dar es Salaam. In addition Sabena introduced a new call at Nairobi and Lufthansa commenced serving Entebbe and Dar es Salaam on a second frequency, with their existing frequency continuing from Nairobi through to Johannesburg. This brought the total number of foreign carriers serving East Africa to eighteen, an indication of the increasing competition which East African Airways faced from international carriers.

Despite the increase in competing services, passengers carried during 1967 improved over 1966 by 22.1 per cent to 344,022 and passenger miles by 38.1 per cent to 375,871,000. With the Super VC10's larger capacity coming into the schedules there was a resultant drop in overall load factor to 48 per cent from 56.3 per cent and the passenger load factor fell to 49.7 per cent from 53.9 per cent.

Aircraft utilisation was maintained at a high level, reaching the year's target figures:

Super VC10 .... 8,487 hours
Comet 4 .... 4,918 hours
F27 .... 9,002 hours
DC3 .... 13,060 hours
Twin Otter .... 438 hours

The Super VC10s experienced very little in the way of teething troubles, although on August 13th the EC723 was first delayed at London until 04.00 the following morning, and further delayed to 12.45 on the 14th, with an unscheduled engine change and on August 16th, 5Y-ADA was delayed overnight at London with serviceability problems with the Elliott-Bendix 200 series gyros. There were charters for widely different groups, from service families departing Aden, German tour groups chartered from Sudflug, to a Comet charter with Congo refugees, which arrived at London on 17th August.

The Super VC10 had shown itself to be a superb example of aeronautical engineering. It was not a demanding aircraft on pilot skills and could, as a result, be regarded as possibly the safest airliner of its class ever built, when in the hands of suitably qualified crew. In an almost text-book case, the Super VC10, 5Y-ADA, gave a lesson one night, on 30th May, 1967, which her crew were never to forget.

The crew, under the command of Captain Peter Brumby, were at Bombay, where they had taken their rest days at the Sun 'n Sands Hotel. On the day they were to take the service to Nairobi, the flight engineer reported to Captain Brumby that

Super VC10, 5Y-ADA, at Entebbe after the pilot had failed to complete a 180 degree turn in order to back-track after landing. The wheels sank into the tarmac. (Mr T. Webb)

The starboard undercarriage bogie of 5Y-ADA, embedded in the soft tarmac. (Mr T. Webb)

he felt unwell and did not think he was fit for duty. It was not uncommon for crew to suffer from various forms of food poisoning and gut complaints on the eastern routes. Brumby was not very happy at the prospect of a delay to their departure, so he made light of the problem, telling the flight engineer that he would be better off returning home on the flight and that he would keep an eye on things.

Peter Brumby was a large, barrel-chested, good natured man, exuding bluff confidence. Born in India during the Raj, he had been an R.A.F. Thunderbolt pilot in the battles against the Japanese during the war. A settler in colonial Kenya, he owned a farm in the Rift Valley, at Naivasha, producing high-quality vegetables for market. The flight engineer was persuaded, and the crew set off together for the airport at the appointed time.

It was a foul night, with tropical storms lashing the airport, accompanied by thunder and lightning. Aircraft were queuing to depart as 5Y-ADA taxied slowly, before taking her turn to line up on the wet runway. Many of the passengers were asleep before take-off. Purser Harry Everitt dimmed the cabin lights soon after they were airborne. Everything was normal, as they settled down in the climb on the first leg to Karachi, on the journey home to Nairobi. As 5Y-ADA climbed past 10,000 ft, the flight engineer was overcome by violent dysentery cramps and told the captain that he was leaving his position to visit the toilet. He told Brumby that he was "leaving his panel safe", indicating that he had switched all the fuel booster pumps ON.

The Rolls-Royce Conway engines had suction pumps incorporated, but they could not cope with climb power demands above about 20,000ft. The booster pumps in the fuel tanks assisted with fuel flow above these altitudes.

They had reached approximately 15,000ft when a warning horn sounded and the pilots noticed that the power on all four engines had decreased rapidly. The aircraft, in airspeed-lock mode, was unable to maintain height and gradually a descent attitude was adopted to maintain airspeed. All four engines were stopped, but one generator remained on line.

Harry Everitt was in the first-class cabin, attending to some of the few passengers who were still awake. He went quickly forward to the cockpit door, just in time to hear Captain Brumby shout, "Someone get the bloody engineer!" Everitt rushed back to the front galley and yelled at the stewardess, "Where is the engineer?" The girl pointed to the toilet door. Everitt hammered on the door, "You are wanted on the flight-deck – quickly!" By the time the flight engineer reached his seat, 5Y-ADA was gliding at a high rate of descent towards the Indian Ocean. It seemed an eternity to those watching him, their faces glistening with fear and apprehension, as the flight engineer went through the re-light procedure, and one by one, succeeded in obtaining full power on all four engines. As power was restored, the aircraft returned to level flight and they quickly regained the several thousand feet which had been lost.

The aircraft had a near-full passenger load and it was a tribute to the quietness of the Super VC10 cabin that only one passenger had noticed that something unusual had occurred. At the rear of the economy cabin, where engine noise was normally higher than elsewhere, a passenger had his attendant call-light on. "Why did the engines stop?" he asked Purser Everitt. He received a standard response, "a minor technical hitch", but he didn't believe it and demanded a large scotch, 'on the house'.

"It's funny how one reacts", said Harry Everitt later, "I felt completely calm and yet I was convinced my last moment had come; in fact, none of the cabin staff panicked".

When they reached Nairobi, they explained that they had run into icing conditions which had flamed-out all the engines. Icing has never been known to flame-out engines in this manner. There will always be a warning before anything serious happens. Brumby had chosen to continue the flight, transitting Karachi. There was no satisfactory explanation as to why he had not grounded the aircraft immediately. Unless the crew knew that, in his distressed state, the flight engineer had switched the booster pumps 'OFF', or even failed to include them on his pre-start checks; but at 10–15,000ft [2] the booster pumps would not have been required.

Perhaps because of the fear of repercussions, the crew stuck to their stories and would not change them. The word soon got around and the E.A.A.C. engineering department was inundated with telexes from B.O.A.C., B.A.C. and Rolls-Royce asking for information. Investigations by E.A.A.C. included flying with the booster pumps switched off on one engine up to 30,000ft. The engine flamed-out at 26,000ft. Tests using the flight-recorder data showed that the engines had flamed-out below 15,000ft. After this the crew were interviewed at length by B.O.A.C., Rolls-Royce and the airframe manufacturer in the United Kingdom. Rolls-Royce tried to simulate heavy icing on the engine test-bed. The engine continued to operate until it exploded, causing thousands of pounds worth of damage. Further tests were carried out by Rolls-Royce, using a chartered VC10 of British United Airways, operating out of Gatwick. The results matched those of E.A.A.C.

Consequently Rolls-Royce brought out a 100 page report on the incident; on the penultimate page it said "The captain was a most unreliable witness to the events that happened". This may have been in response to their inability to reach a clear conclusion to what was an unfortunate episode which, but for the grace of God, would have damaged the reputation of East African Airways beyond saving.

It was Chief Training Flight Engineer Tim Nightingale who, a year or so later, figured out what could have happened. Even under normal circumstances flight-deck crews need to change mentally to 'flight mode' when they come on duty. At home, or in their hotel, the light switches go UP for 'OFF' and DOWN for 'ON'. On the aircraft this is reversed. One day, while his attention was diverted, Nightingale switched the cross-feeds up (open) instead of the fuel booster pumps 'ON'. The fuel cross-feed switches are grouped close to the booster switches. What if the flight engineer, in his unhappy condition had opened the fuel cross-feed (UP) and left the booster pump switches off (DOWN) during his pre take-off checks?

---

[2] The flight recorder tape was read in the E.A.A.C. technical office by means of a high powered magnifier. The height indication ruled out icing or lack of fuel pressure.

Although the booster pumps are always selected as a safety measure for take-off, the normal suction feed could cope with take-off power.

The flight engineer, correctly, would have made his panel safe before going to the toilet, sweeping the booster-pumps up into the ON position. There are four normally accepted reasons for a turbine engine failure: lack of fuel; air instead of fuel; presence of water, and otherwise contaminated fuel. The aircraft had been on the ground at Bombay for many hours, during the hot and humid monsoon season. It was normal to refuel soon after arrival. The kerosine fuel had had several hours to settle in the tanks and, with its peculiar ability to soak up water, and aided by melted condensation within the tanks, there would have been several gallons of water lying at the bottom of the fuel tanks. During the departure checks, the ground engineers will normally perform a drain-check on the fuel tanks. In temperate climates a jar is usually sufficient. During the monsoon in Bombay a bucket or old oil drum would be needed. It could well have been the case, that on this occasion, there was no fuel-drain check carried out before departure.

After start-up and on the subsequent take-off and climb, the suction pumps, alone, would not have drawn in the water; when the flight engineer switched on the booster-pumps, which feed from the bottom of the tanks, gallons of water would have been pumped through the cross-feed system into the engines, extinguishing the power on all four engines simultaneously.

Twenty-five years after the flame-out incident, 5Y-ADA is pictured at Boscombe Down, in service with the Royal Air Force. Now a K3 tanker, ZA148, she is fitted with refuelling drogue attachments which can be seen below the wings and under the rear fuselage. 14th June 1992. (Author)

In September, 1967, a special Super VC10 service was operated beyond Bombay to Hong Kong as a proving flight for a planned extension, as well as to carry the Hong Kong Trade Mission to East Africa. The aircraft, 5X-UVA, left Nairobi at 13.00 on Thursday 7th September, routing via Addis Ababa, Karachi and Bombay. The first sector to Bombay was commanded by Captain Leo Davidson, with Captain George Atchison, N/O Jock Milne and E/O Vic House. At Bombay the crew changed and Captain Reg Cartwright, First Officer Jan Hognerud, N/O Bob Gallon and E/O Andy Welmans took the flight on via Bangkok, to make the first East African Airways landing at Hong Kong's Kai-Tak airport. When Captain Cartwright put 5X-UVA down on the notoriously difficult runway at Hong Kong, it was a doubly notable occasion, the first E.A.A. flight and also the first Super VC10 to be seen at Hong Kong.

After a stay of five hours, the aircraft was ready to return to Nairobi, commanded by Captain George Leslie with Captain G.W. Mitchell, N/O Frank MacNabb and E/O Alan James, who had spent the previous two days as guests of Cathay Pacific, flying familiarisation trips into Hong Kong in Convair 880s. One of their trips had taken them to the Philippines, where Manila was the bad weather alternate for Kai Tak airport.

On the return to Nairobi, en route to Bangkok they flew at altitudes of 36,000ft, within a 30 mile wide corridor overhead the American air base at Da Nang, controlled by the centre below them to avoid the paths of the B52s on their bombing missions from far away Guam. At Bombay, Captain Davidson and his crew took over again and they departed for Nairobi, where they touched down at Embakasi ten minutes earlier than the scheduled time of arrival. In the commercial and operations departments, detailed planning was under way with the intention of commencing scheduled operations to Hong Kong in November, 1988. The plans were, in fact, to extend the route to Japan, with a tentative date for a Tokyo schedule beginning in April, 1970. Financial constraints dictated that the development costs of the new route should be spread over a period, during which it was hoped that the airline would become known throughout the Far East through an established sales organisation.

Passengers arriving from London on the overnight flight would disembark, blinking in the bright African sunlight as they walked to the bus which would take them the short distance to Embakasi's passenger terminal. They would not notice the tall, casually dressed figure standing nearby, unobtrusively observing the post-arrival bustle which surrounded the aircraft, as the holds were emptied of baggage, mail and cargo. David Drummond was the chief of security for East African Airways. Every airline provides a multitude of opportunities for fraud, theft and crimes undreamed of by most honest citizens. By its very nature, an aircraft which traverses the globe can extend the possibilities for criminals to operate on a multinational basis – territories such as East Africa harboured their fair share of smugglers, thieves, illegal immigrants and fraudsters.

Drummond had a background which eminently suited the requirements for his task. Born in Nairobi to Scottish settler parents, he was educated as a boarder at the Prince of Wales school where he took his Cambridge School Certificate. He, like many white Kenyans, had been brought up on a farm, where as a child he had mixed freely with the Kikuyu children of the herdsmen and farm labourers, it was not surprising that he was fluent in their language. Deciding against his initial interest in hunting professionally, although he was a first rate Bisley shot, he doubted that it would provide a decent living, so he studied surveying and worked for a time as an assistant engineer.

He was at the time a part time officer in the Kenya Police Reserve and, in 1952, decided to join the regular police. This was the time of the Mau Mau atrocities. Drummond, with his Kikuyu and Swahili language skills was enlisted as an officer in the Special Branch. The period spent in the Special Branch, involving undercover work, blacked-up as a pseudo Mau Mau terrorist, infiltrating the gangs in the forests of the Aberdares, has been told in Denis Holman's book *Bwana Drum*. He received, in 1954, the Colonial Police Medal for Gallantry from the Governor of Kenya, Sir Evelyn Baring, and later, in 1956, he was invested with the George Medal by the Queen at an investiture at Buckingham Palace.

Drummond was a man with more than the average share of courage. In June, 1957, he was flying on police work in a Piper Tripacer piloted by police pilot Paul Harrowing.[3] They approached a dropping zone at a command post near Mogotio. Drummond was to drop a canister containing maps to the officers below. Harrowing cut the throttle and the little aircraft sank down in a steep descending glide. Unseen to the pilot was a mobile VHF mast, as Drummond leaned out, the canister in his hand, the wing of the Tripacer was sliced through by the radio mast. The aircraft spun down and crashed, coming to rest as a crumpled mass of metal. Drummond survived, but the cost was horrifying. It would take six years of slow and painful work by the surgeons of East Grinstead hospital, to rebuild his face, which had been virtually destroyed.

Bwana Drum, as he was known to the Africans, had played a leading role in the elimination of the Mau Mau gangsters, he had received appalling personal threats to his life during the course of his police work and yet, following independence in Kenya, he never suffered one instance of recrimination, in fact his house in the Ngong Road was often visited by police, just to ensure that all was well.

In view of the disaster which befell him in the Tripacer, it was extraordinary that Drummond went on to learn to fly at Wilson airport, during his off-duty time at E.A.A., in a Cessna 150 and, finally, decided to leave East African Airways in order to gain his Commercial Pilots Licence at Oxford and, subsequently, to fly visitors on safari in Kenya.

Captain Tug Wilson had converted to the Super VC10 under the tutelage of Captain Roberts of BAC in November, 1966. As with his up-grade to the Comet, he felt that he had been passed over in the selection process. Again, he found that

---

[3] Paul Harrowing also suffered severe injuries. He was to become a DC-9 captain with East African Airways.

there were others, who had gone on earlier courses, who were junior to him. He completed his conversion training, flying out of Wisley, Gatwick and Bristol and returned to Nairobi to take up his duties flying the line services. On his first command trip, towards the end of 1966, he was flying the sector into Dar es Salaam. As he commenced the descent, he was suddenly horrified to find gallons of water rushing forward, soaking his feet, as it disappeared beyond the rudder pedals and down into the electrical bay below. Within a few seconds every warning light on the panel was flashing and glowing. On final approach the Dar es Salaam controller assured him that the gear was down, contrary to the warning light indications. He adjusted his approach to produce as slow a landing as possible, as the lights told him that he had no brakes, and the runway at Dar es Salaam was not long at the best of times.

Following their safe arrival, investigations revealed that a first class passenger had visited the toilet just aft of the flight-deck and the wash basin tap had failed to close. After half an hour on the ground with all the doors open, things dried out and on start-up everything was back to normal.

On 28th March, 1967, Wilson commanded his last East African Airways service, from Bombay to Nairobi. After twenty years with the Corporation, his disagreements with management unresolved, he had had enough, and on the date that he

Captain H. 'Tug' Wilson some three years before retirement.

(Capt Wilson)

was eligible to collect his provident fund pension, 31st March, he resigned. It was to be the end of his career, for he was never again to fly an aircraft or take up any other employment. He had seen a great many changes in the years that he had flown for East African Airways. In the twenty years since he had left M.E.A. at Beirut to start a new life in Kenya he had flown 13,688 accident free hours.

Wilson had accumulated over 17,000 hours, somewhere between four and five million miles, without a single accident, although there were incidents and adventures too numerous to mention. He represented the no-nonsense, adventurous, pioneering tradition which made the airline so outstanding in the past.

Tim Nightingale, who had flown with him, both as a navigator and, later, as a flight engineer, remarked upon his uncanny skill in "greasing the Super VC10 onto the runway". "I can see, pictured in my mind, the bogies dangling beneath the aircraft, and, as the runway comes up to meet the wheels, I can see exactly when to check the descent and flare," Wilson told him. To some people it was called 'flying by the seat of your pants'; but with Tug Wilson it was something else; it was a natural skill and an understanding of the elements, in which the pilot and machine reach a degree of harmony which all pilots seek, not always with success.

There was, sadly, less and less need of such captains in the new East African age. Among many of his colleagues there was disappointment and bewilderment at his decision. They could not afford to lose a captain of his stature from their midst.

Another departure occurred in 1967; A.W. (Archie) Watkins, MBE, the last connection with Wilson Airways, who had served East African Airways so faithfully from the very beginning, retired from service with the airline's engineering department.

With the governments of the three partner states contributing to the costs of training young East Africans to become pilots, the programme was gaining momentum. At the end of 1967, twenty-five cadets were being trained, sixteen at the Embry Riddle Aeronautical Institute in Florida, six at the Oxford Air Training School and three at Airwork in Perth. In the engineering department, before 1967, engineering apprentices were recruited at the rate of twelve per annum, this number being the maximum entry that could be accommodated in the engineering base. In 1967, with the offer of overseas bursaries, the number was increased to eighteen. The total number of East African apprentices under training in 1967 was fifty-one, including twelve studying in the United Kingdom and eight in India. Unfortunately, experience was showing a wastage rate of approximately thirty per cent per annum as the young Africans left engineering for more advanced academic training elsewhere, which would lead to 'white collar' jobs in the administration.

The airline maintained its drive to recruit graduates and others of similar standards as a category of staff most suited to accelerate the replacement of expatriate staff in the executive grades. Interviewing boards were held on nine occasions during 1967, involving 112 candidates either of graduate status or non-graduates experienced in appropriate disciplines. Twenty offers were made principally to fill positions in the commercial department, of which sixteen were accepted.

Over 13,000 applications for employment of Cambridge School Certificate standard were received from all over East Africa. Of the 1,400 interviewed, 612 were engaged principally for the sales, traffic and catering divisions of the commercial department and for the accounts department. Others were placed in the administration services of the engineering and operations departments. A total of fifty-seven courses were held with 765 candidates attending, of whom seventy-three per cent passed the course examinations. Additionally, six specialised courses were held and attended by fifty-two staff of travel agencies. Training was given by on-station instructors in traffic and sales routines and procedures at Nairobi, Dar es Salaam, Entebbe and Kampala as well as in mail and cargo functions at Nairobi Airport. B.O.A.C. arranged and conducted advanced courses in London for a further forty-seven staff.

Expatriates were departing in larger numbers from the key office positions. Those posts Africanised during 1967 included: manager, Uganda; station superintendent, Mombasa; official-in-charge, Mbeya; controller sales office, McKinnon Building, Nairobi; controller reservations control office, Nairobi; international relations officer, HQ; and one duty traffic officer post each at Nairobi, Dar es Salaam and Entebbe. African designates were nominated for the posts of sales manager, headquarters; airport cargo manager, Nairobi, and tours promotion officer, Nairobi. In the accounts department, the number of expatriates employed further decreased and recruitment of graduates was maintained providing on-the-job training in executive grade appointments.

Staff figures at the end of 1967 showed a further increase over the previous year with a total of 3,830, an increase of 379. There were 402 expatriates, of whom eighty-five per cent were crew and engineering staff.

Many training and conversion courses were held to speed the Africanisation of cabin crew. In particular, the more senior positions on Super VC10 aircraft became available to locally trained staff, replacing some of the expatriate staff. Of 112 cabin crew working on international routes, sixty-six were African. The domestic flights were served entirely by African cabin crew.

Aircrew training was carried out on simulators installed for all three main aircraft types. The Friendship and Comet simulators were used for some 1,200 hours training for all pilots requiring instrument training and for Instrument Rating training and tests. Cadet pilots received an introduction to instrument flying on the simulators. The Super VC10 simulator, which had been installed in the second half of the year, was used for almost 700 hours. In the air, the DC3 had proved to be a most useful aircraft for training the African cadets. Nearly 4,000 aircraft flying hours of route training were completed on the DC3s, mainly with African cadets.

In ground operations a considerable increase in workload was brought about by the introduction of the Super VC10s. Navigational services moved into the ground floor of the headquarters building and by the end of the year work was well advanced for the move of the operations control centre to the Headquarters building, together with a new single-sideband (SSB) HF station.

At the time the evaluation panel had been considering the Comet 4 replacement, consideration had to be given to improving communications within E.A.A.C., since the operational reliance on B.O.A.C., already largely reduced, had to be replaced by self-sufficiency. It was vital that communication between Nairobi and the Super VC10s should be possible at all times. With this in mind, Ted Boyle and Derek Rhodes rigged up a Collins SSB transceiver at the operations base, slinging a piece of wire out of the window to act as an antenna. They were amazed when, after some test calls produced no results, suddenly, they found themselves in clear contact with a British United Airways VC10 on final approach to Buenos Aires airport.

It was following results of these early tests, conveyed to the evaluation panel, with the enthusiastic support of the panel chairman, chief engineer A.E. 'Robby' Robinson, that negotiations were entered into with Collins, resulting in East African Airways becoming the first carrier in Africa to possess an SSB/Log Periodic communications system. A substantial portion of the £50,000 cost was recovered in co-ordinating from Nairobi an early Super VC10 engine change – although exceeding, at times, the authority for use of the system, which was governed by international telecommunications agreements.

The single-sideband HF radios installed in the Super VC10s enabled them to remain in voice contact with Nairobi operations from almost anywhere in the world. 'Eastaf Radio' at Nairobi and the similar facility at London Airport 'Speedbird London' were manned and operated by International Aeradio Ltd. Sometimes, if reception conditions were suitable, it was possible to speak to base from the flight deck, while parked at London, in order to pass information of delay or engineering requirements.

The station operated by B.O.A.C. through I.A.L., on a permanent licence from the G.P.O. to operate ground/air/ground communications for company use, transmitted from a station at Birdlip in Gloucestershire, controlled by landlines from Heathrow. Consisting of two Marconi 1 KW transmitters (one for standby) feeding into a high-gain directional aerial giving an effective radiating power of 5 KW, the system covered the African continent as far south as Johannesburg. After a period of experimental use, the B.O.A.C. system came into operation during 1968, after being given high priority as a means of effective communication during a period of unprecedented political unrest.[4]

It was not unknown, when Nairobi failed to receive a transmission through atmospheric distortions in the ionosphere, for it to be picked up by 'Springbok Radio' at Jan Smuts Airport, Johannesburg, and relayed back to Nairobi. A practice which the African politicians certainly would have disallowed.

Politics caught up with the general manager, Mr Wilson Kyobe, in November. Kyobe was a Muganda and, it was widely believed, a relative of the Kabaka of

---

[4] 1967/68 saw: The six day war in the Middle East; the independence of Aden after bitter fighting; Soviet invasion of Czechoslovakia; continuing civil war in Nigeria; two Israeli airliners attacked at Athens and the resultant destruction of 13 Arab aircraft at Beirut by the Israelis.

Buganda. Uganda had undergone a period of severe conflict during 1966, during which the Baganda had come very close to civil war with the administration of Milton Obote. Disputing the constitution, they had passed a resolution in the Lukiko, or Baganda parliament, that the central government should withdraw from Buganda territory by 30th May. On 24th May, Obote's forces, led by Colonel Idi Amin, attacked the palace of the Kabaka, who fled once it was obvious that the cause was lost. The Kabaka went into exile in England, from where he would never return. The Baganda people were at the mercy of their despised enemy, Milton Obote and his equally hated Langi tribesmen.

The appointment of general manager in the airline was one of the positions nominated by the partner states. In this case, Uganda. Wilson Kyobe had been summoned to a meeting by the Uganda government at Kampala, during November. This co-incided with an I.A.T.A. meeting in Singapore, at which among other things, new promotional fares to East Africa from the U.S.A., Europe and the Middle East were to be discussed. Kyobe felt that this meeting was of such importance that he should attend. The result of this decision was that an open Telex was sent on the instructions of Chief Fundikira who was acting on orders from the Uganda government, that he was "dismissed from his appointment with immediate effect". Kyobe read the message, which was brought to him at the I.A.T.A. meeting, with shock and disbelief.

The results for 1967 came as a disappointment after the continuous run of increased operating surpluses of the past years. The figures showed that after charging K£1,577,241 for fleet and general depreciation, the net operating profit was K£189,717 compared with K£713,308 in 1966. After various deductions and additions for subvention payments to S.K.A.T. and interest received on Stock, the surplus on operations was K£181,979 from a total revenue of £13,060,458, giving a marginal return of 1.4 per cent.

The leasing commitment for the Super VC10 original project at 31st December, 1967, including the three aircraft delivered totalled £8,864,958 sterling without provisions for payment of future interest. Payments were to be made from revenue over seven years at quarterly intervals from the delivery dates of the aircraft. The commitment for the fourth aircraft and spare engine to be delivered in March, 1969, and a second Twin Otter to be delivered in April, 1969, was K£3,170,838 not including provision for the future payment of interest.

While operations for 1967 had not produced as large a surplus as those of recent years, it was felt that a sound position had been established from which to go forward with a degree of confidence into 1968. Much had been learned during the year of the airline's new and favoured front-line Super VC10 aircraft in the operational, engineering and commercial spheres. The improved traffic loads which had emerged during the second part of the year were encouraging. With the plans for new services to Bangkok, Hong Kong and new European destinations, following the delivery of a fourth aircraft, there were high hopes for further growth.

It could not be ignored, however, that there were clouds on the horizon which could not be circumvented. These included the prospect of declining revenue yields resulting from the growing emphasis in sales promotion being placed upon non-standard lower fares and rates, while having to resolve problems of increasing costs in all spheres. In addition, provision had to be made for financing, at a high rate of initial investment, for the next generation of first-level airliners. In common with airlines around the world, the prospect of financing from revenue the future widebody, high cost airliners, then under construction, without government aid was daunting.

In December, 1967, Kenya introduced new immigration and work permit regulations designed to produce rapid Africanisation of the commercial sector, which traditionally had been dominated by the Asian community, ranging from small shop keepers to international business moguls. The civil service had been completely Africanised, with some key exceptions where expatriate advisors remained temporarily in office. East African Airways employed Asians in considerable numbers, many of the engineering technicians were drawn from the Asian community as were many clerical and supervisory staff. The majority of Asians throughout East Africa had retained their British Colonial citizenship, fearing that events within the East African countries may drive them to seek the protection of Britain, at some future date.

The new immigration regulations, which required Asians to register for Kenya citizenship, if they wanted to retain their trading licences, coupled with the fear that the British government would soon introduce legislation to curb entry to Britain of Asians holding British Colonial citizenship, caused panic among the Asian population, leading to a mass exodus by many thousands of Asians of Indian and Pakistani origin. There were appalling scenes, as Africans gleefully drove the Asians out, appropriating their cars and other property, believing that with their departure the jobs, shops and wealth would fall into their hands.

As a result of the exodus, East African Airways benefitted by virtue of the increase in Comet charters to London, in addition to the one-way bookings on the Super VC10s and aircraft of B.O.A.C. and B.U.A.

For East African Airways the exodus brought a short term gain of minimal value, since the charters and scheduled service bookings were one way – the S.K.A.T. flights all returned to Nairobi empty. On the opposite side of the scale, however, was the loss to the engineering department alone of more than 100 skilled artisans, who now had to be replaced by African recruits, requiring motivation and training, during which time the airline would be hard pressed to maintain efficiency and productivity in those areas of depleted skilled manpower.

A major step to strengthen East African unity was taken at Arusha in Tanzania on 1st December, 1967, when the three partner states signed the Treaty for East African Co-operation, creating an East African economic community of thirty million people. Common services such as railways, harbours, post office and airways hitherto operating wholly or partly under the direction of the East African Common Services Organisation were concurrently re-constituted as Corporations and became Institutions of the East African Community. East African Airways had, under its previous constitutions acted as a Community corporation so very little changed – other than the board of directors, which was renewed by the appointment of fresh nominees.

1968

The Directors and Officers of East African Airways following the institution of the East African Community were, in 1968:

Chairman
Chief Abdullah Said Fundikira

Directors
J. Mawalla
A.J. Nsekela (to May 1968)
Gurdial Singh
A. Tiberondwa
G.W. Gichuki
T.M.C. Chokwe
Wg.Cdr. G.L.W. Boswell
Sir James Simpson, K.B.E.
H.R. Msefya (from September 1968)

Executive Management
W.O. Lutara Director General
M.S. Amalemba Administrative Director
F.B. Mahatane Secretary to the Corporation (from April 1968)
S.G. Choppin Financial Controller
R.E. Young Commercial Director (to June 1968)
A.C. Faraji Commercial Director (from July 1968)
C.E. Smith Chief Engineer
Capt. L.R. Davidson Director of Operations (to September 1968).

This was the team which was to determine the fortunes of the airline in the immediate future. Under their administration, 1968 was to prove an exceptionally good year for East African Airways,

With the delivery of two more Twin Otters, the requirement for S.K.A.T. to be solely concerned with the Zanzibar-Pemba-Tanga-Dar es Salaam route pattern was ended. With ever increasing foreign competition in the charter market, it had been decided that East African Airways would enter the non-I.A.T.A. fare market by means of their ready made subsidiary operator, Seychelles Kilimanjaro Air Transport Ltd. Thus it became possible to market low fare charters, both within East Africa and abroad. S.K.A.T. long-haul charter flights were operated with the Comets, in addition to their use on the E.A.A. inter-city services, for which the Comet 4s were not ideally suited, being designed for longer distance international flights.

Decisions had to be made soon about the replacement of the Comets. There was concern over the continued serviceability of the aircraft, which would require extensive and costly re-building to overcome main-spar fatigue. Continued use of Comet 4s for internal services would bring diminishing returns as they aged. On long-haul charter services, they would soon be overtaken by the large capacity aircraft which were already being presented, offering greatly reduced seat-mile costs in addition to the large wide-body cabins which the travelling public would demand. For the internal routes the types under consideration at the time were the BAC111, the Boeing 737 and the McDonnell Douglas DC-9. (But unlike on previous occasions, a technical committee had not been appointed to evaluate the aircraft). Even the Friendships were now considered inadequate in payload to provide a sufficient number of seats and cargo space to meet all the varying levels of demand on the internal routes.

DHC-9 Twin Otter, 5H-MNK, being turned round at Entebbe, with evidence of full employment. (Mr T.Webb)

The DC3 fleet was reduced from nine to six aircraft by the sale of three aircraft, one each to Zambia Airways and Hunting Aerosurveys in Zambia and one to Air Malawi. Together with the Twin Otters and Friendships, the DC3s shared in over 550 charter flights carrying tourists to the game parks and coastal resorts. There were now seven African first officers flying on the Friendship and DC3 operated services.

For many years E.A.A.'s continued expansion in the number of services and capacity offered in the operation of regional/international routes had kept the overall unit costs of operation at a reducing rate. This had been made possible through the increasingly greater capacity of the aircraft used to operate those routes compared with the capacity offered by the aircraft operating the domestic services. In terms of capacity ton miles performed per aircraft hour, whereas in 1964 each average aircraft hour flown provided capacity of 1,630 ton miles, five years later in 1968, an average hour flown produced 3,427 ton miles.

The influence of the larger aircraft operating the international services in keeping down the overall unit operating costs was plainly apparent, particularly since the principal aircraft such as F27 Friendships and DC3s operating the domestic services in 1964 were generally still the same in effective numbers and type for 1968, but supplemented to a minor degree by Comets.

The effect of the available wider spread of overheads, due to the accelerated rate of expansion on the international services, had only been of assistance to the domestic services in lowering their share of the costs commonly shared by both domestic and international services. There had been no corresponding check on the effect of growth in costs directly incurred in the operation of domestic services, such as labour, spares, supplies and services.

In effect, the international services had been subsidising the domestic routes for eleven years during which domestic fares had remained unchanged. In July, 1968, the domestic fare structure was brought up to date by an increase of 10 per cent in fares and rates. An estimated increase in revenue of K£156,000 during the first six months was expected to go some way in reducing the scale of cross-subsidisation of the domestic services by the remaining operations.

It was not to be, however; the new fares were rescinded in July of the following year, on instructions from the political masters, who regarded the domestic services as a social necessity and the fare increases were seen as inflationary. It was an indication of the gradually spreading perception that the airline was to provide for the economy from its revenue sources, derived from, principally, the wealthy foreign customers.

Apart from increasing services to Europe, the United Kingdom, Malawi, Rwanda and within East Africa, to match demand, new calls were inaugurated during 1968 with Super VC10 aircraft through Athens, once a week, in April, followed by a second frequency in May. The Eastern service was extended from Bombay to Hong-Kong once weekly from November, (with plans already being made for an extension to Tokyo, with an eye on Japanese tourist traffic) and once weekly Comet services were terminating at Cairo with F27 Friendships operating once a week to and from Mogadiscio.

An IBM computer reservations project was systematically phased into the reservations control system and finally superseded the manual system in September, enabling greater efficiency in dealing with the increasing numbers of seat reservations during the period of Africanisation and training in a vital key function of the airline.

A further dilution of the airline's revenue earning base occurred following the conclusion of an agreement between K.L.M. and E.A.A. permitting K.L.M. to operate into East Africa on the route Amsterdam-Munich-Tunis-Entebbe-Nairobi-Dar es Salaam and vice versa on a once weekly basis. East African was permitted to operate to Amsterdam and beyond, on a once weekly basis.

The expansionist policies of East African Airways were fuelled by political desire to have the national airline of the three states seen, by as many of their contemporaries as possible, flying into the capitals of the world. In their vain-glorious enthusiasm to pursue their aim, no one dared whisper negative thoughts or ask uncomfortable questions. Given the choice, for example, would the passengers from Holland, Germany and the United States, (where there was strong loyalty to their national airlines and considerable prejudice in favour of the quality and professionalism of their crews) be comfortable with the idea of flying on a new (to them) airline seemingly crewed and controlled by Africans from newly independent countries? The negotiations which continued month by month with foreign countries for bi-lateral traffic rights and the extension of the route network to distant capitals would be dependent for their success on passenger loyalty to E.A.A. The passenger growth was not going to come out of the impoverished East African countries.

Passengers carried during 1968 rose to 421,989 of which 176,876 flew on the regional/international services. The percentage passenger increase on these routes was 30.7 per cent on the previous year. Comets operating the S.K.A.T. charters made a profit of K£2,288 in an active year during which they competed with foreign charter companies operating at low non-I.A.T.A. fares. Charter package tours from Germany and Scandinavia were gradually becoming a threat to the regional fare structure as they increased at an alarming rate. Malindi was already considered almost a 'German colony', with German replacing English as the primary language on many hotel menus, and the local Moslem people complaining about the women tourists immodest mode of dress and the moral dangers to their daughters; tourist money was attracting the good-time girls from Nairobi, disturbing the old coast way of life.

A Comet was made available for a West African tour by President Nyerere at the beginning of the year and a combined Comet and Super VC10 operation was mounted to and from Karachi and Bombay during President Nyerere's Far East tour in June. Comet and F27 Friendship charters were also arranged for visits by President Obote to Dar es Salaam and Arusha.

Fleet utilisation showed a 25 per cent increase in the Super VC10 fleet and a small increase in Twin Otter utilisation:

Super VC10	10,599 hours	9.71 per aircraft/day
Comet 4	4,898 hours	5.30 per aircraft/day

Friendship	9,726 hours	6.68 per aircraft/day
DC3	11,651 hours	4.84 per aircraft/day
Twin Otter	2,029 hours	3.15 per aircraft/day

A new committee had been formed called the Board's Appointments and Africanisation Committee. There was dissatisfaction at political level concerning the speed of Africanisation. The goal was to have all appointments and departments fully manned by citizens (meaning Africans) with as little delay as possible. With the appointment of Mr F.B. Mahatane as secretary to the corporation and the positions of commercial director; sales manager; manager Tanzania; publicity manager; expenditure accountant; budget accountant and tours promotion manager all Africanised, eyes were turning upon the operations department to come up with pilots. Twenty-seven African pilots completed their courses during the year, of these seventeen came from flight schools in the U.S.A. and ten from the U.K. With seven African first officers flying on the DC3s and F27s and Steve Wanyee, the first African flight engineer, flying on the Comets, it was not regarded as being enough. Pressure was being put on the director of operations and the instructors to get the pilots qualified. This pressure was to build up considerably in the months ahead.

On 26th September, 1968, Captain Leo Davidson was killed while off duty at home. He had been using an electric drill to make a hole in a wall, at the same time clearing the dust with a vacuum cleaner, when he was electrocuted. By the time he was discovered, he was dead. This tragedy was a great blow to everyone who had known him, and he would be deeply missed by his colleagues. At the time of his death he was forty-four years of age. He had come to Kenya with his parents, in 1928, and was educated at the Prince of Wales School, Nairobi. In 1941, he had joined the Royal Air Force and gained his pilot's wings, after training in Rhodesia and Britain. In 1943, he was awarded the DFC for long range operations over Sumatra and Malaya. He joined East African Airways at its inception, flying one of the original DH89A Rapides from England in 1945, and flew every aircraft type, except the F27, as it was introduced by the airline.

The end of 1968 brought about some sombre reflections by the airline:

The duty of the airline as expressed in the East African Airways Corporation Act 1967, is to provide air services both within and to/from the partner states on a commercial basis.

It is considered the airline performed this duty during 1968 in a generally satisfactory manner whilst acknowledging changes could be made to give improved performance. The tasks to be attended to in this respect are seen as:

1. Service to the customer

2. Staff productivity and cost consciousness

3. New aircraft for domestic/regional services

4. Load Factors

The results for 1968 show that the introduction of the Super VC10 aircraft has consolidated East African's position as an operator of repute on the trunk routes to Europe/

Britain and Pakistan/India. The passenger appeal, ease of operation and technical qualities of the aircraft should ensure the viability of the Super VC10 services up to 1973 when the major part of the project will have been paid for.

The choice of a new type of aircraft for the inter-city domestic and the Africa lesser-density regional routes has however to be decided but it is now expected to be made in 1969 for delivery in late 1970. There is now no doubt that the Friendship aircraft are inadequate in payload to meet all the varying levels of demand experienced on these routes, both present and to be expected. Moreover, the Comet 4 aircraft as now employed on the inter-city and the Africa regional services do not return as favourable operational economics as they give on long haul services.

A training school with more advanced facilities is recognised as being necessary to develop staff education, to raise performance and courtesy standards as well as to inculcate the ideals of service and loyalty. This could result in greater productivity and higher load factors and is a feature of the 1968/72 five year plan. Finance, however, has yet to be obtained although the requirement of K£250,000 for the purpose has been **brought to the attention of the donors of development aid.**

For some years now, the major part of East African's production has been directed towards the East Africa/Europe/Britain services. These contribute in similar proportions to the total of the airline's revenues. While, however the market for this traffic continues to expand, it is clear East African is not moving ahead at the rates of growth experienced by many of the more internationally known competitor airlines. The growth in their number intensifies the competition for East African as much now at home in East Africa as abroad. **Every airline securing new traffic rights in East Africa and opening up new services adds further strength to the competition.**

It is also East African's duty to maintain financial viability, this competition has to be met and will be met to the full extent of the airline's resources.

Now with a total of 4,104 employees at the end of the year, including an increase of twenty qualified pilots, eight navigators and two flight engineers. Out of a total of 191 cabin crew, 126 were African. The year had brought more than satisfying results, compared with the disappointing figures of 1967. The three Super VC10s now in operation contributed significantly to the published figures:

Revenue	K£14,890,610	up 14.0 per cent
Expenditure	K£14,438,443	up 12.2 per cent
Net Operating Profit	K£452,167	up 138.3 per cent
Surplus on Operation	K£466,534	up 156.4 per cent
Output – Capacity ton miles	128,349,000	up 22.3 per cent
Seat miles	910,523,000	up 20.5 per cent
Traffic – Load ton miles	60,595,000	up 20.4 per cent
Passenger miles	448,675,000	up 19.4 per cent

The outstanding debt on the three Super VC10s stood at £7,572,643 sterling, without provision for payment of future interest. The purchase commitment for the fourth aircraft and spare engine to be delivered in April, 1969, was £3,591,342 sterling. The outstanding purchase commitment for the four Twin Otters, all delivered by 31st December, 1968, was Canadian $1,256,510 (K£415,085 at the ruling exchange rate). Payments for all the commitments were planned to be made from revenue over seven years at quarterly intervals from delivery dates of the aircraft.

1969

In January, 1969, there had been a Commonwealth Conference in London, attended by all the East African heads of state. On Friday, 17th January, the EC711 was to carry President Obote and his party back to Entebbe. The flight had been rescheduled from the normal 20.00 departure time to 21.30, to enable the president to complete his business in London. The baggage had been sent on in advance and was presented to the check-in clerk together with all the tickets for the party by a member of the Ugandan high commissioner's office. On being assured that the tickets and baggage represented the entire group, the check-in was completed and the bags were tagged and despatched for loading. The president duly arrived and was entertained in the VIP suite by the government representative. Boarding passes for the party were given out, after which it was found that there were three passes remaining. Following some frantic enquiries, it was discovered that three passengers were not travelling on the flight due to altered arrangements. The baggage, however, had all been loaded on the Super VC10.

President Milton Obote had many enemies, quite possibly some among his immediate entourage. The security implications were obvious to the E.A.A.C. traffic liaison officer as he entered the flight deck, where the crew were preparing for departure. Captain Dennis (Jacko) Jackson was not too keen to be further delayed that night, but he agreed that there was some cause for concern, in the circumstances. "We'll have to have all the bags off and checked by their owners", the TLO said. "You had better tell him", said Captain Jackson, nodding towards President Obote, sitting in the front first class seat.

"I'm afraid, sir, that we'll have to take all the baggage off and identify it; your party has checked in baggage for people who are not travelling – there's a security risk". Obote's eyes flashed as he said calmly, "You must do what you think best".

Everyone trooped off the aircraft, as the loaders, cursing their luck on a cold January night, were recalled to undo their work of an hour or more past.

The presidential party returned to the VIP suite, where a full scale trial commenced. Burly Ugandan bodyguards barred the doors as high commission staff were dragged into the room and thrown down to plead their innocence before the seemingly mild mannered Obote whose lieutenants were a great deal less gentle as they beat confessions out of those responsible. Finally all the bags were lined up by the loaders, the passengers identified their bags and the task of re-stowing them began. Finally, at 01.10, Flight EC711 departed, with the unclaimed bags standing forlornly on the now empty Heathrow apron.

Captain Jackson subsequently went to another airline, Gulf Air. One night at Karachi, a similar incident occurred, when he was told by the despatcher that they were one passenger 'light'. On being asked whether he wanted to depart with a loadsheet error, he said "No, I want a baggage check". As the bags were returned to the baggage hall, there was an explosion – one of them contained a bomb.

At the beginning of the year, there had been some changes at the top in E.A.A. It had been decided that the executive management would now be constituted of directors – the term manager had been dropped. Mr Kyobe who had departed in 1967, was replaced at the beginning of 1968 by fellow Ugandan, Mr Wilson O. Lutara (variously described by his secretary, Captain Bill Fumerton's widow, Barbara, as 'a tall, gangling clown' and by Captain Cunningham as 'a fine man – a true gentleman') who would be director-general, with a seat on the board just below the chairman, Chief Fundikira. Captain Peter Cunningham had been appointed director of operations, replacing Captain Leo Davidson. Cunningham had been one of the first pilots recruited as first officers on the early Lodestar services. Prior to his new appointment he had been a Super VC10 fleet instructor before which he was chief pilot regional and domestic fleets, and chief pilot Comet fleet.

There had been efforts made to recruit those expatriate staff and aircrew which were necessary in the absence of qualified Africans, from countries which had no connection with the old 'colonial mentality'. Many of the pilots recruited in the previous year in advance of the fourth and fifth Super VC10 were from Scandi-

Captain Dennis Jackson.

navian countries. In keeping with this policy, a newly created director of planning and development was appointed, Mr T. Isaacson. This appointment was the result of an arrangement with S.A.S., whereby their former manager market and traffic research, on a two year loan, would head up E.A.A. market research, forecast and planning, with particular emphasis on pushing the E.A.A. routes across the Atlantic to the United States. Preceding this, a market survey of Japan was undertaken in the early part of 1969, and plans were made for a preliminary study of the Australian and New Zealand market, where in Australia particularly, it was believed that a tourist potential existed which could sustain a route extension.

Air service agreements were negotiated with the United States to permit East African, at a later stage, to mount services to New York via intermediate points on a frequency and routing reciprocal to that permitted to U.S. designated carriers. The agreed weekly frequency for the U.S. carriers was four services for the first year and thereafter six services for a three year period *after which there would be unlimited frequencies*. By 1970, the American carriers would be operating Boeing 747 Jumbo jets on the Atlantic routes. The fares, which permitted the thirsty Super VC10s to transport their 125 passengers economically, would have to tumble in order to fill the 350 or so seats on offer in each 747. Without further legislation, E.A.A. was at a disadvantage.

Delivery of the fourth Super VC10, 5X-UVJ, which departed London on the evening of 30th April, led to a route expansion in June which added Copenhagen (EC722/723 via Rome on 6th June) and Bangkok to the international network, with increased calls at Frankfurt, Paris, Rome and Hong Kong. New offices were opened in Hamburg, Munich, Copenhagen, Milan and Tokyo during the course of the year. In addition to the introduction of a service to Copenhagen, a Super VC10 service linking Addis Ababa and London was inaugurated, the first regular link of its kind, at the time. The poor condition of the runway at Addis was, however, a source of concern within the operations department. With Comets operating across to Lagos in West Africa, further agreements were concluded to permit operations to Accra. By the end of the year East African Airways would have an international route network encompassing flights to and from Accra; Addis Ababa; Aden; Athens; Bombay; Blantyre; Bujumbura; Cairo; Copenhagen; Dar es Salaam; Entebbe; Frankfurt; Hong Kong; Karachi; Kigali; Lagos; London; Lusaka; Mauritius; Nairobi; Ndola; Paris and Rome.

The Super VC10s of East African Airways, operating into Zambia's prestigious new airport at Lusaka, were proving to be a source of embarrassment and unease to the Zambian government, who were struggling, with the assistance of Alitalia, to maintain a regular international service with the Boeing 707s of their national airline. In November, 1968, Zambia took part in talks concerning her application to join the East African Community. During the year, the Zambian government had commissioned a survey by Arthur D. Little Ltd of New York and London, on the country's tourist industry and communications.

It was with great embarrassment that the government read, in the subsequent report, of Zambia Airways' incompetent management, overbookings and cancellations at short notice, followed by the recommendation that the Alitalia contract should not be renewed and that Zambia should join East African Airways "at the earliest opportunity". The report stated:

> *We seriously doubt whether Zambia has sufficient financial resources to create an effective, profit-making airline on her own...*
>
> *We believe it would be advisable for Zambia to investigate now the feasibility of joining East African Airways, when the current Zambia Airways' contract expires in 1972. East African Airways has been in existence for 23 years. It has a modern fleet. It has a well developed domestic and international route network, which is being aggressively extended to create new links with Europe and the Far East. It is a strong and rapidly expanding airline...*

The Zambian government reacted by claiming fifth freedom traffic rights out of East Africa, which, after prolonged discussions, were refused. Early in 1969, George Morton, the EAA manager in Lusaka, received a letter from the government ordering EAA not to sell tickets to destinations beyond East Africa. EAA had a large number of loyal clients among the expatriates of Zambia's copper-belt. They were not going to be defeated easily. East African overcame the problem by employing 'Flight Clerks' on all Lusaka services, who would apply onward reservation stickers to tickets, produce passenger manifests and, on arrival at Dar es Salaam, re-tag baggage to final destinations in Europe and beyond.

The route network by now produced greatly increased figures:

	1969	1968	Increase
Unduplicated Route Miles	75,711	67,554	12.1%
Miles flown	11.9 mill.	10 mill.	18.7%
Capacity Ton Miles	162.2 mill.	128.3 mill.	26.4%

Operating expenditure was up by 13.5 per cent on 1968, with the cost of operating the aircraft up by 8.5 per cent. The increase in capacity offered by the fourth Super VC10 was of the order of 26.4 per cent, which had the effect of reducing net unit costs by 6.4 per cent to KShs.1/90 per capacity ton mile. As a further result of the increase in capacity, the passenger load factor decreased from 49.3 per cent in 1968 to 43.2 per cent in 1969 although passengers carried went up to 450,273 compared with 421,989 in 1968.

To add to the honour of being the first airline in the world to carry a reigning British Monarch, East African Airways was selected to carry, on the first visit to Africa by a reigning pontiff, His Holiness Pope Paul VI, on 31st July, 1969, from Rome to Entebbe.

The specially modified Super VC10, 5X-UVJ, was provided with a reconfigured cabin giving 24 first class seats in addition to the papal compartment situated in the area normally occupied by the cargo pallets. A luxurious cabin comprising a convertible divan/settee,[5] two first class seats, a dining table and a wardrobe was constructed in the compartment. In the rear of the aircraft were 75 tourist class seats.

The crew selected for this historic flight comprised Captain G. (Mitch) Mitchell, Captain Ian Ainscow, First Officer David Dempster, Flight Navigator D.J.(Griff) Griffiths, Flight Engineer P.L. (Tim) Nightingale. The cabin crew consisted of two Ugandan stewardesses, Ruth Lutale and Mary Muganga, with Pursers Ernest Elkington, Frank Morrison, Chief Steward John Abilla, Danish stewardess Eleonore Salingboe, In-flight Training Instructress Katherine Baguley and Cabin Services Supervisor Roy Parmenter. Nancy Leri, a French-Canadian married to an Italian, was a ground hostess at Rome. She joined the crew in order to give a welcoming address in Italian.

It was a proud moment as Captain Mitchell opened the throttles and 5X-UVJ commenced its powerful take-off from Rome's Fiumacino airport. With the temporal head of the world-wide Roman Catholic Church and twenty four of her Cardinals, departing on a mission of historic importance, the crew of the Super VC10 were well advised not to dwell too much on their responsibilities, but just get on with flying in the professional manner to which they were accustomed. Leaving Rome their route took them parallel to the coast of Italy, passing over the island of Ponza before crossing over the foot of Italy near the town of Catanzaro. They crossed the Mediterranean to be overhead Benghazi after one hour thirty-three minutes.

Their course was carefully monitored at all times by the controlling authorities below them. For additional security they remained in continuous SSB voice contact with B.O.A.C. at London Heathrow and with the Operations Centre at Nairobi.

Pope Paul had been provided with an in-flight guide, written in English and Italian, describing the route. As they passed over Benghazi, commencing the next 2 hour 30 minute leg to overhead Khartoum he would have read:

> *From Benghazi to Khartoum the area is complete desert until approaching the RIVER NILE in the vicinity of the old township of MEROWE. There is evidence to suggest that this town was the most southerly point of penetration by Roman Legionnaires. From that point to Entebbe the route lies approximately over the course of the river. The nature of the terrain begins to change after Khartoum commencing with the great area of cotton plantations between the BLUE and WHITE NILES.* **(Khartoum – Entebbe flight time 2 hours 04 minutes).** *The remainder of the route is scrub or bush country with some forest in the south. The Ethiopian escarpment is visible to the east after passing MALAKAL township. The level nature of the terrain continues until nearing the border of Uganda there changing to rolling hills and plains with forest and grasslands. Farther south near Entebbe lush tropical vegetation may be observed.*

The Pope was given some useful information on route climatology:

> *During the months of July and August the weather is good over the Mediterranean and North Africa except for very occasional depressions travelling along the North Africa coast.*

---

[5] This divan was borrowed from B.O.A.C., who used it for Royal Flights. Thus it could be truthfully said that the Pope and the Queen of England had slept in the same bed.

The main weather band lies approximately between latitudes 6 North and 12 North as a result of the northerly movement of the Inter-tropical Convergence Zone. This band of weather is not necessarily active continuously but follows quite marked cycles.

For passenger comfort a climb to the next upper level will be made if necessary after leaving Khartoum. Weather radar always ensures a smooth flight in this region.

Upper Winds and Temperatures
During the July - August period the West to East jet stream, normally existing over most of North Africa during the winter remains westerly or north westerly varying between 20-40 knots becoming light and variable between latitudes 20 North and 10 North. South of 10 North i.e. from Malakal to Juba the Equatorial Drift is prominent and easterly winds up to 40 knots can be expected. The overall wind component for this route will be in the region of 10 knots.

Ambient temperatures at Flight level 33,000ft will vary from -40C in the North to -37C in the South.

The flight went smoothly, according to plan. The Pope visited the flight deck during the cruise where Captain Mitchell explained the controls and equipment. The Pope asked many questions about the airline, its routes and aircraft and about the crew themselves and their families. Other questions which might arise could have been dealt with by Chief Fundikira who had joined the flight for the journey from Rome to Entebbe.

Pope Paul VI on the flight-deck of 5X-UVJ. Captain Ainscow stands behind as Captain 'Mitch' Mitchell explains features of the aircraft to His Holiness. F/O Dave Dempster is in the right-hand seat.

Passing into the airspace of the countries below, messages would be sent forward from His Holiness for transmission to the heads of state. The first one annotated by the navigator "Passed to Benina 118.1 07.32Z" read:

His Majesty
Mohammed Idris I AL Mahdi AL Sanusi
King of Libya
Tripoli
Libya

We respectfully salute your majesty from the aeroplane bearing us to the commemoration of heroic young Africans in Uganda, assuring you of our goodwill and esteem, and praying that god may grant your majesty and your people prosperity and peace.
PAULUS PP.VI

The special bed, loaned by B.O.A.C., used by the Pope and H.M. the Queen, on different occasions. (Mr Tim Nightingale)

332 · EAST AFRICAN: AN AIRLINE STORY

Pope Paul VI spoke with each of the crew members.
  Above: *With Flight Engineer Tim Nightingale,*
  Below: *with F/O Dave Dempster,*
  Opposite page: *with Captain Mitchell.*

Viewed through the cockpit window, the reception crowd waits for the Pope to disembark.

Nearly four hours later, another message, annotated "Passed to EBB 131.9 11.18Z" read:

His Excellency Doctor A. Milton Obote
President of the Republic of Uganda
Presidential Lodge
Kampala

As the aircraft bearing us to venerate the Uganda martyrs enters your national air space, we anticipate deferential greetings to Your Excellency, looking forward to the honour of our personal meeting.

PAULUS PP.VI

As they made their approach to the 9,875ft main runway at Entebbe, the enormous crowds could be seen, waiting to welcome the man who had come to canonise the first African Martyrs in the history of the church.

A newspaper photograph taken of the Super VC10 after arrival at Entebbe shows Captain Mitchell looking at a figure in the foreground. In full military regalia, swinging his swagger stick proudly, strode Colonel Idi Amin.

Colonel Idi Amin descends the aircraft steps after inspecting 5X-UVJ. It would be another 17 months before he seized power in Uganda. (Capt Mitchell)

Idi Amin dominates this group of Ugandan army officers talking with Capt Mitchell and Flight Navigator (navigation superintendent) Dave Griffiths.

Below:
Prior to the return flight of Pope Paul on 2nd August, 1969, Chief Stewardess Ruth Lutale, Rome ground hostess Nancy Leri and Senior Stewardess Kathy Baguley at Entebbe.

At the completion of the Pope's return flight to Rome, the crew relax at the ENALC hotel. L to R: Chief Steward John Abilla, Chief Stewardess Ruth Lutale, Purser Frank Morrison, Senior Stewardess Kathy Baguley, Captain Ian Ainscow, Stewardess Elleinor Salingboe, Stewardess Mary Muganga, E/O Tim Nightingale, F/O Dave Dempster (back to camera).

As time went by, the pilots and crews of East African would notice more of the Aeroflot Ilyushin IL62 "VC10ski" airliners, as the Soviets made more frequent visits to East Africa. These VC10 look-alikes were to be seen at most of the European and Far Eastern airports on the E.A.A. routes. The Soviets had for many years a very efficient industrial espionage network well entrenched in the British aircraft industry. This was not unknown to the British, who, rather than become embroiled in the inevitable confrontations both with the Soviet government and the British labour unions, would use the Russian spies as a conduit for mis-information (resulting, for example, in a virtually useless Soviet copy of Concorde). In the case of the VC10, the Soviets had obtained detailed information on the early models, which had suffered from engine problems resulting in surging, accompanied by unacceptably high fuel consumption. This had been cured by the Weybridge engineers, by repositioning the four engines in a re-designed mounting, which placed them ten inches further outboard from the fuselage, angled up three degrees, thus avoiding the wash from the wings.

This re-design information had been kept from the Russians, who had produced an aeroplane based upon the early Weybridge designs. They soon discovered that something was wrong and great efforts were made to obtain and examine the British performance and operations data.

Back in 1963, Captain Leslie had obtained a copy of the VC10 Flying Manual and the Engineers Technical Manual from the British Aircraft Corporation. He had been studying the information in advance of the acquisition of the Super VC10 by E.A.A. He kept the bulky manuals together with the other E.A.A. manuals in his flight bag, so that he could read them during off-duty times at slip stations on the routes.

On Friday, 13th December, 1963, Leslie and his crew had just boarded the B.O.A.C. crew bus at the Skyway Hotel for the EC711 Comet departure from London, when a porter ran out to say that the airport operations office was on the phone. Leslie went back into the hotel, carrying his flight bag and picked up the telephone, to learn that there was a technical problem with the aircraft. He finished talking with operations and took from his bag his little black book of numbers and made a call to engineering. He finished his call and bent down to replace his note book, only to find that his flight bag had gone.

The hotel lobby was crowded with arriving and departing crews and other guests. There was no sign of the bag in which he had his passport, licences, medical certificate (required by law to be carried while carrying out his duties), the flight manuals and, on top, a bottle of whisky.

The flight was delayed overnight while the B.O.A.C. engineers dealt with the technical problems. In the meantime the police had been alerted and tracer messages had been sent to all U.K. airports. The next morning, Saturday, 14th December, they departed for Nairobi, Captain Leslie was still without his bag and his documents.

On Sunday evening, Leslie was relaxing at home in Nairobi when a crew bus pulled up outside and the driver brought him his flight case. It was carefully sealed with customs seals and wire, and attached to the handle was a luggage label with the place of origin – Moscow. A scribbled note on the label, by the B.E.A. station manager at Moscow, explained that it had been found abandoned on a baggage counter. No doubt the K.G.B. technical experts had discovered with great disappointment that there was nothing in either of the VC10 manuals which would help them overcome their IL62 problems!

There had been a large increase in staff during 1969, an additional 715 bringing the total up to 4,916 of which 1,277 were expatriates. There was a turnover rate of 7.3 per cent, the actual number newly employed during the year was 1,048.

Africanisation was continuing to move ahead, and many departments were beginning to show strain from over manning – with no related improvements in efficiency. Some of the 'expatriate' (a term which was widely synonymous with 'white') staff were getting concerned that the efficiency of the airline would not survive the speed at which Africanisation was being implemented. It was not, however, an opinion which could be widely aired. In addition to the special courses for instruction of air crew and engineering apprentices, greater emphasis was being placed on the training of local staff of other categories.

At the commercial training centre, forty-three courses were held during 1969, attended by 550 staff from most of the stations. Of these 402, or 72.3 per cent achieved a satisfactory pass mark. Of fifty selected staff who attended B.O.A.C. traffic and cargo courses, thirty-three achieved the required standard. An additional seventy-one trainee stewards and stewardesses were engaged and trained, bringing the total number of African staff in cabin services to 178 out of a total establishment of 234. Special advanced courses were arranged with Lufthansa and T.W.A. for 1970, with the aim of having total Africanisation of cabin services by the end of the year. By the end of 1969, twenty-six African cadet pilots had completed their overseas training and were continuing training as first officers on the DC3 and Friendship fleets.

The end of 1969 had shown a disquieting fall in the level of profits; K£190,000, compared with K£466,534 in 1968. A considerable increase in aircraft capacity still had to be filled and paid for. In addition, there was serious and increasing competition from foreign scheduled and charter airlines operating into East Africa, further aggravated by the proliferation of low promotional fares and cargo rates on the main trunk route to Europe and the United Kingdom. With the withdrawal of the domestic fares, low overall growth in the airline industry, the poor drop in net profit was explained away.

Despite the fact that some airlines must try harder to gain the public's confidence, there was no advance warning to the passengers on the London to Nairobi flight which was diverted to Addis Ababa on 9th September, to pick up President Nyerere and party and was delayed five hours on the ground as a result. The passengers were extremely cross when they discovered what had happened. E.A.A.C. lost a number of future customers on that day alone. Unfortunately it would not be an isolated incident for the airline whose political masters were, with the exception of Jomo Kenyatta, inveterate travellers.

Mr Steve Choppin, the financial controller, was coming up to retirement and 1969 would be the last time that he would prepare the annual accounts. E.A.A.C. had changed beyond recognition since he came from B.O.A.C. to assist with the accounts back in 1951. Apart from its great expansion to parts of the world unthought of twenty years ago, the airline had undergone a great cultural change, no longer British in character, it was aspiring to the emerging Afro-Asian culture of the third world. No longer could the decisions regarding airline policy be taken following discussion between like-minded colonial governors, whose background and grooming for office would have enabled a level of full understanding between them. In Uganda, the leader, Milton Obote, while appearing to be an urbane, westernised statesman, was a tribal politician with a power base dependent upon an illiterate army. Julius Nyerere, in Tanzania had demonstrated his political and cultural preferences by embracing Marxism from eastern and western exponents of the doctrine. Only Kenya showed some pragmatic respect for the ways of the former colonial rulers, but again, tribalism often ruled political actions. Schools and universities were producing newly awakened, ambitious young Africans, hungry for jobs and status. Knowledge and understanding of airline economics and ethos would not feature high among their list of achievements, if at all; for many, the ways and aspirations of the European, western way of life was alien to African goals. The educated elite was still very small. In countries still primarily agricultural, the leaders were often more at home discussing cows. A Kalenjin member of parliament believed, with great conviction, that "a city existed beneath the ground in London" – an impression gained from a ride on the Underground during a visit to England for an agricultural show.

Mr Choppin's accounts for 1969 showed a small profit of K£190,000. But it was achieved in a difficult trading year by creative accounting, avoiding a politically unwelcome loss, gaining time for a return to profits in a years time. The assets of the Corporation were re-assessed "Following other international airline's practice". The fleet depreciation for 1969 was shown as K£1,040,300. By extending the book value of the fleet a saving of K£1,112,500 had been affected. It was the following changes which had reduced the fleet depreciation figures for the year:

1) *Super VC10 Amortisation period extended from 7 to 10 years with a residual value of 10 per cent.*

2) *F27 Friendship Amortisation period extended from 7 to 12 years with a residual value of 15 per cent reduced to 10 per cent.*

3) *Twin Otter Amortisation period extended from 10 to 12 years with a residual value of 10 per cent.*

Had the depreciation for 1969 been on the same basis as in previous years, the charge in the accounts would have been greater by K£1,112,500.

1969 ended with a hidden loss of nearly one million Kenya pounds, yet the airline was being asked to continue with route expansion programmes of great complexity, and with potential for failure at great cost. The chairman was busying himself with negotiations for more new aircraft. Africanisation was being pursued unremittingly, with huge increases in staff and training costs which showed continuing poor returns – staff turnover was 7.3 per cent in 1969. The warning bells were ringing loud and clear, but those who recognised them were branded enemies of the airline, or racists with 'colonial mentality'. Africa had to be given its chance, and those who appeared to be holding it back had better go...

1970

In common with most international airlines, the training and certification of qualified pilots was undertaken by instructors and examiners from the airline, who were licensed by the Department of Civil Aviation. Thus type ratings and instrument flight checks were carried out within E.A.A. by senior captains holding Type Rating Examiner and Instrument Rating Examiner qualifications. One of the difficulties encountered with the Africanisation programme was in the area of pilot qualification. One could quite easily appoint a sales manager or station manager with minimal qualifications, since there was no arbitrary examination and standard of achievement demanded by an outside authority. Pilots were required to meet international standards, there was no way that a responsible airline or governmental authority could gloss over the fact that a pilot was not up to the tasks imposed upon him.

The policy of Africanising the flight-deck was conditioned by two factors. On the one hand there were no East African citizens, other than white settlers, with advanced pilot qualifications or high numbers of hours of flight time. On the other hand, the only pilot instructors, T.R.E.s and I.R.E.s in the airline were white, expatriate senior captains, who were under an obligation, by law, to maintain standards. It soon became apparent that as the inexperienced and poorly qualified African pilots were pushed forward and failed, as they experienced the demanding disciplines of flight instruction, the effect would be to aggravate the sense of frustration among the directors charged with the policy of Africanisation.*

The pressures mounted on the director of operations, Captain Cunningham and his team of instructors. There were accusations of racial prejudice, obstruction of the aims of the East African Community and vague suggestions that "some people were agents of foreign powers or airlines". Efforts were made to recruit pilots from

---

*See *Notes to Second Edition*, page 446.

Mr C.E. Smith, with his wife and daughter, outside Buckingham Palace, following his investiture with the MBE.

other Afro-Asian countries. One pilot arrived from Pakistan. He reported to the flight simulator centre, where he was given a series of tests on the basic procedural trainer. It soon became evident that he had no experience and no real flying ability, he became disorientated and could not maintain headings or heights. The instructor sent him away and wrote a short negative report. Unfortunately, the man had been recruited by Chief Fundikira, short circuiting the normal selection routine. The situation did nothing to improve the relations between the flight instructors and the directors.

Shortly after this event, Captain Leslie, who was a flight simulator instructor at the time, was told by friends in management that *"they* were out to get him". He was due to go on leave, and he took the precaution of withdrawing all his cash from the bank and, together with some other possessions, wrapped them up in oilskins and hid them in a friend's fish pond. Fortunately, when he returned, things had died down and the threat seemed to have faded.

To add to the growing list of VIPs carried by the airline, Captain Cartwright commanded the Super VC10 which brought the King and Queen of Denmark from Copenhagen to Nairobi and Dar es Salaam on 9th/10th January. They took further flights from Nairobi to Addis Ababa returning to Nairobi on 15th. They departed home via Rome on 24th January. During February, President Makarios of Cyprus travelled from Nairobi to Mombasa.

More changes had occurred on the board and within the executive management. There were now, including the chairman Chief Fundikira, thirteen directors on the board. The executive management team consisted of eleven. By comparison, in 1960 there had been seven board members and nine members of executive management.

Chief Engineer C.E. 'Smudge' Smith resigned, after guiding the airline's engineering expansion and success with the Comet and Super VC10. He was unable to accept the manner in which the new chairman was proceeding with the acquisition of new aircraft. Ironically, he was to be invited to Buckingham Palace on his return to England, to receive the MBE, for services to aviation in East Africa. His replacement was Mr P.R. (Ron) Barton.

Mr Isaacson, the Scandinavian director of planning and development had been joined by a newcomer, Mr Nigel Thompson, a British director of marketing. Thompson had initiated a survey into the viability of extending the route network through to the United States. With the new route to Hong Kong failing to provide the passengers so confidently expected, and losing money heavily; and the internal routes dependent upon international revenues, since they were continuing, under government dictat, to operate with a fare structure unchanged for over ten years, it was remarkable that this project was on the agenda for early implementation, considering the financial risks involved. A rosy, up-beat survey report was prepared by the marketing department, which was totally in favour of the route extension. The most outstanding feature of the confidential report was its failure to even hint at the possibility of failure, accepting the glib promises of travel agents upon whom the project depended entirely for its success.

NEW YORK/NAIROBI: SCHEDULED SERVICE TRAFFIC SURVEY, JAN/FEB 70

The first question that needed answering was whether the US travel agents would be prepared to make use of East African Airways over the Atlantic.

Our researches revealed not only was the industry prepared to book on it but new direct one-plane services to Nairobi were welcomed with enthusiasm. More fast one-plane service was not an additional luxury, it was a necessity if the East African tourist potential was to be realised. The reaction to selling East African, previously known and respected within Europe, Africa and Asia, as a scheduled Atlantic carrier was favourable in the extreme – Super VC10 one-plane, fastest elapsed time scheduled service once a week between B.O.A.C.'s new terminal in New York and Nairobi was certainly a marketable proposition.

The next question to resolve was when would be the most advantageous time to inaugurate such a service. Our researches indicated that December 1970 was the ideal time if it was announced the previous April to afford a minimum of seven months for advance selling and image building.

We determined from our own experience and that learned from the industry itself that the following reasons indicated an early entry into this market for E.A.A.

1. For the first time East Africa is on the brink of having sufficient hotel rooms of a suitable standard to appeal to the U.S. tourist.

2. Competition is producing for the first time transport facilities and land arrangements at realistic prices.

3. A fare with appeal to the mass market has been agreed.

4. IATA regulations now preclude the airline picking up pax overnight accommodation charge in Europe.

5. The market to East Africa expanded 50% in the US from 1968-1969.

6. The US sees East Africa as a year-round destination, not a seasonal one.

7. East African Airways being the country of destination (sic) is more focused than any other airline serving East Africa and therefore has a special appeal to travel agents.

8. East African has the domestic flight facilities to service this market.

9. The US market is desperately in search for new destinations for travellers.

10. B.O.A.C.'s unwillingness to compete with Lindblad Travel's East African Safaris, and desire to sell Johannesburg rather than Nairobi out of London, may change with new sales management due to take over in the U.S.A. on 1st April 1970.

11. The immense prestige of being the first African carrier to mount scheduled services on the Atlantic.

If East African Airways postpones entering this market it is doubtful if such a favourable opportunity will occur again for the following reasons:

1. Other carriers will be so well dug into this presently virgin market that the cost and difficulty of cutting out a piece for E.A.A.C. will be immeasurably increased.

2. Presently the industry sees P.A.A.'s Tuesday service as the only comparable competitive service. This may be increased in frequency and T.W.A. may adopt a more direct routing, either of which will increase their identification on the route and reduce E.A.A.C.'s share of the market.

3. The Agents sending tourists to Africa will have developed loyalty to the airlines with whom they pioneered the market, as Cahill Laughlin has with Qantas.

4. Ideally, passengers belong equally to the countries of origin and destination. The US economic wealth provides the traveller, East African attractions provide the motive and destination. If East African Airways evinces no interest in these passengers they are sacrificing East Africa's natural resources, and can hardly complain if they are stolen by the airlines of other countries.

Additional considerations are:

1. Identification on the Atlantic should increase interline sales on other E.A.A. routes by no less than 100%.

2. The Super VC10 has been spectacularly pre-sold by B.O.A.C. as the ultimate in aircraft luxury and has gained them the highest load factor over the past three years – and E.A.A.C. has five such aircraft to employ.

3. The US has a population of 210 million, a travel market on the Atlantic in 1969 of five and a quarter million passengers which showed an increase of almost 15% over 1968's figures.

4. The price of an East African holiday package despite the increased distance from the US is presently, taking the different economic structures of the two countries into account, comparatively less expensive for an American than a Briton.

Lastly, East Africa is suddenly hot property. Books such as "Born Free" and "Serengeti shall not die" and the vast coverage in such magazines as Life and Time has for the first time revealed to the travelling US public that the unknown vast continent of Africa is there ready and waiting to be explored. It is now accessible, it can be seen in comfort, it is within the price range of the vast American middle class and as a holiday destination it has attractions that are unique, unsurpassed and prestigious.

All of the foregoing is just great – unquestionably if the economy of the US doesn't take a dramatic downswing and the political climate of east Africa remains stable, it cannot happen otherwise than that the three countries of Kenya, Uganda and Tanzania will enjoy a tourist boom of immense proportions with the resulting economic advantages. Visas issued in the US by the Kenya government were:

1968	15,000
1969	23,645 – over a 50% increase
Jan 1969	2,313
Jan 1970	3,028 – a further 33% increase

To assume a conservative increase of 25% in 1970, there will be approximately 29,000 passengers and by 1971, some 35,000 US tourists proceeding to East Africa.

However, the intention of this survey is to determine whether East African Airways can mount a profitable service between New York and Nairobi to commence in December 1970. No matter the tourist boom or the economic advantages indicated for East Africa; can the airline qua se profitably utilise its equipment in this market by transporting passengers directly out of the USA rather than picking them up at some point in Europe if the originating carrier will relinquish them.

A scheduled service flying once a week between New York and Nairobi configured to 150 seats would provide 7,800 seats a year. The cost of operating each round trip of 32 hours at £600 an hour ($1440 an hour) would be $46,080. Allowing a margin, this figure would call for 90 passengers at the minimum economy GIT fare of $540 net producing $48,600. The passenger requirement at higher priced excursion economy fares and, indeed, first class fares would be correspondingly reduced but for the purpose of the exercise, it is apparent that with a minimum of 90 passengers per flight, or a total of 4,680 GIT $600 passengers over the calender year the revenue would equal the cost of the operation. This number of passengers is approximately one sixth of the total passengers projected for 1971. There would remain a further 60 seats per flight to be sold to produce profit.

The next step was to go out into the market place and interview the industry, interline airlines, prominent travel agents, tour wholesalers, African safari specialists and those who had the potential to become East African specialists and determine how many passengers we could reasonably expect to obtain.

A cross section of the United States and Canada including the following cities was surveyed:

New York	Seattle	Houston
Boston	Portland	Atlanta
Washington DC	Salt Lake City	Miami
Chicago	Denver	Montreal
Buffalo	Phoenix	Toronto
Baltimore	Dallas	Vancouver
San Francisco	Fort Worth	Victoria
Calgary	Edmonton	Winnipeg

It was quickly apparent that the Canadian market was by nature more inclined to travel over London rather than New York. There is great potential for increasing the London/Nairobi load factors. No Canadian travellers have been included in the figures for the JFK/NBO service. In point of fact there was evidence that somewhere between 400 and 500 passengers could be contracted between London and Nairobi on East African Airways.

From the US cities surveyed we obtained the following regional totals:

	GIT	FIT
East Coast	6330	540
Mid West	1840	470
West Coast	1115	365
	9285	1375

Allowing for the optimism of travel agents, if these total figures are cut in half we still come up with 4642 GIT passengers and 688 FIT passengers giving a total of 5330 passengers for whom interviewed travel agents would like to block space on E.A.A.C.'s New York/Nairobi service. However, it is a requirement that E.A.A.C. and the tourist boards of the three countries promote East Africa and the National Airline. E.A.A.C. will have to participate considerably in brochures.

Additionally, we interviewed many travel agents who were unready to commit themselves until they knew that the projected service was definite and many cities were not covered in the survey at all.

Basically, in six weeks of beating on doors there was evidence that more than enough passengers could be generated in 1971 to cover the cost of operation.

Eight months of hard selling from April to November of 1970 cannot fail to better these figures, though in fairness, the majority of the present large operators have been approached.

Lastly, there is the freight potential from East Africa, a survey of Pyrethrum is available for follow up, and the traffic potential that will originate from East Africa.

Taking into account these findings it is our opinion that a once-weekly scheduled service from New York to Nairobi would from the beginning break even and as the market increased so would East African's share.

There is every indication that this market would in the immediate future become extremely profitable for E.A.A.C.

As a result of this survey, it was decided that an Atlantic service should commence, on a once-weekly basis from December 1970, in order to take full advantage of the American tourist traffic.

The de Havilland Comet 4s were now reaching the stage in their life when major rebuilding was required in order to overcome the effects of corrosion and main spar metal fatigue. It was decided that the cost of repairs was not economically viable, since the aircraft were unsuitable for either the short routes, where they were uneconomic on performance, or the longer routes where they were obsolete on capacity and range. In November 1969 a contract had been arranged, in unusual circumstances, by Chief Fundikira with McDonnell Douglas to lease two DC9-15s, 5Y-AKX and 5Y-AKY, pending a decision on Comet replacement. One aircraft, 5-YAKX, was painted in E.A.A. livery and flown to Nairobi by McDonnell Douglas pilots, much to the surprise of Captain Cunningham, director of operations, who knew nothing about the arrangement, until he saw the aircraft parked on the apron at Embakasi. With no provision made for training and operational acceptance, there was no possibility of continuing with the contractual agreements made by the chairman and the machines were not brought into service. This had been yet another clash between the chairman and management. The Comets 5H-AAF (VP-KPK) and 5X-AAO (VP-KPJ) were withdrawn from service and a Comet 4 (5Y-ALD) was leased from Dan-Air from January to March which operated in Dan-Air colours until another Comet 4 (5Y-ALF) was prepared in E.A.A. livery. The original E.A.A. Comet 4, 5Y-AAA (VP-KRL), continued to operate, together with the leased machine, on the charter services of S.K.A.T.

On 17th February, 1970, the last Super VC10 to be produced left Brooklands on its short flight to Wisley. At the beginning of March, 5H-MOG was delivered to East African, completing the fleet of five aircraft.

The annual Certificate of Airworthiness tests on the Super VC10s were at first undertaken by the manufacturers in England. Subsequently, East African Airways was authorised to carry out these certification tests at their Nairobi base. The test flight would take approximately four hours, with a series of tests being carried out on all the aircraft systems both at low and high level. A minimum crew of four was carried, plus a ground technician who would record the data collected. A cabin window was removed on either side of the fuselage to allow incident meters to be installed, which recorded the number and accompanying data of stall tests undertaken. These were carried out to ensure that, should the unlikely event of a stall occur, the aircraft, which could weigh between 100 and 150 tons, could be recovered. This was the most critical test, sometimes the Super VC10 would lose more than ten thousand feet before full recovery was achieved, Captain Mitchell suffered back injury on one occasion as a result of this manoeuvre, which was eventually abandoned as being unnecessary. With the stall-warning devices set at 10 per cent EAS above the stall speed, the C.A.A. agreed that the requirement to enter full stall could be dropped.

The low level flying, being a rare experience, except in the final stages of normal flight, was regarded as being extremely enjoyable by all concerned. An area to the south of Embakasi was chosen, close to the Athi River. This was remote and very lightly populated, being mostly typical African bush country of low scrub, with several very large farms, consequently there should not be any danger of annoying any humans, regardless of what the wild game may think about it. Here the test crews carried out 'engine slams'. Throttling back one engine at a time to flight idle, followed by 'banging' open the throttle to full bore. The period between idle to full power needed to be within a set time of six seconds. The reason was to ensure that in the event of an abandoned approach, all four engines could provide the

---

Opposite: *East African Airways Super VC10, 5H-MOG, the last VC10 to be built, takes-off for the first time on its short journey from Brooklands to Wisley, 17th February, 1970.*
(BAC)

power demanded for a safe climb and go-around, without delay and subsequent height-loss.

Four Rolls-Royce Conways at full power created an ear-splitting noise with an earthquake effect, which caused severe vibration on the ground over which the Super VC10 was flying. Sometimes, if they were a little lower than was strictly necessary, over this dry and arid country, great dust clouds would rise from the engine's jet blast and the down draught from the wings. It was most exhilarating, flying this great, powerful aircraft, as it swept low across the vast plain.

Returning one day, to write up their reports in the operations department, the crew were surprised to find a big, brawny 'Kenya cowboy', complete with wide brimmed slouch hat and covered in dust. He had barged into the office, shouting at anyone who would listen that "one of your bloody VC10s has flown so low over my farm that my wife, who was on the long-drop[6] fell off when the tin roof ripped off – the dogs have taken off in fright and disappeared into the bush!" He wanted compensation for the damage and for the chickens which he was sure would not lay as a result of the incident.

The operations staff, who were mostly African by then, had no idea what he was talking about, since they were not familiar with the test flight routine. Fortunately, Captain Ted Imison, who was chief pilot at the time, realised what must have happened, and using his diplomatic skills, calmed the farmer down by inviting him and his wife to visit the base and have a conducted tour of the aircraft.

There was another farm which was known to the crews, equipped with a light aircraft landing strip. One day they brought the Super VC10 down, lowered the flaps and gear and made an approach to the grass strip. Just before 'touch-down' the engines were opened up to full power, gear was raised and the huge aircraft thundered upward into the blue. A day or so later a bill was received from the farmer, Bob Cronje, stating: "To Landing Fees for one Super VC10 – Shs 7/50."

1970 saw an increased effort to counter competition by establishing a marketing department independent of the all purpose commercial department. At the same time a customer services department was created which was split into four main divisions – traffic, cabin services, catering and commercial training. The airline communications network was also brought into this department. As handling agents for foreign airlines re-equipping with Boeing 747 'Jumbo' jets, the traffic staff were receiving training on the new aircraft, which would be arriving on the East African routes towards the end of 1971.

Over fifty stewardesses participated in overseas training courses organised by T.W.A. and Lufthansa in Kansas City and Frankfurt respectively. These courses had been arranged as development aid by community minister for communications, research and social services, Mr J.S. Malacela, early in the year. During the year

---

[6] Privy

a total of 104 stewards and stewardesses were recruited, trained and posted to the DC3 and F27 fleets.

In operations, two new instructors were employed, one from Denmark and the other, Captain Joe Prendergast, from the U.S.A. Flying crews now totalled 117 captains, ninety-three first officers, forty flight engineers, twenty-six flight navigators and six cadet pilots. Of these, four captains, forty-five first officers, two flight engineers and the six cadet pilots were East African citizens. 'East African citizen' in this context would include those settlers of European stock who had applied for Kenya passports and citizenship. These included captains Peter Brumby, Ian Cowie, Jerry Sirley, Trevor Hill and his son Terry and Reg Cartwright.

In common with all departments, the operations centre was now largely Africanised with staff of necessarily low experience – on the job training was the only way in which a virtual revolution in staffing could be successfully achieved. Thus it was that on 10th November, 1970, a message was received at London that the Super VC10 which had arrived that morning should return direct to Nairobi as soon as possible due to shortage of equipment. The crew were quickly assembled and the aircraft departed empty, some eight hours before it was scheduled to depart London. It was with shocked incredulity that, half way across the Sahara, they made contact with another East African Super VC10 on the company frequency, and found that he too was empty, en route to London to replace them!

It was not only the inexperienced staff who caused problems with aircraft schedules. At 07.30 on 4th April, Captain Leslie had been preparing Super VC10 5H-MMT for departure from Dar es Salaam with co-pilot, Captain K. Tveiten, when

Captain E. 'Ted' Imison.

a message was received that the flight should be delayed for the President. The flight, EC746 was the new daylight service which terminated at London. There was nothing to be done about it, so they settled down to wait for President Nyerere. When he finally arrived, it was found that he had about fifty people accompanying him, and he did not want to travel to Nairobi or London, but Lagos! Leslie explained that he had no charts or information for a flight coast to coast across Africa, apart from the fact that this was a scheduled service with passengers for Nairobi and Europe already on board, with their luggage stowed in the hold. None of this was of interest to the Tanzanian officials, who demanded that the passengers be off-loaded and the aircraft flown to Lagos. Since a captain could hardly be expected to deal with such an extraordinary situation, Leslie flew the entire delegation to Nairobi regardless. "Let *them* sort it out", he said. There was no daylight EC746 service to London that day and passengers were transferred to other flights.

Captain George Leslie

Negotiations with the C.A.A. in London had failed to permit East African Airways fifth freedom traffic rights through London for the proposed North Atlantic service, due to objections from B.O.A.C. who were not interested in a pool arrangement on the route. An agreement was finally achieved with the Swiss authorities to route the service weekly via Zurich. The inaugural flight into New York took place on 10th December 1970. Captain George Leslie commanded 5H-MOG on the first leg, from Nairobi to Zurich, via Entebbe. The trans-Atlantic leg was commanded by Captain Reg Cartwright.

The flights were operationally successful on the 18 hour journey from Nairobi. A problem which had not been foreseen, however, was the difficulty that the cabin crews would encounter on the long ten hour flight from Zurich. Unused to working continuously for so long on a route which crossed multiple time zones, some of the African stewards and stewardesses could not stay awake. As a result, the demanding requirements of the American passengers could not be met. As the weeks passed, the cabin service standards fell, complaints started to come in from the few American tour organisers who had followed up their optimistic forecasts with bookings. The long flights were operating with less and less passengers, as cabin crews slept or quarrelled among themselves in the half empty cabins.

The New York inaugural had coincided with Kenya Independence Day and the crew were invited to the reception held at the United Nations headquarters building. They arrived, unusually, in uniform, but had already refreshed themselves with 'after landing' drinks. The room held a glittering assembly of diplomats, military officers in uniform and members of the international smart set. Harry Everitt, the purser on the flight, had already downed a couple of Martini cocktails when he told the major domo that his name was the "Honourable Harry Everitt". Introduced as such, he found that none of the VIPs knew how to deal with this uniformed Englishman. The military saluted him and the women curtseyed as Harry got into the swing of things, "Saluting everybody in sight and kissing the ladies hands". Afterwards Captain Cartwright (who was not altogether pleased at the time) and the crew bought him a pewter beer tankard inscribed: "The Honourable Harry Everitt".

The return of the inaugural flight from New York had not been without incident. A new catering manager had been recruited from Scandinavia, Mr Carl Possman. Possman had been in New York to oversee the catering arrangements for the return flight. He had joined the cabin crew on the return in order to ensure that everything went smoothly, there being a large number of members of the Press and travel agents on board. After landing at Entebbe, Captain Ian Ainscow watched from the cockpit window as the passengers disembarked from the first class steps. Among them walked Possman. "Here, what's he doing?" he said to Captain Leslie, seated beside him. In front of a large crowd of dignitaries who had come to meet the flight, Possman had dropped his trousers and pants and, at the foot of the aircraft steps, defecated on the ground. Pulling his pants and trousers up when he had finished, he walked towards the terminal building, ignoring the horrified gaze of the entire assembly. The two captains, with a feeling of despair for the airline which both of them had seen grow from the days of Lodestars and Dakotas, could only wonder at the level to which it had fallen, as they continued the flight to Nairobi. Possman had been arrested and was in jail long before their journey was completed.[7]

During 1970 alone, development expenditure for the Hong Kong and New York routes had amounted to K£192,300. This was marginally more than the expense incurred in training citizen pilots and engineers, K£164,550.

Chief Fundikira had been continuing with his negotiations for replacement aircraft for the Comet 4s. In April, authority for purchase of three McDonnell Douglas DC-9-32 aircraft was given by the Communications Council of the East African Community. During mid May, 1970, Chief Fundikira accompanied by recently appointed Kenyan board member R.M. Douglas travelled to the United States, where they concluded an agreement with McDonnell Douglas for the purchase of three DC-9-32 aircraft, to be delivered at the end of the year. A loan agreement was signed with the Export-Import Bank of the United States amounting to K£2,480,625, for the three aircraft, three spare engines, ancillary equipment and services. East African was to make a cash payment of ten per cent of the cost with the remainder of the loan to be repaid in ten semi-annual instalments, beginning May 15th, 1976, at an annual interest rate of six per cent on outstanding balances. Each of the partner states undertook to guarantee the loan in equal proportions.

At 22.30 G.M.T. on 4th November, 1970, at the Nairobi operations centre the following call was broadcast via the SSB radio: "Eastaf Nairobi, this is Five Hotel Mike Oscar India, how do you read?" It was the voice of Captain Ian Cowie of East African Airways, testing the radio equipment on the first E.A.A. DC-9-32 overhead Long Beach, California, some 8,000 statute miles away. Together with Captain Alan Ratcliffe, chief pilot DC-9s, he had the task of training the initial six captains and accepting and delivering the first of the new aircraft. Arriving on Christmas Day, 1970, the aircraft had left Long Beach on 22nd December, and routed via Kansas City-Montreal-Gander-Keflavik-London-Benina and Khartoum.

Mombasa airport was the scene of great excitement on December 20th, when a Super VC10 landed for the first time on its short runway, still un-prepared for the large aircraft. The flight, ex New York, was inbound from Zurich for Nairobi, where early morning fog had made a landing impossible. Entebbe was also fog-bound, so the captain decided that he must divert to Dar es Salaam. After setting course for Dar, he heard on the radio that a B.O.A.C. aircraft had managed to land at Nairobi. He turned round and began a descent, but learned from the controller that the fog, churned up by the landing aircraft, had brought the visibility below limits again. Now there was insufficient fuel for the flight to Dar es Salaam. The only possibility was Mombasa, where a landing was made on its,

---

[7] Pleading "Guilty" in the Kampala court on 12th December, Possman (age 53) said "I admit it, Your Honour, but I was sick at the time of the alleged offence". He was fined £10 and cautioned.

as yet, unfinished runway extension. Unable to take-off on the short runway with passengers, who were all ferried to Nairobi on other aircraft, the lightened Super VC10 "Took-off like a bat out of hell". Thus Mombasa received its first Super VC10, and a senior captain discovered that it is never too late to learn another lesson in the flying game.

The continuity of the accounts department had been severely disturbed by the retirement of Mr S.G. Choppin and the degree of Africanisation which had taken place. The new financial controller had been recruited on secondment from Pakistan International Airlines. Mr A.Z. Rahman had been the former financial director of P.I.A. and his brief was to train an African to replace him within two or three years. As a result of the lack of expertise in all departments, and the increasing failure to control expenditure and accounting procedures, there were no accounts presented to the East African Community at the end of 1970 – it was not to be until March, 1972, some fourteen months after the death of Mr Rahman[8] following

At the McDonnell Douglas factory at Long Beach, California in September, 1970. Watched by Chief Stewardess Ruth Lutale, Captain Alan Ratcliffe and Captain Ian Cowie demand 'baksheesh' as the MD executive suggests a photograph in front of the prototype DC10. It was widely rumoured that bribes had been paid to E.A.A. board members in connection with the DC-9 purchase.

a heart attack, that the accounts were presented, unapproved by the independent auditors.

1970 would show an operating loss of K£650,000. Although revenues had increased by 22.1 per cent, operating costs had risen by 11.9 per cent over 1969. Low promotional fares were still a problem – with an increase in passengers of 13.3 per cent the passenger revenue earned only went up by 7.9 per cent on the previous year. Payments made for the DC-9s had amounted to K£2,697,700 and the instalment payments on the Super VC10s K£3,304,300.

With five Super VC10s in service, the fleet utilisation increased by 21 per cent over the previous year:

Aircraft Type	Total Hours Flown 1970	1969
Super VC10	16,406	13,557
Comet 4	3,630	5,956
F27	10,365	10,587
DC3	11,388	12,438
DHC6 Twin Otter	6,238	4,457

These figures gave a daily utilisation of:

Super VC10	9.31	10.15
Comet 4	4.89	5.45
F27	7.12	7.27
DC3	5.21	5.69
DHC6 Twin Otter	4.28	3.75

It was remarkable that the old DC3 Dakotas were still providing high hours of utilisation some 21 years after they had been introduced to East African Airways.

The staff establishment increased from 4,816 at 31st December 1969 to 5,116. Available ton miles produced per employee was 30,450 compared with 29,527 in 1969.

The 1970 revenue miles flown were claimed as 130,491,510 which equated to 2,551 fare paying passenger miles per employee. The equivalent figures for 1969 were 119,306,530 revenue miles flown, adding up to 2,477 miles per employee.

It is interesting to compare these figures with the year 1960, when the staff complement was 1,759 and a total of 120,839,104 passenger revenue miles were flown, producing some 6,870 revenue miles per employee. The net operating profit for that year had been £460,683 sterling. The cost of salaries and other staff benefits

---

[8] With a history of heart trouble, it was not possible to effect a life insurance policy for Mr Rahman, and this was agreed by Mr Lutara. Unfortunately for Mrs Joan Odell, who administered the pensions and insurance, Mr Lutara had left when Mr Rahman died, and she was accused of failing to carry out the insurance cover, and was instantly dismissed. It was not until the pilot's association threatened a strike that the matter was put right and Mrs Odell was retired, after 15 years service, with full privileges.

represented 33.4 per cent of expenditure in 1970. Staff costs in 1960, including provident fund contributions, leave passages, housing, insurance, medical expenses, and expenses on duty away from base were 31.3 per cent of total expenditure.

The one outstanding issue, which was raised year after year by the chairman of the corporation was that of under-capitalization. For an airline with an annual turnover of £17,720,000, it was clearly absurd to maintain the share capital available at £450,000. It was an indication of the failure of the leadership of the partner states to co-operate in the manner which was envisaged at the commencement of the East African Community. The future of the Community, with its headquarters at Arusha in Tanzania, depended largely upon political factors. These political factors were about to come very much to the fore, with terrible consequences for East Africa.

CHAPTER 10

A Coup in the Morning

From the Author's Notebook

I HAD ARRIVED in Entebbe on the Super VC10 5H-MOG, commanded by Captain Alan Burkitt, on the Saturday morning of 23rd January, 1971. My intention was to stay with friends in Entebbe, before continuing to Nairobi on the Monday.

I kept some notes of the events which occurred:

25th January, 1971

07.00 – Unusually foggy morning. First indications of abnormality from radio – no expected news broadcasts and usual programmes replaced by military band music (Guards Brigade band!). No voice broadcasts at all. Joking remark at breakfast table that perhaps a 'coup' had taken place, since such broadcasts are the tradition on these occasions! Soon after this, the telephone rings, and my hostess tells us that there is shooting in Kampala and we were right. The house-boy is sent hurrying to bring her husband and daughter back from school, whence they had just departed.

Another telephone call, this time from the East African Airways station manager, Ezra Kyomukama, to advise us not to come to the airport. House-boy returns – Jackie is in school and Dr Lubega has gone to his office (he was Chief Architect of Uganda). Transport arrives to take us to the airport, decide that it's better to go. There was no sign of activity on the roads, the mist still shrouding the trees and hedges. When we arrive at the airport, there are soldiers guarding the entrance, but it is quiet, with an air of expectancy pervading the atmosphere.

The EC717 Super VC10 from London had diverted to Nairobi due to the fog, and the only aircraft on the apron was a DC3, 5H-AAL, scheduled to operate the Murchison Falls – Kasese route. Captain A.J. Burleton, the DC3 commander, was in the operations room, wondering whether to take-off for Nairobi in order to get the aircraft safely out of danger. Finally he decided to cancel and return to the Lake Victoria Hotel, with the intention of operating the next schedule at mid-day.

0900-1030 – Trying to contact Nairobi. Telephones to Kampala are cut, Telex machines dead. The SSB radio link is still working, but unable to raise Nairobi, after repeated calls. Someone says, "The soldiers are coming down the road". A Sabena Boeing 707, alerted by the control tower, passes overhead at about 0945, diverting to Nairobi. After a short interval, a sudden loud explosion in the terminal building. People are running past, some through the office, others running in panic outside, past the windows. We hear rifle fire. Then more, this time automatic, continuous firing. A second shell explodes in the terminal, bringing down plaster and dust from the ceiling. "Let's get out of here", I say to the African service controller, not wishing to have the place fall about my ears. The quickest way was out of the window. Then which way? I was on the apron, with the expanse of the airfield before me.

A large number of people were running into the open, getting away from the targeted buildings, running across to the airfield boundary and over towards the fuel installations. An elderly white man came reeling out of a service entrance, bleeding heavily and fell to the ground. I took cover, behind a cart of some kind, in the company of some Sabena crew; one, a stewardess, was injured with a wound in the back, where shrapnel or a bullet had nicked the flesh close to the spine. Continuous single-shot rifle fire was coming from the direction of the terminal. An incredibly tall Ugandan, dressed in military fatigues approaches, he is holding a heavy automatic pistol, insignia on his shoulders indicates that he is an officer. "You must go and tell them to come down from the control tower", he tells me. "You had better send your soldiers", I reply, "I don't want to get shot". He hesitates for a moment and says: "All right", and walks away. Momentary relief.

The Belgians then stop him and ask for an ambulance for the wounded man lying on the ground, who was now looking bad and bleeding heavily. The stewardess beside me is beginning to suffer shock, and I offer her a cigarette, which she refuses. The firing is continuing, and the thought occurs that the soldiers are killing everybody – we have had it.

The Entebbe terminal building, photographed in 1966. (Author)

The author at Entebbe in 1966, and the control tower as it remained in 1971. (Author)

Some brave men, Belgians, I think, holding white handkerchieves tied to sticks, come forward, crouching, towards the injured man. They carry him away.

People are moving towards the terminal, with their hands above their heads – cannot hear any orders, but assume that everyone is being herded inside and decide that the best course of action is to join them. I put my hands up, feeling rather stupid, but better than getting shot. We are herded through the transit lounge, through the kitchens, pots unattended, boiling over. Up a narrow staircase. Frightened woman wails: "They are going to shoot us". One can smell the fear from the mixed group of American, Belgian and British tourists, who had departed for the airport that morning, with no thought other than the continuation of their journey.

The firing is now sporadic. As we come out into the open, the mist has now burned off, and, in the brilliant morning sunshine, we see a great mass of Africans, the women bright in their varied coloured head scarves and dresses, some with babies on their back. They are seated on the ground, with their hands held high. Surrounding them are the soldiers, each with an automatic FN rifle. There is a Land Rover, with a mounted weapon, maybe an anti-tank rifle, and two armoured personnel carriers, from atop one of which an officer of some sort shouted at us as we ranged on the perimeter of this scene. "Hands up! Don't worry – what are you? You on safari?" He was an extraordinarily ugly and menacing creature, with a wispy moustache. Someone shouted back to him: "Don't shoot us – we are tourists". Another shouted: "We are East African Airways passengers". There is a momentary pause while he undergoes a mental process, then "Go – go over there"

The Lake Victoria Hotel, Entebbe. (Author)

he yells, indicating that we should move away from the unfortunate natives. "We have no cars" shouts someone. "Go!" he yells, "East African Airways take them away!".

At this moment I see my hostess of the week-end, edging round the circle of prisoners, her hands high above her head. I move across to meet her, "Which way do we go, Margaret?" "Come on, let's get in the transport". The transport was the EAA VW Kombi used for running people around. We jump in. It soon fills up with a mixed bunch of Asians, a Belgian, a Ugandan EAA receptionist in uniform. We drive off, the soldiers now behind us – I am still waiting for the bullets, as we must be a tempting target. Margaret wants to go home, worried about her child. She looks bad, scared and grey with shock. The Kombi stops at the bottom of Edna Road, a neat, quiet residential road from former days of British rule. The door slides open and Margaret gets out. I do not know what to do for the best, "Shall I come with you, Margaret?" "Better one of us than two" she says, walking slowly up the road, her hands up high, fearing that there should be soldiers near.

The rules of gallantry must be tempered with common-sense in such situations – she was better qualified to judge whether to be seen in the company of a foreigner would have endangered her more than otherwise. I felt uneasy with my decision for some time after that though.

We continued for a short distance to the Lake Victoria Hotel, where there were a large number of people, African, European and Asians, sitting at the tables which had been set up on the grass beneath the trees. There was a half-scared, half-holiday atmosphere, as waiters hurried to and fro with trays of beers, and some hotel residents splashed in the pool. I find the EAA station manager at one of the tables, drinking Guinness, he is visibly shaking and has removed his gold epaulette bars. I ask him to send the Kombi to collect the Lubegas from their house. There is much confusion. Most people had heard the firing, but do not know what has happened. Everyone is telling his own story. I order a cold beer. The Kombi arrives with the Lubega family, soon followed by Ezra Kyomukama's wife and three babies. We move to a table beneath the shade of a large tree and order beer and lemonade for the party. There is much talk and speculation, trying to piece together the events of the morning.

On our arrival earlier that morning, I had left Margaret at her desk in the station manager's office and gone into the East African Airways operations room. She had seen from her position, at the front of the airport building, the gradual disappearance of airline and airport staff, anxiously fleeing to their homes, as rumours of troop movements came in. At approximately 10.15 the armoured personnel carriers (APCs) and cannon (later seen to be a 105mm rifle) bearing Land Rovers drove through into the airport forecourt, and troops scrambled out. Margaret and one other girl hid beneath their desks as firing started immediately. There were shouted commands that everyone should come outside. A burst of automatic fire was directed at the office door, then they scrambled out with their hands up. They were ordered to join the crowd, cowering on the ground, with their hands raised.

An Ankole officer approached her and asked: "Are you Muganda?" "Yes Sir, Muganda", she cried. "Have you left anything behind?" "Yes Sir, my handbag". "Go and get it".

They were then forced to separate into tribal groups, Baganda, Bunyoro, Acholi, and the Langi, the tribe of Dr Milton Obote, the President. These unfortunates were being forced to raise and lower their arms by the threatening soldiers, "Hands up!", "Down!", "Up!, "Down!", "Up!".

In the meantime the soldiers were rounding up the policemen, loyal army guards, whom we had encountered on arrival that morning, and the government chief of protocol (whom I had last seen talking with the station manager earlier, dressed in the most immaculate fashion). They were herded into a police rondavel by the entrance to the airport, whereupon the soldiers poured rifle fire into the hut, it was not known if anyone survived. It was not clear at the time how many deaths occurred, it was said that two Catholic priests and two Africans accompanying them died, together with two Sabena passengers and a woman, who lay in a pool of blood beside Margaret. Later, it was reported that the parish priest from Entebbe was shot as he remonstrated with the soldiers.

Other troops were within the terminal building, firing wildly at the ceiling, lights, fittings and portraits of President Obote, which adorned each office and the public areas.

The first cannon shell blasted a hole through the toilets (which I had vacated five minutes earlier), the next one, directed at the terminal, destroyed the check-in desks, the only known casualty being the girl on the cash-desk, who was hit in the jaw. The soldiers appeared to be Nubians and men from the northern region of Uganda. The commander was the Ankole, and since a Muganda officer (whom I had encountered earlier) was moving about freely, at least one of them was *persona grata*. To Margaret, it seemed that everyone inside the main building was being slaughtered, and as the group of us slowly emerged, she was relieved to see me still alive. Aware that the soldiers seemed sympathetic to the Baganda, she risked edging round to our group.

The rest of the day was spent at the Lake Victoria Hotel, in the company of various friends of the Lubega's, the hotel manager, Mayanja, and the Kyomukama family. Many residents of Entebbe had poured into the hotel to swell the ranks of guests and 'refugee' passengers, who had been forced to abandon their belongings at the airport. We were told that the sister-in-law of President Obote, who had worked for an airline, was hiding somewhere in the hotel, frightened for her life. At about mid-day, the tall air force officer (his badges of rank now removed) and another soldier, arrived in a commandeered EAA mini-van. They left with packets of cigarettes and packed food.

Fear and consternation gripped the assembled groups as, a little later, one of the APCs rumbled into view, stopping by the hotel entrance. Sinister and menacing, the soldiers, looking particularly ugly wearing tank-helmets, peered down the barrels of their weapons at the fearful civilians, many of whom, until now had seen nothing of the mornings horrors. However, memories of the Belgian Congo were still fresh in the minds of the assorted Europeans. The commander and two soldiers entered the hotel and conducted some interrogations, following which more food was collected. The atmosphere was very tense, no one knowing what they were up to. As they sat at a table outside the hotel, I joined them for a while, in the company of Captain Burleton, who was, rather unwisely, I thought, bothering them about permission to fly away the DC3, which was still standing on the apron at the airport. He had no success. The Muganda officer then spoke quietly to me: "Tell your captain that I have flown Dakotas, and I am telling you that no thirty-year-old aircraft is worth his life – they are getting annoyed with him". I advised Burleton to be very careful, as their mood was quite unpredictable.

It was at about 16.00, when someone in the crowd, listening to his portable radio, turned it up so that we could hear the announcement. It confirmed that a coup d'etat had taken place, conducted by the armed forces led by Maj-Gen Idi Amin Dada, who was proclaimed head of state 'pending future parliamentary elections'. A curfew, from 19.00 to 06.30 was imposed. About an hour later, we decided that it was reasonably safe to drive home. Already in the streets, groups of people on foot and in car loads, waving green branches, were rejoicing. Our experiences of the morning prevented us from sharing their mood. Back at the house, we had a meal and re-told our versions of the day's events. I was still afraid that we had not seen the worst, and this was confirmed when, later in the evening, firing began again. We switched off the lights. Margaret went to her daughter's room, where she slept. Dr Lubega and I sat on the floor, below the window height and filled our glasses from a bottle of Scotch, by torch-light. The firing increased in severity, we could hear the bullets swishing through the leaves of the trees next to the house. I thought the worst, that uncontrolled elements were going from house to house, killing the inhabitants.

To our relief, the sound of gun-fire gradually became more distant, and finally ceased. At about mid-night we turned in, but I did not undress, in case some form of quick escape from the house may be necessary. As I fell into exhausted sleep, the sounds of frantic, distant, drumming filled the night air. Some of the Ugandans, either soldiers or joyful civilians, were celebrating in their traditional way.

26th January, 1971

Morning quiet. No school, but Dr Lubega went to his office, as most Ministries are working. Around mid-day, the Lubegas drove to Kampala, but I did not accompany them this time, as I did not know the mood of the army, so decided to stay in the house. In the afternoon I decided to go for a walk with their daughter and two young friends. Stopped at the Lake Vic for a drink and spoke to several people, including E.K. who had been drinking Guinness steadily. Returned to the house, where, later, the Lubegas reported wild celebrations in Kampala, marred only by the sight of Dr Obote's Mercedes, with dead driver inside, burning by the roadside. In a broadcast in the evening, Idi Amin sounded very reasonable, promising to "return the body of the Kabaka, with a full military funeral at the royal palace at Kasubi".

27th January, 1971

08.00. Left the house to walk to the airport. Picked up on the way by the EAA Kombi. The airport was quiet, with men from the Works Department clearing up and repairing damage. All the offices were ransacked, curtains torn down, drawers and files emptied. The airport keys had disappeared from the station manager's office. Of E.K. there was no sign. No one seemed to be taking any initiatives or decisions. Out on the apron, however, the DC3 was having its Daily Inspection and one engine was running (Tom Webb, the East African Airways station engineer was carrying on as usual). At about 09.15 I decided that something positive should be done, so together with the head EAA receptionist, Miss Nantume, I got the Kombi driver to take us back to the Lake Vic, to collect a full list of passengers and make contact with the crew. I found E.K. by the window, in the upstairs bar. He was still very frightened and was drinking Guinness non-stop. I told him that I was collecting information with a view to getting the DC3 out to Nairobi. He wanted to wait, afraid to take any action at that time.

10.45. People start to arrive from the airport, saying that there had been more trouble and that the army had ordered them out. Rumours are flying about that aircraft are approaching from Tanzania. An air of tension returns. The passenger list is fairly complete.

11.30 The Muganda air force officer arrives, to collect more food and soft drinks. He advises that there is no trouble at the airport. I decide to go with Miss Nantume in the Kombi to the airport to find out what is going on. On walking through to the airside, I find a Land Rover with several fierce looking soldiers aboard. "Where is your commanding officer?" I ask one of them. Pointing, he says "Up there, in the control tower". In the tower, I see a couple of British controllers, who had very little to say, since they were in the presence of the officer, who shook hands and introduced himself as Lieutenant Orombi. "All staff should return to work, no command was given to evacuate the airport", he tells me. I ask him about the possibility of operating the DC3, with passengers, to Nairobi. "The army has no objection at all to any scheduled flights, as long as they are cleared by the Permanent Secretary of the Ministry of Works, Communications and Housing". I tell him that if that is the case, I shall go ahead and organise a 15.00 departure. "The staff are frightened of the soldiers, can you not pull them back from the passenger area?", I ask him. He agrees to do this and I return to the transport.

On returning to the hotel, I asked Capt Burleton to prepare for a 15.00 departure and told the passenger officer to select twenty-four people, preferably women and children first. I asked E.K. to contact the Ministry by telephone, but he had no success. We then decided to walk to their offices, which were close by, but found that the Permanent Secretary had "Gone to a meeting in Kampala". But his deputy agreed to furnish me with a letter to Lt. Orombi, clearing the DC3 for departure. Clutching the letter, together with a copy, we returned to the hotel and asked for arrangements to be finalised (It was at this time that I was approached by a European man who told me that his boss was a very important businessman, who needed to be in Nairobi urgently, "He would be very generous" to me, personally, if I were to ensure that he got on the aircraft. I told him that we intended loading women and children first and that I could not promise him a seat).

14.00 The captain and first officer were ready to depart for the airport. We departed in the faithful Kombi, in my hand the all-important letter. Lieutenant Orombi was still in the control tower and I handed over the letter, which appeared to be acceptable, much to my relief. The passenger officer went in the transport, which returned to the hotel to collect the first passengers. They soon arrived and Miss Nantume prepared a manifest and commenced checking them in. It was a complicated business, most of them had surrendered their tickets on the day of the coup. Some could only speak French or German. Amin, the Asian service controller set about preparing a loadsheet and, following a 'security search' when the soldiers rummaged through all the baggage, the passengers boarded the aircraft at about 16.00. The 'women and children first' idea had not really worked, I had left it to the local staff to select the passengers, since I could not be at the hotel. As it happened, most of them seemed to be retired people on safari, with, I think a couple of missionary women among them. One of these was left without a seat, I found an elderly man whose name was not on the passenger list. He refused to move out of his seat, looking rigidly in front of him. "Never mind, I'll go back" said the lady, and she disembarked.

Tom Webb, standing in front of the Dakota, lifted his fingers, indicating ready to start and the engines burst into life one after the other. A very brief period for checks and the captain waved chocks away. It was 16.30 as we stood and watched our last link with the outside world climb out over Lake Victoria and set course for Nairobi. We had all had enough for one day. Climbing into Tom Webb's ancient Land Rover, which was cluttered up with the tools of his trade, we drove back to the hotel, where Tom dropped us off before continuing home. I had eaten nothing since 07.30 that morning, we had a very welcome tea in the hotel, before I departed for the Lubega's house to telephone Mike Hall, the traffic manager, in Nairobi. E.K. was still drinking Guinness as I left.

28th January, 1971

Everything at the airport getting back to normal. The station manager is in his office and clearing-up is in progress. Made contact with Nairobi via the SSB radio and assured them that the airport was safe for operations. Spoke with Lieutenant Orombi, who assured me that EAA Tanzanian registered aircraft would be allowed to land. Nairobi operations advised that they planned to send a DC3 at 15.00 and a Comet at 15.30.

E.K. now more confident, was becoming unhappy about the presence of a Briton on his patch, without proper authority. I realised that the situation was now fairly normal and it would be better if I left him to it.

Eventually, a DC-9 and a Dakota arrived in the afternoon. The DC-9 carried members of Dr Obote's Commonwealth Conference party, returning from Singapore. At first they were greeted in a friendly fashion by the soldiers, no doubt because the press were in attendance. When the DC9 had departed back to Nairobi, and the press had left, the army commander gave an order, and the unfortunate VIPs were pushed outside, whereupon the soldiers set about them with rifle butts. Mr Ntende (Permanent Secretary to Interior Minister Bataringaya) was kicked repeatedly in the stomach, and struck about the head with rifle butts. It seemed likely that they killed him.

Paul Etiang, Uganda High Commissioner in London, was also beaten, together with the remainder of the party. The onlookers were highly amused and the beatings were accompanied by hand-clapping from those standing around.

1st February, 1971

Yesterday, Sunday, two people were killed by soldiers in the airport VIP lounge. One was reported to be in EAA uniform. Looting at the airport continues, three typewriters stolen, the safe destroyed by rifle-fire, cars and Kombis 'requisitioned' by the army (including a Jaguar sports car, which was in the cargo warehouse in transit, seen driven around Entebbe with reckless abandon by an officer). This morning, it is rumoured that passenger's baggage was stolen between the aircraft and the customs hall. Customs officer reports that the bonded store was broken into last night.

2nd February 1971

Captain Jerry Sirley brought 5X-UVA in from Nairobi this morning, and the graceful, familiar shape of the Super VC10 stood shimmering in the hot sunlight, ready for a 10.00 departure. I was on my way out of unhappy Uganda. As I climbed the steps, I saw, in the doorway of the Super VC10, the diminutive figure of stewardess Ruth Lutale, she smiled and said in astonishment: "Mr Davis, what are *you* doing *here*!" I sat back in my seat, with a feeling of utmost relief, thankful to be alive and out of the madness which, unknown to me then, would engulf the beautiful country of Uganda. Ruth brought me a long, ice-clinking, gin and tonic and I gazed out of the window as Lake Victoria gradually disappeared from my view.

CHAPTER 11

Africa Claims its Own

*Woe to the land shadowing with wings
Which is beyond the streams of Ethiopia.*

Isaiah 18.1

AT SINGAPORE on the morning of 25th January, 1971, the East African Airways Super VC10 5H-MMT, was preparing to depart for Bombay. Captain John Winson and his crew had brought the aircraft into Singapore, diverting from the normal Hong Kong service, in order to convey President Milton Obote and his delegation to Bombay for a state visit, at the conclusion of the Commonwealth Conference held in Singapore. President Obote arrived punctually, and after inspecting the guard of honour boarded the aircraft with his delegation.

Soon after take-off, Paddy Brennan, the E.A.A. chief operations officer, made contact from Nairobi on the SSB radio. He wanted to know whether the President was on board, and whether he was aware of the situation in Uganda. The crew had no knowledge of anything untoward, they had not listened to any news broadcasts. Winson replied that the party did not appear to be disturbed, and he had not made any enquiries. Brennan replied that the president should be informed that all communication with Uganda had been cut, that the army was involved and had surrounded his palace, the airport was closed and Uganda radio was playing martial music.

Obote always travelled with a group of rather ugly looking strong-arm men, the same ones who had dealt with the high commission staff in London. Winson's main fear was that they were almost certainly armed and may, in their desperate haste, hijack the aircraft and its passengers, forcing him to fly directly to Entebbe or, even, to Hanoi.

Despite being reminded that he was directed by the director general of the airline to comply, Captain Winson advised Nairobi that he considered it was prejudicial to the safety of the aircraft and he was not prepared to inform Obote of the bad news while in flight. Finally, after some discussion, it was agreed that he should continue to Bombay, a flight of some three hours, and reveal the news to Obote on arrival. While these messages were being broadcast, the cockpit door was locked, in case the cabin crew, some of whom may have been Ugandans, may have overheard the conversations and passed the news to the President.

On landing at Bombay, Captain Winson advised the tower, after clearing the runway, that he would be off the air for a few minutes, as he had an important duty to perform. He asked the navigator if he would approach the President and ask him if he would mind coming to the cockpit, where he briefed him on the succession of messages which they had received. Winson said: "On behalf of the airline and the crew, I wish to express our hope that your family are safe, and I have been instructed to place the aircraft at your disposal". Obote seemed unduly calm as he heard the bad news. He put his hand on Winson's shoulder and asked him whether he had known at Singapore. Winson told him that they had received the news while in flight, and Obote, thanking him, said: "It is only a section of the army we are having trouble with" and looking through the windscreen at the reception party, said, "Well, I suppose we had better move forward, as it looks as if I have a welcoming party to greet. But would you kindly make arrangements for me to fly directly to East Africa. I will not be staying over in Bombay".

In fact, President Obote had already known about the coup when, at about 6.00 a.m. local time, at the Singapore Hilton, he had been brought the news by Mr Richard Ntende, an hour before their flight departed.

5H-MMT, commanded by Capt David Power, bearing the worried and disconsolate Ugandan party arrived at Embakasi airport at 7.00 p.m. where they were met by Mr Daniel arap Moi, Kenya's vice-president and whisked off to the Panafric Hotel in Nairobi, with little or no ceremony.

Obote had made plans to hire seven limousines in order to drive up the Rift Valley road via Nakuru and Eldoret into Uganda that night. But unknown to him, President Jomo Kenyatta had blocked all means of escape, merely telling him on the telephone that he "would like him to stay". Kenyatta had no liking for Obote, or Nyerere for that matter, being distrustful of their socialist ideas. President Nyerere, on a three-day state visit to Delhi, had been briefed by Obote's aides, as the Super VC10 re-fuelled at Bombay earlier in the day. Through the Tanzanian second vice-president, Rashidi Kawawa, Obote was offered refuge in Tanzania. The following day, an East African Airways Super VC10 was chartered to carry Dr Obote from Nairobi to exile in Dar es Salaam, where he would meet his host, as he arrived from Bombay on another E.A.A. Super VC10 5Y-ADA, with Captain Winson in command, to a tumultuous welcome at the airport.

There were calls for war against Amin from the Tanzanians; "Give us arms to fight" proclaimed banners held high at the airport. Nyerere denied that he intended to invade Uganda in order to re-establish his friend Obote, but these were early days. The East African Community was beginning to look very shaky – and East African Airways was at the very core of it.

Captain Winson and his crew, had expected to be back in Hong Kong, as it was their turn to perform the 'double shuttle', but as a result of flight cancellations, they had found themselves on another Presidential special flight after their rest period in Bombay. As they flew the now empty 5Y-ADA back to Nairobi, they all felt that they had, indeed, had an epic week.

On 8th March, 1971, the new Kenyan station manager arrived to take up his duties at London Airport. Mr Gregory Wangara had very little experience in airline operations or customer service, his main qualification had been in trade union work in Kenya, which was of a more overt political nature than in many other countries.

Unfortunately, it was not generally known that he had used his former position to misappropriate funds for his own benefit and had mismanaged his department so effectively that he had to be removed. The previous station manager, Ray Lambeth, had resigned some months earlier to take up a new position with South African Airways. London station, which ran effectively with the full handling of B.O.A.C., was overseen by two traffic liaison officers with the assistance of African female passenger staff and two male 'trainees'. In addition, two or three African ground hostesses were posted at intervals from the East African airports for familiarisation, training and general experience at London.

Wangara, who was a protege of Chief Fundikira, seemed an affable man, always seen to be extremely well dressed in the best quality English suits. He did not devote a great deal of time to airport duties, he was busy with meetings at the Skyway Hotel, where he resided, or in London, being driven to and fro by a personal chauffeur in a hired Jaguar. It was said that he was something of a ladies man, which was a possible explanation for the frequent nocturnal chauffeured drives to and from Bayswater and the West End of London, the bills being paid by the E.A.A. London office. Uncomfortable with the British officers at Heathrow, ways and means were found to dismiss them, replacing them with East Africans and, ironically, Asians who had settled in Britain following their enforced departure from East Africa. One of these, a bearded Sikh with long service in E.A.A.C., established a very profitable business connection with a travel agent of similar origins to himself. Being responsible for despatching the aircraft, he would, from time to time, tell the captain that there was an L.M.C. (Last Minute Change) on the loadsheet, and a passenger would be shepherded on board just before the door was closed. By carefully failing to amend the accounts copies of the ship's papers, he was able to collect his half of the fare paid to the travel agent. No ticket was issued and a boarding pass and passport was all that was needed to gain access to the aircraft.

But there was to be considerable strife before Wangara could re-arrange London station, dismissing the staff and bringing in his own people from East Africa, including, at the end of the year, sacking his British-resident Ugandan secretary and requesting from the then director of customer services, S.L. Rwebangira, a girl from his own Baluhya tribe, to which the following reply was sent from Nairobi:

Greg, Happy New Year,
   John Muhanuka told me that you are interested in a Miss Margaret Warob for your secretary. If this is so, can I know why? I am trying to send you a girl by mid-January.
   S.L. Rwebangira.

Colonel Bruce Mackenzie had been appointed directly, on instructions from Government House, to the board of E.A.A. in June. As a farmer and former minister of agriculture in an otherwise all black government, his main qualification was his close friendship with President Jomo Kenyatta, who had entrusted him with looking after Kenya's interests in what was beginning to be a struggle for influence by the three states within the airline. Mackenzie could also prove to be useful in negotiations with B.O.A.C. and the British, when necessary, since it was felt that he would gain from his position as a white former government minister.

By mid-summer the activities of at London station had reached the level of farce by the time Colonel Bruce Mackenzie received the following letter from a ground hostess on temporary familiarisation training from Entebbe station, concerning a senior African staff member:

CONFIDENTIAL

<u>Mr ...</u>

I wish to inform you about an incident which happened on the 17th and 18th July and others which have happened up to today, between me and Mr .... Because I must tell you everything and wish to tell you everything it is the truth.

On the 17th July I worked a late shift, 14.30 to 20.00, with B.O.A.C. check-in. At my break time I decided as usual, to go to the E.A.A. office to check whether I had got a letter from home. In the office I found a girl, Erinah was her first name. She told me that she was working in the E.A.A. Nairobi office as a telephone operator. She had been helped to the office by Miss Muema, E.A.A. Receptionist. She was crying very bitterly, and she had been crying since 09.00, when she arrived on Alitalia from Nairobi. She told me she had a free ticket, on Mr ...'s knowledge and she is taking the same flight back. She told me that she had arranged to be met by Mr ... and didn't know London at all and knew no one. I suggested to take her to my room to have some rest and stop crying until I went back after work, then I would take her to reception to get herself a room.

When I went back to the Skyway Hotel at 20.00 and asked her to get her own room, she started crying again, telling me she does not have any money because Mr ... had agreed to accommodate her. I tried to ring Mr ...'s room, but he did not stay in the hotel that night. I had no alternative, I slept with that girl in my room, on one bed, on condition that if Mr ... does not turn up tomorrow, the 18th, she would have to get a flight back to Nairobi.

Fortunately for both of them, we managed to find Mr.... Before he came Mr Masunga (E.A.A. traffic liaison officer, LHR) was talking to the girl in my room, for he had found her crying (so she had been crying for the last two days). Immediately I had entered my room the girl told me that she had talked to Mr ... and he was coming to see her. When Mr ... came in (I was in the room and the girl was inside my bed), he went to my bed and started kissing the girl in my presence and in my room, until I had to tell him that he was my boss and he should remember that, and that this was my room and I was there. He stood up and said that I should excuse him and he asked me to take the girl in his room, after getting dressed, because by then that girl was in her nightie. She got dressed and went to Mr ...'s room. After asking me how I met the girl he asked me to dinner with Mr Masunga, Mr Mmari and another gentleman. During all that time Mr ... was behaving in a very unrespectable manner. Until he started talking about Mr Shipman (acting manager United Kingdom) and Mr Hall (traffic manager, Nairobi), how they don't have any right to write to him. How he wrote and abused Mr Hall about the retaining of two girls from East Africa at London station.

And I have heard him so many times talking to us, that I asked him why he thinks he has all the right to write to those gentlemen and others, and they themselves do not have the right to tell him what they think. That is when Mr Masunga asked whether I knew that I was talking to .... I told him that I fail to understand how Mr ... can talk to us (as a receptionist and the girl friend, a telephone operator) about his and our senior officials in such a manner and in such a place, and how would he expect us to treat him. The subject ended there.

After dinner we went upstairs, the other gentlemen went to their rooms and I asked this girl to come and collect her belongings from my room, as I had already understood that she was to stay with Mr ... in his room, which she is still doing until this today. She agreed to come soon, for I told her I was working early shift, starting at 06.00 the next morning.

I went to my room with Mr Masunga, who wanted to collect an iron from there. We talked about what was said in the dining room while we waited for the girl. When she did not appear, mr Masunga suggested we take the baggage to Mr ...'s room, so that I can sleep. He carried the bag. We knocked at Mr ...'s room, where he and the girl were, and they did nor answer, instead, Miss Rayassa Mbatta, from Tanzania, opened her door, because the rooms are nearly opposite. Mr Masunga said we should ring Mr ... from Rayassa's room and tell the girl to collect the baggage from that room that I could go and sleep. Mr ... answered the phone and agreed to pick the things from there.

At 01.00 in the morning, Mr ... rang me and said he wanted to come and talk to me. I told him that I was already asleep, if he could wait and tell me tomorrow. He insisted that he he must talk to me then. He came in with the girl and ordered me out of my bed, that I must go and take the girl's baggage from where I had put it. I explained to him that he knew where the things were and it was nearer to his room than walking all the way to my room, so late. To this he started shouting, so that all my neighbours came out of their rooms. I called Mr Masunga on the telephone, because I did not see any call for such shouts and orders. Mr Masunga heard from his shouts that he was commanding for the girl's things and he came rushing, in his pyjamas, with them, only to find people in the corridor. One of these was Mr Morand, E.A.A. first officer, occupying room 4132, opposite mine. Before this, when I was phoning Mr Masunga, Mr ... came to my bed and started hitting my nose with his hotel key. This made me nearly to madness, because I didn't see any reason for such treatment.

I have accommodated his girl friend, fed her the night before, and in the end I get them together, and why I deserved that I couldn't understand. I cried and the more I cried the more he shouted at me, holding the girl. Mr Masunga asked him to get out of my room because even security people had started coming (I understood in the morning). When they had gone I was very sick, that Mr Masunga brought me some tablets and asked Miss Rayassa to stay with me for the night. In the morning I managed to go to work. I have been meeting this girl at breakfast, she is staying in Mr ...'s room since then.

On the 19th another friend of the girl, Vasay is her first name and she works for E.A.A. Reservations, Kampala, arrived on Alitalia and Mr ... sent her to the E.A.A. house in Hounslow, where she stayed for a few days then came back to the hotel, where she is sleeping on the sofa of Mr ...'s suite.

From that night Mr ... has been insulting me whenever he finds me in the presence of other people. Until this evening (26th), when I feel I can't bear it any longer, when he shouted at me twice in the afternoon, so wildly that I cried. The last incident was in the presence of Mr Walmsley, E.A.A. London office. He was shouting about my being in the office, when I told him that we always have a supper break, as we have to work up to 23.30, he went on telling me how he is going to put me on the aircraft tomorrow and send me back to Entebbe. I told him that he must have a sound reason for it, but how can he toss around his staff only because he is ...? Every time he insults me he tells me how he is going to throw me out of the hotel room and send me back to E. Africa.

I know he is guilty about what he did that night, to come to my room so late and wake people up. He knows one day Nairobi will know, because the first officer asked me why I was crying and what those gentlemen were doing in my room in pyjamas. I did not tell him because I thought Mr ... would come to his true senses and apologise to me. Instead, he is only continuing his insults.

I have never wanted to tell you this, but I feel I must. The reason behind all this is because Mr ... wanted to use me - which I told him was impossible. First because he is ..., second because I am engaged, third he is married. He kept promising me that he will make Nairobi make me P.H.O. [Passenger Handling Officer] Entebbe, which I told him the post was too high for me at the moment, however much he will put in a recommendation and I told him that if he thinks I am fit for the post then Nairobi can as well find out. Failing all his tricks, he has now turned to insults to make me lose my temper, that he would find a reason for my downfall - for he once told me that my success or downfall is in his hands, which I suspected as groundless since my joining E.A.A. was not for him.

I am sorry that I have had to write this statement, but I have been waiting until it has reached this stage, when I can't stand it any more. I have been crying for the whole of last week.

I wish, Sir, that ... be asked to treat his subordinates like grown-ups, but not just shout at them, with threats to keep everyone miserable. No one can enjoy his or her work when you are expecting someone to buck you anytime for no reason.

I was so much upset that night he hit my nose with his key. I never had such a treatment in my life. And, to make it worse, to have it in my room, so late and for no reason at all.

Now today (27th), he has ordered me to leave for Entebbe and has issued tickets already that I cannot stay another night at London, for he fears that I must tell what he had done to me, and there is no one who can help me.

The letter was signed by the Ugandan hostess and dated 27th July, 1971. There was very little initial reaction to the letter. Much of it could be put down to the over-emotional response of a female to the strange environment and a personality clash with her superior. The combination of the letter and the measures taken to dismiss the London Airport staff, who had as a result of their feeling of insecurity joined a trade union *en masse*, was to cause East African Airways a considerable amount of trouble which would boil over into a great debate in the East African press and, ultimately, reveal the extent of corruption and mismanagement which was destroying a once greatly respected airline.

On 9th August, the first termination occurred, of a British traffic liaison officer. There was no reason given, although it had been engineered some weeks previously, in a letter sent to Nairobi on 12th July. Apart from the desire to break away from any British influence, Wangara was frustrated in his ambition to carve out an environment in which he could feel comfortable. British career airline officers did not fit in with his plans.

The dismissal of the traffic liaison officer resulted in a flurry of activity on the trade union front, demanding his re-instatement. Trade union power at Heathrow was considerable. The Transport and General Workers Union controlled the vital key workers who re-fuelled the aircraft – there was no need to call upon any other airport workers to bring the entire place to a halt.

In Nairobi, the news of imminent strike action at London was received with dismay, since they were already embroiled in a dispute with the Kenya Pilots Association who were threatening a strike of all aircrew, notified on 6th September, over the termination of the pilot's agreement by E.A.A. who 'by coercion' sought to impose a less beneficial agreement and salary negotiations had been broken off with threats to limit backdating of previous agreed settlements.

Strikes were planned to take place every Friday at 15.00 G.M.T until 20.59 G.M.T. on Saturday from 15th October. In London, the Transport and General

Colonel Bruce R. Mackenzie.

Workers Union called upon its members in the refuelling companies to 'black' East African Airways aircraft from 20th October, 1971. The East African Airways Super VC10 departure for Nairobi was cancelled that night and the following morning's arrival terminated at Paris. B.O.A.C. gave no assistance to help despatch the EC service, which could have reached Paris with the remaining fuel on board, since they feared union action against themselves. On the day of departure of an E.A.A. delegation to London, with a brief to end the dispute, the Transport and Allied Workers Union in Nairobi announced a boycott of all B.O.A.C. and Caledonian/B.U.A. aircraft. This resulted in the British aircraft being delayed overnight at Nairobi. "As long as the East African national airline was not served in London, his union would not give way", stated the Kenyan union leader Mr J.N. Chegge. This indicated, to say the least, a confusion of ideas concerning the trade union movement. Colonel Bruce Mackenzie, who had been in London at the end of September and had been fully briefed on the way things were going at Heathrow, remained in Nairobi and chaired a number of meetings at board level to decide on the action to take. There were unconfirmed reports that the Kenya government were discussing with him at the time whether events were leading to the point where their best advantage would be served if the airline should collapse, whereupon plans were already in place to form a Kenyan replacement on a more modest scale.

The dispute was settled on 22nd October, at a meeting in the Skyway Hotel. The British officer was awarded one year's salary and a staff agreement was signed giving the remaining staff protection. The matter, however, did not end there but would rumble on in the East African Press and East African Community for months ahead. The first blow was struck by the *East African Standard* in a leader on Saturday, 23rd October, 1971:

JUSTICE MUST BE DONE

For trades unionists in one country to retaliate with strike action against a strike called officially by a union in another country must be unique. This extraordinary event occurred at Nairobi airport, where the Transport and Allied Workers Union ordered members not to service British Aircraft on Thursday.

The Kenya Petroleum Oil Workers Union promptly promised support. Joint reprisals, because fraternal members of the Transport and general Workers Union were ordered not to handle E.A.A. aircraft, are not the only bizarre acts in this mystifying affair.

The boycott of E.A.A. planes at Heathrow began out of the frustration experienced by the T. and G.W.U. over delay at the Nairobi headquarters of E.A.A. in dealing with a protest against the dismissal of an employee in London... Moreover, the union appealed for support to the International Federation of Transport Workers.

Is this what happens to the solidarity of the workers? The universal trades union slogan seems to have been a little dented. Why? The short answer must be misunderstanding, if not misrepresentation.

> *...Senior officials of E.A.A., who have denied several suggestions during the dispute, began by denying any boycott had been instituted because of the decision to Africanise...*
>
> *...Mr Wangara said the employee was discharged in accordance with the terms of his contract, given proper notice and all salary and allowance paid. Then came the sting: "If he had not acted against the interests of the company, he would still have been in our service today".*
>
> *...it seems the reason could be connected with trying to help a lady in distress. When this proposition was put to Mr Okot, the Director General of E.A.A. the reply was: "There is not a grain of truth in this story. There is nothing to substantiate it at all".*
>
> *... Mr Okot, remember, denied the report... At one stage Mr Wangara admitted there had been a report signed by a girl, but claimed it was out of order because it had not been submitted through him. Two days later, it is said, the Ugandan receptionist was ordered to return to Nairobi.*
> *What is the truth?*

While the events at London had been building up through the early summer of 1971, the airline had been haemorrhaging its life blood in vast sums on the long extensions to Hong Kong and New York, where the flights were carrying less passengers as the weeks passed by and interest by the American travel agents never materialised. Both Mr Isaacson and Mr Nigel Thompson departed during April and a decision was taken to suspend both loss making services with effect from July.

Negotiations had been going on at the end of 1970 with the British cargo carrier Lloyd International Airways, following which an agreement was reached under which E.A.A. would operate a fully palletised freighter service between East Africa and the United Kingdom and Zambia. The service commenced on 28th January, 1971, utilising a Britannia freighter of Lloyd International, offering 16 tons of cargo capacity on eight standard pallets. Announcing the new service at the beginning of the year Nigel Thompson had said: "We in E.A.A. are delighted to introduce this new service for our customers. E.A.A. will now be able to offer a complete freight service including *more than sufficient capacity* for all exports from East Africa." This was to prove a fairly truthful statement, since the freighter would very seldom operate to capacity with East Africa's primary air freight export, fresh fruit and vegetables, and on southbound flights would often fly empty. In its first year of operation the freighter lost K£450,000.

Another change occurred in April, when Malin Sorsbie's romantically named Seychelles and Kilimanjaro Air Transport was reconstructed into a self-managing company and renamed Simbair. The new airline was to operate dedicated non-I.A.T.A. fare charters from Europe to East Africa, competing with the British and German charter operators who were bringing large numbers of cheap-fare tourists to the Kenya coast.

Captain Edward Alleyne received acclaim in the Nairobi newspapers when, on 4th January, he crash-landed an F27, 5X-AAF, in front of hundreds of onlookers at Embakasi. After taking-off at 11.10 for Malindi with 26 passengers and crew, Alleyne and First Officer K. Makinda, noticed low pressure on the undercarriage locking mechanism, where the locking-link had broken, and the port undercarriage warning light was indicating that it was not locked up.

Captain Alleyne decided to return to Embakasi and made a normal approach, until above the runway, when he touched down firmly on the starboard gear, hoping to shake the port undercarriage locking mechanism into place. Unsuccessful, he climbed away for another, final, approach and landing. Touching down gently, to relieve weight on the port gear, as the wheels met the surface, he reduced speed, the wheel collapsed, slewing the aircraft on to its port wing-tip.

Among several cases of shock, only one woman was admitted into hospital and a man suffered an arm injury. It was acknowledged as a case of brilliant handling by the captain, who remained calm, but understandably shaken after the event.

January, 1971, had seen the introduction of the DC-9s on the inter-city routes within the partner states. The first service was operated between Nairobi and Entebbe and return. The DC-9-32 was a standard version of the marque, with uprated Pratt and Whitney JT8D-5 turbofan engines developed for hot and high conditions.[1] Arrangements had been made for all engine overhaul work to be carried out by Swissair. The seating configuration was twelve first class and eighty-five economy class. With a maximum take-off weight of 98,000lb the DC-9-32 had a range of 1,725 miles with maximum cruising speed of 565 m.p.h. This gave it the capacity to operate the African regional routes to Zambia, Malawi, Ethiopia, Somalia, Rwanda, Burundi and the Congo-Kinshasa.

---

[1] As with the Super VC10-1154, this model of the DC-9 was specially designed for East African Airways

MD DC-9s, 5X-UVY (foreground) and 5Y-ALR at Nairobi's Embakasi airport.
(Capt Ricketts)

With the arrival of the third DC-9 in March, the fleet was complete and training was going ahead with the assistance of the manufacturer's pilot instructors. The three aircraft were registered, in order of delivery: 5H-MOI, 5X-UVY and 5Y-ALR.

The engineering base at Embakasi, now under Chief Engineer Ron Barton, continued to perform most of the major airframe overhaul work necessary to keep all fleets flying. With the DC-9 engines being overhauled by Swissair and all engine work on the Super VC10s being undertaken by B.O.A.C. at London and Treforest (a 'fifth pod' engine transporter had been purchased for this purpose), engine repairs were confined to the DC3 Pratt and Whitney piston engines and F27 Rolls-Royce Darts.

Training in all fields in the airline and especially in the engineering and operations departments was carried out as extensively as possible. Fourteen 'citizen' pilots and eleven engineers were sent to Pakistan International Airlines for training where they obtained licences which enabled the pilots to be posted to the DC-9 and F27 fleets and the engineers to jobs including overhauls of F27 aircraft engines and airframes. Thirteen apprentice engineers who were in training with Ethiopian Airlines were expected to complete their courses and take up their duties as qualified engineers at the beginning of 1972. There were an additional seventeen apprentice engineers in training in the United Kingdom. Of a total of 242 non-citizens i.e. expatriate Europeans and Asians, who left the airline during 1971, a large number were skilled engineers and technicians. There was, as a result, a gradual decline in general quality of maintenance, not only on the aircraft but also to ancillary equipment.

On 28th October, the EC745 Super VC10, commanded by Captain Leslie, departed from London, destined for Frankfurt and Nairobi. Leaving Frankfurt just

MD DC-9 5Y-ALR at Chileka airport, Blantyre, Malawi. (Capt Ratcliffe)

The photograph (below) taken in 1948 in the E.A.A.C. hangar at Nairobi West contrasts with the scene (above) twenty-five years later, as Super VC10 5X-UVJ undergoes a major check in the large maintenance facility at Embakasi. The changes which took place in the years since 1948, in East African's engineering workshops, are well illustrated by these photographs.

The DH Dove VP-KEJ at Nairobi West in 1948 (L to R: name unknown, 'Dick' Whittingham, Terry Brown, Ian Keith and Terry McBreaty).

(Mr R.A. Whittingham FRAeS)

before midnight at maximum all up weight, the aircraft had to remain at the lower flight levels, around 30,000ft, until over the Mediterranean south of the Italian mainland. A climb was then initiated to a higher level. On the climb, the captain's HDI failed, followed a few moments later by a number of instrument panel lights. Torches were fished out of flight bags and the flight engineer began leafing through his manual of electrical diagrams. There was no obvious cause for the malfunctions. Then the altimeter, which was electrically operated, on the captain's side began winding down to zero. Something very disturbing was happening. The next event, after some five or ten minutes, was the failure of the captain's electrically operated repeater compass. Now the aircraft could not be flown by the captain, since his primary instruments were inoperative. When No.1 autopilot stopped working the crew became doubly concerned and it was soon decided that they had an emergency situation on their hands which required quick action. The first officer took control of the aircraft and they turned back towards Rome.

They called Rome, requesting immediate clearances for a quick descent. Very soon the first officer's HDI failed. Now they had an unusually difficult task in flying the aircraft, using the standby artificial horizon and tiny magnetic compass, mounted on the panel between the pilots. With no panel lights to illuminate them, they relied upon the flight engineer, who leaned forward, shining the beam of his torch onto the instruments, as the handling pilot stretched over to check his heading and attitude. The flight engineer continued to check the circuit breakers, hoping to find a cause for the failures. While the navigator updated their position, the aircraft was flown manually, a difficult and demanding task in a large airliner at high altitude and high speed. They made the emergency call "Pan, Pan, Pan" on the distress frequency, 121.5, whereupon they were immediately given vectored headings by stations which they had never known existed, the Italian military radar controllers. Approaching Rome, they became more confident, as they spotted the bright lights of familiar towns and cities shining up through the crystal clear night. Picking up the runway lights of Rome's Fiumicino airport, they made a normal descent and straight-in approach and landing.

It was not until several weeks had passed, during which time it was found that a VC10 of British United had suffered similar electrical faults, that the cause was identified in a ground power unit at Entebbe, which due to lack of correct maintenance, had been providing excess power generation (normally 400 cycles/sec), overloading the 210/115 volt systems of the aircraft while they were parked, and during start-up.

In February, The director general Mr W.O. Lutara had been replaced by Mr J.A. Okot on the instructions of Idi Amin. Lutara, an appointee of Milton Obote, was to return to Uganda, where he soon suffered the fate of some 80,000 to 90,000 Ugandans slaughtered within the first twenty-four months of Amin's rule. At the same time, more of the major managerial posts were Africanised, including those of director of customer services, communications manager, cabin services manager, chief stewardess, traffic superintendent and the senior service controllers. African managers were posted to head overseas stations in the United Kingdom and the

U.S.A. in furtherance of the management's policy of filling all key positions in overseas stations with citizens of the partner states.

Even with the loss of over 240 non-citizens, the staff establishment rose to 5,161 at the end of 1971. The staff cost element of total expenditure fell, however to 30.3 per cent. With a total of 534,393,830 revenue passenger miles flown this equates to 10,354 revenue passenger miles per employee. If the un-audited accounts could be believed, the airline was earning K£3,913 per employee per annum during 1971. The New York service had contributed in part to a 22.5 per cent increase in costs during the year, with fuel and oil prices rising by twenty per cent world-wide. During 1971, the figures relating to East African Airways were combined with those of the subsidiary Simbair, thus adding confusion to the already vexed question of the airline's comparative performance.

Statistical information was beginning to become inaccurate, patchy, or, in some cases concerning finances, impossible to obtain. At the end of 1971 the previous year's Annual Report and Accounts still remained unpublished and un-presented to the Authority. Rumours flew about concerning losses of various amounts, some as high as K£3 million. By November the great debate which had been initiated by the London station affair was still in progress.

The matter had been taken up before the year's end by leading Nairobi barrister Byron Georgiadis in a series of letters to the *East African Standard*. The affair of the London strike and its attendant details soon gave way to more direct matters concerning the conduct of the airline. Board member Wing Commander Boswell had replied, on 5th November, in the newspaper, to a letter of Mr Georgiadis in the previous day's paper, in which, among other things, he had stated:

"Today it (E.A.A.) is allowed to continue humbling along only because of the extended tolerance of its creditors. Had it been a commercial organisation, we can hazard a guess as to what would have happened long ere now".

Mr Byron Georgiadis asks what would have happened had East African Airways been a "commercial organisation".

A company achieving continued spectacular and successful growth without its shareholders having contributed one cent of equity (which is in fact the case with this airline) would have been hailed as something of a financial marvel.

G.L.W. BOSWELL.
Nairobi, Nov, 5, 1971

Mr Georgiadis' advocacy skills were in evidence when, on the 9th November his reply was published in the *East African Standard*:

What Mr G.L.W. Boswell does not seem to appreciate despite (until very recently) his many years on the East African Airways Board, is that there can be haphazard growth.

Indeed, if a body has disproportionate growth of some of its limbs, it becomes grotesque and can be an embarrassment, vide the recent lopping-off of the Zurich,

New York run and the Far East route to Hong Kong, and the cancelling of the proposed run to Japan.

Similarly, disproportionate growth can result in inability to sustain the body adequately. Does he know, and would he care to divulge, the ratio of all employees to aircraft of the Corporation, in comparison with its competitors?

I suggest that Mr Boswell takes off his ex-director's rose-coloured spectacles when evaluating the position today. The "financial marvel" is that the Corporation is permitted to carry on, existing from hand to mouth, thanks largely to transfusion of funds by Kenya and the patience of its creditors.

Are there any public documents, apart from the December 1969 audited accounts of the Corporation? Under the East African Community legislation and the Treaty for East African Co-operation, it would appear that the Board of Directors of the Corporation should transmit annually to the Auditor-General proper accounts and records in relation to the revenue and expenditure of the Corporation.

Under Article 78, when such accounts are returned certified by the Auditor-General, the Board of Directors should immediately transmit the statement of accounts and report of the Auditor-General to the Communications Council, which shall then cause the same to be presented to the Assembly without delay and, in any event, before the expiry of nine months from the end of the financial year.

In the case of E.A.A., I understand this to be September 30, 1971, at the latest. Have these audited accounts been so submitted?

Is Mr Boswell speaking with esoteric knowledge when he compares the Corporation to a company..."achieving continued spectacular and successful growth"? Does he dispute that the Corporation is now living from hand-to-mouth? Is he aware that basic supplies are threatened because of the Corporation's inability to meet its financial commitments?

Anyhow, all this is beside the point. I am not looking for oblique references from an ex-director of the Corporation who left the board six months ago. The questions posed in my previous letter related to another aspect altogether (the London affair) which, I would have thought by now merited an official explanation in the public interest.

Lest he misconstrues, let me assure Mr Boswell that my interest and concern are not to criticise and disrupt. Strangely enough, as a constant traveller, I was proud of the airline, which compared very favourably with its competitors, and I would hate to see it sink irretrievably because of bumbledom and ineptitude.

I am further convinced that merely sweeping problems under the carpet and refusing to face and rectify them does not generate public confidence; nor is it an internationally recognised method of inspiring the loyalty and goodwill of its employees.

After all, this is not a domestic airline. It is an international one and the standards it aspires to and should attain are international standards.

BYRON GEORGIADIS
Nairobi, Nov. 9, 1971.

On 11th November the *East African Standard* carried a news item under the headline:

Oil Company denies threat to E.A.A.

Senior officials of East African Airways and an oil company in Nairobi yesterday denied reports suggesting the Corporation was facing a serious financial crisis.

It has been stated that the oil company had told E.A.A. it would discontinue fuel supplies unless substantial arrears in payment were met in a stipulated period. The oil company agreed, subject to a solution being found in that time, to continue services for 24 hours.

However, a senior official of the company said: "We have not foreclosed or threatened to do so."

The Financial Accountant of E.A.A., Mr J.J. Ogwabit, said the suggestion of a serious split was "news to him". He went on to confirm that: "We have this very morning paid a substantial cheque to the oil company concerned".

After a period of changes both in staff and air routes, which included dropping the New York and Hong Kong services, the chairman of the Corporation, Chief Fundikira, said in June that, in spite of recent setbacks, the airline was perfectly solvent.

"Our overdrafts are secured and loan and interest commitments are met on time," he stated.

He explained that financial difficulties being experienced at that time by the airline were the result of a shortage of working capital and the suspension of the new York and Hong Kong services would "restore full viability" to the airline which was passing through a turbulent period.

Chief Fundikira, the director-general of the Corporation, Mr J.A.O. Okot, and the secretary to the Corporation, Mr F.B. Mahatane, were not available for comment yesterday as they had left, with their wives, for Honolulu to attend an I.A.T.A. meeting.

The news report was followed up by an Editorial comment inside the newspaper:

Another E.A.A. Crisis

The future of E.A.A. is of the utmost concern to the East African public. Nobody would deliberately work to the airline's disadvantage. Everybody would wish to see its reputation safeguarded.

What is the use of trying to gull the public by denials of a financial crisis and other troubles? People who are "in the know" are aware of the attitude of the lending banks and suppliers of fuel. A foreclosure has been averted, though nobody seems willing to admit it has been another close shave.

Unless the E.A.A. can keep abreast of payments, there will be renewed difficulties. The Corporation cannot go on like this, with perpetual financial troubles, strike threats by pilots, dissatisfaction among engineers, a dispute about the dismissal of an employee which led to strikes at Heathrow and Nairobi over issues which were utterly misrepresented as opposition to Africanisation but related solely to an expatriate's attempt to help a Ugandan hostess who was in distress.

At the height of this treble crisis, why do the Chairman, Director-General, Secretary, with their wives, fly off to Honolulu, reportedly to attend an I.A.T.A. meeting which, in any case, is irrelevant?

This remarkable open debate in the newspaper was to continue into December and the New Year. In a country governed by a one party system, where the level of parliamentary debate was not generally well informed, it was an apparent credit to the freedom of the press which existed in Kenya that such a deeply critical process was permitted to continue – unless, of course, it was with the full approval of the Kenya government.

The *East African Standard* returned to the subject in a leader, written by the editor, Malcolm Payne, on Monday, 15th November. Headed ***E.A.A. 'action objectives'***, it continued the questioning of the airline's parlous state:

When the Chairman, Director-General and Secretary of the E.A.A. Corporation, with their wives, return from their expensive trip to Honolulu, they ought to do some very hard thinking.

First they should look into the Corporation's financial affairs and administration. On top of various bank warnings, Shell last week demanded payment of debts said to exceed £1,000,000. In default, the company indicated supplies of fuel would be suspended; but it relented after a member of the board had intervened. If the fuel tap is turned off, E.A.A. will be grounded.

But E.A.A. could find its aircraft grounded for a variety of reasons if only some of the allegations being bandied about are true. If the rumours are untrue, whose fault is it that they are believed by the public?

Top officials stay silent, other than deny or evade the issues. The P.R. people, never shy of publicity when there is some gimmick to popularise, keep their mouths shut, obviously on instructions. For any P.R. man knows that just about the surest way to get a bad Press and public image is to issue denials or keep studiously aloof in the midst of grave public disquiet.

After all, the Corporation is owned by the East African Governments, i.e. the people. This is no private concern where anybody can play ducks and drakes without caring. Even a private company, its Board, executives and rank-and-file, have to observe the customary procedures.

The Chairman, Chief Fundikira, the Director-General, Mr Okot, and the Secretary, Mr Mahatane, have a duty to the Corporation, to the E.A. Community and to the public. To explain what is going on. To answer the well founded criticisms of Mr Georgiadis and others in Nairobi, of Mr Davis and others in London. To do what Mr Tyson has suggested: issue a statement giving "the truth, the whole truth and nothing but the truth".

High Life and Low Morals
Readers are asking why this newspaper does not publish the full facts. What is being said about E.A.A. is well known, have no doubt. Employees see to that. But there is an old newspaper axiom - "the greater the truth the greater the libel", when applied to publication of actionable statements on non privileged occasions.

Criticisms mount. A flight engineer has written about deficiencies in maintenance. A Londoner has written about extravagance, high life and low morals, with allegations amounting to a scandal. These can be made available, if the correspondents agree, to an official inquiry, if one is ever mounted. Or to the Air Registration Board, if the Corporation is reported and it might well be because, after independence, E.A.A. asked to continue under its jurisdiction.

At the opening of the I.A.T.A. meeting in Honolulu yesterday, its Director-General, Mr Hammarskjold, gave a disturbing survey of the aviation industry. He concluded with these "action objectives" for the delegates:

"An adequate return on capital. A lean and hard management philosophy, with heavy emphasis on innovation, improved efficiency and productivity. Improved cost controls with particular stress on indirect costs. Greater harmonisation of collective industry marketing policies, including the development of new approaches to meet the demands for low fares at high load factors.

"Improved methods of establishing international fares and rates based on expanded co-operative industry research and analysis. Simplification of fares and rate structures, with differential flexibility to meet passenger and cargo market requirements, while achieving improved profitability. Improved long-term corporate planning, leading to improved matching of capacity with demand and future development on a sound economic basis.

"Finally, emphasis on long-term collective industry strategic planning on appropriate subjects".

The E.A.A. delegates could make their journeys worthwhile if they set about applying these principles. The Corporation is supra-national, which tends to make changes difficult. But changes there will have to be to keep E.A.A. flying, as the public wishes, and resume the profitability known some years ago when this "Friendly Airline" was just about the only international one in the world making a profit.

Mr Georgiadis returned to the fray on 16th November, writing a letter which spelled out, quoting chapter and verse, the responsibilities of the directors of the Corporation - should they have overlooked them:

I regret that, despite the repeated requests for answers to serious questions posed in the public interest, the Board of the E.A.A. Corporation has seen fit to ignore the matter; so that I feel it now to be my duty to point out certain basic facts which may, perhaps, have escaped this Corporation hitherto.

...I regret having to spell things out, but would earnestly ask its Board of Directors, its Director-General and its Chairman, to ponder deeply and to re-evaluate the position

in the light of their duties, responsibilities and mandate under the Act which established the Corporation as an institution of the E. A. Community, particularly as:-

1 - Under the Function and Powers of the Corporation, it is the duty of the Board of Directors...to provide air transport, and in performing that duty to secure... that the undertaking of the Corporation is operated efficiently, economically, and with due regard to safety.

2 - Its accounts, under Section 20 of the Act, are subject to audit by the Auditor General (who, incidentally, cannot be directed by anyone in the conduct of his duties).

3 - Under Section 18, it is the duty of the Corporation to conduct its business according to commercial principles...

4 - Under Section 10, the Director-General has the control and executive management of the Corporation.

5 - Under Section 12, it is the Board's responsibility (subject to general directions from the Communications Council...and the Authority) ... to give directions to the Director-General.

6 - Ultimately, the Authority (which is the three Heads of State through the Ministers) is responsible for the general direction and control of the Corporation...and can give directions to the Board as to the exercise and performance of the functions of the Corporation in relation to any matter which appears to the Authority to affect the public interest.

7 - Under the Treaty of E. A. Corporation, Article 51...it is the responsibility of the E.A. Ministers (appointed) to assist the Authority in the exercise of its executive functions...and to advise the Authority generally.

8 - Under Article 73... the Board of Directors for each Corporation... shall be responsible for its policy, control and management through the Director-General...in accordance with Annex XIII of the Treaty (which is detailed and I commend its careful perusal).

In general, and broadly, the acceptance of the office, e.g. of a "director" of even such a nationalised body, carries with it the acceptance of certain duties which are partly statutory, partly regulatory and partly dependent on the law of agents and trustees or persons in a fiduciary capacity.

Although, for all practical purposes, it is unlikely that an erring member of the board, or the board as a whole inter alien would be looked to by the authority for reimbursement of Corporation funds unnecessarily or negligently expended, it must not be overlooked that directors and other persons in authority (appointed or nominated) are at all times expected to show a certain degree of skill and diligence in the conduct of the Corporations affairs. Should they be found wanting in that regard, the least that can happen is their removal from the board.

In this context, I would remind them that in the conduct of the Corporation's affairs they hold in trust, ultimately, the reputations of the three Heads of State of the three territories that constitute the authority, through their Ministers, who are working hard to serve the public, and are sensitive to public opinion – even if the board appear not to be. Perhaps this thought may have a sobering effect on all concerned.

Hence, because of public conscience, although there may not be always legal accountability, there is, in the ultimate, public accountability because of the Minister's "political accountability".

I estimate (it is the best one can do in the absence of official information) that the ... affair (in London) must have cost the Corporation approximately £15,000, bearing in mind the grounding of its aircraft, re-allocation of its passengers and other related expenditure of the strike. If the Corporation ignores these questions now, I imagine sooner or later accounts..."in accordance with the best commercial standards"... as required by Section 20 of the Act and Article 78 of the Treaty will be submitted to the Auditor-General. I presume these questions, or similar will be asked by the Auditor-General, and they cannot be ignored.

Meantime, it behoves the board to remember that the Corporation should br run solely for the benefit of the Community and the public. It is the public interest which should be the sole criterion in determining the course to pursue in relation to all matters pertaining to the Corporation. It is the public interest that demands that these questions be answered and moreover, answered promptly, fully and truthfully.

It is the public who, in one form or another, ultimately have to pay to enable the Corporation to function and it is the public who have every right to question public expenditure. Disregard of the public and the public interest can only be at best a temporary expedient. Ultimately, it corrodes the public's confidence in the Corporation.

The board can certainly choose to ignore all these questions and factors, but does so at its peril. Public confidence and commercial goodwill can be ephemeral and are usually reflected in direct proportion to the responsibility shown by its board of directors.

As Kenya is, in a sense, a shareholder of this Corporation, the members of its National Assembly are perfectly entitled to question the position under Standing Order No. 35 (1) "Questions to Ministers..." which may be put to a Minister relating to public affairs with which he is officially connected... This, I think, includes matters of the Community and, if the board declines to answer, perhaps the Minister will.

BYRON GEORGIADIS
Nairobi, Nov. 15, 1971

The newspaper correspondence continued through November and into December, with new questions being thrown up by the Editor of the *East African Standard*, until, on 3rd December, in the Kenya National Assembly, the Minister for Power and Communications, Mr Ngala, fielded questions from a rather poorly briefed M.P. from Kitui North, who chose to concentrate on minor and rather insignificant items involving Chief Fundikira's car hire charges abroad and free air travel for him and his wife – quite normal for many categories of airline staff worldwide. Mr Ngala said, however, "Both the management and the control of finance in the Corporation needed to be improved and positive action is already being taken to this end and as the political climate has now cleared I hope the Communications Council will soon be meeting to take further action in the management and financial control".

Following the K£650,000 loss in 1970 a further loss was to come for 1971, amounting to a massive K£2,702,400 on the airline's operation. One of the reasons for this deficit was explained as an 'increase in expenses'. Passenger revenue had increased by a disappointing eight per cent, with a corresponding increase in operating expenditure of 22.5 per cent over 1970. This was explained by unusual hikes in aircraft servicing, landing and ground handling charges. Interest paid on bank overdrafts and charges amounted to K£285,000. The bank overdraft at the end of 1971 was K£3,590,000, compared with K£1,110,000 in 1970. East African Airways had at the end of 1971 depleted its capital structure by some K£3,795,000 through accumulated losses, resulting in a K£50,000 deficit in capital. This underlined the argument so often expounded that the Corporation was undercapitalised and required additional funds from the partner states.

Passengers carried in 1971 rose to 564,229 of which 343,532 were on the uneconomic domestic services. Comparative figures for 1970 were 510,293 with 289,513 being carried on the domestic services. *Over 61 per cent of the total passenger traffic was being flown at fares fixed in 1956* – these loss-making, uneconomic fare and route structures, predominantly favouring the Tanzanian social experiment, were the most significant cause of the economic decline of the airline. Together with the rapid Africanisation policy, which was over-staffing the airline with inexperienced and unsuitable staff, replacing previously loyal and qualified professionals, and the undoubted high level of self-serving and corruption within the executive management, these problems would now be almost impossible to address, since the political climate within the Community would never again permit sensible debate and consensus agreement.

It was Captain Henry Hartley's last trip in command of an E.A.A. Super VC10 (5H-MOG), before he left the airline to join Britannia Airways. They were departing Dar es Salaam on 25th August, 1971, for Lusaka and he generously offered the leg to his co-pilot, First Officer Brian Meadley. Meadley thanked him and said that he would do a 'dead stick' landing into Lusaka, pulling back the power at 39,000ft. and not touching the throttles again until 'over the fence', the same routine which Captain Ainsworth had perfected in the Comets. Hartley was not keen on the idea, but he finally acquiesced, saying, "For every mile you undershoot or overshoot, you buy me a beer".

The rule of thumb is simply to calculate altitude to be lost divided by distance to go, which equals the rate of descent required. Thus, at, say, fifty miles from touchdown (assuming 39,000ft), one would need to set up a descent of 780ft per minute. Meadley had to employ all his skills as, at one stage, the rate of descent approached 6,000ft per minute,[2] with the airspeed climbing towards the maximum full flap speed of 186 knots. With the final stage of flap yet to be selected, Paddy Murray, the flight engineer, warned him to watch his airspeed, as Meadley concentrated on the approach, determined to succeed with his self imposed task. Captain Hartley called "Final approach", to which the tower replied that they could not see the aircraft. "Look higher", he replied, as the Super VC10 seemed to drop like a stone towards the runway threshold. Coming over the fence, Meadley called for 90 per cent power, to check the rate of descent. Paddy Murray, manning the throttles on his engineer's console, said that he "Gave him 110 per cent" [sic], and he made a perfect landing, easing the throttles back to idle then calling for reverse thrust to slow down the aircraft on the runway.

Brian Meadley had shown what an exceptional handler he was of the Super VC10 - but Murray states: "I kept my foot against the cockpit door, in case any disembarking passenger might complain about the highly original approach and landing". There is no record that anyone did.*

Dr Obote, with the full support of Tanzania's President Nyerere, had established a training camp for his supporters at the Tanzanian township of Kingolwira, some 120 miles up-country from Dar es Salaam. Relations between Tanzania and Idi Amin's Ugandan regime were at a very low ebb, with Uganda anticipating an invasion. In August an attempt was mounted to invade Uganda with a force of some 300 well trained men. Having been disarmed for the journey through Tanzania, they expected to receive their weapons on arrival at the border location, near Tabora. On arrival, in the early hours of 5th August, they disembarked from the train and were driven in trucks to their camp at Kigwa. Nyerere had had second thoughts, and the group was to remain, un-armed at the camp for many frustrating months. This, no doubt, led to the improvement in confidence which would lead to an early meeting of the Communications Council. The political climate was not happy in the unfortunate country of Uganda. Stories of such unimaginable horror were emanating from there, that few people were prepared to believe them, dismissing them as typical African hyperbole from the losing side. In June, rumours were being widely circulated that Amin's troops had slaughtered up to 200 Acholi and Langi soldiers at Mbarara barracks. Two American journalists named Nicholas Stroh and Robert Siedle had tried to investigate the rumours, and were themselves killed in appalling circumstances. In July, Amin claimed that 600 troops had been

---

[2] Normally 500-700 ft per minute
*See notes to second edition Page 446

killed in fighting on the border with Tanzania, which although found to be false, was probably an excuse to explain the Mbarara killings. He closed the border and declared a state of emergency with Tanzania.

In July, 1971, incredibly, Amin was entertained at lunch by H.M. the Queen and Prince Philip at Buckingham Palace. The purpose of his trip seems to have been to acquire sophisticated arms with which to invade Tanzania. En route to London, he had visited Israel, where he had had a meeting with Prime Minister Golda Meir. Unsuccessful in his attempts to obtain tanks and Harrier jump-jets from Britain, he returned to Israel to try and persuade them to assist him in his plan to move against Tanzania.

With these events in mind, it is understandable that the Tanzanian newspaper *The Standard* of Dar es Salaam should declare in its 13th December edition **"Plot against E.A.A."**:

> *An International conspiracy is underway to kill the East African Airways Corporation. A special correspondent tells* **'The Standard'** *that influential people in Kenya, Britain and Israel and at least two highly placed men in Tanzania, are out to show that the airline is losing money, allegedly because of mismanagement by African officials.*
>
> *And the imperialist Press represented in Kenya by the British-owned and British-run* **"East African Standard"** *has been used to carry out the muck-racking* [sic] *work against the EAAC Chairman, Chief Abdullah Saidi Fundikira, the secretary Mr Felician Mahatane, both of whom are Tanzanians. This Press has deliberately been fed with false information by detractors of the airline. The aim of all being :*
>
> • *To show that E.A.A.C. is losing money, especially on internal flights in Tanzania.*
>
> • *To show that the airline could be 'saved' by changing the management from African to European (British expatriate) or Israeli.*
>
> • *To pave way for asking the British Overseas Airways Corporation or El Al to manage international flights.*
>
> • *To allow a Nairobi based 'airline' the African International Airways Ltd. to take over management and later complete service of internal flights of E.A.A.C. the phased plan first beginning with cargo and charter business, which E.A.A. is handling perfectly well now.*

The rambling report went on to criticise various aspects of the Press campaign in the Nairobi paper. Eleven days previously, had seen the opening of the new Tanzanian gateway airport, near Moshi, named Kilimanjaro International Airport.[3] An interesting incident, which was misrepresented in print, shows how B.O.A.C. were prepared to come to the assistance of East African Airways, had the political

---

[3]In 1963, with the introduction of the F27, both Arusha and Moshi airfields were considered unsuitable; this upset the local chambers of commerce, resulting in the suggestion from Ted Boyle that a new 4,400ft strip be constructed at Sanya Plains, midway between the two towns. Before the work could commence, President Nyerere vetoed the idea, insisting on a new International Airport to serve northern Tanzania. Thus was Kilimanjaro International Airport conceived.

climate and post-colonial animosity not been against such a plan. *The Standard* reported:

> *The affairs of E.A.A.C. have been shown to be black in the particular Kenya Press which asked for an inquiry and the Western Press by people with vested interests. Some of these are Kenyan nationals. Others are British, and yet others strangely, are Tanzanian citizens or in the Tanzanian payroll.*
>
> *One such Tanzanian politician was approached by a B.O.A.C. official during the opening of the Kilimanjaro International Airport on December 2 to seek redress after another Tanzanian had rebuffed the official for offering the services of a General Manager to E.A.A. The B.O.A.C. man had been told that as his airline and El Al were involved in intrigues against E.A.A., other considerations apart, he should never have raised the matter.*

It was not until Wednesday, 15th December, that the *East African Standard* in Nairobi reacted to the Dar es Salaam report, in a long Editorial it replied:

> *What preposterous nonsense was published by the* **Standard Tanzania** *alleging an international conspiracy to discredit the East African Airways Corporation.*
>
> *The Editor of that newspaper is Mr. S. Mdee, who is also a Tanzanian nominee to the Corporation Board. In the interests of impartiality, it is questionable whether an editor should be a director of any organisation except his own newspaper.*
>
> *The Chairman of E.A.A. is also a Tanzanian, Chief Fundikira. Very recently, he returned from the I.A.T.A. conference in Honolulu. Last night he was due to be off again, flying to London. Why? What is the chairman doing about the current crisis in the airline's affairs?*
>
> *If the Editor-E.A.A. director is blissfully ignorant of unrest, frustration and low morale among many of the Corporation's staff, he ought to make a few inquiries. He might then learn of inefficiency and maladministration...*
>
> *Publicity exposing the Corporation has been chiefly through this newspaper, which is in no fractional part of a cent interested in who runs the airline provided it is operated efficiently, upholding the good name of East Africa and restoring the reputation E.A.A. enjoyed. The three participating countries sit on a gold mine in tourism, provided passengers are flown to and fro with the maximum of ease and the minimum of difficulty.*
>
> *...An inquiry is promised when the Communications Council meets on January 4. Here are some points for consideration before that time:-*
>
> *Why is the E.A.A. Board meeting not being held tomorrow, as scheduled, and as demanded by the nominees from Uganda and Kenya? The National Bank of Kenya, which bears the lion's share of the financial strain, wants to know, by Friday, how it is proposed to reduce the E.A.A. overdraft. Unless a satisfactory answer is received, will it be surprising if further credit is stopped within a few days?*
>
> *In the present circumstances, how will E.A.A. meet its liabilities? There is ground for believing that around £3,000,000 is owed to trading debtors.*

...*The sheer fact is that the airline has lost and is losing money, its accounts are in the red, and all this must be put right whoever is responsible. No campaign is being waged, again as suggested, to show E.A.A. can be saved by, or should be handed over to, British or Israeli interests. They would almost certainly refuse if any such offer were made.*

Most of the Corporation's debts are owed in Kenya. The Board must realise it cannot get very far without support and approval in Kenya and must face up to its responsibilities; all the directors together, not just one or two, and especially the chairman, instead of ducking plain answers.

Chief Fundikira can rightly claim his position is not meant to be executive under the Corporation's constitution. Whether or not it was because the Director-General's appointment remained unratified for ten months, the reality is that Chief Fundikira has undertaken a substantial measure of executive duty.

...He is, however, a non-executive chairman... Neglect strongly indicates that efficient business control is wanted. Business does not mix with politics particularly in the highly competitive world of flying. Experts are needed and it matters not a whiff of paraffin where they come from, provided they apply professional methods and thoroughly train Africans to follow on actively and efficiently.

Among recommendations..is the appointment of a top quality professional as General Manager...Another... is that of Finance Controller...Israel and Britain can be left out, that should dispose of the ridiculous assertion about international intriguing for an "expatriate" take-over.

Why must this cardinal issue be submerged in racism? Why cannot genuine critism be answered, with some self-analysis instead of falling back on nationalistic horror? or the evasiveness of silence? One of these days the accounts will have to be made public. Perhaps an imperialist plot will then be discovered to explain away the parlous state. What is wanted is action now, to protect and preserve E.A.A., not futile excuses later.

The communications ministers of the three partner states met on Christmas Eve 1971, when Mr Rwetsiba, East African Community Minister for Communications, Research and Social Services, from Uganda, calmly dismissed the crisis as being "No cause for alarm" He said that the problems facing E.A.A. were almost identical to those faced by other airlines and "it was pointless treating its case as a special one". It was clear that, with disharmony between the territories, no solution to the problems of East African Airways would be found before the unhappy year ended.

On the eve of 1972 there waited, patiently, the shadowy figure of the Grim Reaper.

❖ ❖ ❖

1972

Since replacing Wing Commander Boswell on the Board in June, 1970, Colonel Bruce Mackenzie had endeavoured to bring the airline back on to course, with high level meetings with the National Bank of Kenya to alleviate their misgivings over an over-run on the Corporation's overdraft of some £3,500,000 sterling; policy meetings concerning the dispute at London and meetings with the Kenya Pilots Association in order to de-fuse the unrest over terms of service and salary levels. During October, he had taken the initiative, with the authority of the Kenya government, in negotiations with B.O.A.C.in London, when Chief Fundikira was unable, as chairman of a Corporation governed by divided partners, to take effective decisions.

One of the paramount ambitions of the more fiercely nationalistic African directors was the Africanisation of the flight-deck. It was believed that "Resistance to the progress of E.A.A.C." was the reason for the perceived reluctance to train African pilots. It was felt that the Kenya Pilot's Association, to which all the Europeans belonged, was an obstacle to the progress of Africans, since the "European pilots feared the loss of their jobs".

In an atmosphere charged with racial overtones, on both sides, it was impossible to convince the Africans that the paramount consideration was safety. Seeing that a number of African pilots had been trained by Pakistan International Airlines and were apparently qualified to command the F27 and Twin Otter aircraft, they could not understand or accept that the European instructors and examiners of E.A.A. refused to pass them as competent. Bruce Mackenzie had urged the Board to appoint an expert European general manager. Africans strongly resisted this move, arguing that "There is danger that the frustrated African pilots could resign from the Corporation – and the Europeans think this is a splendid idea. The E.A.A.C. chairman and other officials are trying hard to counter these efforts by enemies of the airline. Hence the pressure for the position of general manager (European) being exerted by certain Kenya personalities".

The frustrations concerning the up-grading of low time and in some cases, incompetent, pilots came to a head in February, 1972, following an unconnected incident. General Idi Amin had decided that he should fly to meet with some friends at a remote airfield in the Congo. A message had come through to the operations centre at Embakasi that an F27 Friendship should be despatched to Entebbe as soon as possible to take the general to his rendezvous. The duty staff contacted the only pilot available at the time, Captain John Bunstead, telling him to report immediately for the flight. Captain Bunstead explained that he had recently returned from a flight, was running out of legal flight time and, anyhow, he was not feeling well. The duty officer then called Captain Michael Lorenzi, the chief pilot F27 Fleet, who backed up Bunstead, agreeing that he should not be asked to fly the charter. He was not, however, told that it was for General Idi Amin; if he had been, he would have endeavoured, notwithstanding the lateness of the hour, to find another captain who had had adequate rest. At such short notice, regrettably, a last-minute charter could not be despatched. The captains did not know it at the time, but the general could not be accommodated, and the result would be unhappy for everyone concerned.

When the matter was raised the following morning with the director of operations, Captain Peter Cunningham, he could only support the decision of his fleet captain. He was, however, critical of the duty officer who had not told Captain Lorenzi the full story. For Cunningham this came as an additional problem, for he was under increasing pressure in his meetings with Okot, Amalemba and personnel manager Muteshi concerning an ultimatum that six African pilots who had been trained by Pakistan International Airlines, and with further training by Eastern Airlines in the U.S.A., should be given commands within six months. Since they did not have the flight time or qualifications to take command in such a short time, Cunningham had written to director-general Okot refusing, on safety and efficiency grounds.

There had been many difficulties in trying to train Chief Fundikira's recruits (at one time between twenty-four and twenty-six had arrived together, without any prior notification), without any additional equipment. Training had to be conducted sporadically, as and when a spare Twin Otter or DC3 could be made available for a few hours. Captain Cunningham was continually rebuffed by Okot, and previously by Lutara, in seeking a higher priority for flight training. Training sessions frequently had to be cancelled when additional charter flights were accepted, and when engineering was behind schedule. There was no money to purchase additional aircraft for training purposes, and the situation was compounded by the fact that the recruits were very slow to learn, by European standards.

On 2nd February, 1972, Cunningham and Lorenzi were summarily dismissed, without notice or compensation, although the charter flight incident had no connection in Cunningham's case. Captain Bunstead was also dismissed, then reinstated following pressure from the Kenya Pilot's Association, after which he was compulsorily retired by the Corporation.

In the early 1950s, some two years after Peter Cunningham had joined East African Airways, Captain Eric Morris had confidently predicted on his annual confidential report that "Here is a future operations manager of E.A.A.C.". And so he had become, but, sadly, only when the airline's infrastructure was already being weakened by political pressures on inexperienced top management and board. Being primarily responsible for the safety of both passengers and crew, Captain Cunningham had no professional option other than to refuse the instructions given to him. After twenty-three year's service as co-pilot, training captain, chief pilot, and director of operations, this officer was summarily dismissed without notice and with the loss of all rights. At ten o'clock in the morning of 2nd February, 1972, he was handed a letter instructing him to leave his office immediately. He was even refused payment of his out-of-pocket expenses, amounting to only a few shillings.

Captain Cunningham remained in Nairobi, as regional technical representative of the International Air Transport Association and, before leaving East Africa, was presented by the pilots with a silver tray inscribed "May you never be forgotten". He would go on to become a senior official in other international airline organisations.

On 5th January, 1972, Captain Alan Burkitt was in command of Super VC10 5Y-ADA, which, after a frustrating three hour delay, departed Dar es Salaam at 15.00 for Lusaka and Blantyre. Soon after take-off, there was a loud bang and, in Captain Burkitt's words, "One half of No 1 engine turbine came adrift, and fell with a shower of blades on a 'copper' south of Dar es Salaam. He informed the tower at Dar es Salaam that he thought that 'that feller up there had a lot of trouble'!" Burkitt diverted to Nairobi, where, after circling for thirty minutes to burn off fuel, he landed without incident at 18.00. The 135 passengers were visibly shaken as they streamed out of the aircraft and boarded buses to the terminal.

In the first week of the new year, on 6th and 7th of January, a meeting had taken place between the communications ministers of the three countries, to try and resolve the financial crisis, but no agreement had been forthcoming, since the Ugandan and Tanzanian members clashed and haggled with Mr Ngala, representing Kenya. Due to delaying tactics, no conclusions were reached, other than to agree to meet again in February, when the finance ministers of the three countries would be invited to attend. Mid way through the month, the government-owned Kenya National Bank demanded, on government instructions, that E.A.A. should appoint two "Highly skilled advisers". The airline announced that it was seeking persons "Highly skilled and of vast experience", but there was no confirmation that anyone had been located for these posts. In view of the resistance by both Tanzania and Uganda to "imperialists" or persons of "colonial mentality" it was unlikely that Britain would provide expertise to the airline. In fact, it would be to the U.S.A. that the Board turned for management expertise and advice.

When the annual report for 1970 was finally published in 1972, Chief Fundikira wrote, on 30th March, to the chairman of the Communications Council at the Arusha headquarters:

I have the honour to present the Report and Accounts for the East African Airways Corporation for the year ended 31st December 1970.

1970 was a very difficult year for the airline industry generally and the East African Airways was no exception.

For the first time in 13 years the Corporation is reporting a loss of K.Sh 13.541 million on its operations and a further loss of K.Sh. 0.530 million on the operations of its subsidiary company Seychelles Kilimanjaro Air Transport.

It is with deep regret that the accounts are presented with the kind of audit report that accompanies them.

The board fully accepts the responsibility for this in that it appointed men with little experience and inadequate training to senior posts. This was further aggravated by the poor health and eventual death of the Corporation's Financial Controller.

Early remedial steps were taken and are being continued to rectify the situation and the Board assures the Authority of the East African Community that the presentation of correct accounts at all times and control of the Corporation's finances has its constant attention.

CHIEF A.S. FUNDIKIRA
CHAIRMAN

The Auditor General of the East African Community, Frederick Sims, commented on the audit of the 1970 accounts:

Acting under the powers vested in me by section 20 (2) of the East African Airways Corporation Act 1967, I authorised Cooper Brothers & Co. to have access to all books, records, returns and other documents relating to the accounts of the Corporation to carry out the audit. The accounts of the subsidiary Seychelles Kilimanjaro Air Transport Limited, which have been included in these accounts, were audited by Alexander, MacLennan, Trundell & Co. but they have not yet been signed by the directors.

Cooper Brothers & Co. have reported to me that in their opinion the books and records of the Corporation have not been properly kept, and there has been inadequate control over various important sections of the accounting organisation. Numerous large adjustments had to be made to the draft accounts.

In the light of their report I am unable to state that the accounts give a true and fair view of the state of affairs and the results of the Corporation and its subsidiary.

The morning of April 18th, 1972, was bright and clear as the East African Airways Super VC10, 5X-UVA made its approach to the runway at Addis Ababa. After landing, Captain John (Paddy) Vale brought the aircraft gently to taxi speed, and turned off the runway to continue to the parking position. It was an uneventful arrival, their stop-over scheduled to be less than an hour, to pick up a few Rome and London bound passengers, refuel and be on their way. The flight-deck crew comprised the captain, First Officer Ronald Botto, Flight Engineer Brian Twist and Navigating Officer Frank McNabb.

As the passengers boarded EC720, the crew busied themselves preparing for departure. The passenger cabin was unusually noisy, with the excited chatter of schoolchildren, returning to England after the Easter holidays with their parents in Kenya and Ethiopia. Among the children were Alexandra and Helen, the daughters of Frank McNabb and Paddy Murray. The loadsheet was brought to the flight deck by the despatcher and it was immediately examined to find the take-off weight. A perusal of the Addis Ababa page in the operations manual performance tables would then show the crew at what speed on the runway they could fix V_1, at which a decision must be made to continue with the take-off, or if necessary, to abort. It was routine, and the navigator would normally write it on a card which would be placed in front of the pilots.

All was complete, the engines were quickly started and the Super VC10 commenced its slow taxi to the take-off point.

Captain Vale swung the aircraft onto the runway centre-line and with no delay called for full take-off power. The engines thundered as 5X-UVA responded, surging forward. Suddenly, as the speeding aircraft gathered momentum, there was a loud bang, followed by an incredible increase in noise, and vibration so bad that the forward galley literally disintegrated, with doors flying open and locker contents flying out onto the floor. The reaction on the flight-deck was swift and instantaneous. At about 160kts, "Abort take-off!" Wheel brakes were fully applied, throttles were brought back, reverse levers lifted and full reverse thrust employed, as the runway rapidly flashed past them. There was a floating sensation as, in the passenger cabin, it was sensed that the aircraft was being brought to a stop. Even as it continued past the runway's end, the sensation was not yet violent.

The new runway at Addis Ababa did not have an 'over-run,' as recommended by normal I.C.A.O. standards. Where it had been completed was a huge 50ft depression beyond a 6ft deep drainage ditch. 5X-UVA, unable to stop in the runway length available, hit the lip of the ditch at 75kts and the landing gear was stripped off as the aircraft continued, virtually in a glide, until crashing into the approach-light tower, the top of which was level with the runway surface. The lights ripped the inboard fuel tanks and the electrics fired the fuel. The aircraft hit the ground slightly starboard wing down and was swinging to the right. Nose up, in a stalled condition, the tail broke off as she hit the ground, then the cockpit sheared off and was turned under the fuselage as it continued to plough forward.

The aircraft was on fire as it hit the ground, but the flames had not taken hold as the orderly evacuation began. Passengers were even saying, "after you", as they left out of the starboard side. One male passenger, standing under a stream of 'water', helped an African stewardess get people away, down a slope, to safety. On the port side, passengers encountered a barbed wire fence. Some braved the fence and ran clear. It was not until the last live passenger was out of the wreckage that the stream of 'water' ignited – it was kerosine fuel.

The take-off was witnessed by an American, in charge of the reconstruction work. Sitting in his caravan at the side of the runway, he stopped work to watch the take-off. As the Super VC10's engines roared against the thrust reversers, he yelled: "He won't make it!" and, together with his assistant, jumped into a jeep. They reached the scene before the fuel ignited and helped to get some of the passengers away. The fire-service arrived too late to help.

Captain Vale, First Officer Botto, Navigating Officer McNabb (hereditary chief of the clan McNabb) had died instantly. Four cabin crew and thirty-five passengers were killed, most as a result of the fire. There were sixty-four survivors[4] of the horrific fire which consumed the Super VC10. Many people died caught up in the barbed wire, as they tried to scramble free. One cabin crew member, senior stewardess Mariam Fadhil, from Zanzibar, remained in the cabin, with blood pouring down her face, as she helped passengers to safety. Finally she had to be

---

[4] Including the McNabb and Murray children.

pulled clear, but even then she continued to comfort people and lead them to safety. Flight Engineer Brian Twist died, after three days, from terrible burns, but managed to tell his wife, Kathy, briefly, what had happened, when the crew thought that a tyre had burst, which could have led to hydraulic fuel leaks and fire.

There were two remarkable escapes. One woman, in a starboard side first class aisle seat, had not fastened her lap-strap. On impact she took-off and flew head first towards the port side of the aircraft. Whilst she was in the air, the side of the aircraft opened (possibly the freight door), she flew through, over the barbed-wire fence and landed on her feet, running, and she kept on going. The first moments of this escape were witnessed by her husband, who was sitting next to her.

A woman in a first-class bulkhead seat escaped when the ceiling fell, killing her companion and trapping her in her seat. On impact, the window beside her shattered and she was able to climb through. She was an Italian film actress, travelling, with her producer, as husband and wife. As a result, the producer's real wife was not informed of his death until she telephoned E.A.A. later.

The bodies were taken to the local hospital and all the survivors went to the Seventh Day Adventist hospital. Their staff were stretched to the limit, and two nursing sisters were recalled from up-country. The British ambassador, realising the problem, arranged for a Royal Air Force hospital VC10 to fly the injured to the United Kingdom. The ambassador's wife worked tirelessly to comfort the survivors in both hospital and hotels, helping them to overcome immediate problems.

The question on everybody's lips was how could it have happened? The Super VC10 was acknowledged as the safest airliner in service anywhere in the world. There had been only one previous fatal accident, to a Nigeria Airways VC10, when the British captain had "probably" descended below his decision height in fog at Lagos, and hit the ground, killing all 87 people on board.[5]

The cause of the bang was soon found to have been a light aircraft jacking-pad, which had fallen onto the runway and become embedded in the new surface. One of the nose wheels of 5X-UVA had hit this small metal object, ramming the nose-wheel assembly on to full lock, bursting a tyre. The self-centring mechanism slammed it back, and with one tyre missing, it hit the stop and slammed back the other way, causing the unprecedented vibration.

It was not until some time later that, although the crew did everything correctly, the full extent of the compound of ingredients leading to the accident came to light. It was found that the primary cause of the accident was the inability of the aircraft to stop on the runway, because the only available information and data used to calculate V_1 was incomplete, thereby causing the aircraft to over-run the runway and also the emergency stop-way. In addition, it was found that braking depended on, effectively, only five and a half of the eight brakes. The half was lost when a main-wheel tyre burst; the loss of the two remaining brakes was another story. The official findings were summarised as follows:

---

[5] ex-E.A.A.C. First Officer John Wallis died in the crash of WT925 on November 20th, 1969, just one month after leaving Kenya.

The cabin window frames above the wing centre-section of 5X-UVA stand out above the burned-out wreckage of the once proud airliner. *(E.A. Standard.)*

The tail-plane and engines of 5X-UVA remained intact. *(E.A. Standard)*

1. The information promulgated on the new runway was incorrect, since the figures (Take-off distance available and gradient) had not yet been revised.

2. The aircraft performance graphs for the aerodrome were wrong, as a result of lack of data, resulting in a stopping distance in excess of that shown.[6]

3. Braking action was considerably reduced, due to incorrect re-assembly of the brake systems following repairs.

It was not until many months later that the implications of the incorrectly re-assembled brakes came to light.

The young wives of the flight-deck crew had not received any insurance money from E.A.A.C. With mortgages and school fees to pay, some of them were getting

Captain Trevor Hill, operations director, surveys the wreckage of 5X-UVA.   E.A. Standard

[6] V_1 calculated by the crew was never known. Estimates indicated a speed of 163kts.

desperate. Sunny McNabb, representing them, approached Tim Nightingale, who had deputised for his chief flight engineer, Paddy Murray, at the crash inquiry, to help with the technical details of their case.

Nightingale discovered, among the mass of papers, evidence which showed that the braking system had been worked on at Nairobi, where it had been snagged on a flight from Dar es Salaam. The work had been done out on the ramp and not in the hangar. There was more evidence to show that a subsequent, identical, snag had been dealt with by B.O.A.C. at Heathrow, this time in the hangar. On the first occasion the brake-assembly had been re-fitted the wrong way round. The fault was overlooked by B.O.A.C. engineers on the second occasion. It was impossible, said the manufacturers, B.A.C., to fit the brake unit incorrectly, "the entire aircraft needs to be jacked up and, furthermore, the axle is splined, so that it will not fit if reversed."

Nightingale, who was by this time no longer with E.A.A.C., took the problem to a British Airways flight engineer friend and, over a couple of pints, explained the details. The result was that British Airways engineers at Heathrow jacked-up a VC10 undercarriage with a bottle-jack, withdrew the axle and then replaced it the other way round. A good blow with a hammer would drive it home.

Calculations made by the British Aircraft Corporation showed that 5X-UVA would have stopped in the distance available on seven and a half brakes. The incorrectly installed unit was an important component of a tragedy constructed of a chain of events from which no pilot could have escaped.

B.O.A.C. (by then British Airways), B.A.C. and E.A.A.C. paid funds into the court. At the last minute, the case was settled out of court, and the widows received compensation in equal shares.

Addis Ababa's runways had been under criticism for many years, even the new runway was so rough that pilots reported: "It is sometimes difficult to read the instrument panel accurately while accelerating for take-off". B.O.A.C. inspectors had turned down the runway for their operations, delaying a proposed service to the Seychelles via Addis Ababa.

Only two days after the tragedy, an East African Airways DC-9 ran off the same Addis runway, when turning for take-off, the nose-wheel slid off the slippery, new-laid tarmac into soft ground and stuck in the mud. The eighty passengers were disembarked while a tractor was employed to pull the aircraft free. The ghastly wreckage of 5X-UVA stood close by, observed by both passengers and crew. At least one of the DC-9's passengers had been a survivor of the Super VC10 crash; seven of the DC-9 passengers refused to fly East African again and were re-booked on an Air India flight to Nairobi.

The Press interest moved from East Africa to London, when just over one month after the Addis crash, the London *Daily Mail* published, on Saturday, 20th May, 1972, a feature by Harry Longmuir on East African Airways entitled *"Why a once-proud airline faces collapse":*

JOHN VALE, 41, from Manchester was an airline captain with a distinguished flying record. He was also, with good cause, a disgruntled, disillusioned man.

He died at Addis Ababa Airport, Ethiopia, in the blazing wreckage of his East African Airways Super VC10 jetliner along with 40 other people, including 16 British men, women and children. For doing it he got paid a good deal less salary than a flight captain in nearly every other international airline.

When news of the disaster reached the world's civil aviation safety experts, many said: 'it had to happen. With the kind of morale they have got, an E.A.A. crash was a certainty.'

This time they were wrong. It was caused by the million-to-one chance of a steel cargo-loading hook [sic] lying undetected on the runway. ...Next time the experts could very well be right.

For East African, once in the top ten of the airline league and used by thousands of British passengers, is on the verge of complete financial collapse. Some millions of pounds could probably stall the ruin ahead.

NO HOPE FOR THE FUTURE

Nothing short of a miracle will save it from the total disintegration of morale and confidence that has already set in among its senior pilots and engineers. A **Daily Mail** *investigation in Kenya and Britain has disclosed an alarming situation in the East African Airways Corporation...*

It has men in command of planes carrying thousands of people on the Britain – Africa air routes who have lost all pride in the many past achievements of their airline and all hope for its future.

Hundreds of British children will be flying at cheap rates on those ten hour hauls this summer. For E.A.A. handles much of the 'lollipop specials' charter traffic carrying children between schools at home and their parents in Kenya.

The airline is in such a financial mess that it cannot afford enough vital spare parts such as replacement engines. Top engineers responsible for maintaining the line's aircraft to accepted international standards feel just the same as the pilots. Flight Engineer Brian Twist, who died from burns after the Addis Ababa disaster, had told colleagues he was looking for another job.

Until the Addis Ababa crash, E.A.A. had a very high safety record, but pilots and maintenance men alike, fear that this reputation is being endangered by too-rapid Africanisation of the airline's key jobs. These posts, they accept, must be taken over eventually by nationals of the three countries running the Corporation – but only when the right candidates are fully ready, and neither safety, nor efficiency, is imperilled. But they claim that their expert opinion is being ignored. For expressing it, Captain Peter Cunningham, the Corporation's top pilot and director of operations, was recently fired.

...Some of the recommendations for speeding up Africanisation of piloting strength came from American Captain Joe Prendergast during a brief spell as the airline's training manager.

His 18-month career in E.A.A. came to an abrupt end earlier this year when he was ordered to be deported from Kenya. It had been discovered that a number of people in various parts of the world were anxious to trace Captain Prendergast, former pilot for a Swiss charter company, and a big-time gambler.

...Two senior British pilots were summarily fired... because they did not send a special plane... for the use of Ugandan President General Idi Amin.

NO FAITH IN BROTHERHOOD

...Such treatment of men who helped make E.A.A. an efficient airline has been a shattering blow to more than 100 key Europeans still flying and maintaining its planes. In Kenya, I found that they have not only lost confidence in their airline, but also any faith they may have had in a democratic, East African, multicoloured brotherhood. One senior captain, trained in the R.A.F. to give of his best and 100 per cent loyalty as well said: 'Morale has already sunk below the level at which safety could be endangered.

Three years ago, despite poor pay and conditions, no company had more loyal flight deck crews than East African. We were efficient. We were respected. We made a profit.

'Now the state of this airline is quite frightening. It is being reduced to a third rate status by a policy of full-speed Africanisation regardless of the consequences.

'There has been a mad, tribal, jobs-for-the-boys scramble which has financially damaged the Corporation, probably beyond recovery. We have about 5,000 staff, including fewer than 800 expatriates, for nearly 1,500 passenger seats. That ratio is about 3,000 jobs too many.

'First - class passengers were recently being issued with paper cups, yet at least one African executive was demanding and getting a bigger luxury home with furniture and a limousine to match.

'When we dare say anything about it we are accused of race prejudice. None of us is against proper Africanisation as basic policy.

'The truth is that Kenya, Uganda, and Tanzania each wants to run the airline its way - and on some kind of tribal basis. They are incapable of handling anything so complex as an international air network without expert guidance.

'The accounts division is in such a mess that they have even asked Pakistan International Airlines to second people to sort it out. Air Canada has been asked to help in other ways.'

One of the main worries is the airline's chronic shortage of maintenance engineers, leading to long delays and cancellations of services. In less than two years, 45 European ground engineers have left E.A.A. Of the 90 remaining, 13 are working out notices of resignation, including the British chief engineer, Mr Ron Barton.

NO CASH FOR SPARE PARTS

The engineers have warned the airline that safety standards are being placed in jeopardy because maintenance men work such long hours under pressure and face a constant shortage of spare parts.

For nearly a year Chief Abdullah Fundikira of Tanzania, chairman of E.A.A., was claiming that the airline was 'perfectly solvent'.

Although the 1970 accounts have still not been published, it is known to be about £6 million in the red, including large sums owed for fuel, landing rights and catering, and E.A.A. has admitted it cannot afford the hire-purchase payments on some of its planes. Two months ago the three controlling countries each agreed to advance another £1.3 million to save E.A.A. The Kenyans paid their share, but Tanzania and Uganda have so far not provided the agreed cash.

In Nairobi I asked to see E.A.A.'s director-general Mr Okot about disturbing facts disclosed by the **Daily Mail** *inquiries. The airline's chief spokesman later said: 'Mr Okot is too busy to meet you'.*

On the 5th August 1972, Idi Amin announced that the British government was to be held responsible for all Ugandan Asians, who "Were sabotaging the economy". The next day, he announced that all 80,000 citizens of Asian origin had ninety days in which to leave the country. "If they still remain, they will soon see what happens to them" he threatened.

On Tuesday 12th September, 1972 the House of Lords, in London, debated the question of aid to Uganda. Lord Barnby had posed the question ". . . why, in view of the action taken by that country, headed by a rebellion-installed dictator, Britain had not taken the step of cutting off all aid for the present as an indication of her indignation". Speaking for the government, Baroness Tweedsmuir rejected the notion, saying that the greater part of the aid went to British suppliers. The figures involved were very large indeed, in total. In the four years prior to 1972 Uganda had received £16,296,000; Kenya had been in receipt of £42,639,000 and Tanzania £7,749,000. In addition, a further £11,517,000 was given to the East African Community.

On 17th September, Amin started his mass deportation of Asians. Some 30,000 were to be flown to Britain, the remainder were scattered across the world, to Canada, the U.S.A., India and Pakistan. East African Airways scheduled and charter flights were fully employed in this migration. On one Super VC10 flight chartered by an Asian group, 172 passengers named Patel flew to London, providing the immigration authorities with a headache never to be forgotten.

By the end of 1972, East African Airways had earned, from the Asian exodus alone, K£1,800,000 in additional revenue.

Two days before the Asian exodus from Uganda began, on 15th September, Captain Richard Carne and his crew left the Kilimanjaro Hotel in Dar es Salaam for the ride out to the airport. They had stopped overnight after handing their inbound aircraft over to another crew and were now due to fly the morning DC-9 service to Nairobi in an aircraft which had arrived at about midnight and parked overnight.

Arriving at the airport, the crew were mystified to find the apron bare. No DC-9. The airport officials would not help, they seemed churlish and unfriendly, refusing the captain permission to telephone Nairobi for information. From a public callbox in the terminal, Carne managed to get through to Eric Molberg, at the hotel. The captain of the arriving DC-9 who, not pleased to be woken before 07.00 after a late-night arrival, could not explain where the aircraft had gone.

After an unsuccessful attempt to contact Nairobi using the SSB radio in a Twin Otter parked on the apron, the whole crew retired to the restaurant, as there seemed to be nothing better to do. Leaving the rest of the crew to their breakfast, Captain Carne decided to visit the control tower to see if the staff there could throw any light on the extraordinary situation. The controller on duty was an old acquaintance and, after exchanging greetings, Carne asked him if he had news of his aeroplane. The controller was reading a magazine, which lay open on his desk and instead of replying he wrote one word on the open page 'Police' and an arrow pointing behind him. Carne then noticed a surly looking person glowering at him. Sensing a potentially uncomfortable situation, he withdrew and returned to the restaurant.

There had been rumours emanating from Kenya that the British were planning to fly troops into Uganda on or about the 17th September, the weekend prior to the first Asian departures. President Nyerere and Milton Obote had been laying careful plans for an invasion of Uganda to topple Amin and restore Obote to his former position. The British, if the rumours were true, were about to throw all the carefully laid plans awry. There were good reasons to believe that they would not favour Obote, and the idea of British intervention in African affairs was anathema to Nyerere, who had avoided any form of military contact with the former rulers (unlike Kenyatta, who allowed a battalion of British troops "on training exercises," out of sight in Kenya)[7]. Something had to be done – quickly. The guerrillas and anti-Amin forces were warned by coded radio messages that an invasion would take place on the night of 15th/16th September. A central item of the invasion plan was the airlifting of some 190 trained Obote troops into Entebbe to take the airport and secure the perimeter, after which army units loyal to Obote would show their support. The obvious means of transport lay parked overnight at Dar es Salaam airport! The entire operation, ferrying the 190 soldiers could be carried out before the DC-9 was required for the morning departure to Nairobi.

Soon after midnight, police and plain clothes officers moved into Dar es Salaam airport. They overpowered the airport security guards and moved into the control tower, holding up the controllers at gun-point. All telephone and telex communications were cut off. Two Africans, one of them a former East African Airways first officer, who had been dismissed recently for incompetence, boarded the DC-9 – which by the random vagaries of chance, was Ugandan-registered 5X-UVY, and, after an interval, the engines were started and it taxied out and took-off.

The destination was the new airport at Kilimanjaro, where the invading troops were waiting to be picked up. The pilot, understandably, given the stressful circumstances, overlooked a couple of items on his check-list. One of these was to the setting of the circuit-breaker which controlled both the pressurisation and the flight

---

[7] Kenyatta's security was guarded by the S.A.S. provided by the British government. *Vide: Who Dares Wins* by T. Geraghty.

recorder – normally pulled on the ground to prevent the recorder running off the batteries. As a result, pressurisation was not applied and the 'rubber jungle' of emergency oxygen masks in the cabin fell from the ceiling panels at about 12,000ft. This must have alerted the pilot, since he dutifully re-set the circuit-breaker, starting the flight recorder, at 13,000ft.

Another important check-list item was selection of anti-skid, normally tripped manually after landing. A red light indication shows if unselected, but goes out after take-off. The pilot did not select anti-skid 'on' prior to departure. After a flight which wandered close to Nairobi and back onto a course for Kilimanjaro, he commenced his approach, no doubt aware during his pre-landing checks that the entire flight had been conducted with the landing gear down. The approach was fast, approximately 40 knots higher than the ideal 110 knots required for an empty aircraft. His touch down was very smooth – it could not later be detected on the flight recorder – then he ran into trouble, the anti-skid not being selected, as he braked at speed the brakes locked, blowing the tyres, the aircraft drifted and then swung almost 90 degrees to the runway centre-line, still at speed, bouncing sideways down the runway, finally coming to rest in the middle of the airfield. It is thought probable that the pilot, never having used the nose-wheel steering on the left-hand captain's side of the cockpit, attempted to use the device, which is normally only used at low speed in confined areas and is thus high-geared. When used at speed, the slightest touch would produce a wild swing to left or right. The violent motion had emptied all the passenger ashtrays but, apart from the burst tyres, there was only suspected damage to the undercarriage.

This disastrous flight by an incompetent, inexperienced (yet undeniably bold) pilot put paid to the plan to get troops quickly into the heart of Amin's territory. A half hearted attempt by Obote's troops was made to invade Uganda, but the soldiers were soon disheartened and after less than a week they were routed by Amin's troops.

The DC-9 was examined and found to be fit to fly back to Nairobi. On the afternoon of 15th September, Captain Alan Ratcliffe, the chief pilot of the DC-9 fleet, flew to Kilimanjaro in a DC3. He had brought his camera to record evidence for the inquiry, which would invariably follow the incident. One of the things which he photographed was the pilot's flight-log, which lay on the cockpit floor. He picked it up and read the entries which the pilot had made, with headings and fuel states entered, quite correctly and professionally, and at once recognised the writing of the young Ugandan pilot, Tom Olalobo, whom he had trained, and so often cautioned about his habit of excessive braking on the DC-9. After all the wheels were replaced and with locking pins inserted in the undercarriage, Captain Ratcliffe flew the aircraft back to base, with the landing gear locked firmly down.

The photographs were confiscated by the director-general and were never seen again. At the end of November the East African Legislative Assembly was still debating a motion "That this house notes with dismay the continued absence of an official statement by the Tanzanian government relating to the DC-9 aircraft which was stolen by a person or persons from Dar es Salaam International Airport and subsequently found damaged at Kilimanjaro Airport..."

Captain Carne later wrote:

The incident had a sequel some time later, when I was flying a charter for the Ugandan government delegation attending the ceremonies to mark the (belated) 10th anniversary of Somali independence in Mogadishu. During the course of the flight a colonel of the Ugandan army came up to the cockpit. He evidently knew my name and my connection with the coup attempt, for it was with great relish that he told me that his government was fully aware of the plot long before it was put into operation - and most of the details of it, into the bargain. When he told me that among the precautions taken was the sighting of anti-aircraft weapons at both ends of the runway at Entebbe, I was more than thankful that the plotters had relied on the claims of an over-confident young pilot, rather than dig me out of bed to do their flying for them.

❖ ❖ ❖

It had been another year of losses. With total revenue of K£238,800,000, and 564,000 passengers carried, the airline incurred a loss for 1972 (according to the figures it produced to the Authority), of K£1,635,000.

But, at last, remedial action was promised. At its second session held in Kampala, in the months of May and June, 1972, the East African Legislative Assembly passed the following motion:

"That the Annual Report and Accounts of the East African Airways Corporation for the year ending 31st December, 1970, be noted with dissatisfaction and that a Select Committee of this House, empowered to summon and examine witnesses, be appointed to summon and examine such witnesses as it shall deem necessary for the purpose of scrutinising the Annual Report and Accounts of the Corporation now being debated by the House and any other documents connected therewith and relevant thereto and report to the House at a later Session and that such a Select Committee as appointed by the House shall exercise the powers conferred upon a Standing Committee in so far a such powers relate to the summoning and examination of witnesses and production of documents".

1973

It was 13th March, 1973, and the Super VC10 operating EC624 from Nairobi arrived on schedule at Rome, before continuing on to London. It was 5.15 in the morning, and Captain Leslie and his crew were anxious to hand over the flight to the London-bound crew and be on their way to the hotel to get some rest. The station manager, Bruno Riggi, was very apologetic when he explained to Leslie that the station had run out of money and, as a result, he could not pay them any stopover meal allowances. He had repeatedly sent messages to the London and Nairobi offices, but had received no response.

The idea of spending two hungry days in Rome did not appeal to the eleven crew, now standing disconsolately around, waiting for their captain to come up with an answer to the problem. The idea of continuing to London on the aircraft was put forward, but the aircraft was full, and they could not throw passengers off.

After the aircraft had departed, and they had explored almost every avenue, Riggi realised that the town office would soon be open. A telephone call a few minutes later revealed that the ticket receipts for the previous day were still in the safe. If there was enough money, they could use that. En route to the hotel, the crew bus waited outside the town office while the weary crew collected their cash-allowances from the proceeds of the ticket sales. It was an indicator, if they needed one, of the way things were going.

The flight of Super VC10, 5X-UVJ, from London's Gatwick airport had been uneventful, and Captain Tony Britchford was anticipating a routine hand-over to the new crew at Entebbe, from where they would continue to the destination, which was Bujumbura in Burundi. The charter flight had departed that morning, Saturday, 7th July, 1973, with 110 American passengers, members of the Peace Corps, destined, via Bujumbura, for their training camp at Bukavu, in Zaire. As the engines wound down on the Entebbe airport ramp, facing the terminal, they noticed a raised platform and red carpets, evidently in wait for some VIP.

Captain Mitch Mitchell and his crew settled into the aircraft after hand-over and called the tower for start-up clearance. This was refused, due to the imminent arrival of President Albert Bongo of Gabon, on a state visit. The clearance was subsequently changed, since a British United VC10 had just landed and was approaching the hard-standing on which all the parking bays were occupied. 5X-UVJ was cleared for an immediate start-up and taxi to the holding-point. This involved a tight left turn to avoid the VIP platform. The blast from the Super VC10s jets could have played havoc with the arrangements.

They waited at the holding-point for Bongo's DC8 to land and clear the runway before being cleared to enter and take-off. They climbed away and set course for Bujumbura, some 260 miles to the south-west on the shores of Lake Tanganyika. They had been airborne for approximately 15 minutes and at about 20,000ft, when Entebbe transmitted a message that they should return. No reason was given. First Officer Di Piero, a newly recruited American pilot, looked questioningly at Captain Mitchell as he queried the reason and the authority, telling the controller that his instructions from E.A.A.C. were to ignore such instructions unless confirmed by an authorised member of the E.A.A.C. management (This had been found necessary because on a number of occasions aircraft had been ordered to return by airport managers in order to pick up friends, or self-important civil servants and others who had arrived late, without any thought for the expense and operational problems entailed).

After some argument with a clearly embarrassed controller, he advised, very quietly, that the order had been issued by the "very highest authority" (Idi Amin) and if they ignored it they would be intercepted by the air force. The Mig 21 fighters did not worry Mitchell, as the Super VC10 could easily outpace them, with their 15-20 minutes lead; but with the need to transit Entebbe on future occasions, to disobey Idi Amin would be foolish in the extreme. So they turned back, puzzling over the reasons for the instructions. Had they, inadvertently, blown over the VIP platform and red carpets, causing embarrassment to Amin?

As soon as they arrived, even before the aircraft could be stopped on the ramp, it was surrounded by approximately a hundred armed troops. They shut down again and waited for some explanation. They sat for ninety minutes, as the temperature climbed in the cabin to 100 degrees Fahrenheit. Finally a pair of senior army officers boarded the aircraft and rather sheepishly explained to Mitchell that they were not sure why the flight had been recalled. They were vaguely apologetic about everything.

The passengers and crew were ordered off the aircraft and kept in the airport transit area until the following afternoon, when the aircraft was permitted to depart for Nairobi at 15.00, after some 27 hours on the ground, leaving the 110 Peace Corps members at Entebbe, where they were transported under guard to the Lake Victoria Hotel, following the departure of the president of Gabon.

In the meantime, Idi Amin had sent a bizarre telegram to the Secretary-General of the East African Community, with copies to President Kenyatta, President Nyerere and the director-general of East African Airways. The telegram said:

> *Today, July 7, 1973, at about 1700 hours G.M.T., an East African Airways VC-10 plane landed at Entebbe en route to Bujumbura from London with over 100 American passengers, who claimed to be Peace Corps, on board. It was reported that the aircraft landed at Entebbe due to bad weather over Nairobi where it was scheduled to land.*
>
> *In view of the current troubled situation in Burundi and Rwanda, I decided to stop the plane and passengers from proceeding as there was a possibility that those aboard were mercenaries or even Israelis who might have come to engage in subversive activities against sister African States taking advantage of the troubled situation there.*
>
> *It is claimed that this aircraft was on charter to the American Peace Corps. Before we can allow it to proceed I would like to receive from you the circumstances of the plane's flight and passengers. The point of interest to us is to establish the status of these passengers.*

The next day, Sunday, Amin sent a welter of telegrams to the presidents of Rwanda, Burundi and Zaire, saying that he 'Feared the Imperialists, especially Zionists could be planning an intervention in Burundi and Rwanda, taking advantage of the new situation created by the new regime in Rwanda... Before we can allow these Peace Corps members to proceed, I would like to receive from President Mobutu and President Micombero confirmation whether their countries expected these 110 American Peace Corps'.

The weary and unshaven crew never really knew what it was all about, whether Amin had fallen into a rage when he heard that the dais and chairs had been blown over (they had not, in fact, been affected by the manoeuvring aircraft), or whether he simply wanted to impress his visitor with a quixotic gesture against the American giant, from the safety of his equatorial bunker, there was no way of telling. However, it was another blow to East African Airways and to the vital East African tourist industry, already suffering under the stress of Amin's mis-rule. The young Americans went on their way, after a delay which would provide them with food for thought about the Africa which they had come to serve.

The beginning of 1973 saw the arrival of the American experts, brought in at the insistence of the National Bank of Kenya. The Board had determined that management assistance should be sought only from airlines which would never be considered a competitor at any time in the future. Subsequently, three carriers, Aer Lingus, Air Canada and Eastern Airlines had been contacted. Following discussions and negotiations with the three airlines, each of which had shown willingness to provide expertise, Eastern Airlines was finally chosen and was awarded a three year Management Services Contract to be effective from December 1st 1972. So it was that from E.A.L. to E.A.A.C. that came one of their vice-presidents, Captain R.W. Rivenbark, technical adviser and operating director, Mr C.F. Nichols, controller-finance, Mr W.S. Lush, manager marketing and Mr A.L. Pogue, computer manager. Free of the 'colonialist' taint, it was hoped that these knights in shining armour would reverse the disastrous slide of the airline.

On the departure of Captain Cunningham there had been a problem in finding an acceptable operations manager, who would have the ability to progress Africanisation on one hand while remaining true to the professional demands required in the interests of safety. Captain Tom Dornan had held the fort as acting director of operations, but he had encountered similar difficulties to Captain Cunningham, finding it impossible to come to terms with accepting lower standards in the interests of Africanisation. He was ordered by the director-general to take the 78 days leave owing to him, with effect from 1st April, 1973.

Not all the senior captains were interested in the position. There were, however, two contenders for the job, both, by then, holding Kenya citizenship and passports. One was Captain Reg Cartwright, whose seniority and credentials could not be denied. The other was Captain Trevor Hill. Hill was a friendly, non-assuming Australian[8] settled in Kenya, whose son, Terry, also flew as a captain with E.A.A. As a line captain and training manager there was no doubting his ability. It was thought by some, though, that he was not the type to fit in easily with the administrative regime demanded by the position. He had one remarkable card up his sleeve, however. Trevor Hill was an international amateur boxing referee at Olympic level. As such he had been in the ring, as referee, with Idi Amin, who

---

[8] This should not have deceived the unwary. A Judo Black-Belt, he once encountered three burglars in his room at a hotel in Lagos. After a scuffle, he sauntered to the reception and asked them to have three bodies removed from outside his door.

was a boxing champion of both the British colonial and Uganda army. With this one common interest, Idi Amin regarded Trevor Hill as a 'friend'.

Captain Hill was appointed operations manager, probably the only airline captain to have been depicted on a postage stamp, when he was shown, together with President Jomo Kenyatta and the Kenya Commonwealth Games boxing team, on the one shilling commemorative stamp to be issued in July, 1978.

During May the East African Legislative Assembly debated the report of the select committee on East African Airways' mismanagement. The committee of six, under Mr J. Ssebaana Kizito presented its findings to the Legislative Assembly creating a storm of indignation at the extent of its revelations. At last the stone had been turned over and all the worms were opened up to the light.

What emerged from the report was not just evidence of petty fiddling, fraud and embezzlement but of total chaos within the administration which allowed such behaviour to be undetected. The evidence came to light almost immediately, as the committee visited the revenue section. Thousands of files were piled in the corridor apparently unreferenced and uncared for. Some of the documents were seen to be loose and many of them could have been lost before they were accounted for. While the audit of the 1971 accounts was being carried out, it was discovered that a stock of coupons from other airlines worth over £100,000 had been thrown into a dustbin. The committee discovered that of all the 304 permanent employees of the finance department, not a single one had a final professional qualification. A senior officer who had been promoted "since he had been there the longest", had made two unsuccessful attempts to pass elementary correspondence courses in accounts. The

Captain Trevor Hill.
(Capt A. Ratcliffe)

chief accountant, William Mbuvi, resigned on 11th May, 1973, saying that he wanted to go overseas to complete his professional accounting course.

As they delved into the remotest depths of the airline's structure, the committee continued to uncover more unsavoury facts. The IBM computers which were introduced in 1967, were, six years later, running with no staff trained in computer operation. In this way, the accounts data was lost or misdirected, on one occasion six whole batches of cheques worth over £1 million were never posted. Much of the failure to satisfy the auditors in earlier years was due to the inability of staff to handle the computer database.

The failure of the finance department was mirrored elsewhere. There was, for a long time, no proper tender board and purchases were made and deals struck at the discretion of a few individuals. The 1970 agreement to lease a freighter, on the advice of the marketing director, from Lloyd International, was a prime example. Lloyd's Britannia had a break-even load factor of 65%, whereas, should a rival bid from Trans Meridian been properly considered, it would have been seen that their CL-44 would break even at 46%. A fully laden Britannia would earn £3,500 for a round trip from London to Nairobi, compared with Trans Meridian's CL-44 returning £9,700 - £10,000.

In another deal made by F.B. Mahatane, corporation secretary, acting on behalf of the director-general, a Simbair charter contract was signed with an Asian business, Acharya Travel, for a series of 78 Super VC10 round trip charters from Nairobi to London at £5,500 per flight. This price represented a loss to the airline of £1,900 on each charter.

The most highly publicised of these deals was, however, made by Chief Fundikira with the McDonnell Douglas Aircraft Corporation. The extraordinary event which culminated in the arrival, unannounced, of a MD DC-9-15 at Nairobi was finally explained. With the withdrawal of the E.A.A. Comets, a stop-gap solution had to be found. Two quotes were received, one was for a DC-9 from McDonnell Douglas at £125 per hour, the other from Dan-Air for a Comet 4 at £100 per hour. Chief Fundikira unilaterally opted for two DC-9-15s, a completely unsuitable variant for the hot and high East African environment. The aircraft, the second of which was turned round at Rome, were never flown on an E.A.A. service for this reason and also because the board repudiated the decision, on which it had not been consulted; the deal was too favourable to McDonnell Douglas, and there had been no technical evaluation.

The select committee recommended that Chief Fundikira be made personally responsible for the $40,000 paid to McDonnell Douglas for two aircraft which had at no time been utilised.

A Ugandan member charged that "most of the mess" in the East African Airways' report being discussed "was caused by the chairman Chief Fundikira". Mr Kihuguru told the Assembly that the committee, of which he was a member, was of the opinion that he should be retired. A long list of examples of misappropriation of funds and illegal claims for expenses followed. Citing other airline officials, he said: "Mr Donald Owuor sold tickets to Kianda College girls and denied having seen the money... Mr Onyango, who had a criminal record, was promoted... A Mr Wangara, who had been involved in defrauding a certain trade union, had been selected to man a London post... Mr Wangara had messed up the London office and made the corporation lose 96,000/-. He was advised to retire. The money had not been recovered. Mr Kileo, a Tanzanian member of the committee said: "It is interesting to note that this particular officer was sent to London with the full backing of... Chief Fundikira... even after the officer had proved a failure". Mr Joseph Nyerere, of Tanzania added: "It is a fact that the chairman of the corporation told us that he personally appointed Mr Wangara to the London office because he was a good man. We in the committee did not have the time to go into what is a good man or a bad man".

Committee member Mr Mkapa, observed that every chapter in the 120 page report indicated that in not one area of the corporation's operations were commercial principles observed.

Decisions made in all matters relating to the corporation "had been totally unscientific, very bad and backed by no logic at all."

He added: "In the light of these outstandingly bad decisions, it becomes evident that a large section of the management in the corporation was either made up of fools or very incompetent people. I would, however, not like to think that they are fools, otherwise they would not have been appointed to the executive positions they hold now".

Mr Mkapa said that: "as things stand now, from the revelations by the committee, there was no alternative but to get rid of the incompetent 'hands' from the corporation. If you leave them to change the situation, in the next three months we shall be in the same, or even worse muddle. We must adopt a new approach and find new hands to operate our airline".

Mr Wamunyu, from Kenya, stated: "earlier excuses that E.A.A. was having financial problems because it was unable to make profits had been proved entirely wrong by the committee... the problem lay in the rate of uncontrolled expenditure, fraud and employment of excess staff who had no work to do". He went on to report: "according to the report the rate of growth in the past five years was 13 per cent... This is a very reasonable growth rate of a viable commercial organisation. Most organisations of this nature would be doing very well with a 5 per cent rate of growth in the light of competition in the industry".

Turning to the matter of competition, Mr Kihuguru explained to the Assembly that traffic rights had been permitted without restraint to foreign carriers, too many charter flights had been permitted into East Africa. The East African economy was not gaining any benefit from the tourists who "pay their fares at home, use a foreign carrier to East Africa and stay in hotels owned by their own nationals. There were altogether too many scheduled airlines operating into East Africa".

A week after the report was debated at Arusha, Mr Rwetsiba, the Community minister for communications announced, on 28th May, that the documents were to be handed to the Kenya police for further investigation. Mr Kizito said that senior management had obstructed the investigation, "We had a lot of problems with Chief Fundikira", a member of the committee said, "He adopted the attitude of 'I do not care' and would not give us the information we wanted... The director-general (Okot) was also very difficult with information, either because he had been in the corporation only a short time or he had vested interests", he alleged. He ascribed the unwillingness of the airline's legal adviser, Mahatane, to give information either to the fact that he had low qualifications for the job or because he had an interest in concealing the facts. Some of the documents referred to in the report had subsequently been destroyed. The East African Legislative Assembly was, at the same time, advised that the airline was £3,750,000 sterling in the red, and owed £2,875,000 instalment arrears on its aircraft. No payments on the Super VC10 fleet had been made to the British Aircraft Corporation, it was discovered, since 1971. Interest was now accumulating on the debt.

The first to go was F.B. Mahatane, the secretary and legal adviser, who cleared his desk and returned to Tanzania on 11th May. Chief Fundikira held on long enough to save face and departed at the end of June. J.A. Okot, the director-general was replaced in mid October by Idi Amin's former air force chief, Colonel G. Wilson Toko. His previous job in East African Airways had been considerably less important – he had been employed as an engineering apprentice, prior to leaving for a commission in the Uganda military. He then rose to become commander

DHC-6 Twin Otter, 5X-UVN at Tanga. (Capt Ricketts)

of the Ugandan Air Force. One of three senior officers in the defence council who demanded Amin's resignation in February, he was fortunate that the general, preferring not to incur the wrath of the air force, removed him from office, sending him to exile in Nairobi rather than have him killed.

Chief Fundikira's replacement was Mr A.B. Kilewo, who took up the chairman's position on 1st July, 1973. A Tanzanian lawyer, Mr Kilewo was, prior to his appointment, Assistant Attorney-General of Tanzania. He had been a former secretary and counsel for the National Bank of Commerce and Commissioner for Lands and Registrar of Buildings. He was a member of the Board of the East African Posts and Telecommunications from 1967 to 1973.

Ted Wray, the chief engineer, who had taken over following Ron Barton's resignation in 1972, was, tragically, killed when his car hit an elephant, at night, on the road to Mombasa in July. He was replaced by Mr J.H. (Jock) Glass.

A decision was reached, in June, to phase out of operation the four Twin Otter aircraft during 1973. Their capacity was almost entirely booked by the 'Wing Safaris' of Lindblad-Irwin Travel, for groups wishing to visit the game-parks. Based upon safari flights started in 1964, a regular two week charter programme had been newly contracted with the New York travel company, Lindblad Travel and the Kenya operator Tony Irwin, back in November, 1969. The charters had been very

Turkana people pose in front of Twin Otter 5X-UVP during a Wing Safari stop at Lake Rudolf (Turkana). 1969.

popular with the well-to-do American tourists, who would be collected from Nairobi by the Twin Otter, for a night at the famous Treetops hotel near Nyeri. The next day, after a leisurely breakfast, they would leave for Ferguson's Gulf camp on Lake Rudolf, now known as Lake Turkana. Two nights were spent there, bird watching and fishing. Nile perch weighing up to 300-400lbs were common. On the fourth day they would be flown from lake Rudolf to Chobe game lodge, on the Nile, in the Murchison Falls National Park, in Uganda. After two nights at Chobe, the group of nineteen would continue down to Cottars camp in the Tsavo, then to Bamburi, on the coast, followed by a long flight up to Mount Kenya, staying at the little known, but beautiful, Lady Kenmere Lodge. It was a short hop to the famous Mount Kenya Safari Lodge at Nanyuki, for a night of luxury, then off to Keekerok Lodge in the Mara. A final night was spent at the Lake Manyara Hotel, before returning to Nairobi's Embakasi airport for the flight back to New York.

It was on one of these flights, in June 1969, that Captain 'Rusty' Bowker-Douglass and his passengers had an experience which none of them would ever forget.

Bowker-Douglass had picked up his group in Twin Otter 5X-UVN, at Embakasi from an incoming British Airways flight, on 8th June. He departed for Nyeri, where everything went smoothly. The next day, they made their way up to Ferguson's Gulf

Captain Russell 'Rusty' Bowker-Douglass

camp, where the safari followed the enjoyable routine which was, by then, well established. They departed Lake Rudolf on the 11th June, for the fascinating flight west, across the Turkana and Karamoja country, to Chobe.

As he circled the lodge, Bowker-Douglass noticed three elephant in the tall grass, between the airstrip and the lodge, close to the taxi-way, which enabled pilots to park their aircraft in the hotel car park. After landing and taxying along the twisting taxi-way, they suddenly saw one of the elephant facing them, quite unafraid of the Twin Otter's whining PT6 engines. The elephant, a cow, was obviously very curious about the aircraft, and walked steadily and determinedly towards it.

The captain of the Twin Otter was faced with a problem for which his training had certainly failed to prepare him. He considered shutting down the engines and waiting out the encounter. His concern for the safety of the aeroplane and his passengers made him decide on another course of action. Unable to turn in the narrow space, he could do only one thing, as the giant form began to fill the windscreen, to the alarm of the passengers. Putting the propellers into reverse, he backed the Twin Otter down the narrow, twisting, taxi-way, unable to see anything other than the edge outside the left-hand window. As the taxi-way widened onto the runway, Bowker-Douglass quickly selected take-off flap and, with feelings of great relief, they were airborne again within seconds.

A quick buzz over the heads of the elephant sent them off into the surrounding bush, and the area was clear for landing. They were soon all in the hotel bar, celebrating their escape from what must be the one and only occasion when an elephant has chased an aircraft back into the air – and when reverse pitch has been put to such use.

A Twin Otter operated the Tanzania coastal services, which were gradually being upgraded to F27 standard. The F27s were also being used, as their capabilities were explored, for flights into the game reserves, enabling larger tour groups to be flown more economically. The four Twin Otters were flown by E.A.A. pilots to Toronto in August, where they were sold to a Canadian company for almost one million dollars.

1973 had been a remarkable year in many ways. With the acceptance that there must be change, the airline's performance had improved dramatically.

The Eastern Airlines management team had set the following objectives:

I. Establishment of strong financial and administrative controls;

II. Development of aggressive marketing and customer services;

III. Extensive training of the E.A.A.C. staff to improve efficiency;

IV. Implementation of Africanisation of the airline as soon as possible;

V. Development of a viable and practical five-year development plan for the E.A.A.C.;

VI. Improvement of airline operations.

During August the final terminations and resignations occurred, consequent upon the clean-up of the mainly accounts oriented frauds, corruption and general incompetence. The following categories were affected:

Chief Accountant, E.A.A.C.

Accountant, Simbair

Chief Financial Accountant, E.A.A.C.

Accountant, E.A.A.C.

Corporation Secretary, E.A.A.C.

Manager, Properties, E.A.A.C.

Chief Revenue Accountant, E.A.A.C.

Wages Accountant, E.A.A.C.

Purchasing Officer (2), E.A.A.C.

Revenue Accountant, E.A.A.C.

Chief Budgets & Reports Accountant.

The communications manager had been dismissed in March for "Utilizing Corporation's assets for his private use".

The vexed question of the domestic fares was again tackled and the new administration finally succeeded in gaining permission for a five per cent fare increase, effective 1st July, 1973, after much discussion with the appropriate governmental agencies. This was the first domestic fare increase since 1956.

Passengers carried were down on 1972, at 553,800 compared with 564,000. However, by reducing the overall expenditure by some K£257,000 an operating surplus of K£770,000 was achieved, compared with the previous year's loss of K£1,635,000. The figures (which were presented in September, 1974) were further enhanced by the new financial controller by the expedient of revaluing materials and assets to the tune of K£475,000 and the disposal of other assets amounting to K£30,000.

December, 1973, was the best month in the airline's history with total revenues for the month of K£235,000. During September, the fitting of additional first class seats in the Super VC10s for the use of delegates to the International Monetary Fund Conference in Nairobi netted the airline an additional K£140,000. The total operating revenue for the year had been K£23,715,000 offset by expenditure of K£22,945,000.

Staff strength had been reduced to 4,644, a dramatic reduction of 517 on 1971s high of 5,161. A total of forty-five expatriate aircrew left during the year – thirty-five of those being from the Super VC10 fleet.

In London, the airline had, in December, inaugurated its own Heathrow passenger handling facilities, ending the twenty-seven year old handling arrangement with B.O.A.C. (now, since 1972, British Airways). Twenty-three new employees were engaged, bringing the total Heathrow staff to forty-five. In the London town-office a large number of forged tickets were discovered and two employees were dismissed for their participation in fraudulent ticket sales.

The airline's parlous financial situation was patched up by means of overdraft facilities, guaranteed by the three partner states of K£750,000 and a new agreement concluded with the National Bank of Kenya to convert K£2,250,000, part of the overdraft of K£3,250,000, into a long term loan of seven years, effective from December 31st, 1973. The Corporation was, in effect, now in the hands of the government owned National Bank of Kenya.

On the evening of December 3rd, 1973, the Super VC10 5H-MOG, commanded by Captain George Leslie, left London on the EC615 service for Frankfurt and Nairobi. With the Christmas holidays coming up, the flight was heavily booked out of Frankfurt and every seat was taken.

After arrival at Frankfurt, the E.A.A. traffic liaison officer came to the flight-deck together with the Lufthansa flight planner. There was a problem – high winds were forecast on the nose for the entire southbound seven hour flight. With a full load, they would not be able to carry sufficient fuel for the non-stop flight to Nairobi. There was no question of off-loading passengers as there was no alternative flight to offer them until the following day. They would have to flight-plan the trip via an en route re-fuelling stop. It did not take long to decide that Tripoli would provide the ideal place to re-fuel.

The flight proceeded to Tripoli, where after landing and taxying to the terminal area, they shut down and waited for the Shell refueller to drive up with the thirty tons of fuel that had been requested by Frankfurt.

After some minutes, during which time the only action was the placing of passenger steps against the door, the crew decided that some investigation was called for. The navigator 'went ashore' to find the refueller's office. It was after midnight and he was away for quite a long time. When he returned to the aircraft, together with the Libyan refuelling crew-chief, it was with bad news. Evidently the Shell head office in London had sent a signal to all stations that E.A.A. fuel carnets were not to be honoured due to non-payment of fuel accounts. All future fuel must be paid for on a cash basis. The telex had been sent soon after their departure from Frankfurt.

This did not come as a complete surprise to the crew, who had been reading about the airline's cash flow problems in their Nairobi daily newspapers for many months. But the situation could not have arisen in a worse place. Tripoli was not on their regular route, they were virtually unknown there. There was no B.O.A.C. representative who may (or may not) have helped them out of their dilemma. Captain Leslie had, with passengers and crew, very nearly two hundred people to get out of the predicament and on their way to Nairobi. Stirring himself from his seat, while the first officer called Nairobi operations on the SSB radio, he went with the Arab to the Shell office.

The Shell manager had told his staff that under no circumstances should E.A.A. uplift fuel from them, or any other company. Leslie spoke to the manager on the telephone, he was not pleased at being woken up, but regretted that he could not ignore his company's instructions. No credit – cash only.

Back on board the aircraft, the first officer had made contact with operations. It was 03.00 in Nairobi and the African night-shift were aware of the problem, but reluctant to call their boss until he came into the office at 09.00. They were terrified of the consequences of calling the executive management at home during the night. The plight of a full Super VC10 load of passengers, stuck for over six hours at a desert airfield was, it seemed, not their problem.

By now the passengers were getting restless, they had been told by the cabin staff that there would be a short stop for re-fuelling and they would be on their way. Not wanting to use the public address system, since many were asleep, the purser had moved through the cabin telling the passengers that as Tripoli was not a usual stop, the Libyans were reluctant to supply fuel and that they wanted cash.

On the flight-deck, the crew were examining every avenue of escape. They thought about going to Malta, which would just be possible with the fuel on board. But the situation could be the same there. As they were talking, the purser came in, saying that a first class passenger wanted to speak with the captain, to see if he could help in any way. He handed over a business card, which indicated that the passenger was a French speaking African from the Ivory Coast, no less than the president of the Bank of Abidjian.

Captain Leslie asked the purser to bring the gentleman to the flight-deck, where it was more private, and after shaking hands they sat at the navigator's table, where Leslie explained the predicament. Opening his briefcase, the gentleman said he could probably help them out of their difficulty. The open briefcase revealed closely packed wads of high denomination U.S. dollar bills.

Another telephone call was made to the Shell manager, who this time gave up the idea of sleep to deal with these crazy people who now wanted to pay for thirty tons of fuel with dollar bills. There was more than enough money. Captain Leslie signed a receipt for the 'loan', promising their benefactor, who was travelling to Nairobi for a meeting with President Jomo Kenyatta, that E.A.A.C. would repay the money on arrival.

Refuelled at last, 5H-MOG showed Tripoli a clean pair of heels and they were on their way. Their belated mid-day arrival at Embakasi was met by a high level government delegation – to greet the president of the Bank of Abidjian.

Bruce Mackenzie, using his established lines of contact, endeavoured to ease the problem soon afterwards and, in the short term, B.O.A.C. agreed to guarantee all further fuel uplifts.

Chapter 12

The End of a Dream

*O! that a man might know
The end of this day's business, ere it come;
But suffice it that the day will end,
And then the end is known.*
                    William Shakespeare
                    Julius Caesar v.i.

THE NEW BROOM from Eastern Airlines had swept away many of the loss making trends which had culminated in the disastrous results of 1971/72. With many of the criminal elements cleared out of the accounting organisation, where at least two of the original staff were serving long jail terms for theft of Corporation funds, the financial affairs of the airline seemed to be emerging into a more manageable state. Loan repayments on the Super VC10s were restructured, being re-scheduled to seven-year-loans at an interest rate of five and three-quarter per cent; a similar arrangement for the DC-9s, which were also in arrears, was arranged with East African banks over seven years, at an interest rate of seven and a half per cent.

The fuel crisis of 1973, occasioned by the Arab-Israeli war and the subsequent OPEC cut in production, carried over into 1974, causing restrictions to fuel uplifts at several stations. This necessitated making technical calls at Tunis or Algiers and also forced a reduction in flights. This crisis ended in March, with fuel costs having soared by 145.9%.

On 20th March, 1974, East African experienced its first hi-jack, when an F27, commanded by Captain Eddy Penfold, operating the EC301 service from Nairobi to Malindi was forced to alter course after two Ethiopians, one of them female, demanded that the aircraft be flown to Libya. On arrival at Entebbe, where refuelling was to take place, the male hijacker held a gun at Captain Penfold's head and demanded to speak to President Idi Amin. Amin duly arrived, dressed in a smart grey suit, and was brought to the aircraft in an armoured vehicle, which drew up close to the aircraft, its heavy calibre machine gun almost poking through the cockpit window. Everyone, including the passengers, then trooped off to the terminal, where they witnessed an extraordinary scene, as Amin chaired an impromptu enquiry into the affair.

Finally, leaving the Ethiopians to their fate, the F27 and its passengers returned to Nairobi that evening.

Operations into Kinshasa were resumed by DC-9 aircraft during April, following suspension of services due to problems regarding alternate airfields. The DC-9s also opened up new routes to Lourenco Marques and the Seychelles.

After twenty-four years service, the chief engineer, J.H. 'Jock' Glass, finally retired during February, after finding himself at variance with Captain Rivenbark, and was replaced by Mr F. Gillett. The airline was having considerable difficulty in maintaining its previous high standards of engineering skills, due to the high rate of resignations by expatriate engineers and technicians. During 1973 twenty-one had submitted their resignations. To counteract this trend, revised wages and working conditions were implemented during March.

The overall maintenance reliability compared favourably with industry standards. Resulting largely from partial re-organisation of the engineering department and the separation of line maintenance from base maintenance for aircraft in service, the delay rate per 100 departures was reduced from 4.4% in 1973 to 3.4% in 1974.

An on-time performance target of eighty per cent was set for the year 1974; an above target percentage was achieved for eight months during the year. January was the worst, with seventy-two per cent on time, while May was the best, with 89.1 per cent on time. The average on-time for the whole year was 82.4 per cent.

Average fleet daily utilisation for 1974 was:

	1974 Hours	1973 Hours
SVC10	9.5	9.8
DC-9	5.8	5.0
F27	5.6	4.8
DC3	3.5	2.3

All airframe maintenance was performed in-house, with engine overhaul being conducted on the Rolls-Royce Dart and Pratt and Whitney 1830 engines. The basic training scheme was completely overhauled and the former apprentice training scheme abandoned in favour of a more practical orientated curriculum, utilising the facilities of the flying training school which had been established at Soroti, in Uganda, in November 1970. A number of courses were conducted overseas, including avionic training at Ethiopian Airlines, DC-9 training at S.A.S., as part of a Danish government aid package, and supervisory and instructional technique courses at the I.C.A.O. training school in Beirut. Seventeen engineers won scholarships to study for part III of the City and Guilds Aeronautical Engineering course at Southall College, in the United Kingdom.[1]

At the time of his appointment as chief engineer, Jock Glass was asked to examine the question of selecting a suitable candidate for Africanisation of the position, following his retirement. He had no hesitation in nominating Julian Lyatuu. Lyatuu was born in Tanzania and had taken a Bachelors degree in Mechanical Engineering at the University of Nairobi followed by a Masters degree in Air Transport Engineering from the Cranfield Institute of Technology in England. He held Catagory A licences on Super VC10 and DC-9 aircraft and Catagory C licences on Rolls-Royce Conway and Pratt and Whitney JT8D-11 engines. He had been station engineer at both Cairo and Dar es Salaam.

---

[1] Of these, 16 returned with City and Guilds Diplomas in Air Transport, Part III.

A period of two years grooming, first as deputy production manager, under Cliff Sarginson, followed by six-month periods under the chief inspector and chief technical officer before a final six months as deputy chief engineer, would have brought this most qualified and well suited African into the key position dominating the airline's technical strength.

Sadly, it was not to be, as so often is the case. On the departure of Jock Glass, his protege was out of favour and was appointed to a dead-end job in maintenance planning. Justin Lyatuu eventually resigned to join Shell in Kenya before departing for Tanzania.

Clifford (Cliff) Sarginson had been appointed Production Manager at the time of Jock Glass' confirmation as chief engineer. Sarginson, born and educated in Kenya had joined E.A.A.C. as an engineering apprentice on 24th June, 1946. He was to become the longest serving member on the staff of the corporation, finally sharing the task of running the engineering department with Ray Kearns, following the departure of Mr F. Gillett in 1976.

On 30th March, 1974, another historic milestone in the history of East African Airways was reached, when a Super VC10 landed at Peking on a charter from Dar es Salaam with 145 Tanzanian students. On the return flight, the Tanzanian president, Julius Nyerere, foreign minister Malacela and a party of thirty-five returned to Tanzania's Kilimanjaro airport, stopping over en route at Calcutta, where they were received by Mrs Indira Gandhi, the Prime Minister of India.

The number of personnel at year end 1974 was 4,674. The level was thirty employees above the 1973 year end level. While the number of personnel increased in 1974, the capacity tonne kilometres per employee was 57,764 in 1974 compared to 48,256 tonne kilometres per employee in 1973, a significant increase. A system of employee time clocks for checking in and out of the engineering base were introduced during the year. In addition, attendance registration books were installed in other departments. The purpose of these measures was to improve attendance record keeping and control. The result of these controls was a two-and-a-half day wild-cat strike at Nairobi airport during July, which was solved by resorting to original procedures. The objective of reducing overtime to the absolute minimum, in order to achieve necessary savings, was the paramount driving force.

Captain Rivenbark, with typical American directness, had called on all E.A.A. staff to work hard in order to make the airline prosperous, "For a day's pay we expect a day's work. If we don't get a day's work, then we should stop the pay", he said at the closure of a United Nations Development Programme management training course.

During 1973, the sales and marketing effort had produced a remarkable coup in concluding an agreement with two of the largest tour wholesalers in Germany. The program, scheduled to start during the winter months of 1973-74 was expected to generate 4,000 passengers. With Kenya becoming one of the leading destinations for package tours, the airline was now experiencing a boom in passenger traffic. Revenue passengers carried in 1974 would add up to 651,045, compared to 554,803 carried in 1973. Passenger load factors were 53.2% for 1974 compared with 43%

for 1973, the break even figure was 47.9%. Although the average figures were showing barely half-full, during the peak winter holiday months capacity could not cope with the demand. The solution, which also had the advantage of raising the image of E.A.A.C., was to be found in negotiating the wet-lease of a Boeing 747 from Aer Lingus for the three winter months from December to February. The 747 was to operate once weekly on the London-Frankfurt-Nairobi route with a combined Aer Lingus and E.A.A.C. cabin crew; a number of the East African stewardesses were sent to Dublin to complete type training.

On the morning of December 14th, 1974, the first E.A.A.C./Aer Lingus aircraft, EI-ASJ, named *St Patrick*, touched down at Embakasi to a welcome by a huge crowd of E.A.A.C. and Kenya government officials and many curious spectators. The aircraft brought nearly 300 tourists, one of the largest groups ever to land at Nairobi.

In 1974 E.A.A.C. flew the first VC10 to be seen in Australia and New Zealand, since the scheduled services of British Airways used the Boeing 707 on this route. The occasion was the Commonwealth games, which were held at Christchurch in New Zealand. The Super VC10 was chartered by the Kenyan government to carry their team to the games. The flight was routed via Perth in Australia, where the crew slipped, staying at the Sheraton hotel. After checking-in and the African cabin crew had disappeared, the reception clerk turned to Captain Tony Britchford and said "Hey, Blue – where did you get the *Abbos* from?" The sight of a smartly turned out group of African cabin crew was unknown in those parts.

Captain Reg Cartwright had resigned at the beginning of the year, his last flight being London-Rome-Nairobi in command of 5Y-ADA on 12/13th February. After a period when he was managing director of aircraft distributor C.M.C. Aviation, he went on to fly the HS125-700, as chief pilot of Coca-Cola, (Africa and Middle East). He had seen nearly twenty-five years service with East African Airways, and all the indications had shown that it was time to leave.

Captain George Leslie resigned at the end of the year. He commanded his last Super VC10 flight on 22nd December, 1974, after which he settled in South Africa, flying Lockheed C130 Hercules freighters, prior to retirement. The airline which he so proudly joined back in 1950 and had seen grow into a great international airline had, it seemed, become a pitiful shadow of its former self. Stumbling along from month to month, unable to pay its bills, riven by distrust, complacency, corruption, intrigue and – more worrying for a pilot, inefficiency in all departments; it was time for him to remember the good times, draw a final line under it all, and leave for a new start.

Profitability on operations had continued its upward trend, as the figures for 1974 were to show. Total revenues for E.A.A.C. and its subsidiary Simbair were a record K£31.58 million, an increase of 33.2% on 1973. The net profit was K£2,053,800, compared with the previous years K£1,278,800. Losses carried forward from previous years amounted to K£1,773,300. One outstanding item was the sum of K£515,000 representing the airline's insurance claim on the loss of 5X-UVA at Addis Ababa. The insurance monies had been paid to the British Aircraft Corporation, the nominal owners of the aircraft, who refused to release the E.A.A.C. share due to the outstanding unpaid loan instalments.

It was a Saturday afternoon, 7th December, 1974, and they were still working in the main hangar at Embakasi. Super VC10, 5Y-ADA was undergoing routine maintenance, which involved gear retraction tests. The empty aircraft, weighing some eighty tons, was supported by three high-lift jacks, positioned under the specially integrated jacking points, one under each wing and a third under the rear of the aircraft, below the engines.

A team of men were to adjust each jack, until the aircraft was level, it was a fairly routine performance and had been done many times in the past. Unfortunately, on this occasion, the mechanic operating the rear jack was inexperienced and failed to concentrate properly, resulting in his releasing the hydraulic pressure fully, causing the jack's cylinder to descend to its stop. The aircraft slipped off the jack tail-first, remained on the wing supporting jacks, and crashed to the floor of the hangar in a parody of the take-off attitude. The tail supporting jack had not fallen but, slipping, had penetrated the main engine beam which held two of the four Conway engines, damaging it beyond repair. Miraculously, no one had been hurt, as might have been the case if it had not been a Saturday afternoon, with few people on duty.

This was a blow to East African Airways in more than just an engineering sense. In 1974 the *Hajj* season occurred during December, together with the seasonal Christmas heavy bookings. Apart from the financial losses and immense loss of face when it became known that E.A.A. 'had dropped a Super VC10 on the hangar floor', the logistics of repairing the aircraft were overwhelming. It became probable that the damage may even be beyond the airline's capability to finance repairs when it was discovered that the British Aircraft Corporation did not carry such a major component in their spares inventory. The VC10 jigs had long been dismantled and the cost of a one-off engine beam would be astronomical.

Then someone remembered 5X-UVA. They had buried the remains of the burned out aircraft at Addis Ababa by the simple expedient of filling in the ditch in which she lay. What if the engine boom was still intact? Sadly, the suggestion was countered by Cliff Sarginson, now assistant chief engineer, who had been responsible for blowing up the tangled debris of 5X-UVA with dynamite, before the bulldozers covered up the remains. The explosions had completed the destruction of the tail and engine assembly, which had survived the fire.

In the best engineering traditions, it was proposed that, since the right side of the 'spectacle-shaped' frame of the engine mounting was undamaged, a new left side might be made at Weybridge. With brilliant engineering skills on the part of the team led by an ex-BAC Weybridge engineer, who was brought out of retirement to lead the project, the new piece was joined to the existing half by splicing and plating. With a slightly heavier empty weight and requiring an adjustment to trim, 5Y-ADA rejoined the fleet, some weeks later than planned.

Simbair, under the management of Mr Earnest 'Woody' Woodward, of Eastern Airlines, had proved to be a profitable enterprise, after a weak period during the early part of 1974. A total of 5,316,000 kilos of cargo was uplifted, an increase of 2,208,000 kilos on 1973. One contract, for the transportation of 1.7 million kilos of flowers, on 152 flights, from Nairobi to Frankfurt, netted K£1,000,000. A total of seventy-four flights carried 20,526 non-I.A.T.A. pool affinity charter passengers. During December alone four average trip flights to London operated with an average load factor of 79.2% northbound and 98.3% southbound. All other charters were carried out by E.A.A.C.

A major highlight of the year was the approval by both the Simbair and East African Airways Boards as well as the Communications Council for the purchase of a Boeing 707 freighter for the use of Simbair. This aircraft was scheduled to become operational by the second quarter of 1975.

The year 1974 ended on a high note; with the prestige of the 'Jumbo-jet' operations and overall increases in productivity and efficiency, December ended with a monthly profit of K£645,000; the highest in the history of E.A.A.C.

1975

Marketing was the name of the game both within the airline and to the world at large. The American team brought the concept of 'programs' to procure better performance, discipline and attitudes within the Corporation. It was necessary to improve, in particular, the attitude of staff towards clients both on the ground and in the air. The maintenance of staff morale was made difficult by the layers of national, racial, and tribal differences which, at all times, were compounded by the political posturing of the three East African countries. By bringing into focus the importance of management objectives and airline performance goals, the company-wide conferences sought to overcome the differences between individuals.

A theme based upon 'The Ticket is a Contract' was developed and stressed throughout 1975. A staff booklet was published for all staff and a training film with this title was produced to be shown to all customer contact personnel. In order to receive service improvement suggestions from airline staff, an incentive scheme was developed. The person submitting the winning suggestion each month received a cash award of 500 shillings.

A major marketing effort was commenced in 1975 to secure business in the U.S.A. and Europe. As a major part of this effort, a new twenty-seven minute colour film entitled "Karibu" was made covering the tourist attractions of Kenya, Tanzania and Uganda. In conjunction with the DC-9 manufacturer McDonnell Douglas,[2] the film was made with the expectation of being shown on 950 U.S. television channels and was to be distributed to 3,000 travel agents and 1,200 travel clubs throughout North America.

A new Safari Digest in-flight magazine was published in 1975 and marked the first time that E.A.A.C. had its own in-flight publication covering the services offered by the airline and the tourist attractions to be found in the East African states. The newly contracted advertising agents, Ogilvy and Mather, had produced a 'Flying Jumbo' advertising campaign in connection with the Boeing 747 services from Europe on Friday night and from East Africa on Saturday night during January to March and December, 1975. Under a Disney-like flying elephant cartoon character, the East African media carried the message:

Fly to Frankfurt and London
in Jumbo style
with East African Airways

If you're bound for Europe take a
fabulous flight in Jumbo comfort. Take
of on EAA's Special Safari Service
747 any Saturday evening up to
March 27th 1976

EAST AFRICAN AIRWAYS 747 Special Safari Service

It was with no regrets that Captain 'Mitch' Mitchell commanded his last flight, the EC615, from Rome via Cairo destined for Nairobi, on 8th April, 1975. He could not get off the aircraft quickly enough, after the final paper work was completed. He felt that the airline was disintegrating around him; after so many dedicated people had given every thing they had to make East African Airways a respected and popular international airline, it was all coming apart at the seams. The new management advisers were doing their best, but it was too late to be effective, and now politics were in control.

After twenty-five years of service and over 15,325 hours logged with the airline, in which he had served as route check captain DC3s, Canadair instructor, chief instructor Comets, Instrument Rating examiner, chief instructor and Fleet Captain Super VC10s, Mitchell departed. As with so many others – no one said so much as "thank you" as he made his departure.

---

[2] McDonnell Douglas had hopes, since the DC-9 contract, of orders from E.A.A.C. for the DC-10 as a wide-body replacement for the Super VC10s.

He returned to South Africa to join George Leslie flying Hercules freighters in Captain Jeff de Jager's company Safair Freighters. He went on to fly a HS125-600 for Rio Tinto, followed by almost ten years as manager of Air Botswana Cargo, involved in famine relief programmes for international organisations, such as the International Red Cross, World Food Programme and Caritas.

The travel industry, long used to subtly portraying, in their promotions of third-world airlines, pilots of obvious Caucasian good looks, had now to accept that Africanisation on the flight-deck was here to stay.

One of the major activities of the flight operations department in 1975 was training the flight crews for the Boeing 707-323CF freighter, 5X-UWM, which was acquired from American Airlines in May. Twelve pilots and six flight engineers successfully completed the Boeing 707 training course at the American Airlines Academy at Fort Worth, Texas. Intensive training was concentrated upon the citizen crews to qualify them for promotion to higher fleets. As a result of the acquisition of the Boeing 707 and due to the fact that twenty-four qualified air crew left the airline, it was necessary to recruit a total of fifty-six air crew during the year. The majority of these recruits were citizen second officers and cadet flight engineers. The second officers came primarily from the graduates of the Soroti and Perth flying schools, with flight engineers being recruited from the ranks of the ground engineers.

A total of ninety-one pilots checked out in the various fleets. Of these, sixty-two, or 68% were citizens. Six flight engineers checked out on the Super VC10 and a further seven on the Boeing 707. Seven pilots qualified for a senior pilot's licence after training at Copenhagen, under a technical assistance programme offered by the Danish government.

By early 1976, some thirty years after E.A.A.C. came into being, there were some ninety-nine 'citizen' pilots in the airline. Of these, seventy-five were first officers, nineteen captains and a further five were in training prior to receiving their commands. Gradually, as the years passed, the African pilots were accumulating hours and experience. Contrary to some predictions, there had been no major catastrophes. Colonel Toko, the director-general, had said "We will not have citizen pilots at the expense of safety... the required standards are the same for all pilots regardless of their racial or ethnic origin".

The first African to achieve command of the Super VC10 was Captain Joseph C. Roy, having accumulated 6,000 hours on the DC3, F27, DC-9 and Super VC10. His first command flight was in January 1974, from London to Nairobi. He was followed, a week later, by Captain Sandy Buruwari Newman, a former instructor and check-captain on the F27, with 5,000 hours total flying time. Together with American Captain Porter, Captain Faustin Sabai, with 4,000 hours, crewed the delivery flight of the Boeing 707-323CF, 5X-UWM, which arrived in Nairobi on 15th May, 1975, from Fort Worth, Texas. The 707, fully palletised and equipped with an electrically driven loading system, was acquired for Simbair solely for freight operations. A number of E.A.A.C. crews (among them Captain Ian Cowie and Captain Jerry Sirley – both non-African 'citizen' pilots) carried out training on the Aer Lingus flight simulator at Dublin.

Captain James Kiwanuka was the first African to qualify as a captain with East African Airways, on the DC3. He upgraded to command of the DC-9 in 1973 with 6,500 hours. By early 1976, ten per cent of the pilots of E.A.A.C. were 'citizens' – although many of these were still Kenya citizens of European extraction.

Uganda's tourist industry had been virtually eliminated. In 1972, there had been 100,000 visitors. Of the European population of 10,000, by 1975 there were a mere 700 still braving the terrors of daily life in the country, in which murder, robbery and violence were common occurrences. Small groups of brave tourists still travelled to the Murchison Falls and the Queen Elizabeth National Park in the west. But travel was dangerous by road, the journey to Kasese was only safe by air.

The effect of Idi Amin's despotic rule in Uganda was to concentrate the tourist industry in East Africa even more within the bounds of Kenya, with the added 'safari' excursion into the Serengeti region of Tanzania.

Within Kenya, 1975 was a crisis year, with the murder of a prominent M.P. and potential future candidate for president, Josiah Mwangi Kariuki, whose body was found outside Nairobi on 3rd March. Twenty-four hours prior to this a bomb explosion at the Nairobi bus terminus killed twenty-seven people and injured many more. On 11th April, two bombs exploded near the President's residence at Bamburi near Mombasa.

With a population which had risen by 50% in the past ten years to some 12 million, of whom only 1.3 million had a cash income and with male unemployment levels of 29%, political elements agitating the urban poor of Kenya were thought to be behind the upsurge of discontent. Inflation and soaring import costs were hitting the economy. Kenya's external reserves, which had reached $314 million in 1973 stood at $192 million a year later. At the end of 1974, there was a visible trade deficit with non-Community countries of £220 million sterling. The major external cost factor was the price of petroleum, total imports of which, in 1973, stood at 327,220,000 shillings had soared to 1,341 million shillings in 1974, following the cuts in supplies made by OPEC producers, and the consequential rise in prices, world-wide. Petroleum import costs in Tanzania had risen from 92,000,000 shillings in 1972 to 640,000,000 shillings at the end of 1974.

Tanzania had, for several years, been embarked upon the construction of a railway connecting the port of Dar es Salaam with the Zambian copper-belt. The so called Tanzam railway was financed and built by the Chinese. Unfortunately, for the success of the project, the port of Dar es Salaam had received little or no attention to its outdated sheds and equipment. The resultant congestion caused ship owners to route their vessels to Mombasa, from where the consignments were trucked to Tanzania and Zambia.

Preceding the forthcoming opening of the railway, in June, 1975, Tanzania announced, in December 1974, that all Kenyan lorries of 18.75 tons or more were prohibited from crossing the border. Kenya had some 200 45-ton trucks operating on the route from Mombasa to Zambia, carrying, among other products, sulphur imports required in the production of refined copper and returning with Zambia's exports of copper. With the deportation of 812 Kenyans and their families from Tanzania in December 1974, the gradual disintegration of communications within the Community continued into 1975. Tanzania was looking to the Zambian connection and the Tanzam railway, and no longer paid its dues (the amount owing in June 1975 was £1,366,000 sterling) to the East African Railways Corporation. While debts of £2 million were owed by the E.A.R.C. to the U.K. Crown Agents for spare parts, Tanzania was unilaterally ordering spares from Canada for its own region.

In Uganda, President Amin had stated that he would not approve payment of funds owed to the East African Airways Corporation unless and until the three presidents had met at a session of the East African Community. There was no prospect of such a meeting while the road traffic dispute continued between Kenya and Tanzania, and the confrontation between Uganda and Tanzania remained. Due to the inability to freely transfer funds between the partner states, East African Airways was suffering an additional burden amounting to approximately 8.4 million U.S. dollars, which lay on deposit and which it was unable to utilise.

In June, 1975, Mr Charles Njonjo, the Kenyan Attorney-General stated in Parliament in Nairobi that "the Community had failed for lack of political goodwill... the concept of eventual political federation between the three partner states should be forgotten and buried... the Community should be dissolved".

With the political union of the three partner states falling into disarray, the East African Airways accounts for 1975 showed some heartening improvements. It was to be the last time that the Corporation's accounts would be presented and is therefore worthy of examination:

EAST AFRICAN AIRWAYS and its subsidiary SIMBAIR
Consolidated Profit and Loss Account for the year ended 31st December 1975

Revenues	1975 K.Sh/000	1974 K.Sh/000
Passenger	466,454	397,128
Cargo, Mail, excess baggage	76,853	70,735
Charter operations	32,423	28,692
Pool receipts	22,909	14,481
Total Traffic Revenue	598,639	511,036
Incidental Revenue	59,638	57,621
Dividends Received	806	1,768
Total Revenue – E.A.A.C.	659,083	570,425
Simbair Revenue	74,969	61,317
Total Revenues	**734,052**	**631,742**

Expenses		
Aircraft operations	297,092	241,157
Engineering support	74,969	73,035
Marketing, Administration & other	234,232	193,824
Interest on aircraft & loans	20,551	16,612
Misc. expense charges (credits)	(1,939)	5,353
Total Operating Expenses-E.A.A.C.	624,728	529,981
Simbair expenses	72,651	60,685
Total Expenses	697,379	590,666
1975 Net Profit	36,673	41,076

Losses Brought Forward Summary

Losses brought forward at 1.1.75	(35,466)	(76,542)
Profit (losses) carried forward 31.12.75	1,207	(35,466)

Charlie Nichols had done a good job. The accounts were coming out right; at last he could carry forward a small profit of K£60,350. If only the politicians could settle their affairs, the airline might just have had a chance.

But whatever the chance may have been, it would have commanded a high price. An item not shown on any of the Corporation's accounts was the cost of the management advisers. With initial salaries of £17,500 per annum for the two leading Eastern executives, plus Kenya withholding tax (£10,000), accommodation, cars (£5,000 plus £100 per month) and a secondment fee to Eastern Airlines of £35,000 per annum – to be paid in advance, the total cost was to bite deeply into the airline's borrowing capability. Interest alone was calculated at £3,000 per annum.

The initial contract presumed that up to nine Eastern staff would be required, all to be paid Eastern's overseas salaries and allowances. The contract specified that E.A.A.C. would train staff on Eastern's equipment in the U.S.A. and purchase DC-9 spares from Eastern, an operator of up to eighty of these machines. A 'Potential Fee Reduction' clause allowed for E.A.A.C. to save $25,000 for every $100,000 over $400,000 spent with Eastern on goods and services. Insurance had to be taken out to the sum of $25,000,000 for comprehensive public liability for personal injury and property damage involved in any single accident by E.A.A.C., indemnifying their employees, before Eastern would go ahead with any agreement.

Although Eastern Airlines gave a warranty that it would endeavour to give the same service as in its own services, to E.A.A.C., there was a proviso that: "Eastern makes no guarantee as to the results of East African's operations or the safety thereof."

There was speculation at the time that the advisers would seek to dispose of the Super VC10s and replace them with DC8s or Boeing 707s from Eastern. There were emphatic denials, which led to increased speculation. In fact, a team led by two Guinness Peat negotiators and including Super VC10 Fleet Captain, Ted Imison and engineering adviser Ray Kearns were to visit Havana in February, 1976, in a week-long attempt to sell the four aircraft to the Cubans. A similar attempt to sell them to South Korea had earlier failed. There was, however, little chance of success, since the market for four Super VC10s existed mainly in the imagination.

The comfortable life-style, which had brought many of the E.A.A.C. expatriates to Kenya, was no longer something to be taken for granted, as the country underwent social change, accompanied by a serious increase in lawlessness. On 15th September, 1974, senior Super VC10 captain, E.F. 'Nobby' Clarkson was killed at his farm by panga wielding thieves. It was thought that they knew of a recent sale of cattle and they attacked the farm in search of the cash. Eight months later, on 30th May, 1975, Captain Peter Pettit died from terrible wounds received three months previously in another panga attack.

1976

Tom Webb, E.A.A.C. station engineer, had been at Entebbe for some thirteen years. He had been in East Africa since 1949, when he worked on the B.O.A.C. flying-boats at Lake Naivasha.[3] When the flying-boat era ended, in January 1951, he moved to E.A.A.C. at Nairobi West, followed by a posting to Dar es Salaam and finally to Entebbe in mid-1963. Although most of the Europeans had departed, he had stayed on, not wishing to leave the country which he had come to love. In July, 1975, he had been the only white man to meet the R.A.F. VC10 which arrived with Mr Callaghan, who was then the British Foreign Secretary, on his mission to rescue Mr Dennis Hills, a British writer detained by Amin. He was well aware of the dangers of his situation, and had made provision for escape, by keeping a motor boat, which he shared with his future wife, Jenny Briggs, deputy chief pharmacist to the Uganda government, ready at its mooring on Lake Victoria. With food and fuel hidden on a nearby island, he was certain that a high speed dash across the lake to the Kenyan shore would outwit any pursuing Ugandan soldiers.

In a surprise move however, they picked him up at lunch time on 8th April, 1976, at his bungalow in Mugulu Road, with the accusation that he was reading a Kenyan newspaper – all Kenyan newspapers had been banned throughout Uganda

---

[3] Captain Cartwright first met Tom Webb at Lahore. "He was then in B.O.A.C. and armed with a shot-gun keeping the approach to the runway clear of vultures and kitehawks. Several aircraft had been damaged by bird-strikes. The next time I saw him was at Port Bell in Uganda. He was working on the engine of a flying-boat at anchor off-shore. I recognised him by his language when he dropped a spanner in the lake! It must have been one of the last flying-boat services."

by Amin. They took him to the airport, where he was locked up for three days. At 21.00 on the third day, Saturday, he was collected by the military police and incarcerated in a verminous cell in the Kampala central police station. The following day he was transported to the Luzira prison, where he was placed in the top

TELEPHONES KAMPALA 58631 AND 34700

S. 10156

IN ANY CORRESPONDENCE ON THIS SUBJECT PLEASE QUOTE NO.

THE REPUBLIC OF UGANDA

OFFICE OF THE MINISTER.
MINISTRY OF INTERNAL AFFAIRS,
CRESTED TOWERS.
P.O. BOX 7191.
KAMPALA, UGANDA.

DETENTION ORDER

I, ARPHAXAD CHARLES KOLE OBOTH-OFUMBI, Minister of Internal Affairs, being satisfied that Mr. THOMAS WALTER WEBB of Entebbe is conducting himself in a manner dangerous to the peace and good order of the Republic of Uganda, I order his arrest and in pursuance of this my order I DO HEREBY authorise and order the detention of the said THOMAS WALTER WEBB in Luzira Prison or in any prison established under the Prisons Act as may from time to time be directed.

Therefore in pursuance of this order I DO HEREBY authorise any Officer-in-Charge of a prison established under the Prisons Act to detain the said THOMAS WALTER WEBB until his lawful release.

This order is made in exercise of the Powers conferred upon me by Decree No. 7 of 1971 as amended by Decree No.15 of 1971.

Given under my hand.

(A.C.K. Oboth-Ofumbi)
MINISTER OF INTERNAL AFFAIRS.

DATE: 11th April, 1976.
KAMPALA.

security wing, together with a former Ugandan ambassador to the Soviet Union and several of the country's top businessmen.

On 3rd May, after the horrors of his windowless, solitary cell, with little to eat, and only the stone floor to sleep on, his pillow being a cherished volume of English poems which he had managed to bring with him,[4] he was rescued by Jim Horrocks, the acting British High Commissioner, and diplomat Peter Chandley. He remained with the Chandleys until deported to London on the midnight, 7th/8th May,

THE REPUBLIC OF UGANDA

THE IMMIGRATION ACT, 1969

DEPORTATION ORDER

(Under sections 8 and 14 of the Act)

WHEREAS MR. THOMAS WALTER WEBB ....
of (address in Uganda) .... Entebbe ....

Passport No. C421476 ...... Nationality ... BRITISH ....

Home address ...... U.K. ....

has been deemed to be an undesirable immigrant by virtue of section 8 (1) of the Immigration Act,

AND WHEREAS by virtue of the said deeming, the said .... THOMAS WALTER WEBB ....

has become a prohibited immigrant;

Now THEREFORE by virtue of the powers vested in me by section 14 of the Immigration Act,

I HEREBY DIRECT that the said ... THOMAS WALTER WEBB ....

be deported from and remain out of Uganda indefinitely;

AND I FURTHER DECLARE that this Order shall be carried into effect by the removal of the said .... THOMAS WALTER WEBB ....
by deportation and while awaiting to be conveyed to the place of departure shall be kept in custody.

GIVEN UNDER MY HAND this 30th .... day of ... May ...., 1976.

MINISTER OF INTERNAL AFFAIRS.

northbound Super VC10, commanded by Captain Alan Burkitt, who was not the least bit pleased at having to land at Entebbe, which was by now avoided wherever possible. Webb had been fined £600 for possessing an old air pistol, and a couple of pellets, which were found when his house was searched. His fine was paid by Alan Smith, the manager of Barclays Bank, Kampala, with the boat taken as collateral.

On June 10th, 1976, Idi Amin narrowly escaped assassination, when three handgrenades were thrown at his car as he left a parade at the Nsambya police barracks. Proclaimed 'President for life' by the Uganda Defence Council, Amin had earlier in the year, in February, claimed that parts of Kenya were Ugandan territory and warned that should Uganda's access to the sea be threatened, he would go to war to reclaim the land, "appropriated by the British" in the nineteenth century. This outburst resulted in the cancellation of East African Community scheduled meetings and dockers at Mombasa boycotted Ugandan cargoes. An agreement between Kenya and the Sudanese government to construct a new road between Kitale and Juba, in Sudan, which would by-pass Ugandan territory was greeted by Amin as "a Zionist Imperialist plot".

But the gradual fragmentation of the treaty agreements between the partner states would pale into insignificance as a forthcoming outrage brought Uganda and the name 'Entebbe' to the forefront of world news.

Captain Marcel Bacos brought his Air France A300-B into Athens on 27th June, 1976, no doubt anticipating nothing worse than the air traffic control delays which were commonplace on the busy summertime Mediterranean routes. He did not know it, as he landed on arrival from Tel Aviv, but it was to be a very bad day indeed. His aircraft had been targeted by terrorists of the Popular Front for the Liberation of Palestine. Led by German Wilfried Bose, the terrorists hi-jacked the Airbus after departure for Paris, and forced the crew to fly to Benghazi. After nine hours on the ground at Benghazi, in appalling heat, the aircraft took off again for another destination – Entebbe.

The world had by now become accustomed to what was, unfortunately, regarded as the 'antics' of Idi Amin. No one was prepared to believe that he would support the act of air piracy which brought a civilian airliner with twelve crew and 247 passengers to Entebbe airport. After six hours waiting on board, the passengers and crew were escorted by Ugandan soldiers to the now deserted old passenger terminal. They were held there, guarded by thirty armed Ugandan soldiers, during which time Amin visited them and chatted with their captors. There was every indication that they were expected.

The unfortunate passengers and crew remained for six days in that dreadful place, while the world wrung its hands and wondered what to do about it.

---

[4] The Collins Albatross Book of Verse. Webb kept up his spirits by memorising Chaucer's *Ballade of Good Counsel*, translated into modern English by Henry Van Dyke.

At 23.00 on 3rd July, the equatorial night of Entebbe airport was shattered by the sudden arrival of three military C-130 Hercules, followed closely by a Boeing 707. Fifty-three minutes later, twenty Ugandan soldiers and seven of the terrorists were dead, the Israeli aircraft, with all the hostages but one old lady, killed by the Ugandans, were disappearing across Lake Victoria, en route to their refuelling stop at Nairobi's Embakasi airport.

Countering charges by Amin, Kenya's Foreign Minister, Munyua Waiyaki, denied that Kenya had collaborated in the Israeli raid. But Kenyans were no longer *persona grata* in Uganda. By 16th July some 3,000 Kenyan refugees had been counted crossing the border. There had been hundreds of killings in the aftermath of the raid. Many Ugandans were suspected of assisting in the rescue. At Entebbe airport the director of civil aviation Peter Kalanzi and the officer in charge of air traffic services, Tobias Rugambi were murdered, among some 245 Kenyans working in the country.

East African Airways was by now having difficulty with its image. The credibility of an airline which represented and carried the flag of a regime which countenanced air piracy was very difficult to maintain. In effect, on international routes, E.A.A.C. remained acceptable by virtue of its Kenyan power base. With no remittances of revenues or financial support forthcoming from either Uganda or Tanzania, it was becoming increasingly obvious that Kenya could not support the cost of maintaining an airline which was effectively bankrupt and was, furthermore, far too large for its own requirements.

With Uganda in the grips of madness, Tanzania was in decline. President Nyerere had been travelling throughout the year in search of funds to prop up his extraordinary socialist doctrine which cut deeply against the grain of African traditions. He had just outlawed privately owned shops, forcing his people to buy only from co-operatives. In March he dismissed 9,496 civil servants, in order to save £4 million per annum (the previous year he had sanctioned a 125% pay increase to members of parliament). Villagers and nomads alike were being forced onto co-operative farms, where there was little co-operation and less production. Hoping to benefit from cheap coal and iron ore mining, West Germany had come up trumps with some DM292 million, and his visit to Sweden netted $58 million for education, health, water supply and industry.

During 1975, Tanzania had collected from the World Bank loans of $21,000,000 in May and $9,000,000 in September. From the International Development Agency $17,500,000 in January, $6,000,000 in February, $20,200,000 in August and a further $9,000,000 in September. In addition, Britain donated £13,250,000 (£3 million of which was to buy out British owned farms in the Kilimanjaro region). A further £17,300,000 came from Denmark for investment in the sugar industry and from Holland $11,000,000. None of this aid money would be allocated to paying agreed contributions to the airline.

THE END OF A DREAM · 435

Amid the gathering political crisis, E.A.A.C. celebrated its 30th anniversary, with another set of commemorative stamps and optimistic supplements in the newspapers. Eastern Airlines, nearing the end of their management contract, brought in another six senior staff to assist with finance, customer services, reservations and passenger handling.

With pilots coming in from the partner states and world-wide, the connections with BALPA were becoming tenuous. When the Kenyan Ministry of Labour insisted that E.A.A.C. must formally recognise the East African Pilots Association, a situation arose whereby two competing unions represented the cockpit crews. This did nothing to ease the already unhappy situation, whereby the expatriate crews were

EAST AFRICAN AIRWAYS – SENIORITY LIST
17th APRIL 1969

Burkitt	Garland	Molberg	Proctor
Atchison	Walker	Dostrup	MacVicars
Payne	Johnson	Cook	Hewett
Ratcliffe	Close	Cosgrave	Heckman
Parker	Brewer	Poulsen	Morriss
Jackson	Vale	Sawbridge	Alexander
De Jager	Waerness	Hetherington	Crosse
Pettit	Harrowing	Bowker-Douglas	Kiwanuka
Grace	Kerstens	Wallis	Carton
McMullen	Connington	Tierney	Drummond
Methley	Dempster	Burleton	Charlton A.P.
Von Berg	Flynn	Karlsen	Simpson
Britchford	Robson	Wilson	Parker
Batt	Sutherland	O'Rourke	Charlton A.D.F.
Rose	Skillet	Svendson	Whelan
Hill (jnr)	Tveiten	Smith-Christenson	Mitchell
Power	Lund	Pearman	Ricketts
Waugh	Martin	Kinsey-Jones	Bond-Smith
Peacock	Viig	Preston	Donovan
Mounter	Dahl	Kennedy	Skjoldboel
Winson	Tudor	Alleyne	Penfold
Scott	Kanne	Disson	Adams
Cowie	Hognerud	Carne	Dunsford
Webster	Frank	Veseley	Clemmow
Knight	Burton	Dalhoff	Murphy
Hartley	Meaden	Cartwright (jnr)	Kennaway
Rae	Quene	Hopkins	Reed
Trent	Dudley-Owen	Berg	Lambert
Sirley	Tilling	Westwood	Llewelyn-Beard
Turk	Noon	Lorenzi	Rommen

becoming increasingly isolated. Later, the low salaries agreed by the EAPA caused many of the African pilots to seek work in other third-world airlines which paid international-scale salaries.

A comparison between the pilot's seniority lists of 1969 and 1976 shows clearly how the airline had suffered from the loss of experienced pilots. (Management captains are not included on the seniority tables):

EAST AFRICAN AIRWAYS CORPORATION
PILOTS SENIORITY LIST AS AT 1st MARCH, 1976

Hill (jnr)	Meadley	Frank	Masao
Waugh	Masud Ghani	Morey	Kung'u
Cowie	Conway	Calnan	Ng'andile
Sirley	Saidanha	Hussein	Jessani
Kerstens	Roy	Kinanjui	Hudson T.
Connington	Kuhne	Maksud	Minault
Dempster	Newman	Mwangi	Kiboi
Hognerud.	Gegin	Turuka	Makyeli
Noon	Morand	Mwendwa	Kassa
Molberg	Tierney	Rapuoda	Kadama
Dostrup	Hopkins	Mwankusye	Babu
Cook	Simpson	Mrikaria	Ndavu
O'Rourke	Quene	Kitta	Bera
Kinsey-Jones	Bolton	Muya	Gachoya
Preston	Shier	Munyi	Okweyo
Carne	DiPiero	Haguma	Njilima
Alleyne	Porter	Opere	Kabucho
McVicars	Sparkes	Ndorosey	Colpoys
Carton	Purdy	Tarnowka	Frost
Ricketts	Gordon	Pyetan	Grumbley
Penfold	Hewitt	Gathecha P.	Willilo
Adams	Brown	Musyoki	Spouse
Clemmow	Smit	Forsyth	Malikita
Martin	Gomes	Mwabukusi A.	Dalhoff
Harrowing	Singh	Wanjau	McTavish
Tveiten	Saleh	Bulhan	Allison
Burton	Chepkonwy	Omar	Allen
Berg	Uriyo	Patel	Berglund
S-Christensen	Tarkhan	Kaweesa	Tijburg
Kiwanuka	Makinda	Munyua	Stols
Drummond	Gathecha J.	Thuo	Young
Berthelsen	Mbaga	Mapunda	Mbuga
Escher	Leask	Dolasia	Parker D.J.
Sabai	Kiniti	Mwaura	Ririani
Turnbull	Dean	Gandi	

THE END OF A DREAM · 437

In April, 1976, E.A.A.C. had discussions with Aer Lingus in Dublin, leading to a three-year management services agreement. The effective date was 1st June, 1976, which allowed for a thirty day overlap with the outgoing Eastern Airlines team.

The East African Community, by the end of 1976, was in its death-throes. President Nyerere had made a speech in Zanzibar on 4th December, 1976, in which he stated that: "The East African 'common market' agreed upon the 1967 treaty had always been used to the advantage of Kenya, which refused to re-organise the common services". The Kenyan government, in a vigorous retort on 7th December, replied "All along, Tanzania had systematically undermined the working of the common market by banning from the Tanzanian market goods manufactured by partner-states, in order to be able to import Chinese goods to offset costs incurred in the building of the Tanzam railway". In accusing Tanzania of exploiting Community institutions for its own benefit and of: "sabotaging Kenya's trade efforts in other countries", the Kenyan government stated "that for reasons of their political circumstances neither Tanzania or Uganda had attracted industrial invest-

Ugandan registered F27 Friendship, 5X-AAP, takes-off from Zanzibar, late 1976. The Kenyan flag has been removed from the fin logo. (Capt Ricketts)

ment, and that Kenya was not prepared to hold back its own development in the interests of the other two partner-countries."

On 16th December, 1976, Kenya revealed that the Tanzanian region of the East African Harbours Corporation had losses amounting to 551,000,000 shillings[5] during the years between 1969 to 1975 and that Tanzania had constantly blocked the transfer of funds to E.A.R.C. headquarters. On the same day Tanzania accused Kenya of seizing the Community's ships on Lake Victoria, unilaterally closing the railway training school and 'nationalising' the E.A.R.C. headquarters.

Tanzania reciprocated by refusing to return 1,000 railway wagons, stating that: "it was un-economical to send them back empty to Kenya".

Mr Gitau, regional director of the East African Posts and Telecommunications Corporation, said that: "Owing to unfavourable conditions in Kampala", the Corporation's headquarters, which should be in Uganda's capital, had had to operate from Nairobi, and that Tanzania had, between 1972 and December, 1976, contributed only 3,900,000 shillings to the Corporation, whereas the Kenya region had spent 220,000,000 shillings to sustain the headquarters in Nairobi.

In the background, Dr Milton Obote remained, exiled in Tanzania, biding his time. His time would come, but it would not be for another three years that Tanzanian soldiers would take Kampala and the obscene tyrant who ruled Uganda would flee with his life.

The board of East African Airways met on 14th December, 1976, and unanimously recommended that the airline should be broken up unless Tanzania and Uganda immediately paid to headquarters their debts totalling 30,700,000 shillings. This decision was over-ruled by a meeting of the Community's Finance and Communication Council's ministers, when agreement was reached, on 16th December, that all the partner-states, and in particular Tanzania and Uganda, should remit funds promptly, and that the airline should continue to be operated "as a single entity".

On 7th January, a decision was taken by East African Airways to suspend all uneconomical services within Tanzania, affecting some nine destinations.

On 19th January, Uganda declared that the 38 million shillings owed to the airline would only be handed over if Kenya allowed Ugandan engineers and other staff to work at Nairobi airport and Ugandan goods permitted to pass unhindered through the port of Mombasa.

The crisis peaked on Wednesday, 26th January, 1977, when eight E.A.A.C. aircraft were refused permission to take-off from Nairobi Embakasi due to non-payment of landing fees. The 7 a.m. deadline had passed without the bill of some 35,000 shillings, being paid. While 300 passengers waited in the departure lounge, officials argued about new terms. Finally, on instructions from the Office of the President, the airport authority allowed a new deadline of noon.

---

[5] The rate of exchange in 1976 was approximately 14 shillings = £1 sterling or 8.16 shillings = US$1.

On Thursday, 27th January, a DC-9 departed Cairo for Khartoum and Nairobi. Bad weather forced a diversion to Luxor and a lengthy delay of twelve hours at Khartoum before it was discovered that there was insufficient fuel to continue. Once again, a passenger came to the rescue when the refuelling company at Khartoum refused credit to E.A.A.C. An Italian passenger paid $1,500 dollars cash after being reassured by the captain that he would be reimbursed at Nairobi.

The day finally came when the National Bank of Kenya would no longer underwrite the continual creeping losses which could only be supported by the bank's overdraft facility, the Kenya government stating: "it could no longer channel funds into the E.A.A.C. while more than K£13,000,000 of debts were outstanding". On Friday, 28th January, 1977, all further credit was frozen. With K£1,635,000 owing to the Shell Oil company, this was immediately followed by suspension of credit facilities world-wide by the fuel suppliers. Insurance premiums of £500,000 were unpaid to the London brokers. With insurance cover now withheld, and unable to re-fuel its aircraft, the airline was grounded.

The announcement by the Corporation was issued in a statement which read:

"The cash flow problems facing East African Airways at its headquarters in Nairobi have forced the airline to temporarily suspend some of its services with immediate effect.

International, regional and domestic services will be affected by this action.

EAA cash problems were triggered by the demands of some of its suppliers that goods and services were paid for in cash. The largest and most single item required to be paid for in cash is the aircraft fuel.

EAA has been paying for its fuel requirements in advance for some time now but found itself unable to do so at midday today (Thursday, January 27), thus forcing it to curtail its operations drastically.

...EAA cash problems stem from three areas: debtors who owe the airline some KShs 100 million; under-capitalization, and lack of transfer of funds from a number of countries..."

The aircraft which were inbound on the route system returned to Embakasi; crews were abandoned at their slip stations, until they could make arrangements to fly home with concessional tickets issued by sympathetic airlines. Captain Ted Imison and his crew had taken 5H-MOG on its last outward flight to Bombay, on 21st January. Marooned in the Taj Hotel, where they were afforded normal hospitality, they were given free tickets by Air India "to anywhere in the world except Nairobi". The withdrawal of East African's three services a week resulted in overbookings on Air India's Nairobi services for months ahead. They finally flew to London, from where they continued on British Airways to Nairobi.

At London, Captain Ian Cowie, after paying for fuel with travellers cheques, had received ATC clearance to depart with the Simbair Boeing 707, when a CAA Land

Rover was driven up against the nose-wheel, preventing him from taxying forward. There were landing fees and other bills unpaid at London, as elsewhere.

The announcement which came from Nairobi, suspending all flights, was predictably greeted by hysterical condemnation by Tanzania, where the government said that Kenya was entirely to blame for the grounding of the airline, alleging that: "a clique of profiteers within the Kenya government wants to shut down the airline so they can start their own airline".

East African Airways flights from Dar es Salaam and Entebbe were cancelled early on the morning of 28th January when the Tanzanian authorities refused permission for a DC-9 and two F27 Friendships to depart. As the news reached Nairobi, E.A.A.C. immediately wrote a cheque for fuel for the grounded aircraft, so that they could be flown to Nairobi, but the Tanzanians refused to respond, putting the two F27s on internal services.

Three Super VC10s were towed to a parking bay outside the E.A.A.C. hangar at Embakasi, to join the fourth aircraft, which was undergoing maintenance.

Uganda Radio, announcing the closure, described it as: "the work of Israeli bandits". An emergency board meeting held in Nairobi on 31st January continued without the Tanzanian members, since they were unable to travel due to the grounded flights. On the same day, all sporting links with Tanzania were broken off by Kenya following their "provocative and indecent attacks". One of the outstanding factors in the financial difficulty which had beset the airline for several years, had been Tanzania's failure to remit its share of funds which were agreed for support of E.A.A.C.'s capitalization.

There would be no solution this time. East African Airways was something which belonged to the past, in common with the people and the dreams which, long ago, brought frail wings and the sound of Gipsy-Six engines across the East African skies.

East African Airways aircraft stand idle on the tarmac at Nairobi Airport on 26th January 1977, when all flights were refused permission to operate due to non-payment of landing fees.

It had outlived its time, a time during which a small colonial airline, formed to connect the far flung communities within the territories bounded in the east by the Indian Ocean, to the west by the Mountains of the Moon, the Ruvuma river to the south and Sudan – Ethiopia to the north, had emerged to compete successfully with the best, across the air routes of the world.

It had failed, not because of any weakness in those who faithfully served it, but because of political failure in the evolutionary post-colonial states, which could not maintain the form which Britain had imposed upon them, stricken by ideology and inter-tribal feuding, in the straight-jacket of the national borders invented in Europe a century ago. It could only be known with hind-sight; but East African Airways' death knell began to toll at the time of independence. With the passing of Kenya Colony and British withdrawal from Uganda and Tanzania, the unifying element within the territories was removed.

As long as Kenya could sustain its development without the support of the other two countries, they would remain dependent for their economic survival within the East African Community on Kenya's dynamic, capitalist economy. Landlocked Uganda depended entirely upon Mombasa for its bulk imports and exports. With only one airport with sufficient runway length, it depended upon the airports at Nairobi or Mombasa as weather diversions for its air traffic. Kenya depended upon Uganda only for a proportion of its electricity, purchased from the Owen Falls power station. Tanzania hardly counted, as far as Kenya was concerned. Although a vast and beautiful country, in economic terms it was almost irrelevant.

The combination of nation building and ignorance; racial intolerance (but by no means as terrible as the internecine intolerance which had destroyed Uganda); human weakness by those entrusted with power and position – and the pressures of external ideology, whether for political or financial ends, brought East African Airways down. There was to be nothing left but the memories of a pioneering colonial airline and of those aviation-minded people who, for a time, set standards not only in Africa, but across the world.

Postscript

"IT ALL ENDED in 1977, after 30 wonderful years". Captain Bob Ainsworth was one of those who had seen it out to the end:

"I was flying with Dave Dempster (I always seemed to be flying with Dave Dempster when encountering the worst of the cumulo-nimbus), and I could not have been with a better man. He is perhaps the most controlled person I know. During one of our early flights together, we were going into Rome, and, as I said: "Approach check", we were struck by lightning, a huge, noisy, blue flash that ran along the centre-line of the aircraft. To an aircraft, being a 'Faraday cage', the lightning is not usually dangerous, but it can damage the compasses. The experience is frightening, especially in the dark, when the flash is dazzling and the noise of the strike is like being in a car with a dozen people striking the roof with the flat of their hands. At the same time the crash of thunder can be heard. Well, Dave simply answered: "Approach check" and did not even blink an eyelid as he proceeded to call the checks from his list, as if nothing had happened at all.

"This time we were on our very last flight. We had taken the Super VC10 into Milan and it snowed. Wet, soggy, snow. I decided to night-stop, until the runway could be cleared the next morning. The passengers were more than a little unhappy about this, they wanted to be in sunny Mombasa with as little delay as possible. The next stop was Rome and before take-off a hail storm caused slush to build up, and again the runway was unusable. I stopped engines and decided to sit on the ground until the runway was cleared, or we ran out of flight-time limits. The passengers were kept on board and they were fed-up and complaining.

"The station manager wanted me to go, and even offered the crew a free dinner next time we were in Rome if we would take-off, regardless! We waited and waited for hours until, just before we ran out on flight-time limits, the runway was announced clear. We started the engines again and taxied out, stopping at the take-off point. Sure enough, it was clear. We were half way down the runway when a huge cumulo-nimbus, not visible on our radar, nor advised by the airport, which had no storm-warning radar, burst its contents onto the runway, which almost disappeared under the volume of water.

"The situation was now dangerous. The flaps can be damaged and the engines can be flamed-out, but V_1 was near and to try and stop with those braking conditions would have been disastrous, so we rotated into the worst turbulence I have ever known.

"Turbulence is always frightening, especially when accompanied by lightning. Control is difficult but possible with changes in speed and or height. At 30,000ft it doesn't matter much, as long as the wings stay on (whenever I was in turbulence at altitude I thought of the VC10 wing at Wisley in England. It had been fastened to a wall and one jack pushed the centre up perhaps 6ft and another jack bent the wing-tip the same distance in the opposite direction. They were testing it to destruction, but when I saw it they had already been doing it for years). But now, so close to the ground there was no room for such comforting thoughts. The igniters were on, but would the engines keep going? Fortunately they did and I battled with the controls. The turbulence was so frightful, I wondered if we would survive. Undoubtedly the passengers felt that way too; perhaps their prayers helped - after all, it was Rome. The complainers who were so anxious to get airborne regardless must now be wishing they were having a quiet drink on the Via Veneto.

"Dave Dempster was his usual calm self. The only remark he made was: 'you are going a shade left, I don't suppose it matters'. I do not know how long this lasted - it was more than five minutes because we had reduced power from full to maximum continuous and still we were pounded and struck repeatedly by lightning and hail smashed against the windscreen as St Elmo's fire illuminated the entire aircraft.

"Quite suddenly it was calm. We were enveloped in the star studded night, beautiful and serene. The trembling tour leader came forward to the flight-deck. 'What has been happening?' The passengers had been clinging to their seats and to each other, the same question on their lips. Now all was calm, there were smiles - their captain had brought them through".

Shortly before midnight on 31st January, 1977, the following signal was sent round the world from British Airways (Overseas) in London:

LONRTBA   312330LG
    REF OUR INTERLINE AGREEMENT WITH EAST AFRICAN AIRWAYS STOP. WITH EFFECT MIDNIGHT GMT 31 JAN ACCEPTANCE OF EAA DOCUMENTS IS TEMPORARILY SUSPENDED STOP
    UNTIL FURTHER NOTICE EAA DOCUMENTS ARE NOT RPT NOT ACCEPTABLE FOR TRVL OR AS EXCHANGE DOCUMENTS FOR BA TKTS REGARDLESS OF WHETHER TRVL HAS STARTED OR IS TO START STOP BA TKTS ISSUED IN EXCHANGE FOR EAA DOCUMENTS PRIOR TO MIDNIGHT GMT 31 JAN MAY BE HONOURED STOP
    WOULD RECEIVING ADDRESSEES PLEASE ENSURE THAT ALL STAFF ARE MADE FULLY AWARE CONTENTS THIS SIGNAL STOP END

After thirty-two years B.O.A.C.'s successor had finally withdrawn its support for the airline it had nurtured into existence, and which had failed to survive in the new world order.

The last Super VC10 service, on 28th January, 1977, from Frankfurt to Nairobi was commanded by Captain Willi Kerstens, a Dutch pilot. Flight Engineer Paddy Murray was horrified to hear him announce to the passengers, as they made their descent to Nairobi: "Ladies and gentlemen, you are on the last flight of East African

Airways, as the company has gone bankrupt". There was pandemonium in the cabin as the, predominantly German, tourists asked: "how do we get back?" Fortunately, Lufthansa agreed to fly them home.

They all thought they would be re-hired the next day, to start the new Kenyan airline. But although Kenya Airways commenced operations, with a leased British Midland Boeing 707, on February 3rd, it didn't happen. Every day some would congregate at the old aero club at Wilson airport, waiting for the news. There was no news, so they all got blind drunk. It went on for day after day until finally it dawned on everyone that it was all over – *Kwisha kabisa!* Some retired, never to fly again, others dispersed to the four corners of the earth, picking up flying jobs wherever they could. Among these were people who would go on to hold senior positions in the most prestigious international airlines. A small handful joined Kenya Airways.

The four Super VC10s stood forlornly on the tarmac at Embakasi for four months, while the legal mess was sorted out by David Coward, the Registrar-General of Kenya, who was delegated the task of liquidating the airline as Official Receiver. One day, former East African Airways captain Arthur Ricketts, together with co-pilot Charlie McVickars and navigator Claude Scott, a scratch crew recruited by him from ex-E.A.A.C. aircrew, boarded 5H-MMT, the first to be returned to the British Aircraft Corporation in England. It was 05.30 GMT on 16th May, 1977, and as they taxied out past the old East African Airways hangars, the ground engineers, who had been brought back to prepare the aircraft for the flights, had turned out to watch the sad departure. There were not many dry eyes around on that morning.

Paddy Murray was hired to crew that first departure of the Super VC10s. As soon as they were airborne, a call came through on the SSB from Filton. Please could they list all the snags, as the British Aircraft Corporation wanted to get cracking as soon as the aircraft arrived. They refused to believe him when he passed only one fault – after four months sitting on the ground – a warning light had failed to illuminate.

Arthur Ricketts was not so lucky with the following flight, of 5Y-ADA. It was 06.30 GMT on 31st May, when they lifted off from Nairobi for the ten-and-a-half hour flight direct to Filton. Almost immediately, 5Y-ADA protested with a total hydraulic failure. The subsequent flapless, slatless landing at Filton was uneventful.

A long time had passed since the test-pilots of BAC had flown the now out of production VC10s. By special permission of the CAA, Arthur Ricketts renewed type ratings for both Eddie McNamarra and Concorde chief test-pilot Brian Trubshaw on training flights from Filton in 5H-MMT on 24th and 25th May. Captain McNamarra had flown supernumerary on the first ferry flight and as co-pilot on the second flight.

McNamarra, with BAC pilot John Cochran, N/O Claude Scott, F/E Denis Akery and supernumerary F/E Alan Hayward brought 5X-UVJ back to Filton on 26th July.

Finally, the last of the beautiful aircraft which had been the pride of East African Airways made its early morning departure from Nairobi. Captain Ricketts lifted 5H-MOG off at 06.30 GMT on 3rd August, 1977, and, for the last time, set course, high above the Great Rift Valley of Kenya, for England and Filton airport near Bristol.

On the 24th May, 1978, a light aircraft was approaching Wilson Airport from the north-west. As it descended over the Ngong Hills, there was an explosion and the aircraft disintegrated, crashing to earth near the airport. On board were three passengers and the pilot. One of the passengers was Colonel Bruce Mackenzie. He had been on a business trip to Entebbe. Before leaving, he had been presented with a magnificent lion skin, a present from President Idi Amin. In the lion's head had been secreted a bomb. Amin had extracted his revenge for Mackenzie's part in the planning of the Israeli raid on Entebbe.

Some fifteen years after these events, Captain Alan Ratcliffe was waiting to take his turn on the Boeing 757 simulator at Gatwick. As the crew emerged from their training session, he saw that they were Africans. Realising that they were from Kenya Airways, he went forward and introduced himself to the captain. He was, Ratcliffe realised, talking to a charming, urbane and fully professional pilot. The years had, after all, completed the task. After a few minutes conversation, the African pilot revealed that he lived at Naivasha, beside the lake. He had bought Peter Brumby's farm.

The End

Notes to second edition

With the passage of time, some accounts of incidents, which occurred many years ago, may have acquired embellishment in the re-telling, or may have suffered due to failing memory on the part of those who experienced them. This must certainly be the case in connection with the approach and landing incident at Lusaka described on pages 386-387 of the first edition. Although changes have been made in this edition, the reader is advised to regard some of this account as being in the tradition of a typical air crew 'line shoot'. The author would like to apologise to both Captain Henry Hartley and Captain Brian Meadley should he have mistakenly given the impression that this flight was conducted in any other than a correct and prudent manner, in accordance with the flight manual and the Corporation's published operations procedures.

Captain Tug Wilson has pointed out that on the first scheduled flight of the DC3 on 5 November, 1949 (page 83), he was the captain of the aircraft. Wing Commander Francombe acted as co-pilot. At the time of this flight Francombe did not have the DC3 on his licence. This edition has been corrected accordingly.

The incident at Lumbo (page 94) describes Captain Wilson's condition after a party. It should be made clear that this was due to food-poisoning, not to an over indulgence in alcoholic beverages, and that his insistence on continuing with the flight was in the best interests of the Corporation and his passengers. Although George Leslie, his first officer, kept a concerned eye on him, he was by no means unable to fulfil his duties as captain.

Again, the passage of time and unreliable memories of some sources have conspired to incorrectly identify a number of persons in the first edition. Together with spelling of some names, these errors have been corrected, where possible, in this edition. Some particulars of events and place names have been altered for the same reasons.

It has been suggested to the author that clarification would be desirable in references to Africanisation of senior positions and, in particular, the flight-deck. The high failure rate of air crew candidates was not necessarily indicative of failure in the Africans as a group. Success in selection for these positions often depended upon political and tribal influence, which was beyond the control of the Corporation's operations management. Many potentially suitable candidates were excluded, since they were unable to obtain preferential treatment prior to selection by E.A.A.C.

Captain John 'Ginger' Brewer retired from E.A.A.C. in 1970 and was appointed Technical Secretary of IFALPA. He settled in New Zealand and formed the Government Technical Correspondence School for pilot's licences. In retirement he continues to teach pilots ground subjects as an off-campus consultant tutor and examiner for the Open Polytechnic.

Peter J Davis
February 1994

Appendices

The first page from the log of de Havilland DH51 VP-KAA. The first flights were conducted by Captain Geoffrey de Havilland on September 11, 1925 at Stag Lane. John Carberry first flew the aircraft at Nyeri on April 7, 1926.

(Courtesy of the Shuttleworth Collection)

APPENDICES · 449

AIRCRAFT G-K.A.A.   ENGINE A.D.C. (Renault type)

Date	Crew Name	Duty	Journey	Depart.	Arrive.	In Air.	Approx. Mileage	No. of Passengers	Wt. of Cargo (lbs.) Goods	Mails
					Brought forward	57 10				
26·9·28	T.C. Black, Mr Basso		Nairobi to Naivasha	4 09	4 42	0 33		2.		
26·9·28	T.C. Black, Mr Basso		Naivasha to Gilgil	6 42	6 53	0 11		2.		
29·9·28	T.C. Black, Mr Basso		Gilgil to Kisumu	7 30	8 31	1 01		2.		
27·9·28	T.C. Black, L. Basso		Kisumu to Nairobi	1 21	3 30	2 09		2.		
28·9·28	T.C. Black, Mr. Cartland		Nairobi	5 31	5 43	0 12		2.		
29·9·28	T.C. Black, J. Abbott		Nairobi	5 46	5 56	0 11		2.		
29·9·28	T.C. Black, Mr Eager		Nairobi	6 03	6 15	0 12		2.		
29·9·28	T.C. Black, Mrs Eager		Nairobi	6 17	6 27	0 10		2.		
30·9·28	T.C. Black, Mr Eager		Nairobi to Naivasha	12 15	12 45	0 30		2.		
30·9·28	T.C. Black, Mr Eager		Naivasha to Gilgil	3 10	3 20	0 10		2.		
30·9·28	T.C. Black, Mr Eager		Gilgil to Nairobi	3 50	4 40	0 50		2.		
7·10·28	T.C. Black	Test	LOCAL: TEST	5 30	5 36	0 06				
7·10·28	T. Black, J. Simpson		NAIROBI	6 05	6 18	0 13		2		
7·10·28	T. Black, Graham Bully		Nairobi	6 30	6 42	0 12		2		
13·10·28	T. Black		Nairobi to Nakuru	4 55	5 55	1 00		2		
15·10·28	T. Black, Mr Wood		Nakuru to Nairobi	7 30	8 45	1 15		2		
					Carried forward	66 05				

*A page from the log of VP-KAA showing entries by Tom Campbell Black in 1928, after he had acquired the DH51 **Miss Kenya** from John Carberry. The aircraft is now maintained in flying condition as part of the Shuttleworth Collection, in England. It has been restored to the British register as G-EBIR, its original registration prior to export to Kenya Colony.* *(Courtesy of the Shuttleworth Collection)*

AGREEMENT BETWEEN THE GOVERNMENT OF THE UNION OF SOUTH AFRICA AND THE GOVERNMENT OF THE UNITED KINGDOM OF GREAT BRITAIN AND NORTHERN IRELAND, IN CONNECTION WITH THE ESTABLISHMENT OF CIVIL AIR SERVICES BETWEEN THE UNION AND THE UNITED KINGDOM.

For the Government of the Union of South Africa:
Field Marshall the Right Honourable Jan Christian Smuts, C.H.,K.C.,D.T.D.,M.P. Prime Minister, Minister of External Affairs and of Defence for the Union of South Africa.

For the Government of the United Kingdom of Great Britain and Northern Ireland:
The Honourable Sir Evelyn Baring, K.C.M.G.,High Commissioner in the Union of South Africa for His Majesty's Government in the United Kingdom.

It being in the interest of public convenience and necessity that direct air communications should be re-established as soon as the military situation permits between the Union of South Africa and the United Kingdom of Great Britain and Northern Ireland;

And it having been recommended at the International Civil Aviation Conference held at Chicago in November and December 1944, that Agreements for the operation of air services should contain clauses substantially in conformity with those set out in the draft form of standard agreement incorporated in Section VIII of the Final Act of the Conference entitled "form of Standard Agreement for Provisional Air Routes".

The Government of the Union of South Africa of the one part and the Government of the United Kingdom of the other (hereinafter called the Contracting Parties) have agreed as follows:-

(1) Each Contracting Party grants to the other for the purpose of the establishment of the civil air services herein described, the rights specified in the Annex to this Agreement.

(2) Each Contracting Party grants within its territory to the designated airline of the other shown in the Annex to this Agreement the operating permission designated therein, along the route therein described.

(3) The Contracting Parties agree that-

(a) the charges which either may impose or permit to be imposed in the designated airline of the other for the use of airports or other facilities shall not be higher than would be paid for the use of such airports and facilities by its national aircraft engaged in similar international services;

(b) fuel, lubricating oils and spare parts introduced into the territory of either Contracting Party by the other or by the nationals of the other and intended solely for use by aircraft of the designated airline of the other party operated on the Air Service described in the Annex shall be accorded national and most favoured nation treatment with respect to the imposition of customs dues, inspection fees or other national duties or charges by the Contracting Party whose territory is entered;

(c) the fuel, lubricating oils, spare parts, regular equipment and aircraft stores retained on board aircraft of the designated airline of either Contracting Party, authorised to operate the routes and services described in the Annex shall, upon arriving in or leaving the territory of the other Contracting Party, be exempt from customs inspection fees or similar duties or charges, even though such supplies be used or consumed by such aircraft on flights in that territory.

(4) Each Contracting Party agrees to recognize as valid the certificates of airworthiness, certificates of competency and licences issued or rendered valid by the other, for the purposes of operating the air services described in this Annex, providing that

(a) such certificates and licences satisfy the minimum standards set out in the Annexes to the Convention for the Regulation of Aerial Navigation, Paris, 1919, or such other International Convention as may take its place and,

(b) either Contracting Party may refuse to recognize, for the purpose of flight above its own territory, certificates of competency and licences issued or rendered valid to its own nationals by the other or any other country.

(5) The Contracting Parties agree that:-

(a) the laws and regulations of each relating to the admission to or departure from its territory of aircraft engaged in international air navigation, or to the operation and navigation of such aircraft while within its territory, shall be applied to the aircraft of the other without distinction as to the nationality and shall be complied with by such aircraft upon entering or departing from or while witin the territory of the Contracting Party;
(b) the laws and regulations of the one Contracting Party as to the admission to or departure from its territory of passengers, crew or cargo of aircraft, such as those relating to entry, departure, immigration,passports, customs and quarantine shall be complied with by or on behalf of such passengers, crew or cargo on board aircraft of the other upon entrance into or departure from or while within the territory of the first mentioned party.

(6) Each Contracting Party reserves the right to withhold or revoke a certificate or permit in respect of the designated airline of the other if when operating in or over the territory of the first Contracting Party it fails to comply with the laws mentioned in Article 5 which are in force in that territory or to perform its obligations described in the Annex to this Agreement.

(7) Each Contracting Party agrees that this Agreement and all contracts concerned therewith shall be registered with the Provisional International Civil Aviation Organization.

(8) Each Contracting Party agrees that if any matter in dispute under this Agreement, whether of interpretation or of application cannot be settled by negotiation, it shall be referred for decision to an Arbitral Tribunal. The composition of this Tribunal shall be determined by agreement between the Contracting Parties.

(9) This Agreement may be terminated by one Contracting Party giving one year's notice to the other. Such notice may be given at any time after a period of two months to allow consultation between the two Contracting Parties. This Agreement shall also be subject to review upon the entry ito force of a general multilateral convention to which the Contracting Parties have adhered.

Signed in duplicate at Pretoria on the twenty-sixth day of October, 1945, in the English and Afrikaans languages, both texts being equally authentic.

For the Government of the Union of South Africa:-
J.C. SMUTS.

For the Government of the United Kingdom of Great
Britain and Northern Ireland:-
E. BARING.

ANNEX

1. The airlines designated for the purpose of the operation of the air services on the route specified in paragraph 2 below shall be:-

For the Government of the Union of South Africa:-
 South African Airways (S.A.R. & H.)

For the Government of the United Kingdom of Great Britain and Northern Ireland:-
 The British Overseas Airways Corporation.

2. The route to be followed by the designated airlines of the Contracting Parties and in respect of which the rights set out in this Agreement are accorded shall be:-

 A United Kingdom airport - a Mediterranean airport - Cairo - Khartoum - Nairobi - Salisbury - Johannesburg.

 The Contracting Parties may, however, vary the intermediate stopping places or the terminals of the route by mutual agreement and subject to the consent, as necessary, of other countries whose territory is traversed.

3. Each Contracting Party grants to the other in respect of its own territory the right to pick up and set down traffic for or from any destination on the route.

4. The Contracting Parties shall agree to the type of aircraft to be operated by the designated airlines for the air services on the route specified in paragraph 2 above. Initially the aircraft shall be of the York type.

5. Having regard to public convenience and necessity, to the traffic offering for carriage between the United Kingdom on the one hand and the Union on the other and to the maintenance of broad equililibrium between capacity and traffic offering on the route, the

Contracting Parties agree that the capacity to be operated from time to time shall be related to traffic requirements, and that the frequencies determined between the operators subject to the approval of the Contracting Parties.

6. The Contracting Parties further agree that the total route capacity provided by aircraft of the type specified operating the agreed number of frequencies shall be divided equally between the designated airlines of the two Contracting Parties. If, however, actual traffic interest no longer justifies such equal division, it shall be competent for either proportions as may be agreed upon to accord therewith. If, further, one of the Contracting Parties may decide that its designated airline will not, permanently or for a defined period, operate, in full or in part, that number of services which would provide capacity on the route equal to that to which under this paragraph it is or may be entitled, that Contracting Party may arrange with the other Contracting Party, under terms and conditions to be agreed between them for the designated airline of such other Contracting Party to provide the additional capacity on the route necessary for the operation of the full schedule of services agreed between them from time to time.

7. The Contracting Parties shall arrange for the designated airlines to confer with a view to reaching agreement with each other and with the airlines of any other States that may also be operating along the whole or any part of the route designated in paragraph 2 of this Annex concerning the tariffs to be charged for the carriage of passengers and cargo. Any tariffs that the airlines concerned may agree among themselves shall be subject to the approval of the Contracting Parties. In the event of disagreement between the designated airlines of the Contracting Parties, the tariffs shall be agreed between the Contracting Parties themselves.

8. Each Contracting Party shall arrange for the provision in its own territory of the ground organization and facilities required for the operation of the air services.

9. The revenue (other than revenue from mails) accruing from the operation of the air services shall be pooled and allocated between the respective airlines in proportions agreed between them and approved by the Contracting Parties. Revenue from conveyance of mails shall be dealt with under arrangements to be agreed, from time to time, between the Contracting Parties.

10. Expenditure incurred by the designated airlines in the operation of the services covered by this agreement shall be dealt with under arrangements to be agreed from time to time between the designated airlines, subject to the approval of the Contracting Parties.

11. For the purposes of this Agreement the territory of the Contracting Party in relation to -

    (a) the Government of the United Kingdom of Great Britain and Northern Ireland shall be regarded as including the United Kingdom, Malta, Uganda, Kenya, Tanganyika, Northern Rhodesia,Nyasaland, and the Bechuanaland Protectorate; and

    (b) the Government of the Union of South Africa shall be regarded as including the mandated territory of South West Africa.

WILSON AIRWAYS FLEET LIST, 1929-1939

Reg'n.	Type	c/n.	Previous Identity	Remarks
VP-KAC	D.H.60G Gipsy Moth	1004	–	"Knight of the Mist"
VP-KAD	Avro 619 Five	436	–	"Knight Errant" broken up 10/32
VP-KAE	Avro 619 Five	228	–	"Knight of the Grail". Sold back to Avro 7/10/30
VP-KAG	D.H.60G Gipsy Moth	1137	G-AALD	Impressed
VP-KAH	D.H.80A Puss Moth	2061	G-AAZS	British reg'n. not taken up. Later sold abroad as G-ABNV.
VP-KAK	D.H.80A Puss Moth	2118	–	"Knight Crusader". sold abroad as G-AFKV
VP-KAL	D.H.60G Gipsy Moth	1108	G-A AJV	Broken up 23/11/32
VP-KAM	D.H.80A Puss Moth	2153	–	Sold abroad Congo 1934. Restored as VP-KBI. Impressed in Kenya Auxiliary Air Unit as K.3 5 7 or 17
VP-KAS	D.H.60G Gipsy Moth	1911	–	Crashed 16/10/32
VP-KAT	D.H.80A Puss Moth	2059	G-AARF	"Knight of the Garter". To VP-KBO SU-ACN G-AARF. Impressed as HK-866
VP-KAW	D.H.84 Dragon 1	6047	–	Crashed Mombasa 8/12/33
VP-KAY	D.H.80A Puss Moth	2076	G-AAZU VR-TAI	Withdrawn from use 1939
VP-KAZ	D.H.80A Puss Moth	2160	G-ABMC	Impressed as K.3 K.5 K.7 or K.17
VP-KBA	D.H.84. Dragon 1	6059	–	Impressed as K.15
VP-KBB	Klemm L.25A	4	–	Impressed as K.21
VP-KBE	D.H.85 Leopard Moth	7055	–	Crashed 8/6/38
VP-KBG	D.H.84, Dragon 11	6079	G-ACRO	Crashed 14/4/37
VP-KBP	D.H.85 Leopard Moth	7107	–	Crashed Iringa 25/1/39
VP-KBR	D.H.87A Hornet Moth	8034	–	Sold abroad
VP-KCA	D.H.90 Dragonfly	7528	–	Impressed as K.13 or K.14
VP-KCD	P. 10 Vega Gull	K.39	–	Impressed as K. 18 or K. 19
VP-KCE	P.10 Vega Gull	K.44	–	Impressed as K.18 or K.19
VP-KCG	D.H.89A Dragon Rapide	6357	–	Impressed as K.4 10, 11 or 16.
VP-KCJ	D.H.B9A Dragon Rapide	6366	–	Impressed as K.4 10, 11 or 16. To E.A.A.C. 1946
VP-KCK	D.H.89A Dragon Rapide	6267	K5070	Impressed as K.4 10, 11 or 16.
VP-KCL	D.H.89A Dragon Rapide	6394	–	Impressed as K.4 10, 11 or 16.
VP-KCO	D.H.85 Leopard Moth	7095	ZS-AFI	Impressed as K.12 or K.6
VP-KCP	D.H.60G 111 Moth Major	5100	G-ACYD	Impressed as K.22?
VP-KCR	D.H 89A Dragon Rapide	6413	–	Impressed as K.8
VP-KCS	D.H 90 Dragonfly	7554	G-AEXI	Impressed as K.13 or K.14

EAST AFRICAN AIRWAYS FLEET LIST, 1946-1977

Reg'n	Type	C/N	Previous identity	Acq'd	Remarks
VP-KCJ	DH89A Dragon Rapide	6366	VP-KCJ, K? (K.A.A.U.)	1946/1955	Ex Wilson Airways. Sold 1948. Repurchased 1955. Sold to Caspair 1960. Written off Entebbe 7/10/62
VP-KCT	DH89A Dragon Rapide	6803	NR715, G-AGNH	1945	Restored as G-AGNH 17/8/49 for Civil Air Attache Baghdad. Subsequently sold as VR-AAP.
VP-KCU	DH89A Dragon Rapide	6848	NR772, G-AGOX	1945	Written off after forced landing near Garsen 28/6/46
VP-KCV	DH89A Dragon Rapide	6849	NR773, G-AGOW	1945	Sold 1951 to Caspair. Restored as G-AGOW 1956. Cancelled 1957
VP-KCW	DH89A Dragon Rapide	6875	NR799, G-AGOU	1945	Sold to Sir Alexander Gibb & Partners 9/49. Sold abroad 11/55 as VP-YNN
VP-KCX	DH89A Dragon Rapide	6876	NR800, G-AGOT	1945	Sold to Jivrais Air Services Ltd. 18/10/48. Broken up 1950.
VP-KCY	DH89A Dragon Rapide	6874	NR798, G-AGOV	1945/1953	Sold to Noon & Pearce Air Charters Ltd. 8/51. Repurchased 6/53. Sold 1960
VP-KDE	DH104 Dove Series 1	4117	none	1948	'Masai' later 'Chagga'. Sold 1951 as G-AMFU. Converted to Srs 6. Sold as OO-SCD
VP-KDF	DH104 Dove Series 1	4118	none	1948	'Buganda' later 'Kikuyu'. Sold 1951 to Gulf Aviation as G-AMJZ. Cancelled 1962
VP-KDG	DH104 Dove Series 1	4119	none	1948	Chagga' later 'Wakamba'. Sold 6/51 to Mandated Air Lines as VH-MAB. Subsequently VH-AWF, converted to Srs 5. VH-RAJ, VH-TLU, VH-RCI, and VH-CTS. Written off after heavy landing near Geelong, Vic, 17/11/68
VP-KEA	DH89A Dragon Rapide	6890	NR814, PH-RAA	1947	Written off 23/1/54
VP-KEB	DH89A Dragon Rapide	6891	NR815, PH-RAB	1947	Written off after landing accident at Kasese, 15/10/51
VP-KEC	DH89A Dragon Rapide	6893	NR829, PH-RAC	1947	Written off after accident at Mafia 12/5/50
VP-KED	DH89A Dragon Rapide	6895	NR831, PH-RAD	1947	Sold to Israel 1951 as 4X-AEH (?)
VP-KEE	DH89A Dragon Rapide	6496	X7323, G-AJFM	1947	Sold to Israel 1951 as 4X-AEI (?)
VP-KEF	DH89A Dragon Rapide	6831	NR743, PH-RAF	1947	Transferred to S.K.A.T. 1960. Re-registered 5H-AAN.
VP-KEJ	DH104 Dove Series 1	4120	none	1948	Swahili' later 'Masai'. Sold 6/51 to Mandated Air Lines as VH-MAL. Subsequently VH-AWE, VH-GVE, and VH-GVM. Sold to Nicholson's Air Service, N.S.W.

Reg'n	Type	C/N	Previous identity	Acq'd	Remarks
VP-KFA	Lockheed L18-56 Lodestar	2076	G-AGBT	1948	'Lake Victoria'. Sold as SE-BUU
VP-KFB	Lockheed L18-56 Lodestar	2071	G-AGBS	1948	'Lake Nyassa'. Sold as SE-BUX. Crashed Jonkoping 11/1/53
VP-KFC	Lockheed L18-56 Lodestar	2091	G-AGBV	1948	'Lake Albert'. Sold as N94536
VP-KFE	Lockheed L18-56 Lodestar	2070	G-AGBR	1948	'Lake George'. Sold as SE-BUF. To Kar-Air for spares 1961.
VP-KFF	Lockheed L18-56 Lodestar	2095	G-AGBX	1948	'Lake Edward'. Sold as N94537. Crashed New Jersey 28/1/52
VP-KHA	Lockheed L18-56 Lodestar	2013	F-ARTM, OO-CAY	1949	Sold as N5381N
VP-KHB	Lockheed L18-56 Lodestar	2420	42-32226, OO-CAS	1949	Broken up for spares 1951
VP-KHE	Lockheed L18-56 Lodestar	2421	42-32227, OO-CAV	1949	'Lake Naivasha'. Sold as N94537
VP-KHK	Douglas C-47B Dakota 4	14654/26099	43-48838, KJ928, G-AGKI	1949	'Kongwa Pioneer' later 'Sagana'. Sold USA 4/53 and subsequently French Air Force
VP-KHN	Douglas C-47B Dakota 4	15276/26721	43-49460, KK139, G-AGNE	1949	'Iringa Pioneer'. Sold 1/53 as G-AGNE. Subsequently sold (possibly French Air Force)
*VP-KHV	Lockheed L18-08 Lodestar	2029	ZS-ASO, SAAF 1350, ZS-ASO	1950	'Mtwara Safari'. Sold in USA
*VP-KHW	Lockheed L18-08 Lodestar	2035	ZS-ASI, SAAF 1373, ZS-ASU	1950	'Tanga Safari'. Sold as ZS-DHK, subsequently SE-CDR and N6064V
*VP-KHX	Lockheed L18-08 Lodestar	2038	ZS-ASX, SAAF 239, ZS-ASX	1950	'Uganda Safari'. Sold as N94550
*VP-KHY	Lockheed L18-08 Lodestar	2047	ZS-ATB, SAAF 242, ZS-ATB	1950	'Kenya Safari'. Sold as N94547
*VP-KHZ	Lockheed L18-08 Lodestar	2049	ZS-ATC, SAAF 1375, ZS-ATC	1950	'Tanganyika Safari'. Sold as N94548 (not taken up), re-sold as CF-FYR. Destroyed at St Eugene, Ont. 26/12/54. (c/n wrongly quoted as 2048 by EAAC, perpetuated in Canadian records)
*VP-KIA	Lockheed L18-08 Lodestar	2050	ZS-ATD, SAAF 243, ZS-ATD	1950	'Mombasa Safari'. Sold as ZS-DHL, then VP-WCN.
*VP-KIB	Lockheed L18-08 Lodestar	2051	ZS-ATE, SAAF 244, ZS-ATE	1950	'Zanzibar Safari'. Sold as N94546.
VP-KIF	Douglas C-47B Dakota 4	14161/25606	43-48345, KJ822, G-AKDT	1950	'Mbeya Pioneer'. Returned as G-AKDT. Subsequently F-BGOU and ET-ACZ
VP-KJD	Macchi MB320	5910	none	1952	Sold 1955, then abroad as ZS-CBA.
VP-KJE	Piper PA-20 Pacer	20-820	none	1953	Sold 1954. Subsequently re-registered VR-TCE and 5H-AAS.
VP-KJG	Macchi MB320	5911	none	1952	Sold 1955, then abroad in Somaliland as I-MSO. Scrapped Milan 3/65.
VP-KJJ	Macchi MB320	5912	none	1952	Sold 1954. To Air Safaris Arusha 1955. Written off in crash at Mbeya 1962.
VP-KJP	Douglas C-47B Dakota 4	16077/32825	44-76493, KN402	1952	'Seyyid Said Bin Sultan'. Re-registered 5Y-AAD
VP-KJQ	Douglas C-47B Dakota 4	16096/32844	44-76512, KN418	1952	'Lord Delamere'. Re-registered 5Y-AAE.

* All converted by E.A.A. to Model 18-56 with Wright Cyclone G.205A engines

Reg'n	Type	C/N	Previous identity	Acq'd	Remarks
VP-KJR	Douglas C47B Dakota 4	16097/32845	44-76513, KN419	1952	'Sir John Kirke'. Re-registered 5X-AAQ.
VP-KJS	Douglas C47B Dakota 4	16463/33211	44-76879, KN581	1952	'J. Hanning Speke'. Re-registered 5X-AAR.
VP-KJT	Douglas C47B Dakota 4	16530/33278	44-76946, KN625	1952	'Joseph Thomson'. Destroyed by fire at Francistown 29/8/63.
VP-KJU	Douglas C47B Dakota 4	16577/33325	44-76993, KN638	1952	'Sagana II'. Re-registered 5Y-AAF.
VP-KKH	Douglas C47B Dakota 4	16820/33564	44-77236, KP266, G-AMSO	1953	'David Livingstone'. Crashed Mwenzi peak, Mt Kilimanjaro, 18/5/55.
VP-KKI	Douglas C47B Dakota 4	16207/32955	44-76623, KN478, G-AMST	1953	'Sir Richard Burton'. Re-registered 5H-AAL.
VP-KKJ	Consolidated Catalina 3	?	44-34082, VR-HDS, VT-DEX, SE-XAD, SE-BUB	1953	'Nannagani'. Survey flight to the Seychelles. Chartered for 'Mogambo' film. Sold in USA 1954.
VP-KLA	Douglas C47B Dakota 4	15880/33628	44-76296, KN322	1953	'James A. Grant'. Re-registered 5H-AAJ.
VP-KLC	Douglas C47B Dakota 4	14370/25815	43-48554, KJ876	1953	'Alexander M. Mackay'. Re-registered 5H-AAK.
VP-KMI	Airspeed AS65 Consul	5106	LB572, G-AIUX	1954	Ex-BOAC, used for twin-engined conversion training. Broken up 1957.
VP-KNS	DH89A Dragon Rapide	6492	R5964, G-AKOS	1955	Transferred to S.K.A.T. in 1960. Re-registered 5H-AAM.
VP-KNU	Douglas C47A Dakota 3	12166	42-92373, FZ611, ZS-BXI	1956	Leased from S.A.A. Restored as ZS-BXI in 1966.
VP-KNY	Canadair DC4-M	161	G-ALHO	1957	Crashed at Embakasi 4/11/62.
VP-KOI	Canadair DC4-M	152	G-ALHF	1957	Sold to Britair (E.A.) Ltd
VP-KOJ	Canadair DC4-M	159	G-ALHM	1957	Sold to Britair (E.A.) Ltd. Restored as G-ALHM. Broken up at Redhill 1966.
VP-KOT	Canadair DC4-M	156	G-ALHJ	1958	Restored to BOAC 2/2/58. Used for apprentice training at Heathrow. To Fire Section 1970.
VP-KOY	Canadair DC4-M	146	G-ALHD	1960	Registration not taken up. Re-allotted to a PA-22 Tri-Pacer.
VP-KPJ	DH106 Comet 4	6431	none	1960	Re-registered 5X-AAO.
VP-KPK	DH106 Comet 4	6433	none	1962	Re-registered 5H-AAF.
VP-KRL	DH106 Comet 4	6472	none	1962	Re-registered 5Y-AAA.
VP-KSA	Fokker F27 Friendship 200	10211	PH-FEA (Test reg'n.)	1962	Re-registered 5Y-AAB.
VP-KSB	Fokker F27 Friendship 200	10212	PH-FEB (Test reg'n.)	1962	Re-registered 5Y-AAC.
VP-KSC	Fokker F27 Friendship 200	10213	PH-FEC (Test reg'n.)	1962	Re-registered 5H-AAI.
VP-KTK	Fokker F27 Friendship 200	10241	PH-FFG (Test reg'n.)	1963	Re-registered 5X-AAP.
VP-KTS	Douglas C47B Dakota 4	15908/32656	44-76324, KN341, ZS-DHX, VR-TBJ	1963	Re-registered 5X-AAS.

E.A.A.C. Aircraft registered in Tanzania

Reg	Type	C/n	Prev ID	Year	Notes
5H-AAF	DH104 Comet 4	6433	VP-KPK	1960	Transferred to S.K.A.T. 1968. Sold to Dan-Air 11/70. d/d 6/1/71.
5H-AAI	Fokker F27 Friendship 200	10213	PH-FEC, VP-KSC	1962	To Kenya Airways 1977.
5H-AAJ	Douglas C-47B Dakota 4	15880/32628	44-76296, KN322, VP-KLA	1953	To Caspair re-registered 5Y-BBU.
5H-AAK	Douglas C-47B Dakota 4	14370/25815	43-48554, KJ876, VP-KLC	1953	
5H-AAL	Douglas C-47B Dakota 4	16207/32955	44-76623, KN478, G-AMST, VP-KKI	1953	To Caspair, re-registered 5Y-BBM
5H-AAM	DH89A Dragon Rapide	6492	R9564, G-AKOS, VP-KNS	1955	Registered to S.K.A.T. Burnt out Dar es Salaam 13/9/66.
5H-AAN	DH89A Dragon Rapide	6831	NR743, PH-RAF, VP-KEF	1947	Registered to S.K.A.T. Sold to A.D. Aviation, Nairobi 1967.
5H-MMT	Vickers Super VC10 1154	882	none	1966	Delivered 11/66. To RAF 30/9/78. Converted to VC10 K3 Registered ZA147.
5H-MNK	DHC-6 Twin Otter	40	none	1967	Sold in Canada 1973.
5H-MNR	DHC-6 Twin Otter	106	none	1968	Sold in Canada 1973.
5H-MOG	Vickers Super VC10 1154	885	none	1970	Delivered 3/70. To RAF 30/9/88. Converted to VC10 K3. Registered ZA150
5H-MOI	McDonnell Douglas DC-9-32	47430	none	1970	Delivered 12/70. To Kenya Airways 1977

E.A.A.C. aircraft registered in Uganda

Reg	Type	C/n	Prev ID	Year	Notes
5X-AAO	DH106 Comet 4	6431	VP-KPJ	1960	Transferred to S.K.A.T. 1968. Sold to Dan-Air, d/d 8/2/68.
5X-AAP	Fokker F27 Friendship 200	10241	PH-FFG, VP-KTK	1962	
5X-AAQ	Douglas C-47B Dakota 4	16097/32845	44-76513, KN419, VP-KJR	1952	Sold to Caspair (Sunbird Aviation). Re-registered 5Y-BBN.
5X-AAR	Douglas C-47B Dakota 4	16463/33211	44-76879, KN581, VP-KJS	1952	Sold to Air Malawi 31/1/68 as 7Q-YKN.
5X-AAS	Douglas C-47B Dakota 4	15908/32656	44-76324, KN341, ZS-DHX, VR-TBJ, VP-KTS	1963	Sold to Hunting Surveys 10/68 as 9J-RHZ. Re-registered A2-ZFD, 1970
5X-UVA	Vickers Super VC10 1154	881	none	1966	Delivered 9/66. Written off Addis Ababa, 18/4/1972.
5X-UVJ	Vickers Super VC10 1154	884	none	1969	Delivered 4/69. To RAF 30/9/88. Converted to VC10 K3 Registered ZA149.
5X-UVN	DHC-6 Twin Otter	181	none	1968	Sold in Canada 1973
5X-UVP	DHC-6 Twin Otter	182	none	1968	Sold in Canada 1973

5X-UVY	McDonnell Douglas DC-9-32	47478	none	1971	Delivered 2/71. To Kenya Airways 1977.
5X-UWM	Boeing 707-323CF	18689	?	1975	Delivered 15/5/75. To Simbair. Sold to Tradewinds and re-registered G-BFEO.

E.A.A.C. aircraft registered in Kenya

5Y-AAA	DH106 Comet 4	6472	VP-KRL	1962	Transferred to S.K.A.T. 1968. Sold to Dan-Air, d/d 8/2/71.
5Y-AAB	Fokker F27 Friendship 200	10211	PH-FEA, VP-KSA	1962	To Kenya Airways 1977.
5Y-AAC	Fokker F27 Friendship 200	10212	PH-FEB, VP-KSB	1962	To Kenya Airways 1977.
5Y-AAD	Douglas C47B Dakota 4	16077/32825	44-76493, KN402, VP-KJP	1952	Sold to Zambia Airways 6/2/68 as 9J-RGY.
5Y-AAE	Douglas C47B Dakota 4	16096/32844	44-76512, KN418, VP-KJQ	1952	Sold to Caspair/Sunbird/ Air Kenya
5Y-AAF	Douglas C47B Dakota 4	16577/33325	44-76993, KN638, VP-KJU	1952	
5Y-ADA	Vickers Super VC10 1154	883	none	1967	Delivered 3/67. To RAF 30/9/88. Converted to VC10 K3 Registered ZA148
5Y-ADD	DH106 Comet 4	6413	G-APDL	1965	Leased from BOAC 10/65-3/67.
5Y-AFU	DHC-6 Twin Otter				Registration not taken up.
5Y-AKX	McDonnell Douglas DC-9-15	45787	HB-IFE, N1793U, D-AMOR, N1793U	1969	Leased from McDonnell Douglas 11/69. Leasing contract cancelled before delivery of 5Y-AKY. Registrations re-alloted.
5Y-AKY	McDonnell Douglas DC-9-15	45785	HB-IFC, N1790U	1970	Leased from Dan-Air 9/1/70 - 21/3/70.
5Y-ALD	DH106 Comet 4	6412	G-APDK	1970	Leased from Dan-Air 22/2/70 - 12/70.
5Y-ALF	DH106 Comet 4	6406	G-APDE, 9M-AOE, 9V-BAU	1971	Delivered 2/71. To Kenya Airways 1977.
5Y-ALR	McDonnell Douglas DC-9-32	47468	none		
5Y-AMT	DH106 Comet 4	6405	G-APDD, 9M-AOD, G-APDD	1970	Leased from Dan-Air 28/12/70 - 22/2/71

List of Illustrations

1. Alan Cobham's Short Singapore 1, G-EBUP, on the River Medway near Rochester, prior to departure for Africa. November, 1927. .... Page 8

2. The Short Singapore 1 at anchor on Lake Victoria off Entebbe, with Baganda war canoes. February, 1928 .... Page 8

3. Armstrong Siddeley 'Genet' powered Avro Avian IVM of the Tanganyika Government Survey. One of two IVMs, G-AAUN, re-registered VR-TAA in September, 1931, this was the first civil aircraft to be imported into Tanganyika. This photo was annotated by Aubrey Francombe "Roberts doing a job of work!". Mr Roberts, seen swinging the prop' was one of three engineers working for the Survey Department. Circa 1930. (Mr Ian Francombe) .... Page 11

4. Imperial Airways Armstrong Whitworth XV, G-ABTI, *Atalanta*, (the fourth of its class), at Mbeya, Tanganyika Territory. This aircraft, commanded by Capt H.G. Brackley, flew the first proving flight to the Cape, departing Croydon 31 December, 1932. .... Page 15

5. Imperial Airways Handley Page HP 42, G-AAGX, *Hannibal*, being refuelled at Entebbe, Uganda. Circa mid-1930s. .... Page 16

6. Avro 619 'Five', VP-KAE, Knight of the Grail at Nairobi, with Tom Campbell Black (nearest aircraft). Circa 1929. (Capt Alec Noon) .... Page 21

7. Kisumu aerodrome, Kenya Colony. Handley Page HP 42, G-AAUC, *Horsa*, and Armstrong Whitworth AW XV, G-ABTH, *Andromeda*, in front of the Imperial Airways hangars. Prior to the introduction of the 'C' Class flying-boats in 1937, passengers for South Africa transferred from the HP 42s to the AW XVs for their onward journey. Mail for East African destinations was collected by Wilson Airways. .... Page 25

8. A DH84 Dragon, VP-KBA, of Wilson Airways at Zanzibar. Circa mid-1930s. .... Page 25

10. A DH89A Dragon Rapide of Wilson Airways. (Mr I. Francombe) .... Page 27

11. A DH90 Dragonfly takes off from a typical bush strip. .... (Mr I. Francombe) Page 27

12. The sign-post near Mbeya aerodrome, Tanganyika Territory. Circa 1930s. (Mr I. Francombe) .... Page 28

13. Aubrey Francombe stands beside VP-KCA, first of the two DH90 Dragonfly, four-passenger aircraft which Wilson Airways utilised for government charters in Uganda. There is no record of the identity of these officials, photographed at Masindi, together with members of the Verona Fathers mission. Circa 1938. (Mr Ian Francombe) Page 29

14. Watched by an askari, Aubrey Francombe fills in the paper work. The aircraft is the Wilson Airways DH84 Dragon 1, VP-KBA. Circa mid-1930s. (Mr Ian Francombe) .... Page 30

15. A DH90 Dragonfly of Wilson Airways lands in fading light.
    (Mr Ian Francombe) .... Page 31
16. DH80A Puss Moths VP-KAK and VP-KAY and DH85 Leopard Moth VP-KBP of Wilson Airways, on the beach at Lindi. Circa late 1930s
    (Wg Cdr A. Francombe) .... Page 32
17. The Short 'C' Class Empire flying-boat RMA *Canopus*. This aircraft departed Southampton on 2nd June, 1937 on the first Imperial Airways flying-boat service through to South Africa. .... Page 33
18. Wilson Airways advertisement, circa 1932. .... Page 34
19. Maasai warriors find shade beneath the wing of a DH85 Leopard Moth of Wilson Airways, circa 1935. .... Page 34
20. Imperial Airways advertisement for Armstrong Whitworth XV Atalanta services ex-Nairobi, circa 1934. .... Page 35
21. The 1938 advertisement for the Empire flying-boat services. .... Page 35
22. The African routes of Imperial Airways, South African Airways and Wilson Airways, circa 1938. .... Page 38
23. With a few months before outbreak of war, there was still time for an off-duty flight with the ladies. Aubrey Francombe with a Wilson Airways Puss Moth.
    (Mr I. Francombe) .... Page 39
24. DH85 Leopard Moth, VP-KBP after a crash at Iringa, 25th January, 1939.
    (Mr I. Francombe) .... Page 39
25. On 1 July, 1937 a DH90 Dragonfly of Wilson Airways carried the first "all-up" or unsurcharged air mail from Nairobi to connect with the northbound "C" class Empire flying-boat at Kisumu. At Nairobi aerodrome, for the occasion are: (l.to r.): Mr F. Birkitt, deputy postmaster-general; Mr M.C.P. Mostert, manager of Wilson Airways Ltd; Mr V.G. Crudge, Central African area manager, Imperial Airways; H.E. the Governor of Kenya, Air Chief Marshal Sir Robert Brooke-Popham; Mrs F.K. Wilson, OBE, chairman of Wilson Airways; and Lady Brooke-Popham. .... Page 40
26. A DH89A Dragon Rapide, or Dominie, of East African Airways. The photograph has been autographed by the pilots who flew these aircraft.
    (Capt R. Cartwright) .... Page 43
27. Captain Malin Sorsbie. (Baron Studios) .... Page 49
28. DH Dove Series 1, VP-KDF and VP-KDE, at Hatfield prior to delivery to East African Airways. February, 1948. (BAe Hatfield) .... Page 53
29. Lockheed L18 Lodestar, VP-KFC, RMA *Lake Albert*, on arrival at Entebbe from Nairobi. August, 1949. (Mr Tom Webb) .... Page 53
30. DH Dove, VP-KDE, at Mombasa. March, 1948 (BAe Hatfield) .... Page 55
31. DH Dove, VP-KDE, is refuelled at Nairobi West. March, 1948
    (BAe Hatfield) .... Page 55
32. A DH Dove at Nairobi West in 1948. The maintenance crew are L to R: Ian Keith, Terry Brown, R.'Dick' Wittingham, (not known), and Jack Marsh.
    (Mr R.A. Whittingham, FRAeS) .... Page 57

33. Engineer 'Dick' Whittingham attends to a troublesome engine on DH Dove, VP-KDF, while Captain Walter Hillary, R/O and young passengers seek shade under the wing. Tabora, December 16th, 1948. (R.A. Whittingham, FRAeS) .... Page 57

34. Archie Watkins in the war time rank of flight lieutenant in the Royal Air Force. His pilot's wings show that he was a member of the Auxiliary Air Unit. (Mr Cliff Sarginson) .... Page 58

35. DH89A Dragon Rapide, VP-KED. Tanganyika, 1948
   (R.A. Whittingham, FRAeS) .... Page 59

36. DH89A Dragon Rapide, VP-KEA and L18 Lodestar at Kongwa, October, 1948. (Mr R.A. Whittingham, FRAeS) .... Page 59

37. Captain Reg Cartwright with DH89A Dragon Rapide at Tororo, Uganda in 1950. (Capt R. Cartwright) .... Page 67

38. The Lockheed L18 Lodestar, VP-KHX, RMA *Uganda Safari*, on the dry bed of Lake Amboseli, on 14th February, 1950. This aircraft was purchased from South African Airways. The vehicles in the photo are ex-WW2 trucks converted to safari cars, with racks on the roof to carry luggage and stores. The flight was carried out to inspect the landing strip before bringing in a group of American tourists the following day. This was, perhaps, the first tourist promotion in East Africa - prior to this, only big-game hunters were catered for. The vehicles pictured belonged to Kerr and Downey, pioneers of safaris and game-park tours. The figure on the right, with his arm on the propeller, was professional hunter Eddie Grafton; one side of his face was paralysed after being mauled by a buffalo, which hunted him after being wounded. The hoof tracks are from Maasai cattle. B.O.A.C./Capt Morris. .... Page 70

39. The East African Airways servicing crew, Nairobi West, Christmas Eve, 1950. Back row: Sid Cox, Wally Plunkett, Dick Wright, Terry McBreaty, (not recognised), Eric Smith. Front row: Tosh Green, Dickie Maidens, Al Bennett, Gus van Schalkwyk, Ginger Brewer, Ron Herbert(?). (Capt Brewer) .... Page 75

40. East African Airways engineers at Dar es Salaam, 1953. Standing, L to R: George Templeman, Sid Cox. Seated: Edwin 'Tubby' Hobday, Tommy Webb, together with five African helpers. (Mr T. Webb) .... Page 76

41. Viewed across the four Bristol Hercules 637 engines of a B.O.A.C. Short Solent class flying-boat moored in Dar es Salaam harbour, the Lutheran church can be seen in the background. E.A.A.C. engineer Tom Webb would accompany the flight from Lake Naivasha for the Thursday night-stop. Circa 1950.
   (Mr T. Webb) .... Page 78

42. Airborne from Lake Naivasha, the last B.O.A.C. Short Solent service, commanded by Captain Deadman, departs for Southampton. September, 1950.
   (Mr T. Webb) .... Page 79

43. At Tananarive, 3rd February, 1951. L to R: R/O from Prince Aly Khan's Dove, F/O G.W. 'Mitch' Mitchell, R/O Derek Rhodes, Captain Benjamin (of the DH Dove). (Capt Mitchell) .... Page 81

44. Rita Hayworth with her husband Prince Aly Khan at Tananarive, 4th February, 1951. (Capt Brewer) .... Page 82

45. Rita Hayworth poses for Ginger Brewer at Nairobi West. (Capt Brewer) ...... Page 82

46. At Mombasa, 15th August, 1954. L to R: Steward Duffell, Capt G.W. Mitchell, Prince Karim Aga, Prince Amin Aga, F/O Pieter van Emmenis, Captain 'Dickie' Bird. (Capt Mitchell) .... Page 82

47. At Lumbo, 22nd September, 1954, prior to departure for Lindi—Dar es Salaam-Nairobi. L to R: Capt G.W. Mitchell, F/O Alan Handford-Rice, D.E.T.A. airport manager 'Louie', R/O Russ Blakely. (Capt Mitchell) .... Page 84

48. The Dakota, VP-KIF, stuck firmly in the mud, with the local labour preparing to start work. (Capt Leslie) .... Page 88

49. The problem is assessed by the experts while the convicts and their guards look on. (Capt Leslie) .... Page 88

50. Dakota VP-KHK, RMA Sagana, with the crew of the royal flight: Captain A.N. Francombe, Captain W. Watson, Radio Officer Ivan Morris, Steward George Matthews. Behind them the engineering personnel who had completely overhauled and prepared the aircraft. (Capt E.Morris) .... Page 101

51. Dakota VP-KLA, RMA *James A. Grant*, at Moshi, Tanganyika, 1953. Mt Kilimanjaro visible in the background. (Capt Leslie) .... Page 103

52. Ginger Brewer with Macchi test pilot Commandante Carristiato, and the MB320 VP-KJD, at Varese. February, 1952. (Capt Brewer) .... Page 106

53. Archie Watkins and Douglas Stewart at Nairobi West. .... Page 107

54. ...They were to proceed to the most northerly part of Kenya, to position 'X'... it was north-east of Lokitaung... and a couple of miles from the borders of Ethiopia and the Sudan. (Map) .... Page 122

55. Pages from Captain Leslie's Log Book, with the entry for 15th July, 1953. .... Page 124

56. DH89A, VP-KCY, shown at Dar es Salaam, with engineer Tommy Webb and local helpers. Circa mid- 1950s. (Mr T. Webb) .... Page 126

57. Dakota VP-KKI, RMA *Sir Richard Burton*, being refuelled at Hargeisa, British Somaliland, 1953. (Capt Mitchell) .... Page 128

58. At Chingola copper mine, Northern Rhodesia. The Dakota was chartered by a United Kingdom Parliamentary group touring Central Africa. The crew used the DC3 wing as a diving-board. Seated by the pool: R/O Curly Payne, Stewardess Dora Young, F/O Alan Burkitt. 5th September, 1954. (Capt Leslie) .... Page 130

59. The acceptance of DC3 VP-KJR at Tollerton on 3rd June, 1952. Captain Pat Travers shakes hands with Captain G.W. 'Mitch' Mitchell, accompanied by N/O Paddy Murray. Two Field Aviation staff look on. (Capt Mitchell) .... Page 136

60. Dakota VP-KJT, RMA *Joseph Thomson*. The eternal snows of Mt Kilimanjaro (19,340ft), in the background. (Capt Brewer) .... Page 137

61. The cockpit of DC3, VP-KJU *Sagana II*, photographed during a demonstration flight to Salisbury in July, 1954, two months after the royal flights. (Capt Morris) .... Page 143

62. The Royal Flight aircraft VP-KJU, RMA Sagana II, at Jinja, Uganda, on 29th April, 1954. The crew L to R: E/O Cawthorne, F/O Pat Travers, Captain Eric Morris, R/O Derek Rhodes, Steward George Matthews. Although the Royal

Standard is flying, the Queen was inspecting the 5th Battalion, Kings African Rifles at the time the photograph was taken. (Capt E. Morris/B.O.A.C.) ... Page 143

63. The royal party including the Governor of Uganda, Sir Andrew Cohen (in full dress), followed by his ADC, board *Sagana II*. They are seen off by Captain Malin Sorsbie, Sir Alfred Vincent and Mr Hugh Dawson (airport manager, Entebbe). A security officer stands near the tail.
(B.O.A.C./Capt Morris) .... Page 144

64. Her Majesty the Queen and Prince Philip board *Sagana II* at Entebbe, saluted by E.A.A.C. senior station officer Entebbe, 'Robin Grant. 29th April, 1954.
(B.O.A.C./Capt Morris) .... Page 144

65. Chocks away, as *Sagana II*, Royal Standard flying, prepares to taxi at Entebbe, bound for Jinja. 'Spud' Murphy supervises the ground-crew. For moments during take-off, Lake-birds and shrike, seeking worms after a series of showers, presented a hazard to Captain E. Morris. 29th April, 1954.
(B.O.A.C./Capt Morris) .... Page 145

66. The internal territorial ticket issued to Her Majesty the Queen. Written in the days before ball-point pens, it was completed in indelible pencil. The fare paid is shown as 'Free'! (courtesy of Capt E. Morris) .... Page 145

67. The interior of *Sagana II*, looking forward. The telephone intercom to the cockpit can be seen, between the Queen's and the Duke of Edinburgh's seats.
(Capt E. Morris) .... Page 146

68. The interior looking aft. The Queen sat facing forward, opposite the Duke of Edinburgh (left of picture). Decorative pictures can be seen in the window recesses. The linen head rest covers were embroidered with the ER monogram. Steward Matthews served only canned orange juice during the flight, opened in the cabin, as a security precaution against poisoning. (Capt E. Morris) ..... Page 146

69. The passenger manifest issued on the occasion of the Royal Flight from Entebbe to Jinja, 29th April, 1954. (courtesy of Capt E. Morris) .... Page 147

70. George Leslie bought this 1951 Standard 8 tourer at a bargain price - £75, in Tanga. With no seats fitted in the Dakota, he was able to bring it home to Nairobi as 'crew baggage'. 12th September, 1954. (Capt Leslie) .... Page 150

71. Dickie Waters supervises the off-load of the Standard 8 at Nairobi West.
(Capt Leslie) .... Page 150

72. The crew of VP-KJU at Durban during 'Wings Week' in July, 1954. L to R: R/O Paddy Murray, F/O Pieter von Emmenis, Captain Eric Morris. "By this time Sagana II (VP-KJU) was part of me" said Morris "She seemed to have accepted me and we just throbbed a singular beat together. She seemed to glide herself to a 'kiss' landing, quite differently to that first at Jinja with the Queen on board, when she (Sagana) made it known that it was neither Her Majesty nor the fellow controlling her that was playing the most important part of the whole Pageantry."
(Capt Morris) .... Page 152

73. Snow covered Kibo and Mwenzi, the twin peaks of Mt Kilimanjaro. The crash site is on the top of the left-hand ridge of Mwenzi. (Capt Brewer) .... Page 156

74. A photograph of the snow clad crater of Kibo, taken from a Lancastrian (4 Rolls-Royce Merlins) of Skyways of London, by C.E. Smith, at that

time a flight engineer with the airline. Circa 1947.
(Mr Tim Nightingale) .... Page 157

75. The scene of the wreckage of VP-KKH, at about 17,000ft up on Mwenzi peak. The separated tail-plane can be clearly seen. (Capt Brewer) .... Page 158

76. DC3 Dakota 4, VP-KLC, RMA *Alexander M. Mackay*, at Dar es Salaam.
(Mr T. Webb) .... Page 165

77. The main highlight of the year 1956 was the visit of Her Royal Highness the Princess Margaret to the East African Territories. Months of detailed planning by E.A.A.C. and the Government ensured that the successful programme of charter flights and airport arrangements gained high praise. A Royal Air Force Heron of the Queen's Flight is seen at Mwanza, where the Princess was greeted by Sir Edward Twining, Governor of Tanganyika. The senior officer responsible for E.A.A.C. ground handling arrangements was Bill Ainscough, seen here presenting a smart salute. (Mr W. Ainscough) .... Page 167

78. Captain Roger Drew and F/O Ginger Brewer at the controls of Dakota VP-KKI, RMA *Sir Richard Burton*. The panel indicates that the aircraft was in flight.
(Capt Brewer) .... Page 169

79. Photographed at Dar es Salaam in February, 1956, Edward Onyango Were was the first African steward to be employed on international services. He is shown with Captain Roger Drew and F/O Ginger Brewer. .... Page 171

80. Captain Phil Henn, enjoying the luxury of first class travel, accompanied by Diana Howard-Williams (E.A.A. public relations officer). The steward is Arthur Street. (Capt A. Ratcliffe) .... Page 172

81. Nairobi West airport, looking north. The cars indicate that the photograph was taken on the occasion of an annual air-show. (*E.A.Standard*) .... Page 175

82. The B.O.A.C. Constellation back-tracks past the Nairobi West control tower.
(Capt A. Ratcliffe) .... Page 176

83. The giant airliner in front of the E.A.A.C. maintenance hangars, workshop and administration building at Wilson airport. (Mr John Hudson) .... Page 177

84. The East African Airways DC4-M Canadair, VP-KNY, starting engines at Dar es Salaam. (Mr T. Webb) .... Page 179

85. Passing Mt Kilimanjaro, the view from the cockpit of a Canadair.
(Capt Brewer) .... Page 182

86. First Officer Ginger Brewer in the right-hand seat of a Canadair.
(Capt Brewer) .... Page 183

87. Captain G.W. 'Mitch' Mitchell in the new B.O.A.C. style uniform which was introduced for the overseas Canadair services. (Capt Mitchell) .... Page 184

88. Captain Peter Cooke. .... Page 185

89. Engineer Officer Franz Margadant .... Page 185

90. Captain Tug Wilson (1960) .... Page 189

91. Looking across Nairobi towards Ol Donyo Sabuk, which rises 2,144ft above ground level. Author. .... Page 195

92. ...pilots used the AA road maps, compiled after the war... .... Page 197

93. The road junction familiar to passengers and crew driving from the airport at Embakasi during the 1950s and 60s. (Author) .... Page 201

94. Col M.C.P. 'Mossie' Mostert stands between Mrs Gay Ainscough and the millionth E.A.A.C. passenger, Mr Stan Young, who was presented at a small reception with a silver cigarette box. On the right stands E.A.A.C. Chief Engineer, Mr A.E. 'Robbie' Robinson. Circa 1958. (Mr W. Ainscough) .... Page 202

95. The de Havilland Comet 4, VP-KPK, of East African Airways, airborne from Hatfield prior to delivery. The new E.A.A.C. logo style had not yet been fully decided. A mixture of B.O.A.C. and E.A.A.C. styles is evident. (de Havilland) .... Page 211

96. Members of the East African Airways course at Hatfield, March, 1960. L to R: (Partially obscured) Capt Bill Fumerton, (leaning on wheels) ex-N/O Frank Warren, ex-N/O Tim Nightingale, DH Instructor, Capt Roger Drew, Capt Leo Davidson, F/E Bill Cawthorne, ex-ground engineer Derek Taylor, ex-N/O Paddy Murray, F/O Larry Allen, Capt Reg Cartwright, F/O Dave Dempster, F/O Ginger Brewer. F/O Ivan Morris stands hidden behind Brewer. The N/Os and Derek Taylor had been selected for training as flight engineers. It was thought navigators would become redundant with the advent of the Comet. (de Havilland/Capt Brewer) .... Page 212

97. Comet 4, VP-KPJ, landing at Shannon during crew training. August, 1960. (Capt Brewer) .... Page 213

98. de Havilland Comet 4, VP-KPJ, showing the definitive E.A.A.C. blue and white livery and logo style. (BAe Hatfield) .... Page 214

99. Passengers disembark from VP-KPJ, the inaugural Comet 4 arrival at Nairobi on 18th September, 1960. (E.A. Standard) .... Page 215

100. Captain Jack Bicknell. (Capt Ratcliffe) .... Page 216

101. The crew of VP-KPJ, the first East African Airways Comet into Johannesburg. L to R: Steward J. Malyon, Steward P.J. Maclaughlin, E/O Watts, Stewardess Barbara Seymour, F/O J.H. 'Ginger' Brewer, Captain Roger Drew, Stewardess L. Strang, N/O D.J. Griffiths, N/O R.A. Foster. .... Page 216

102. Comet 4, VP-KPK, airborne from Entebbe. 1964. (Mr T. Webb) .... Page 217

103. Comet 4, VP-KPJ, at Entebbe. 1964. (Mr T. Webb) .... Page 217

104. Captain Pat Travers. (Capt Ratcliffe.) .... Page 219

105. A DC4M Canadair of E.A.A.C., VP-KNY, at Plaisance airport, Mauritius, where, prior to independence from Britain, trooping contracts were undertaken in 1960 to fly British officers and NCOs and 250 soldiers of the Tanganyika Battalion of the Kings African Rifles, and their families, back to Dar es Salaam. VP-KNY flew ten 14 hour round trips on ten consecutive days without a minutes delay. This remarkable achievement by an elderly aircraft was tribute to the airline's maintenance excellence and the work of Ron Gander and his crew who carried out the daily maintenance at Dar es Salaam and Plaisance. Ground Engineer Jock Glass, in white overalls, supervises the departure. (Mr J.H. Glass) .... Page 222

106. H.E. the Governor of Kenya, Sir Patrick Renison, awards Captain Peter Cunningham with the Queen's Commendation for Valuable Services in the Air, at Government House, Nairobi, 27th May 1961. .... Page 225

APPENDICES · 467

107. The third production East African Airways Fokker F27 'Friendship', VP-KSC (re-registered 5H-AAI). This photograph was taken prior to delivery, the aircraft being test flown with the Dutch registration PH-FEC. (Fokker).. Page 241

108. Captain Tom Dornan. (Capt Ratcliffe) .... Page 244

109. East African continued to provide charter aircraft for the spiritual leader of the Ismaili community. The new Aga Khan is shown shaking hands with Asian Stewardess Zarina Keshavjee after a two-week charter covering some 2,560 miles and 15 hours flying throughout Kenya, Uganda and Tanzania. The remainder of the DC3 crew are: L to R: Captain Alan Ratcliffe, F/O Jim Cole and Purser Roy Prout. May, 1961. (Capt Ratcliffe) .... Page 246

110. Colonel M.C.P. Mostert and Mr A. Gill represented E.A.A.C. at the Tanganyika independence celebrations. Shown at Dar es Salaam, a Comet 4 in the background, are L to R: Capt R. Drew, Mrs Gill, Col M.C.P. Mostert, Mrs Joan Mackenzie, Mr A. Mackenzie (manager Tanganyika) Capt P. Cooke, Mr A. Gill. (Mr A. Mackenzie) .... Page 247

111. At Schipol, following the signing of the F27 acceptance, L to R: Captain Lou Starling, Mr Ron Gander (EAA Engineering), Captain Tom Dornan, Mr C.E. Smith. November, 1962. (Fokker) .... Page 253

112. Fokker F27 Friendship, VP-KSA, at Dar es Salaam, 1962. .... Page 254

113. Mrs Florence K. Wilson receives a tribute from Mr Muliro, Kenya Minister for Commerce, Industry and Communications, at the unveiling ceremony at the renamed Wilson Airport. Sir Alfred Vincent stands on the left of the picture. 25th January, 1962. (E.A. Standard) .... Page 256

114. The plaque which was unveiled by Mrs Wilson. E.A. Standard .... Page 256

115. Captain Bill Fumerton (Mrs Barbara Fumerton) .... Page 258

116. Under a darkening sky, the gleaming white upper surfaces of Comet 4, VP-KRL, are displayed in this photograph taken at Embakasi in 1963. Parked alongside is F27 Friendship, VP-KSA, which had been delivered the previous year. (Mr Tim Nightingale) .... Page 261

117. HRH the Duke of Edinburgh takes leave of the crew at Khartoum, following the Fokker Friendship flights associated with independence celebrations in Zanzibar and Kenya. L to R: Captain Peter Cunningham, Captain Lou Starling, licensed ground engineer Ray Kearns, (in uniform for the occasion, on which he accompanied the aircraft to Khartoum, in case repairs were necessary), Purser Gordon Evans, Steward John Muthiani. The obscured figure last in line was David Drummond, the EAA chief of security.
(Capt Peter Cunningham) .... Page 264

118. Captain Leo Davidson at the controls of the Comet 4. .... Page 270

119. A highly polished Comet 4 is admired by three young passengers. Nairobi, 1964. .... Page 272

120. Stewardesses Rosie Chettyar, Naomi Amakowa and Sheila Smith in the B.O.A.C. style uniform in April, 1964. Note experimental logo on the fin of F27, 5H-AAI. .... Page 273

121. After a Comet night-flight from London, stewardesses Janet Chamberlain and Mary Loe on arrival at Nairobi. (Mrs Mary Breuker née Loe) ...... Page 274

122. The Dakota, VP-KJP, at Kilwa following the accident on 27th April, 1964, in which the propeller blades sliced through the fuselage, killing Captain Gene Brokensha. The aircraft was repaired by East African Airways and was later sold, in 1968, to Zambia Airways. (Mr Cliff Sarginson) .... Page 282

123. As at Tanga, thirteen years earlier, convicts were employed to assist the engineers in pulling VP- KPJ out of the soft ground on the verge of Kilwa's grass runway. (Mr Cliff Sarginson) .... Page 282

124. The new uniforms, shown by Iris Breidenbend and an Asian and African stewardess. The sign-post was a familiar land mark to travellers, as was the waving base above the departure gate at Nairobi's old Embakasi airport. .... Page 284

125. With a Comet 4 in the background, stewardesses: Mary Muganga, Jennie Dickson, Chief Stewardess Una Buchanan and, showing the specially designed sari uniform for the Asian girls, Priscilla De Souza. Mrs Jennie Hartley née Dickson) .... Page 285

126. The contract for the Super VC10's is signed at Nairobi, March, 1965. L to R, seated: Mr A.V. Gill, Capt P.A. Travers, AVM Sir Geoffrey Tuttle (vice-chairman BAC), Chief Fundikira, Mr P.K. Jani. Standing are members of the British Aircraft Corporation, including Mr Ron Bailey and Mr R. Phillips next to Mr S.G. Choppin, E.A.A.C. financial controller, on the extreme right. (E.A.A.C.) .... Page 293

127. East African Airways' first Super VC 10, 5X-UVA, lands at Wisley on its maiden flight from Brooklands. 15th September, 1966. 5X-UVA was fitted with a set of Conway 540 engines, borrowed from a Standard VC10, for the maiden flight, as her 550-B engines were not ready in time. (BAC/E.A. Standard) ...... Page 294

128. At Brooklands, 1966. 5X-UVA prior to completion. (Capt Leslie) .... Page 295

129. The interior, looking aft, of 5X-UVA, prior to the fitting of seats. The cargo door lifting arm can be seen above the windows on the right of the picture. (Capt Leslie) .... Page 296

130. Super VC10, 5X-UVA lands at Entebbe's lake-side airport. 1966. (E.A. Standard) .... Page 298

131. Captain Bob Ainsworth at the controls of Super VC10, 5Y-ADA. .... Page 299

132. Comet 4, 5H-AAF, at Blantyre, Malawi, 17th February, 1966. (E.A. Standard) .... Page 300

133. A Comet 4 arrives at Entebbe from London. 20th May, 1966. (Author) ..... Page 301

134. DC3 Dakota, 5H-AAJ (formerly VP-KLA, RMA *James A. Grant*) at Entebbe, May, 1966. (Author) .... Page 303

135. A Twin Otter, Comet 4 and two Super VC10s on the apron at Nairobi's Embakasi airport. 1967. .... Page 305

136. Super VC10, 5Y-ADA, at Entebbe after the pilot had failed to complete a 180 degree turn in order to back-track after landing. The wheels sank into the tarmac. (Mr T. Webb) .... Page 307

APPENDICES · 469

137. The starboard undercarriage bogie of 5Y-ADA, embedded in the soft tarmac. (Mr T. Webb) .... Page 307

138. Twenty-five years after the flame-out incident, 5Y-ADA is pictured at Boscombe Down, in service with the Royal Air Force. Now a K3 tanker, ZA148, she is fitted with refuelling drogue attachments which can be seen below the wings and under the rear fuselage. 14th June, 1992. (Author) .... Page 310

139. Captain H. 'Tug' Wilson some three years before retirement. (Capt Wilson) .... Page 313

140. DHC-9 Twin Otter, 5H-MNK, being turned round at Entebbe, with evidence of full employment. (Mr T.Webb) .... Page 320

141. Captain Dennis Jackson. .... Page 326

142. Pope Paul VI on the flight-deck of 5X-UVJ. Captain Ainscow stands behind as Captain 'Mitch' Mitchell explains features of the aircraft to His Holiness. F/O Dave Dempster is in the right-hand seat. .... Page 330

143. The special bed, loaned by B.O.A.C., used by the Pope and H.M. the Queen, on different occasions. (Mr Tim Nightingale) .... Page 331

144. Pope Paul VI spoke with each of the crew members: With Flight Engineer Tim Nightingale. .... Page 332

145. With F/O Dave Dempster .... Page 332

146. With Captain Mitchell .... Page 333

147. Viewed through the cockpit window, the reception crowd waits for the Pope to disembark. .... Page 333

148. Colonel Idi Amin descends the aircraft steps after inspecting 5X-UVJ. It would be another 17 months before he seized power in Uganda. (Capt Mitchell) .... Page 334

149. Idi Amin dominates this group of Ugandan army officers talking with Capt Mitchell and Flight Navigator(navigation superintendent) Dave Griffiths. .... Page 335

150. Prior to the return flight of Pope Paul on 2nd August, 1969, Chief Stewardess Ruth Lutale, Rome ground hostess Nancy Leri and Senior Stewardess Kathy Baguley at Entebbe. .... Page 335

151. At the completion of the Pope's return flight to Rome, the crew relax at the ENALC hotel. L to R: Chief Steward John Abilla, Chief Stewardess Ruth Lutale, Purser Frank Morrison, Senior Stewardess Kathy Baguley, Captain Ian Ainscow, Stewardess Elleinor Salingboe, Stewardess Mary Muganga, E/O Tim Nightingale, F/O Dave Dempster (back to camera). .... Page 336

152. Mr C.E. Smith, with his wife and daughter, outside Buckingham Palace, following his investiture with the MBE. .... Page 340

153. East African Airways Super VC10, 5H-MOG, the last VC10 to be built, takes-off for the first time on its short journey from Brooklands to Wisley, 16th February, 1970. (BAC) .... Page 347

154. Captain E. 'Ted' Imison. .... Page 349

155. Captain George Leslie. .... Page 350

156. At the McDonnell Douglas factory at Long Beach, California in September, 1970. Watched by Chief Stewardess Ruth Lutale, Captain Alan Ratcliffe and Captain Ian Cowie demand 'baksheesh' as the MD executive suggests a photograph in front of the prototype DC10. It was widely rumoured that bribes had been paid to E.A.A. board members in connection with the DC-9 purchase. .... Page 353

157. The Entebbe terminal building, photographed in 1966.(Author) .... Page 357

158. The author at Entebbe in 1966, and the control tower as it remained in 1971. (Author) .... Page 358

159. The Lake Victoria Hotel, Entebbe. (Author) .... Page 359

160. Colonel Bruce R. Mackenzie. .... Page 372

161. MD DC-9s, 5X-UVY (foreground) and 5Y-ALR at Nairobi's Embakasi airport. (Capt Ricketts) .... Page 375

162. MD DC-9 5Y-ALR at Chileka airport, Blantyre, Malawi. (Capt Ratcliffe) .... Page 376

163. The photograph below, taken in 1948 in the E.A.A.C. hangar at Nairobi West contrasts with the scene twenty-five years later, as Super VC10 5X-UVJ undergoes a major check in the large maintenance facility at Embakasi. The changes which took place in the years since 1948, in East African's engineering workshops, are well illustrated by these photographs. .... Page 377

164. The DH Dove VP-KEJ at Nairobi West in 1948 (L to R: name unknown, 'Dick' Whittingham, Terry Brown, Ian Keith and Terry McBreaty). (Mr R.A. Whittingham FRAeS) .... Page 377

165. The cabin window frames above the wing centre-section of 5X-UVA stand out above the burned-out wreckage of the once proud airliner. (E.A. Standard) .... Page 397

166. The tail-plane and engines of 5X-UVA remained intact. (E.A. Standard) ...... Page 397

167. Captain Trevor Hill, operations director, surveys the wreckage of 5X-UVA. (E.A. Standard) .... Page 398

168. Captain Trevor Hill. (Capt A.Ratcliffe) .... Page 409

169. DHC-6 Twin Otter, 5X-UVN at Tanga. (Capt Ricketts) .... Page 412

170. Turkana people pose in front of Twin Otter 5X-UVP during a Wing Safari stop at Lake Rudolf (Turkana). 1969. .... Page 413

171. Captain Russell 'Rusty' Bowker-Douglass. .... Page 414

172. Ugandan Detention Order: Mr Tom Webb .... Page 431

173. Ugandan Deportation Order: Mr Tom Webb .... Page 432

174. Ugandan registered F27 Friendship, 5X-AAP, takes-off from Zanzibar, late 1976. The Kenyan flag has been removed from the fin logo. (Capt Ricketts) ...... Page 437

175. East African Airways aircraft stand idle on the tarmac at Nairobi Airport on 26th January, 1971, when all flights were refused permission to operate due to non-payment of landing fees. .... Page 440

COLOUR GROUP

176. Super VC10, 5X-UVA (BAC)
177. Super VC10, 5X-UVA (BAC)
178. Fokker F27 Friendship, 5Y-AAB, at Moshi, Tanzania, 15th Sept 1969. (Author)
179. McDonnell Douglas DC-9, 5H-MOI (MD/Capt Ratcliffe)
180. Super VC10 5H-MOG at Filton after delivery to BAC, the last flight in East African Airways colours. 3rd August, 1977. (Capt Ricketts)
181. 5H-MOG parked beside a British Airways Concorde at Filton. (Capt Ricketts)
182. Formerly 5X-UVJ, one of four ex-East African Airways Super VC10 K3 tankers in service with the Royal Air Force. (C British Crown copyright 1992/MOD reproduced with the permission of the Controller of her Britannic Majesty's Stationery office)
183. Flanked by a Tornado, Super VC10 K3 tanker ZA 149 (5X-UVJ)takes up station to receive fuel from a Tristar tanker of the Royal Air Force. (C British Crown copyright 1992/MOD reproduced with the permission of the Controller of her Britannic Majesty's Stationery office).

INDEX

A
Acharya Travel: 410
Addis Ababa: 274, 283, 311, 327, 338, 341, *crash of SVC10, 5X-UVA*: **394-395, 399-401,** 423, 424
Adeane, GCVO KCB Lt-Col Rt Hon Sir Michael: 142
Aden: 50, 95, 98, 113, 178, 183, 184, 188-191, 193, 199, 203, 209, 227,234, 242, 250, 265, 285, 287, 298, 306, 316, 327
African Queen, The :115, 139
African Wharfage Company: 30
Aga Khan, HE The: 80,81, 229
Ahamed Bros, Nairobi: 69
Ainscough, Mr W.T. 'Bill': 167, 202, 230
Ainscow, Capt Ian: 130, 238, 329, 330, 336, 351
Ainsworth Capt Bob: 49-52, 174, 220, 238, 239, 299, 386, 442
Aircraft:
  A300-B, Airbus: 433
  Atalanta, Armstrong Whitworth XV: 12, 15, 25, 36, 37
  Avian, Avro: 10, 12, 22, 45
  Avro 619 *'Five'*: 20, 22
  Avro 621, *Tutor*: 12
  Avro 748, 240
  BAC 111: 320
  Boeing 707: 276, *VC10 comparisons*: **290-293**, 327, 356, *B707-323CF freighter*: **424-426**, 430, 434, 444
  Boeing 737: 320
  Boeing 757: 445
  Boeing 747: 293,348, *wet lease from Aer Lingus*: 422
  Britannia, Bristol: 104, 203, *charter of BOAC Britannia 312*: **205, 221,** 238, 290, 374, 410
  Calcutta, Short flying-boat: 13, 14
  Canadair CL-44: 410
  Canadair DC4-M (*Argonaut*): 102, 126, 153, 166-168, 174, 178, 179, 181-185, 187-195, 199, 203, 205, 207, 208, 209, 213, 219, 220, 221, 222, 231, 242, 243-245, 266, 280, 288, 425
  Caravelle, Aerospatiale: 291
  Catalina, Consolidated flying-boat (amphibian): 109-117
  Comet airliner: see DH106
  Constellation, Lockheed: 79, 175, *at Nairobi West*: **176-178**, 188, 200, 207
  Consul, Airspeed: 49, 130
  Convair 240: 153
  DC3, Douglas (C-47) *Dakota*: 63, 64, 66, 67, 76, *first operated by EAAC*: **83**, 85, 94, 95, 96, 100, 102-104, 108, 109, 116, 119-121, 123, 125-134, 135, 136-138, 142, 143, 149, 150, 151, 152, 155, 157, 159-163, 165-168, 169, 170, 172, 176-178, 185, 187, 188, 191, 194, 196, 198, 199, 203, 219, 220, 221, 223, 224, 229, 231, 234, 237, 238, 240-242, 246, 250-252, 259, 265, 266, 268, 276, 279, 281, 282, 288, 302, 303, 305, 306, 315, 321, 323, 338, 349, 354, 356, 362-365, 376, 392, 404, 420, 426, 427
  DC4, Douglas (*Skymaster*): 58, 65, 79, 174
  DC6, Douglas: 65, 136, 174, 175, 207
  DC8, Douglas: 276, 406, 430
  DC-9, McDonnell Douglas: 312, 320, 352, 353, 365, 375, 376, 399, 402-405, 410, 419, 420, 425-427, 429, 439, 440
  DC-10, McDonnell Douglas: 353, 425
  De Havilland:
    DH51 (*Miss Kenya*): 18, 19, 201
    DH60 *Moth Major*: 7, 39
    DH60G *Gipsy Moth*: 22, 23, 26, 39
    DH66 *Hercules*:12, 13
    DH80A *Puss Moth*: 13, 21, 22, 23, 24, 26, 30, 32, 35, 39, 40, 45
    DH84 *Dragon*: 25-27, 30, 40
    DH85 *Leopard Moth*: 28, 32, 34, 39, 40
    DH88 *Comet* racer: 21, 35

INDEX · 473

DH89A *Dragon Rapide* (*RAF name Dominie*): 21, 26, 27, 39, 40, 43, 46-47, 48, 50, 51, 59, 60, 62, 63, 64-67, 68, 69, 91, 106, 108, 126, 137, 196, 203, 271, 288, 304, 305, 323
DH90 *Dragonfly*: 26, 27, 29, 31, 40, 91
DH104 *Dove*: 53, 54, 55, 56, 57, 63, 64, 65, 80, 81, 377
DH106 *Comet* airliners: 98, 104, 118, 129, 186, 201, 204, 205, 207, 209-221, 223, 226, 227, 229, 230, 233, 234, 235,237, 239, 242-245, 247, 249, 250, 252, 254, 255, 257, 258, 259, 261, 265, 270, 272, 274, 275, 276, 277, 280, 281, 283, 285-289, 290, 291, 299-302, 304-306, 312, 313, 315, 316, 318, 320-324, 326, 337, 341, 345, 346, 352, 354, 364, 410
DHC-6 *Twin Otter*: 305, 306, 317, 320, 322, 323, 339, 354, 391, 392,403, 412-415
Empire, Short 'C' Class flying-boat:14-15,16-17, 25,31,32,33,36-37,40,85,203
Friendship, Fokker F27: 240, 241, 251-255, 261, 263-265, 268, 273, 274, 279-281, 301, 302, 304, 306,315, 321-324, 338, 339, 349, 354, 374, 376, 391, 415, 419, 420, 426, 437, 440
Harvard, North American T6: 207
Herald, Handley Page: 240
Hermes, Handley Page: 67, 77, 79, 80, 104, 105, 129
HP42, Handley Page: 12, 14, 16, 25
IL62, Ilyushin: 336-337
Kent, Short flying-boat: 14, 32
Lancaster, Avro: 207
Lancastrian, Avro: 157
Lockheed 10, *Electra*: 90
Lockheed 14, *Hudson*: 90
Lockheed L18, *Lodestar*: 53, 54, 58, 59, 63-65, 66, 68-70, 73, 74, 75, 76, 78, 80, 81, 83, 91-97, 101, 108, 109, 117, 118, *last service:*125, 129, 130, 137, 138, 288, 326
Lincoln, Avro: 207
Macchi 320B: 105-107, 108, 162
PA-20, Piper *Pacer*: 68, 138
Solent, Short flying-boat: 58, 78, 79
Super VC10/VC10, Vickers (BAC): 276-278, 281, 283, 287, 289, 290-300, 302-305, *four-engine flame-out*: **306-310**, 311, 313-317, 321-329, 334, 336, 337, 339, 341-343, *last production aircraft*: **346**-349, 352-354, 356, 365, 366, 367, 373, 375-377, 386, 387, 393-396, 399, 400, 402, 405-407, 410, 412, 416-418, 420-423, 426, 430, 433, 442, 443, 444
Swift, Comper: 30
Universal, Fokker: 19
Vickers *Valiant*: 290, 291
Vickers V1000 *(project)*: 290
Vickers *Victoria*: 6, 48
Vickers *Viking*: 125
Vickers *Viscount*: 153, 200, 229
Vickers *Vimy*: 5, 6
Vulcan, Avro V-Bomber: 201, 291
Aircraft Research Association: 291

Airlines:
Aden Airways: 95, 99, 199, 209, 234, 265, 298
Aer Lingus: 408, 422, 427, 437
Aeroflot: 306, 336
Air Canada: 401, 408
Air France: 58, 260, 433
Air India: 79, 99, 260, 286, 298, 301, 399, 439
Air Rhodesia: 251
Alitalia: 283, 327
American Airlines: 426
Bahamas Airways: 278
B.E.A.: 97, 243, 278, 286, 337
B.O.A.C.: *assistance with formation of E.A.A.C.*:**41-46**, *sale of Lodestars to E.A.A.C.*: **54**, 56, 58, 66-67, 76,77, *flying-boat service*: **78-79**, 80, 85, 90, 91, 98, 100, 102, 103-105, 118, 126, 129, 130, 138, 148, *negotiation of Argonaut sale to E.A.A.C.*: **153**, **154**, 162, 163, 166, 174-176, *Canadair training assistance*: **178**, 181, 186, *a Canadair engineering problem*: **191-192**, 204, 205,*Comet training assistance*: **209-211**, 218, 219, 221, 230,231, 234, 235, 237, 238, 240, 245, 257-260, 265, 267, 271, 273, 276, 277, 281, 283, *an appreciation*: **288-289**, 290, 292, 297-299, 302-304, 309, 315, 316, 318, 329, 331, 337, 338, 342, 343, 351, 352, 368, 369, 373, 376, 388, 389, 391,

399, *ground handling agreements cease*: **416**-418, 430, 443
B.O.A.C. Associated Companies: 43, 288, 289
B.S.A.A.: 50
Britannia Airways: 386
British Airways: 96, 260, 399,414, 416, 422, 439, 443
British United (B.U.A.): 276, 299, 309, 316, 318, 373, 378, 406
Cathay Pacific: 311
Central African Airways: 58, 98, 125, 128, 151, 153, 181, 185, 229, 234, 259, 278
Dan Air: 346, 410
D.E.T.A.: 84, 85, 137
Eagle Airways: 159, 170
Eastern Airlines: 392, 408, 415, 419, 424, 429, 435, 437
El Al: 79, 98, 388, 389
Ethiopian Airlines: 98, 283, 298, 376, 420
Hunting Clan Air Transport: 163
Imperial Airways: 6,7,9,12-16, 26, 31, 33, 36, 37-40, 43, 51, 203, 238, 288, 291, 304
Iraqi Airways: 90
Kenya Airways: 444, 445
K.L.M.: 175, 322
Lloyd International Airways: 374
Lufthansa: 298, 306, 338, 348, 417, 444
M.E.A., Middle East Airlines: 91, 314
Misrair: 235
Pan American World Airways: 153, 283, 298
Pakistan International Airlines (P.I.A): 192, 199, 298, 353, 376, 391, 392, 401
Rhodesia and Nyasaland Airways: 41
Scandinavian Airlines System (S.A.S.): 58, 98, 148, 298, 327, 420
Seychelles and Kilimanjaro Air Transport (S.K.A.T.): 110, 221, 227 305, 317-320, 322, 346, 374, 393, 394
Sabena: 98, 129, 154, 224, 298, 306, 356, 357, 361
Simbair: 374, 379, 410, 416, 423, 424, 426, 428, 429, 439
Skyways: 58, 63, 66, 83, 157
South African Airways: 14, 38, 54, 58, 70, 75-76, 79, 98, 108, 126, 129, 148, 151, 159, 175, 204, *Quadripartite pool*: **234**, 239, 259, 289, 368
Syrian Arab Airlines: 235
Trans Meridian Aircargo: (TAC): 410
Trans World Airlines (TWA): 306, 338, 343, 348
United Arab Airlines: 235, 283
Wilson Airways: 20, 21, 22, 23-28, 29, 30-40, 41-46, 48, 56, 80, 203, 255, 257, 288, 314
Zambia Airways: 282, 298, 321, 328
Airwork: *see also Perth* 181, 270, 314
Akery, F/E Denis: 444
Aly Khan, Prince: 80-82, 251
Allen,'Bunny': 116
Allison, Capt T.H.C.'Harry': 43, 44, 51, 135, 136
Allen, F/O Larry: 212
Alleyne, Capt Edward: 374, 375, 435, 436
Althorp, Lord: 142
Antsiranana: 114
Amin Aga, Prince: 82
Amakowa, Stdss Naomi: 273
Amalemba, Mr M.S.: 271, 273, 278, 319, 392
Anderson, Miss Robin : 142
Anderson, Capt L.N,: 268
Armstrong Whitworth: 12, 15, 25, 36, 37
Arthur, Capt Laurie: 174
Arusha: 23, 65, 196, 234, 262, 280 318, 322, 355, 388, 393, 411
Associated Companies, BOAC: 37, 43
Atchison, Capt George: 244, 311, 435
Australia: 21, 35, 89, 100, 200, 289, 290, 327, 422
Aviz Hotel, Lourenco Marques: 138
AVTUR (*refuelling accidents*): 243, 244

B

Babu, Abdul-Rahman Mohamed (Zanzibar): 269
Bacall, Miss Lauren: 115
Bacos, Capt Marcel (Air France): 433
Baines, Mr J.W.: 234, 257
Baghdad: 90, 91
Baguley, Stdss Katherine: 329, 335, 336
Bailey, Mr Ron: 293
BALPA: 208, 435
Banks, Capt 'Monty' (BOAC): 54
Barclays Bank: 205, 433

INDEX · 475

Baring, H.E. Sir Evelyn, Governor of Kenya: 200, 312, 450
Barnard, Capt C.D.: 9, 10
Barnard, F/O Bruce: 181
Barton, Mr P.R. 'Ron': 244, 341, 376, 401, 413
Bates, Mr E.F. 'Ted': 252, 268, 273
Baudet, Mr G.: 44
Bazzochi, Sr. Eng.: 105
Bearcroft, Commandant Michael 'Punch': 158
Bedford, Mary, Duchess of:: 9, 13
Bedford *(Aircraft Research Est)* England: 291
Beech, Miss Connie: 288
Beirut: 91, 118, 314, 316, 420
Bembridge, I.O.W.: 10
Benghazi (Benina): 5, 49, 94, 95, 111, 181, 190, 191, 192, 203, 235, 258, 259, 280, 329, 433
Benjamin, Capt: 81
Bent, Miss Mayence: 164
Bentley, MC; Capt R. (Dick): 7, 9
Berenice Hotel, Benghazi: 181
Betts, Mr John: 285
Bicknell, Capt Jack: 68, 80, 81, 131, 192, 194, 210, 212
Birdlip, Glos. *(GPO radio station)*: 97, 316
Bird Capt D.R. 'Dickie': 44, 82, 138, 244, 252
Blackbushe: 96, 97, 109, 110, 138, 170
Blakely, R/O Russ: 84, 170
Blantyre: 63, 128, 151, 168, 229, 300, 327, 376, 393
Block Hotels: 164-165
Bogart, Mr Humphrey: 115
Bombay: 5, 79, 178, 180, 181, 189-193, 196, 199, 203, 209, 212, 234, 242, 283, 285, 286, 298, 302, 306, 310, 313, 311, 321, 322, 327, 366, 367, 439
Bongo, President Albert of Gabon: 406
Bordeaux: 23, 97
Boswell, Wing Commander, G.L.W.: 319, 379, 380, 391
Botto, F/O Ronald: 394, 395
Boursnell, Std George: 94
Bowker-Douglass, Capt R.'Rusty': 414, 415, 435
Brammah, Mr 'Taffy' 162
Brancker, KCB AFC; AVM Sir Sefton: 13

Brand, KBE DSO MC DFC; ACM Sir Quintin: 6
Brazzaville: 206
Brennan, Mr Paddy: 366
Breidenbend, Stewardess Iris: 284
Brewer, Capt John 'Ginger': 75, 80-82, 94, 96, 97, 100, 105-109, 116, 128, 129, 137, 156, 158, 161, 162, 168-173, 212, 213, 215, 216, 250, 251, 266, 280, 281, 435, 446
Britair (E.A.): 266
Britchford, Capt Tony: 406, 422, 435
British American Tobacco Company: 30
British Aircraft Corporation (BAC): 293, 296, 297, 301, 312, 337, 399, 412, 423, 424, 444
British East Africa Association: 3
Brokensha, Capt Gene T.: 276, 282
Brooke-Popham, Air Chief Marshal Sir Robert: 40, 41
Brooklands: *Vickers (BAC) factory (see also Weybridge)*: 5, 6, 294-296, 346, 347
Broome, Capt F.C.: 5
Brown, Mr Terry: 57, 377
Brumby, Capt Peter: 308, 309
Buffalo Springs: 116
Bujumbura: 250, 283, 327, 406, 407
Bukavu: 223, 224, 406
Bunstead, Capt John: 176, 391, 392
Burkitt, Capt Alan: 130, 356, 393, 433, 435
Burleton, Capt A.J.: 356, 362, 363, 435
Burundi: 375, 406, 407
Butiaba: 6, 32, 52, 115, 139, 149
Butler Capt C. (BOAC): 174

C

Cairncross, F/O: 155
Cairns, Mr Bill: 297
Cairo: 5-7, 12-14, 32, 33, 36, 45, 49, 54, 56, 64, 79, 91, 96, 105, 160, 181, 203,204, 232, 235, 274-276, 280, 283, 285, 297, 298, 321, 327, 420, 425, 439
Callaghan, Rt Hon Mr James, MP *(later Lord)*: 430
Campbell Black, Mr Tom: 18-22, 33-35, 37, 43, 56, 260
Campling Brothers: 105
Cape Town: 5-7, 9, 13, 14, 166
Carberry, Mr John *(formerly Lord Carbery)*: 18-20, 73, 74, 201
Careful, F/O Bill: 286, 287

Carristiato, Commandante: 105, 106
Carne, Capt Richard: 402, 403, 405, 435, 436
Carpenter, Mr Charlie: 67
Cartwright, Capt T.R. 'Reg': 43, 52, 66, 67, 105, 107, 115-117, 138-142, 149, 178, 212, 244, 311, 341, 349, 351, 408, 422, 430
Caspair: 95
Caspareuthus, Capt R.F.: 13, 14, 17, 194, 260
Caterair, *(later NAS-Caterair)*: 165, 230
Cawthorne, F/E Bill: 143,149, 212
Chadwick, Mr Roy: 22
Chalmers Mitchell, Dr Peter: 5
Charles Butler Associates: 290
Chamberlain, Stdss Janet: 274
Chandley, Mr Peter: 432
Chegge, Mr J.N.: 373
Chesham, Lord: 72
Chettyar, Stdss Rosie: 273
Chicago Field Museum: 20
Chingola: 130
Chokwe, Mr T.M.C.: 319
Choppin, Mr S.G.: 202, 257, 288, 293, 304, 319, 338, 339, 353
Christchurch, NZ: 422
Churchill, Sir Winston: 232, 285
Clarkson, Capt 'Nobby': 430
Close, F/O Brian: 435
Cobham, Sir Alan: 6, 7, 260
Cobham-Blackburn Air Lines: 9
Cockerell, Capt S.: 5
Cochran, Mr John (BAC): 297, 444
Cohen, Sir Andrew: 142, 144
Cole, F/O Jim: 246
Coleman, Harry: 266
Collins Radio:111, 316
Colls, Mr Stacey: 50
Colonial Development Corporation: 99, 205
Communist: 98, *(post-colonial influence Zanzibar)*: 267-269
Congo: 1, 63, 69, 115, 129, 154, 206, *refugee airlift*: **221, 223-225**, 227, 241, 242, 306, 361, 375, 391
Continental engines: 105
Cooke, Capt Peter: 184-186, 247, 250
Cooper Bros (Auditors): 394
Cooper, Stdss Dorothy 'Dot': 275
Copenhagen: 327, 341, *Danish govt. aided pilot training*: **426**
Corby, Mr C.: 5

Coward CMG, OBE; Mr David : 444
Cowie, Capt Ian: 349, 352, 353, 426, 435, 436, 439
Cox, Mr Sid: 75, 76
Cox, Mr Johnny: 138
Crewdson, F/O John: 52, 136
Crown Agents: 428
Cull, Flt Lt John Tullock: 5
Cunningham CBE, DSO**, DFC*; Gp Capt John 'Cat's Eyes': 204, 209
Cunningham, Capt Peter: 52, 68, 95, 136, 224, 225, 237, 238, 240, 252, 263, 264 326, 340, 346, 392, 393, 400, 408

D

Daily Mail: 141, 399, 400, 402
Daily Telegraph: 218
Damascus: 151, 173
Dar es Salaam: 1, 4, 6, 10, 12, 13, 15, 21, *experimental mail service*: **24**, *route development*: **26, 29, 30**, 32, 40, 45, *Auster mail flights*: **47**, 48, 52, 54, 58,60,63, 72, 73, 76, 78, *snake in cockpit*: **92-93**, 131-133, 208, 212, 219-222, 227, 240, 247, 250, 251, 254, 259, 263, 266, 268, 280, 281, 283, 298, 300, 306, 313, 315, 319, 322, 327, 328, 341, *President Nyerere requisitions SVC10*: **350**, 352, 367, 386-389, 393, 399, 402, *a DC-9 is stolen*: **403-405**, 420, 421, 427, 430, 440
Davidson, DFC; Capt Leo: 43, 51, 162, 174, 190, 212, 270, 271, 305, 306, 311, 319, 323, 326
Dawson, Mr Hugh: 144
Deadman, Capt: 79
De Gaulle, General Charles: 206
De Jager, Capt Jeff: 212, 250, 426, 435
De Souza, Stdss Priscilla: 285
Deedes, Lord W.F. (Bill): 218
de Havilland engines:
Ghost: 204
Gipsy Major: 26
Gipsy Queen: 54
Gipsy-Six: 26, 140, 440
Delves Broughton, Mr John 'D.B.': 67, 191
Dempster, F/O David: 119-121, 123, 192, 212, 220, 329, 330, 332, 336, 435, 436, 442, 443
Denmark: 341, 349, 434

INDEX · 477

Diego Suarez: 114
Di Piero, F/O: 406
Directorate of Civil Aviation: (DCA): 14, 50, 69, 107, 114, 157, 162
Dodoma: 9, 12, 13, 24, 32, 39, 100, 104, 151
Donovan Maule Theatre: 218
Dornan, Capt Tom: 172, 173, 244, 252, 253, 408
Douglas, Mr R.M: 352
Drew, DFC*; Capt Roger: 52, 95, 109-113, 125, 169-171, 193, 212, 216, 243, 247, 249, 275
Drigh Road: 190
Drummond GM, CPM(G); Mr David: 264, 311, 312
Duff, Capt Peter: 51, 161, 210, 215, 245
Duffell, Std: 82
Duke of Edinburgh (*see also* Prince Philip): 100, 101, 142, 146, 148, 149, 264
Duke of Gloucester: 22
Duke of Kent: 22
Durban: 4, 7, 15, 32, 46, 63, 66, 68, 69, 83, 85, 86, 94, 95, 100, 114, 129, 133, 134, 137, 138, 151, 152, 153, 155, 161, 168, 178, 180, 194, 203, 218, 250, 259, 289
Dykes, Mr J.C.: 240

E
East African Common Services Organisation: 249, 287, 304, 318
East African Community: 218, 271, *Arusha Treaty*: **318**, 319, 327, 340, 352, 353, 355, 367, 373, 380, 390, 394, 402, 407, 428, 433, 437, 441
East African Standard: 23, 272, 304, 373, 379, 381, 382, 386, 388, 389
Eastleigh Airport, Nairobi: 43, 47, 56, 64, 65, 74, 77, 79, 91, 95, 104, 107, 108, 133, 163, 164, 175-178, 199, 207, 220
Egglesfield, Capt L.A.: 32
Eldama Ravine: 18
Eldoret: 26, 31, 46, 47, 51, 54, 108, 119, 220, 367
Elkington, Purser Ernest: 329
Embakasi Airport, Nairobi: 104, *under construction:***176**, 199, *opening ceremony:***200-201**, 207-209, 218, 220, 234, 243, 244, 252, 261, 263, 284, 305, 311, 346, 367, 374-377, 391, 414, 415, 418, 422, 423, 434, 438-440, 444
Embry Riddle Aeronautical Institute: 314
Emmenis, F/O Pieter von: 82, 152
Entebbe: 2, 6, 7, 8, 16, 23, 26, 47, 51, 53, 56, 66, 67, 76-79, 83, *new airport opened:* **95**, 98, 101, 102, 104, 105, 108,186, 188, 191, 200, 203 210, 212, 217, 219-221, 223, 224, 228, 238, 239, 255, 280, 283, 298, 300, 301, 303, 306, 307, 315, 320, 322, 325, 327-329, 330, 334, 335, 351, 352, *the military coup*: **356-366**, 369, 371, 375, 378, 391, 403, 405-407, 419, 430, *the Israeli raid*: **433-434**, 440, 445
Equator: 2, 10, 46, 90
Erasmus, Mr Carl: 86
Ethiopia: 1, 121, 122, 161, 273, 298, 366, 375, 394, 400, 441
Etiang, Mr Paul: 365
Evans, Purser Gordon: 263, 264
Everitt, Purser Harry: 308, 309, 351

F
Fadhil, Stdss Mariam: 395
Faraji, Mr Abdu C.: 257, 319
Farnborough *(Royal Aircraft Establishment)*: 204
Ferguson's Gulf: 414
Fiddian-Green, Mr R.R.: 23
Field Aircraft Services Ltd: 103, 136
Flame-out *(SVC10 5Y-ADA)*: 306-310
Flight magazine: 33, 186
Ford, Mr John: 116, 117
Fort Jesus, Mombasa: 2, 85
Fort Victoria: 185-188
Fort Worth, Texas: 344, 426
Foster, N/O R.A.: 216
Fowzi Hoss, Mr: 91
Francistown: (*Dakota VP-KJT burned out)* 259
Francombe MBE, DSO; Wg Commander Aubrey: 10, 11, 12, 14, 26-32, 39, 41, 48, 50, 83, 101, 102, 109, 118, 135, 162, 260
Fuller, Capt Ken: 125, 131, 155
Fumerton, Capt Bill: 51, 114, 162, 174, 195, 212, 257-259
Fumerton, Mrs Barbara: 258, 326
Fundikira, Chief Said Abdulla, *Chairman EAAC 1964-1973*: 271, 276, 277, 293, 296,

317, 319, 326, 330, 341, 345, 352, 368, 381, 382, 386, 388-394, 402, 410-413
Furniss, Mr Joe (DCA): 50, 51, 69, 114

G
Gable, Mr Clark: 116, 117, 118
Gabon: 406, 407
Gallon, N/O Bob: 277, 311
Gander, Mr Ron: 222, 236, 253, 467
Gandhi, Mrs Indira: 421
Gardner, Miss Ava: 116, 117
Garsen: 47, 48
Gascoine, G. Company: 67
Georgetown, British Guiana: 154
Georgiadis, Mr Byron: 379, 380, 382, 383, 385
Gethin, Mr P.E.L. (*Director of Surveys 1928*): 10, 12
Ghibli: 236
Gichuki, Mr G.W.: 319
Gilbert Lee, Mr: 271, 303
Gilda (The film): 81
Gilfillan, Mr 'Gilly': 131
Gilgil: 51, 52
Gill, Mr A.V.: 203, 247, 257, 277, 288, 293, 303
Gillett, Mr F.: 420, 421
Gladstone, AFC; Capt T.A.: 7, 9
Glass, Mr 'Jock': 68, 222, 413, 420, 421
Gothic: 100, 102
Grafton, Mr Eddie: 70
Grand Hotel, Beira: 168
Grand Hotel, Khartoum: 170
Granville, Mr Keith: 271
Griffiths, N/O D.J. 'Griff': 216, 239, 329, 335
Griffiths, Mr H.T.: 44
Groundnut Scheme: 99, 100, 108, 110, 132
Goddard, Lord Chief Justice: 125
Goodlin, Mr 'Slick': 109, 154
Guinness Peat Aviation: 430
Gurdial Singh, Mr: 319

H
Haeufl, Mr: 19
Haines, Barry: 291
Hajj pilgrim flights: 76, 95, 127, 128, 151, 159, 161, 170, 172, 227, 283, 423
Hall, Mr Michael: 285, 364

Hall, Capt Peter: 116
Handford-Rice, F/O Alan: 84, 92, 105, 135
Hannaford, Mr Syd: 178
Hargeisa: 128
Harrowing, Capt Paul: 312, 435, 436
Hartley, Capt Henry: 386, 387, 436, 446
Hartley, Stdss Jenny: 285
Hasham, Mr: 268
Hatfield: de Havilland factory: 53, 204, 209, 211, 212
Hawkins, Capt (Skyways): 83
Hayley Bell, Mr Dennis: 297
Hayward, F/E Alan: 444
Hayworth, Miss Rita: 80, 82, 251
Heathrow Airport, London (*see also London Airport*): 174, 191, 192, 205, 236, 245, 285, 297, 306, 316, 325, 329, 368, 372, 373, 381, 399, 416, 417
Hemingway, Mr Ernest: 138-142, 151
Henn, Capt Phillip: 54, 63, 69, 105, 109, 135, 159, 172, 210, 218, 220, 240, 245, 252, 257, 265, 271
Hennesberger, Leutnant: 4
Hepburn, Miss Katherine: 115, 116
Herbert, Mr Ron: 75
Hill, Capt Trevor: 349, 398, 408, 409
Hillary, Capt Walter: 52, 57
Hinchey, Hon H.J.: 202, 257
Hobday, Mr Edwin 'Tubby': 76
Hognerud, Capt Jan: 311, 435, 436
Holmes, Capt Peter: 110-115
Hong Kong: *Super VC10 proving flight:* **311**, 317, 327, 341, 352, 366, 367, 374, 380, 381
Horrocks, Mr Jim (*British High Commission, Uganda*): 432
Houlder, Capt C.P. (BOAC): 174
House, E/O Vic: 311
Howard-Williams, Mrs Diana: 172
Howes, Mr A.M.D.: 12
Howes, Mr Bobby: 50
Huston, Mr John: 116
Huxley, Miss Elspeth: 48

I
Idi Amin, Maj-Gen, President: 317, 334, 335, 362, 367, 378, 387, 402, 403, 404, 406-409, 412, 413, 419, 430, 431, 433, 434, 445
Illari, General: 105, 106

Iliffe, Capt Howard: 138, 159, 162, 168, 178, 234
Imison, Capt E. 'Ted': 348, 349, 430, 439
India: 10, 14, 17, 47, *first services to:* **190, 199,** 227, *introduction of Comet services:***234, 242, 252,** *operations during Indo-Pakistan war:***285-287,** 289, 308, 314, 324, 402, 421
International Aeradio Ltd (I.A.L.): 281, 316
Isaacson, Mr T.: 327, 341, 374
Ismaili: 80, 81, 229, 246

J
Jackson, Capt Dennis: 325, 326, 435
James, F/E Alan: 244, 311
Jani, Mr P.K.: 257, 293
Jeddah: *first Hajj flights:* **76, 95,** *problems encountered with charters to:***127, 128,** 131, 151, 161, 172, 173
Jenkins, Mr A.R.: 44,
Jenkins, Capt (BOAC): 209
Jet Stream winds: 235
Jinja: 7, *construction of hydro-electric dam:* **66,** *Royal visit to:*142, 143, 145, 147, 152
Johannesburg: 23, 37, 45, 49, 79, 118, 129, 164, 178, 184, 186, 210, *inaugural EAA Comet service:***212, 216,** 221, 242, *suspension of services to:* **259,** 289, *foreign carriers transit E.A. to:* **306,** *SSB station:* **316,** 342
Johnson, Johnny, *Chief Technical Officer:* 240, 252
Jones, Capt O.P.: 238
Jordan, Hashemite Kingdom of: 170
Jordan, Stdss Heather: 258

K
Kabaka of Buganda: 3, 206, 316, 317,
Kagera river: 116, 117
Kai-Tak airport: *SVC10 proving flight to Hong Kong:* 311
Kakamega: 46
Kalanzi, Mr Peter: 434
Kampala: 2, 78, 255, 302, 315, 362, 371, 405, 438
Kanza, M.: 206
Karachi: 178, 183, 188-190, 192, 196, 199, 203, 212, 234, 242, 283, 285, 286, 298, 308, 309, 311, 322, 326, 327
Karim, Prince Aga: 81, 82
Karume, Mr Abeid: 269

Kasavubu, M. Joseph: 222, 223
Kasese: 52, 66, 67, 95, 109, 220, 223, 356, 427
Kasenye (*emergency landing strip*): 219
Kearns, Mr Ray: 264, 421, 430
Keekerok Lodge: 414
Keith, Mr Ian: 57, 377
Kelly, Mr D.: 44
Kelly, Miss Grace: 116, 118
Kenyatta, President Jomo: *political meetings:* **99,** *detained; flown into exile:***118-125,** 207, *freed from detention:* **232,** *President of Kenya:* **267,** 269, 338, 367, 368, 403, 407, 409, 418
Kenya Auxiliary Air Unit: 41, 45
Kenya Farmer's Association: 218
Kenya Pilot's Association: 391, 392
Kerstens, Capt Willi: 435, 436, 443
Keshavjee, Stdss Zarina: 246
Khartoum: 6, 7, 12, 13, 24, 31-33, 46, 48, 49, 94-96, 106, 107, 118, 128, 131, 138, 151, 159, 210, 212, 235, 236, 238, 264, 265, 277, 280, 329, 330, 352, 439
Kigwa: 387
Kilewo, Mr A.B. (*chairman EAA wef 1 Jul 1973*): 413
Kilimanjaro, Mount: 69, 103, 131, 132, 137, 'Snows of Kilimanjaro':**141,**(*VP-KKH crash*): **156-159,** 170, 182, 200, 203, 209, 220, 277, 295, 434
Kilimanjaro Hotel, Dar es Salaam: 402
Kilimanjaro International Airport: 388, 389, 403, 404, 405, 421
Kilindini: 2, 114
King HM George VI: 100
King Solomon's Mines: 115, 117
Kingolwira: 387
Kirkham, Capt Norris: 26, 44, 45, 51, 73, 74
Kisumu: 5, 7, 9, 10, 12, 14, 15, 24-26, 31-33, 39, 40, 46, 47, 49, 51
Kitale: 40, 46, 47, 51, 52, 54, 108, *Kenyatta flight to exile:***119-121, 123, 125,** 433
Kiwanuka, Benedicto: 232
Kiwanuka, Capt James: 279, 427, 435, 436
Knight of the Grail (Avro 'Five' VP-KAE): 20, 21
Knowlden, Wg Commander: 45
Koenigsberg: 4, 85
Kongwa: 52, 59, 78, 79, 83, 94, 99, 100, 108, 132
Kyobe, Mr Wilson: 271, 278, 317, 326

Kyomukama, Ezra: 356, 360, 361

L
Lady Kenmere Lodge: 414
Lake Albert: 6, 115, 139, 224
Lake Edward: 224
Lake George: 67, 113, 219
Lake Jipe: 155, 159
Lake Kivu: 224
Lake Magadi: 196
Lake Naivasha: 78, 79, 119, 430
Lake Rudolf: 121, 124, 161, 413, 414, 415
Lake Tanganyika: 7, 406
Lake Victoria: 2, 5-7, 9, 31, 116, 138, 196, 364, 365, 430, 434, 438
Lake Victoria Hotel, Entebbe: 102, 116, 238, 356, 359-361, 407
Lambeth, Mr Ray: 201, 368
Lavers, Capt Douglas: 43-45, 47, 48, 51, 106, 107, 130, 162, 174, 178
Leri, Mrs Nancy: 329, 335
Leslie, Capt George: 68, 69, 71, 87, 88, 94, 100, 108, 119-121, 123, 124, 129, 134, 136, 137, 150, 223, 243, 244, 249, 277, 286, 311, 337, 341, 349-351, 376, 405, 417, 418, 422, 426
Lettow-Vorbeck, Maj-Gen von: 85
Lewin, Brig-Gen A.C.: 15, 17
Lewis, Capt Lou: 87
Lindblad Irwin Travel (*Wing Safaris*): 413
Lindi: 15, 24, 30, 32, 46, 52, 63, 65, 80, 81, 84, 99, 266
Little, Mr R.F.: 9
Llanstephan Castle :10
Lloyd, Mr Charles: 50
Lloyd, Mr Dennis: 131
Lloyd Triestino: 86
Lockhart, Sir Charles: 43
Lodwar: 161, 235, 267
Loe, Stdss Mary: 274
Lokitaung: 121-123, 125
London Airport (*see also Heathrow*): 174, 239, 258, 295, 302, 316, 367, 372, 439
Lorenzi, Capt Michael: 391, 392, 436
Lourenco Marques (Maputo): 7, 32, 63, 85, 137, 419
Lovemore, Capt R.B.: 26, 45
Lubega, Dr and Mrs Anthony: 356, 360-362, 364

Lumbo: 80, 84-86, 94, 95, 155, 168, 195
Lusaka: 32, 39, 128, 161, 286, 327, 328, *SVC10 'dead-stick landing:* **386**, 393
Lush, Mr W.S.: 408
Lusinde, J.M., *Minister Home Affairs, Tanganyika*: 268, 304
Lutale, Stdss Ruth: 329, 335, 336, 353, 365
Lutara, Mr W.O.: 319, 326, 354, 378, 392
Luxor: 46, 173, 439
Lyatuu, Mr Julian: 420
Lyttleton, Rt Hon Oliver: 142

M
Maasai: 2, 34, 70, 117, 142
MacAdam, Dr Ian: 139
Mackenzie, DSO DFC MLC; Col Bruce: 202, 368, 369, 372, 373, 391, 418, 445
Mackinnon House, Nairobi: 78
Maclaughlin, Std P.J.: 216
MacNabb, N/O Frank: 95, 239, 275, 311, 394, 395
Macmillan, Mr Harold, M.P.: 221
Macphail, Mr (*Acting Governor, Malakal*): 17
Macpherson, Mr (*engineer, Tanganyika Survey*): 12
MacRobertson Trophy Air Race: 21
Madagascar: 41, 94, 114, 251
Mafia Island: 4, 5, 30, 78, 266
Maggidi Mr : 268
Mahatane, Mr F.B.: 319, 323, 381, 382, 388, 410, 412
Mahe: 114, 115
Maidens, Mr 'Dickie': 75
Maison Blanche: 70
Maitland Aerodrome, Cape Town: 9
Majendie, Capt A.M.A.: 118
Makarios, President: 341
Malta: 5, 96, 138, 170, 200, 236, 243, 258, 280, 418
Malyon, Std J.: 216
Mamba (*snake in cockpit*): 91-93
Margadant, E/O Franz: 178, 185
Markham, Miss Beryl: 20, 22, 56
Markham, Hon Sir Charles: 165
Martin, F/O Alan: 281
Marseilles: 49, 97, 110, 111
Marsh, Mr Jack: 57
Marsh, Capt Roy: 139
Marshall-Field, Mr: 22

Masindi: 138, 139, 141
Matthews, Purser George: 68, 101, 102, 133, 143, 146, 149
Mau Mau: 99, 104, 118, 119, 124, 152, 153, 159, 199 207, 232, 312
Mauritius: 3, 114, 200, 208, 221, 222, 327
Mawalla, Mr J.: 319
Mbarara Barracks, Kampala: 387
Mbeya: 13, 15, 24, 39, 46, 47, 54, 76, 250, 251, 259, 280, 315
McBreaty, Mr Terry: 57, 75, 376, 470
McCrindle, Maj J.F.: 202
McIvor, Stdss Sheila: 83, 125
McNamarra, Capt Eddie: 444
McVickars, F/O Charlie: 444
Meadley, Capt Brian: 386, 387, 436, 446
Medway River, *Short Bros seaplane factory, Rochester* : 6, 8
Meir, Prime Minister Mrs Golda: 388
Mervyn Hill, Mr: 18
Metro-Goldwyn-Meyer: 116
Milan, Italy: 105, 106, 327, 442
Mildenhall: 21, 35
Milne, N/O 'Jock': 311
Miss Kenya (DH51): 19, 201
Mitchell, Capt G. W. 'Mitch': 68, 80-84, 108, 129, 136-138, 155, 156, 162, 170, 181, 183, 184, 209, 224, 243, 296, 297, 302, 303, 311, 329, 330, 332, 334, 335, 346, 406, 407, 425
Mitchell, Sir Philip: 29
Mobutu, President Joseph: 223, 407
Mogadishu (Mogadiscio): 321, 405
Mogambo: 116, 117, 128
Moi arap, Mr Daniel (*later President*): 367
Molison, Mr A.G. : 202, 234, 252, 257, 268
Molyneux, Purser 'Russ': 302
Mombasa: 1-5, 15, 18, *first landings:* **21**, *Puss Moth airmail service:* **24**, *DH89s introduced:* **26**, 30, *flying-boat services:* **32**, *last Wilson Airways pre-war service:* **40**, 46, 47, 51, 52, *first EAA Dove service:* **54-55**, 64, 65, 68, 73, 77, 82, 84, 85-87, 94, 100-103, 114, 115, 129, 131, 132, 141, 153, 161, 163, 164, 166, 199, 207, 219, 221, 234, 235, 240, 248, 250, 261-263, 274, 280, 315, 341, *first SVC10 lands:***352-353**, 413, 427, 433, 438, 441, 442
Moon, Mr Frank (DCA): 69

Morris, MVO; Capt Eric E.:44-46, 48, 50-52, 69, 96, 109-112, 123, 129, 138, 143, 145, 147, 149, 151, 152, 174, 194 218, 232, 240, 243, 392
Morris, F/O Ivan: 101, 102, 106, 212
Morton, Mr George: 328
Moscow (*flight bag returned from*): 337
Moshi: 5, 12, 13, 32, 39, 47, 48, 65, 103, 157, 158, 388
Mostert, Col. M.C.P.: 23, 24, 26, 28, 40, 41, 45, 91, 178, 202, 203, 205, 247, 257, 260, 288
Mount Kenya Safari Lodge: 414
Mountains of the Moon (Ruwenzoris): 223, 224, 232, 441
Mounter, Capt Malcolm: 251, 435
Mount Royal Hotel, London: 239
Mozambique: 32, 63, 80, 85, 86, 137, 251
Mpika: 24, 39
Msefya, Mr H.R.: 319
Muganga, Stdss Mary: 285, 329, 336
Mundy, Mr J.C.: 178, 202, 205, 257
MUNITALP Foundation: 288
Murray, E/O (N/O) Paddy: 94, 136, 152, 173, 190, 194, 212, 237, 239, 275, 277, 387, 394, 399, 443, 444
Murray-Brown, Mr Jeremy: 123
Murchison Falls: 113, 115, 138, 139, 141, 356, 414, 427
Murphy, Mr Michael 'Spud' (DCA): 114
Murphy, 'Spud' (EAA traffic): 144, 145
Muteshi, Mr A.G.: 302, 392
Mwanza: 5, 6, 12, 13, 24, 26, 31, 54, 104, 151, 167, 234, 280
Mweya Lodge: 148

N

Nairobi West: (*see also Wilson Airport*): 21, 46, 55-57, 64, 65, 68, 72, 74, 75, 77, 81-84, 86, 96, 104, 107-109, 119,129, 133-135,150,155-157,162,163, *Constellation lands by mistake*:**175-177**, 198, *re-named Wilson aerodrome*:**201**, 377, 430
Naivasha: 21, 51, 52, 58, *BOAC flying-boat services*:**78-79**, 107, 119, 308, 430, 445
Nasser, Col Gamal Abdel: 170, 171, 173
Natchingwea: 100, 108
National Physical Laboratory: 291
Newman, Capt 'Sandy' Buruwari: 426, 436

New Stanley Hotel: 69, 78, 116, 164, 195, 199, 207
New York: 76, 141, *Lodestar ferry to*: **154-155**, 208, 210, 290, 327, 342, 344, 345, *SVC10 inaugural flight*: **351**, 352, 374, 379-381, 413
New Zealand: 89, 90, 289, 327, *SVC10 flight to*: 422
Ngong Hills: 51, 104, 445
Nichols, Mr Charlie: 429
Nicol, Mr G.D.H.: 178
Nightingale, E/O (N/O) P.L. 'Tim': 63, 212, 277, 309, 314, 329, 332, 336, 399
Nile Hilton, Cairo: 275
Nile Hotel, Wadi Halfa: 112
Njonjo, Mr Charles, Kenya attorney-general: 428
Nkrumah, President Kwame: 99
Noon, Capt Alec: 21, 26, 28, 44, 47, 115
Noon, Capt Chris: 436
Norfolk Hotel: 19, 69, 262
North Sea Aerial and General Transportation Ltd: 9
Nottingham, Tollerton aerodrome: 95, 136
Nsekela, Mr A.J.: 319
Nyerere, President Julius: 206, 232, 269, 271, 322, 338, 350, 367, 387, 388, 403, 407, 411, 421, 434, 437
Nyeri: 18, 19, 31, 40, 46, *Treetops hotel*: 100, 262, 414

O

Obote, President Milton: 232, 317, 322, 325, 334, 338, 361, 362, 365, 366, 367, 378, 387, 403, 404, 438
O'Connell, Mr Ted: 75
O'Donoghue, Mr Tony: 285

Olalobo, F/O Tom: 404
Okot, Mr J.A.O.: 374, 378, 381, 382, 392, 402, 412
Oram, N/O Barry: 277
Order-in-Council (*enabling formation of E.A.A.C.*): 42, 43
Orombi, Lieutenant (*Entebbe Coup*): 363, 364
Overseas Food Corporation: 78, 79, 100, 108
Owen Falls: 142, 441
Oxford Air Training School: 314

P

Parfitt, Mr: 12
Park View Hotel, Durban: 86
Parker, Capt Joe: 102, 174, 178, 190, 288
Parmenter, Roy *(Cabin Services Supv.)*: 329
Payne, Mr Malcolm: 382
Payne, Capt T.F. 'Curly': 83, 94, 118, 129, 130, 154, 155, 435
Peace Corps (USA): 406, 407
Pearson, Capt: 26
Pemba Island: 1, 60, 160, 161, 166, 221, 227, 319
Penfold, Capt Eddy: 419, 435, 436
Perth, Australia: 422
Perth (Airwork) Scotland: 270, 301, 314, 426
Pettit, Capt Peter: 430, 435
Phillips, Sir Charles: 178, 202
Phillips, Mr R. (BAC): 293
Pink, Capt Leslie: 191, 192
Plunkett, Mr Wally: 75, 68
Pogue, Mr A.L.: 408
Pomfret: Capt Ruthven 'Pommy': 60, 61, 74, 75, 95, 157
Pope Paul VI (*flight to Uganda*): 328-333, 335, 336
Port Bell: 6, 14, 31, 32, 79, 430
Port Florence: 2
Port Reitz, Mombasa: 73
Possman, Mr Carl: 351, 352
Power, Capt Dave: 250, 367
Pratt and Whitney:
engines:
90C Double Wasp: 54
R1830: 75
sent to B.O.A.C. Treforest for overhaul:103
90Ds sold in Sweden:109
R-2800-2SD13-G Twin Wasp (*DC4*): 174
overhaul at Nairobi: 209, 265, 376
difficulty obtaining spares: 254
engine failure en route to Lindi: 266
PT6A-27 (*Twin Otter*): 305
JT8D-5 (*DC-9*): 375
JT8D-11: 420
Prendergast, Capt (*flying-boats, Imperial Airways*): 14
Prendergast, Capt Joe: 349, 400, 401
Prince of Wales, HRH: 22, 35
Prince of Wales School, Nairobi: 312, 323

Prince Philip, HRH (see Duke of Edinburgh): 144, 263, 388
Princess Margaret, HRH: 108, 131, 167
Pritt, Mr D.N. QC: 123, 125
Privy Council: 125
Proctor, Stdss 'Nicky': 131
Prout, Purser Roy: 246

Q
Quadripartite Pool: 234, 259, 260, 289, 298
Queen, HM The (Elizabeth II): *honeymoon in Kenya curtailed by death of the King:* **100, 102,** *Royal visit to Uganda:***142-146, 148, 149,** 152, 263, 312, 329, 331, 388
Queen Elizabeth National Park, Uganda: 142, 148, 427
Queen Mary: 155
Queen Mother, HM The: 200
Quelimane: 95
Quill, Stdss Mary: 236
Quirk, Capt Jack Neville: 155, 156

R
Radio LM: 85
Raisman, GCMG GCIE KCSI; Sir Jeremy: 248
Ratcliffe, Capt Alan: 246, 280, 352, 353, 404, 435, 445
Reuters: 139, 141
Rhodes, R/O Derek: 80, 81, 83, 96, 97, 143, 149, 170, 174, 316
Rhodesia: 1, 24, 41, 45, 96, 100, 130, 135, 151, 161, 186, 188, 206, 227, 228, 250, 251, 266, 285, 287, 323
Richer, Mr W. (Bill): 201
Richter, Capt 'Laddie': 157, 173, 188
Ricketts, Capt Arthur: 435, 436, 444, 445
Rift Valley: 18, 203, 367, 445
Rigby, F/O Mike: 238
Riggi, Mr Bruno: 405,406
Rivenbark, Capt R.W.: 408, 420, 421
Roberts, Capt Lew: 297
Robinson, A.E., 'Robbie', *chief engineer EAA:* 142, 159, 202, 245, 252, 257, 281, 316
Robins, Sir Reginald: 43
Rolls-Royce : 5, 6, 157, 174, 181, 195, 204, 209, 216, 240, 250, 255, 265, 279, 288, 290, 292, 293, 297, 301, 308, 309, 348, 376, 420

Factory:
Derby: 209, 279
Engines:
Avon: 204, 205, 209, 216, 250, 254
Conway: 290, 292-294, 297, 308, 348 420, 423
Dart: 240, 255, 265, 376, 420
Eagle: 5
Merlin: 157, 174, 181, 195, 209, 243
Rome: 5, 105, 118, 138, 178, 181, 203, 204, 210, 212, 215, 216, 221, 235, 242, 255, 266, 277, 278, 283, 286, 287, 291, 297, 298, 327, 329, 331, 335, 336, 341, 378, 394, 405, 406, 410, 422, 425, 442, 443
Rose, Flt Lt T.: 12
Ross-Marsh, Mr Andy: 142
Royal Air Force (R.A.F.): 4, 6, 7, 10, 17, 35, 41, 43, 45, 47-49, 58, 62, 74, 103, 108, 136, 141, 154, 156, 167, 175, 178, 188, 199, 200, 201, 204, 213, 243, 263, 271, 289, 290, 308, 310, 323, 396, 401, 430
Ruaha River: 52
Rufiji River Delta: 4, 85
Rugambi, Mr Tobias: 434
Ruwenzori Mountains (see *Mountains of the Moon):* 223
Rwebangira, Mr S.L.: 368
Rwetsiba, Mr *(E.A. Community Minister for Communications):* 390, 411

S
Sabai, Capt Faustin: 426, 436
Sack, Capt Tommy: 47
Sagana I (VP-KHK): 101, 102
Sagana II (VP-KJU): 142-146, 149, 152
Sagana Lodge: 101
Salingboe, Stdss Eleonore: 329, 336
Salisbury, Rhodesia: 24, 76, 125, 128, 134, 138, 143, 151, 161, 168, 178, 184, 186-188, 218, 229, 243, 285
Samburu: 117, 288
Sandford, Sir George: 66
Sao Hill: 71
Sarginson, Mr Clifford: 253, 421, 423
Sarjit Singh, Mr: 133
Saudi Arabia: 128, 171, 173
Schneider Trophy: 18, 105
Schubert, Mr 'Schuby': 132, 133
Scott, N/O Claude: 444

Scott, C.W.A.: 21, 35
Semiramus Hotel, Cairo: 275
Semogerere, Mr Charles: 302
Seremai: 18, 37
Serengeti: 22, 196, 198, 228, 250, 343, 427
Seronera: 196, 198 228, 250
Seymour, Stdss Barbara: 216, 258
Seychelles: 110, *Catalina survey of:***114, 115**, 399, 419
Seyyid Said, Sultan: 3
'Shervic': 99
Shifta: 161
Sibson, Capt Rex: 50
Siedle, Mr Robert: 387
Silverlock, Mr Reg: 133, 155, 177
Silver Wings Club: 278
Simpson, Sir James, KBE: 202, 257, 319
Sims, Mr Frederick: 394
Sinatra, Mr Frank: 116
Sindbad the Sailor: 3, 84
Singapore : 204, *Kyobe dismissed at IATA conference:* 317, *Commonwealth Conference:* **365**, 366
Singapore Hilton: 367
Sirley, Capt Jerry: 277, 349, 365, 427, 435, 436
Skinner, Mr G.T.: 19
Skyway Hotel, Heathrow: 239, 259, 337, 368, 369, 373
Slade, Capt: 43
Smallpeice, Mr (*later Sir*) Basil: 153
Smith, Mr Alan (Barclays DCO): 433
Smith, MBE; Mr C.E., *chief engineer EAA* : 75, 157, 253, 319, 340
Smith, Stdss Sheila: 273
Smith, Mr Ian M.P.: 285
Soltau, Capt V. 'Lynx': 10, 12, 26, 28
Soroti, Uganda: 66, 420, 426
Sorsbie, CBE Kt; Capt Sir Malin: 48-50, 58, 63, 66, 74, 75, 83, 96, 102, 105, 110, 114, 118, 144, 149, 153-155, 159, 174, 203, 288, 374
South African Air Force: 7, 14, 23, 24, 41, 203
Southern Highlands Club (SHC): 71, 72, 251
Soviet: 165, 267, 316, 336, 432
Spiegel, Mr Sam: 116

SSB Radio: 316, 329, 352, 356, 364, 366, 403, 417, 444
SS Caronia: 102
SS Kinfauns Castle: 4
SS Tabora: 4
Stamford Hill Airport, Durban: 68
Stanleyville: 23, 223
Starling, Capt Lou: 68, 252, 253, 263, 264
Stewart, Mr Douglas: 69, 107
Strang, Stdss L.: 216
Street, Std Arthur: 172, 174
Stroh, Mr Nicholas: 387
Suez Canal: 170, 173
Sultan of Zanzibar: 3, 83, 206, 207, 269
Sun 'n Sands Hotel, Bombay: 306
Swensen, Mr Swen: 109-112, 116
Swoffer, Flt Lt F.A.: 21
Symes, Sir Stewart: 29

T
Tabora: 5, 6, 23, 57, 78, 79, 83, 85, 104, 135, 151, *DC3 ad hoc engine repair:* **160**, 387
Tagart, Capt Alan Weston: 54
Tait, KBE CB; AVM Sir Victor: 174
Tananarive: 80-82, 94, 251
Tanganyika Government Survey: 10-12, 28, 132
Tanga: 12, 24, 30, 32, 40, 46, 51, 60, 64, 69, 73, *Dakota stuck in the mud*: **87**, 89, 125, 129, 132, *a Standard 8 loaded as crew baggage*: **150**, 161, 221, 227, 250, 282, 319, 412
Tanga Club: 87, 89
Tanner, Mr J.H.: 12
Taylor, Mr Derek: 212
Templeman, Mr George, 'Temp': 12, 29, 76, 132
Thomas, Sir Miles: 153
Thompson, Mr Nigel: 341, 374
Thousand and One Nights: 3
Tiberondwa, Mr A.: 319
Todenyang: 124, 125
Toko, Col G. Wilson: 412, 426
Tokyo (*schedules planned to*): 311, 321, (*office opened*): 327
Tollerton aerodrome, *see Nottingham*: 136, 138
Tonnet, Mr Jack: 72, 131
Transport and General Workers Union: 372, 373
Travers, Capt F. Dudley: 37

Travers, Capt Pat: 51, 116, 117, 128, 136, 138, 143, 149, 202, 218, 219, 252, 257, 270, 278, 293
Treetops Hotel: 100, 262, 288, 414
Treforest: 103, 376
Tripoli: 5, 235, 331, *passenger pays fuel bill:* **417, 418**
Trubshaw, Mr Brian (BAC test pilot): 297, 444
Tshombe, M. Moise: 222
TUFMAC: 219
Turk, Capt Tommy: 276, 436
Tuttle, AVM Sir Geoffrey: 276, 293
Tveiten, Capt K.: 349, 435, 436
Tweedsmuir, Baroness: 402
Twist, F/E Brian: 394, 396, 400

U

Uganda Communications Flight: 66, 107
United Nations: 1, 206, 259, 351, 421

V

Vale, Capt John 'Paddy': 394, 395, 400, 435
Vincent, Sir Alfred: 19, *appointed chairman of EAAC:* **56**, 144, 153, 154, 162, 166, 202, *Comet contract:* **205**, 237, 242, 249, 255-257, 267, *retires from EAAC:* 271
Varese *(Macchi factory)*: 105-106
Vasco da Gama: 1-3

W

Wadi Halfa: 32, 46, 49, 96, 111, 113, 138, 159, 170, 173
Waiyaki, Mr Munyua, *Kenya Foreign Minister:* 434
Walsh, Mr J.: 142
Wangara, Mr Gregory: 367, 368, 372, 374, 411
Wanyee, E/O Steven: 323
Warder-Griffin, Capt Bob: 100, 127, 137
Warren, N/O Frank: 174, 212
Waterpark, Lord: 105, 106
Waters, Mr R. 'Dickie': 150
Watkins MBE; Mr A.W. 'Archie' E: 19, *employed by Mrs Wilson:* **20**, 41, 44, 56, 58, 76, 108, 117, 203, *retires from EAA:* 314
Watson, Mr D.: 44
Watson Capt Bob: 51, 101, 102
Watts, F/E Des: 209, 216
Webb, F/O Johnny: 83, 94
Webb, Mr Tom: 78, 126, 363-364, *detention and deportation:* 430-433

Welmans, E/O Andy: 311
West End Hotel, Bombay: 180
Westlake, Sir Charles: 66
West-Thomas, Mr Charles: 148, 198
West with the Night: 20
Weybridge: *Vickers (BAC) factory (see also Brooklands)*: 296, 297, 302, 336, 424
Whittingham, Mr R.A. 'Dick': 57, 377
Williams, Maj-Gen D.A.: 153
Williams, Mr S.G.H.: 186
Wilson Aerodrome (*see also Nairobi West*): 152, 201, 220, 255, 256, 312, 444, 445
Wilson, OBE; Mrs Florence: 19, 23, 28, 255-257, 260, 304
Wilson, Capt H. 'Tug': 54, 63, 83, 89, 90-95 108, 154, 155, 188, 189, 242, 313, 314, 446
Wilson, F/O John: 244
Wilson, Capt Peter (DH): 242
Winson, Capt John: 366, 367, 435
Wisley, *Vickers/BAC aerodrome and works:* 294, 297, 313, 346, 347, 442
Wood, Mr C.F.W.: 20
Woodward, Mr Earnest 'Woody': 424
Wray, Mr E. 'Ted': 413
Wright Engines:
 Whirlwind: 19
 Cyclone: 54
 R1820: 75
 used in Mogambo film: 117
Wright, Mr 'Bunny': 108
Wright, Mr R. 'Dick': 75
Wright, Mr P.D.: 44,
Wyatt, Sgt-Maj James: 5

Y

Young, Stdss Dora: 130
Young, Mr R.E.: 272, 297, 319

Z

Zanzibar: 1, 3, 4, 21, *survey and first mail flights:* **23-25**, 30, 32, 36, 37, *last Wilson Airways service:* **40**, 42, 46, 51, 52, 60, 61, 63-65, *pilots sleep as Lodestar overflies:* **73, 74**, 76, 77, 83, 87, 89, 92, 129, 132, 160, 163, 201, 205, 207, 221, 224, 227, 230, 232, 250,*HRH Duke of Edinburgh attends Independence ceremonies*: **263-265**, *revolution; EAAC aircraft requisitioned:***268-269**, *visit of Chou En-lai:* **280-281**; 319, 395, 437

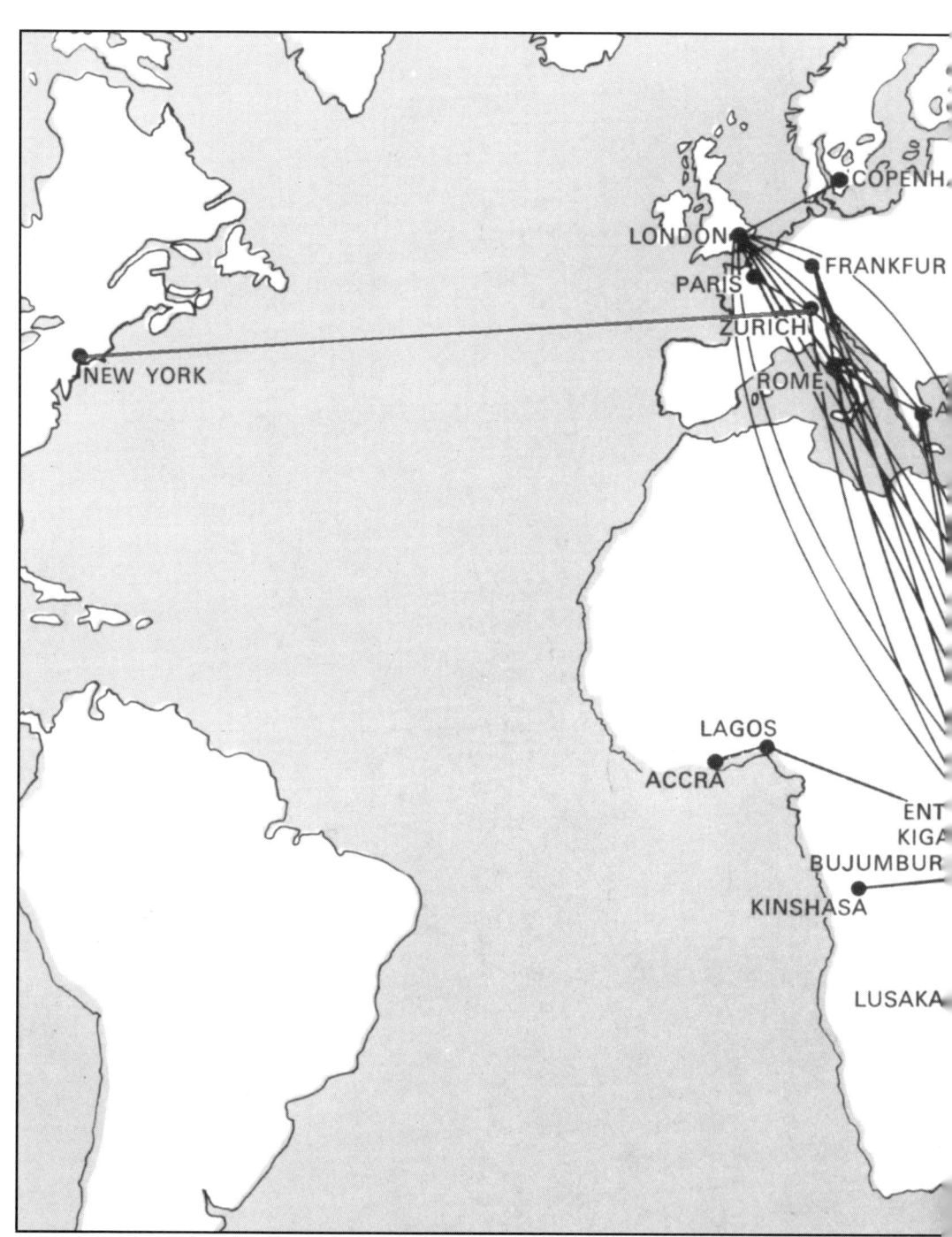